ITALY'S SORROW

By the same author

NON-FICTION:
Fortress Malta: An Island Under Siege, 1940–1943
Together We Stand:
North Africa, 1942–1943 – Turning the Tide in the West
Heroes: The Greatest Generation and the Second World War

FICTION:
The Burning Blue
A Pair of Silver Wings

ITALY'S SORROW
A Year of War, 1944–1945

JAMES HOLLAND

Harper
Press

HarperPress
An imprint of HarperCollinsPublishers
77–85 Fulham Palace Road,
Hammersmith, London W6 8JB
www.harpercollins.co.uk

Visit our authors' blog: www.fifthestate.co.uk

Published by HarperPress in 2008

1

A catalogue record for this book
is available from the British Library

ISBN 978-0-00-717645-8

Maps drawn by HL Studios
Prelim picture © NARA

Set in PostScript Linotype Minion by
Rowland Phototypesetting Ltd, Bury St Edmunds, Suffolk

Printed and bound in Great Britain by Clays Ltd, St Ives plc

Mixed Sources
Product group from well-managed
forests and other controlled sources
www.fsc.org Cert no. SW-COC-1806
© 1996 Forest Stewardship Council

FSC is a non-profit international organisation established to promote the
responsible management of the world's forests. Products carrying the FSC
label are independently certified to assure consumers that they come
from forests that are managed to meet the social, economic and
ecological needs of present and future generations.

Find out more about HarperCollins and the environment at
www.harpercollins.co.uk/green

For Daisy

ITALIAN PENINSULA

0   50
MILES

Milan

Genoa

Bologna

Rimini

Leghorn

Elba

CORSICA

ROMA

Anzio

Foggia

Bari

Naples

Taranto

Salerno

SARDINIA

SICILY

Gela

Pantelleria

TUNISIA

By the spring of 1944, the vast reach of Hitler's Third Reich, achieved so spectacularly in the early part of the war, was diminishing. In the East, the Soviet Red Army was clawing back land lost and was about to regain the Crimea, while in the West, the Western Allies were poised to invade France. Already the Axis powers had lost North Africa and, the previous summer, Sicily. Mussolini, the Fascist dictator of Italy, had been deposed, and on 8 September 1943, the Italians surrendered to the Allies. With British troops already on the southern toe of the peninsula, the main Allied invasion force landed at Salerno, south of Naples, the morning after the Italian armistice. Thus began a long and bloody campaign that would cause untold suffering. Seven months of fighting, mostly in the intractable terrain around the town of Cassino, would wreak appalling destruction.

By May 1944, with the Italian winter behind them, the Allies were ready to renew their drive towards Rome. As the battle rolled north, the rest of Italy would become consumed by the campaign raging up its narrow leg. That year, from May 1944 to the war's end almost exactly twelve months later, would be one of the most terrible in Italy's history.

CONTENTS

List of Illustrations   xi
List of Maps   xv
Note on the Text   xxvii
Principal Personalities   xxix
Prologue   xxxiii

Part I: The Road To Rome   1
 1 The Eve of Battle: May 1944   3
 2 Battle Begins: 11–12 May 1944   18
 3 Churchill's Opportunism   23
 4 The Slow Retreat   32
 5 Frustrations   42
 6 Between the Devil and the Deep Blue Sea   53
 7 Masters of the Skies   70
 8 The Battle Rages: 13–16 May 1944   81
 9 New Order   92
10 Breaking the Gustav Line: 17–18 May 1944   103
11 *Achtung Banditen!*   111
12 The Fog of War: 18–23 May 1944   125
13 Break-out: 23–26 May 1944   139
14 General Clark and the Big Switch: 26–30 May 1944   152
15 The Fall of Rome: 1–5 June 1944   169

Part II: The Brutal Summer   185
16 The North   187
17 The Problems of Generalship: June 1944   202
18 The Typhoon Rolls North   215
19 Breaking the Albert Line: 20–30 June 1944   225

20 The Politics of War   241
21 Differences of Opinion   252
22 Summer Heat: July 1944   264
23 Crossing the Arno: July–August 1944   279
24 A Change of Plan: August 1944   291
25 Despair: August 1944   305
26 The Gothic Line: 25 August–1 September 1944   317
27 The Tragedy of Gemmano: 1–12 September 1944   333
28 Mountain Passes and Bloody Ridges: 12–21 September 1944   345

    Part III: The Winter of Discontent   365
29 Death in the Mountains: 22–29 September 1944   367
30 The Reason Why   383
31 Rain, Mud and Misery, Part I: 1–14 October 1944   393
32 Rain, Mud and Misery, Part II: 15–31 October 1944   411
33 The Infantryman's Lot: November 1944   425
34 The Partisan Crisis: November–December 1944   441
35 White Christmas: December 1944   453

    Part IV: Endgame   471
36 Stalemate: January–February 1945   473
37 Getting Ready: February–April 1945   487
38 The Last Offensive: 9–20 April 1945   504
39 The End of the War in Italy: 21 April–2 May 1945   516

    Postscript   528

    References   541
    Bibliography   547
    Acknowledgements   573
    Abbreviations and Glossary   577
    Guide to ranks   581
    Index   583

LIST OF ILLUSTRATIONS

First Plate Section:

General Sir Harold Alexander. © *Imperial War Museum NA14719*.

Hans-Jürgen Kumberg at his machine gun post on Monte Cassino. © *Hans Kumberg*.

Ray Saidel. © *Raymond Saidel*.

Monte Cassino taken before the war. © *Cassino*

Monte Cassino towards the battle's end. © *Cassino*.

General Sir Oliver Leese, General Sir Harold Alexander and Lieutenant General Mark. W. Clark. © *NARA*.

A US Baltimore attacks a railway line.© *NARA*.

Charles Dills. © *Charles Dills*.

Sketch of the Liri Valley as seen by Ted Wyke-Smith from atop Monte Trocchio. © *Ted Wyke-Smith*.

The Liri Valley from Monte Cassino with Monte Trocchio on the right. © *NARA*.

Kesselring and General Fridolin von Senger und Etterlin. *Taken from Neither Fear nor Hope by General Frido von Senger Und Etterlin (Presidio Press, 1989)*.

Ted Wyke-Smith in his dug-out. © *Ted Wyke-Smith*.

Wladek Rubnikowicz. © *Wladek Rubnikowicz*.

Jupp Klein. © *Joseph Klein*.

Santa Maria Infante. © *NARA*.

One of the twenty-six bridges built by Ted Wyke-Smith in the Liri Valley. © *Imperial War Museum NA 15042*.

The Canadian, Stan Scislowski. © *Stan Scislowski*.

A Nebelwerfer – or 'Moaning Minnie'. © *Imperial War Museum NA 15590*.

US troops in Formia, 19 May 1944. © *Corbis*.

Moroccan Goumiers. © *Imperial War Museum NA 14434.*
Fallschirmjäger retreating northwards. © *Ullstein Bild.*

Second Plate Section:
Willi Holtfreter. © *Willi Holtfreter.*
Ion Calvocoressi with other ADCs from Eighth Army Tactical HQ. © *Ion Calvocoressi.*
Indian Sikhs greeting British troops in the Liri Valley. © *Imperial War Museum NA 14966.*
Starving Italian boys in Naples. © *Corbis.*
An elderly Italian lady on the steps of a church. © *NARA.*
A woman from southern Italy being publicly deloused. © *Corbis.*
Harold Macmillan with Alexander. © *Ion Calvocoressi.*
Italian troops of the CIL, who fought alongside the Allies, April 1944. © *Getty Images.*
Mark Clark.© *Getty Images.*
Marquesa Iris Origo with some of the evacuees and orphans taken into her care at La Foce. © *La Foce.*
A fighter-bomber over German lines. ©. *SANMMH.*
Young Italian partisans.© *SANMMH.*
Gianni Rossi. © *G. Lippi.*
William Cremonini and the men of the Bir el Gobi Company in Milan. © *William Cremonini.*
Carla Costa. © *TNA.*
The 8th Garibaldi Brigade of partisans. © *Iader Miserocchi.*
GNR militia carrying out an execution of Romagnan partisan, Aldo Palareti. *Author's Collection.*
Half Palareti's head blown away by the Neo-Fascist firing squad. *Author's Collection*
Kendall Brooke. © *Kendall Brooke.*
A convoy of trucks from Eighth Army take a brief break north of Rome. © *Imperial War Museum NA 18399.*
Men of the 16th Waffen-SS Division at Cecina on the Tuscan coast. © *Im gleichen Schritt und Tritt.*
Reg Harris. © *Reg Harris.*

Third Plate Section:
The Guards Brigade in Montepulciano. © *Imperial War Museum 16549.*

'Germany is truly your friend', German propaganda poster. © *Istituto Storico della Resistenza Forlì.*

Walter Reder, commander of the 16th Waffen-SS Reconnaissance Battalion. *Author's Collection*

Feldmarschall Kesselring – or 'Smiling Albert'. © *Corbis*

The San Terenzo massacre. © *Paulo Cozzi / taken from a leaflet published by Nuova Graphica.*

Karl Wolff. *Author's Collection.*

Partisans from the 29th GAP Brigade in Ravenna publicly strung up. © *Istituto Storico della Resistenza Forlì.*

Iris Versari strung up on a lamppost in the centre of Forlì. © *Istituto Storico della Resistenza Forlì.*

Victims of the Sant' Anna massacre. *Author's Collection.*

Tanks from the 6th South African Armoured Division pushing through Impruneta. © *Imperial War Museum NA 17572.*

Florentine partisans firing on the Via de Serragli. © *Imperial War Museum NA 17584.*

Fallschirmjäger defending the northern half of Florence on the banks of the River Arno. © *Ullstein Bild.*

General Oliver Leese. © *Ion Calcovoressi*

Ken Neill. © *Dennis Bray.*

Spitfires of 225 Squadron lined up at Florence airfield. © *Dennis Bray.*

An infantryman 'digging in'. © *NARA.*

Mario Musolesi, better known as 'Lupo'. © *G. Lippi.*

The Monte Sole Massif from the Setta Valley. © *Imperial War Museum.*

One of the many bridges built by the Allies.© *NARA.*

An anti-tank ditch along the Gothic Line. © *NARA.*

British troops walk through the shattered remains of Gemmano, September 1944. © *Imperial War Museum.*

Sam Bradshaw. © *Sam Bradshaw.*

Peter Moore with a friend whilst on leave in Rome. © *Peter Moore.*

Fourth Plate Section:

German soldiers receiving mail from home.© *Ullstein Bild.*

Ernest Wall and his crew from 24 SAAF Squadron. © *Ernest Wall.*

A 24 SAAF Squadron's B-26 Marauder, W-E6. © *Ernest Wall.*

The Allies grind to a halt in thick, glutinous mud. © *NARA.*

Eighth Army tanks cross the Savio. © *Imperial War Museum.*

Franz Maassen.© *Franz Maassen.*

Sketch by Ted Wyke-Smith of Allied infantry on the front. © *Ted Wyke-Smith.*

Members of the 8th Garibaldi Brigade in Forlì. © *Iader Miserocchi.*

Emilio Sacerdote's identity papers. © *Imperial War Museum.*

US troops walk back down the mountain. © *NARA.*

Albert Burke, Master Sergeant of the 92nd 'Buffalo' Division. © *Albert Burke.*

Hans-Jürgen Kumberg. © *Hans-Jürgen Kumberg.*

Bill Mauldin cartoon, based on his own experience in Italy. *Taken from* Bill Mauldin's Army (Ballantine, New York, 2003). © *Bill Mauldin.*

Lieutenant General Mark. W. Clark and General Sir Harold Alexander. © *Imperial War Museum NA 14296.*

Mussolini in Milan and, behind him, Alessandro Pavolini, in December 1944. © *Parabola.*

Major Stephen Hastings with men from the XIII Piacenza Partisans. © *Sir Stephen Hastings.*

Wrecked German vehicles and war materiel along the banks of the River Po. © *Imperial War Museum.*

Friedrich Büchner. © *Friedrich Büchner.*

US infantry climbing into the mountains in the final days of the war. © *NARA.*

A long column of German prisoners at the war's end. © *NARA.*

The cemetery at Casaglia as it is today. *Author's Collection.*

Endpaper illustrations: *The Ambulance, Evening on Route 16* and *Dust on Route 9* by Edward Seago, courtesy of the Estate of Edward Seago and Thomas Gibson Fine Art.

While every effort has been made to trace the owners of copyright material reproduced herein, the publishers would like to apologise for any omissions and would be pleased to incorporate missing acknowledgements in any future editions.

MAPS

Italy showing German defensive lines   xvi

Cassino front, 11 May 1944, and Alexander's battle plan for
DIADEM and the destruction of AOK 10 south of Rome   xviii

The Monte Sole massif   xix

Operational zone of the 8th Garibaldi Brigade of Partisans, also
showing the river network Eighth Army had to cross, September
1944 to April 1945   xx

The Val d'Orcia   xxi

Northern Italy, Lake Como and Lake Garda   xxi

Main Italian rail network and ports   xxii

Allied Control Commission Organisation of Italy, 1 September 1944   xxiii

The Winter Line, January 1945   xxiv

DIADEM: The battle for Rome and German lines of retreat for
AOK 10   154

The Allied pursuit from Rome to the Albert Line, 5–20 June 1944   204

From the Albert Line to the River Arno, July and early August 1944   260

Alexander's battle plan for the Gothic Line, August 1944   296

Eighth Army's attack on the Gothic Line, August to September 1944   322

Fifth Army's assault on the Gothic Line, 10–18 September 1944   350

The German attack on Monte Sole   376

Fifth Army's attempt to break through the Apennines,
1–15 October 1944   402

The final offensive, April to May 1945   506

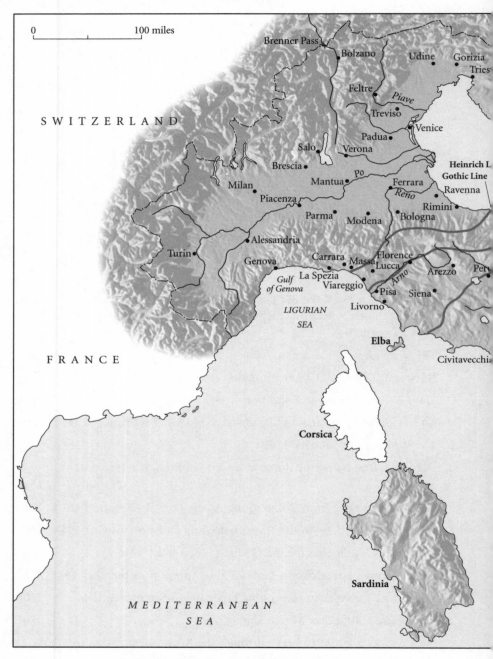

Italy showing German defensive lines

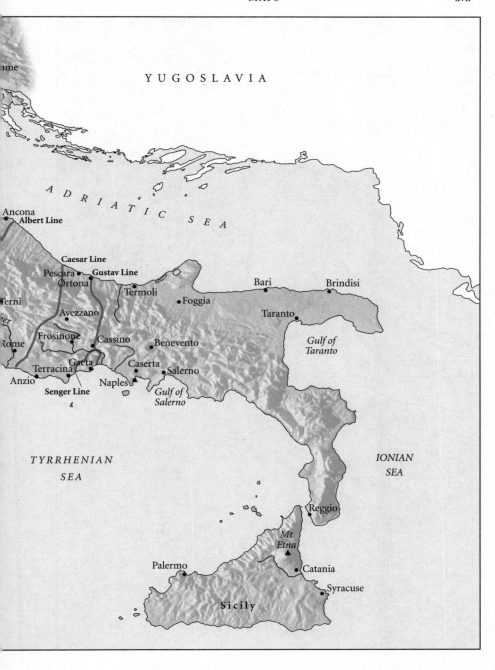

YUGOSLAVIA

ADRIATIC SEA

Ancona
Albert Line

Caesar Line
Pescara **Gustav Line**
Ortona
Bari Brindisi
Termoli
Terni Foggia
Taranto
Avezzano
Gulf of
Frosinone Taranto
Rome Cassino
Benevento
Gaeta Caserta
Terracina Salerno
Anzio Naples
Senger Line Gulf of
Salerno

TYRRHENIAN
SEA
IONIAN
SEA

Reggio

Mt
Etna ▲
Palermo Catania
Syracuse
Sicily

ITALY'S SORROW

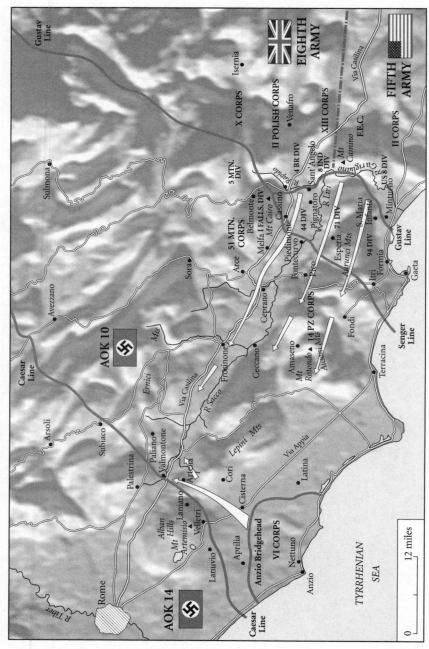

Cassino front, 11 May 1944, and Alexander's battle plan for DIADEM
and the destruction of AOK 10 south of Rome

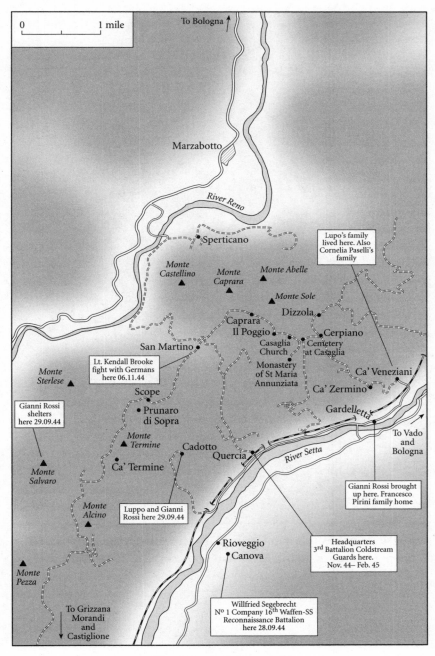

The Monte Sole massif

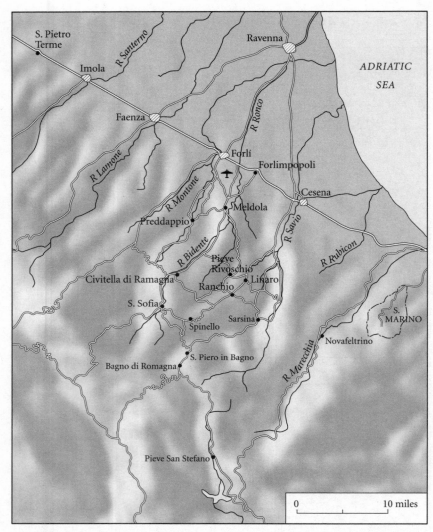

Operational zone of the 8th Garibaldi Brigade of Partisans, also showing the river network Eighth Army had to cross (Sept. 1944–April 1945)

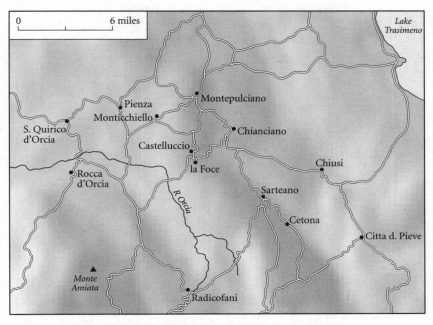

The Val d'Orcia

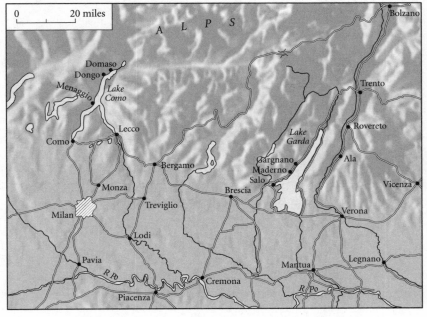

Northern Italy, Lake Como and Lake Garda

Main Italian rail network and ports

Allied Control Commission Organisation of Italy, 1 Sept. 1944

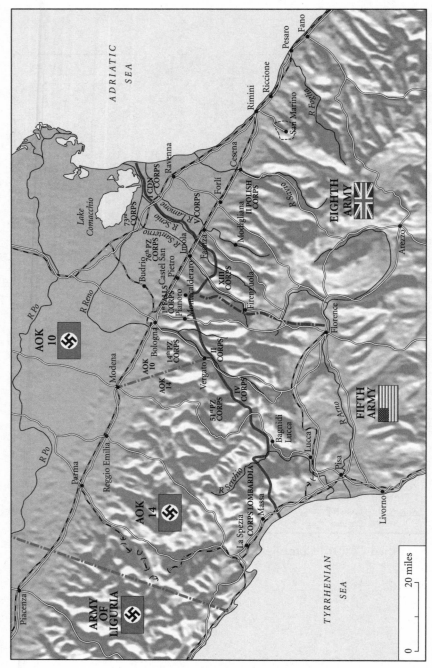

The Winter Line, January 1945

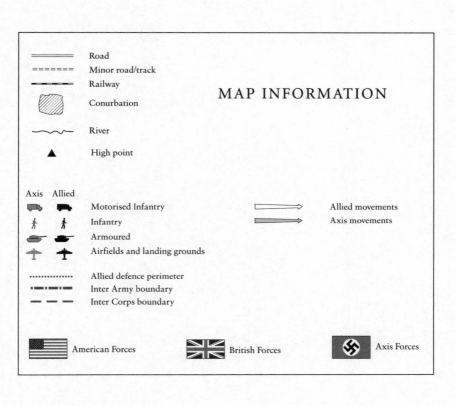

MAP INFORMATION

Road

Minor road/track

Railway

Conurbation

River

High point

Axis Allied

Motorised Infantry

Infantry

Armoured

Airfields and landing grounds

Allied defence perimeter

Inter Army boundary

Inter Corps boundary

Allied movements

Axis movements

American Forces   British Forces   Axis Forces

NOTE ON THE TEXT

One of the difficulties faced when writing about different armies of different nationalities is that many units have similar names. Furthermore, many American servicemen also have Germanic-sounding names. So in an effort to avoid any confusion, I have used the German spellings for the names of military units and ranks. For example, the German name for an army was *Armeeoberkommando*, or AOK as it was known; paratroopers were called *Fallschirmjäger*; armoured divisions were called panzer divisions. I have also included as an appendix to the book a comparison of military ranks.

On the other hand, I have translated Italian ranks, but have kept certain Italian words in their true form where there is no appropriate translation, such as *contadini*, who were Italian peasant farmers, and *rastrellamento*, the word to describe a military operation to clear an area of partisans.

Traditionally, army numbers are spelled out, and corps numbers given in Roman numerals. However, I have used numerical figures to describe German corps, purely because LXXVI Panzer Corps seems unnecessarily long-winded. I hope readers will accept these inconsistencies and anomalies in the spirit in which they were intended.

PRINCIPAL PERSONALITIES
(ranks as at end of war)

Cosimo Arrichiello Italian former soldier with Fourth Someggiata Field Battery; agricultural labourer hiding in the Stura Valley south of Turin

John Barton British officer and agent with SOE, Italy

Sam Bradshaw British reconnaissance trooper with 6 Royal Tank Regiment, 7th Armoured Brigade

Kendall Brooke South African subaltern with A Coy, Royal Natal Carbineers, 6th SA Armoured Division

Friedrich Büchner German trainee artillery officer with 98th Infantry Division

Albert Burke American master sergeant with Divisional HQ, 92nd 'Buffalo' Infantry Division

Ion Calvocoressi British senior aide-de-camp to General Sir Oliver Leese, Tactical HQ, Eighth Army

Carla Capponi Italian civilian and member of Rome-based resistance movement GAP Central

Eugenio Corti Italian lieutenant with 184th Artillery Regiment, Nembo Division, CIL, later Folgore Combat Group

Carla Costa Italian civilian spy with German Intelligence Service (Abwehr)

William Cremonini Italian sergeant with Bir el Gobi Company, Alessandro Pavolini's personal bodyguard

Antonio Cucciati Italian teenager paratrooper with Nuotati e Paracadutisti Battalion, Flottiglia Decima MAS

Elena Curti Italian civilian and illegitimate daughter of Benito Mussolini, working for government of the RSI

Charles Dills American fighter pilot with 522nd Squadron, 27th Fighter Bomber Group

Group Captain Hugh 'Cocky' Dundas British airman serving as wing commander, HQ Desert Air Force, 244 Wing; commanding officer, 244 Wing, RAF

Clara Duse Italian civilian living in Trieste

Tom Finney British trooper with 9th Queen's Royal Lancers, 78th Division

Dick Frost South African lance corporal with D Squadron, Royal Natal Carbineers, 12th Motor Infantry Brigade, 6th SA Armoured Division

Martha Gellhorn American freelance journalist and war correspondent with *Collier's Magazine*. Estranged wife of the writer Ernest Hemingway

Tini Glover Maori sergeant with 28th Maori Battalion, 2nd New Zealand Division

Hans Golda German commanding officer serving with 8th Battery, Werfer Regiment 71

Reg Harris British sergeant with 3rd Battalion, Coldstream Guards

Stephen Hastings British liaison officer with No 1 Special Force, SOE in Piacenza

Willi Holtfreter German fighter pilot with fighter group III/JG 53

Hamilton Howze American commander, 13th Armored Battalion; later commander Combat Command B, 1st Armored Division

Jupp Klein German commander with Pioneer Company, 1st Fallschirmjäger Division

Hans-Jürgen Kumberg German paratrooper with 4th Parachute Regiment, 1st Paratroop Division

Norman Lewis British intelligence officer with 412th Field Security Service

Franz Maassen German NCO with 2nd Battalion, 994th Infantry Regiment, 278th Infantry Division

Iader Miserocchi Italian partisan commander of 2nd Battalion, 8th Garibaldi Brigade; later served with 28th Garibaldi Brigade

Peter Moore British officer with 2/5th Battalion, Leicestershire Regiment

Ken Neill New Zealander flight commander with 225 Tactical Reconnaissance Squadron, RAF

Marchesa Iris Origo Irish/American/Italian civilian living in Val d'Orcia, southern Tuscany

Cornelia Paselli Italian civilian living near Monte Sole

Francesco Pirini Italian civilian living near Monte Sole

Pasua Pisa Italian civilian farmer living on Monte Rotondo, near Amaseno

Italo Quadrelli Italian civilian living at Onferno, near Rimini

Walter Reder German commanding officer, 16th Reconnaissance Battalion, 16th Waffen-SS

Gianni Rossi Italian partisan; served as second-in-command, Stella Rossa, Monte Sole

Wladek Rubnikowicz Polish troop leader with 2nd Squadron, 12th Lancers Reconnaissance Regiment, 3rd Carpathian Division, II Polish Corps

Emilio Sacerdote Italian Jew and partisan in Piemonte

Ray Saidel American private first class with G Coy, 1st Armored Regiment, 1st Armored Division

Rudi Schreiber German engineer with Pioneer Battalion, 16th Waffen-SS Panzer Grenadier Division

Stan Scislowski Canadian private with Perth Regiment, 11th Infantry Brigade, 5th Canadian Armoured Division

Willfried Segebrecht German commanding officer, 1 Company, 16th Reconnaissance Battalion, 16th Waffen-SS

Eric Sevareid American broadcast journalist and war correspondent for CBS

Hans Sitka Czech German NCO with East Regiment

Carlo Venturi Italian partisan with Stella Rossa and later 62nd Garibaldi Brigade

Roberto Vivarelli Italian volunteer with Bir el Gobi Company

Ernest Wall British wireless operator/air gunner with 1 Squadron, South African Air Force

Bucky Walters American sergeant with H Coy, 135th Infantry Regiment, 34th 'Red Bull' Infantry Division

Bob Wiggans American commanding officer with 'D' Coy, 1st Battalion, 338th Infantry, 85th 'Custer' Infantry Division

Ted Wyke-Smith British officer with 281st Field Park Company, 214th Field Company, 78th Division Royal Engineers

Georg Zellner German commanding officer with 3rd Battalion, 'Hoch-und-Deutschmeister' Reichs Grenadier Regiment (44th Infantry Division)

PROLOGUE

A few minutes before two o'clock on the afternoon of Thursday, 23 March 1944, Rome was a city bathed in spring sunshine and temperatures that were easily the warmest so far that year. But while the promise of summer may have lightened the mood of the majority of Romans, the heat brought no such cheer to twenty-two-year-old Carla Capponi, or 'Elena' as she was known amongst her fellow partisans. Clasping a pistol in her pocket, she was already feeling conspicuous for carrying a man's raincoat on such a beautiful day.

A couple of hours before, she had been too nervous to have any of the beer and potatoes on offer for lunch. Instead, she and her boyfriend, Rosario 'Paolo' Bentivegna, and two other partisans of the Roman resistance group GAP Central – the *Gruppi di Azione Patriottica Centrale* – had left their meal and hurried over to the hideout near the Colosseum. There Paolo had collected the old dust cart that had been stolen the day before, in which there was now hidden a homemade bomb of 18 kilogrammes of TNT topped by a 50-second fuse. While the bomb was big enough to destroy an entire building, the Gappists had planned to bolster their attack with mortars and gunfire. It had been Carla's job to pick up four mortars from the hide-out and deliver them to 'Francesco', a fellow partisan, waiting in the Via del Traforo. Carrying the mortars in nothing more than a shopping bag, she had managed safely to deliver them to Francesco, and then, as she had walked past, had glanced down the Via Rasella. It had been quite deserted; Paolo, with his heavy bomb-laden dustcart, had not yet reached his appointed position.

Passing the bottom of the Via Rasella, Carla had continued up the Via del Traforo and was now waiting by the offices of *Il Messaggero* newspaper. She spotted Pasquale Balsamo, another partisan, standing by a news-stand. Perhaps he could sense her nerves in the taut expression in her face, because as he looked across he gave her a reassuring wink.

At least they were both now in position. It was Pasquale's job to give Carla the signal to let her know that the German troops were on their way. She would then turn right onto the Via del Tritone, a main thoroughfare that ran roughly parallel to the Via Rasella, and after 300 yards, turn right again onto another main street, the Via delle Quattro Fontane, until she reached the top end of Via Rasella. There she would wait for Paolo with the raincoat – the overcoat that was to cover up his dustman's uniform as they attempted to make good their escape.

Standing by *Il Messaggero,* Carla paused to look at the newspaper pinned in a display case outside the entrance, keeping half an eye out for Pasquale's reflection in the glass in front of her. Nearby, far too close for comfort, were two men – very obviously plainclothes policemen. The newspaper was full of news about the eruption of Mount Vesuvius five days earlier, but as her eyes flickered over the newsprint she was conscious that too much time was going by. Why hadn't Pasquale given her the signal? And where were the SS troops? The whole operation had been built around the Germans' unvarying Teutonic routine: every day, without fail, the same column of around 160 men of the 11th Company of the 3rd Battalion of the SS Police Regiment Bozen would march through the centre of the city on their way back to their barracks after a morning's training at a shooting range near the Roman bridge, Ponte Milvio. As they marched, singing '*Hupf, Mein Mädel!*' – 'Skip, My Lassie' – they would pass up the length of the comparatively narrow and enclosed Via Rasella.

A quarter past two came and went. Then 2.20 p.m., 2.30 p.m., 2.45 p.m. and still no sign of the troops. The plainclothes policemen approached her. As they did so Carla gripped the pistol in her pocket. 'Excuse me, *signorina,*' one of them said to her. 'Are you waiting for someone?' For a split second she froze, then said, yes, she was waiting for her fiancé, who, she explained, worked at the Palazzo Barberini. She then began talking to them about the eruption of Vesuvius and the potential disaster this might cause for Naples. This seemed to work. She felt calmer suddenly, so that when one of them asked her sharply why she was carrying a raincoat on such a hot day, she told them that it was her fiancé's and that she had had a stain removed from it and was going to give it back to him.

She then saw Pasquale start towards her. What was the time? She asked the policemen: 2.47 p.m. one of them told her. In that case, she said, it was time for her to go. Hurrying away from them, she passed Pasquale who muttered something she could not make out, but knowing she could not look back and believing Pasquale's message was the signal for her to move, she turned into the Via del Tritone and then down Quattro Fontane to take up her position for the attack.

At the top of Via Rasella, Carla saw Paolo sweeping the road half way down the street, the dustcart in the middle of the road. She had been expecting to see the SS column marching into the bottom of the street but there was still no sign. She could not think what had gone wrong. One of only twelve partisans from GAP Central, she was well aware that their chances of pulling off such an attack and then successfully escaping were not high. Life in Rome was becoming increasingly dangerous with not only the Gestapo closing in on them but also the Neo-Fascist secret police. There was also a particularly vicious gang of Fascist vigilantes, which had been set up soon after the German occupation the previous autumn as a counter-partisan 'Special Police Unit'. Known as the Koch Gang after its leader, Pietro Koch, the band was already a byword for ruthlessness and brutality, known for the particular vindictiveness with which they tortured those who fell into their grasp.

The growing dangers had done little to deter the Gappists, but all of the partisans in GAP Central, Carla included, were very aware that their planned attack in the Via Rasella was the most daring strike attempted yet. The night before, lying next to Paolo in their hide-out, she had needed to remind herself why she was taking part in such an action. In the silence and dark, she had thought of how unjust the war was, and of the destruction and devastation it had caused to her country. She thought of her compatriots who had already been shot and tortured and of all those who had been deported and who had not been heard of since; and she thought of all those friends of hers who had already died in the fighting in Russia, in Greece, in Yugoslavia; she remembered her cousin, Amleto, killed fighting the Allies at El Alamein. But while such thoughts had helped stiffen her resolve, her fears remained. If they were caught, she knew they would be killed.

At the top of the Via Rasella, in the garden of the Palazzo Barberini, Carla spotted some children playing football. Imagining the horrors of the children being caught in the bomb blast she walked over and shouted at them, 'You can't play football in this garden. Go home and do your homework!' Recognising something in her tone, they all immediately scurried off.

The minutes ticked by. Still nothing. What could have gone wrong? As she waited by the gates of the Palazzo Barberini the same two plainclothes policemen approached her again. It was now just after 3.30 p.m., more than an hour and a half after the bomb was supposed to have gone off. 'You still here?' they asked her. Her fiancé was at the Officer's Club in the Palazzo, she told them, desperately hoping they would not see Paolo and his rubbish cart a hundred yards up ahead. She couldn't go in there, she explained, as it was men only, and so had to wait. 'We'll wait with you,' they told her.

Carla was almost at her wits' end when she spotted an elderly friend of her mother's on the other side of Quattro Fontane. Excusing herself from the two policemen, she hurried across the road and after a very brief conversation, whispered to her to get away as quickly as possible.

It was at that moment that she saw one of the other partisans walking down the street towards Paolo. As he passed, Carla finally spotted the head of the column of SS men turn into the bottom of the Via Rasella. Her heart in her mouth, she watched them gradually fill the entire street, tramping rhythmically – though not singing as usual – towards Paolo and the dustcart, until he was lost from view, engulfed by the marching column.

She was still straining to see him when he suddenly appeared by her side. The front of the column was now near the top of the Via Rasella. She gave him the raincoat, which he hastily put on over his overalls, just as Carla saw the two plainclothes policemen, who had not stopped watching her, begin to cross the street. She pulled out her pistol but a passing bus came between them.

And then the bomb detonated.

The explosion rocked the entire city centre. A violent blast of air followed, pushing Carla and Paolo forward and knocking the bus, directly in front of the Via Rasella, across the street. The policemen fled and Carla and Paolo sprinted in the opposite direction, gunfire and bullets from the troops at the head of the column pinging and ricocheting all around them and bits of stone and stucco from the buildings showering them as they ran. Behind them mortars exploded, but they both kept running, sprinting for their lives until the sounds of the inferno at last began to die down.

That same Thursday in March 1944 was proving to be a significant day on the main front line as well. Just over sixty miles to the south-east of

Rome, lay the town of Cassino, and towering above it, the remains of the sixth-century Benedictine monastery of Monte Cassino. Emerging from the high and jagged peaks that stretched east to the Adriatic coast and overlooking the flat Liri Valley before the mountains rose once more to the western coast, Monte Cassino held the key to the route to Rome and was the single most important point in the German 'Gustav Line', a defensive barrier than ran like a belt across the waist of Italy.

Since January, the Allies had repeatedly tried to force their way through, but the formidable defences had prevented them. Indeed, as the dust and debris of the blast in the Via Rasella began to settle that sunny spring afternoon, the Allies were about to call a halt to their third attempt to break Cassino and Monastery Hill above.

That the Allied attack was now almost beaten had much to do with the tenacious defending by the German 1st Parachute – or *Fallschirm-jäger* – Division. Amongst these defenders was Hans-Jürgen Kumberg, a nineteen-year-old paratrooper born in Ventspils, Latvia to German parents. In 1939, as Russia was soon to occupy the Baltic States, the family moved to Posen in German-occupied Poland, and it was here, in June 1943, that Hans finished school. Inspired by a film about the Fallschirmjäger's action over Crete in May 1941, he promptly, aged just seventeen, volunteered to become a paratrooper himself. Before Christmas, having successfully completed his training, he was posted to the Adriatic where the Fallschirmjäger were still defending Ortona. It had been a month since Hans and the division had arrived at Monte Cassino, in time for the Third Battle of Cassino.

The German defenders had fought with almost insane bravery and determination since the moment the Allies had landed at Salerno the previous September. Almost every yard had been bitterly contested as the defenders had fallen back across rivers, through mountains and networks of mines, booby traps and wire. Through November and December, they had successfully held the Allies at bay along the narrow Mignano Gap, a mere ten miles south-east of Cassino, before retreating in January to their well-prepared defences of the Gustav Line, along which Cassino was the key position. Helped by a particularly wet and cold winter, they had in that first month of the new year, and again in February, barred the Allies from bludgeoning their way through to the wider valley beyond that led to Rome. The first two battles of Cassino had seen some of the most bitter and bloody fighting of the war to date.

In the four long weeks since his arrival at Cassino, Hans had not had a chance fully to grasp just how high up he was in the mountains, or how dominant was the monastery that overlooked the Liri Valley below. His division had reached the town in the dead of night on 20/21 February. Arriving at the foot of Monastery Hill, they had then disembarked from their trucks and walked as silently as they could – despite their heavy packs and equipment – up through a steep gully to a ridge about a mile beyond and above the remains of the monastery. It was wet underfoot and bitterly cold and the climb a difficult one; yet, whatever the difficulties of hauling equipment and supplies high into the Cassino massif, there was no denying that such an imposing landscape was an enormous advantage to the defender. Monastery Hill itself rose sharply from the town below, standing sentinel and, at 700 feet, a formidable feature for any attacker. Compared with the range of mountains stacked behind it, however, Monastery Hill was just that – a hill – dwarfed by the 5,475-foot-high giant that was Monte Cairo.

In the Liri Valley, the defenders had smashed dikes and diverted water courses to flood large parts of the valley floor and so make it impassable to vehicles, especially heavy trucks and tanks. South of the valley, as far as the sea fifteen miles away, were more mountains: the Aurunci range rising to 5,000 feet – almost as high as the mighty range of the interior. It was along these positions that German engineers and their Italian press-ganged labour force had built a network of bunkers and gun emplacements and laid intricate webs of wire and mines. And it was from here that the defenders had blocked the Allied advance to Rome for more than two months.

When daylight broke the following morning, Hans could just about see the scree-like ruins of the monastery emerging through a thick mist, but the valley floor below and Monte Cairo behind remained completely hidden. As Hans was soon to discover, he had come to one of the most desolate and violent places in the world. The hard rock and precipitous slopes of the mountains and the flooded valley below had blunted the Allies' superior fire power. At Cassino, each yard – each foot – had to be won or defended by the men unfortunate enough to find themselves thrown into this battle of attrition.

The monastery had been just one of the victims, obliterated by the Allies a week before Hans' arrival. Other victims from the previous months' fighting lay scattered and strewn in front of Hans' machine-gun post; the dead were everywhere. The stench of rotting corpses, bloated and noxious, was overpowering. Hans' regiment occupied a small ridge known as Hill 445, some 400 yards to the north of the obliterated monastery. By day, Hans and his comrades remained at their post, the constant smoke and dust from shellfire and from British fog canisters shrouding the top of the mountain. By night, they would be able to cautiously slink their way back to the ruined farmhouse that served as company headquarters, or back down the hill to collect ammunition and supplies.

Although Hans' arrival had coincided with a lull in the fighting, shell and mortar fire, bombing and sniping continued incessantly. Neither side could ever afford to relax; as the German paratroopers had soon learnt, they had to be on their guard at all times. Opposite them were the 1/9th Gurkha Rifles, notorious for their proficiency with *kukri* knives. Sometimes at night, when less ordnance was hurled back and forth, Hans could hear the screams of his fellow paratroopers as Gurkhas stealthily infiltrated a German outpost, killing – often decapitating – the men with their curved knives. Hans and his comrades hardly dared sleep at night for fear of meeting such a fate: on edge all the time, the strain was immense.

A week before, the battle had begun again in earnest. The morning of 15 March had been clear and sunny, but at around 8.30 a.m. Hans and his unit heard the sound of massed aero engines and then watched open-mouthed as the sky filled with Allied aircraft. They had come to pulverise Cassino town: nearly 800 planes in all, dropping over 1,000 tonnes of bombs. When they had gone, and the dust had settled, the town lay utterly and completely destroyed. The ruins had since proved easier to defend than when the town had been standing, as the New Zealand troops sent in afterwards had discovered at great cost – the Corps losing around 4,000 men. At the same time, the British 4th Indian Division had failed to make headway around Monastery Hill. Hans-Jürgen Kumberg and his comrades had fought hard and valiantly – and had even earned a certain respect from their enemy, who had started to refer to the paratroopers as the 'Green Devils'.

That evening, 23 March, the British general, Sir Harold Alexander, Commander-in-Chief of Allied Armies in Italy (AAI), drove up to the front line to see the battlefield for himself. The New Zealand commander, General Freyberg, and the US Fifth Army commander, General Mark Clark, had both recommended that the Third Battle of Cassino be called off without delay. Agreeing that any further offensive action was indeed futile, Alexander concurred. The Germans had scored another defensive victory. Difficult though it was to accept in this age of highly mechanised modern warfare, the harsh winter conditions and formidable natural defences of this thin, mountainous country had ensured that the Allies would henceforth have to return to the old summer campaigning season of centuries past.

Curiously though, along the Anzio bridgehead, thirty miles to the north-west, the German Supreme Commander South-West, Feldmarschall Albert Kesselring, was drawing much the same conclusion as his opposite number as he drove along the front and talked with his commanders. It was now two months since the Allies had made their landing at Anzio in Operation SHINGLE. On 22 January, 36,000 American and British troops under the command of US VI Corps had come ashore on the flat land thirty miles south of Rome. Although intended as a means of outflanking the main front along the Gustav Line to the south-east, the shortage of available shipping had ensured that not enough men and equipment had been landed quickly enough to take early advantage of the surprise that had been achieved. The initiative was quickly lost as German troops were hurriedly sent to counterattack, and Allied hopes of forging a link to their forces further south were subsequently dashed.

Anzio, however, had proved equally frustrating for the Germans who had recognised the importance, both psychologically and strategically, of forcing the Allies back into the sea. Generaloberst Eberhard von Mackensen, commander of the German AOK (*Armeeoberkommando*) 14, whose area of operations included both Rome and the Anzio bridge-head, had for some weeks been suggesting to Kesselring that they should give up any hopes of such a goal. Repeated German counterattacks had been forced back, blunted by the Allies' superior fire power. Indeed, the night before, as Carla Capponi had lain with Paolo in their hide-out in Rome, they had heard the distant muffled thunder of the guns along the Anzio bridgehead to the south.

The Allies may have managed to cling on to their small gains, but for the American and British troops trapped there, the Anzio bridgehead had proved a hellish place, with the men enduring conditions akin to those of the Western Front in the previous war. The landscape all along the front was now witness to a terrible desolation. Villages and towns lay utterly flattened. Areas of thick pine forest stood splintered and shorn. The earth was pockmarked by shell crater after shell crater; the soil churned into thick, glutinous mud by the sheer scale of exploding ordnance and labouring Allied vehicles. As Ray Saidel – a nineteen-year-old private with the US 1st Armored Regiment – had discovered, artillery dominated every aspect of their lives. His friends and comrades around him all shared the same look: deep-set hollow eyes from lack of sleep, and the 'Anzio Crouch' – the way they walked so as to be ready to throw themselves flat on the ground the moment a shell whistled nearby.

For the troops trapped in the Anzio enclave, there were two ways of existing and both were underground. The first was in large dugouts each holding about five men, where there was plenty of company but only a comparatively thin roof because the hole was too wide to support anything heavy. The second option was to dig a tiny foxhole about six-feet long, like a coffin, but with an entrance at an angle at one end. Ray liked his buddies well enough but he also wanted to stay alive, so he opted for the one-man foxhole, dug beside a felled pine tree. He covered it with branches and wood and mud, and discovered that at the end of every night's shelling, as more and more branches and debris landed on top, his roof became thicker and thicker, and therefore more secure.

However, although he felt safe enough in there, at just three feet deep it was hardly comfortable; any lower and the water level would have flooded the floor. He could just about lie there and read a book by the light of a small candle dug into the side. Sharing this miserable shelter was a stray puppy. The dog had become something of a lucky mascot as it could hear approaching shells coming long before Ray and his comrades could, and would immediately take cover.

By day, Ray would travel by jeep down the notorious 'Bowling Alley', a long, highly exposed and extremely hazardous disused railway line that led to the forward area. There, in a sunken road, were five tanks from his own Company G, hunkered down amongst the infantry. Ray's task was to take messages from the tanks to an observation post in a small, squat, one-storey shell of a building on the junction of the Bowling Alley and the sunken road. Message carrying was an extremely dangerous occupation, as any movement would attract German fire. There was never any room left in the GIs' foxholes along the sunken road, and so, in between running errands, Ray and his colleagues would take whatever cover they could between the tanks and the dirt bank. As he was well aware, Anzio was an easy place to get yourself killed.

The one consolation was that the Allies were firing greater amounts of ordnance at the Germans than the Germans were firing at them, and it was for this reason that, as the partisans' bomb shattered the spring

calm in Rome, Feldmarschall Kesselring agreed to call a halt to any
further offensive action along the Anzio front.

So it was that on that March day, a renewed stalemate developed
along the two fronts. The Germans had achieved a victory of sorts during
the third battle at Cassino; the Allies at Anzio. For Ray Saidel and
Hans-Jürgen Kumberg, and for the many thousands of other troops
opposing one another, this merely meant a lessening in the intensity of
the fighting. They still had to keep their wits about them and do their
best to make sure they survived this war of attrition. And that meant
concentrating on what was happening immediately around them. Their
war was one being fought on a very narrow front; and the lives of
innocent men – whether Italian or German – far away in distant Rome
were of no concern to them at all.

It was, however, of great concern to Feldmarschall Kesselring as he
arrived back at his headquarters north of the capital at around seven
o'clock that evening. The terror attack at the Via Rasella that afternoon
had caused fury and outrage among the German occupiers. It had also
given an ugly foretaste of the menace the guerrillas would present from
that day until the end of the war. Miraculously, not only had Carla and
Paolo safely escaped, so too had the other eleven Gappists involved in
the Via Rasella attack. The SS troops had suffered 60 per cent casualties.
Twenty-eight had been killed immediately in the initial attack and during
the following day that figure would rise to thirty-three. As an effective
unit, the 11th Company of the 3rd Battalion SS Police Regiment Bozen
had ceased to exist. Two civilians, a middle-aged man and a thirteen-
year-old boy, had also been killed. The street itself was now wrecked by
a massive thirty-foot crater and littered with debris.

The German response was swift. Moreover, the conversations that
followed between Rome, Germany, and the German command in Italy
late that afternoon and evening of 23 March were to have far-reaching
consequences for the remaining fourteen months of the war in Italy.

It was General Kurt Mälzer, the German Commandant of Rome, who
had first informed German Supreme Command South-West (SW) of
the attack, even though the SS troops had been policemen and therefore
came under the direct command and jurisdiction of General Karl Wolff,
the senior SS officer in Italy. Since Kesselring and his Chief of Staff,
General Siegfried Westphal, were still not back from the Anzio front at
this time, Mälzer had spoken to a staff officer at Supreme Command

SW, Oberst Dietrich Beerlitz. He had then informed the German High Command in Berlin, the OKW, who in turn informed Hitler.

The Führer had been spending the day quietly at the *Wolfsschanze* ('Wolf's Lair') – his underground bunker complex near Rastenburg in East Prussia – when he was interrupted with the news soon after the attack had taken place. He flew into a rage and demanded the kind of retribution that would 'make the world tremble'. He would, he vowed, destroy an entire quarter of Rome with everyone in it; a moment later he demanded the shooting of at least thirty Italians for every German killed. During the same rant this figure rose to fifty Italians to be shot for every slain SS man.

Hitler's reaction reached Beerlitz before Kesselring and Westphal's return and so he rang Generaloberst von Mackensen at AOK 14 head-quarters. Mälzer, Beerlitz and von Mackensen all recognised that the Führer's demands were excessive, but they also realised that something drastic and urgent had to be done. Partisan actions in Rome had, until then, largely targeted Neo-Fascist Italians rather than Germans. Neither these nor earlier German casualties had prompted any form of reprisal, but there was a feeling now that anti-partisan measures had been too lenient. Moreover, the events of that afternoon seemed to signal a depar-ture from previous partisan activities: this attack had been more violent and destructive, and it was close to the front line. A strong and speedy display of force was necessary. But what did von Mackensen consider was necessary? Beerlitz asked him. Mälzer had suggested shooting Italians at a ratio of 10:1; and now von Mackensen agreed, but stipulated that only those already sentenced to death and awaiting execution in prison should be proceeded against. Beerlitz duly reported this decision back to OKW in Berlin, who in turn presented the suggestion to Hitler.

When Kesselring finally reached his headquarters based at Monte Sorrate, a mountain north of the capital, he was quickly informed of the news and then spoke with SS Obersturmbannführer Herbert Kappler, the head of the *Sicherheitsdienst* (SD) – the SS intelligence service – in Rome, and asked him whether he had enough people awaiting execution to fill the ten to one criterion. Both Kesselring and Beerlitz, who was listening in, heard Kappler say that yes, he did have enough prisoners already condemned to death. The Field Marshal then received a call from the High Command in Berlin stating that Hitler definitely wanted ten Italians shot for every German killed that afternoon in Rome, and that that was a direct order. Later, some time between ten and eleven o'clock

that night, Westphal spoke with General Jodl, Hitler's Chief of Operations, in Berlin. Jodl repeated Hitler's order, and stressed that the
executions were to be carried out by the SD under Kappler's supervision.
'The Führer wishes that thorough action should be taken this time,' Jodl
told Westphal. 'Tell that to your *Feldmarschall*.'[1] The implication was
clear: Kesselring's Wehrmacht officers could not be trusted to carry out
such a brutal reprisal. Soon after this conversation, Kesselring confirmed
the order: ten Italians would be killed for every German soldier killed in
the Via Rasella, and the executions were to be implemented immediately,
within twenty-four hours.

The die had been cast.

The problem for Kappler was that despite his claim to the contrary, he
did not have anything like 280 prisoners already awaiting execution and
certainly not the 330 that were needed by the following afternoon. In
fact, there were only three prisoners in the whole of Rome already
sentenced to death. A looser classification was then hastily adopted:
candidates would be drawn from those 'worthy of death', but this still
only produced sixty-five Jews and a handful of known Communists.
Other criminals were rounded up, as were men from the Italian armed
forces who had been detained after the German occupation of Rome the
previous September. During the day more were frantically added to the
list, including a priest and a number of people detained by Neo-Fascist
authorities on largely spurious charges.

The dazed and disorientated prisoners were taken in butchers' lorries
to the Ardeatine Caves, just south of the city near the ancient catacombs
on the Appian Way. The first arrived shortly before 3.30 on the afternoon
of Friday, 24 March. The men, in groups of five, were then taken deep
into the dark caves, told to kneel and turn their heads to one side. They
were then shot.

To begin with, the executions were carried out with some semblance
of order, but as the bodies began to mount and the caves began to
fill with corpses, discipline, made worse by the amount of drink the
executioners had taken to help steel themselves for the task, began to
waver. The firing grew wild; moreover most of the executioners were
clerks rather than soldiers, and members of the SS and SD, who, like
Kappler, had only limited military training. Nearly forty of those killed
were completely decapitated by the wayward firing. Others were beaten
to death. More still were not killed instantly and were left to die through

suffocation and loss of blood. Somehow, an extra five men had been rounded up earlier that day. As witnesses to the executions they could not be spared, and so they too were shot, making the final tally of those slain that afternoon 335.

The massacre at the Ardeatine Caves was the first reprisal carried out by the Germans against the Italian people. It would not be their last; rather, it signalled the start of a policy to counteract partisan activity that was to cast a terrible shadow over Italy and which would fan the flames of a bloodbath that would last beyond the end of the war.

PART I

The Road to Rome

ONE

The Eve of Battle
May 1944

There were many nationalities and differing races in the two Allied armies waiting to go into battle. The British and Americans formed the largest contingents, but there were also French, Moroccans, Algerians, Canadians, New Zealanders (whites and Maori), Poles, Nepalese, Indians (all faiths), South Africans (white, Asian, black, Zulus), and in the air forces, Australians, Rhodesians and others beside. Whatever their differing creeds and wide-ranging backgrounds, they all were relieved to see that on this day, the eve of battle, the weather was being kind. Thursday, 11 May 1944, was a glorious day: warm, with blue skies, and, by the afternoon, not a rain cloud in sight, just as it had been for most of the month. By evening, the temperature had dropped somewhat, but it was still warm, with just the faintest trace of a breeze – even near the summit of Monte Cassino, some 1,700 feet above the valley below. In their foxholes, the men of the 45,600-strong II Polish Corps waited, repeatedly checking their weapons; eating a final meal; exchanging anxious glances. The minutes ticked by inexorably slowly. It was quiet up there, too; quieter than it had been for many days. Not a single gun fired. The mountain, it seemed, had been stilled.

It was now three weeks since the Poles had taken over the Monte Cassino sector and since then, almost every minute, both day and night, had been spent preparing for and thinking about the battle ahead. By day, the men had trained; they had held exercises in attacking strongly fortified positions, practising rock climbing and assaulting concrete bunkers. New flamethrowers were also introduced, while each squadron and platoon* was given clear and detailed instructions as to what they were supposed to do when the battle began.

---

*Although they were now operating as infantry, the Polish cavalry and armoured units kept their usual structure and formation.

By night, the Poles had been even busier. Vast amounts of ammunition and supplies had to be taken up the mountainside, a task that was impossible during daylight when the enemy would easily be able to spot them – secrecy was paramount; so, too, was saving lives for the battle ahead. It was also a task that could only be achieved by the use of pack mules and by the fortitude of the men, for there were just two paths open to them – both old mountain tracks, which for more than six miles could be watched by the enemy. A carefully adhered-to system had been quickly established. Supplies were brought from the rear areas by truck. Under carefully laid smoke screens, they were loaded onto smaller, lighter vehicles, then, as the mountain began to rise, they were transferred onto mules and finally carried by hand and on backs by the men themselves, slogging their way up the two mountain tracks that led to the forward positions. All this was done in the dark, without any lights, and as quietly as possible. Even so, the men were often fired upon. The German gunners around Monte Cassino would lay periodic barrages along various stretches of these mountain paths and despite their best efforts, casualties mounted – casualties II Polish Corps could ill-afford.

Now the waiting was almost over, and as the sun slipped behind the mountains on the far side of the Liri Valley, and darkness descended, the Poles knew that at long last the moment for which they had endured so much in the past four-and-a-half years was almost upon them.

In what had once been a lovely mountain meadow, the men of the 2nd Squadron, 12th Lancers, were now dug in. Part of the Polish Corps' 3rd Carpathian Division, they were some 600 yards from the crumbled ruins of the monastery, and the ground ahead of them was pock-marked and churned by shell holes, and strewn with twisted bits of metal and remnants of the dead. Not that twenty-seven-year-old Wladek Rubnikowicz had had much chance to examine the area that was to be his part of the battlefield. In an effort to keep their presence a secret, Wladek and his comrades had been forbidden to send out patrols to reconnoitre the area. In fact, since arriving in their positions on the night of 3 May, Wladek had done little but bring up more supplies by night and brace himself for the attack by day.

The Lancers were cavalry, trained to use armoured cars and to operate as a fast-moving reconnaissance unit, but for the battle they had become infantrymen, foot-sloggers like almost every other soldier that had fought across this damnable piece of land for the past four months. The armoured cars now waited for them miles behind the line with the rear echelons. Only once the battle was won, and the men were out of the mountains and into the valleys below, would they get their vehicles back.

For the vast majority of Polish troops now lying in wait on the mountain, their journey there had been long and tortuous – an epic trek that had seen them travel thousands of miles, crossing continents and enduring terrible losses and hardship – and Wladek was no exception. It was a miracle that he was alive at all.

The blitzkrieg that followed the German invasion of Poland on 1 September 1939 had lasted just twenty-eight days and on 29 September, the country was carved in two by the month-old allies, Germany and the Soviet Union. What had been a beacon of democracy was now subjugated under fascism in one half and Stalinist communism in the other. Its cities and towns lay in ruins, while its stunned people wondered how this apocalypse could have happened in such a short space of time.

Wladek, then a cadet with the Polish Army, had been wounded in the shoulder in the final days before the surrender. Left behind in a disused schoolhouse, he was helped by some local girls who tended him and brought him food and water and, once fit enough to walk, he began the long journey back home to Glebokie, a small town in what had been north-east Poland, but which had now been consumed by the Soviet Union.

His older brother had been killed in the fighting, leaving a wife and two small children, while his home town had been devastated by the war. 'I could see that every thing that made life worthwhile had come to standstill,' Wladek recalled. Nor could he stay at home. Russian troops were everywhere, arresting Poles in their droves. He eventually managed to get to Warsaw after travelling most of the way by clutching to the buffers of a train in temperatures well below freezing, and despite being arrested at the German–Russian border. Temporarily locked in a barn, he quickly escaped and made his way through the snow into the German-occupied half of Poland.

For a while Wladek worked for the Polish resistance movement, but on a mission back into Russian-occupied Poland, he was arrested at the border once again. This time he did not escape.

For thirteen long months, Wladek was held at Bialystok prison. He was one of fifty-six prisoners crammed into an eight-man cell. Occasionally he would be interrogated and beaten. Eventually he was sentenced to three years in a Siberian labour camp. In June 1941, he and 500 others were loaded onto a goods train, fifty to a wagon, and sent to a labour camp in the Arctic Circle.

Ventilation for the wagon came from a small, barred hole and an opening in the floor used as a toilet. There was not enough air and they all struggled to breathe properly. Each prisoner received 400 grammes of bread and one herring at the start of the journey, but the salty herring made them thirstier. They were eventually given a small cup of water each, which, they were told, had to last until the following day. Dysentery soon gripped many men, and most had fever. A number died, their bodies remaining where they lay amongst the living. 'Can you imagine?' says Wladek. 'We didn't realise then that of course the Soviets hoped these conditions would kill off many of us on the way.'

The journey lasted two weeks. The further they travelled the more bleak and desolate the surrounding country became. Eventually they halted at a railhead on the Pechora River. Staggering off their wagon, they were herded towards a transit camp before continuing their journey by paddle steamer. This took them a further 700 miles north. They disembarked a week later at Niryan-Mar Gulag, in one of the most northern parts of Russia.

Conditions had been bad at Bialystok, but Niryan-Mar reached new depths of deprivation. The men were housed in large marquee-like summer tents, each sheltering around 180 men, and although they each had a rough wooden bunk to sleep on, there were neither mattresses nor blankets and the prisoners slept fully clothed at all times. They kept their clothes stuffed with cotton wool and although they just about managed to keep warm, they were soon plagued by lice.

Every day the prisoners were put to work at the nearby port on the mouth of the Pechora for twelve-hour days of physically demanding labour, sustained only by meagre rations of water and hard bread. As Wladek says: 'We worked as slaves.'

The camp was surrounded by barbed wire and watchtowers, but there was nowhere a prisoner could go even if he did escape: they were miles from anywhere and the surrounding forests and marshes were home to wolves. Even so, Wladek did make one bid for freedom. A Swedish vessel came into port and thinking the crew seemed friendly and sympathetic, he managed to slip away and hide in the hold. He misjudged them, however. Soon discovered, he was handed back to the Soviets. 'The punishment I received I shall never forget,' he says; Wladek was beaten to within an inch of his life.

Inevitably, many prisoners succumbed to disease. Illness, however, was no excuse not to work. Despite high fevers and crippling dysentery, prisoners had to keep going, as 'the alternative to working was death'. Wladek's malnutrition caused him to start to go blind. His affliction was worse in the evening and to ensure that he did not step out of line and that he made it safely back to camp each night, he depended on others to guide him.

This hell did eventually come to an end, however. Months after the German invasion of the Soviet Union in June 1941, he and his fellow prisoners were released and, armed with a free rail pass and some meagre rations, were told to head south. As they did so, Stalin had already begun to renege on his promises and large numbers, Wladek included, were forcibly detained on collective farms. He and several others managed to escape by stealing and pilfering, and, weeks later, they finally reached the Polish camp at Guzar in Uzbekistan, one of the most southerly points in the Soviet Union.

Even before Wladek had left the gulag and set out on the journey that would take him eventually from the Arctic Circle to the edge of Persia, he had been in a weakened physical state – and just a fraction of his normal body weight. Several thousand miles later, having travelled by rail, boat, and on sore and bloody feet, he was seriously ill. Struggling with a high fever, he staggered to the Polish camp's registration office and was then sent to the first aid station, where he was told he had contracted typhoid.

Meanwhile, General Wladyslaw Anders in the southern Soviet Union, and General Sikorski, the Commander-in-Chief of the Free Polish Forces, in London, had been having a difficult time with the Soviet leaders. It had been the Poles' hope and intention that the reconstituted Polish Army should fight as a whole against Germany on the Eastern Front, which would send out a strong signal to the world about Polish solidarity and their fighting spirit. Stalin, however, who had designs on Poland if and when Germany was beaten, had no intention of allowing this to happen, and so had been making life as difficult as possible, giving the Poles mustering areas and camps in inhospitable parts of the Soviet Union where disease – such as typhoid – was rife, and waylaying potential Polish troops by forcing them to work on collective farms.

Eventually, however, Stalin decided he wanted to free himself of any obligations to arm and provide for the Polish Army, no matter how useful they might one day be. Churchill had let it be known that he wanted Polish forces fighting alongside the Allies in the Middle East, and so under pressure from both Britain and America, Sikorski agreed that Anders' Polish Army should be evacuated to Persia, from where they would train under British guidance.

Wladek Rubnikowicz was still making his miraculous recovery from typhoid when the first evacuation to Persia was made, but he joined the next one a few months later, only to contract malaria. After a couple of weeks the fever subsided leaving him with recurrences of the disease that would plague him for years to come. Things were looking up, however. He made his way to Iraq, where he joined General Anders' camp at Quisil Ribat Oasis and where training began in earnest. It was whilst there that Wladek also heard good news about his parents. They too had escaped from the Soviet Union and were at a camp in Iran. He even managed to get leave to see them.

Now with the 12th Polish Lancers of the newly formed II Polish Corps, Wladek moved with his regiment to Kirkuk. With plentiful rations and a moderately balanced diet, he and the rest of his Polish comrades gradually began to build up their strength. 'We all felt anxious to get to the front,' he says, 'and begin fighting for the liberation of Poland. That may sound strange, but it's true.'

After further training in Palestine, the 12th Lancers, part of the 3rd Carpathian Division, reached Italy in December 1943. Several months were spent carrying out final training and acclimatising, until, in the middle of April, they were moved up to the Cassino front.

In fact, General Sir Oliver Leese, commander of the British Eighth Army, under which II Polish Corps served, had visited General Anders on 24 March and proposed that his troops be given the task of taking the Monte Cassino heights and then the hill-top village of Piedimonte, several miles to the west in what would become the fourth battle of Cassino. 'It was,' noted Anders, 'a great moment for me.'[2]

The Polish commander had suffered as well in the previous years of war. Captured by the Russians in September 1939, Anders had been imprisoned in Lubianka after refusing to join the Red Army. Released after the German invasion of the Soviet Union, he was given permission to trace and recruit Polish POWs held in the gulags. It was largely thanks to his tireless efforts that he managed to muster some 160,000 men in Uzbekistan and Kazakhstan who were then trained to continue the fight for Poland. Now, at Cassino, he had a small corps of two divisions and an armoured brigade made up of 45,626 fighting men. It was an incredible achievement by the dashing and charismatic fifty-two-year-old.

For a few moments only, Anders had considered Leese's suggestion.

He was well aware that Monte Cassino had not been taken in two months of bitter fighting; that it had hitherto eluded the efforts of battle-hardened and highly experienced troops. The task that Leese was putting forward was an awesome proposition for his men in what would be their first battle since the fall of Poland. 'The stubbornness of the German defence at Cassino and on Monastery Hill was already a byword,' Anders observed. 'I realised that the cost in lives must be heavy, but I realised too the importance of the capture of Monte Cassino to the Allied cause, and most of all to that of Poland.'[3] And so he accepted.

Now, on the evening of 11 May, the moment had almost arrived. Wladek and his comrades had been thoroughly briefed. The messages of Generals Alexander and Leese to their troops had been translated into Polish and the single sheets of thin paper passed around. So too had Anders' own message. 'Soldiers!' he wrote, 'The moment for battle has arrived. We have long awaited the moment for revenge and retribution over our hereditary enemy . . . The task assigned to us will cover with glory the name of the Polish soldier all over the world.'

Wladek and the men of 2nd Squadron, 12th Lancers were as one behind their commander. Certainly, Wladek was scared, but he was excited too. 'We all wanted to be able to fight for our country,' he says. 'All of us, 100 per cent and 100 per cent more, felt a sense of honour at going into battle for Poland.'

It was not only the Poles who felt ready for the coming battle. Operation DIADEM, the codename for the battle for Rome, had been launched by the Commander-in-Chief of Allied Armies in Italy at a commanders' conference on the last day of February 1944.* Since then, General Alexander, his staff, and commanders had been working flat out, reorganising and training troops, planning and making sure that nothing was left to chance; they were not going to be caught short for want of a horseshoe.

All of the commanders felt tense. For every single one involved, whether at divisional, corps or army level, this was to be the biggest battle of their careers: more men, more guns; more aircraft above them. Each was acutely aware of how much was at stake. Despite the build-up of men and materiel, and despite the improved weather, there was unlikely to be any easy victory. The flooding in the valley had receded but the Liri Valley, only six miles at its widest and just four at the greater

*Allied Central Mediterranean Forces had become Allied Forces in Italy on 9 March 1944.

part of its length, was narrow for a two-corps assault. The serpentine River Liri was too wide and deep to ford, while numerous other tributaries and water courses cut across the valley and hence the path of the attackers. There were also heavy German defences: concrete dugouts, gun turrets, machine-gun posts, mines and wire. Furthermore, overlooking this softly undulating valley of pasture, cornfields and broken woodland – slow going for wheels and tracks – were the imposing mountain ranges, filled with yet more carefully positioned guns, machine guns and troops. Indeed, the mouth of the Liri Valley, the gateway to Rome, was protected by two superb artillery positions, Monte Cassino to the north, and Monte Maio to the south. In four months of fighting these 'gate posts' had not been cleared. Few of the Allied commanders, however, could have felt this pressure more keenly than Lieutenant-General Mark W. Clark, Commander of the US Fifth Army.

The planning for Operation DIADEM largely complete, Clark spent a final few days touring the front, briefing his commanders and inspecting his troops, many of whom would be going into battle for the first time. Earlier that morning of Thursday, 11 May, Clark had inspected also the US 36th Division, pinning a number of medals on the chests of Texans and addressing them briefly. It was the 36th Division who had been involved in the first disastrous attempt to break into the Liri Valley back in January, when they had tried to cross the narrow Rapido River that runs south through the town. Even before that attack, the auspices had not been good. The British 46th Division had already failed to cross the wider River Garigliano further south – an operation designed to help the Texans in their task to cross the Rapido – and had warned the Americans that the ground on the far side of the river was heavily defended. Moreover, they had insufficient river craft with which to do the job. Yet Major-General Walker, 36th Division's commander, had assured Clark, despite considerable private doubts, that the operation was still achievable. Clark, who had urgently needed to divert German troops away from the Anzio beachheads for the Allied landing that would take place two days later, had consequently given the go-ahead.

In the forty-eight hour operation that followed, some 1,700 men were killed or wounded. Rather like the men on the Somme on 1 July 1916, the Texans had been cut down in swathes. The river had run red with blood; the bodies stacked six high in places. In America, the pressmen had labelled the 'Bloody Rapido' the worst disaster since Pearl Harbor.

General Clark had taken his share of the blame, but within a few days it became apparent that the American-led operation at Anzio, Operation SHINGLE, had also fallen short of its aims. Neither the Rapido disaster nor the setback at Anzio had been entirely Clark's fault and both operations had been executed because of pressure higher up the chain of command. But an army commander lives and dies by his successes, and by the spring of 1944 – on the battlefield at any rate – these had been all too few. Clark was unaware that his position was under threat and that discussions had taken place about whether to remove him, but he nonetheless keenly felt the frustrations of his comparative lack of success.

Mark Clark – or 'Wayne' as friends knew him – had just turned forty-eight at the start of May. Standing six foot three inches tall, he was lean and muscular, his hair still dark, and despite a prominently hawkish nose, he was a youthful-looking and handsome three-star general who towered over most of his subordinates and superiors alike. One of the few American commanders who had seen action in the last war, he had led a battalion in France in 1917, until wounded when a shell had exploded nearby. He spent the rest of the war as a captain carrying out staff duties. It was a rank he kept for sixteen years, sitting out the post-war doldrums with mounting impatience.

In 1933 his fortunes had finally begun to change, with promotion followed by time spent at both the US Command and General Staff College and the Army War College, so marking him out for future high command. By the summer of 1937 he had joined the 3rd Division, where he renewed his friendship with his old West Point friend, Dwight D. Eisenhower. By 1940, he was a lieutenant-colonel and was appointed chief of staff to General Lesley McNair, the man commanded to expand, train, and reorganise the US Army ready for war. Clark immediately showed his exceptional aptitude for planning and organisation, demonstrating great resources of energy, intelligence, enthusiasm, and an ability to get things done, and done fast.

Catching the eye of General Marshall, the US Chief of Staff, Clark was sent to Britain in 1942 along with Eisenhower to arrange for the reception and training of American troops and to begin preparations for the invasion of Continental Europe. When immediate Allied plans were redirected towards an invasion of northwest Africa, Eisenhower was made Commander-in-Chief with Clark as his deputy. As head of planning for Operation TORCH, Clark deservedly won a great deal of credit for pulling off what was the largest seaborne invasion the world had ever known. It was also no small thanks to Clark and his pre-invasion discussions with Vichy French commanders that the resulting landing was a comparative walkover.

But however much Clark had proved himself as a planner and diplomat, he desperately wanted the chance for operational command but, as Eisenhower's official deputy, he knew he was in danger of spending the rest of the war as a desk man. Consequently, he began to badger his chief for his own command until he was eventually appointed commander of the newly created US Fifth Army, the first American army headquarters to be formed overseas. Although for the first few months it was little more than a training organisation, it was then that he began to develop a deep affection for Fifth Army, a force that he nurtured and considered his own. Together, he believed, they were destined to achieve great victories.

Not until the invasion of Italy was Clark finally given the chance he so craved, of leading his men in battle. Given the task of planning the main Allied landings at Salerno, VI Corps from his Fifth Army duly landed on 9 September 1943. It was almost a massive failure. Heavily contested by Kesselring's AOK 10, it had been a far more bitter fight than either the North African or Sicily landings. Clark, however, had showed resolve and courage, quickly getting himself onto the beachhead and taking firm and decisive command. At one point, during the second and most threatening German counterattack, he took personal charge of an anti-tank unit and turned back eighteen German tanks at almost point-blank range. The Allies regained their footing, a bridgehead was firmly established, and as Axis forces withdrew north towards the defences of the Gustav Line, Clark and his Fifth Army quickly took Naples, a key port on the route to Rome.

Despite this success, however, Clark suffered the mutterings of some. At the height of Salerno, with defeat a distinct possibility, Clark realised he had made no provision for an evacuation should the worst occur. Quickly trying to rectify this, he ordered his staff to make the necessary plans for a withdrawal. Although purely a contingency plan, news of these orders spread; to some, this was not seen as Clark's pragmatism shining through, but rather a sign that he had momentarily lost his nerve.

In fact, at Salerno and in the fighting in Italy since the Allied invasion, Clark had proved himself an extremely able battlefield commander. He possessed a thorough understanding of modern all-arms tactics, an ability to grasp and see the bigger strategic overview, and was not afraid of taking difficult decisions or the rap if things did not go according to plan. However, many found him overly blunt, arrogant even; he could be prickly – and brusque and heavy handed with his subordinates. He was the boss – and no one was allowed to forget it. If that made him unpopular to some, well to hell with it; winning battles and the war was what counted, not worrying about telling people some harsh home truths. Again, in many respects, there was nothing wrong with this approach, but unfortunately Clark also suffered from a deep-rooted hang-up that many of his fellow commanders, whether Alexander or Leese, or the British corps commanders attached to his Fifth Army, had considerably more battlefield experience than he and he suspected that they looked down on him because of this. There is no evidence that anyone regarded this as a defect at all, but it niggled him considerably and made him far too quick to see the decisions of Alexander and others as an attempt to undermine him, his authority, and to belittle the efforts of his Fifth Army.

Just six days earlier, on 5 May, this paranoia had come to the fore when Alexander made a visit to the Anzio bridgehead, from where the US-led VI Corps was to make its break-out once the southern front had been sufficiently broken in the forthcoming battle. There, Alexander had spoken with Major-General Lucian Truscott, the VI Corps commander. After hearing Truscott's plans, Alexander suggested he should be concentrating on only one course of action, namely to spearhead north-eastwards towards Cisterna, Cori and Valmontone, as had been previously agreed with Clark and all concerned. Truscott then informed Clark of this conversation. Outraged, Clark rang Alexander's headquarters and demanded to speak with the British commander. 'I told Alexander,' Clark wrote in his diary, 'that I resented deeply his issuing any instructions to my subordinates.' Alexander, by now used to Clark's occasional fits of over-sensitiveness, assured him he had not intended to undermine his authority in any way, and that he had merely made the point lightly in the course of his conversation with Truscott, gently reminding Clark that he was only telling Truscott what had already been agreed. It seemed to be what the American wanted to hear. 'This is a small matter,' Clark noted later, his honour sated and his feathers smoothed once more, 'but it is well that I let him know now, as I have in the past, that he will deal directly with me and never with a subordinate.'[4]

However, on the eve of battle – 11 May – that day of days, Clark was playing the part of army commander perfectly. It is typical of him that he should have chosen that morning to address the men of the 36th Texas Division – the men who blamed him above all for the Bloody Rapido – looking them in the eye and stirring them for the battle to come, a battle in which yet more of them would lose their lives.

News that the offensive would at last begin that night was given out to men along the line throughout the day, in the form of thin paper fliers. In the case of those in Eighth Army, one was from General Alexander and the other from General Leese. Then, in the afternoon, battalion commanders gathered their officers around them and gave them a general as well as a more specific brief. The 19th Indian Brigade, for example, part of 8th Indian Division, had a key role that opening night of the battle. 'Tonight,' the Brigade Commander, Major Parker, told his officers, 'we're attacking the Gustav Line across the River Rapido here. We'll have the Poles and 4th Division on our right and French troops on our left. The Fifth Army are making a push at the same time. This is the first blow of the Second Front. It will be closely followed by the invasion of Western Europe and a general attack by the Russians in the south-east.' The attack, Major Parker continued, would begin with a massive barrage at 11 p.m. using just under 1,700 guns – almost double what had been used at the Battle of Alamein in November 1942. To begin with, the fire would be counter-battery, that is, falling behind the German forward positions in an effort to hit the enemy's own artillery. Then it would be directed against targets on the front. After this opening barrage, the infantry would begin their attack. In their own sector along the Liri Valley, the division would make their assault alongside the 4th Division, crossing the River Garigliano under cover of continued artillery fire, while the Poles assaulted Cassino and the *Goums* and part of the French Expeditionary Force attacked the Aurunci Mountains on their left, 'with instructions to cut off the heads of every German they meet'. Furthest to the south, along the Minturno Ridge that runs to the sea, the US II Corps would attack with the new boys, the 85th and 88th Infantry Divisions.

The task of 19th Infantry Brigade was twofold. The Indian battalions were to get themselves across the river, whilst the Argyll and Sutherland Highlanders were to invade what was known as the 'Liri Appendix', a narrow finger of land between where the Garigliano turned sharply and ran parallel to the River Liri before actually joining it. From the moment the barrage began, the Appendix would be covered by machine-gun fire to keep the Germans' heads down. 'So if you hear close machine-gun fire,' the Brigade Major told them, 'you'll know it'll be our fellows pumping lead into this Appendix.' The barrage would not finish until 4 a.m., and would then be followed by wave after wave of Allied bombers and fighter planes – 'as many as we'll want'.

Having given his brief outline, Major Parker paused, folded away his map, then smiled dryly at his men. 'We hope,' he told them, 'this will do the trick.'[5]

Although any infantry heading into battle obviously faced extreme danger, amongst those men most at risk were the junior officers. American Lieutenant Bob Wiggans was a platoon commander with Company D of the 1st Battalion, 338th Infantry Regiment – part of the 85th 'Custer' Division.* The 85th had reached Italy less than seven weeks before, sailing into Naples under the smoke and pall of the still-erupting Mount Vesuvius, and had only been sent up to the front in the middle of April. The entire division, along with the also newly arrived 88th Division, were the first American all-draftee divisions to go into combat. Bearing the brunt of the Americans' initial assault in the coming battle, their performance would be the first proper test of the US Army's wartime training and replacement system – a system that had been set up in some part by General Mark Clark.

A twenty-six-year-old farmer from upstate New York, Bob Wiggans had undergone reserve officer infantry training whilst at Cornell University – an activity that was compulsory for all male students – and so when he was given his draft notice just a couple of weeks after the Japanese attack on Pearl Harbor on 7 December 1941, he was immediately sent to Camp Shelby in Mississippi to join the cadre that would help form and train the brand-new 85th Infantry Division.

Bob regarded 7 December 1941 as one of the saddest days of his life. The war would not only take him away from the farm he had bought less than a year before, but also from Dot, his wife of five months. Leaving home was a terrible wrench, but he believed that the United States was doing the right thing, and that Nazism had to be defeated.

*The 85th was given the association 'Custer' because the division was activiated in 1917 at Camp Custer in Michigan, so named after the Civil War and Indian Wars general who had led the Michigan Cavalry Brigade at the Battle of Gettysburg.

In the two years in which Bob had served with the 85th, it had grown from nothing to a fully-formed and trained combat division. However, the division showed its inexperience during its first few days on the Cassino front, when it took over positions from the British in the rubble and remains of the town of Minturno, the most westerly point of the front line. Most of the 85th's men found the whole experience of being on the battlefield and close to the enemy and of coming under shellfire deeply unsettling. Bob had been called out one night offering to help 3rd Platoon who were convinced there were Germans crawling around in the rubble above them. It turned out the 'enemy' were just rats scurrying about. Bob had found that hurtling through the ruined town in his jeep, distributing mail, ammunition and supplies, was enough to get his heart racing. 'These night missions were harrowing enough with the interdictory artillery fire,' he noted, 'but the awful smell of decaying flesh from under the rubble made it infinitely worse.'[6]

That the 'Custermen' were a little jumpy is no wonder: all the draftees, officers and enlisted men were entirely new to war, with no battlefield experience to draw upon. And like the Poles and so many of the assaulting troops, their first battle would be one of the biggest their countries had ever taken part in.*

That afternoon, back in his caravan at Fifth Army headquarters, General Clark dictated a message of best wishes to his fellow army commander, General Sir Oliver Leese – happy, on this occasion, to observe inter-army protocol. The British commander promptly replied in kind. 'We all in Eighth Army,' wrote Leese, 'send your Fifth Army our cordial good wishes and look confidently forward to advancing shoulder to shoulder together.'[7]

Leese was impatient for the battle to begin, and though apprehensive was quietly confident. 'Ultra' intercepts of German Enigma codes passed on by the Government Code and Cypher School at Bletchley Park, Buckinghamshire, suggested that the Allies' elaborate deception plans

---

*There were 158,805 men in AOK 10 and AOK 14, while Alexander could call on 602,618 Allied troops in Italy at this time, of whom 253,859 were British, 231,306 were American, 71,827 were French and 45,626 were Polish. Although nothing like this number would take part in the coming battles, Alexander was still able to have the three to one advantage in manpower along the main battle line that he believed was necessary for victory. Even so, when one considers the air forces and men in reserve, the best part of a million men were to be directly and indirectly involved in the offensive.

had worked and that the Germans were not expecting a major attack until the following month. Leese had more than a quarter of a million men under his command – 'an immense army' – all of whom were fully trained and briefed. Ammunition and petrol were ready in dumps at the front line. Everyone was agreed on the battle plan, and from his manic tours around the front, Leese believed his troops to be in good heart. 'It has been a vast endeavour and it will be a huge battle,' he wrote. 'All we want is fine weather and a bit of luck.'[8]

As the evening shadows lengthened, infantrymen along the front furtively began moving up to their start lines and forming-up positions. In the Liri Valley, men uncovered assault boats; bridging parties moved trucks of Bailey bridge sections forward, while other sappers reeled out long lines of white marker tape to later guide the troops in the dark towards specific river crossing points.

Dusk soon gave way to the darkness of night, and the first desultory shelling of Cassino began just as it had every night for weeks since the end of the third battle of Cassino in March. Partly as cover, and partly to give the impression that this was just like any other evening along the front, the shelling gradually died out, so that at ten o'clock, when General Leese sat down to write to his wife, Margie, the front seemed eerily quiet.

'In sixty minutes,' he scrawled on the thick blue writing paper Margie Leese had sent out to him, 'hell will be let loose, the whole way from Monte Cairo to the sea. At 11 p.m. on 11 May, 2,000 guns will burst forth.'* It had, he added, been a lovely day, and it was now a glorious night.

A huge weight of responsibility rested on Leese's shoulders and those of his fellow commanders, not only for the men under their command but also because there was so much at stake with this, the biggest battle the Western Allies had yet attempted in the war. A sweeping, crushing victory promised untold riches, yet defeat would not only be a blow to Allied chances of success in launching an invasion of northern France, but it would also wreck the future of the Italian campaign and with it British credibility in particular. No wonder General Leese was counting down the minutes.

---

*Leese was never particularly accurate with his facts and figures when writing to his wife. In fact, there were around 1,660 guns in action: 1,060 along Eighth Army's front, and 600 along that of Fifth Army.

TWO

Battle Begins
11–12 May 1944

Manning his machine-gun post amongst the rubble near what had once been the Via Casilina – the main road to Rome – was Hans-Jürgen Kumberg. The 4th Fallschirmjäger Regiment had moved down from the heights of Monte Cassino a month earlier. Although the ruins provided excellent defensive cover, the place was a hell hole, swarming with malaria-infested mosquitoes and reeking of death and sewage. The men were short of just about everything: water, food, cigarettes; reinforcements that had been promised but had not materialised. And they were exhausted: living like sewer rats and being pummelled by relentless Allied harassing fire was not conducive to sleep. Only the Pioneer – engineers – battalion of the 4th Regiment had arrived to help, having joined them alongside the Via Casilina just the day before.

Amongst them was twenty-three-year-old company commander Lieutenant Joseph 'Jupp' Klein, a battle-hardened veteran of the Eastern Front, Sicily and the second and third battles of Cassino. His company's recent leave had been the first since arriving in Italy the previous August following the Sicily campaign and had done much to revive their spirits, but after a day back at the front they still had much to do. There were more machine-gun positions to be built, more tunnels to dig and retreat routes to be prepared.

On the night of 11 May, at eleven o'clock, Jupp Klein was standing on the debris-strewn Via Casilina, talking to one of his corporals, when 'suddenly from heaven to hell the night became as bright as day'.⁹ As the shells screamed overhead, Jupp immediately recognised that the sheer scale of the barrage could only mean one thing: the offensive had started – and sooner than any of them had expected.

A few miles north in a concrete bunker along a narrow valley between the mountains above Cassino, Major Georg Zellner, commander of the

3rd Battalion *Hoch-und-Deutschmeister* Reichs Grenadier Regiment, gathered around him a few of his officers. Throughout the day he had been receiving the best wishes of his men on this his thirty-ninth birthday. Some of his staff had even brought him some flowers picked from the mountain. The major, however, was not in good spirits. Desperately homesick, he hoped for a letter or card from his wife and two young daughters back home in Passau in south-east Germany, but nothing had yet arrived. All day, he'd waited, praying there would be some word from them on the evening's ration cart but nothing came.

Two bottles of *sekt* – sparkling wine – had arrived for him and he and a few of his officers were about to share them. Having eased the cork from the first of the bottles, Georg was about to take a birthday gulp when the world seemed to be ripped apart as the massed Allied guns roared the opening salvo of the battle. 'We drink the *sekt* anyway,' he noted drily.[10]

Watching the barrage from the safety of Monte Trocchio, behind the Allied lines, was twenty-eight-year-old Lieutenant Ted Wyke-Smith, a former steel engineer from Sheffield now serving with 78th Division Royal Engineers. As commander of a bridging unit, his job was to be amongst the division's spearhead as it advanced, once the 4th and 8th Indian Divisions had made the initial breakthrough, and build Bailey bridges over the numerous rivers and anti-tank ditches that barred the Allied progress. Ted had been sitting in his tented dugout listening to nightingales in the trees nearby when the guns opened fire. 'It was terrific,' he remembers. 'The noise was incredible and even where we were, several miles behind the lines, the ground trembled.' Curiously, however, the nightingales began singing again shortly after. 'It was most extraordinary,' says Ted, 'a concerto of nightingales and cannons.'

The first infantry to attack were the unblooded Americans of the 85th Infantry Division, who set off from their start positions the moment the barrage began. None of the French and American troops of Fifth Army had any rivers to cross, but they faced formidable obstacles nonetheless. The 1st and 3rd Battalions of the 338th Infantry Regiment had been ordered to assault a 400-foot high ridge studded with knolls, known as Spigno Saturnia. Terraced and dotted with farmhouses and occasional olive groves, the forward slopes were well defended by the infantry regiments of the German 94th Division.

Company D of the 1st Battalion had been given 'Point 131' as their first objective – the most imposing and best-defended height along the ridge. Lieutenant Bob Wiggans had been impressed by the scale of their barrage and had begun the advance through the wheat fields and olive groves with a certain amount of confidence. As the barrage lifted, however, he realised to his horror that the Germans, hidden in their well-constructed concrete bunkers, were almost completely unharmed.

'We moved forward and immediately drew all kinds of fire,' he noted, 'machine gun, automatic weapon, rifle, mortar, and artillery. So many men were killed.'[11] Although the Custermen had briefly gained the crest, they became pinned down and with reinforcements unable to reach them, they were forced to fall back halfway down the slopes. As Bob paused, he glanced at a ditch next to him where five men of his company were already lying dead. For two years they'd been training for this moment, yet for so many of them it had all been over in a trice.

It was not only the 1st Battalion that were being stopped in their tracks. Elsewhere along the southernmost part of the front, other American units were coming up against a wall of enemy fire and finding it almost impossible to make any headway. On their right, the French were also struggling. The *Goumiers* managed to take the heights of Monte Faito, but other objectives could not be taken as the colonial troops had been confronted with German flamethrowers as well as heavy mortar and machine-gun fire.

Meanwhile, in the Liri Valley, barely anything had gone right for the Allies. After the warm day and suddenly cool night, river mists had developed along the River Garigliano and then mingled with the intense smoke caused by the biggest barrage of the war. Despite weeks of endlessly practising river crossings, no one had considered the effect the smoke from the guns would have on visibility. Nor had the planners appreciated just how strong the current would be in the 'Gari'. Many of those crossing in assault boats were swept away, while others were destroyed by machine-gun fire and mortars. Meanwhile the sappers who had been due to lay six Bailey bridges under the light of the moon had found the fog as thick as the worst kind of London pea-souper. Their task had been almost impossible. Only by a miracle and enormous ingenuity was the first successfully built by 9 a.m. on the 12th. Another was open for business an hour later, but attempts to build the others failed amidst enemy fire and appalling fog.

The Poles had not fared much better. They had not launched their assault until 1 a.m., two hours after the barrage had opened up and some time after the 8th Indian and 4th Divisions had attacked in the valley below. As a result, the German paratroopers were already alert to the possibility of an attack. To make matters worse for the Poles, the 3rd Fallschirmjäger Regiment, whose positions they were attacking, were in the process of relieving a number of their troops, so in the cross-over there were many more enemy forces opposing them than there might have been. This extra German fire power proved decisive. Although the Poles reached their first objectives, they were soon pinned down, and, like the Americans, struggled to get reinforcements and further supplies forward. By evening the following day, they had suffered 1,800 casualties – nearly a quarter of their attacking strength – and had been driven back to their starting positions.

Wladek Rubnikowicz and the 12th Lancers, in their positions below the rubble of the monastery, had been given the task of sending out reconnaissance parties across no-man's-land, while the main force attacked the high ground to the north of the monastery. It was the first time they had ventured from their positions and although not part of the main attack, they had still come under heavy enemy machine-gun and mortar fire. It was merely a taste of what was to come.

News of the unfolding battle was patchy. Visibility, through the thick blanket of mist and cordite smoke that smothered the valley, was no more than ten yards and only snippets of information trickled in to HQ. Despite the paucity of news, the Signals Office was a hub of activity, with exchanges and calls coming through constantly. The Argyll and Sutherland Highlanders had been cut to pieces at the Liri Appendix, but the division as a whole had captured a small but critical bridgehead. RAF Spitfires were soon patrolling overhead; then USAF bombers came over to paste the German positions. Reinforcements arrived for the Appendix, but the enemy mortaring did not let up.

At his Tactical Headquarters near Venafro, less than ten miles west of Cassino, General Leese appeared to be as unaware of the situation as most of the attacking troops, noting 'there is a vast smokescreen like a yellow London fog over the battlefield'. Yet the Germans couldn't see very clearly either. As General Alexander had intended, Feldmarschall Kesselring's forces had been caught completely off guard. On the morning of the 11th at AOK 10 headquarters, Generaloberst von Vietinghoff's chief of staff had reported to Kesselring's headquarters 'nothing special is happening here'.[12] Allied air superiority had prevented the Luftwaffe from carrying anything but the sparsest of aerial reconnaissance, while carefully executed deception plans had convinced the German commander that the Allies intended to make another amphibious landing, either to reinforce the troops at Anzio, or further north of Rome, near the port of Civitavecchia. Kesselring also had it in mind that the Allies might try an airborne assault in the Liri Valley near Frosinone. Moreover, German intelligence suggested that the Allies had far more troops in reserve and fewer at the front than was the case – which was also considered to be evidence that the Allies were preparing another attack north of the Gustav Line.

Because of this, Kesselring had left the front line relatively thinly defended. Most of his reserves were either north of the Gustav Line or around Rome. Both German armies had been in the process of regrouping since the beginning of May, but once again, thanks to Allied air dominance, movement by day had been all but impossible and so this reorganisation had not yet completely finished.

The Werfer Regiment 71, for example, had been withdrawn from the front line a couple of weeks before and moved back into reserve to give it a chance to regroup and rest. An artillery regiment of six-barrelled rocket mortars – *nebelwerfer*, or 'moaning minnies' as the Allies called them – the Werfer Regiment 71 had needed this break after a long stint of front-line duties. Eighth Battery commander, Oberleutnant Hans Golda, had heard the muffled noises from the front and seen flashes of light to the south, and had gone to bed that night feeling restless. His unease had been well founded. In the early hours he had been woken by Major Timpkes who telephoned with the news that the Allied offensive had begun and that they were to get going to the front right away. 'Calmly and seriously we got ready to march,' he noted. 'Our recovery time had been cut short after two weeks.'[13]

But German troops in Italy were mostly a stoical bunch. They recognised that while the attacker could dictate the timing of his assault, it was the role of the defender to do his best – to respond as well as he could, whether properly rested or not.

THREE

Churchill's Opportunism

On the morning of 11 May, the British Prime Minister had dictated a letter to Alexander, his commander in Italy. 'All our thoughts and hopes are with you in what I trust and believe will be a decisive battle, fought to a finish,' wrote Churchill, 'and having for its object the destruction and ruin of the armed force of the enemy south of Rome.'[14]

Ever since the agreement to invade southern Italy the previous summer, Churchill had been looking forward to the day the Allies captured Rome. 'He who holds Rome,' he had told President Roosevelt and Marshal Stalin the previous November, 'holds the title deeds of Italy.' This was perhaps overstating the case, but there was no doubting the enormous psychological fillip that the capture of Rome – which would be the first European capital to be taken – would provide.

Yet despite the considerable commitment of the Allies – and Britain in particular – to the Italian campaign, their presence there had never been part of any long-agreed master plan. Rather, it had been purely opportunistic, a decision born of a series of unfolding events, each one bringing Italy closer and closer to the typhoon of steel that would rip through it.

The seeds of this momentous decision date back to a meeting between a US general and the Russian Foreign Minister in Washington DC in late May 1942. Normally wary of promising too much, the US Chief of Staff General George Marshall, America's most senior military figure, nonetheless assured Vyacheslav Molotov that the United States would start a second front before the end of the year. Three days later, speaking to Molotov on 1 June, President Roosevelt reiterated his determination to help the Soviets by engaging German troops on land some time during 1942.

What Roosevelt and Marshall had in mind was an Allied invasion of

Continental Europe. America's commitment to a 'Europe-first' rather than a 'Pacific-first' policy had been agreed with Britain more than six months before, in December 1941, at the hastily arranged Washington Conference following the US's entry into the war. The Americans agreed that Nazi Germany, rather than Japan, posed the greatest immediate threat, especially since the Soviet Union appeared to be a hair's breadth away from defeat. Such a collapse would have been catastrophic for the Western Allies, with the weight of the Nazi war machine turned against them. Furthermore, Germany would then have had access to all the oil and minerals it needed; indeed, it was for these essential raw materials, above all, that Hitler had ordered the invasion of the Soviet Union. Britain and the United States, not the USSR, were regarded as the most dangerous enemy by the Führer.

There was thus considerable urgency to help the Soviet Union as soon as possible. Broadly, they agreed on a policy of 'closing and tightening the ring around Germany',[15] which was to be achieved in a number of ways: by supporting the Russians materially; by beginning a campaign of aerial bombardment against Germany; by building up strength in the Middle East and wearing down Germany's war effort; and then striking hard with a punch that would see a combined Allied force make an invasion of Continental Europe, preferably in 1942, but otherwise certainly in 1943.

Yet despite this agreement, Britain and America approached the task of winning the war from completely different strategic viewpoints. Britain's tactic was to gather the necessary forces and wait for events to dictate where the decisive engagement would take place. The Americans, on the other hand, began with deciding where they should attack and then, working backwards, preparing the forces required for success. The British viewed the American approach as naïve, born of their lack of experience in war and international affairs. Conversely, the Americans thought the British lacked decisiveness and the willingness to make the necessary sacrifices to see the job done.

To begin with, however, these differences in approach were smoothed over. Britain was happy to agree in principle to America's avowed intention to invade northern France, while it soon became apparent that America was physically unable to stick to its desired timetable. Despite its rapidly expanding manufacturing capabilities and massive mobilisation, in 1942 the United States was still some way behind the times and its armed forces were just a fraction of the size they would balloon to by the war's end. In September 1939, for example, America's standing army comprised just 210,000 men – only the nineteenth largest in the world. By the time of Pearl Harbor, this figure had only slightly more than doubled. From there on, the figure would rise exponentially, but there could be no seaborne invasion of Nazi-occupied Europe just yet and most certainly not of France. Nor could Britain be relied on to mount such an operation. With their forces already overstretched in the Far East, in North Africa and the Middle East, the Allies accepted that the proposed invasion would have to take place in 1943 instead – although, as General Alan Brooke, the British Chief of the Imperial General Staff, pointed out during a visit to Washington in June 1942, it was important that no alternative, lesser operation should be undertaken in 1942 that might affect the chances of a successful large-scale assault into Europe the following year.

However, Roosevelt was determined to see his promise to Molotov fulfilled. 'It must be constantly reiterated,' he told his Chiefs of Staff on 6 May 1942, 'that Russian armies are killing more Germans and destroying more Axis material than all the twenty-five nations put together . . . the necessities of the case called for action in 1942 – not 1943.'[16] Moreover, he was all too aware that the American people, having been led into war, would not tolerate a long period of apparent inaction.

It was following the talks with Molotov that Churchill suggested the Allies invade northwest Africa as a means of Roosevelt keeping his word. There were, he argued, all sorts of good reasons for making such a move: the British Eighth Army was already fighting in Egypt and Libya – and in strength – and securing Vichy-French-held Algeria, Morocco, and Tunisia would be a less demanding task than an assault anywhere on the Continent. Furthermore, securing the Mediterranean would ease British shipping for future operations in Europe, would enable Allied bombers to attack Germany and Italy from the south, would hasten Italy's exit from the war, and tie up Germany's forces – all of which would help Russia.

General Brooke and the British Chiefs of Staff, despite their concerns, soon fell in line with their prime minister. But both the American Chiefs of Staff, and General Eisenhower and his planning team in Britain – Mark Clark included – were deeply sceptical, believing an invasion of north-west Africa would be a major deviation from their main goal – and one that could, if undertaken, see hopes for an assault on France dashed even in 1943. Roosevelt, however, saw some merit in the plan,

and having accepted there was no other viable place they could successfully bring about a second front, supported Churchill's proposals. The
misgivings amongst his military commanders may have continued, but
Roosevelt had made up his mind and his word was final. The invasion
of north-west Africa was on.

This, then, was how the Mediterranean strategy was born. In a remarkably short time, Eisenhower, together with General Clark as his chief
planner, diverted their attention to an invasion of north-west Africa
instead of France. In November 1942, as the Eighth Army was soundly
beating Rommel's German-Italian army at El Alamein, a joint British
and American invasion force landed in Morocco and Algeria. The landings were an astonishing achievement and produced a rapid and overwhelming victory. Admittedly, the opposition had hardly been very stiff,
but conception to execution had taken a little over three months. It
showed what could be achieved, logistically at any rate.

It certainly got Churchill's mind whirring. Suddenly he began to see
a wealth of opportunities emerging in the Mediterranean. With the
whole of North Africa secure, he realised that Britain and America would
be 'in a position to attack the underbelly of the Axis at whatever may
be the softest point, i.e. Sicily, southern Italy or perhaps Sardinia; or
again, if circumstances warrant, or, as they may do, compel, the French
Riviera or perhaps even, with Turkish aid, the Balkans'.[17]

This memo to his War Cabinet in October 1942 showed that Churchill
was beginning to think in terms of a double second front – one that
could be opened alongside the cross-Channel invasion. Churchill has
often been accused of putting his designs for the Mediterranean above
those of the invasion of France, but this was not the case in the autumn
of 1942. There were few people more determined to see, for instance,
the cross-Channel invasion take place in 1943, something Churchill stuck
to longer than most. But he *was* the arch-opportunist, a man who never
lost sight of the ultimate goal, but who was always open to new ways
and different approaches to achieving that final victory.

By January 1943, with the defeat of Axis forces in North Africa looking
to be inevitable – even if it was taking considerably longer than originally
envisaged – a more concrete Mediterranean strategy was agreed. At the
Casablanca Conference that month, the decision was made to follow
success in North Africa with an invasion of Sicily. This, it was argued,
would knock out Axis airfields threatening Allied shipping in the Medi-

terranean, but more importantly would provide the Allies with the greatest chance of forcing Italy out of the war, and, for the time being, was considered the best way to continue closing the ring around Germany – even if that meant postponing the invasion of northern France for yet another year.

This time it had been General Brooke who successfully manipulated the Americans into following the British way of thinking, and with the subsequent capture of more than 250,000 Axis troops in Tunisia, Churchill finally began to start looking towards the long and mountainous leg of Italy.

The news of the victory in North Africa in May 1943 came as the Prime Minister was steaming his way across the Atlantic for yet more talks, and in the flush of so emphatic a triumph both he and the British Chiefs of Staff were unsurprisingly gung-ho about what might still be achieved that year. German forces, they argued, were now widely stretched, not just in Russia, where the tide seemed to be turning in the wake of the Red Army's victory at Stalingrad in February, but elsewhere too: trouble was brewing in the Balkans; in France, which since the Allied invasion of North Africa was now entirely, rather than partially, occupied; resistance was also growing in Norway; and Italy appeared to be on the point of collapse. If and when Italy was out of the war, Germany would have to replace the half-million Italian troops in Greece and the Balkans, not to mention the figure that would surely be diverted to Italy itself, as well as the French Riviera and other borders now vulnerable to Allied attack. This kind of dispersal of forces, they suggested, was just what was needed to help the Allies get a toe-hold in France for 1944.

With this in mind, the British pressed their case to follow an invasion of Sicily with an invasion of southern Italy. This would open up yet further airfields from which to attack the German Reich, and could lead to exploitation eastwards into the Balkans and Aegean. At the very least, they argued, this use of their massed forces would be of greater help to the cross-Channel invasion than transferring most of the troops in the Mediterranean back to Britain. And in the best-case scenario, who was to say such operations might not prove decisive?

If the British were getting carried away with themselves, it was hardly surprising. Not only had they fought through a long, three-and-a-half-year campaign in North Africa, they had had interests in the Mediterranean dating back to Nelson's day, nearly a hundred and fifty years before. The Americans, however, had none of these emotional attachments and had so far played a far smaller role in the theatre. 'The Mediterranean,' General Marshall said at a meeting of the Combined Chiefs in May 1943, was 'a vacuum into which America's great military might could be drawn off until there was nothing left with which to deal the decisive blow on the Continent.'[18] They had agreed to North Africa, and had been persuaded there was sense to the invasion of Sicily, but they were damned if British over-enthusiasm for the Mediterranean was going to get in the way of the stated and original Number One Goal: the invasion of France.

Determined not to be outmanoeuvred, as they had been at Casablanca, General Marshall insisted that a date for the cross-Channel invasion be decided upon and that this should be the priority over and above any other operations. Only when the British had agreed to 1 May, 1944, for what he now appropriately renamed Operation OVERLORD, and had accepted that a certain number of troops would have to be withdrawn back to Britain to help with that task, would Marshall acquiesce to any further Allied action in the Mediterranean, whether it be the invasion of Italy or anywhere else.

The British agreed with the American terms – after all, they still believed in the invasion of France too – but to Churchill's great frustration, no definite plan was made about what should follow the successful conquest of Sicily and by 10 July 1943, the day the Allies made their landings on the southern Italian island, the matter had still not been resolved.

The decision to go on and invade southern Italy was finally taken on 16 July. It had, in fact, been prompted by none other than Marshall himself, who proposed an amphibious operation to take Naples and then to push on as quickly as possible to Rome. Needless to say, the British Prime Minister jumped at this suggestion. 'I am with you,' Churchill cabled to Marshall on hearing this plan of action, 'heart and soul.'[19]

No one was under any illusion, however, that Italy would be an easy place to fight a campaign should the Germans make a stand – not since Belisarius in the sixth century had Rome been captured from the south. Yet despite General Marshall's lack of enthusiasm for any further Mediterranean strategy, he recognised the necessity of both knocking Italy out of the war for good and drawing German troops away from northern France and Russia; and Italy was the only feasible place in which they could do this. Air superiority was a prerequisite for any seaborne landing, so this ruled out southern France; capturing Sardinia and Corsica were possibilities but would not draw enemy troops or necessarily prompt Italy's collapse; while an invasion of Greece and the Balkans carried the same risks as Italy, the roads and lines of communication there were considerably worse, nor would there be the benefits of a sizeable launch pad such as Sicily close at hand.

And anyway, both Marshall and the Allied chiefs had good cause for optimism. Momentum was with them, and the gutful of intelligence at their fingertips suggested Germany had no plans to defend southern Italy at all. Rather, it looked as though they intended to fall back to a line more than 150 miles north of Rome. With luck, the invasions would be as lightly defended as those on Sicily. Italy's southern airfields would be captured and there was no real reason to doubt that some time before Christmas, Rome would be theirs.

All too quickly, however, these high hopes were dashed. Only the occupation of the islands of Sardinia and Corsica – two of the pre-invasion objectives of the Allies – had brought any cause for cheer and these had both been abandoned by the Germans as part of their plans to deal with the Italians' collapse. In Italy itself, the strong and determined resistance shown by the Germans at Salerno in September 1943 had demonstrated there would be no easy victory. The Italian armed forces – with the exception of a large part of the navy and some of the air force – had been swiftly and efficiently disarmed by the Germans, not just in Italy but throughout the Balkans, Greece and the Aegean as well. In fact all but a few of the Dodecanese islands were soon in German hands, and most of those that were not were quickly taken back from the Allies. In Italy itself the Allies had discovered that it was a truly terrible place to fight a war. Running down three-quarters of the narrow peninsula were the Apennine Mountains – for the most part, high, jagged peaks that in places rose more than 10,000 feet. All too frequently sheer cliffs and narrow ridges towered over the narrow valleys below. And where there are mountains, there are always rivers, which in Italy generally ran down towards the sea and across the path of the Allied advance. Even where there were no mountains, there were still plenty of hills, such as in Tuscany, and although there were some flat coastal plains – like that around Anzio – these were criss-crossed with yet more rivers, canals, dikes and other water courses. In the north, there was the open country of the Po Valley, but then the mountains rose again – this time the even higher Alps. Furthermore, despite being a Mediterranean country, the winter climate was harsh – often freezing cold and wet, and to make matters worse, the winter of 1943/44 was especially bad.

Compounding the problem was Italy's relative economic backwardness and poor infrastructure. Certainly, there were the great industrial cities of the north, but much of Italy was dotted with tiny villages and walled mountain-top towns, a reminder that not so long ago Italy had been a place of city states and warlords, not the unified whole it had become less than a century before. Mussolini may have improved the railways, but few proper roads linked these isolated towns and villages. Indeed, large parts of the mountainous interior were joined by nothing more than tracks.

By the beginning of October, the Allies had taken both Naples and the Foggia airfields, after three weeks of hard fighting, but then it began to rain. Bad weather in 'sunny' Mediterranean Italy had not really been considered by the Allied chiefs before the campaign began. It did not seem possible that a bit of rain and cold could affect modern armies. Yet with almost every bridge and culvert destroyed by the retreating Germans, and with rivers quickly rising to torrents, the Allies, with all their trucks and tanks and jeeps and countless other vehicles, soon found themselves struggling horribly in thick, glutinous mud where roads used to be.

So it was that increasingly stiff resistance, bad weather and the onset of winter, and, above all, a severe shortage of men and equipment, ensured their advance ground to a halt. A hard-fought-for foothold in the southern tip of Italy now seemed like a small reward for their efforts.

And yet, and yet. More than fifty German divisions – the best part of a million men – were now tied up in Italy, the Balkans and the Aegean. By the end of October there were nearly 400,000 German troops in Italy alone. It began to dawn on the British especially, and Brooke and Churchill in particular, that if Italy was anything to go by, OVERLORD was going to be an incredibly tough proposition. If the cross-Channel invasion was to have any chance of success – and Churchill was remembering Gallipoli all too clearly – then it was imperative that even more be done to keep up the pressure on German forces throughout the Mediterranean.

With this in mind, at the Tehran Conference at the end of November 1943, the British pressed the Americans to agree to continue the advance up the leg of Italy to a line that ran from Pisa in the west to Rimini in the east. By overstretching Germany in southern Europe, they reasoned, the invasion of France would have a greater chance of success. However, in terms of strategy, the gulf between the United States and Britain was widening. As far as America was concerned, Britain had had its own way far too long. Increasingly suspicious about British intentions in Italy and the Mediterranean, the American chiefs only very reluctantly agreed to British proposals. OVERLORD would be postponed for the last time, and by a month and no more, and only in order to give the Allies more time to take Rome and reach the Pisa-Rimini Line. And there was to be one very strict caveat: in July 1944, a significant amount of Allied resources would be diverted from Italy to be used in an operation that would give more direct support to OVERLORD. This was to be the Allied invasion of southern France, codenamed Operation ANVIL.

With this now an agreed and approved strategy, General Alexander was given a little under eight months in which to achieve this latest Allied goal. After that, he had been told emphatically, the tap would be turned off.

General Alexander now had just two months left. He had guessed the present battle would last three to four weeks. Replying to Churchill's message on the morning of 11 May, he had signalled that everything was now ready for the battle ahead. 'We have every hope and intention of achieving our object,' he wrote, 'namely the destruction of the enemy south of Rome. We expect extremely heavy and bitter fighting, and we are ready for it.'[20]

Throughout the night and into the morning of 12 May, the cipher clerks at AAI headquarters in the vast Reggio Palace at Caserta were busy transcribing signals as news of the opening of the great battle began to pour in. Even for a man of General Alexander's imperturbability, these must have been tense times. There was much at stake.

FOUR

The Slow Retreat

Dense smoke and mist may have confounded the British Eighth Army's opening attack into the Liri Valley, but the fog of war was every bit as thick on the German side. Not only had they been caught off guard, they were without a number of their senior officers. Incredibly, Generaloberst von Vietinghoff, commander of AOK 10, was away, as was General von Senger, commander of 14th Panzer Corps that opposed the Allies from the Liri Valley to the coast, as well as his Chief of Staff, Oberst von Altenstadt; so too was Generalmajor Baade, commander of AOK 10 Reserve. Kesselring's Chief of Staff, General Siegfried Westphal, was also away sick at the time. Von Senger's temporary substitute was new to Italy and comparatively inexperienced, as was the other corps commander in AOK 10, General Feuerstein of the 51st Mountain Corps, which covered the Cassino massif.

General Fridolin von Senger und Etterlin – or 'Frido' von Senger as he was known – had been called away from the front on 17 April at the personal behest of Hitler for the investiture of the Oak Leaves to his Knight's Cross at the Führer's Obersalzberg headquarters in Berchtesgaden in the Bavarian Alps. Von Senger, a learned Catholic from Baden in south-west Germany, was something of an intellectual and a keen student of warfare. A former Rhodes Scholar, he had served throughout the First World War and remained in the much-reduced post-war Reichswehr. Rising steadily through the ranks, he had been an armoured brigade commander during the Blitzkrieg and had then been sent to Italy as Chief German Liaison Officer with the Franco-Italian Armistice Commission, a two-year post that had given him a deep understanding of Italy and its people. By late 1942, he was commanding a Panzer Division in Russia, but after the collapse at Stalingrad was posted back to the Mediterranean as Chief Liaison Officer to the Italian Army in

Sicily, a difficult task that he performed extremely well. After then extricating German troops from Sardinia and Corsica, he was given command of 14th Panzer Corps, covering the western side of Italy. It was von Senger's troops who met the Allied invasion at Salerno.

Despite his growing reputation and experience, von Senger was known to be no admirer of either Nazism or fascism and his experience at Hitler's headquarters that April had done little to change those views. The Führer, von Senger thought, looked tired. His uniform was drab and scruffy, his handshake clammy, and his pale eyes seemed glassy rather than hypnotic. Only his voice, so loud and forceful during his speeches, seemed soft and steady. He had, noted Frido, 'a pitiful and scarcely concealed melancholy and frailty'.[21]

Von Senger, one of the more senior officers present in Berchtesgaden, wondered what the more junior officers and NCOs must have thought of their leader, especially when Hitler began to list a string of defeats, and to describe the critical situation they now found themselves in. No mention was made of the few recent successes they had achieved in Italy. 'The impression gained by General Baade, who had been summoned to the reception to receive an even higher decoration,' noted von Senger, 'was the same as mine, namely that this political and military regime was coming to an end . . . and Hitler knew it.'[22]

Hitler was certainly not the man he had once been. There had been too many defeats, too many setbacks, and by the spring of 1944 he had realised he had lost the unshakeable belief of his people. He had consequently become more and more withdrawn and was hardly seen at all in public or in newsreels or heard on the radio. He was also, as von Senger had seen with his own eyes, a sick man. Ageing fast, he had a heart condition, stomach and intestinal problems, and, it seems, was suffering from Parkinson's, which caused uncontrollable trembling in his left arm and leg.

His all-consuming prosecution of the war was undoubtedly impairing his health. By nature, he was an idle man, and throughout the 1930s and the early years of the war he had been content to spout forth his ideas and let others put them into action. Now, though, trusting fewer and fewer people, he took increasingly direct control of every matter of state, be it military or domestic. His authority and power were absolute, and every decision required his authority and his alone. Because of this obsessive need to control, he subjected himself to a punishing work schedule, which allowed little or no time for relaxation and nowhere near enough sleep. Even then, he was unable to cope with such a vast workload, and the stress and strain accordingly took their toll. Although he was prone to violent mood swings and outbursts of anger at the best of times, these had recently become more frequent and severe.

And yet, although the war was spiralling out of his control, Hitler remained in deep denial about the catastrophic changes in German fortunes, and continued to preach the same unvarying message to his generals: that there should be no retreat and no surrender; that if they just held firm, the tide would be turned once more. The fragile alliance between Eastern and Western Allies would collapse; new German wonder weapons would come to their rescue. Massive self-deception and delusion were part and parcel of the Führer's world. Occasionally, as von Senger had witnessed, doubts would creep in, striking him with a crippling depression; but there was never any question of surrender. If Hitler was going to fall, then all of Germany would fall with him.

Nor did he ever accept responsibility for any mistake or misjudgement. Failings and disasters were always because of other people's treachery, disobedience or weakness. To his mind, the Italians were shining examples of this. They had waited too long to join the war and had bungled everything since then, starting with the failed invasion of Greece in October 1940. Since then, despite the large numbers of Italian troops fighting in Russia, they had been little more than a millstone around Germany's neck. German troops had come to their rescue in the Balkans, elsewhere in the Mediterranean, and in North Africa. By the autumn of 1942, with Rommel's men routed at Alamein, and with the Allies advancing towards Tunisia, Hitler began to realise that the great victory in North Africa that had seemed so tantalisingly possible in the summer of 1942 was rapidly turning into a catastrophe. He had considered the Mediterranean theatre peripheral so long as it had been restricted to North Africa; but like the British, he had begun to see all too clearly what would follow should they be defeated there. With this in mind, he had resolved to pour troops and equipment into Tunisia in an effort to forestall Italy's collapse and any subsequent – and suddenly far more serious – threat to his southern flanks.

Hitler's aim had been to keep the campaign in North Africa alive until the autumn of 1943 at the very least, by which time the conditions would be unfavourable for an Allied invasion of Sicily. The plan, however, had backfired spectacularly: the subsequent Axis defeat in May 1943 had been even bigger than that suffered at Stalingrad three months earlier, and only served to weaken Italy further.

With the collapse in North Africa, Hitler and the German High Command had very clearly read the writing on the wall, and so had hastily begun working on contingency plans for when Italy pulled out of the war. For some, there had been relief that they would soon be rid of the Italians, as many Germans felt little more than contempt for their less well-trained, poorly equipped, and mostly reluctant ally. No doubt Hitler could have defended the Alpine passes with only a handful of divisions, but an Allied-occupied Italy would have left Germany horribly exposed elsewhere. The Führer's overriding fear, for example, had been the loss of the Balkans, a rich source of oil, bauxite, and other key minerals essential to his war effort – and it was this that the German High Command had believed was the most likely target for the Allies' Mediterranean strategy. As a result Hitler had demanded that Italy should be hastily occupied and then defended.

Despite the warnings, however, Hitler had still flown into a severe rage when he heard, on 25 July 1943, the news that Mussolini had been dismissed as head of the Italian government and replaced with Marshal Pietro Badoglio, formerly Chief of Staff of the Italian Army, who had always been against Italy's alliance with Germany and who had resigned following the disastrous campaign in Greece in 1940. Hitler now declared the Italians the 'bitterest enemy. They say they'll fight but that's treachery . . . this bastard Badoglio has been working against us all the time.'[23] He had demanded that German troops occupy Rome immediately, and that Badoglio and the King, Vittorio Emanuele III, be taken captive. In this kind of paranoid and irrational mood, the Führer was hard to placate, and both Generalobersts Keitel and Jodl, the German Chief of Staff and Chief of Operations, had only been able to listen with mounting concern as Hitler appeared ready to elevate the urgent needs of the Mediterranean above all others – even Russia, where the situation was worsening.

Hitler had eventually conceded that the storming of Rome might be impracticable, but he had refused to waver over the need to act in Italy; he had screamed for revenge for Italy's 'betrayal' and he was going to get it. By committing his forces to the Italian peninsula, he had condemned his old ally to a terrible fate.

Feldmarschall Rommel had been hastily called in and given command of the newly formed Army Group B, and on 28 July had been ordered to begin seeping troops into northern Italy and securing the Alpine passes that fed into Austria. Then, when Italy surrendered – as Hitler had been convinced it would – his troops would disarm all members of the Italian armed forces and take over all areas of southern France, northern Italy, the Balkans, and the Aegean, which up to that point had been held by the Italians, in a carefully planned operation that was given the codename AXIS. Meanwhile, from 12 August, Kesselring, in agreement with Jodl, had begun evacuating all German troops from Sicily back to the mainland. With typical efficiency, he had managed to get more than 60,000 troops across the Straits of Messina, the last safely making their way across just a few hours after the Allies took Messina town and with it all of Sicily.

The problem was that despite the lightning efficiency with which these plans had been put into effect, Germany simply did not have the capacity either to mount a major front in Italy or to occupy the Balkans and the Aegean. When Feldmarschall von Kluge, commander of Army Group Centre in Russia, complained forcibly that the removal of key troops from the Eastern Front to Italy would be disastrous, Hitler had replied, 'Even so, Herr Feldmarschall: we are not master here of our own decisions.'[24] By September, the German southern flank in Russia had begun to collapse. With it came the loss of key strategic areas, including the Donets Basin with its vast reserves of coal. Every setback had knock-on effects and Germany could not afford any one of them.

No clear-thinking leader would have demanded that four senior commanders leave the Italian front at a time when a new enemy offensive was expected to be launched at any moment – even if intelligence suggested it would happen a couple of weeks after it actually began. Rather than being hurried back to the front after their investiture, Generals von Senger and Baade were sent on an indoctrination course at the Ordensburg in Sonthofen, the Nazi party school that had been set up in 1936 to train instructors in Nazism for the rising generation. While this was a complete waste of both men's time, it was also followed by a short stretch of leave that ensured that both were far away from Italy when the Allies launched Operation DIADEM; in the meantime von Vietinghoff – the army commander – had been summoned to yet another of Hitler's investitures.

And yet there was no suggestion that Hitler's *mental* capacity had been in any way damaged by his worsening health. Rather, his irrational behaviour was merely part of his character. Furthermore, despite his often woeful lack of judgement, he did, on occasion, demonstrate a certain clear-headedness and lucidity. This was certainly true with regard to Italy, for, little as he could afford a campaign there of any kind, having made the decision he had soon recognised there was sense in fighting the Allies as far south as possible. That he had come to this conclusion had been largely due to his man at the front line – Feldmarschall Albert Kesselring.

Kesselring had demonstrated to Hitler what the Germans might yet achieve in Italy. Moreover, this Luftwaffe field marshal had clearly shown his aptitude as a battlefield commander. During almost two years in the Mediterranean, Kesselring had been dogged by a troublesome partner and an overmighty subordinate. Once free of those constraints, his true worth had rapidly emerged.

In many ways, Kesselring was a rather untypical German field marshal. There was none of the patrician austerity, for example, that was a feature of many of the highest-ranking German commanders – no monocled scowl or stiff-backed swagger. Rather, he was known for being genial and good-humoured: not for nothing was he nicknamed 'Smiling Albert'. He was also diplomatically adept, getting on well with his Italian partners and doing much more than most of his fellow Germans to forge a good working relationship with them. Shrewd both tactically and strategically, he fully understood modern warfare in all its facets, far more so than Rommel, for instance, his subordinate in North Africa. Yet there were paradoxes to Kesselring. Despite his obvious skills as a commander, he had a reputation for over-optimism. In September 1940, for example, he mistakenly believed that the Luftwaffe had all but destroyed RAF Fighter Command, while at the height of the Siege of Malta in the spring of 1942, as Commander-in-Chief of Axis Forces in the Mediterranean, he believed he had successfully brought the tiny British island to its knees only for it to recover more quickly than he had anticipated. In Tunisia, he repeatedly told Hitler the Axis forces could hold on long after his commanders had realised the game was up, and his optimism came to the fore again during the crisis of the Italian collapse, when he had refused to accept that the Italians would betray them. 'That fellow Kesselring is too honest for those born traitors,' Hitler said of him.[25] Fine diplomatic skills had been offset by political naïvety.

Yet Kesselring always claimed he was nothing more than a simple soldier. Unlike many of the German senior commanders, his background was far from aristocratic and nor did he come from a family steeped in military tradition. Indeed, despite becoming one of the first three Luftwaffe officers – after Göring – to be made a Feldmarschall in July 1940, his had been an unremarkable upbringing, and it says much about the man that his rise was so comparatively rapid.

Born in Bayreuth, Bavaria, in 1885, where his father was a schoolmaster and town councillor, Kesselring came from solid middle-class stock. From an early age, however, he was determined to pursue a career in the army, and after matriculating from his local grammar school in 1904, he became a *Fahnenjunker* – an aspiring officer – in the 2nd Bavarian Foot Artillery Regiment. Serving in the unglamorous foot artillery during the First World War, he gained valuable battlefield experience, and then in 1917 became a staff officer first at divisional, and by the war's end, at corps level – a sure sign that he was beginning to stand out.

Indeed, he was one of comparatively few officers – along with Frido von Senger – to keep their jobs in the tiny post-war army, where he demonstrated his further aptitude as a staff officer, and where he rose to the rank of colonel with the command of a division. In 1933, Hitler came to power and immediately announced the clandestine formation of the Luftwaffe. Kesselring was retired from the army and given a civilian post in the new air force where he set to work running the administration and airfield development of the Luftwaffe. He also learnt to fly and worked hard to develop the Luftwaffe strategically and tactically. By 1936, he was back in uniform, both as a general and as the Luftwaffe Chief of Staff.

At the onset of war, Kesselring was in charge of the 1st Air Fleet that helped launch the blitzkrieg on Poland with such devastating results. He took over the 2nd Air Fleet, commanding it with great success in the Netherlands and France, and against Britain in 1940, and in Russia in 1941. During this time, he pioneered the theory of mass air assaults and did much to develop the use of the Luftwaffe as a tactical air force working in close co-operation with the German ground forces.

In December 1941, he was appointed Commander-in-Chief of Axis Forces in the Mediterranean, but despite his elevated position he had had a difficult time handling both his Italian partners and his subordinate, General Rommel. No inter-Axis staff had been established, while the chain of command had remained typically muddled, so that Rommel, commanding the Axis army in North Africa, had been, officially at least, under the command of the Italian Commander-in-Chief in North Africa, General Bastico, who in turn had been subordinate to the Italian Chief of Staff, General Cavallero. Further complicating matters had been Cavallero's deep resentment of Kesselring's appointment. Undeterred, however, Kesselring, from his base in Rome, had worked hard to improve relations with his allies, and in this had been highly successful. Showing both respect and sensitivity towards them, his diplomacy and brilliant organisational skills had done much to ease the difficult supply situation faced by the Axis forces in North Africa.

His inability to tame Rommel had had disastrous results for the Axis, although the blame had hardly lain with Kesselring. Whilst Rommel was directly appealing to Hitler to allow him to make his dash for Alexandria and the Suez Canal in the summer of 1942, Kesselring had been urging the Führer to first capture Malta and secure the Axis supply lines. Hitler deferred to Rommel with fatal consequences. As it happened, neither Kesselring's subsequent misjudgement of the situation in Tunisia nor his gullibility over Badoglio had made much difference to the course of events. It had been Hitler who had insisted on pouring troops and supplies into North Africa, not Kesselring; and it had also been Hitler and the German High Command who had ordered the steady flow of troops into Italy from the moment Mussolini was forced from power.

Yet it was Kesselring who had done so much to confound the Allied assault on Italy the previous September. After extricating the majority of his troops from Sicily, he had begun to see that there was much to be gained by making a firm stand in the south of Italy, rather than retreating far north of Rome as favoured by Rommel and the High Command. He had already seen that Britain had become 'the aircraft carrier from where powerful attacks were launched against northern Germany' and feared what would happen if the Allies were to take a firm grasp of most of Italy.[26] He had also correctly recognised that Italy's economic capacity was important for the German war effort, but that it would be harder to sustain the further the Allies climbed up the leg of the peninsula. Furthermore, he had argued that other parts of Germany's southern domains would be far more vulnerable if much of Italy were to be lost. All were sound arguments.

With regard to the Allies' intentions, he had also correctly guessed that General Alexander would choose the Gulf of Salerno with the nearby major port of Naples as their objective. Nonetheless, at that point, with Hitler vacillating, the view of the High Command that they should withdraw north of Rome still held firm, so that despite repeated requests for urgent reinforcements from Rommel's Army Group B in northern Italy, Kesselring's pleas had been ignored. He had been left to defend the Allied invasion with only those troops still in the south.

Had Rommel come to his aid, events might have been very different in Italy. As it was, Kesselring had only retreated from Salerno once it had become clear the Allies had established a firm foothold. He had then begun a careful and highly effective retreat, blowing up much of Naples' infrastructure and leaving barely a single bridge or road intact. In addition, the advancing Allies had been greeted at every turn with a network of minefields and debilitating booby traps. And while his troops had fought this rearguard action, Italian labourers had been set to work building up a defensive system across Italy – a series of lines that had originally been singled out by the Italians but which had then been massively strengthened on Kesselring's orders.

These orders were based on three entirely correct assumptions – first, that Rome must surely be the Allies' next goal, and second, that a modern army in winter could only effectively reach it from the south using one of the main Italian roads as the axis of their advance. There was no such road through the mountainous middle of the peninsula, and if the Allies attacked up the Adriatic, they would then have to cross back to the west coast to reach Rome. This meant that realistically there were only two routes open to them, either Route 7 – the Via Appia – or Route 6, the Via Casilina. The Allies, he guessed, would be unlikely to use the former as the Via Appia ran along the coast, was narrow and easily defendable as it passed around the Aurunci Mountains, and then cut through the now-flooded Pontine Marshes. The Via Casilina, however, ran into the Liri Valley and so his third assumption was that this offered the most likely route of advance for the Allies.

Nonetheless, Kesselring felt sure the Via Casilina could be successfully blocked. Ten miles south-east of the Liri Valley, the road passed through a narrow defile, ideal for mounting artillery, and known as the Mignano Gap. Then, at the mouth of the Liri, were the twin guardians, Monte Cassino and Monte Maio and the mighty ranges beyond. It was for this reason that first the Mignano Gap, and then the main Gustav Line at Cassino, at the mouth of the Liri Valley, were to be the strongest and most heavily protected points of these new defensive systems. And there was another advantage to the Gustav Line: it ran across the narrowest point of the peninsula. Because the Allies would have to channel most of their forces along a comparatively narrow point, it would require, in theory, fewer men to defend it than the wider, more accessible Pisa–Rimini position further north.

'Smiling Albert' had, in early September, set out clearly his arguments for heavily defending southern Italy, but in this case it had been his actions that had spoken louder than his words. While Rommel had continued to urge Hitler to fall back as far as the Alps, on this occasion it had been Kesselring who had won the debate. Not only had Grand Admiral Dönitz, of whose views Hitler had been increasingly taking note, agreed with Kesselring's view, the High Command had even begun to come round to his way of thinking. Sure enough, on 4 October 1943, Hitler had ordered Kesselring to continue his defence south of Rome. He had impressed to such an extent that by the third week in November, Rommel had been moved to northern France, his lustre further dimmed by suspicions of defeatism – something that could never be directed at Kesselring. Nor was his loyalty in question: Kesselring had made his oath to serve Hitler and he would stick to it; honour and obedience were part and parcel of the soldier's creed.

After Rommel's dismissal, Kesselring was, on 21 November 1943, appointed Commander-in-Chief Southwest and Army Group C, with direct command of all German forces in Italy. Furthermore he no longer had to weave his way through a political minefield, since the defence of Italy had become his show, and his alone.

Yet by May 1944, Feldmarschall Kesselring faced one of his toughest challenges thus far. His troops had been caught off guard by Alexander's new offensive, his HQ had been badly bombed, and the phone lines to headquarters AOK 10, who were bearing the brunt of the Allied attack, had been destroyed.

And too many of his senior officers were far, far away.

FIVE

Frustrations

For the best part of two years Kesselring's opposite number had been General Sir Harold Alexander. No two commanders had battled it out for longer in the European war, and they would be pitting their wits against each other for a while longer yet. They were certainly aware of each other, although neither had ever tried to make the kind of mileage Montgomery had done from his professed rivalry with Rommel, and nor would they; both were far too modest. Self-glory was not their game at all.

There were other similarities. Alexander, or 'Alex' as he was universally known, was every bit as genial as Kesselring and he shared the German's unflappability, but in many other ways they had little in common. Kesselring, for example, despite more than thirty years in the armed forces, had limited experience of battlefield command – he was a Luftwaffe field marshal, after all. Alexander, on the other hand, was one of the most experienced Allied battlefield commanders of the entire war. In a long and distinguished career he had fought in more battles in more countries and alongside more nationalities – including German – than any contemporary commander with whom he served.

And unlike Kesselring, his background was distinctly aristocratic. Born in December 1891, the third son of the Earl of Caldeon, he spent much of his childhood at the Caldeon estate in Northern Ireland, where he indulged in his lifelong passions of shooting, fishing and painting. At Harrow he excelled at sports, and then seamlessly progressed to Sandhurst, passing out in July 1911. As a fiercely proud Ulsterman – he carried an Irish flag with him throughout the war – he joined the Irish Guards, a regiment created by Queen Victoria only eleven years before, and although in those final pre-war years he had little opportunity to show his promise as a soldier, he did develop into the perfect gentleman, a tag he would never lose. Handsome, charming and athletic, he played polo, boxed, raced motor-cars at Brooklands and, at Easter 1914, entered Ireland's most famous run, the Irish Mile, and won quite effortlessly.

The First World War developed him as a soldier and revealed extraordinary bravery and leadership. In November 1914, he was seriously injured in the thigh and was invalided home, but was determined to get back to the front as quickly as possible. To prove his fitness, he walked and ran sixty-four miles in one day, and by February 1915 he was back in France. Later that summer Alexander led his company at the Battle of Loos. He was wounded twice more, survived the Somme, Cambrai and Passchendaele, and in 1917, still only twenty-five, became acting lieutenant-colonel commanding the 2nd Battalion Irish Guards. By the war's end, he had won a DSO and bar, an MC, the French Légion d'Honneur, and had been mentioned in despatches five times. Adored by his men, he combined courage and compassion with ice-cool composure and decisiveness: in combination, rare gifts in a soldier.

There was no sign of Alexander's career faltering with the end of the war. In 1919, he was sent to command the Baltic Landwehr, part of the Latvian Army, in the war against Russia. Most of the men under his command were of German origin, so he had the unique distinction amongst Allied commanders of having commanded German troops in battle. Staff College and subsequent staff appointments were followed by stints along the North-West Frontier in India, experience that would not be forgotten in the equally mountainous terrain of Italy.

By the outbreak of war in 1939, 'Alex' was one of the youngest major-generals in the British Army and commanding the 1st Division. In France, he supervised the final withdrawal of British troops from Dunkirk and was the last senior officer to leave – on the penultimate day of the evacuation.

Remaining in England for the next two years, Alexander did much to revolutionise the way British troops were trained, developing battle schools in which troops were taught simple combat drills and, by using live ammunition, were given a much-needed dose of realism. It was during this time that he began increasingly to catch the Prime Minister's eye, and in early 1942 Alex was posted to Burma to oversee yet another retreat from defeat. This time, with his usual unflappability, he safely oversaw the British crossing of the Irrawaddy River, and with it – for a time at any rate – saved British forces from the threat of annihilation at the hands of the Imperial Japanese.

In August 1942 he was sent to Cairo to become British Commander-in-Chief, Middle East, with Montgomery, as Eighth Army commander, as his subordinate. While Monty commanded on the battlefield, Alex improved the administrative and supply situation, played a vital buffering role between his forces and London, as well as adding his military advice on the ground; El Alamein was his victory too. By the beginning of 1943, with the Allied campaign in Tunisia stalling badly, Alex was given command of the newly formed 18th Army Group and took over direct control of the campaign. In a little over ten weeks after taking command, he had improved almost every aspect of the Allied war effort in Tunisia and had won a great victory, with the capture of more than a quarter of a million troops.

When he had taken over in Tunisia, Alex had been justifiably concerned about the greenness of American troops, but had handled the firebrand, General Patton, with firmness and skill and had earned the respect of not only Patton, but another future star, General Omar Bradley. By the time of the Sicily invasion, however, he had still had certain reservations about the effectiveness of American troops, and this had led to a potentially damaging dispute in which he had allowed Montgomery and Eighth Army to gain a priority over the American troops that they did not deserve. That it was Montgomery who bore the brunt of understandable American grousing says much about Alex's personal charm and charisma. To Bradley, Alex carried 'the top rating among Allied professionals',[27] while to General Eisenhower, the Allied Supreme Commander in the Mediterranean, he was not only an outstanding soldier but also personable and easy to get along with. 'Americans,' he noted, 'instinctively liked him.'[28]

So did almost everyone else. He had an ability to speak freely with anyone and to make them feel at ease. He never swore – describing something as 'tiresome' was the closest he came to cursing – and only once was he seen to have lost his temper, and that apparently was when some of his men refused to give two dying Germans a drink of water during the Battle of Passchendaele in 1917. He drank but was never drunk; he liked to sketch and paint whenever he had the chance, spoke a number of languages including German, French, and Russian, and when in Burma even made an effort to learn Urdu.

Moreover, he looked the part. Despite his modesty – bragging was anathema to him – he had something of the dandy about him. Dressed immaculately at all times, he liked to wear a high-peaked cap, with its visor dropping over his eyes – a style he had spotted on a Russian officer in 1919 and which he had liked so much he had asked his hatter in St James's to copy.

He was universally admired by his men. General John Harding, his Chief of Staff, wrote that Alex's soldiers 'thought of him as one of themselves, as a soldier. That's what I call the magic; he'd got that.'[29] During some of the darkest moments at Salerno, he had joined Clark, striding amongst the troops and exuding a sense of unruffled calm and resolve. Never one to stay stuck away miles behind the lines, he was seen at the front most days, talking to commanders and troops and surveying the battlefield for himself. Whilst maybe not a brilliant tactician, he developed a very sound judgement and understood the men under his command, from privates to generals, and how to get the best from them all. He understood how much men could endure and what could be expected of them. He understood that armies need confidence and experience in combat, and that the approach to battle – the preparation and the removal of potential stumbling blocks – was the key to success. And he understood that any attacking fighting force needs both balance and momentum.

The problem facing Alex in Italy had been that right up until the late spring of 1944, he had had neither balance nor momentum, and far too many stumbling blocks, none of which had been of his making. From the moment Allied troops had landed at Salerno, Alex had been plagued by the slow build-up of his forces. In Italy, the German build-up, begun way back in July, had been far faster than anything the Allies had been able to achieve. Supplying their forces by land – on rail and by road – was a huge advantage. The Allies, on the other hand, had only been able to do so by air and sea – and mostly the latter. The frustration was that the shipping that was so desperately needed simply had not been available; nor had there been enough landing craft. 'The reduction in craft,' Alex had written, 'already decreased by wear and tear, has been so serious as to preclude us from taking advantage, other than with minor forces, of the enemy's inherent weakness, which is the exposure of his two flanks to turning movements from the sea.'[30] In other words, rather than playing to the advantages Italy offered the attacker, the Allies had been forced to play to its massive disadvantages instead. As any German commander was aware – not least Kesselring – there were more than 2,000 miles of Italian coastline for them to defend. Fortunately for them, the Allies simply did not have the shipping to make the most of this defensive weakness.

The Allies were fighting in far more corners of the globe than Germany. Not only had there been the continuing build-up of troops and supplies in Britain, there had been their commitments in the Far East, and, at Churchill's urging, in the Aegean, where British forces had humiliatingly lost the battle for the Dodecanese Islands. With the huge losses of shipping so far in the war – in the Pacific, the Atlantic, Arctic and Mediterranean – resources had been stretched to breaking point.

Furthermore, the US Chiefs of Staff had decided that the build-up of an effective bomber force in Italy at the airfields around Foggia in central southern Italy should be the first priority. Six heavy bomber groups of around forty-eight aircraft each had been sent over the moment Foggia had been captured at the end of September, forming the embryonic US Fifteenth Air Force, with twelve more and a further four fighter groups operating from Italy by the end of 1943. By March 1944, there had been twenty-one heavy bomber groups in Italy and seven long-range fighter groups – some 1,300 aircraft.

On the face of it, this had been a sensible idea, especially as part of the reason for invading Italy had been the prospect of bombing Germany from the south. However, transporting the men, parts, ammunition, ordnance and fuel necessary for such an air force took up vast tonnages of shipping that could have otherwise been used to strengthen the ground forces. Alex had requested that the Fifteenth Army Group be built up properly first. This had been refused.

Compounding the problem had been the removal of a large number of his more experienced troops to Britain in preparation for the invasion of France. Their transfer had long been planned for November 1943, but even so, when it took place it had been felt particularly keenly because German resistance was stiffening all the time. The slow build-up and shortage of Allied troops had put a greater strain on those already in place in Italy. Clark's Fifth Army had struggled to recover quickly from the losses they had suffered at Salerno and the fighting that had followed first at the River Volturno and then as they had struggled through the Mignano Gap. Unfortunately, however, as pressure on the Germans had lessened, so the enemy had been able to spend more time on improving defences and making the Allied troops' task even harder, thus creating a vicious circle. For the kind of speedy campaign the Allies had envisaged, far greater commitment had been needed. Yet because Italy had always been seen, by the Americans at least, as a secondary theatre, this commitment had not been forthcoming. Although the

Normandy invasion had not yet occurred, the Allies had – in logistical terms – already begun fighting on two fronts in the West. Had they hit Italy hard with everything they had from the outset, the situation by the spring of 1944 might have been very different.

As it was, Montgomery's Eighth Army had won important but costly and hard-fought gains on the Adriatic coast, and the US Fifth Army had continued to push northwards, eventually breaking through the first German line of defence, the so-called Winter – or Bernhardt – Line, before running out of steam around Cassino where in January they hit the more formidable Gustav Line. In the mud, cold, and rain, the fighting had suddenly seemed horribly familiar to all those who had experienced the Western Front in the First World War – and that had been the majority of British commanders. For Churchill and the British chiefs, the opportunity for glorious exploitation in the Mediterranean and Balkans had passed; it was as though a glittering prize had somehow slipped through their hands. Meanwhile, as far as the American chiefs had been concerned, Italy had become the millstone of their worst fears, a drain that was distracting their efforts from the most important operation of all: the invasion of France.

In the middle of December 1943, General Alan Brooke had toured the Italian front on his return from the Tehran Conference, meeting with Generals Alexander, Montgomery and Clark, and other commanders. Already depressed about the slow Allied progress in Italy, Brooke saw nothing to improve his mood. Monty, he had thought, looked tired and in need of a rest, while it seemed as though there was no real plan for the capture of Rome, the goal for which they were supposed to be striving.

This was not quite true. Back in October, Alex had begun to formulate ambitious plans for Italy, recognising the need for the Allies to force their way north of Rome, clear of the Apennines, and break out into the Po Valley and the plains of the north. While he had not conveyed this far-sighted strategy to the Allied chiefs, just a few days later he had presented a very clear picture of Allied prospects and had urged greater ambition and direction in Italy. Churchill had been so impressed that he had cabled this 'masterly' document in full to Roosevelt and Stalin. But at this stage the Tehran Conference was still over five weeks away. Alexander and his commanders could only be expected to do so much without clear policy and direction from the top.

As far as Brooke had been concerned, it was clear to him that Alex had not been 'gripping this show'.[31] His comments had been an expression of his disappointment and frustration at Allied progress thus far in the campaign; throughout the war, generals not doing as well as hoped were often accused of 'lacking grip'. Sometimes, the accusation was justified; sometimes not. Certainly what Brooke failed to appreciate was that fighting on a battlefield such as Italy, with its horrendous geography and, in winter, truly atrocious conditions, had less to do with fire power – or even air power – and more to do with manpower; and in this area the Allies did not have the overwhelming advantage needed by any attacking force. Even by May 1944, when Alex would at last begin the great battle for Rome, the Allies had only twenty divisions available in Italy to pit against Kesselring's twenty-six.

The 'division' tended to be the military unit commanders used when analysing their strength, and at full strength usually meant around 14,000–17,000 men. However, although German and Allied military units were similar in composition, only recently had the Allies closed the gap in terms of tactics and training. Not until Alexander and Montgomery's arrival in North Africa did British forces begin to work out how to beat German forces on the ground, and in this they were greatly helped by the massive material contribution of Britain's new ally, the United States.

America was not a naturally warring nation, and its people were insular and inexperienced in the ways of continental politics and warmongering. However, America did have three important factors in its favour: it had enormous resources of manpower, a rapidly expanding and large-scale industrial capability, and a willingness to learn. Britain, on the other hand, could claim maybe only the last of these attributes. These three potential war-winning facets had been clearly demonstrated in the final six months of the campaign in North Africa. US equipment – from tanks right down to the tiniest nuts and bolts – had given the British Eighth Army technological parity with Germany for the first time and had played an important part in the victories at Alamein and those that had followed. In Tunisia, American greenness had been horribly shown up during their first battles with German troops, but despite several knocks and one particularly humiliating setback, they had bounced back, and in the closing stages showed how much they had progressed and learned.

Yet just as the Allies seemed to have caught up with the Germans, they had found themselves flung against topography and conditions that required a different, almost retrogressive, approach. The possession of high ground has been an advantage in warfare since the dawn of time, and in Italy the German defenders were able to choose where they defended, making the most of the best observation points. Guns, mortars and machine-gun posts could be hidden whilst maintaining a clear view of the enemy, while troops could hide amongst rocks, caves and in cellars that were often a feature of the countless towns and villages that dotted the mountains. Kesselring had discovered that a rearguard of only company strength could hold up an Allied division for as much as a day, taking pot shots, and then silently slipping away under the cover of darkness. The Allies could not pass through the valleys until the surrounding high ground was taken – otherwise they would have been sitting ducks as their massed equipment tried to rumble along the few metalled roads that would support them. This meant assaulting often viciously steep slopes, where they would find the Germans dug in on the reverse side where they were impervious to all but a few lucky mortar strikes.

In the winter the situation had been made worse because only the very best roads – which were few and far between – could be used; the rivers were high and difficult to cross; and the Germans had flooded the low ground of the Liri Valley that lay beneath the Monte Cassino massif.

So it was that while the ground was largely impassable to trucks, tanks and other vehicles, the onus lay with the Allied ground troops, the foot-sloggers, to make any significant progress. Around Cassino, and at Anzio, they had been all but halted. Suddenly the men had to unlearn the lessons of this new, highly mechanised war and return to the tactics of the 1914–18 war – a life of perpetual bombardment, trenches and dugouts and night-time patrols into no-man's-land, and morale-sapping battles that achieved small pockets of ground in return for all too many casualties.

Yet from the Allied point of view, these small gains were important. They had kept up the pressure on the Germans so that Kesselring had been forced to keep troops at the front at all times. It would also make their task that much easier when the big offensive was finally launched at the beginning of the summer. The Anzio bridgehead, for example, seen as a failure back in January, now gave Alexander a huge advantage, forcing Kesselring off-balance in his efforts to protect both fronts. It also meant that Alexander had the launch pad for a double blow, a right and then a left punch, when the battle began.

By the beginning of May 1944, an already severely overstretched Germany had pushed around half a million troops into the peninsula, which was precisely what the Allies had hoped for when first considering Italy. And, as Alexander pointed out, 'All this was achieved without our once having that numerical superiority usually considered necessary for offensive operations, with a mixed force of many nationalities and with little opportunity of flexibility in their employment.'[32]

Even so, there was still a feeling during those long winter months of 1943 and early '44 that Alexander and his forces had lost a sense of direction. Because of the lack of shipping – above all – the landings at Anzio had had neither the scale nor conviction ever to cause a significant breakthrough, while the battering at Cassino suggested the Allies were not using what resources they did have to the best of their potential, despite the enormous limitations imposed by both weather and geography.

There had been a number of changes amongst the command in Italy as 1943 had given way to 1944. General Eisenhower, the Supreme Allied Commander in the Mediterranean, had been given command of OVERLORD, and Montgomery had left Eighth Army to command Eisenhower's land forces into northern France. Eisenhower had in fact specifically asked for Alex as his commander, but had been overruled by Brooke, less because of his doubts about Alex but more because he had believed it would have been a mistake to remove both senior commanders in the theatre in one stroke. Furthermore, he had recognised that no other British general got on better with or was more highly regarded by the Americans; and while it was now recognised that OVERLORD was predominantly an American show, it was equally considered that the campaign in Italy was being largely run by the British. In the interests of future Allied policy in the Mediterranean, Brooke had understandably wanted the most popular British general to help maintain influence over their American ally.

General Alexander had also been kept on as battlefield commander in Italy. General Sir Henry 'Jumbo' Maitland Wilson, at the time British C-in-C in the Middle East, had been appointed Supreme Commander in Eisenhower's place, which had been a sound decision. The role of the Supreme Commander was largely political and administrative. It was far better that Alex remain in command of the battle. He did, however, have a new Eighth Army commander in Lieutenant-General Sir Oliver Leese, and, crucially, he had a new Chief of Staff in Lieutenant-General John Harding.

Harding, an experienced staff officer and commander, had only recently recovered from serious wounds suffered in North Africa when he had arrived in Italy at the beginning of the year. Good staff officers were worth their weight in gold. From army group to brigade level, every commander had a team of them, whose job was to assist him in the task of command. And most important of all was the Chief of Staff, who was the commander's right-hand man: his adviser, his confidant; the man who ensured the smooth operation of logistics and planning; and the conduit between the headquarters and the HQs down the chain of command. It is no coincidence that the best generals almost always had excellent Chiefs of Staff. Eisenhower, for example, had found his ideal partner in General Bedell-Smith; Montgomery in General Freddie de Guingand; Kesselring had General Westphal. In North Africa, Alexander had been well served by Lieutenant-General Dick McCreery, now commanding X Corps. But since Sicily his Chief of Staff had been Alec Richardson, who was perfectly competent but lacked vision and had been unable to bring about a partnership of minds with Alex.

All this had changed with Harding, who had been a platoon commander at Gallipoli and who had developed a deep and studied understanding of warfare. Together he and Alexander had immediately begun to plan for a large-scale offensive that would shatter the German defences for good. By constant discussion between the two, Harding had drawn up a new appreciation of Allied aims in Italy, in which he had suggested that capturing Rome was not a big enough goal. Instead, German forces in Italy had to be completely destroyed, so much so that only by massive reinforcement would the German southern front avoid complete collapse.

For this to be achieved, Harding and Alexander had recognised that three things had to happen. First, there needed to be a superiority of manpower of at least three to one at the main point of attack. Second, the weather needed to be sufficiently dry to allow the Allies' great mechanical superiority to play its part; and third, there needed to be enough time to properly rest, refit and retrain those forces exhausted by the bitter winter fighting.

Throughout the spring, the battle plan had been refined and preparations made. Exhausted troops were moved out of the line and to a quieter sector, while new divisions, both American and British, had arrived and made their way towards the front. A major and extremely complicated regrouping had taken place, with army boundaries changing and a number of corps crossing over from Eighth to Fifth Army and vice versa. In this new battle, Alex was going to use both armies, supported by more artillery and aircraft than had ever been used before by the Allies in a single battle.

There were to be three distinct phases in the battle. First, the Allies had to break through and destroy the Gustav Line before Kesselring realised the threat of an amphibious landing further up the coast was nothing more than a deception plan. Second, the Allies had to break the second line of defence, the Hitler or Senger Line as it was variously called.* Finally, once Kesselring was fully occupied trying to hold the main line in the south, and the Allies were surging north towards Rome, a reinforced US-led VI Corps would burst out of the Anzio bridgehead and cut off the retreating German AOK 10. Surrounded, it would then be destroyed.

The date for the launch of the battle, originally April, was moved to May, while from the middle of March, Allied air forces had been carrying out Operation STRANGLE, which aimed to destroy all German lines of communications – roads, bridges, and railways – from Cassino to 150 miles north of Rome.

By the beginning of May 1944, the stage had almost been set. General Alexander had got his three-to-one advantage around Cassino, his guns were primed and ready, and overhead he had complete command of the skies. But only time would tell whether this enormous battle would wash away the disappointments of the winter and bring about the decisive victory that promised the Allied armies in Italy so much.

---

*The Germans initially labelled it the Führer Line, but then, realising this might have an adverse psychological effect should it be overrun, changed it to the Senger Line. The Allies, however, continued to refer to it as the Hitler Line.

SIX

Between the Devil and the Deep Blue Sea

Although the main Allied attack that started on 11 May would be flung against the 20-mile stretch between Cassino and the western coast, there were troops on both sides loosely holding the line all across Italy to the Adriatic. In the centre of the country, for example, in the Abruzzi mountains, were a number of Italian troops of the Royal Army, loyal to Vittorio Emanuele III, now esconsed in Brindisi and the man who had been King of Italy throughout the century, even during the Fascist era. Attached to the British X Corps, the Corpo Italiano di Liberazione – or CIL – found themselves opposite their former ally and on a different side to a number of their fellow countrymen. As such, the Italian civil war was already under way.

Further to the south, in a tented reorganisation camp near Lecce, were a number of artillerymen due shortly to join the reconstituted Nembo Division, CIL. One of the lieutenants of the 2nd Group – or battery – of the 184th Artillery Regiment was twenty-three-year-old Eugenio Corti, a highly experienced and capable officer who was only gradually coming to terms with events since the previous September.

Eugenio had been one of only around 4,000 of an original corps of 30,000 Italian troops to have escaped the Soviet encirclement along the River Don in early 1943. He had reached Nettuno, near Anzio, just a week before the armistice was signed on 8 September 1943, but as an officer, had been living out and therefore had been asleep – and safe – when, at dawn on 9 September, a force of German troops attacked the barracks and rounded up the survivors. Local civilians, already desperately short of food and just about any other conceivable supplies, subsequently looted the barracks. Three days later, any Italian officers still in or around Nettuno were ordered to convene at a small palazzo in town for a 'clarifying report' by the Germans. Unlike most of his colleagues, Eugenio had, in Russia, developed a serious distrust of their former ally, and so had tried to dissuade his fellow officers from attending. Few, however, had listened to his entreaties. 'I saw with my own eyes,' he wrote, 'the kind of blindness that strikes men, as they lose even the most ordinary capacity for discernment that could dissuade them from following an already formed opinion.'[33] Appalled, Eugenio had only been able to watch as the Germans kicked and shoved the Italian officers into the backs of trucks and drove them away.

Eugenio had managed to dissuade just one of his colleagues, a fellow lieutenant, Antonio Moroni, from handing himself over to the Germans. Having shed their uniforms for civilian clothes, the pair had watched distraught as columns of German troops poured southwards. The initial relief on hearing the news of the armistice had gone. Instead they had wondered whether Italy would soon share the fate of Poland. 'As soon as they feel sure of themselves,' Eugenio had suggested to Antonio, 'they'll begin the massacres.'[34] Both had agreed they could not return home to Lombardy, in the north; but nor would they idly endure German violence and occupation. Antonio suggested heading for Rome. In a large city, he reasoned, it would be easier to remain anonymous until the Allies arrived – and that was bound to be soon. Eugenio, however, said he preferred the high ground and sparsely populated mountains to the south. Here he was certain the mountain people would resist the German occupation. Because he had been right about the Germans earlier, Antonio had agreed to join him in the mountains. Neither, however, had had any idea what to expect, or how their fellow Italians would respond to German occupation.

Eugenio and Antonio had made their way across Allied lines in the middle of October and presented themselves at the garrison of Potenza in central southern Italy straight away. From there, they had been sent to a reorganisation 'camp' – a requisitioned school building – near the Adriatic, where remnants of the Italian Army still loyal to the King were supposedly being reconstituted with a view to fighting on the side of the Allies. The reality, however, as Eugenio soon became aware, was that royalist Italian forces were in a desperate state. Most of those trapped in southern Italy at the time of the armistice had been under-trained troops who had never been in action; their discipline was terrible, as was their morale. Equipment was almost non-existent, and Eugenio and his comrades were all too aware that the Allies had little respect or use for them. Rations were also meagre. Some days, Eugenio was given no more than two biscuits on which to survive. Many lacked proper uniforms. 'Those were very bitter days,' wrote Eugenio, 'when it seemed as though we could lose all hope in the fate of Italy.'[35]

Life had improved, however, albeit very slowly. In the subsequent months more men and materiel had arrived and talk of mutiny had died down. Training had become more organised and with it the enthusiasm of the men had grown. Even so, by the beginning of May 1944, Eugenio had little to cheer about. Rumours of disputes between the British authorities and their own superiors reached them, while there was still no sign of the Nembo paratroopers they, in the artillery, were supposed to be supporting; apparently, they were still in Sardinia. 'The sense of our uselessness,' wrote Eugenio, 'which had never completely vanished, came back again.'[36]

If Eugenio and his colleagues felt side-lined, it was because they had been. Part of the armistice deal had been that Italian armed forces, more than 3 million strong throughout Italy, the Balkans and the Aegean, should fight on the side of the Allies, and indeed, the government had been assured of more favourable treatment if they ensured this. Unfortunately Badoglio had managed to make a spectacular mess of such plans when the armistice had been finally announced the previous September.

Admittedly, Badoglio and the non-Fascist government had found themselves in a very troublesome position during the forty-five days between Mussolini's dismissal and the announcement of the armistice. As German troops had begun to pour into the north of Italy, they had been all too aware that if they turned on their ally, they could expect the full wrath of a jilted partner. But equally, they had realised their future position might be much improved if they could be seen to have helped the Allies. Judging which side to back had proved an extremely thorny problem, and so throughout most of August they had earnestly avowed their unswerving loyalty to Germany, whilst secretly negotiating peace terms with the Allies.

No one, apart from Kesselring, had been fooled by any promises from the Italians, however. The Allies, without ever revealing their hand, had allowed Badoglio to believe they had a far larger invasion force than was the case; they had also agreed to send in the US 82nd Airborne Division to help the Italians secure Rome. Had the Italians known that Clark's Salerno invasion would see only three landing divisions and two close behind – rather than fifteen as they had been led to believe – they might never have signed at all. Nor had the Allies allowed the Italians to know the timing of the Salerno landings. Consequently, when Eisenhower had made his own announcement of the Italian surrender on the afternoon of 8 September and then sent a signal to Badoglio to do likewise by 8 p.m. that same day, it had caught them completely off guard. They had been expecting the invasion to be as much as a week later.

This had left the Italians in the position of their worst nightmare. Although they had been due to become 'co-belligerents', they had not had time to organise their armed forces properly. Badoglio had further complicated matters by failing to tell the Italian armed forces to begin fighting the Germans; instead, he merely told them they should no longer fight the Allies, which was not the same thing at all. Moreover, the Allies' plan to drop the 82nd Airborne into Rome had been shelved just as the paratroopers were being loaded onto their planes. Badoglio had realised with mounting horror that they could not possibly expect to defend Rome. A far more realistic expectation had been that they would soon be rounded up, along with the King, and most probably shot for their perceived treachery.

With this in mind, fleeing to safety had seemed a better option than martyrdom. 'For me, one question was of capital importance and overmastered all the others,' wrote Badoglio; 'that was the necessity to maintain at all costs a close and continuous contact with the Allies, so that the armistice might continue in operation.' If the government remained in Rome, he reasoned, this could not happen. And so, the following day, 9 September, Badoglio, King Vittorio Emanuele III and the royalist government had fled the capital, first to Pescara and then on to Bari on the southern Adriatic coast, far, far away from the fighting.[37]

Whatever their motives, the flight from Rome had been appallingly handled and had left the country rudderless. Gripped by panic and fearing for his life, Badoglio had failed to keep a clear head. In the early hours of 9 September, he had even issued orders to all Italian military headquarters not to 'take the initiative in attacking the Germans'. This had hardly been helpful to their new allies, especially since around Rome the Italians had been numerically superior to the Germans, and in the Ariete Division had had their best-armed units led by General Raffaele Cadorna, a highly experienced commander. How effective the Italian forces could have been against the Germans will never be known, but there were plenty of people who saw both the armistice and the abandonment of Rome as terrible acts of treachery and betrayal, including many of the officers and men surrounding Eugenio Corti in the Royal Army; their disenchantment had played its part in the breakdown of authority and discipline.

Finally, in his haste to flee, Badoglio had also completely forgotten to take Mussolini from his captivity on Gran Sasso in the Abruzzi Mountains and hand him over to the Allies as had been agreed. Instead, on 12 September, 120 crack German paratroopers had sprung him without a shot being fired and flown him, via Vienna, to Munich and then to an audience with Hitler himself.

If the Allies had taken a pretty dim view of the fighting qualities of the Italians, then this was doubly so in the opinion of the Germans, and the ease with which they had disarmed the vast majority of the Italian armed forces in the days that followed the armistice had only confirmed that opinion. Indeed, the Germans had been primed and ready and no sooner had the surrender been announced than Operation AXIS had been put into swift effect. German officers had reached the majority of Italian barracks within a few hours of the news of the armistice with instructions for the Italians to co-operate or else face German fire. A number of telephone lines had been cut to isolate the Italians further and misleading propaganda had been hastily spread about.

Cosimo Arrichiello, a twenty-three-year-old soldier based in northern Italy, had witnessed this utter confusion first hand. Brought up a good Catholic, he had gone to bed on the night of 8 September and had prayed hard that God would save Italy and especially those in the south around Naples, where he had been brought up and where much of his family still lived. He had also asked the Lord to restore peace and stability, not just in Italy but around the whole world. Having done this, he had felt better and had been dozing off to sleep when he heard a bugle. Glancing sleepily at his watch, he had seen it was half past eleven at night – perhaps, he had thought, it was an air raid. Within moments he and his colleagues had been ordered to hurry downstairs. Bleary-eyed, Cosimo and his fellow soldiers at Pellizzari barracks had fallen in, whereupon the captain, in an emotional voice, told them that the Italian government had signed an armistice with the Allies. 'This is no time for rejoicing,' he had warned them, however. 'This is not the end of the war. We have a German army in Italy, which is determined to fight the Allies at any cost, and this will not make our lives easier.' With that, they had been ordered back to bed.[38]

Cosimo's feeling of relief at the news had been mixed with a sense of bewilderment which was in no way assuaged the following day. At dawn they had been ordered on a march and given emergency rations. After three hours on the road, they were brought to a halt, their mules unloaded and their ageing First World War-era howitzers assembled. Having eaten some lunch in the early afternoon sun, they had then been ordered to pack up once more and return to their barracks. By the evening they were told they were confined to barracks, although rumours had begun to spread that a number of troops garrisoned nearby had already disbanded and left, fearing otherwise that they would be captured by the Germans.

Cosimo had hardly known what to think, although it had begun to occur to him that it might be up to each individual to use his own initiative; certainly the officers had appeared to be in as much turmoil and confusion as everyone else. Shortly after he had gone to bed, a commotion had developed, with people running around outside. From the courtyard, someone had shouted 'Hurry! The sentries have gone! Quick! The Germans are coming!' His heart racing, Cosimo had hurriedly dressed, cursing as the laces on his shoes snapped in his haste. Grabbing his wooden suitcase he had run to the barracks gate, peered outside, and seeing no Germans, had sped off towards a friend's house in town.

By the middle of the following morning, there were still no Germans in sight, but there had been plenty of notices from the barracks commander ordering his men back without fear of recrimination, and warning that they would be shot as deserters if they did not. Reluctantly, Cosimo had done as ordered and was shocked to discover that Pellizzari barracks had been looted. Officers were standing around gloomily amidst the pervading air of apathy and sudden listlessness. No further orders had been given. Moreover, as Cosimo realised, he was among only around 40 per cent who had returned – the others being still at large.

His return had been short-lived, however. In the early afternoon, reports had arrived that the Germans really were on the edge of town. Once again, mayhem had followed, but this time most of those still at the barracks had left for good, and Cosimo was one of them.

The Pellizzari barracks were in Bra, a small town south of Turin, and although his friend in the town had agreed to hide him for a short while, Cosimo had been unsure what he should do next. His father and two of his brothers were in Java, in Indonesia, where they had moved before the war in an effort to find much-needed work, but though he had desperately wanted to get back to his mother and remaining brothers and sisters – there had been eleven in all – he had felt it was simply too risky to travel all the way from Bra, in the north-west of Italy, back home to Naples.

A few days later, he had thanked his friend and left, heading for the village of Bardo in the hills some miles away, where he knew his former captain's batman lived and whose family had a farm. No German had spotted him leaving Bra and no one had bothered him as he walked through the seemingly peaceful countryside. 'There was so much free-dom around me in that world of nature,' he noted; 'yet deep in my heart I knew that I wasn't quite free.' Far from it: Cosimo was now on the run, an outlaw in his own country, and like many hundreds of thousands being rounded up all over the country, he faced, at worst, execution for desertion and, at best, servitude as manual labour for the Germans deep within the Third Reich itself – a role for which Germany considered the average Italian male was far better suited.

In fact, in under a week from the moment the armistice was signed the Italian Army had ceased to exist – all fifty-six divisions dissolved – and while there had still been a number of troops at large, Cosimo included, more than half a million had become POWs. By February 1944, there were some 617,000 former Italian troops interned in Germany and working in armaments factories. A large part of the navy had sailed to Malta and given itself over to the Allies, but the air force had also been disbanded and vast amounts of equipment requisitioned by the Germans. This booty included 9,986 guns, 15,500 vehicles, 970 tanks and self-propelled guns* and no less than 4,553 aircraft. Not a bad haul, all things considered.

Even so, there had been some resistance. The Italian Motorised Corps had fought with conviction outside Rome, and the Ariete Division had also moved to help a mass of some 10,000 civilians who had spon-taneously taken up arms throughout 9 September.

One of those had been twenty-four-year-old Carla Capponi. From her mother's flat near the Forum, she had seen flashes of artillery fire from the south-west throughout the night of the 8th/9th. Early on the

*An artillery piece mounted onto tracks or sometimes wheels. Unlike a tank, it does not have a revolving turret.

morning of the 9th, she had heard excited voices in the streets below, and looking out had seen a group of men, armed with rifles. They beckoned her to join them – the Germans were coming and they needed everyone to help defend the city. Without much hesitation, Carla told her mother she was going to join them.

At the Pyramid of Cestius by the Porta San Paolo, Carla had joined the growing resistance. Unarmed, she had spent the day tending the wounded and carrying food and provisions to the Italian troops and armed civilians. The fighting around the Pyramid had gone on throughout most of the 9th and on into the 10th, with high casualties on both sides. Realising he was the highest-ranking officer left in Rome, the ageing Marshal Enrico Caviglia had taken charge of the resistance, only to receive a severe ultimatum from Kesselring: surrender, or Rome would be carpet-bombed into dust. Unwilling to test the threat, Caviglia had ordered his ad hoc force to lay down their arms. They had done so, but for many – Carla Capponi included – the two-day battle had given them a taste for resistance. The seeds of Rome's partisan war had been sown at the Porta San Paolo.

There had also been smatterings of resistance outside Italy – on Corfu, for example, and on Cephalonia. Of nearly 12,000 Italian troops on this latter island, more than a thousand had been killed in ten days' fighting against the Germans, while nearly 5,000 had then been subsequently executed in one of the worst crimes of the entire war. Cephalonia had become a 'carpet of corpses'.*[39] The 4,000 who had laid down their arms and survived the massacre had then been given starvation rations before being shipped to Germany. Cruelly, all three vessels had hit mines and sunk. Those who had jumped to safety had been machine-gunned in the water. In all, 9,406 soldiers out of 11,700 were killed. Almost the entire garrison had been wiped out.

Not all Italians wanted to see the back of the Germans, however. Far from it: the bulk of the Nembo Division in Sardinia, and units of the Folgore Division, veterans of Alamein, had sworn their allegiance to Hitler and had continued to fight on the side of the Germans and under German command; so too had the Decima MAS, a semi-autonomous group of elite naval commandos led by the charismatic Prince Valerio

*The massacre of Italian troops on Cephalonia was worse even than that in Katyn Forest, but although the German commander who ordered it, General Lanz, was later tried for war crimes, he was given just twelve years in prison.

Borghese. And not by any stretch of the imagination had there been universal cheering on the signing of the armistice. Twenty-one-year-old William Cremonini, for example, had been appalled on hearing the news. 'I was disgusted,' he admits. 'It was a shameful thing.'

He was an only child, and his father had died when he was five, so William had been brought up solely by his mother. Both she and most of their neighbours had been supporters of Mussolini, and as a boy William had joined the *Balilla,* the Fascist youth organisation that had been established in 1926. Like the Hitler Youth that followed, it served as a means of *fascistizzazione,* of reinforcing Fascist doctrine amongst the younger generation. Boys joined the Balilla between the ages of eight and fourteen and the *Avanguardisti* from fourteen to eighteen. William had enjoyed it – the sports, the discipline, and the sense of camaraderie that developed amongst them, so that by the time war broke out in June 1940, he and his friends had been excited by the prospect of winning glory for their country, and eager to do their bit.

Although still not quite eighteen, William, with his mother's assent, and a number of his friends had joined the *Giovani Fascisti* – Young Fascists – Bologna Battalion that was being formed at that time. Soon after, they had taken part in the 'March of Youth' across Italy, a grand military parade in which the Young Fascists marched sixteen miles a day for three weeks. In Padova, they had even been greeted by Mussolini himself.

In the summer of 1941, the Young Fascists had been sent to North Africa, and there they had remained until the very end of the campaign, having been one of the few Italian divisions to have repeatedly distinguished themselves on the battlefield. William had somehow survived until two weeks before the Axis surrender, when on 29 April, as they attacked a British position at Enfidaville, he had been shot in the chest. By good fortune, he had been evacuated on the last hospital ship back to Italy before the campaign's end, and so had avoided the fate of so many of his colleagues who were to spend the rest of the war as POWs.

William had lost a lot of friends in North Africa. So many lives had been given for Italy, nearly his own too. Having been shot, he had recovered consciousness only to find himself in the middle of a minefield. Whilst trying to cross it back to his own lines, he had been tended to by some Germans. 'They took my jacket off,' he recalls, 'and then the blood started glugging out.' He was taken to a field hospital where a priest arrived to hear his confession: 'It gave me the feeling that I was dying.'

Somehow, however, he survived. His feelings on hearing the news of the armistice were understandable. 'Suddenly we were told we should be shooting Germans,' he says. 'Until the day before, we had been fighting with them. The first medical aid I received when I was wounded was given to me by Germans. We fought side by side. How were we expected to make such a change so suddenly?'

Still convalescing at home in the village of San Pietro in Casale, north-east of Bologna, William had in fact been on a train in the station at San Pietro when he heard the news of the armistice and had immediately taken himself to the nearest German unit in Poggio Renatico, a Luftwaffe base, and offered his services. Sent home again, he soon after met one of his former officers, who had also been wounded in North Africa. 'Don't join the Germans,' he told William. 'It's ugly to fight in someone else's uniform. Let's hang on a bit and see what happens.' William had done just that, and had soon learned that his old battalion commander, Major Fulvio Balisti, was back in Italy thanks to a prisoner exchange of badly and permanently disabled prisoners at the end of the North African campaign, and was serving as the new Fascist Provincial Head of Brescia. William had gone to see him and had immediately been offered the chance to stay in Brescia, serving with Balisti. However, he had also learned that the core of the surviving Young Fascists were now based in Maderno on Lake Garda, where they were serving with the personal bodyguard of Alessandro Pavolini, the Neo-Fascist Party Secretary in the newly formed Fascist Republic. Without much hesitation, William had gone to join them.

By May, William was a sergeant with the Bir el Gobi Company, as the bodyguard were known. Named after the Italians' most famous stand in North Africa, they wore Italian grey-green uniforms and Fascist black shirts. It wasn't soldiering as William had known it in North Africa, but he was happy enough – pleased to be with some of his old comrades and glad that his own sense of honour remained intact.

Others had been equally concerned about the betrayal and dishonour of the armistice, including Marchese Antonio Origo. At their beautiful country palazzo in the Val d'Orcia in southern Tuscany, the marchese and his wife, Iris, had spent the evening of 8 September in grim silence, listening with mounting unease to the locals rejoicing and lighting bonfires in celebration. Iris, on the other hand, had been more concerned about what would follow. She had been filled with a sense of foreboding, guessing – quite correctly – that Germany would continue fighting.

Iris had been born in England the daughter of an English mother and American father, and had had a particularly peripatetic yet privileged childhood. Around the time of her birth, in August 1902, her father contracted tuberculosis, and so the family had gone in search of warmer climes and clean air: Italy, then California, then Switzerland, then back to Italy again, where despite his TB, her father became American Vice-Consul in Milan. Iris was eight when her father died, but between holidays with her grandparents in Ireland, she remained with her mother in Italy. Her father's wish had always been that she should be brought up in France or Italy or 'somewhere where she does not belong', so that she would grow up both cosmopolitan and free of the normal tug of patriotism.[40]

Consequently, she was still based in Florence when, in 1920, she was 'launched' as a debutante into Anglo-Florentine society. It was during this time that she met her future husband, Antonio, the illegitimate son of an Italian aristocrat and a man ten years her senior. They married in 1922 and a little over a year later bought a large estate south of Pienza and Montepulciano, in southern Tuscany, called 'La Foce'. Antonio had no desire for either business or diplomacy – for which he was trained – and instead yearned to farm; and in this still wild but beautiful part of Italy, some sixty miles south of Florence and a hundred north of Rome, they realised they could create a new and worthwhile life for themselves.

The Val d'Orcia had, like many parts of rural Italy, been neglected over the centuries. Soil erosion and misuse had left large parts of the estate resembling a lunar landscape, but Iris and Antonio soon breathed new life into it, and by the late 1930s they had re-landscaped much of the land, established around fifty tenant farms, and introduced more modern farming techniques. While Antonio oversaw the running of his tenant farms, Iris set up a health centre and a school for the estate children, which also provided evening classes for the adults.

Antonio had never had much of a taste for politics, and consequently had never openly opposed Mussolini and the Fascist regime, nor had he denounced it; neither had Iris, although both had been privately opposed to the war. Their concerns had been the safeguarding of Italy, and more specifically, La Foce and all the people for whose lives they were responsible. At the outset of war, Iris had gone to Rome to work for the Italian Red Cross, but two years later, expecting her third child, she had returned home for good. Soon after, the Allies had begun regularly bombing Italian cities and so Iris and Antonio began taking in a number of refugee children, both orphans and evacuees, from Turin and Genoa.

With the war now having reached Italy itself, the futures of these children and the many families in Val d'Orcia had seemed under an even greater threat. In the days that had followed the armistice, the Val d'Orcia, as elsewhere, had been flung into a state of chaos. News had been scarce, with no guidelines about what to do or what the Italian people could expect. The gates of the nearby prisoner of war camp had been opened, and the neighbouring countryside had become flooded with POWs. On the morning of 8 September, there had been 79,543 Allied POWs interned throughout Italy. Two days later around 50,000 of them were loose in the Italian countryside in what had been the biggest mass-escape ever. Iris had found a large number in a creek near Castelluccio, hiding from any Germans that might pass by, and clearly feeling rather bewildered and unsure what to do next. She had given a British corporal a map and a few Italian phrases and then on her return home had met one of their *contadini* – peasant farmers – in his uniform and on his way back to his regiment from leave. 'What am I to do now?' he had asked her.[41] He had just met a number of other soldiers, now in plain clothes, who had left their barracks in Bologna and Verona. All those able to run away had been doing so, he had been told, while the word on the street was that the rest had been rounded up by the Germans and packed off to concentration camps. Wild rumours and a mounting sense of panic had been rife. 'Later in the day,' Iris had noted, 'yet other fugitive soldiers turn up.'[42]

By the beginning of May, the Origos, like the vast majority of Italians, were doing what they could to keep a low profile, trying to safeguard everything that was dear to them, and praying they would safely make it through the war. Yet Iris's fears on 8 September had been well founded: Italy had become a place of suspicion and menace. 'Nothing has been uglier in the story of these tragic months,' she noted in her diary on 5 May, 'than the avalanche of denunciations which have been showered on both the Italian and German officials. Professional rivalry, personal jealousy, the smallest ancient spite – all these now find vent in reports to the Fascist police, and cause the suspected person to be handed over to prison, to questioning by torture, or to a firing squad. No one feels safe.'[43]

Another doing his best to get by was Cosimo Arrichiello, who had been living in the small village of San Bernardo in the Stura Valley, south of Turin ever since fleeing the Pellizzari Barracks the previous September.

He had been fortunate that the Bolti family had taken him in. Harbouring former Italian soldiers and Allied POWs was a crime punishable by death, yet there had never been any question of him being turned away. In return, Cosimo worked on the small family farm. For this, he was very thankful, and did his best not to let them, or himself, down.

He found the work extremely tough, however. A sickly child, he had not developed into a particularly physical person, and was far more interested in culture and the arts than sport and the great outdoors. Nor had he been a natural soldier, and in more than two-and-a-half years in uniform had barely moved from the barracks at Bra and had seen no action whatsoever. For a man who had been vehemently against the war from the outset, this lack of action had suited him well, and since his desertion he had had no further interest at all in fighting, whether it be for the Germans, the Allies, or the embryonic bands of partisans that had gradually emerged in the weeks and months that had followed the armistice.

Yet Cosimo had been luckier than many in finding San Bernardo, a quiet village in a low-lying valley in north-west Italy. Most German troops were in the cities or further south near the front, while the local partisans tended to stay in the mountains for much of the time. Consequently, the village and nearby town of Marene attracted less attention than some places. For the most part, local law and order was left to two members of the Carabinieri, the police force in Italy.* Both men soon became Cosimo's friends, and although they knew he was a disbanded soldier, they made no effort to betray his real identity. Neither Giacomo nor Dino was from the Piemonte region, and rather like Cosimo, they had little taste for politics and preferred to do their best to see out the war as quietly and peaceably as possible. Officially, as Carabinieri, they were German and Neo-Fascist collaborators. In practice, however, they had no real authority, no means of enforcing the law, and in fact made an effort to tip off Cosimo if there were any German or Fascist raids being planned. If the partisans appeared, they would do their best to avoid confrontation by remaining firmly in their quarters.

Even so, Cosimo had to be careful. He could rarely stray far from the farm and had to be on his guard most of the time. It was an existence he found monotonous in the extreme. Almost every day was unwaveringly

---

*The *Carabinieri* was a police force, but strictly speaking were military police, since they were part of the army. Their role was to maintain law and order like any other police force.

the same: he would get up at dawn, have a hot drink made from roasted barley, then set to work – picking grapes, loading hay, mending fences, or attending to any other odd jobs. There might be something to eat at lunchtime – perhaps soup or polenta with some salad – and then a further meal in the evening of much the same but with a couple of glasses of homemade wine. Pasta and meat were scarcities, although they would usually manage to have tagliatelle on Sundays. As Cosimo admits, he felt more at home in an urban environment – and one that was southern too. Desperate to go home to Secondigliano, a small town near Naples, he struggled to find much in common with his hosts.

Italy might have been one of the most homogeneous countries in Europe, where 99.61 per cent of the population were Roman Catholic, but in other respects it was extremely diverse. It had only been unified since 1870, when the *Risorgimento* – 'revival'– was completed. Before that time, it had been made up of a patchwork of city and sovereign states. Indeed, the drive for revolution and national unity had only really emerged following Napoleon's invasion in 1797.

Yet even throughout the age of fascism, which had been dominated since 1922 by Mussolini, most Italians felt a far greater sense of local and regional, rather than national, identity and loyalty. Italy, for example, still had innumerable regional dialects, probably more than any other country in Europe. Cosimo Arrichiello, as a Neapolitan, could barely understand his Piemontese hosts. 'They spoke their dialect,' he noted. 'I could communicate with them only when they made the effort to speak Italian, their knowledge of which was very limited indeed.'[44]

In the countryside, life was primitive, so much so that Cosimo, from a poor background himself, had been genuinely shocked. There had been no agricultural revolution in Italy, for example, and the system of rural existence had barely changed in centuries. Most farmers were contadini, impoverished peasant farmers, most of whom worked as share-croppers for big landowners, or *padroni* – such as Antonio Origo, for example. This system was known as the *mezzadria*, and, naturally enough, benefited the padroni far more than the contadini, who frequently struggled to deliver their share of crops and profit. Few contadini were educated or could read or write, so there was little chance of betterment; only by working like a slave and having a big slice of good fortune could the farmer create a secure existence for his family.

Living conditions were basic: no electricity, no running water, and only limited sanitation. There was a toilet, but it was only a hole in the ground, and it was not near where Cosimo slept. If he needed the toilet in the night, he would excrete on to a piece of paper and then bury the faeces the next morning. Most contadini lived in houses that doubled up as barns: the animals would be in stalls on the ground floor, while the family lived above. It meant there was always a strong smell of animals and animal dung, but their heat helped warm the rest of the house. Cosimo also found he suffered terribly from bed bugs. 'I was a complete fish out of water,' he admits. 'For them this was all natural, but for me it was a form of slavery.'

In this battle for survival against over-mighty landlords and the ever-capricious Italian weather, religion, myth and superstition played important roles. Most people went to church regularly, and religious feast days, or *feste*, were important landmarks in the calendar and were celebrated by the whole community. But while the priest was an elevated figure in any community, the local witch, or *strega*, was also respected. With life as precarious as it was, few dared risk the *strega's* curse.

It was a very insular world and few ever thought of escaping it. A small number had a radio – the Bolti family had an aged set – but most news travelled by word of mouth and had it not been for the war, most Italians living in rural backwaters would have had only a rudimentary idea of what was going on beyond a few miles from where they lived. Except in times of war, few needed to. Most accepted their lot, had little ambition, and fully expected life to continue in much the same way it had for centuries before. The men and women worked on the land, the women bred the next generation. Only in wartime, with the men gone, was this pattern suddenly threatened. The Bolti, for example, had four daughters, all of whom worked and lived on the farm. Cosimo struggled to find them attractive. 'They were not at all romantic,' he says. 'They had bad breath, and were not very clean. Their only ambition was to find a strong and hard-working husband, have lots of children, and then bow to his undisputed authority.'

Cosimo would perhaps have been surprised to know, however, that this pattern of existence was repeated throughout much of rural Italy. In the Ausoni Mountains, for example, some fifty miles south of Rome, there were a number of mountain communities that were far more cut off from the rest of the world than the Stura Valley in Piemonte. Some 5,000 feet high, on a verdant plain near the summit of Monte Rotondo, Pasua Pisa lived and farmed with her family. In May 1944, Pasua was twenty-eight; she had lived on the mountain all her life. They were a small community – just a few farmhouses of around ten families – although unlike most contadini, Pasua's family owned their own farm; not that it was much – little more than a hayloft above the animals. This scarcely made their life any easier, however, and like most peasant farmers, everyone had to work long and physically demanding days.

They were largely self-sufficient up on the mountain. They grew crops, made their own wine, and reared buffalo from which they had milk and made mozzarella cheese. Once a week, they would go down the mountain with the donkeys to the small market town of Amaseno, a journey that took a little over an hour on the way down, but well over an hour and a half on the way back. 'We didn't sell much of our produce,' says Pasua, 'just the odd calf or sheep, as we only needed to buy a very few things, like salt. We would take our grain to the mill and get it milled, and our grapes pressed.' There was, of course, no electricity up there, or drains. Water was collected when it rained, or could be drawn with the help of a donkey from a nearby spring. On feast days they would sometimes go down into the valley; more often, they would stay on the mountain and hold a dance there.

'I was beautiful,' she says, although she had left it until she was twenty-three to get married, quite late for most young country women. 'Lorenzo,' she says suggestively, 'was born straight away.' It was a simple life, yet Pasua had always been happy enough; after all, she had known nothing else.

For the most part, Mussolini, fascism and national and international affairs had passed her by. Only when war came did Pasua take notice, for with it came conscription: being a farmer was not a reserved occupation, as it was in Britain. Suddenly, the young men on the mountain were gone, her husband included, leaving her with their only child. Her husband had been posted to North Africa, where he had been taken prisoner by the British. Pasua had heard nothing except a telegram informing her that he was now a prisoner of war in Canada.

Without the young men around, life had been considerably harder: it had meant even longer hours and more work for everyone, but there was no point complaining; Pasua, like everyone else, simply got on with the task of existing and making sure the farm kept running. She was also lucky that her father was still alive and there to help her. Furthermore little four-year-old Lorenzo adored him and followed him everywhere. 'We always used to say he was his grandfather's shadow,' says Pasua.

It had been nearly four years since Italy had joined the war. Now the fighting was just fifteen miles away, and although Pasua had absolutely no idea what the military commanders had in store, in a few days' time the front line would cut a swathe right through the Aurunci Mountains. Even high on the mountains, Italians were discovering they were not safe. Soon it would be Pasua's turn to face the whirlwind of war.

SEVEN

Masters of the Skies

By the beginning of May, the US General Ira Eaker, commander of the Mediterranean Allied Air Force, (MAAF), could call on no fewer than 3,960 operational aircraft in Italy alone, a formidable air force. In sharp contrast, his counterpart, Feldmarschall Wolfram von Richtofen, had just a little over three hundred. How the tables had turned. In the first two years of the war in the Mediterranean, the Luftwaffe, along with their Italian partners, the Regia Aeronautica, had all too often ruled the skies. Their fighter planes, especially, had frequently overwhelmed the tired and battered Hurricanes and Kittyhawks of the RAF. Since then, however, better aircraft, increased production, and the arrival of the Americans in the theatre had coincided with lessening German production and shortages of fuel. All aspects of the German war machine were now being hugely stretched and the Luftwaffe were among the hardest hit. Those aircraft destroyed in the air or on the ground by the Allied air forces were no longer being replaced in kind.

So it was that every time Leutnant Willi Holtfreter took to the skies, he invariably found himself surrounded by hordes of Allied fighters. Rather as the beleaguered RAF pilots had discovered two years before over Malta, Willi found that instead of actually shooting down any enemy planes, he was doing well just to get back to base safely.

Just turned twenty-one, Willi was from the village of Abtshagen, near Stralsund on the Baltic coast. Before the war, the village had been dominated by the timber works, renowned for its manufacture of parquet flooring, and Willi's father was a foreman there. The third child of a family of two boys and two girls, he had a sheltered but happy upbringing. Like most children, he left school at fourteen and immediately went to work at the timber factory as an apprentice. But while he was quite content with this line of work, he developed a passion for aircraft. Not far from his home was an airfield and he and his friends would often watch planes there. Then, with the Hitler Youth, he learned to fly gliders. 'It was incredible that you could do this for free,' he says. 'To have that opportunity was very exciting.'

At the outbreak of war he was studying woodwork technology in Dresden, but returned home to register for the Luftwaffe before he was due to be conscripted into the army. 'You had to volunteer to fly,' he explains. 'And I was happy to do so. Like most people, I wanted to do my bit for the Fatherland.' On registering he stated his desire to become a fighter pilot, but as with the RAF or US Army Air Force, whether a potential pilot ended up flying single- or multiple-engine aircraft tended to be decided on as flying training progressed. As it turned out, however, he was indeed singled out to fly fighters, and after more than a year of 'pretty thorough' training, he was posted to the Fighter Reserve in France in November 1943, before being sent to join the celebrated fighter group, JG 53, in Italy at the end of March.

Jagdgeschwader 53 was one of the oldest Luftwaffe fighter groups. Known as the 'Pik As' – the Ace of Spades – the group had become one of the top-scoring fighter units, having served in France, over Britain, in Russia, North Africa and over Malta. Like all German fighter groups, it was divided into *gruppen* – or wings, and was, by the spring of 1944, split up, with just III Gruppe left in southern Italy. By the beginning of May they had just over thirty single-engine Messerschmitt 109s left.

One of these had been lost by Willi on 1 May. Flying over the Cassino front, he and his three other colleagues had soon been pounced on by hordes of Spitfires. Badly hit, he had been forced to bail out for the second time in eight days. He was not alone. Since the beginning of March, III/JG 53 had lost no less than thirty-eight aircraft, destroyed either in the air or on the ground.

But with such a dearth of resources, all the Luftwaffe in Italy could do was send up men like Willi Holtfreter on a fool's errand in the vain hope that they might achieve *something*, however slight.

This was not the case for the Allies, however, who spent much time and soul-searching trying to master the opportunities offered by air power. Mediterranean Allied Air Forces was now a vast behemoth of an organisation, with British and Commonwealth units operating hand-in-hand with American. By May 1944, it was the biggest air force the world had ever seen, with more than 12,500 aircraft throughout the Mediterranean theatre. To ease potential clashes of nationality, the system of commander and deputy commander that had been implemented by the Allies in all theatres extended to the air forces too. Thus the American, General Eaker, was commander of MAAF, with Air Marshal Sir John Slessor, British, as his deputy. Defining these roles, however, was no easy matter, because in the case of Slessor, his responsibilities extended beyond those of MAAF, since he was also Commander-in-Chief, Royal Air Force Mediterranean and Middle East, and therefore in charge of subordinate commands in Egypt, East Africa, the Levant, Iraq and Persia, which meant that west of Greece he was responsible, through Eaker, to the Supreme Allied Commander Mediterranean, and east of Greece to the British Chiefs of Staff only.

It was an odd and potentially fraught set-up but happily for the Allies it caused few difficulties. 'It worked all right,' wrote Slessor, 'because I had in Ira Eaker an Allied Commander-in-Chief who was not only an old friend but a great airman and a splendid chap who stood on no dignities, trusted me to serve him loyally in the sphere where he was responsible and left me to get on with it – and gave me all the help he could – where he was not permitted by his directive from Washington to have a direct interest.'[45] Eaker was every bit as warm in his praise of Slessor. 'Nothing could have pleased me more,' he told Charles Portal, the British Chief of the Air Staff on hearing of Slessor's appointment in January. 'I also wish to assure you that without question he and I will work together in perfect harmony.'[46]

That these two men were able to operate so well together was enormously fortunate because both were experienced and highly able commanders, whose close partnership was much needed in Italy – a theatre where air power was able to give the Allies an essential and decisive edge. Although both had started their careers as fighter pilots – Slessor had made the first ever aerial attack on a Zeppelin during the First World War – more recently their backgrounds had been with bombers. Eaker had commanded the US Eighth Air Force in Britain, overseeing the daylight strategic bombing of Germany, until getting the top job in the Mediterranean. Slessor, on the other hand, had commanded 5 Group, RAF Bomber Command, in England, and had then taken charge of Coastal Command where he had played no small part in the destruction of the U-boat threat in the Atlantic.

Although both men had been hoping to play major parts in the upcoming invasion of France, they recognised that a considerable challenge faced them in Italy. With such an enormous force, spread over such a wide area, theirs was a massive responsibility. The two biggest components were the Mediterranean Allied Strategic Air Force – MASAF – and the Mediterranean Allied Tactical Air Force – or MATAF. The former consisted of one group of RAF heavy four-engine bombers and the US Fifteenth Air Force, predominantly made up of heavy long-range bombers but also a fighter component largely used for escorting the bombers. Their task was to continue the strategic bombing campaign both within and outside Italy. In contrast, MATAF's role was more directly to support the ground forces. This consisted of the US 57th Bombardment Wing of twin-engine bombers; of the US 12th Tactical Air Command; and of the Desert Air Force, the battle-hardened force that had fought throughout the North African campaign, and which was a polyglot mixture of RAF, South African Air Force, Royal Australian Air Force, and Polish bomber and fighter wings. In addition were the Mediterranean Allied Coastal Air Force, the Mediterranean Allied Photographic Reconnaissance Wing, and the US 51st Troop Carrier Wing. The guiding principle was to have joint operational staffs but separate administrative staffs. In other words, at MAAF headquarters, in matters of operations, signals and intelligence, the staffs were mixed, but otherwise American and British forces were left to get on with their tasks on their own. For example, the 12th Tactical Air Command was a purely US Army Air Force show, while the Desert Air Force remained entirely in the hands of the RAF.

In 1944, air power was in many ways still in its infancy and, despite their overwhelming numerical superiority, the Allies were still feeling their way with regard to its use, both in terms of its potential as a means of long-range strategic bombing, and in the way it could support troops on the ground.

Fortunately, however, there were not only extremely experienced and capable men at the top, but also a wealth of young, dynamic, and operationally seasoned men at both squadron and wing levels of command. This was especially true of the Desert Air Force, whose headquarters and flying units were liberally sprinkled with men who had been combat flying almost since the beginning of the war.

One of these men was Wing Commander Hugh 'Cocky' Dundas who, despite being only twenty-three, had seen action over Dunkirk back in May 1940, and then had subsequently flown throughout the Battle of Britain. So, too, had his adored older brother, John, a young man who had seemed destined for great things. He had been killed in October

1940, having shot down and killed the great German ace, Helmut Wick. It had thus been left to Cocky to fly the family colours, and it seemed the gods had decided to shine on him. By the age of twenty, he was commanding 56 Squadron at Duxford, Cambridgeshire, before being given the task of forming the first Typhoon fighter-bomber wing. He had then been posted to Tunisia in January 1943 to lead 324 Wing, which included five squadrons of Spitfire; and when still aged only twenty-two, had led the wing to Sicily, and then to the Salerno beach-head, before finally, in January 1944, joining the Desert Air Force Staff.

Standing well over six foot, with a mass of blond hair and a somewhat goofy expression, he cut an unlikely and gangly picture as a fighter pilot, yet he had repeatedly risen to every challenge. Working directly for Air Vice-Marshal William Dickson, the CO of the Desert Air Force, Cocky acted as his eyes and ears in all the fighter and fighter-bomber wings. Young, experienced men like Cocky were also there to help bring new ideas and innovations into the operations of the Desert Air Force (DAF) and to create an atmosphere where opportunities for improvement were always encouraged.

Great steps had already been made in recent times, especially in the North African campaign with the development of army–air co-operation. This meant positioning air force and army headquarters next to each other, respective commanders working closely together, and using an entire air force – known as a tactical air force – in direct support of the army.

However, with almost no aerial opposition whatsoever over Italy, this level of co-operation had recently been taken a step further with the development of what was known as the 'Cab-Rank' and 'Rover David' systems, enabling the air forces to reduce the time it took to respond to a request by the army for air support. These had been the brainchild of another young fighter commander, a South African, Group Captain David Heysham. The systems were simple. On the ground, an RAF officer would act as the controller, directing aircraft on to a target using a VHF radio transmitter. Assisting him with a clear picture of the situation on the ground and helping to establish the target would be an officer of the Army Air Staff. These 'Rover Davids' would drive around a given area of the front in an armoured car, or truck and jeep, in what was termed a Mobile Observation Room Unit. Meanwhile, up above would be six or more bomb-laden fighter aircraft circling the same pre-arranged area, gridded maps and aerial photographs stuffed down their flying boots, waiting to be directed onto a target by the Rover

David. This was the Cab Rank, and it enabled pilots to bomb and strafe with machine-gun and cannon fire moving or static targets in a matter of minutes after being detected. 'This "Rover" technique was tremendously successful,' noted Cocky Dundas. 'It not only achieved very much more effective tangible results than the old system, when all targets had to be selected before the aircraft left the ground; it was also a wonderful thing for the morale of the soldiers fighting on the ground.'[47]

On the broader, more strategic view of how air power should be employed, there remained, however, notable differences of opinion, especially with regard to the campaign in Italy. Air Chief Marshal Sir Arthur Tedder, previously C-in-C Mediterranean Air Command before it evolved into MAAF, had been a proponent of his scientific adviser, Professor Solly Zuckerman, who believed that the best way to stop enemy rail movement was by destroying marshalling yards and the rolling stock based at big railway centres. But a new theory had more recently developed, known as 'interdiction' – which meant blowing up bridges, blocking tunnels and cutting tracks, and keeping them cut.

On the face of it, Slessor was a supporter of Zuckerman's views because he had written as much in a book on the subject of air power that had been published in 1936. However, it also occurred to him that it wasn't really a question of favouring one view over the other, or following a rigid operational doctrine. Following on from further discussions with Eaker, Slessor drew up a new bombing directive, in which the heavy bombers of MASAF would concentrate on bombing marshalling yards, while the medium bombers and fighter-bombers would make every effort to fulfil the interdiction policy. Where Slessor now took exception was to the idea of using air power to bombard the enemy's defensive positions. 'It was perhaps memories of the old Western Front many years before,' he wrote, 'where bombardments really were bombardments, going on for days and weeks on end and blasting almost every identifiable feature of the landscape out of recognition that led me to doubt whether a concentrated air bombardment, however heavy, would prove to be the key to unlock a strongly prepared position in the face of resolute and skilful resistance.'[48]

The bombing of Monte Cassino and Cassino town underlined this belief. The two attacks, on the monastery in February and on the town in March, had certainly pulverised the targets but had hardly helped the Allied troops on the ground. Rather, the Germans had found defending amongst the rubble easier than when the buildings had still been standing. The failure of these attacks did, however, enable Eaker and Slessor instead to launch Operation STRANGLE on 19 March. This was a direct preparation for the DIADEM offensive, but rather than trying to obliterate the Gustav Line, its object was to destroy German supply lines and thus throttle them where they stood.

While the medium bombers and fighter-bombers concentrated on this 'simultaneous interdiction' policy, the heavy bombers of MASAF pounded marshalling yards in northern Italy, but also, throughout April, attacked targets in the Balkans with particular ferocity, the aim being to continue their strategic bombing work, interrupting the flow of oil and other materiel into all parts of the Reich. By taking the strategic bombing campaign into Romania and other areas of Eastern Europe as well as enemy-controlled ports around the Eastern Mediterranean, the Allies hoped to debilitate the German war effort in general, which included that in Italy.

Amongst those taking part in Operation STRANGLE were the pilots of the single-engine aircraft of the US 27th Fighter-Bomber Group. Operating from airfields around Caserta, the men of the 27th FBG were now highly experienced in the art of dropping bombs on specific targets, having been one of the first US outfits to be designated specifically in the role of fighter-bombers.

Lieutenant Charles Dills flew his forty-sixth combat mission the day Operation STRANGLE was launched, and in the weeks that followed was flying almost daily – sometimes twice daily – hitting German columns of vehicles, enemy supply dumps, railway lines, railway viaducts and bridges. He and his colleagues might not have had to worry too much about the likes of Willi Holtfreter, but low-level combat flying was extremely hazardous. There was always plenty of small-arms fire and flak* to contend with. And at such low heights there was little chance of bailing out. If a plane came down, then more often than not, the pilot came down too, and very few survived.

It had taken a while for Charles to realise this. 'To begin with it was all kind of a lark and I didn't really think of the dangers,' he admits. But back in early February, Charles had been flying as wingman to his flight leader. They were flying at around 300 mph, just 200 feet above the

---

*The word 'flak' is a German abbreviation of *Flugabwehrkanone*, meaning anti-aircraft gun, which was adopted by the Allies and is now universally accepted as meaning the shell-burst from an anti-aircraft gun, rather than the weapon itself.

ground looking for anything to strafe. Charles had been looking around – behind him and either side, and then suddenly had turned back and seen his flight leader in a steep dive. A second later he had exploded on the ground. 'It was a shock,' admits Charles. 'I just couldn't believe it.' In a state of numbed confusion, he had circled over several times, calling for him on his radio, but then there had been flak all around him and he had managed to pull himself together and head home. Later, it had been concluded that the flight leader had been hit in the head by a freak rifle shot. 'That's when you realise this is a pretty serious business,' says Charles, 'and you start getting a bit mad and you realise you're only going to survive if there's nothing else alive to shoot at you.'

From La Moure, in north Dakota, Charles had had, like many of those growing up in the 1920s and '30s , a tough childhood. He was the third of four children, two girls and two boys, although his younger brother had tragically died at birth. Despite this, the 1920s were his family's 'happy time', with father and uncle running a successful drug-store business and the family living comfortably. The tide would soon change, however. In 1930, his father died of cancer; the business had to be sold and Charles and his mother and sisters moved to Fargo. For the next few years, with America in the throes of the Depression, she did her best to keep the family by running a small lingerie business, but then she also contracted cancer and died. An orphan at fourteen, Charles was sent to live with his uncle, who looked after him and ensured he went to good schools. It paid off because after leaving high school, he went to North Dakota Agricultural College.

Charles had, however, always had a passion for aircraft, and in his second year at college, in 1941, he was given the chance to learn to fly. This was thanks to Roosevelt's Civilian Training Program, a scheme designed to speed up the rate at which pilots could be prepared for war, and Charles enrolled even though he was against America joining the war. By January 1942, he had his civil pilot's licence; six months later he had joined the US Army Air Force. A little over a year later, he was on his way to Italy.

Charles had joined the 27th Fighter-Bomber Group the previous November and since then had become one of the most experienced pilots in his squadron, although he was yet to lead a mission himself. 'I was relatively small,' he says, 'and I looked like I was perhaps nineteen. I always looked younger than my real age. The senior guys in the squadron always used to think of me as a bit of a kid brother.'

His part in Operation STRANGLE came to an end on 24 April. Loaded with fuel and armed with six 20lb fragmentation bombs and a 500-pounder strapped underneath, he taxied his P-40 Kittyhawk over to the runway as normal. But there was a strong crosswind and as he sped down the runway a heavy gust blew him sideways towards the left of the runway where a trench had been dug. Giving the engine some emergency boost he felt the undercarriage lift off the ground, but unfortunately his tail wheel had snagged into the ditch as the front of his plane lifted into the air – and this took away just enough speed to prevent him from climbing further. In a trice, his Kittyhawk began roll to the left. 'It's amazing how quickly you think in an emergency like this,' says Charles. 'I remember thinking, if my left wing-tip clears the ground, I'll land on my back. If it doesn't, I'll cartwheel. Either of these seemed a sure death. So I pulled back the mixture control and killed the engine. The plane straightened up and slammed to the ground, wiping out the landing gear.'

It was nonetheless a heart-stopping moment, especially with seven live bombs strapped underneath. The aircraft tilted to the right, tearing off much of the wing as it dug into the ground. As the plane slewed heavily, the bombs fortunately rolled away from underneath him, but the pierced-steel plating runway bowed upwards with the force of the crash and slammed against the rear of his fuselage, knocking the tail ninety degrees from the cockpit. Incredibly, Charles walked away with nothing more than a scratched thumb, but his commanding officer felt the time had come to give him a break. The next day he was sent to the American rest camp on Capri for a week.

By that time, however, Eaker and Slessor had realised that Operation STRANGLE had not fulfilled its objective of making it impossible for the Germans to remain south of Rome. On paper the interdiction policy was sound, because the railway system in Italy was highly vulnerable to aerial attack, with its multitude of tunnels, bridges, viaducts and embankments. The limiting Italian terrain also meant the Germans were predominantly using only three main rail routes – the western, central and eastern – all running roughly north–south down the leg of the country.

Early results had been promising. By 4 April, Kesselring's Army Group was receiving just 1,357 tons of supplies per day, rather than their minimum daily requirement of 2,261 tons. From 22 March, the eastern route was almost entirely impassable, while large parts of the central and western routes were also almost continuously blocked. By the end of April, the central route was cut in sixty-nine places, and by the end of the first week of May, 155 more had been added. When STRANGLE officially ended on the eve of the battle on 11 May, 22,500 tons of bombs had been dropped – more than during the entire London Blitz.

Yet despite this the Germans had not withdrawn. With the kind of efficiency and improvisation that prompted awe from the Allies, the Germans managed to repair large parts of track and numerous bridges, while also making good use of lesser roundabout routes and moving goods between trains across damaged parts of track. Overseeing this work was a 'General with Special Responsibility for the Maintenance of Rail Communications in Italy' newly appointed by Kesselring. German engineers provided the skills; the Organisation Todt, the German military labour force made up of mostly press-ganged Italians, provided the workers. It also helped that Kesselring had ensured that considerable stocks had been built up at the front during the winter, and that, with a stagnant front, he was using up little of his stocks of fuel and ammunition. As Slessor recognised, German troops seemed to be hardier than many of the Allies. 'He doesn't worry about ENSA shows or V cigarettes,' he noted, 'Coca-Cola or chewing gum, the masses of motor vehicles, or all the luxuries without which it is assumed that the modern British and American soldier cannot wage war.' Germans, it appeared, could survive four or five days on the same tonnage the Allies consumed in a day. Furthermore, they had managed by moving greater volumes of traffic by road and by sea, using coast-hugging lighters at night, and taking what they could from the land. 'The fact is,' noted Slessor in a report written on 16 April 1944, 'if you don't care a damn about the civilian population and are prepared to use all the transportation resources to hand (and, incidentally, forced civilian labour) for purely military purposes,' then only a small proportion of a transport potential needed to be used to achieve a minimum requirement.[49]

These were important lessons and were duly noted – both in Italy and by those preparing for D-Day. Air power alone could not destroy the enemy in the field. Alexander, on the other hand, was delighted by the efforts of the air forces in the weeks before his offensive had been launched. 'I never felt,' he said, 'that these air attacks would force the Germans to withdraw.' Rather, he had hoped they would be able seriously to hamper German supply and reinforcement. In this aim, STRANGLE had been an unquestionable success.

Air power had played an integral part in the Allies' success in both North Africa and Sicily. It would continue to do so in Italy – but it could never do the job of the men on the ground.

EIGHT

The Battle Rages
13–16 May, 1944

As General Oliver Leese's senior aide-de-camp, Captain Ion Calvocoressi was able to view the unfolding events of the battle with a far greater clarity than the vast majority of men who shared his rank. Recently turned twenty-five, Ion was not, as his surname suggested, Italian, but half Greek. His upbringing, however, had been thoroughly English: born in India, he had then been sent to prep and public school in England and at the outbreak of war had joined the Scots Guards, subsequently serving with them in North Africa. Wounded at the First Battle of Alamein in July 1942, where he had won a Military Cross, he had later been called for by General Leese, then XIII Corps commander under Montgomery, just prior to the second battle. As was often the way with such appointments, there had been a connection: Leese had known Ion's uncle and having heard of his wound and MC, and needing a new ADC, had sent for him.

They had been together ever since: through the remainder of the North African campaign, through Sicily, and in Italy since Leese had taken over as Eighth Army commander. And in that time Ion had met more generals and politicians – not to mention kings – than he could ever have imagined, and had become privy to the kind of intelligence that was often extremely sensitive – including information he should not have heard, such as when, during the Sicily campaign, Admiral Mountbatten had visited Leese's HQ and Ion had attended the ensuing dinner. In the course of conversation, Leese had asked Mountbatten about what was going on in England and had then been told in great detail about a floating 'Mulberry' harbour they were planning to take across the Channel when the Allies invaded northern France. 'Afterwards,' says Ion, 'General Oliver said to me, Mountbatten should never have talked about that. It was an appalling security breach.'

Not that Ion would ever have dreamed of betraying the trust placed in him. Nor would he have ever wished to let his chief down, for not only did he greatly admire 'General Oliver' as a commander, but also liked him enormously as a man. Although Leese was prone to brief outbursts of temper and irritability, for the most part he was good-humoured and informal, and took great care of his men. His Tactical HQ was always a lively and entertaining place to be. A cricket-obsessed Old Etonian, Leese was also known for his mild eccentricities of behaviour. His appearance, for example, was often most unbecoming for an army general; unlike the sartorial Alexander, he tended to wear baggy corduroy breeches and big sweaters, the effect of which was to exaggerate his large frame; like Clark, he was a tall man, some six foot three. Most of the staff at his HQ had nicknames – Ion's was 'Tante', which Leese pronounced 'Taunt'– while Leese had also introduced another in-joke, namely 'Eighth Army French', which helped lighten the atmosphere. This had developed during the planning of Operation DIADEM, when General Anders had asked for more guns. Leese spoke no Polish except '*Oscryzakrit*', meaning 'hairpin bend' and '*Poska ney darlecco*', meaning 'Poles not far away', while Anders had only a small command of English, so they tended to converse in French. Leese, how-ever, was not quite as fluent as Anders and on this occasion he had replied to the Polish commander that there was '*non beaucoup de chambre*' when trying to explain that there was not enough room for the guns Anders was demanding on the mountain. At this, Anders had fallen about laughing. Since then, Leese had continued to sprinkle in further howlers whenever he spoke with Anders. As Leese realised, it helped them to understand one another better.

On the evening of 12 May, however, Leese needed all his charm to calm the Polish commander after their disappointing opening attack at Monte Cassino. Accompanying him was Ion Calvocoressi. 'The Poles were very gloomy,' he noted in his diary. Leese had done as much soothing and reassuring as possible, but the Poles would now have to hold fire for a few days, regroup and then, on his signal, try again.

General Leese could not, of course, let on to his commanders his own feelings of anxiety. In Eighth Army's sector, the news on the morning of 13 May was only slightly more encouraging. By great endeavour, another Bailey bridge – 'Amazon' – had been built across the Garigliano. The three bridges now open were not enough, but it did mean that bridge-

General Sir Harold Alexander, or 'Alex' as he was known to all. Beloved by his men and the most experienced Allied battlefield commander of the entire war, he was also utterly imperturbable and extremely adept at handling his commanders, who represented a multitude of egos and wide-ranging nationalities, and who often had different and potentially problematic agendas.

Hans-Jürgen Kumberg at his machine gun post on Monte Cassino. Just nineteen at the time, Hans was one of the elite troops from the 1st Fallschirmjäger Division – men who earned the grudging respect of many of the Allied attackers for their stoic and courageous defence of Cassino.

Ray Saidel. Already a veteran of the Tunisian campaign, Ray served with the US 1st Armored Division and managed to survive two winters, the fighting at Anzio, the battles north of Rome, those along the Gothic Line, and the final offensive in April 1945. He had his fair share of close calls, but was nonetheless one of the few lucky ones to emerge without a scratch.

Monte Cassino taken before the war …

… and from the same spot toward the battle's end, by which time it looked more like the shell-blasted lunar landscapes of the Western Front in the First World War. The Allies were extremely proficient at obliterating Italian towns and villages.

Leese, Alexander and Clark, the commanders of Eighth Army, Allied Armies in Italy and Fifth Army respectively. Leese, jovial and eccentric in appearance, stands beside the ever-immaculate Alexander, while Clark – 'the American Eagle' – stands tall in his pristine yet casual US uniform. Each man understood the importance of looking the part and of cultivating an image.

ABOVE: Interdiction. With Operation STRANGLE, the Allied Air Forces aimed to cut off all German supplies to the front by destroying railways, roads and bridges. Although it made life very difficult for the Germans it failed in its original objective and proved that wars on the ground could not be won by air operations alone. Here a US Baltimore attacks a railway line.

LEFT: Charles Dills, a pilot in the US 27th Fighter–Bomber Group. Charles played a full part in Operation STRANGLE and then, on the eve of the battle, found himself seconded to Fifth Army Headquarters to fly General Mark Clark to and from Anzio and the Southern Front.

ABOVE: The Liri Valley as seen by Ted Wyke-Smith from atop Monte Trocchio. As a bridging engineer waiting in reserve with the rest of 78 Division, Ted was here on 11 May 1944, which gave him a grandstand view of the start of the DIADEM battle.

BELOW: The Liri Valley from Monte Cassino with Monte Trocchio on the right. Never more than six miles wide, this gentle, open valley offered the Allies the only real route to Rome.

LEFT: Kesselring (*left*) and one his ablest commanders, General Fridolin von Senger und Etterlin. It was disastrous for Kesselring that von Senger – amongst other commanders – was absent when the battle commenced. Although a brilliant strategist, Kesselring was a Luftwaffe – rather than an Army – Field Marshal – and had little experience of commanding troops in battle. As he desperately tried to plug gaps and split up regiments and divisions in the process, this inexperience began to show.

BELOW: Ted Wyke-Smith in his dug-out. Wherever the front stabilised, troops found themselves spending large amounts of time living half-submerged out in the open like this.

BELOW RIGHT: Wladek Rubnikowicz, one of the victors of Monte Cassino. Like most Poles fighting in Italy, Wladek had suffered an extraordinary journey before going into battle for the first time at Cassino – one that had taken him from Poland to a gulag in Siberia, then south to Uzbekistan, across Persia, Iraq and Palestine.

FAR RIGHT: Jupp Klein, an engineer in the 1st Fallschirmjäger Division. Another veteran of the Eastern Front, not to mention Sicily and the battle for Ortona, Jupp was able to use his enormous experience to very good effect during the fighting in the Liri Valley.

LEFT: Santa Maria Infante, one of the Americans' first objectives in the battle, which fell on 14 May. Like nearly every single town and village in the battle zone, Santa Maria was almost entirely destroyed.

BELOW: Eighth Army's progress in the Liri Valley was severely hindered by the weight of traffic and the large number of rivers and waterways that had to be crossed. This is Ted Wyke-Smith's first of twenty-six bridges built in twenty-eight nights, over the River Piopetta. His jeep is in the foreground.

LEFT: The Canadian, Stan Scislowski. Every man had his own way of coping with the stresses and strains of battles. Stan's was an uncontrollable urge to scavenge for 'loot', picked from the dead or left behind by fleeing Italians.

BELOW: A Nebelwerfer – or 'Moaning Minnie' as the Allies called them. A six-barrelled rocket mortar launcher, this was the weapon used by Oberleutnant Hans Golda and his men of Werfer Regiment 71.

BELOW: US troops trundle through Formia on 19 May 1944. The vast majority of the town's inhabitants had already been evacuated but as this picture shows, there would not be much of a home to return to once the cyclone of war had passed through.

Moroccan Goumiers. There is no doubt that the French Expeditionary Corps performed brilliantly in the DIADEM battles, but the behaviour of the Goums – raping, murdering and pillaging more than 3,000 Italians in the flush of victory – was a terrible stain on the Allied victory and one that has since been largely swept under the carpet. Medieval in appearance and attitude, they were justifiably feared by Germans and Italians alike.

Fallschirmjäger retreat northwards. For most of these men there was only one means of getting away and that was by foot.

heads were being slowly but surely established on the far side of the river. Progress, albeit slow, was being made.

No less anxious was the Fifth Army commander, General Mark Clark, who, having spent the first half of the morning reading reports and studying maps, then set off to tour his units along the front. Visiting the command post of the 85th 'Custer' Division, he learned that in the first thirty-six hours of battle the new boys had suffered 956 reported casualties – a heavy toll for one division. In the afternoon, he hurried over to see General Juin at the French Expeditionary Corps headquarters. There, however, the news was much better. Following on from their success the day before, the French had now captured the key position of Monte Maio, the southern bastion of the Gustav Line. Using pack mules and travelling over ground previously considered impassable, they had managed to make the first major breach of the German defences.

Few battles ever go exactly according to plan, no matter how meticulous the preparation. No one amongst the highly experienced Allied staff, for example, had considered the effect of a cocktail of river mists, smoke canisters, and a thousand guns in the Liri Valley; after all, nothing like it had ever been attempted before in such a location. Equally, no one had guessed that the first to break through the Gustav Line would be the French. But such was the capricious nature of battle, as General Alexander and his Chief of Staff, John Harding, were all too well aware. The key, however, was to have that 'balance' which Alex believed was so important, which enabled them to make the most of sudden and unexpected developments and to limit the effects of any potential setbacks. And balance meant having the right number of troops and materiel in the right areas – both at the front and in reserve. Furthermore, communication between commanders and units had to be good, ensuring that any change of orders could be acted upon quickly and precisely.

And so, on the evening of 13 May, Clark was in a position to act swiftly and decisively. Having realised the Germans opposite the French divisions in the Aurunci Mountains were in complete disarray, he recognised that it was imperative that the Americans to the south keep up, rather than allowing the French to penetrate too deeply and narrowly on their own. If they could bring about a major thrust forward between the mountains and the coast, then the whole German right-hand front would collapse. With this in mind, he ordered the two new divisions of the US II Corps – despite the heavy casualties they had taken so far –

to speed up their own attacks that very night 'regardless of previous
schedules or plans'. This way, Clark noted, they could make the most of
the Germans 'being off-balance'.[50]

And off-balance they certainly were. In many ways it was a miracle the
Germans were able to defend so much of the line at all. Communication
between units was terrible. Not only had AOK 10's HQ been bombed
out, Allied bombers had also hit the headquarters of the 1st Fallschirmjäger, 44th Infantry, and 15th Panzer Grenadier Divisions and in so
doing, seriously interrupted their ability to communicate with one
another. And although AOK 10 eventually managed to set up a new
HQ with 14th Panzer Corps, it still had not established an advanced
headquarters close to the front.

All this meant that information from the front was patchy to say the
least. As Kesselring was forced to admit, they were floundering in the
dark, unable properly to evaluate the scale of the Allied attack and
lacking the kind of 'data on which to make a far-reaching decision' on
how best to respond.[51]

Inevitably, the absence of too many senior commanders was hardly
helping. Neither General Feuerstein, the commander of the 51st Mountain Corps, nor General Hartmann, von Senger's stand-in at 14th Panzer
Corps, had much experience of command in a major battle. Nor were
they especially familiar with the terrain. To make matters worse, Kesselring had, for once, made some crucial tactical errors. The lack of sound
intelligence caused him problems on two scores. First, he had an unclear
picture of the troops opposing him. For example, only one French
division had been correctly identified and he had no idea the massed
French Expeditionary Corps was lined up below the Aurunci Mountains,
a mistaken appreciation that would cost him dear. Second, he had been
forced to cater for every eventuality, leaving a number of troops north
of Rome in case of a seaborne landing, as well as around the Anzio
bridgehead. Although his build-up of troops and ammunition had gone
better than the Allies would have liked, he was still under-strength in
almost all his units, while the fighting performance of his divisions
varied massively.

To counteract this problem, he began splitting up his reserve divisions,
and placing them in 'penny-packets' all along the line. One of his best
was the veteran 15th Panzer Division, which had been split into battalions rather than kept as a whole. Similarly, Major Georg Zellner's 3rd
Battalion 'Hoch-und-Deutschmeister' Reichs Grenadier Regiment was

part of 44th Infantry Division, but while he and a few other units were in the mountains north of Cassino, the rest of the division was sprinkled in the Liri Valley.

The problem with this approach was that it reduced the fighting capacity of the division; a smaller unit, such as a battalion, was obviously easier to overwhelm than an entire division. This was the kind of mistake the British used to make in North Africa before Alexander and Montgomery arrived and put a stop to it. Furthermore, it meant unit commanders were constantly faced with differing chains of command and different superiors. In battle, there is much to be said for familiarity and trust.

Struggling their way into this mayhem was the Werfer Regiment 71. They had been part of General Baade's Army Group Reserve, but had now been hastily attached to the 90th Panzer Grenadier Division, which in turn had also been split up and posted to 51st Mountain Corps. The division's progress to the front was piecemeal and too slow, although Werfer Regiment 71 were among the first to hurry south; Oberleutnant Hans Golda's 8th Battery were nearing the front by the evening of the 12th. Artillery shells screamed overhead as he reached the staff post and was given his orders. With the light going, he and his unit set off again, to a bunker along the Gustav Line between Pignataro and Pontecorvo, and halfway from the ruins of Cassino town to the River Liri. 'We were driving into a witches' cauldron,' noted Hans. 'The night was pitch dark. Only the flash of the artillery broke through the darkness. The crashing, roaring and screaming was first of all in front of us and then all around us.'[52] Nervously, they inched their way forward, the drivers dodging shell holes, the men lying flat on the ammunition and trying to make themselves as small as possible. Hans prayed they wouldn't receive a direct hit.

Eventually they reached their new position. Hans was pleased to see that the Organisation Todt had built the bunkers reasonably well. Ammunition was stored and the *werfers* assembled and readied for firing. Soon after, a report arrived that enemy tanks were uncomfortably close: Hans's battery was now firing into the shallow bridgehead made by 8th Indian Division. Ahead was the wreck of the village of Sant' Angelo, which had been completely pulverised. 'I set up an OP [observation post],' noted Hans, 'got it manned and detailed the anti-tank troop to man it.'[53] With luck, these men would be able to provide a brief delaying action should the enemy completely break through.

*   *   *

To the south, US II Corps were now renewing their assault on the troublesome 400-foot-high and well-defended Spigno Ridge. It was another costly effort, although this time Lieutenant Bob Wiggans and his Company D were not part of the main assault on Hill 131. Rather, that honour went to Company I of the 338th Infantry. At the end of their attack, just sixteen men were left standing. Nonetheless, despite further setbacks and a certain amount of confusion by two new divisions fighting at night, the Americans stuck at their bloody task and in the early hours the Germans began to pull back. By morning on the 14th, most of the Spigno Saturnia Ridge, including Hill 131, was in US hands. By the following afternoon, Santa Maria Infante – another village utterly obliterated – was taken too.

On the Americans' right, the French were also continuing their extraordinary advance. On the 14th, they broke into the Ausente Valley and captured Ausonia, a key town, before pushing on towards Esperia. And as they retreated, the German 71st Division was becoming more and more separated from the 94th Division opposing the Americans. For once the Italian landscape was working to the Allies' advantage, for dividing the retreating Germans was the wedge of an almost trackless ridge of the Aurunci Mountains.

On the night of the 14th, Bob Wiggans led his platoon over Hill 131, picking his way through the American and German dead who lay thick across the ground. He'd not slept a wink since the battle had begun and yet now his men's spirits were soaring. They felt they were at last on the road to Rome. So, too, did Mark Clark, even though he felt the two rookie divisions had been fortunate. 'My fears,' he noted in his diary, 'that the enemy might react to our lack of aggressive attitude toward Spigno did not materialise.'[54] In fact, much to Kesselring's chagrin, the 94th Division opposite the Americans had disobeyed a direct order, and had placed their reserve troops along the coast rather than in the mountains ready to plug the gaps. Perhaps in the confusion the order never reached them – at any rate, once German losses began to mount, and it became clear there were no large-scale reinforcements available, General Hartmann, von Senger's deputy, ordered his men to fall back. Clark expected a lot from everyone under his command, not least American troops new to battle, but the fact remained that the Americans had bludgeoned the German 94th Division to 40 per cent of its fighting strength on and around the Spigno Ridge. With the French leading the way, the breakthrough *had* been achieved. With the Gustav Line now broken in the US II Corps sector as well, the entire southern half of the Allied push was surging forward.

In the Liri Valley, however, XIII Corps were still struggling to make any serious headway. The stumbling block was the River Garigliano. Only by nightfall on the 14th was the full quota of nine pre-planned Bailey bridges completed, but even these represented major bottlenecks through which men and materiel had to pass. And where there are bottlenecks there are greater targets for the enemy. While it had been 8th Indian and 4th Division that had been given the job of leading the assault across the Gari, 78th and 6th Armoured had been kept in reserve. On the 15th, Leese and his XIII Corps commander, Lieutenant-General Sidney Kirkman, decided the time had come to send 78th Division into the breach, combined with the Poles' second assault on Monte Cassino. Unfortunately, traffic congestion, along with German mines and concentrated shelling, ensured that 78th Division was unable to cross the river in time – and so the attack was postponed until the morning, as was that of the Poles.

This breather for the Germans was greatly welcomed, not least by Oberleutnant Hans Golda and his men, although he himself was in trouble with Dink, one of his gunners. During a moment of comparative peace, Hans had spotted a rabbit hopping about not far from their position. Taking a rifle, he drew a bead and shot it dead, then proudly showed his men their next meal. Dink, however, was appalled. 'He explained to me that I had killed one of his rabbits that he had been fattening up with a lot of effort,' noted Hans, 'and that it had been completely tame.' Needless to say, Hans was the subject of much ridicule, although as he admitted, 'We polished off the object despite all the laughter that went on.'

The mirth did not last long. That evening, 15 May, their position was once again under fire. What Hans termed 'bunker breakers' were whistling over. He and his men could only cower in the corners, staring at the roof. After every explosion the entire bunker shook. Soon there was a loud crash followed by a scream. 'One of our young lads had been hit,' wrote Hans, 'an open wound between the shoulders.'[55]

Also cowering in their bunker a few miles to the north, in a narrow valley between the mountains, were Major Georg Zellner and his battalion staff of the 3rd Battalion of the H und D Regiment. Opposite them were the New Zealanders of X Corps, and although this stretch of the line was not part of the main thrust of the attack, the Kiwis were still keeping up the pressure. 'Planes and crashing of bombs,' noted Georg. 'We can't get out of our bunker.'

Every time a shell whistled through the air towards them, Georg wondered whether it was their turn to get a direct hit. His nerves were stretched and he was feeling as miserable as he had done four days before on his birthday. The early sounds of summer – the nightingales singing, insects buzzing – had gone. 'Death is creeping over everything,' he scrawled in his diary. 'Tonight they carried the dead down to the valley. It looked ghostly and we stood in front of our bunker watching the sad procession with heavy hearts.'[56] Nearby a badly wounded soldier was screaming horribly. Georg could barely stand it. And to make matters worse, he had still not received any post from home.

Meanwhile on the Allied side of the line, it was Lieutenant Ted Wyke-Smith and his team of sappers' turn to construct their first Bailey bridge – in anticipation of 78th Division's attack the following morning. Ted had been expecting to move soon after the battle had started, so having felt somewhat pent-up in anticipation, was relieved finally to get going. The place they needed to bridge was the River Piopetta, a tributary of the Garigliano, near the hamlet of Piumarola, just north of Pignataro. Getting there was no easy matter, however. Leading in his jeep, Ted had behind him several lorries full of bridging gear, but rather than heading over 'Amazon' – the nearest of the newly built bridges – they were sent on a fairly lengthy route and ended up crossing over 'Oxford' right down by the Liri Appendix. Eventually, however, despite the detour and despite the fact that it was night-time and dark, they reached the right spot. As they began unloading, shells screamed overhead, and small arms fire chattered nearby. On the far side of the river – which was only twenty yards or so wide – infantry had been clearing the far banks of enemy troops and laying down smoke screens to protect Ted and his men.

Bailey bridges were a new and ingenious invention, designed by Donald Bailey, an engineer at the British War Office, and had only been used since the previous autumn. Prefabricated, they were transported in steel panels that could be carried by six men and easily fixed together. The panels, each 10-foot long, made up the walls – or sides – of the bridge. Stood on rollers, the two small panels were then linked together with 19-foot transoms – or girders – strung between them. 'When you've got three or four panels built,' explains Ted, 'you've got to bring it to a point of balance. It's then a case of hands on, and everyone pushes it forwards until the front begins to tip over the edge of the river bank. Then you put two more panels on the back and more transoms between them and everyone pushes again.' This process was repeated until the bridge spanned the river. Wooden planking was then placed across the structure and the bridge was ready: a 12-foot-wide roadbed strong enough to carry tanks, trucks and anything else in the Allied armoury.

It was a simple construction but there were all sorts of factors to consider. 'A bridge could weigh anything from 20 to 40 tons,' says Ted, 'and then you might have a 30-ton tank going over it. That's a lot of pressure on the bank.' It was up to men like him to decide exactly where the banks were strongest and thus where the bridge should be sited. It was a decision they could not afford to get wrong, even when, as at the River Piopetta, they were often coming under repeated enemy fire. Even so, by morning, the bridge was open to traffic. 'It was,' admits Ted, 'very exciting, frankly.'

With this and other crossings now made, 78th Division finally launched their attack, supported by an armoured brigade of 6th Armoured Division. The idea was to push through the bridgeheads made by 4th Division, then wheel round northwards and cut the Via Casilina – or Route 6 as the Allies called it. This, they hoped, would isolate Cassino and would give the Poles the opportunity to renew their assault on Monte Cassino itself. Meanwhile, the 1st Canadian Division, which had, like 78th Division, been held back for the second wave of the assault, also joined the battle, passing through the 8th Indian Division further to the south. Slowly but surely, the Allies were now pushing the Germans back in the Liri Valley as well.

Facing this new onslaught was Fahnenjunker Jupp Klein and his company of Fallschirmjäger Pioneers. They were one of a number of random units from the 51st Mountain Corps flung almost willy-nilly into the line to plug the gaps in the Liri Valley – gaps that were supposed to have been filled by 90th Panzer Grenadier Division. Much of the 90th, however, had still not reached the front, having been harried all the way from Rome by relentless Allied air attack.

Although they were engineers, it was in the infantry role that Jupp's company of Fallschirmjäger were now to be used. In fact, they had been given a very specific task: to accompany a section of self-propelled guns and protect them once they dug in. Mid-morning on the 16th, Jupp led his men, along with the section of self-propelled guns, across the Via Casilina and south towards Pignataro. The renewed Allied assault had already begun, with their artillery pounding the German positions. Finding a suitable position, Jupp led his men forward and found an isolated farm on a slight, shallow hill that was still held by a few infantry and which had been reinforced and converted into a kind of redoubt. The windows had been filled in to become nothing more than loopholes, the lower walls had been strengthened and the cellars converted into a passable bunker. Zig-zagging away from either side of the house were trenches. 'The whole thing,' says Jupp, 'impressed us as a kind of fortress.'

Even so, how much they would be able to achieve against a concerted enemy attack was uncertain. Jupp's company consisted of thirty-eight men, less than a quarter of its full strength, and all that was left after three months at Cassino. 'It was just a platoon really,' says Jupp. 'We hadn't had any reinforcements for a long time.' Nor had they been expecting to defend their outpost against an enemy tank attack, but as Jupp discovered to his horror that same afternoon, the gunners had been warned to prepare themselves against such an assault. Sure enough, as Jupp crept forward to recce the British positions, he could see on the hill opposite, just over half a mile away, a whole tank brigade boldly pointing towards them. Without further ado, he hurried back to the gunners and asked them to send an urgent message to the headquarters of the 1st Fallschirmjäger Division warning them that his company had no anti-tank weapons whatsoever and would be defenceless if and when the British tanks attacked.

Fortunately for him and his men, the British tanks did not attack either that afternoon or evening. It was just the respite they needed, for before nightfall an anti-tank crew with three *Ofenrohre** – bazookas – arrived and reported to Jupp. During the night, a further infantry battalion of reinforcements also joined them. These were men who had been posted from Yugoslavia, where they had been fighting partisans, and who had little battlefield experience. The battalion major immediately proved this by insisting on placing a troop of machine-gunners in a shed to the front of the farmhouse, facing the enemy. 'But the attacking tanks will cut them down at once,' Jupp warned him, 'and they'll have no chance of pulling back.' The major insisted, however. 'We could only feel sorry for the poor machine-gunners,' says Jupp, 'for we knew they were dead men.'

---

*An Ofenrohre was a bazooka-like anti-tank weapon, not to be confused with the better-known *Panzerfäuste*.

While Jupp Klein and his men were bracing themselves for the Allied attack, General Leese had decided the time had come for the Poles to renew their assault on Monte Cassino. And with the Fallschirmjäger reserves being swallowed up in the Liri Valley there were none spare for Monte Cassino. This time, Leese hoped, the valiant Poles would have the victory he believed they so richly deserved. More to the point, with this new all-out attack, he hoped to smash the accursed Gustav Line, the scene of five months' bloody fighting, once and for all.

NINE
New Order

In his villa at Gargnano overlooking Lake Garda, Benito Mussolini still governed the new Fascist Republic this May, 1944 – on paper, at any rate. He was well aware, however, that he was effectively Hitler's prisoner, and that despite the resurrection of the Fascist Party under the leadership of its Party Secretary, Alessandro Pavolini, Italy was now, to all intents and purposes, ruled and governed by the Germans.

Mussolini was sixty. He had always been a bull of man: square-jawed, barrel-chested, and with piercing eyes; yet he was thinner now, his face lacking the lustre that had always radiated from him. Italy's and his own decline had, unsurprisingly, affected him both physically and psychologically.

Following his 'rescue' by German SS and Fallschirmjäger troops from Gran Sasso the previous September, his ambition had been at its lowest ebb and he had said as much to Hitler, telling him he did not believe in the possible resurrection of fascism and that he wanted merely to retire quietly. The Führer, however, had swept aside such concerns. 'Northern Italy will be forced to envy the fate of Poland,' Hitler had warned him, 'if you do not accept to give renewed vigour to the alliance between Germany and Italy, by becoming head of the state and of the new government.'[57] The following day, Mussolini had reluctantly agreed to do as Hitler asked, although he had been fully aware of what that meant. 'The Germans will find a way to administer Italy according to their habits,' he had said, 'and the only outcome will be the loss of that little respect that Italy still has as a nation.'[58] In this instance, he had hit the nail on the head.

There were those in Germany who had believed Hitler had made a mistake in giving the Italians any form of self-rule at all: Kesselring, for one, had felt it would be better for Italy to be treated as an occupied country, and that an Italian government, in whatever form, would be a hindrance to the freedom of action of his troops in the country. Dr Rudolf Rahn, the newly appointed German ambassador, had also agreed with Kesselring. He had recognised that there was little enthusiasm within Italy for a return to fascism, especially after it had dissolved so spectacularly as a political movement after 25 July. Hitler, however, had not wanted to waste valuable German resources carrying out civil administration when there were a number of Italian Fascists willing and ready to carry out his wishes for him. Yet he had been unimpressed with the Fascists who had fled to Germany the previous summer, and quite apart from his fondness for his old friend, had known that Mussolini was the only possible candidate to head up a Neo-Fascist government.

Most of those who now rallied round the Duce were either diehard fanatics or men for whom it had been too dangerous to remain in Italy following Mussolini's overthrow. Alessandro Pavolini, a charismatic forty-year-old Florentine poet and former editor of the newspaper *La Stampa*, was something of an intellectual but also an increasingly fanatical Fascist. His drive and determination to see fascism back in Italy had made him the obvious candidate for secretary of the Neo-Fascist Party, the PRF, or Partito Repubblicano Fascista. There were a handful of others from the Fascist hierarchy of the pre-war heydays. Roberto Farinacci, for one: a former party secretary in the 1920s, and the most outspoken of those who had urged Italy to fight alongside Germany to the bitter end. Another was Renato Ricci, founder of the Fascist *squadristi*, or hit squads, and later head of the Fascist Youth Organisations and Minister of Corporations until fired in February 1943. And there was Guido Buffarini-Guidi, another Fascist of the old school, albeit one who had been previously discredited for a number of frauds.

From this core, a Neo-Fascist government had emerged. Such had been the shortage of able candidates, Pavolini had persuaded Ambassador Rahn to accompany him to Rome back in September to try and recruit others to rally to the cause. As Rahn had suspected, it had proved something of a fool's errand: most former Fascists had wanted nothing to do with it. This had not overly worried the Germans, who had never had any intention of allowing the new government any real power. However, Rahn had felt there was a need for a competent Minister of War to rally support for the continuation of the war, and in desperation had turned to Marshal Rodolfo Graziani. This sixty-one-year-old marshal had been a successful commander in Ethiopia in the 1930s but after being defeated in North Africa at the hands of the British in 1941, he had resigned and returned to Italy. More soldier than politician, he nonetheless carried both the gravitas and the fame Rahn believed was needed.

Mussolini was back, but although physically his health had greatly improved within a few weeks of his return, he found it hard to rekindle the strutting arrogance of old when Germany was piling one humiliation upon him after another. There had, for example, been no return to Rome. Hitler had refused to allow the seat of government to be centred there; it was, as Kesselring had announced, now an 'Open City', and thus supposedly politically neutralised. A good excuse, but one that had scarcely hidden the real reason: that Hitler did not want the Neo-Fascist government getting above itself, which was far more likely had it been based in Italy's largest and most historic city. Milan had also been rejected for the same reason.

Rather, the new seat of government was now based around the tiny town of Salò, on the western banks of Lake Garda in the foothills of the Alps. Government offices were to be established in towns all along the lake. With fuel scarce and only narrow roads connecting them, effective government had been deliberately made harder. Moreover, by setting up in Salò, a small and insignificant place of little note, the prestige of the new government was undermined from the outset.

As if this wasn't bad enough, the new government's sphere of control had also become increasingly depleted. Quite apart from land already lost to the Allies, the Brenner Pass and the Ljubljana Gap – the two main access routes from Greater Germany into Italy – had been annexed into the Reich, in what was yet another stinging blow to Mussolini's power and prestige. The first now became an area known as the Alpine Approaches, incorporating the Tyrol – the Dolomites and towns of Bolzano, Belluno and Trento. The second was the Adriatic Coastland, which consisted of an area that spread through north-east Italy – including Trieste, Fiume, and Istria – and into Croatia. As in other areas of the Greater Reich, two *Gauleiters* – military governors – were appointed, Franz Hofer for the Alpine Approaches, and Dr Friedrich Rainer for the Adriatic Coastland. Both were confirmed Nazis, and ruled as such. The Italian legal system there was abolished and all Italians in those areas came directly under German military law. It was not lost on Mussolini that the annexed areas were more or less those that had been taken from Austria at the end of the First World War.

There were still further disappointments for the man Hitler had once looked up to as a role model. One of the Duce's first jobs had been to order Renato Ricci to re-form the Fascist militia, which now became the Guardia Nazionale Repubblicana, or GNR, and which would work alongside the Carabinieri, the military-based police force, as a means of enforcing fascism once more. Yet although political militias were a useful means of imposing a regime's will, Mussolini knew that for him to regain any kind of reputation, he needed an army, a New Army, with which Italy could once more rise from the ashes.

It was, of course, never to be. The first blow came following Marshal Graziani's visit to Germany in early October 1943, where it had quickly become clear that there was considerable distrust amongst many of the German High Command of Mussolini and Graziani's plans. 'The only Italian Army that will not be treacherous,' Feldmarschall Keitel had noted, 'is one that does not exist.'[59] And anyway, they had already decided that able-bodied Italian men would be more useful as labourers, while those Italians who did want to fight willingly were encouraged to join the German armed forces instead – and did so: by May 1944, there were more than 200,000 Italian soldiers serving directly under the Germans. Even leading Fascists were against the New Army; both Pavolini and Ricci had been against it, as they distrusted Graziani and feared he might then use such a force against them.

Hitler, however, had agreed to the raising of a mere four Italian divisions, which he believed would be useful, not as front-line troops, but as guardians along the coast and behind the lines. He had also eventually agreed to release 12,000 former officers and NCOs from camps in Germany, but the rest of Mussolini's New Army had to come from entirely new recruits and from those who had returned home but had not been interned by the Germans. Dampened but undeterred, he issued a conscription order for all those born in the years 1923, 1924 and 1925 and started a major propaganda effort to draw in volunteers. By the beginning of 1944, some 50,000 young men had responded to Mussolini's call to arms – but a mere four divisions was small fry indeed compared to the fifty-six divisions eradicated by the Germans following the armistice.

The reality was that Mussolini had fallen a long, long way – from more than twenty years of absolute power to almost no power at all. Everything he tried to do was blocked or watered down, not only by the Germans but also by the Neo-Fascists. Most of the leaders of the new Fascist Party had been previously sacked by the Duce – Pavolini included – and although they openly professed their unswerving loyalty towards him, it had become apparent, over the eight months of the RSI's – Repubblica Sociale Italiana's – existence, that Mussolini and the Neo-Fascists were singing from different ideological hymn sheets, and not just over the formation and handling of the New Army.

The previous November, while the Germans and Allies were still fighting south of the Gustav Line, Pavolini had called the Neo-Fascists together to Verona, where a new 'manifesto' had been thrashed out. Mussolini had chosen to remain absent, yet despite his marked non-appearance the Neo-Fascists had, during a highly charged gathering, agreed in principle to holding elections, restoring the power of the judiciary, allowing freedom of the press, and a number of other measures. None of these things had since happened, however. Rather, it was following the Congress at Verona that Pavolini, in particular, had insisted on revenge for those Fascists who had 'betrayed' Italy and Mussolini the previous July. Most of the nineteen members of the Fascist Grand Council who had voted against Mussolini had since gone to ground, but six had been arrested and flung into jail, including Count Galeazzo Ciano, Mussolini's son-in-law and former Foreign Minister, who had been extradited, at Pavolini's behest, from Germany. Rather than restoring the rights of the judiciary, an 'Extraordinary Special Tribunal' had been set up, overseeing a sham trial in which the six were accused on trumped-up charges of treason. They were, of course, found guilty, and rather than being given any chance to appeal, all but one – and Ciano included – were hurriedly executed by a cack-handed firing squad who made a complete mess of their task early the following morning. The executions had been carried out swiftly so as to limit the Duce's opportunity to intervene.

Mussolini could – and should – have stopped the executions at the very least, but he had been warned that it would damage his standing with Hitler if he interfered. He at first dithered and then let it happen, just as he had allowed the Neo-Fascists to arrest other former Fascists, four generals, and several admirals. The admirals had also been executed without mercy.

So much of the key to fascism's success in Italy in the 1920s and 1930s had been the spectacle it offered: the rallies, the speeches, the songs and the marches, and in this regard Mussolini had always been a particularly visible leader. How different it was now in the early summer of 1944. The Duce had barely been seen in public for months, instead cosseting himself away at the Villa Feltrinelli in Gargnano; but he had not been idle, nor had he entirely lost his political verve.

Mussolini's political life had really begun as a journalist and as a socialist before he had broken away from the party, and it was to these roots that he had now returned. Since becoming head of the RSI his journalistic output had been extraordinary, and although he had not restarted his old paper, *Il Popolo d'Italia,* he had opened a new press agency, Corrispondenza Repubblicana, for which he wrote a large number of uncredited articles. Most of his pieces focused on *Socializza-zione* – or socialisation – as he called it. Not for nothing had he insisted on calling the new republic the Socialist Republic of Italy – just about the only concession he had gained from Hitler. Neo-fascism, he believed, was merely the political structure through which his brand of socialism could best be implemented – a brand that still valued the notion of a nation state and the heroism of Italians. Yes, the war was surely lost, despite Hitler's talk of secret weapons; but he still believed there could yet be a new revolution in Italy, and indeed across all of Europe, one that united those who mistrusted communism – a movement that was growing in Italy – and which loathed, as Mussolini did, the middle classes, the bourgeoisie. He began to see a future where Europe was united, and whereby a bridge could be made that linked the ideology of socialism and fascism together. This renewed political passion gave him hope. Mussolini was not completely beaten yet.

From the moment the Duce had lost his virginity to an elderly prostitute at the age of seventeen, he had maintained a voracious sexual appetite that had not dimmed over time. He had slept with hundreds of women, but although he remained married to his wife, Rachele, he had also always kept at least one principal mistress. This honour now belonged to Claretta Petacci, twenty-eight years his junior, and the daughter of a Vatican doctor.

There was another young woman who played an important part in his life. Elena Curti was twenty-one, intelligent, and highly vivacious, and one of Mussolini's few trusted confidantes. There was, however, nothing sexual in their relationship. Rather, Elena was his illegitimate daughter, the offspring of another of the Duce's favourite mistresses, Angela Curti Cucciati.

Elena had been born in 1922, soon after Mussolini had become prime minister. However, in a sense her origins date back to the birth of fascism, to the turbulent years immediately following the First World War when an embittered Italy struggled to come to terms with failure and its hollow victory in the war. The emerging fascist movement, led by Mussolini, had repeatedly clashed with the growing number of socialists. During a fight in Milan, a communist school teacher had been killed and all the Fascists involved flung into prison. One of these was the man Elena had grown up calling her father. Her mother had then contacted Mussolini, who at the time had been editor of *Popolo d'Italia*, and had asked for his help in trying to get her husband out of prison. How much Mussolini had been able to help is uncertain – probably not much, because he soon began an affair with Elena's mother. Signor Curti had not been released from prison until after Elena had been conceived.

Elena had grown up knowing none of this, however, although she had witnessed her parents' marriage disintegrate. 'My father [Signor Curti] had a tendency towards violence,' she says. 'My mother used to tell me he was a bad man. She put great fear into me.' Aged eight, she was abducted by Curti and kept locked up with a distant relative in Mantova, far from her home in Milan. After five months, she was sent away to the Convent of the Ursuline Sisters in Milan. 'I remember I hadn't even gone through the doors,' says Elena, 'but I was standing in the magnificent Bramante courtyard and I was greeted by a tiny nun with shining blue-green eyes. She listened to my story and then said, "So now you know what real suffering is like."' Only later did she discover that her mother had turned to Mussolini for help – help that had resulted in Elena being taken from both parents and placed in the convent instead. But it had been a happy place for her. With the love and security shown her by the nuns, she had blossomed both artistically and academically.

It was when she came of age at eighteen that her mother had taken her to Rome to meet Mussolini and that she finally learnt the truth. Understandably, this was deeply traumatic for her, although having slowly but surely come to terms with her dramatically changed circumstances, she began to feel rather proud of her true parentage. Nor did Mussolini forget her; rather, he continued to help both her and her mother. Whilst at university, following the establishment of the Repubblica Sociale Italiana, Elena began to work for the new government.

Until the spring of 1944, Elena had been living in a requisitioned hotel in Maderno, a few miles north of Salò, and working as a secretary in the Ministry of Popular Culture. Now a favourite not only of her father, Mussolini, but also of a number of the young officers and officials of the new republic, she was enjoying life and the attention she was being given.

She had a new job, too, as the 'Eyes of Mussolini Within the Party'. Every fortnight, a car would collect her and take her to see Mussolini in his villa, and she would tell him frankly about what she had observed in the intervening two weeks, as well as the general state of morale.

In this new role there were also other assignments for the Duce. It was in early May that Elena was contacted by an Italian Air Force officer named Virgilio Pallottelli Corinaldesi. 'The Duce has sent me,' he told her. 'He's charged me with a secret mission and you must accompany me. A couple,' he explained, 'does not get noticed so easily.' Intrigued, Elena did as she was asked. Their task was to go to Gorizia on the Yugoslav border to gauge the political and military climate there, even though this was now part of the Greater Reich. Mussolini had been told that Italian officers and officials there were working with the enemy – the Yugoslavian Communists – and he wanted them to find out the truth and report back.

It was no easy task getting there. They were given a car, a considerable luxury by that time, but they were repeatedly harassed by enemy aircraft, and time and again had to stop and hurl themselves on to the roadside. Elena was surprised by the number of ruined bridges and abandoned fields she saw as they travelled across northern Italy. Once they had to ford a river because the bridge had been destroyed. Despite this and several punctures along the way, they made it to Gorizia, where they found little evidence of any Italian collusion with the Yugoslavs.

'And when I got back to Maderno,' says Elena, 'I did not go straight to Mussolini but visited him as usual when I always did. He asked what I had been up to and I told him, "A friend of yours visited me, and together we went to Gorizia." And all he said was, "Ah yes, Corinaldesi is an intelligent young man." But it had been an adventure. The risk involved, the fact that we were on a secret mission for the Duce. I was young, and it was all very exciting.'

Despite the awe in which she held her father, Elena was all too aware that Mussolini was now an isolated figure. 'Italians thought that he was separate from the government,' she says. 'That was the way I saw it too. He used to refer to himself as a prisoner on this accursed lake.'

He was, however, living in something of a gilded cage. The Villa Feltrinelli in Gargnano had belonged to a wealthy Milanese business family before being requisitioned. Overlooking the beautiful Lake Garda, with the mountains rising behind, it had over thirty sumptuously decorated rooms. A curving driveway and a number of carefully positioned trees hid the house from the road. German SS – rather than Italian – troops guarded the gateway, while further SS men patrolled the grounds and stood sentinel at other posts around the property. All servants and any visitors were vetted and checked by the SD – the *Sicherheitsdienst* – while even the Duce's housekeeper was German. All telephones were tapped. Mussolini could say or do almost nothing within the villa without the Germans knowing about it.

Responsible for these draconian measures and for placing Mussolini there in the first place was General of the Waffen-SS and Highest SS and Police Führer in Italy, Karl Wolff, a smooth-talking charmer and highly intelligent senior Nazi. There were supposed to be four principal Germans running the show in Italy. First, there was Kesselring who, as Commander-in-Chief of Italy, was the most powerful man in the Axis-controlled half of the country, and to whom all others were subordinate. Immediately under him there was the German ambassador to the RSI, Rudolf Rahn, who, Iago-like, hovered over the Duce as his political 'adviser', a euphemism if ever there was one. Then there was General Rudolf Toussaint, 'Plenipotentiary General of the German Wehrmacht to the Italian Fascist Government'. And finally there was the aptly named Wolff.

In reality, however, Kesselring tended to meddle little in specifically civilian or political affairs, especially while he had the military campaign to run. Rather, the day-to-day governing of Italy was left to Ambassador Rahn and Wolff, whose power was so complete and expertly executed that General Toussaint's authority was continually and increasingly undermined. Both men, with Kesselring's blessing, made sure the authority of not only Mussolini but also the Neo-Fascist government was kept to a minimum, and that every decision made by the RSI was carefully monitored. As Rahn had pointed out to Kesselring in October 1943, 'the government consists of men who are willy-nilly bound to Germany, and above all, if need be, we have the means of intervening. In addition, we have delegates in each Ministry, whose task is precisely to bring our wishes before the Ministries.'[60]

It was Wolff, however, who ran the police and security forces for all Axis-controlled Italy. There were SS police and SD units throughout northern Italy. Sub-units of the SD included the Gestapo and the Security Police – or Sipo* – but there were also in Italy units of the military counter-intelligence and espionage service, the Abwehr. Under Wolff's command and control were a large number of SS police troops, Wehrmacht – German army – units, and also the 140,000 members of Ricci's Fascist militia, the GNR. With these highly visible and intimidating forces at his fingertips, it is no surprise that Wolff's authority and power in Italy should have been so obvious. It says much about Wolff's position that it was to him that Mussolini had turned just hours before his son-in-law had been due to be executed. 'What would you do in my position?' the Duce had asked him. Wolff had told him he should remain firm. To do otherwise, he suggested, would do much harm to his reputation with the Führer.

13 May 1944 was Wolff's forty-fourth birthday. Thin-lipped, and with a wide, receding forehead, and pale, grey eyes, he nonetheless had a genial, humorous-looking face that enhanced his natural charm. After serving as an infantry officer in the First World War, Wolff studied law, later ran his own advertising agency, and then joined the Nazis and SS in 1931. He rose steadily through the SS hierarchy, becoming an increasingly close confidant to Reichsführer Heinrich Himmler, commander of the SS. From June 1939 he had been Himmler's Chief of Staff and representative in Hitler's military headquarters, a post he still officially held, despite his move to Italy, and despite incurring Himmler's wrath in February the previous year for divorcing his wife and marrying Countess Ingeborg Maria von Bernstorff; at least he and the Duce had a love of women in common. By the autumn, however, Himmler had forgiven his friend and approved the elevated title of 'Highest SS Chief' rather than just 'Higher SS Chief' – a distinction shared by only one other SS supremo, General Prützmann, who held the same post in the Ukraine.

Wolff's HQ in Italy was just a few miles south of Gargnano in Fasano, another small town on the banks of Lake Garda. The interior of the villa was noticeably calm and tasteful. Opulent carpets lined the corridors; plain-clothed young women – SS secretaries – discreetly passed by before disappearing into a different room. Wolff's own office was filled with

---

*Both Gestapo and Sipo are abbreviations: the former for *Geheime Staatspolizei*, the German secret state police; the latter for *Sicherheitspolizei*, the Nazi security police.

comfortable chairs, a small table, and a well-stocked cocktail cabinet. Works of art hung on the walls, while the room glowed with soft, subtly positioned lighting. Wolff himself spoke with a gentle, yet husky voice. Like that other Nazi 'charmer', General Reinhard Heydrich, Wolff understood the benefits of winning others over, of putting people at ease and becoming a trusted confidant.

Wolff was also prepared to take risks. Just three days before, on 10 May, the Highest SS and Police Chief in Italy, wearing a civilian suit, had had an audience with Pope Pius XII at the Vatican, in which he had asked for the Pontiff's help in making contact with the Allies with a view to opening peace negotiations. Although no one had witnessed the conversation, there were a number of people – including Germans – who had helped set up the meeting, and were aware of Wolff's reasons for wanting the audience.

Little came of the talks, but Wolff had begun playing a dangerous game, making peace feelers – however tentative – without higher authority. His motivation, however, had been simple. He had begun to doubt that Germany could win the war, but hoped it could in some way dictate the peace that would follow. So Wolff, the arch-Machiavel, wanted to find a way out – a way in which Germany could end the war while there was still a chance of bargaining. The battle had only just begun again on the ground, but one of the most powerful men in Italy hoped words, rather than more bullets and bombs, might end the bloodshed. And if that was the case, he might have a chance of surviving the judgement day that would inevitably follow.

TEN

Breaking the Gustav Line
17–18 May 1944

Near a village not far from Route 6, the Via Casilina, and about fifteen miles behind the front line stood rows of pup tents, trucks, jeeps, and canvas stores belonging to the Canadians of the Perth Regiment. They were infantrymen, part of the 11th Infantry Brigade, but attached to the Canadian 5th Armoured Division. All knew they would soon be joining the battle they had heard raging to the north-west.

Since listening to the opening barrage and seeing the night ripped apart by the flash of the guns, large numbers of the Perth men had regularly hovered around the Intelligence Officer's tent, scanning the bulletin board for updates on the progress of the battle. Among them was twenty-year-old Stan Scislowski, a private with 'Dog Company'. A bright young man from Windsor, Ontario, Stan had been working for the car manufacturers, Chrysler of Canada, before being drafted into the army. After basic and then advanced infantry training, he had been posted overseas to Britain with the No 3 Canadian Infantry Reinforcement Unit, and then assigned to the Perth Regiment.

The Perths had shipped out to Italy at the end of October 1943, and at the beginning of January had been sent to the Adriatic Front. At the River Riccio they had gone into battle for the first time, a sobering experience in which they had been criticised by the divisional commander, Major-General Vokes, for not showing enough determination. 'It had been a rough baptism of fire no one had expected,' noted Stan, 'an ass-kicking that we'd have to face up to and live down over the months ahead.'[61]

Although they had manned a section of the Cassino Front in April 1944, the Perths had not been in battle since. Not that Stan personally felt a sense of trepidation just yet. He'd been terrified that first time he'd gone into combat, but although they could now hear the battle raging fifteen and more miles away, he was too far back to feel fear. And anyway, roaring overhead almost incessantly were reams of fighter-bombers, flying back and forth between the front and their bases nearby. 'At times,' noted Stan, 'the roar of engines was so loud as the low-flying planes flew northward with their bomb-loads that conversation was out of the question.' But Stan found it comforting to know that their air forces had such complete mastery of the skies.

The Allied air forces had not let up their effort once the battle had begun. This was why 90th Panzer Division was having such a difficult time getting to the front: daylight travel was out of the question. Increasingly, there were fewer vehicles available as more and more trucks and cars were left burning and riddled on the side of the road. Petrol was in ever-shortening supply. So too was ammunition. And there were other important side effects too. The men were badly undernourished: Jupp Klein and his men felt hungry all the time. It also made it harder for post to reach the front – which was why Major Georg Zellner had still not received any letters from home.

One of those contributing to the massed swarms of aircraft over the battlefield that day was Lieutenant Charles Dills of the US 27th Fighter-Bomber Group. He had begun the battle seconded to Fifth Army headquarters for a few days to fly General Clark and other senior commanders around and in and out of the Anzio bridgehead. On his first flight with the army commander, Charles had found himself flying with Clark sitting next to him in the co-pilot's seat. Knowing Clark flew, he offered the general the chance to take the controls for a while. 'He agreed,' says Charles. 'He was a pretty nice guy. I had a lot of respect for him.'

His stint as a courier pilot with Fifth Army headquarters had finished a few days before, however, and he had immediately returned to the 27th Fighter-Bomber Group at their airfield near Caserta. On 18 May his flight was taking part in an armed reconnaissance over the Ceprano area, a town on the Via Casilina, some fifteen miles north-west of Cassino. Their task was to look out for any significant troop movements and to shoot up and bomb anything they saw while they were about it. The day before they'd been sent up with a more specific target: a mortar position north of Aquino. The drill was always the same: fly towards the target at around 14,000–15,000 feet, high enough to avoid the countless enemy flak batteries, then nearing the target, the leader would waggle his wings and the rest of the pilots would fall in line behind him, turn on their backs and, one by one, follow him down in a dive. 'From a distance,' says Charles, 'this procedure might resemble a number of balls on a slightly tilted table following one another, coming to the edge of the table and then dropping straight down.' Once over the target they would level out of the dive then drop their bombs – usually one 500lb bomb and six 20lb fragmentation bombs – and then flatten out, usually at around 5,000 feet, but often higher depending on the intensity of flak. 'You drop the bombs as best you can,' explains Charles, 'and then get the hell out of there!'

Also flying that day was Leutnant Willi Holtfreter. After bailing out of his Messerschmitt on 1 May, he had luckily landed well behind German lines. Although he had not been seriously injured he had, nonetheless, been packed off to hospital in Montefiascone, near Lake Bolsena, 'for observation', and had been kept off flying duties ever since. On the 18th, however, he was finally back on operations with the 9th Staffel – or squadron. That morning he was up before dawn, as the fighter pilots always were, stumbling out of their quarters and then taking a short ride to the airfield. Breakfast would be eaten at the dispersal tents and then they would sit out on deck chairs, dozing or playing the card game *Doppelkopf*, waiting to be scrambled. 'Our hearts would always beat faster whenever the telephone rang,' admits Willi. If it was a scramble, they would hurry to their planes where their groundcrew would be waiting for them, their Messerschmitt 109Ks ready.

On that day, Willi was scrambled and took off at 11.35 a.m. Orders were to cover the Via Casilina: troops were on the move and they were to do their best to protect them from Allied bombers and strafing fighter-bombers – the dreaded *jabos** as the Germans called them – although how one flight of 109s was supposed to make much difference was anyone's guess. 'We knew how outnumbered we were,' says Willi. 'It was obvious. Whenever we spotted any bombers there were always so many fighters accompanying them that we couldn't get at them at all.' It was fortunate for Willi that he was such a naturally calm, clear-headed person. 'We had a job to do,' he says, 'and we had to do it, whatever the odds.' Just over an hour later, he landed back at their base at Tuscania, south of Lake Bolsena, his Messerschmitt free of bullet holes. For once, they had avoided the massed swarms of Allied aircraft.

*   *   *

*'*Jabo*' was an abbreviation of *Jagdbomber* – literally, 'fighter-bomber'.

At least by now the senior German commanders were back at the front. Generaloberst von Vietinghoff had returned to take command of AOK 10 once more, while so too had General Frido von Senger, who had finally resumed command of 14th Panzer Corps on 17 May. He had been shocked by what he had found. AOK 10 was still sharing his HQ at Castel Massimo near Frosinone, so after getting himself up to speed with the situation he had hurried down to the southernmost part of the line to see for himself the parlous state of his Corps.

The Americans had reached Formia, while further inland, the French were now overlooking a critical German line of communication, namely the road that ran south from the Via Casilina at Ceprano to the coast. In his absence and with his deputy, General Hartmann, failing to show proper 'grip', Kesselring had fed penny packets into gaps in the front between the two retreating German divisions. With bullets pinging around him, von Senger discovered a detachment of the 44th Infantry Division (to which Georg Zellner, still in the mountains north of Cassino with his battalion, belonged), already being forced back. As he was all too aware, these replacement units were far too small to be able to make much difference; he simply couldn't understand how this had been allowed to happen. It had been almost a week since the start of the offensive – ample time in which to send a reserve division in its entirety to plug the gap between the 71st and 94th Divisions. It was incomprehensible folly, especially as, when he had left Italy, 15th Panzer Grenadier Division had been positioned perfectly as a reserve behind the right wing of the corps. Now he had returned to discover the division had been committed by battalions across the front. 'This,' noted von Senger, 'is a classic example of the way conduct of operations degenerated under Hitler's influence.'[62]

Meanwhile, up on Monte Cassino, the Poles had launched their second attack, and this time there was no German changeover taking place. Moreover, they had not attacked blind as before. Wladek Rubnikowicz and the 12th Polish Lancers had remained dug in along the meadow below Snake's Head Ridge between the two attacks, but although they had been unable to move by day, they had patrolled aggressively by night, as had the rest of the Polish troops on Monte Cassino. What had made their life marginally easier had been the amount of mines around the monastery that had been detonated by Polish shell and mortar fire. Shells and mortars rained over the narrow battlefield day and night. On one occasion, Wladek had been standing behind three men. 'A shell came over and exploded right on top of them,' he recalls. 'Two of the men disappeared into thin air. There was nothing left. But on a bush nearby I saw the ammunition belt and the stomach of the third. That was all that was left.' Soon after Wladek saw a soldier sitting down nearby, simply staring into space. The man was covered in dust and had a glazed expression on his face. Wladek bent over and touched his back and saw that it was covered in blood. The man, he realised, was dead.

Although the Fallschirmjäger defending the monastery and mountain had been further depleted in number during the intervening days, they continued to hold out with almost messianic determination. The fighting was brutal. 'It was often a case of kill or be killed,' says Wladek. 'Bullets were flying everywhere. One simply had to pray the angels made those bullets go around you.' Despite this, however, the Poles were not going to be denied a second time. A key position had been captured during a preliminary assault on the night of the 16th/17th, and by dusk the following evening, Point 593, a pinnacle overlooking the monastery that had seen so much bloodshed, was finally in Polish hands.

In the Liri Valley, meanwhile, the British and Canadians had been making steady progress too. On the same day, realising the Gustav Line could no longer be held, von Vietinghoff finally gave the order for AOK 10 to fall back to the next line of defence, namely the Senger Line, or the Hitler Line as the Allies named it. The withdrawal was to take place that night under the cover of darkness.

At their small farmhouse redoubt, Leutnant Jupp Klein and his small band of men had been up before dawn that day. Having made some coffee they then chewed what they believed must surely be the last meal of the condemned. Jupp was worried about the NCO in charge of the bazookas. He had looked nervous on his arrival the previous evening, but now appeared even more terrified. 'My corporals and I,' noted Jupp, 'felt forebodings of the worst kind.'

The son of a coal mine manager from the Saar region of west Germany, Jupp had left school and become an apprentice carpenter. During his time with the Hitler Youth, however, he had trained as a pilot and had even got his licence. Aged eighteen when war broke out, he immediately tried to become a paratrooper with the Fallschirmjäger, but because of his flying experience, he was sent off to become a pilot instead. Had he been made a fighter pilot, he might well have remained one, but much to his annoyance, on finishing his training, he was sent to the Channel coast as an air-sea rescue pilot. Once again, he applied to join the Fallschirmjäger, and this time, to his relief, he was accepted.

With his carpentry skills, he was placed with the Pioneers and having completed his training, joined the 1st Division. After proving himself repeatedly in Russia, Sicily and southern Italy, he was made a Fahnenjunker and then later promoted to lieutenant and given a company of his own. Both he and his men were by this time highly experienced soldiers, who had all had their fair share of close calls. Even so, this current situation seemed particularly perilous. Jupp could not see how they could possibly avoid annihilation, or, at the very least, capture.

But the morning passed quietly, his men keeping under cover while the inexperienced reinforcements that had arrived the night before busied themselves in front of and around the farmhouse. Jupp could hear the sounds of fighting around them but directly opposite he watched shirtless British tank men sunning themselves on top of their machines. It frustrated him, watching them. His sharpshooters itched to use their long-range telescopic-sighted Mauser rifles.

Midday came and went, then the afternoon. Not until around seven in the evening did the whistle and explosion of British artillery start to fall around them, followed soon after by the tell-tale grinding and creaking of approaching tanks. Suddenly they emerged, around twenty-five Shermans cresting a slight ridge in front of them. Behind were considerable numbers of infantry. Immediately the heavy machine gun in the shed in front of the farmhouse opened fire. With horrible inevitability, moments later the inexperienced machine gunners were hit by enemy tank fire.

Jupp looked around for the bazooka men, but could no longer see them. By now the forward tanks were rolling right next to their farmhouse. A shot rang out, followed swiftly by one more – two of the Shermans had been hit; Jupp need never have doubted the bazooka team. At the same time, the Pioneers opened fire with their own machine guns. The bazooka men continued to fire – and with good accuracy. So long as the bazooka – or Ofenrohre – was used at short ranges, it could be a deadly weapon, and so it was proving now. More tanks had been knocked out while the remainder began hastily retreating. Jupp watched as the crews of the burning tanks piled out of the wrecks, running wildly, a number of them ablaze. And as the tanks departed so, too, did the British infantry, who disappeared back behind the ridge ahead.

Once again, a tiny force of carefully concealed men had beaten off a concerted Allied assault by men from 78th Division's 38th Infantry Brigade. Meanwhile, Jupp and his men ran from their positions and gratefully flung their arms around the bazooka men. 'At this point it struck me,' noted Jupp, 'that the commando leader, the senior NCO, at the present moment was the picture of tranquillity itself.' The fear in his eyes of the previous evening had gone. As they counted the burning Shermans, they realised they had knocked out no less than thirteen, more than half the force. Then they saw the mangled remains of the machine-gun crew. 'A senseless death,' wrote Jupp, 'for these young soldiers.'

Orders for the retreat had not reached the Pioneers' now isolated redoubt, but the 4th Fallschirmjäger Regiment, who had remained in Cassino town throughout the battle, had received theirs. Getting away safely, however, was no easy task. The town was tucked into the side of the Monte Cassino massif, but the area directly to the south was already in British hands. The only escape route was to climb back up the mountain and then down the other side. Hans-Jürgen Kumberg had been preparing himself for the move all day, with his comrades gathering together every bit of equipment they could – even empty ammunition cases. Then at around 10 p.m., they began climbing up Monastery Hill along a narrow path. Hans found it an extremely tense experience. It was pitch dark, they were heavily laden, but they had to try and walk as quietly as possible. Even so, as they neared the top of the mountain, they began to hear Poles call out in German, 'Come this way, come here!' Like all other units in the 1st Fallschirmjäger Division, their numbers had diminished massively, but they now lost a further third of their number as men, confused on that dark mountain, fell for the ruse. Hans, however, stuck closely to the man in front and to the path that eventually began to lead them back down the mountain again. 'Amazingly, not a single shot was fired,' he says. 'Perhaps both sides were worried about hitting their own men.' Those that remained struggled all night, weighed down by their loads. 'We were under orders to take everything with us,' adds Hans, 'but gradually you could hear men dropping things to the ground. You just couldn't handle it any more.'

Hans finally reached the town of Pontecorvo, some seven miles behind Cassino, the following morning. He was utterly exhausted after his night trek up and over the mountain but relieved to have made it safely.

Meanwhile, dramatic events were about to take place on Monte Cassino itself. At around ten that morning a battered white flag was hoisted above the monastery. A dozen men from Wladek Rubnikowicz's regiment, the 12th Lancers, cautiously picked their way through the minefield and approached the ruins. They found only a handful of German paratroopers left, who all surrendered without firing a shot. The Poles, unable to find a Polish flag, attached a 12th Lancers pennant to a branch and stuck that into the rubble instead. It was 10.20 a.m. and the Battle of Monte Cassino was finally over.

It was a triumph for the Poles but came at a bitter cost. 'Of course we were thrilled to have taken Monte Cassino,' says Wladek. 'When we captured it we all felt as though we had shown everyone what we were capable of. But a lot of people died.'

So they did. Polish casualties were 3,779 – and most of those were men who had, like Wladek, already endured the loss of their homes and their country, had been imprisoned, beaten and starved, and who had then travelled thousands of miles in order to continue the fight for their freedom.

ELEVEN

Achtung Banditen!

Despite the cool efficiency with which Germany had occupied much of Italy and the way it had disarmed the Italian armed forces, these actions had begun to cause something of an own goal. By May 1944, German forces in Italy were faced with a major partisan – or 'bandit' as they liked to call them – problem. Still comparatively few in number in the big scheme of things, these guerrillas were nonetheless already becoming a serious thorn in Kesselring's side and greatly loathed by the German soldiers, who felt it was one thing to fight against a uniformed enemy at the front, but quite another to be shot at from behind by men and women who looked like civilians. Unsurprisingly, this threat did much to fuel the already prevailing attitude of most Germans towards Italians – which was one of contempt for their perceived collective cowardice, treachery, and poor fighting qualities. Italy had let them down and so deserved everything that came its way.

It was a vicious circle because it was largely due to severe German measures that a number of young Italians were now actively engaged in guerrilla warfare. 'Everything in occupied Italy must be exploited by us for our war effort,' wrote Ambassador Rahn – and that meant bleeding the country dry. Nearly all Italian gold reserves had been handed over. The Repubblica Sociale Italiana was denied the right to an economic and trade policy of its own. The north's factories were turned over to Albert Speer, the Armaments Minister. As the Allies advanced, any industry at the front line was shut down, the equipment packed off to Germany and then the factory or plant blown to bits. Food was also siphoned off to Germany, even though there was not enough to go round in Italy. The Italians were also expected to pay for German war-related costs, an expense which proved impossible. Even so, by May 1944, the RSI was handing over a staggering 10 billion lire a month – roughly £2,500,000 in today's money. 'I am perfectly conscious of the sentiment of violent aversion nourished by the German soldiers against the Italians,' Rahn continued, 'including those Italians who for one reason or another continue to fight at our side.' Yet, he warned officers of the German Propaganda Section, 'This negative attitude damages our war effort. It is an emotional impulse which must be better hidden.'[63]

It was a bit late for that. Germany's disdain for those countries it occupied was all too evident to their inhabitants. Of course, very few Italians knew the details of these measures, but their effects were keenly felt. Moreover, for a nation that had briefly thought the war was over the previous autumn, it did not help seeing German troops all over the place, their continuing presence preventing the peace that the majority so strived for; or reading repeated notices warning that infringement of the new laws was punishable by death.

Moreover, Germany was not only bleeding dry Italy's wealth and resources, but also its manpower. The Third Reich had become expert at plundering occupied territories for labour, and no one was better at foreign labour recruitment than Fritz Sauckel, the General Plenipotentiary for Labour Mobilisation. By May 1944, there were more than 7.5 million foreign workers in Germany. As soon as Italy surrendered, Sauckel packed off his subordinate, Hermann Kretzschmann, to organise labour recruitment, whether it be voluntary, coerced or compulsory. Most workers were sent to Germany, but a large number were also used by the Organisation Todt, founded by Albert Speer's predecessor as Armaments Minister, Fritz Todt, as a labour force that was used for the construction of military defences. It had been the Organisation Todt, full of forced Italian labourers, which had made most of the German defences around Cassino and which was now also reinforcing the next major line of defence north of Rome, the Pisa–Rimini Line.

A number of men were recruited by regular round-ups not dissimilar to the press gangs used by the British Royal Navy of old. Others were creamed off from Mussolini's conscription drives, much to the Duce's chagrin. Initial conscription had not been too bad: 50,000 men had responded to their call-up papers by the beginning of 1944. But thereafter numbers fell dramatically. Those who had not reported for duty were given several amnesties: a date in March was declared by which they had to report and then a further date in May. Those who still did not present themselves were threatened with execution and reprisals against their families. The only alternative for many was to go into hiding, within the city or in the mountains, where a large number joined the growing bands of partisans.

This was precisely what happened to Carlo Venturi, an eighteen-year-old from the tiny village of Fondazza, south-west of Bologna. By May 1944, as one of those born in 1925, Carlo had received his call-up papers. His family, contadini, had never had much interest in politics. 'They were neither anti- nor pro-Fascist,' says Carlo. 'My father didn't want to get involved.' Since the armistice, however, Carlo had instinctively felt opposed to the German occupation and the new Fascist government. A factory worker in nearby Casalecchio di Reno, Carlo had, along with a number of other young men, raided a barracks immediately after the surrender and had stolen some arms. They viewed the Germans as the aggressors, and after the end of the Fascist regime the previous July, no longer wanted to live under the authority of a totalitarian state. 'We loved our country,' he says, 'and we wanted to live in freedom.' Not that they did anything much with the weapons except hide them; Carlo had a number of rifles stashed away in his attic.

But Carlo soon found himself on the wrong side of the Fascist militia, the GNR. One day he was on his way to Bologna when the tram he was on was stopped. A Fascist had been killed nearby and the GNR were carrying out a search. Carlo and two other men were immediately hauled off, and Carlo was accused of having a hand-grenade in his pocket – in fact, it was simply a bread roll. After being taken to prison, he was beaten up then released a few hours later. 'From that time,' says Carlo, 'I told myself I had to make them pay.'

In early May, with the deadline for presenting himself for service drawing near, he was brought to the GNR barracks in Casalecchio, and accused of stealing and hoarding weapons. Among his questioners was a Fascist who lived on the same staircase as him. 'He lived above me,' says Carlo, 'and the arms were right beneath his feet! They said, "If we find the weapons, we'll send you to Poland"'. Somehow, Carlo managed to convince them he was innocent. But he was now beginning to feel seriously in danger, and so tried to join a nearby band of partisans. Unable to find them, however, he then went to look for another group of rebels in the mountains south of Bologna.

At five in the morning of 16 May, Carlo left his flat and headed first to Sasso Marconi at the confluence of two rivers, the Reno and the Setta, then headed south down the Setta valley to the small town of Vado, lying beneath the Monte Sole massif. He hadn't told anyone where he was going, not even his parents. It was dark by the time he reached Vado, but he soon spotted four young men sitting outside a house by the side of the road. 'What are you doing here?' one of them asked.

'I was looking for you,' Carlo replied, tentatively.

'And who are we?'

Carlo felt a wave of panic. What if they were Fascists out of uniform? But to his great relief the men then admitted to being 'rebels' and invited him into their house, a short way up the mountain above the eastern banks of the River Setta. There he spent the night, along with them and another man they had picked up that day. Early the next morning, at about half past four, he was woken and they headed out in the early morning gloom back across the river and up into the mountains to the band's headquarters at a farmhouse called Ca' Bregade.

As the sun rose, Carlo saw the ancient mountain landscape of the Monte Sole massif for the first time. Above him, standing sentinel, was the summit of Monte Sole itself. Either side were further peaks, wooded with small oaks and chestnuts, but with sheer escarpments too. There was also a high mountain plain, dotted with tiny farming communities, here a small village and church, elsewhere, as at Ca' Bregade, just a few barns and buildings. And either side of the massif, the mountains fell away into the two river valleys of the Reno and Setta. Monte Sole was indeed an ideal place to hide a partisan band: plenty of woods and foliage, sandwiched by the two valleys, but with far-reaching views that would warn of any attack from below.

However, Carlo had not yet been welcomed with open arms. The partisans were deeply suspicious of anyone new: trust had to be proved and earned. No sooner had they arrived at Ca' Bregade than the other new man was ordered to dig a pit, which Carlo assumed was to be a trench. A number of partisans, with Sten guns hung over their shoulder, gathered round to watch him. Suddenly Carlo understood what was about to happen. So too did the other man, who threw down his shovel and took off. He did not get far, as a volley of machine-gun fire cut him down. Carlo was horrified. A spy, they told him, sent to infiltrate them by the Fascists. They then turned to Carlo. His blood froze. In desperation, he told them to ask about him at Casalecchio. 'I've stolen weapons,' he told them, 'and given them to the rebels. They'll tell you about me.'

For the time being it did the trick. Carlo was locked in a cave, where he spent the next few days waiting for word from Casalecchio. It gave him time to think. He'd never seen a man cut down before, and the reality of the life he had entered upon began to sink in. 'Something that up until then had been fundamentally a romantic and ingenuous ideal,' he noted, 'had run up for the first time – but not the last – against the harshness of the clandestine fight.'[64]

Guarding him were two Allied POW escapees, who repeatedly quizzed him about his life, his beliefs and the choice he had made. It soon became clear to Carlo that they believed his story. They also knew that their leader, Lupo, disliked killing, and would avoid taking lives whenever he could. 'They told me to have faith,' says Carlo, 'and that once information had reached headquarters that my story was true, all would be well.'

Three days later, he was finally taken to see the commander, 'the famous Lupo who provoked fear in Germans and Fascists alike'. Lupo shook his hand and told him the information they had sought was just as Carlo had said. Also there to welcome him was the vice-commander, Gianni Rossi. He was given a Sten gun, five magazines, and two hand grenades and assigned to the company led by a partisan called Golfieri. For better or worse, Carlo was now a member of the 'Stella Rossa' – the 'Red Star' brigade. There could be no turning back.

'There were three crystal clear choices,' says Carlo about his decision to become a partisan. 'Either go with the Fascists, the Germans, or choose to fight with the partisans.' In making his choice, however, he had to discard his former life. He was given a new nom de guerre, de rigueur for any partisan: 'Ming', the name of a villain in a comic strip called *L'Avventuroso*, destroyed any means of identification, and cut himself off entirely from his family, a harsh necessity for their safety and his own.

Failure to report for conscription was seen as desertion, and desertion was punishable by death. In reality, such action was comparatively rare – after all, an executed twenty-year old was no use to Kretzschmann's labour effort. But there *were* executions. Only a few weeks before, for example, three young men, one of them a nineteen-year-old boy, were shot in Florence for failing to report for military service. Word of such executions spread rapidly, exactly as the Fascists and Germans hoped, and men like Carlo and many others were not prepared to put the threat of execution to the test. But this did not mean they flocked to report for duty. Rather, large numbers fled to the hills and became partisans instead.

*   *   *

While undoubtedly a large number of men became partisans because of the stark choice that seemed to face them, there were a number who did so from a more pronounced political conviction.

Some forty-five miles to the south-east of Monte Sole, in the mountains of Romagna, south of the city of Forlì, the 8th Garibaldi Brigade of partisans were recovering from a devastating battle against the Germans in which, over Easter, a combined force of more than 10,000 German and Fascist troops had swarmed into the area, trapped the one-thousand-strong 8th Garibaldi Brigade and all but destroyed them.

At the beginning of May, however, the 8th Brigade began reforming once more with around 600 men. The commander of the 2nd Battalion, in an operational area known as the First Zone around the small town of Sarsina, was twenty-year-old Iader Miserocchi, a passionate young man who had already repeatedly cheated death, both in prison and during the Easter battle.

It was often the case in Italy that sons – and daughters – followed the political convictions of their parents, and especially their fathers. This was certainly the case with Iader, whose father had always been vehemently anti-fascist. Iader, the second of four sons, followed his father's example. As someone who was strongly against the war, he only very reluctantly joined the Regia Aeronautica, the Italian air force, when he was called up in 1942, and then, when his squadron was posted to Libya, he refused to go, claiming illness. Promptly arrested, he was sent to a military hospital in Bologna, where, by good fortune, he met a doctor who had served with his father in the First World War. The doctor chastised him, but agreed to help, declaring Iader unfit for active service and citing a 'varicose problem'.

With that, Iader returned home to the ancient city of Ravenna, on the Adriatic coast. So many men were away that he managed to get plenty of labouring work. It was during this time that he joined the clandestine Italian Communist Party – the PCI (Partito Comunista Italiano) – a deeply illegal organisation. It was with a sense of mounting despair that he had witnessed German troops flooding into Italy that summer, and following the armistice, he was denounced by a neighbour for being 'a Red'. On 14 September, six days after the armistice, his house was searched by German soldiers, his papers confiscated and his books and belongings destroyed.

Armed resistance was an inevitable next step for him, although initially the rebels in Ravenna had been poorly organised and largely ineffective. On 12 November, Iader and some others had started lobbing grenades into an RSI officer training school. Caught in the floodlights, Iader found himself being arrested by one of his former classmates from school and was flung into prison. Held there for forty-five days, he suffered nine days of twenty-four-hour interrogations, eight days without food, and a beating every two hours. His cell was big but had no furniture at all. Next door, a tap was kept running continually so that the floor of Iader's cell was permanently wet and he had no means of keeping dry. Eventually he took a shutter off one of the window hinges and lay on that. 'I was beaten even more for doing that,' he recalls.

Eventually, Iader could stand it no longer, and so wrote a declaration that he was a member of the Communist Party and that he would never, ever adhere to the RSI. In doing so, he knew he was signing his own death warrant. 'There was no other way out for me,' he explains. 'I was too ill to carry on in there. I had a very high temperature and could no longer continue with the torture.'

His family were informed that the following day he would be shot and then hanged in the main square in Ravenna as an example to others. The man charged with his execution was called Zanelli, a senior Fascist from nearby Faenza with a reputation for ruthlessness and as a torturer. Iader was taken from the prison and driven towards the town square. However, he then shocked Zanelli by reeling off a list of names of anti-fascists and draft dodgers whom he knew the Fascist had had imprisoned, tortured and even executed. 'What happens to me will happen to you,' Iader had told him. 'I have plenty of friends. We know your movements and you will be killed.'

Alarmed by these threats, Zanelli began to dither, driving Iader around Ravenna. Iader continued his defiance, demanding a trial and pointing out places where Zanelli and his henchmen had murdered civilians. Eventually, Zanelli ordered the driver to slow the car, clearly hoping Iader would try and make a run for it, so that they could then shoot him as he tried to escape. 'Of course, I wasn't going to fall for that,' says Iader. Zanelli had taken fright, and sensing Iader was not making idle threats eventually took him back to Ravenna prison, rather than carry out the execution.

There Iader remained another month, jailed with a number of other, mostly older, political prisoners, who looked after him and helped him regain some of his strength. Eventually, at Zanelli's bequest, he was taken to the police station and questioned by a Fascist official and a judge. No sooner had the grilling begun than the air-raid siren rang out and bombs began to fall on the city. In great haste, the judge pronounced that he was either to join up or join the Organisation Todt. Understandably keen to hurry for cover, the judge bailed him on the understanding he report the following day to the Questura. Iader did no such thing. Instead, through the help of local Communists, he headed to the mountains of Romagna, south of Mussolini's birthplace, and joined the partisans.

The 8th 'Romagna' Garibaldi Brigade, as it had become by March 1944, was led by Communists, most of whom had fought with the Republicans in the Spanish Civil War, but not all its members were Communist. Nor was Iader what he considered a 'Soviet-style Communist'. Rather, he and his comrades dreamed of a more Utopian form of equality. 'It was more like pure socialism, really,' he says. 'Also, communism was the antithesis of fascism.'

Like Iader, Gianni Rossi, the second-in-command of the Stella Rossa, also came from a background of anti-fascism. It is often forgotten that during the late 1920s and for much of the thirties both Mussolini and fascism were hugely popular in Italy. Even those who remained less convinced tended to sign up for their *tessera*, the Fascist Party membership card; it made life easier. Those who stuck their neck above the parapet and denounced the Fascists were comparatively few and far between. But Signor Rossi was one of the few, refusing the tessera and continually finding himself in trouble with the local Fascists. 'If there was a Fascist dignitary due to be visiting the area,' says Gianni, 'my father would be picked up beforehand and put in jail for a few days.' He had been put in prison and out of harm's way before Hitler's visit in 1937.

Despite this, the Rossi family lived in relative comfort in their family home in the village of Gardelletta, along the banks of the River Setta beneath the Monte Sole massif. Being self-employed was the only real option for those who refused to carry the tessera: when not in trouble with the Fascists, Gianni's father, a decorated veteran of the First World War, managed to be a successful builder and property developer.

Gianni – or Giovanni as he had been christened – had been born in February 1923. At twelve, he had left school and had become an apprentice mechanic in Bologna. Soon after, he had moved there, living with an aunt until just before the war, when the whole family moved into a large apartment in the city. Although the family had kept the house in Gardelletta, Gianni's father, Brazilian mother, and younger brother had continued living in Bologna throughout the war. In 1941, Gianni had been called up for military service and had joined the navy. Fortunately for him, he had been ill during the summer of 1943, and so at the time of the armistice had been at home in Bologna, convalescing. And it was during this time that he met up again with his old childhood friend, Mario Musolesi, always known to everyone as 'Lupo' – Wolf.

Like Gianni, Lupo came from a family that had always been firmly anti-Fascist. Several years older than Gianni, Lupo had also returned to Bologna, having successfully avoided capture following the armistice. It was during meetings with Gianni and a few others that the seeds of the Stella Rossa were sown. Lupo had in fact been approached by the local Fascist *federale* (party secretary) to become involved with the Repubblica Sociale Italiana. As a popular local figure who had served in North Africa, he was seen to be just the person they needed. But Lupo vehemently refused, believing that fascism was dead and that a German-controlled Italy had no future.

Two incidents, however, pushed him and Gianni towards active resistance. In October, anti-fascist posters had been put up around Vado, and Lupo was accused of being behind it. Finding out his denouncer, Lupo then beat him up and was promptly arrested. Although released soon after, he was seen as an anti-fascist agitator and was becoming a marked man.

The second incident occurred soon after while Lupo was at the Musolesi family home at Ca' Veneziani. The house lay near a bend on the railway line that ran alongside the River Setta. Trains had to slow at the bend and Lupo and Gianni watched five POWs jump off in a bid for freedom. One was injured as he jumped; another was shot and killed, but three managed to get clear. Lupo ran to their aid and after taking them first to Ca' Veneziani, hid them in the mountains as RSI and German patrols continued to hunt for the escaped men.

The die had effectively been cast. The POWs – a Scot known as Jock, and two South Africans, Steeve and Hermes – were kept hidden in the mountains, but along with his friend Gianni, and a few others, Lupo decided to go underground permanently. They began by raiding some of the army barracks that were still largely deserted. With arms, they could actively resist Germany and the new Fascist regime. 'We didn't have much of a plan,' Gianni admits. 'We borrowed a lorry, raided one of the barracks, and took a stash of rifles and ammunition.' They then headed back to their homes in Gardelletta and Ca' Veneziani and hid their cache.

The Stella Rossa was formally consecrated in the crypt of Vado's church, overseen by the parish priest, Don Eolo Cattani, with Lupo elected as the band's leader and Gianni as his second-in-command. Following this they recruited the three escaped POWs and put the word about to any draft-dodgers and to the mountain contadini. That first winter they did little, merely meeting up nightly, continuing to gather numbers and trying to carry on with their lives as best they could. The baptism of fire came at the end of November when they blew up a freight convoy that had halted on the railway. For Gianni, there had been no crisis of conscience. 'I opened fire without emotion,' he says. 'It was just something I had to do.' There were now about twenty of them in all. Each one had now crossed their own personal Rubicons, and with it came the usual hazards outlaws have faced throughout the ages: a price was on their heads; and they were forced to take to the mountains for good, living in the barns of sympathetic contadini, or in caves, never in one place for long. Following threats, even Gianni's parents were forced to keep constantly on the move.

By the spring of 1944, their numbers had swelled to several hundred, as the first two deadlines for joining the New Republican Army passed and more and more young men avoiding the draft headed to the mountains instead. Most were frightened young men, but as the band grew so did the dangers – dangers that Lupo was initially slow to act upon.

At the end of the following January, Olindo Sammarchi – known as 'Cagnone' – one of the original members of the band, betrayed Lupo to the Fascists. On his information Amedeo Arcioni, a Republican spy, was sent to infiltrate the Stella Rossa. Although Arcioni's real motives were soon discovered, Lupo dithered over what to do with him, refusing to accept his old friend Cagnone's treachery. Instead, that night Arcioni was taken to a hide-out along with Gianni, Lupo and a third partisan called Fonso. Lupo was on watch while Gianni and Fonso slept. It was a cave they used regularly and to make it more habitable, they had lined it with wood. Lupo had stuck his dagger into the wood above them and was watching at the edge of the cave when Arcioni went out to relieve himself. On his return, he snatched the knife and lunged at Lupo, catching him in the arm. Lupo's shouts for help woke Gianni instantly. Jumping up, he tried to pull off the traitor, but in the resulting tussle, Arcioni managed to get the better of him and was forcing the dagger ever closer to Gianni's head until the point pierced the skin on his forehead. Just at the moment when Gianni thought his time had come,

Lupo, together with Fonso, who had by now also woken, managed to come to his rescue and between them they were able to pin him down. After that there was no more hesitation. 'We took him outside,' says Gianni, 'and we killed him.'

Another blow came on 6 May when Lupo's brother, Guido Musolesi, was arrested. Since the previous autumn, he had been helping his brother's fledgling band of partisans by working undercover with the local Fascist headquarters – the *fascio* – and feeding information back to the partisans. On the same day, a squad of GNR went to the Musolesi family home at Ca' Veneziani, arrested Lupo's parents and burnt the house to the ground. All were later sprung from jail, but these events had hardened the partisan leader. Unsurprisingly, he developed an often excessive distrust of others – one that on occasion led to a 'shoot first, ask questions later' attitude, as Carlo Venturi discovered almost to his cost on his arrival on Monte Sole a fortnight later. The life of a partisan was brutal, and on Monte Sole there was now only one law and that was the say-so of the Stella Rossa and Lupo.

If the Stella Rossa gave the impression that they were making it up as they went along and somewhat preoccupied with fighting vendettas against local Fascists, then that was because that was precisely what was happening. Nor were they alone. Lots of groups of partisans had been emerging all over German-occupied Italy, learning as they went along and often paying for their mistakes with great casualties in the process – just as the 8th Garibaldi Brigade had done in April 1944. What was needed was guidance and a system of control and unified organisation. This was beginning to emerge, however, thanks in the first place to the undercover anti-fascist parties that had come to life once more.

Although political opposition had been banned during the Fascist era, underground parties had continued, albeit in extremely clandestine circumstances. The largest of these was the Italian Communist Party, and during the months before Mussolini's fall the PCI and these other differing political groups had begun to organise themselves more actively in Rome and in other major cities. No sooner had Mussolini been deposed than six anti-fascist parties declared themselves. In addition to the Communists, there were the Socialists – once a major force in Italy before the Fascists took power; the Christian Democrats; the Liberals; the Labour Democrats; and the Action Party – a new organisation that took its name from Giuseppe Mazzini's party during the age of Italian unification. None, not even the Communists, had any great strength and they held little sway during the days before the armistice. Furthermore, they all had quite different agendas. The Communists, Socialists and the Action Party, for example, were all vehemently anti-monarchist as well as anti-fascist, while the other three were far more divided on this issue. The Liberals were even positively right-wing. However, despite these differences, following the flight of Badoglio and King Vittorio Emanuele III on 9 September, delegates of these six parties came together in Rome to form the Committee of National Liberation – Comitato di Liberazione Nazionale, or CLN – with the aim of leading the resistance against German occupation and the Neo-Fascists. The president of the CLN was the former Socialist prime minister and now leader of the Labour Democrats, Ivanoe Bonomi.*

Throughout the autumn the CLN helped set up clandestine committees in northern Italy, and in January, the main Rome committee gave the Milan CLN the authority to become the 'official' clandestine government of the north and the supreme organ of the resistance movement. With this change, the Milan CLN became the National Committee for the Liberation of Upper Italy – Comitato di Liberazione Nazionale per l'Alta Italia – otherwise known as the CLNAI.

Yet although the CLN was a coalition, individual parties continued to jockey for influence and support. In particular, it was the Communist and Action Parties who successfully took political control of a number of emerging partisan bands. Communist-backed bands, like the one Iader Miserocchi joined, were known as 'Garibaldi' brigades.† Since many of the leaders of the Communist-backed partisan bands were initially Spanish Civil War veterans, the moniker continued; while bands supported by the Action Party were called 'Justice and Liberty' brigades (*Giustizia e Libertà*). In practice, this meant the leaders would be party members, as would the political commissars – usually older figures who acted as go-betweens for the party and the partisan band, and guided young partisans in the ways of party ideology.

Lupo and Gianni, however, wanted nothing to do with party politics in the Stella Rossa, despite being called the 'Red Star' brigade. Admit-

---

*Bonomi had been War Minister before the election of June 1921, when he became Socialist Prime Minister. His government collapsed in February 1922.
†Garibaldi was the name taken by the battalion of Italian volunteers who went to fight alongside Republican forces in the Spanish Civil War – and was used in honour of Giueseppe Garibaldi, the Italian patriot and soldier of the Risorgimento.

tedly, they were both – and always had been – die-hard anti-fascists, but Lupo in particular felt very strongly that it was important they concentrate purely on defeating fascism and trying to drive Germany out of their country, and for this task he believed politics were irrelevant. It was with this in mind that he had rejected early approaches by both the Communist and Socialist parties. Only when representatives of the CLN came to talk to him did he listen and accept their offer of help.

As spring had come and the numbers of the Stella Rossa had swelled, Lupo had made renewed contact with the Bologna CLN, pleading for more weapons and ammunition. The paltry stashes they had stolen were simply not enough. The shortages were severely limiting what they might achieve. But the CLN had barely been able to help. Their problem, of course, was an equally severe shortage of money. All they could offer Lupo and his fledgling band was support, advice and a few limited arms. It was not enough.

Then in April, there had been some good news: the Stella Rossa had made contact with an Italian agent working for the Office of Strategic Services, or OSS, the American secret warfare agency and forerunner of the post-war CIA. Lino Rocco had been a naval radio/telegraphy instructor at Fiume in the north-east of Italy before the surrender. During the previous summer he had met and fallen in love with a Bolognese girl called Liliana Nicoletti, who had been holidaying in Fiume with her mother. Since then, the two had not seen each other, but after the armistice, Rocco had managed to escape to the south, where he had been recruited into the OSS at its base in Brindisi, and had then been landed by submarine behind the lines along the Adriatic coast. From there Rocco and another agent headed north, but reaching close to Bologna decided to head to the city to find his girlfriend. To his great disappointment, she and her family had moved – but, he discovered, only to Vado, some fifteen miles to the south. Having made his way there, the two lovers were at long last reunited. More importantly, through Liliana, Rocco was put in touch with the Stella Rossa, who persuaded him theirs was a partisan band worth American support.

Thanks to Rocco, in early May 1944, on the eve of battle 200 miles to the south, the Monte Sole partisans received their first supply drop from the RAF's 344 Wing, based in Bari. Although the OSS and British equivalent, SOE, operated separately, they did co-operate over supply drops, which were carried out by 344 Wing's predominantly British squadrons and tended to contain an assortment of mostly British – but some American – kit. Consequently Rocco had given them specific instructions: they were to tune in their simple radio set to the BBC's Radio London every day and wait to hear the words, 'Mario, get ready, Mario, get ready.' This was the signal for them to prepare a field for the drop. When they heard the words, 'the birds are singing', they would know the drop was due to arrive at 10 p.m. that night.

Sure enough, as they waited in the dark, high on an open clearing in the mountains, their signal beacons burning as instructed, they heard the low thrum of aero engines. Soon a Liberator from 334 Wing was circling overhead and they began to see small parachutes open as canisters of supplies drifted down towards them.

By the middle of May the band had received three supply drops. To the rebels each canister was more than worth its weight in gold. From having almost nothing, they now had an assortment of Bren, Breda and Browning machine guns; Sten sub-machine guns; rifles; a number of British army uniforms and boots, ammunition, explosives, charges, mortars, medical supplies and grenades. It was because of these drops that the partisans Carlo Venturi had met on his first foray into the mountains had been so well armed. It was why he had been given a Sten and ammunition of his own.

Lupo and Gianni were delighted. Their band was now some 250 strong, and they could at last begin to take the fight to the enemy – and start causing serious havoc.

TWELVE

The Fog of War
18–23 May 1944

Later on the same day that Monte Cassino finally fell, Kesselring held a commanders' conference in the comparative safety of the Upper Liri Valley north-west of Cassino, attended by von Vietinghoff and the AOK 10 Corps commanders. By this time, Kesselring had only just discovered that the Canadians were not, as they had been led to believe, embarking from Naples for a seaborne invasion north of Rome, but were, in fact, fighting in the Liri Valley. Nonetheless, he was still uncertain that the seaborne threat was over; on the other hand, as Frido von Senger pointed out to him, the right flank had now collapsed so completely that the French and Americans threatened to move around the rear of his troops still staving off the Allied threat in the Liri Valley and encircle them completely.

After the overnight move, the majority of troops in the Liri Valley were now either behind or in the process of moving in behind the Senger Line, the next line of defence. This defensive network began near Piedimonte, only a few miles behind Cassino, and ran in a south-westerly direction to Terracina on the coast. It had been developed on von Senger's own initiative during the winter, and although not as formidable as the Gustav Line, it was nonetheless another serious obstacle, linked by bunkers and concrete gun emplacements. Von Senger's original plan had been to use it to swivel 14th Panzer Corps when the time came to begin a retreat. The problem was that until the previous night, the 1st Fallschirmjäger Division and other units of the 51st Mountain Corps had been doggedly holding out at Monte Cassino and along their stretch of the Liri Valley. Von Senger's troops in the Liri Valley, however, had already been pushed back from the Gustav Line, but instead of scuttling back in some order behind the Senger Line, had been forced to fight in front of it in order to maintain the junction with the 51st Mountain Corps.

This is exactly what had happened to the Werfer Regiment 71. On the night of the 16th, Hans Golda and his 8th Battery had been ordered to move back – but only about a mile, between the Gustav and Senger Line defences. As dawn broke, they had found themselves standing in the middle of a cornfield. Their command post was an old Italian Army post, but this was no more than a poorly camouflaged shed, with a shallow dugout. Sure enough, they'd not been there long when they heard an enormous crash; suddenly it was dark and they were covered in dirt and dust. Hans soon realised they had been buried alive. Frantically he and the three men with him began digging themselves out with such fury that their fingers bled. They had been fortunate – no one had been seriously hurt, and later that evening they had, along with the rest, moved behind the Senger Line.

But as far as von Senger was concerned, the moment to make full use of the Senger Line had already passed. Making no secret of his views, he complained to Kesselring that using penny packets from various divisions to plug gaps had been deeply misguided; that by doing so they had only been chewed up as they entered the line and that divisional commanders had lost control because their units had been split up so widely. This was amply demonstrated by the stand of Jupp Klein and his band of Pioneers, who had been separated from the rest of the division, and who were cut off from the senior commanders to such an extent that Jupp had still not received any orders to fall back to the Senger Line.

Von Senger accepted that everyone had been caught off guard by the Allied offensive, but because so many senior commanders had been away, Kesselring had felt obliged to take a greater part in running the battle than he would have normally done. And while he was a highly experienced, even brilliant, commander at a higher level, he had never commanded a corps or even a division in battle – and it had showed.

Von Senger now suggested to Kesselring and von Vietinghoff that they abandon both the Gustav and Senger Lines entirely, and instead fall back, carrying out the kind of delaying actions at which they were so adept, to the next line of defence, the Caesar Line. The Allies, as they were all aware, would, at some point soon, almost certainly make a break-out from the Anzio bridgehead with the aim of cutting off AOK 10's line of retreat. The advantage of the Caesar Line was that it was still south of Rome, but north of the probable Allied line of attack from Anzio. This way, he argued, instead of trying to defend two fronts, as they were still doing, they could defend one and with both armies linked together.

However, despite the obvious merits of his arguments, there was not to be such a drastic retreat yet. Kesselring was going to defend the Senger Line, not abandon it, and with the support of the Führer and the German High Command, who had been equally surprised and not a little concerned by the Allied offensive, troops were already hurrying to the rescue. Two divisions had been ordered from the Adriatic coast, while another from the Trieste area was ordered south as cover. 26th Panzer, currently barring the Alban Hills south of Rome, had been sent south from AOK 14 to join AOK 10. Meanwhile, the 16th Waffen-SS Panzer Grenadier Division had been ordered from Hungary, while some units of the Brandenburg Division, currently on the Eastern Front, were also on their way to Italy. Not only were the Allies currently winning the battle, the Germans were now further reinforcing Italy. In so doing they were fulfilling one part of General Alexander's plans perfectly.

Some twenty miles to the south, Lieutenant Ted Wyke-Smith and his band of bridging engineers had been watching the monastery on Monte Cassino through his binoculars and saw the Polish pennant now flying above the rubble. 'Have a look, boys,' he told his men, passing round his binoculars. 'It was an extraordinary feeling to see that flag,' he remembers. 'We suddenly felt as though the monastery, Cassino, the Rapido – none of them mattered any more. They were all done with. Our problems now lay up ahead.'

In Cassino town itself, Captain Ion Calvocoressi was accompanying General Leese on a visit to the ruins that afternoon, 18 May. The town was now completely in the hands of the British 4th Division. As with the monastery above, so the fighting at this infamous spot had finally come to an end. As they approached this hell hole, Ion was struck by how, from a distance, it looked rather like a fairytale town, with its stalagmites of remains and towers of rubble. Looming massively above was the tumbled debris of the monastery. 'The town is a complete shell,' noted Ion, 'full of holes and rubbish.' They paused by the command post of the 1st Grenadiers and 2nd Coldstream Guards, which was situated in the crypt of a church near the edge of the town. Since the beginning of April, when they had moved there, they had received no less than 127 direct hits on the church. The men were pallid and drawn after spending so long underground. In the crypt it had been hot, sweaty and stifling. 'Sanitary conditions were ghastly,' recounted one Guards officer dryly, 'and it was almost impossible to comply with the simplest rules laid down in the *Manual of Military Hygiene*. This, together with decaying unburied bodies aided by warm weather, which increased during our time there, did not make Cassino resemble a scent factory.'[65] Ion was shocked by what he witnessed. 'The town of Cassino,' he says, 'was more utterly destroyed than any other I saw during the war.'

It was indeed 100 per cent destroyed: not a single building remained intact. The inhabitants had long gone, compulsorily evacuated by the Germans months before. Some Italians had remained in the area, but the surrounding villages and towns were almost as badly devastated as Cassino itself. Nearby Pignataro, for example, was 93 per cent destroyed. Belmonte Castello, close to where Major Georg Zellner was dug in, had been 95 per cent destroyed. Esperia, in a valley beneath the Aurunci Mountains, had not been evacuated until the last minute but now lay 92 per cent destroyed. The village of San Giorgio, halfway between the Gustav and Senger Lines, was 89 per cent destroyed.[66] So it went on, and so it would continue. Soon, Pontecorvo and Piedimonte, two key towns along the Senger Line, would share Cassino's fate with not one single building left standing.

Fallschirmjäger Pioneer Jupp Klein had not really expected still to be alive on Thursday, 18 May, but he was and it was a fine glorious morning for him and his comrades. Having fended off one attack successfully, they were determined to stand firm, even though the sounds of battle to the north suggested the front was already beginning to bypass their tiny redoubt. Across to the far ridge in front of them, however, they could still see British tank crews and infantry busying themselves. Jupp could not understand why they weren't attacking. Not until the afternoon did the British tanks open fire, their shells whooshing over and smacking into the upper walls of the farmhouse. Jupp and his men hurried down into the bunker below the house, listening to the muffled tumbling of roof and walls above them.

Suddenly rubble crashed down into the entrance of the cellar, blocking them in. The air was filled with fine dust. One of the men called for a match, but Jupp stopped him. 'It'll use too much oxygen,' he told them. 'Everyone will sit quietly in one place, breathe gently and behave sensibly.' Quietly, Jupp then called out the names of all his men – they were all there. Then he told the strongest to start clearing away the rubble. 'Think about what you're doing,' he told them; 'be prudent and we will survive this and not suffocate all together like guys in a coffin.'

The men were still clearing the debris when Jupp realised they could no longer hear the sounds of battle around them: no shells crashing, no machine-gun fire. 'What this meant no one had to tell us,' noted Jupp. 'We had been overrun by the enemy.'

Eventually enough rubble was cleared for them to be able to climb out of the bunker. Outside it was evening with dusk just beginning to fall. The roof of the farmhouse had collapsed entirely, as had several of the walls, but their observation platform that they had used on first reaching the house, and the wall in front of it facing the British, still stood, some ten-feet high. Jupp was just about to clamber up onto it when he saw a number of infantry moving towards them. With his Italian Beretta sub-machine-gun already on his shoulder, Jupp opened fire. This was enough to make the British Tommies drop to the ground and take cover. In the meantime, his men hurriedly joined him on the platform and prepared for a fight.

To a man, his men were highly experienced and crack fighting troops. Together they had six heavy MG 42 light machine guns, while the rest had an assortment of assault rifles, Mauser rifles with telescopic sights, machine pistols, other pistols, and hand-grenades. Jupp himself was armed with his trusted Beretta MAB 38 and a Walther-PPK. It was a tidy arsenal, especially since they had both the platform for observation and the wall to protect them.

From an embrasure in the wall, Jupp looked out towards Cassino. He could see infantry and vehicles of advancing enemy and realised that their only chance was to try and wait for darkness then head back through the enemy lines to their own positions. He had not, however, been conscious of a young Tommy approaching his loophole. Evidently, the soldier must have climbed a pile of rubble, for now they stood no more than a metre apart. 'We stared at each other steadily,' noted Jupp, 'and I could still today draw the features of his face, so indelibly are they imprinted on my mind.' Jupp hoped the Tommy would drop down and out of the way, but instead the young man reached for his rifle. Tearing out his Beretta, Jupp was quicker to react, and fired first, riddling the man with bullets. He felt considerably shaken by this exchange, although he did not let his men see it. 'I still think about that young Tommy,' he says. 'His death affected me deeply.'

Following this incident, there was quiet for a while until they saw

around two hundred British troops getting ready to make an assault.
Sure enough, immediately after they rose up the six MG 42s opened fire.
'The last time I had seen the effects of this weapon was during our
operations in the Soviet Union, and I had observed them with horror,'
noted Jupp. 'This time was no different and in a few seconds it was
all over.' The survivors still moving were finished off by the Pioneer
sharp-shooters, until Jupp called for them to stop.

Soon after, darkness fell. With one of his corporals, Jupp made a recce
of the area, and realised their best chance was to try to reach the railway
lines that ran south of the Via Casilina. As they were examining the
trenches that ran from the farmhouse, they heard more British infantrymen approaching. Opening fire with their machine pistols, they then
scurried back to the farmhouse, and then, after telling the others the
plan, waited until after midnight to make their break-out.

All was now quiet, although the air was not filled with the scents of
early summer, but of cordite and smoke and the smell of corpses already
rotting from the heat of the day. Slowly, and as quietly as possible, they
made their way towards the railway line and continued along the narrow
gap between the road and the railway. As the gap widened, they suddenly
heard a British soldier call out to them. Jupp froze then shouted back
in English, 'Polish soldiers.'

'All right,' the Tommy replied and on they continued.

Three hours later, having seen what appeared to be German flares,
they began to think they must have successfully reached their own lines.
When, some time later, they saw a group of soldiers, they felt bold
enough to call out. 'They answered us in German,' wrote Jupp. 'In the
next moment each man was yelling for joy and all the tension was
released.' Incredibly, not a single one of his men had been either wounded
or killed. The only man missing was a medic, who had been captured
at the farmhouse.

Not unnaturally, Jupp felt proud of his achievement and when he later
reported to his battalion commander he had expected congratulations.
Instead the major merely looked at him and said, 'I'd expected you much
earlier, for there are 2,000 anti-tank mines to be laid, and I don't have
any other Pioneers available.' For the Fallschirmjäger, the battle was still
far from over.

But the battle for the Senger Line was finished almost before it had
begun, just as General von Senger had feared. At least, it was in much

of the middle part of the line, where in the French and American sectors it had already been overrun. On the afternoon of the 18th, General Alexander, along with his Chief of Staff, John Harding, had arrived at General Mark Clark's headquarters. Clark, by now delighted with the progress of Fifth Army, told them with no small amount of satisfaction that Formia was in the bag, that he expected the town of Itri to fall the following day, and that Esperia had also fallen. 'General Alexander showed great elation,' noted Clark, 'as he should.'

Alex then raised the subject of the US 36th Division. This now battle-hardened division had been deliberately kept in Fifth Army reserve, ready to be deployed wherever Alex saw fit. He had, in fact, always intended to send it to the Anzio bridgehead to play its part in the eventual break-out, but until now had kept it behind the southern front just in case. It was all part of maintaining balance. Now, however, with the Gustav Line smashed, the time had clearly come to send them on a short sea voyage north. Moreover, Alex, like von Senger, was by now convinced the Senger Line could not possibly hold. 'I agree,' noted Clark, 'but the only reason it will not is because of the flanking action of the Fifth Army.'[67]

By nightfall the following day, Clark's optimism had proved justified. The French Expeditionary Corps had captured another key feature, Monte della Mandrone, which overlooked both Pontecorvo to the north-east, and Pico to the north-west. Ahead of them lay the Liri Valley and the strongest defences of the Senger Line. Further to the south, the key Pico–Itri road, so important to the maintenance of the German line, had also been cut and as Clark had predicted, Itri had also fallen. Between Itri and the coast, the US 85th 'Custer' Division had also continued to push forward. By evening Lieutenant Bob Wiggans and the men of the 338th Infantry had reached the headland of Gaeta, over-looking the Tyrrhenian Sea, capturing a couple of hundred surprised Germans in the process, and also a huge German artillery gun that had been mounted on rails and which was hidden in a tunnel. In fact, it was so big that Bob and his pals had taken photos of each other with just their legs sticking out of the end of the barrel.

The following day, the 338th Infantry continued their advance, for once down a proper road. As evening neared, Bob was sent on an errand back to their rear echelons. Taking a jeep, he set off, then completed his task and headed back. By this time it was dark and as he was driving back someone took a pot-shot at him, which fortunately missed. A little further on, another soldier, clearly a German, also levelled his rifle and ordered him to halt. Bob promptly took out his own weapon and captured him and then radioed back to find out where the battalion was. 'It seems they had left the road and gone into bivouac,' wrote Bob, 'and I was seven miles behind German lines.' Making a swift about-turn, Bob headed back in darkness, his prisoner perched on the bonnet of the jeep with Bob pointing his .45 Colt pistol at his back.

Yet despite the brilliance of General Juin's French Expeditionary Corps in the Aurunci Mountains, and despite the determined and gutsy performance by the two US rookie divisions, it was German mistakes more than anything that had caused the collapse of the southern German flank. They had been ill-prepared for the initial assault and caught completely off guard. The 71st Division opposite the French was no longer functioning as a fighting force; 94th Division fighting the Americans was not much better. Fifteenth Panzer Grenadier had been devoured piecemeal as it had been fed into gaps that had sprung like a leaking dam. It was not surprising that Fifth Army were now finding opposition to be so light.

It was a somewhat different story in Eighth Army's sector, however. Now entrenched behind the Senger Line were the remainders of the 1st Fallschirmjäger Division, as well as the 90th Panzer Grenadier Division, which was at last fully involved with the battle. Entering the fray was the 305th Infantry Division from the Adriatic, as was the 26th Panzer, on loan from AOK 14 and under command of von Senger at 14th Panzer Corps.

However, the fact that so much of AOK 10 – as well as one division from AOK 14 – was now massed behind the Senger Line in the Liri Valley, gave the Allies an opportunity to rout the Germans there and then. The Allied plan was a simple one. Thirteenth Corps would assault the Senger Line towards the town of Aquino, just south of the Via Casilina. The Canadians would attack towards Pontecorvo. Meanwhile, the Poles, still flushed with their success on Monte Cassino, would come round the mountain and try and outflank the northern edge of the Senger Line through the village of Piedimonte.

To the south-west, however, lay the main chance. There was a clear geographical gap between Pontecorvo and Pico, which lay around six miles due west. This axis marked the boundary between the mountains and the Liri Valley. If the Allies could get sufficient forces through this gap, and push on to the town of Ceprano on the Via Casilina, then they would be able to cut in *behind* the bulk of AOK 10 at the Senger Line.

During Alex's meeting with Clark the previous day, the Fifth Army commander had suggested just this, an idea that Alexander understandably jumped at. Suddenly it appeared as though the bulk of AOK 10 might be entrapped along the Senger Line. It was an enticing thought.

Thanks to the bridge-laying efforts of the sappers – Ted Wyke-Smith had completed his third bridge in as many nights – Eighth Army began storming the Senger Line on 19 May. Among those awaiting them was Hans-Jürgen Kumberg and the remnants of his company of Fallschirm-jäger. He'd not slept a wink since leaving Cassino, and after reaching the German lines had continued his march, heading south along the line to an orchard between Aquino and Pontecorvo. 'We were so tired,' says Hans, 'and we thought we could have a rest, but then the artillery fire came in.' They were not dug in at all – those bunkers were further back – but rather were surrounded by apple and pear trees, a welcome sight to Hans after the desolation of Cassino. There were, however, a number of concrete bunkers spaced at regular intervals nearby, and mounted with 75mm high-velocity Panther tank turrets, machine guns and rocket projectors. While the barrage continued, Hans could do little but lie flat and hope for the best. Then, after about three hours, Canadian infantry began to emerge through the orchards ahead of them, accompanied by a lone tank that had managed to cross the anti-tank ditch that barred the attackers' way.

Near to Hans was a German anti-tank crew from a different unit. 'The gunner was in shock, I suppose,' he says, 'because he wasn't firing it. I didn't know how to operate it myself, so I went over to him, pointed my pistol at him and said, If you don't load it immediately, I'm going to shoot you.' The terrified gunner did so, and after aiming the gun as best he could, Hans pulled the firing pin. The gun rebounded and cracked against his wrist. 'I don't know whether I hit the tank or not,' he confesses, 'but it stopped firing at us.' While he bandaged his wrist, Allied fighter-bombers – the dreaded 'jabos' – appeared overhead, bombing and strafing their positions. These were followed by Canadian infantry once more. 'We just kept firing at them,' says Hans. For more than three hours, the makeshift and mixed German force kept the enemy at bay. Unable to break through, the Canadians eventually pulled back again and called upon their own artillery. 'Finally nightfall came,' says

Hans. 'And that saved us.' Utterly exhausted, Hans embarked on his second night of retreat.

Hans and his comrades may have fallen back, but along the narrow stretch of the Liri Valley, the Senger Line had not yet been overrun. Leese had hoped to rush the defences before the Germans had properly established themselves, but the attack had failed. 'A disappointing day,' noted Ion Calvocoressi at Eighth Army Tactical HQ. 'In the early morning we had hopes of breaking through the Hitler Line without a battle, but now it is evident that we shall have to fight for it.'

In his caravan, Leese was jotting down much the same in a letter to his beloved wife, Margie. They had, he admitted, underestimated the strength of the Senger Line, or the will of the Germans to defend it. 'All along the line we came up against strong defences with barbed wire, ditches and with boxes and anti-tank guns. It will be a tough nut to break.'[68] Frustratingly, it had also rained that afternoon, causing problems for the flow of traffic that depended so heavily on dirt tracks for quick movement. Overnight it rained once more, making the situation worse.

Leese still hoped that Fifth Army might come to the rescue, but so far only two French divisions had been thrown into the breach between Pontecorvo and Pico, and they had come up against stiffer opposition than they had been used to so far in the battle. Aware that Alexander had hoped for a quick breakthrough at the Senger Line – they all had – Leese nonetheless believed that small, piecemeal attacks would cost a lot of lives with no guarantee of success. Far better, he argued, would be to make thorough preparations for a set-piece attack against the line. That meant bringing up more men, more ammunition, more artillery, and more tanks. And that was not going to happen overnight. Zero hour for the renewed assault on the Senger Line was accordingly set for 6 a.m. on 23 May.

There may have been a pause in the fighting in the Liri Valley, but Kesselring was conscious that his southern flank was still continuing to be overrun at an alarming speed. True, the French were now being halted south of Pico, but that was only two divisions. The rest of Juin's force was continuing to make great strides through the mountains to the south-west. US II Corps' drive was also continuing with gathering speed, so much so that they had now begun to overtake the French to their north.

On 21 May, Bob Wiggans' 1st Battalion of the 338th Infantry were even put to sea in DUKW amphibious trucks in order to outflank a ridge of troublesome mountains that rose out of the sea to the west of Gaeta. 'Believe me,' noted Bob, 'I was apprehensive. Any 88mm gun could have knocked us all out of those slow-moving vehicles.'[69] He need not have worried, however. They landed without a shot being fired, and immediately headed, with speed, inland through a shallow, flat plain.

The reason for this lack of resistance was that in the south, Kesselring's forces were in as much disarray as they had been several days before. He had still not banished his fears of an Allied seaborne landing north of Rome, which was why he *still* had two of his best divisions coast-watching there. However, by the 19th, he had accepted that the more pressing crisis was on the southern front, and so at long last ordered Generaloberst von Mackensen to release 29th Panzer Division from AOK 14. This done, he fully expected 29th Panzer to have been in position and able to stem the flow of the French and Americans by the following morning. However, when he reached his command post on the 20th, he was shocked to discover that von Mackensen had objected to the decision, believing the greater threat lay with an Allied break-out from Anzio, which he felt sure was imminent, and so had disobeyed the order. Incensed, Kesselring immediately altered the boundary between the two armies so that the southern section of the line now came under AOK 14's jurisdiction, and reiterated his original order for 29th Panzer to move south immediately.

By the following day, however – 21 May – it was already too late. Although 29th Panzer were now on the southern front, the positions to which Kesselring had ordered them originally had already been overrun and Bob Wiggans and the men of the 338th Infantry had outflanked the mountains and taken the key town of Fondi. 'An area ideally suited for defence had been given away,' noted Kesselring bitterly, 'and an almost impregnable position had been opened to the enemy between Terracina and Fondi.'[70] In other words, precisely the area the Americans had just captured.

Amongst those now being brought up from Eighth Army reserves was the Canadian 5th Armored Regiment, whose role in the attack on the Senger Line would be to follow through the breach that was made and then continue the advance towards Rome. Stan Scislowski and his mates in the Perth Regiment were in high spirits when they finally got going on 20 May, part of a long column that stretched all the way from their camp to the front. 'The mostly one-way traffic was a herky-jerky, bumper-to-bumper affair,' noted Stan, 'with the smell of exhaust fumes thick in the air.' It was extremely uncomfortable, and a journey that was particularly painful for Stan thanks to five boils that had developed on his lower back, right along his belt line. As the truck jolted, so his boils chafed. Soon he was groaning like a man being tortured.

By night they had managed only around fifteen miles and camped at the mouth of the Liri, with the desolate ruins of Cassino on their right. The next day, they stayed where they were getting ready for the 'big push'. Boxes of grenades had to be degreased and armed with fuses, Bren guns had to be loaded and magazines clips filled; weapons had to be cleaned and tested. They moved out again in the evening of 21 May, winding their way until they were ordered to debus and continue down a dirt track on foot, and being careful to keep between the strips of white tape that marked out where the road had been cleared of mines.

Soon they reached the main battle area. Stan was stunned by the level of destruction. 'On the road, in the ditches, in the fields, and in the farmyards,' wrote Stan, 'everywhere lay scattered the wreckage left behind by the whirlwind of shellfire.' Gingerly, they stepped round strands of barbed wire and past jagged tree stumps. Stan paused briefly to stare at an abandoned German anti-tank gun. Nearby, from a farmhouse, came the cloying smell of rotting flesh.

They camped again for the night, and the following morning, whilst waiting for orders, Stan took himself off, hoping to scavenge a few souvenirs. He'd not gone far when he stumbled upon two decomposing German bodies. 'One, a burly red-headed fellow, had the back of his head blown away,' noted Stan, 'inside which pulsed a mass of maggots. The other, close by his comrade, lay on his left side, his right hip gone.' Although repulsive to look at and the stench overpowering, Stan still couldn't resist the urge to rifle through the corpses' pockets, and after much difficulty, managed to extricate a wallet full of snapshots of one of the dead men's family and soldier mates. They were off again later that afternoon, passing through the ruins of Pignataro. 'Craters by the thousands, everywhere you looked,' he noted. 'Every tree in the olive groves and orchards along the way had been so shattered and blasted that not a single branch remained.' Stan thought the whole region looked like the face of the moon.

By the evening of 22 May, they had almost reached the front, halting just behind the Canadian 1st Division. Their latest home was a field thick with poppies, although rather than feeling cheered by such a sight, Stan could only think of what those wild flowers had come to symbolise. Moments later German shells began landing intermittently. Stan started digging his foxhole a little more intently. The day before he'd been eager to get into action again, but now he was praying his troublesome boils might get him out of it. 'The reality of where I was,' he noted, 'and what I was getting into hit home with a wallop.' Scared and anxious about the battle that was to begin the following morning, Stan decided to do what he always did whenever he felt tense: go on a search for loot, a nervous compulsion he found hard to control. To his frustration, however, he came back a short while later empty-handed.[71]

Stan Scislowski was far from being the only troubled soul on that eve of the renewed battle. 'Now the enemy is a long way behind us on our right wing, but we are holding out,' noted Major Georg Zellner from his bunker still in the mountains north of Cassino. Outwardly, he knew he had to be strong, and look after his men, but to his diary he confessed his true feelings of misery. 'I'm overcome with homesickness,' he scribbled. 'I think of my little one, of the kids, and there's only death all around us. It's enough to make you crazy. The world could be so beautiful but for a few criminals . . . In the meantime we fight on to the last battalion or the last man. Only laughing and swearing helps. Swearing at the people who order this idiocy. I want to get back to my life. My family is my life's dream – I don't care about anything else.'

Away to the south, young Pasua Pisa was in a greater turmoil. Earlier that day, the war had finally reached her farm on the top of Monte Rotondo. They had heard the guns getting steadily closer, but that day their tiny community found themselves on the edge of the boundary between the French and the Americans, and with shells whistling over them as they came up against the units of 29th Panzer.

It should have been so different. If only von Mackensen had obeyed Kesselring's order, the war might have eventually passed either side of Monte Rotondo; but as it was, shells began landing nearby, then troops appeared, using the piles of freshly cut hay as cover. 'They were shooting over our heads,' she says; 'there were aeroplanes too. We were scared.' Then her four-year-old son, Lorenzo, found an unexploded mortar shell. The boy, still glued to his grandfather, picked it up and he and the old man took it to back to the house where they all now lived. Neither had the slightest idea what it was – they'd never seen anything like it before.

Had Pasua known what they were up to she would have warned them, but she had been busy – with her husband gone and so few men about, she was flat out working from dawn until dusk. The explosion rocked the farm. When Pasua rushed back both her father and adored son were dead.

THIRTEEN

Break-out
23–26 May 1944

Leutnant Jupp Klein and his small company of Pioneers had been promised a spell out of the line by the battalion commander, Major Frömming, the moment they had finished laying 5,000 mines in front of the remainder of the 3rd Fallschirmjäger, now dug in on the Senger Line. With the task completed, Frömming was as good as his word, sending Jupp's men all the way back to Arce, a good few miles behind the lines on the Via Casilina. Jupp, however, had remained behind at battalion headquarters in order to write up a report about the previous few days' fighting. It was a rare luxury, but when he finally went to join the rest of his company, Frömming gave him a *Kübelwagen** and a driver.

It was, of course, tempting fate to drive during the day and, sure enough, Jupp and his driver were creeping round a mountain road when they were strafed by a US P-38 Lightning. The driver was hit and the car swerved from the narrow mountain road and began tumbling down the slopes. Jupp was flung out of his seat, rolling several yards until bushes and a fir tree checked his fall. There was a piercing pain in his arm – he had broken his collarbone. He crawled over to the remains of the car and saw the driver was dead, with several shots in the head and chest, then staggered back up to the side of the road, sat down, pain searing through his body, and wondered what he should do. Luck was now on his side, however. He'd not been waiting long when a lorry full of mountain troops trundled towards him. A medic treated him by the side of the road and from there he was taken to hospital. For the time being, at any rate, the war for Jupp was over.

*   *   *

---

*The Kübelwagen was designed by Dr Ferdinand Porsche at Hitler's behest and was essentially a Volkswagen Beetle modified into an all-purpose military car. A staggering 51,334 were manufactured.

Oberleutnant Hans Golda and his 8th Werfer Battery had been quite impressed by the Senger Line fortifications; they were certainly an improvement on the almost non-existent defences between the two lines. Now near Pontecorvo, his command post was a decent bunker and on either side were further well-covered bunkers for the six-barrelled rocket mortar firing nebelwerfers, with ramps down which they would run when not firing. His only complaint was that the concrete stands outside the entrance to the bunkers did not allow enough movement to swivel the 'werfers. 'Our first job therefore,' he wrote, 'was to blow up the beautiful werfer stands in order to get enough turning space.'

Above Pontecorvo loomed the edge of the Aurunci Mountains, and the Germans at that part of the line found themselves in the unnerving position of being shelled from the mountains behind them to the south by French gunners. In a very short time, the small oak trees around Hans' position were torn to pieces. Soon there were French machine gunners peppering them too. Schütze Schmidt, his communication man, was hit and lay screaming in the cornfield next to them; but Hans and his men could only push themselves further back into their bunkers. Then one of his men, during a pause in the firing, hurried out of the bunker, ran to Schmidt, and carried him on his back safely back into the bunker, where he lay writhing in agony. Only the day before, Hans had awarded Schmidt the Iron Cross 2nd Class. He was a young, cheerful soldier, and Hans hated to see the lad in such a state.

More shells rained down until suddenly there was a huge explosion, bigger than all the others – a shell had hit their ammunition store. Later, once the light began to fade, they crept back out and looked at the devastation. One nebelwerfer was completely destroyed. 'Everything was torn to pieces,' noted Hans.[72]

Having sent Schmidt off to the field hospital, Hans radioed for relief. That same night Werfer Regiment 56 arrived and took over their positions and he and his men fell back. They had left the line not a moment too soon.

At 6 a.m. the following day, 23 May, the Allied guns opened up their barrage along the Senger Line. Stan Scislowski had been many miles back for the opening of the battle twelve days before but even though he was not in the first wave of the attack, he was now in front of the guns, and could only clutch his hands over his ears as thousands of shells whistled and screamed over his head. 'It was mind-numbing!' he noted. 'It was a cross between a howling coyote, a car running on its rims, and the banshee wail of a London Blitz air-raid siren.'[73]

A minute or two after the barrage ended, the assaulting battalions went forward. As expected, they were greeted with a hail of bullets, shells and mortars. But this time, although they had to fight hard all day, the attack prevailed. A concerted, carefully planned assault with overwhelming fire power was the only way to crack a German fixed defensive position. 'A great day!' General Leese wrote to his wife that evening. 'It was a very hard fight all the morning but after lunch we broke in deeper with tanks and infantry.' There had been more rain, which, frustratingly, had prevented them from pushing through further tanks and armour before dark, but he could not feel too disheartened. 'The Germans are in complete chaos: units mixed up everywhere and nearly all serving under command of any division except their own,' he added with no small amount of truth, 'whereas we are all tidy and present and the army is eager to get on.'[74]

Of Fifth Army's effort to cut in behind the Senger Line, however, there was little sign. In his instructions to Clark on the evening of 18 May, Alexander had been quite clear, ordering Fifth Army to strike northwards through the Pico area and cut off the withdrawal of enemy forces opposing Eighth Army. There was absolutely no scope for any kind of misunderstanding, and in any case the order was based on Clark's own suggestion, and presented a golden opportunity for a stunning early rout of the bulk of AOK 10. Clark confessed as much to his diary on 20 May: 'I believe,' he noted, 'if Eighth Army will attack the Hitler [Senger] Line in the Pontecorvo region in the next two days; if we hit it north from Pico all-out with all our forces and the bridgehead next morning, we will fold up the German Army in Italy.'[75]

This was not wishful thinking at all, but a highly realistic assessment of the situation. This fear of being trapped at the Senger Line was precisely why its architect, General von Senger, had so forcefully suggested to Kesselring and von Vietinghoff that they fall back to the Caesar Line right away. As it was, the two French divisions pushing through the Pontecorvo–Pico gap at the time of Leese's first assault on the line on 19 May, had captured the village of Santa Maria lying midway between this gap, and in the process had knocked back a highly experienced Panzer Grenadier Regiment and captured more than forty German field guns. Pico itself had fallen on 22 May. The delay on the renewed attack on the Senger Line, had, in many respects, been a blessing in disguise because in that time not only had Leese brought up more forces to the line, so had Kesselring. By 23 May, the bulk of AOK 10 was now crammed into the Senger Line in the Liri Valley, not to mention the reserve divisions that had been brought in too. The pause would also have given Fifth Army plenty of time to amass an overwhelming force to push through the Pontecorvo–Pico gap. 'I expected and wanted II Corps and the FEC to attack,' said Alex later, 'in such a way as to put the greatest pressure on the Germans in the Liri Valley.'[76]

This had not happened, however. Clearly Clark's interpretation of an 'all-out' attack in the Pontecorvo region was not the same as Alexander's. 'We Americans,' he commented after the war, 'tend to be what I would call broad front men.'[77] In contrast, he added, he had noticed that the British preferred to concentrate a jab at one smaller point, their massed formations behind them. This can be the only explanation why, despite on the face of it being of one accord with Alexander, he made no effort at all to channel the bulk of his troops into the Pontecorvo–Pico gap. Instead, most of the French Expeditionary Corps had continued to thrust west through the Ausoni Mountains, as had US II Corps, where because of weak, disorganised opposition they had carried on making great strides. As a result, just two French divisions had been left to carry out a task that could – and should – have proved a decisive turning point in the battle had a more concentrated effort been made by Fifth Army. And so a golden opportunity to rout AOK 10 had been missed.

Perhaps the commanders had been too distracted by the dramatic events that were brewing in the Anzio bridgehead. Certainly Clark was very occupied with the planning and preparation of the break-out, for although it was always, from the outset, going to be a key moment in Alexander and Harding's plans for the battle, its execution was a Fifth Army show, and Mark Clark was determined to oversee every part of it. The highly experienced Major-General Lucian Truscott might have been VI Corps commander, but Clark was not going to leave anything to chance: every command decision was to go through him; nothing was to happen without his stamp of approval.

This included the timing of the break-out. Clark and Alexander had been in almost constant communication over the past few days, including several face-to-face meetings. When Alex had visited Clark on 18 May, they had agreed to launch the break-out 'when timing seems appropriate'. With news reaching him that Kesselring had thrown more divisions south into the Liri Valley, Alex felt, on the evening of 19 May, that that time had come and so had issued orders to Clark to begin the break-out on the night of 21/22 May or on the morning of 22 May, whichever the Fifth Army commander felt was most appropriate.

This prompted Clark to succumb to another of his fits of umbrage. 'I was shocked,' he confessed in his diary, 'when I received it – to think that a decision of this importance would have been made without reference to me. I sent that word back to General Alexander.' Alex, the most patient of men, replied calmly that he felt they had discussed it for the previous three days. At any rate, a new date for the break-out was agreed: 23 May, the same as Eighth Army's attack on the Senger Line.

Recently arrived into the bridgehead in anticipation of the break-out was journalist Eric Sevareid, a thirty-one-year-old reporter for the American television news network, CBS. The night before the assault, Sevareid, along with a number of other reporters and journalists, was ushered into illuminated catacombs at Nettuno and briefed about the plans. It was customary for the assembled correspondents to rise whenever a general walked into the room, but to Eric's slight irritation the arrival of General Clark was always preceded by an officer striding in and ordering them to attention. 'Just as we got to our feet,' noted Eric, 'General Clark would stride in, cut the air laterally with his palm, and call: Sit down, gentlemen! in a tone which indicated that this was all a mistake, we were all men of parts together, and that he was embarrassed by his colonel's unjustified command. We frequently wondered if they rehearsed it beforehand – it went off with such dramatic flourish.'[78]

Clark then proceeded to tell them the plan of attack exactly as had been discussed for several months and exactly as Alexander had envisaged in his Operation Order No 1 issued on 5 May. In other words, the aim would be to break out and take the town of Cisterna first, then carry on in a straight line northwards to Valmontone, where they would cut the Via Casilina, and thus cut off AOK 10 – all things being well – as it was retreating back down the Liri Valley. In this way, a large part of the German forces in Italy would be destroyed. Capturing Rome thereafter would then be a matter of course. The US-led VI Corps consisted of five US divisions now that the 36th Texas Division had been shipped in, as well as two British divisions and the 1st Special Force, made up of three regiments of picked US and Canadian troops trained for long-range sabotage work. The US 1st Armored, 3rd Infantry and

1st Special Force would launch the attack. Opposing them would be five German divisions, most of which were under strength, but which included the elite paratroopers of the 4th Fallschirmjäger Division. As correspondents and broadcasters they would, naturally, be limited in what they could say about the aims, but it was perfectly all right to say that Mark Clark was personally in command of the operation.

Eric had been recruited to CBS News in 1939 by Edward R. Murrow, by then already a well-known figure in America. A somewhat reluctant broadcaster, Eric always felt more comfortable as a writer. Indeed, after graduating from high school in 1930, he and a friend had canoed up the River Minnesota and on to Hudson Bay, a trip of more than 2,000 miles that he had written up – aged eighteen – and published as *Canoeing With the Cree*. At university he began working as a political journalist and wrote for the *Minneapolis Journal* before joining CBS and being sent to Paris to begin his broadcast career. He was still in Paris when the city fell and had been the first person to report the surrender in June 1940, before heading to London to join Murrow in reporting on the Battle of Britain. Subsequently sent to the Far East to cover the war in Burma and China, he had been fortunate to get out of there alive after the plane he was on developed engine trouble and he and his companions were forced to parachute out behind Japanese lines. Missing believed dead, after three weeks and a 140-mile trek through the Burmese jungle, he and his fellow survivors made it to India and safety. It was with these credentials, and having become something of a household name in America for his pioneering broadcast journalism, that Eric had reached Italy in March 1944. He had been broadcasting what he'd seen ever since, and intended to continue doing so as he followed the fortunes of VI Corps when they began their assault.

At dawn on 23 May, Eric was standing on a slight rise in the flat plain of the bridgehead amongst the olive drab tents of a field aid station attached to the 1st Armored Division. There was a chill in the air and cloud covered the sky; the rain of the past few days had yet to clear. Eric could hear larks singing nearby and see a layer of fog covering the German positions ahead of him. At 5.45 a.m. sharp, flashes could be seen from the clusters of guns away to the right and left, followed by an ear-cracking cacophony and a trembling of the ground below his feet. As shells screamed overhead causing his jacket to ruffle, planes roared by too, followed shortly after by the clank and squeal of tanks trundling forward.

Although the 1st Armored Division was going into action that day, Private First Class Ray Saidel was not amongst them – he was on a radio course near Naples. Nor, much to his frustration, was Colonel Hamilton Howze, commander of the 1st Armored's 13th Armored Regiment and second in command of Combat Command B (or CCB as it was known), which had only recently joined the rest of 1st Armored Division in the bridgehead.*

Colonel Howze was by this time an experienced senior officer in the division. Having been with 1st Armored since it was shipped overseas back in 1942, he had remained with it throughout the North African campaign and the recent winter battles in Italy. A divisional staff officer for much of their time in Tunisia, he had taken over command of the 13th Armored towards the end of the campaign. His tanks had also been supporting the 36th Texas Division when they had made their ill-fated attempt to cross the Rapido back in January – not that they had ever been called upon to help with the crossing. At the time, Hamilton had been shocked to discover the infantry battalion commanding officers he spoke with had had no real idea of what artillery plans there had been, and was even more astonished that neither his tanks nor those attached directly to the Texans had been called upon to help take out the German machine-gun nests on the far side of the river. 'In a word,' he noted, 'so far as I was able to determine, six infantry battalions of the division attacked without the artillery and tank fire support they needed to succeed.'[79]

Fifth Army had learnt much since then, however, and Hamilton was confident that VI Corps would achieve their objectives. On that first day, his job was to command a reserve made up from the 13th Armored and a number of other remaining tank and infantry battalions, with orders to send reinforcements up to the leading armoured formations when required. But he was far from idle. The leading elements of CCB soon came unstuck in the thick minefields between the two lines; they managed to make their way through the narrow passages cleared by engineers of the 34th Infantry Division, but then discovered no routes had been marked out once they pushed deeper into no-man's-land. They were paying for not using any of the elaborate mine clearing contraptions that could be attached to the front of their tanks, and which Combat Command A used with good effect. The result was that Hamilton's

---

*The Combat Command was roughly equivalent to a British armoured brigade.

armoured reserve spent most of the first day and night, and all the
following day, retrieving crippled tanks that had lost tracks and wheels.

Accompanying CCA were the 135th Infantry Regiment, loaned from
the 34th Red Bull Division for the assault. The 135th had come a long
way since the first green and poorly trained troops had left America at
the beginning of 1942. One of those who had been with them all the
way was Sergeant Edward 'Bucky' Walters, part of the forward observation team of Cannon Company. As Bucky was the first to admit, they
had reached North Africa in the autumn of 1942 hopelessly ill-equipped
for the battles ahead; he had never even seen a tank before he reached
the front in the spring of 1943, let alone trained alongside one. At
Fondouk in Tunisia, the Red Bulls – including the 135th – had been
routed, their poor training and lack of battle experience tragically
exposed. But like most rookie US divisions, they learnt from their mistakes and learnt quickly. Just over a month later, they showed their
mettle and new-found resolve in the capture of Hill 609, a key feature
in the final battle for Tunisia. At the subsequent victory parade in Tunis,
it was the Red Bulls who had led the way.

They had missed out on Sicily, but had landed at Salerno and had
been involved in some of the heaviest of Fifth Army's fighting since then,
becoming one of Clark's most battle-hardened and trusted units. It was
for this reason that the 135th had been sent to join the armour of CCA
for the opening assault from the bridgehead. 'Our officers had really
matured,' says Bucky, 'and when replacements came in – and we always
had a lot – we made sure they got all the secrets we had, how to stay
alive and so on. I think we were entirely different from when we'd been
at Fondouk.'

Cannon Company's job was to accompany the infantry with 75mm
pack Howitzers, field guns that could, if necessary, be broken down and
carried in pack form onto high or difficult terrain. Their role was to
give close artillery support for the infantry. Bucky was the 'recon' –
reconnaissance – sergeant, accompanying either Captain Barman or a
lieutenant and leading the way with the infantry and setting up a forward
observation post from which, via a radio, he would help direct artillery
fire.

He was carrying out the same role as the assault began, setting off in
a jeep around 6.30 a.m. once the opening barrage had died down. It was
dangerous work, being among the first to head out into the fray, but he
and Captain Barman managed to get ahead and establish a forward

observation post when the tanks of CCA began rumbling up alongside them, led by Sherman tanks attached with demolition snakes for mine clearing. These were essentially torpedoes, consisting of 3-inch diameter piping, made in segments up to 400 feet long, and loaded with explosives. They were pushed across the minefield, the explosives detonating the mines ahead of them. 'I'd never seen anything like it,' admits Bucky, 'but they were doing a good job of clearing all the mines and wire.'

Meanwhile, Eric Sevareid had watched the first German prisoners being brought in and interrogated, and then had headed up towards the front lines, joining the men of 1st Special Force as they pushed along the Mussolini Canal at the southern end of the advance. The cloud had gone and the sun was now out. Lying by a bunker, he watched enemy shells whining over as they headed for targets in the American rear. 'There was no use denying it,' the correspondent noted, 'I was happy here; I enjoyed it.' Nearby a bazooka gunner from Chicago was wondering whether they would be in Rome by the weekend, while another passed round chocolates sent to him by his Rotary Club back home.

Later, Eric joined his fellow reporters at the press villa. They were all coated in dust and talking eagerly. Eric listened, piecing together the events of the day, which had broadly been good. A wide hole had been blown in the centre of the German defences, although the opposition had been stiffer along the northern shoulder of the American breach. There had been heavy fighting all day. To his shock, Eric learnt that a number of the pressmen were either dead or in hospital. One colleague, Gregory Duncan, an artist for the Forces newspaper, *Stars & Stripes,* had been sketching next to Eric as he'd prepared to make his broadcast the previous night. Now he was dead, killed when his jeep crashed into a newly made shell hole at speed. 'With this news,' noted Eric, 'the exhilaration of the day drained out of me at once.'[80]

There had been no let-up for the Allied air forces, which had continued to bomb and strafe German positions and anything that attempted to move during the day. On 24 May, MATAF alone flew nearly 2,000 sorties,* the biggest effort in a single day since the start of the battle two weeks before. Roads and motor transport north of Rome were attacked; enemy artillery were heavily pasted in the northern sector of the Anzio

---

*A sortie is a flight by an individual pilot or aircraft. For example, if a squadron of twelve aircraft flies a mission, that equates to twelve sorties.

bridgehead; the Via Casilina was repeatedly sprayed with bombs and bullets, as German forces hurried south from the north of Rome, with the fighter-bombers claiming as many as 563 enemy vehicles south of Valmontone. Sixty-one P-40 Kittyhawks and thirty-five P-47 Thunderbolts blasted the towns of Lanuvio and Cori in support of VI Corps. One of those attacking Cori that day was Charles Dills and pilots of the 27th Fighter-Bomber Group. It was his seventy-fifth combat mission since his arrival in Italy. He was leading White Flight, while the 522nd Squadron CO, Major Emil Tanassy, was leading Red Flight and their formation. Their mission was to bomb Cori and then look around for any further targets. Having safely dropped their loads over Cori, however, Major Tanassy got a 20mm flak shell in his engine. 'The engine didn't stop,' says Charles, 'but there was oil all over the place. He couldn't see because there was oil all over his goggles.' Hearing this over the radio, Charles flew up alongside the Major's wing and talked him through the flying until the CO had had a chance to wipe his goggles clear and jettison his Perspex canopy. They then headed for the emergency landing strip at Anzio, where Tanassy belly-landed, sliding with grinding metal beyond the end of the runway. Incredibly, however, the CO walked away unscathed.

Charles then re-formed the squadron of seven remaining P-40s and took over the lead, heading back down the coast. Little did Charles realise at that time how far US II Corps had progressed. Over the Pontine Marsh north of Terracina he spotted a large truck convoy, out in the open and close packed, bumper to bumper. They were within an area that was well beyond the bomb line, but Charles was still suspicious – he realised it was unlikely that the Germans would have allowed themselves to have been caught out in daylight in such a large formation. 'We buzzed them and saw that they were ours,' says Charles, and so a potential tragedy was averted. During their subsequent debriefing, they learned that the Major had been warned about the dramatic advance of II Corps. 'The only one that knew it,' says Charles, 'had been shot down!'

Things had been progressing well in the Anzio bridgehead. Despite continued heavy fighting, the Germans were falling back, especially in the centre of the line, in the direction of the main thrust. On the evening of the 24th, Colonel Hamilton Howze was given command of 'Howze Force', principally his own 13th Armored Regiment, less one company, and placed directly under divisional control. Cisterna was now all but surrounded, but Hamilton's specific job was to push on past the town towards the long valley that led directly to Valmontone, while CCA pressed on across the valley in the direction of Velletri and the Alban Hills.

Having assembled during the night, Howze Force got going early the following morning, 25 May. Almost immediately one of the light reconnaissance tanks received a direct hit, killing all its crew instantly, but pushing on, the other tanks managed to encircle one of the fearsome German self-propelled 88mm guns, and incredibly, forced the crew to surrender despite the gun's phenomenal 7.5-inch thick armour. 'I looked at it closely later,' noted Hamilton. 'Our little 37mm guns had hardly dented it.'[81]

Hamilton's force continued to make good progress all day, with his Sherman tanks reaching the key road that linked Cori with Valmontone, VI Corps' ultimate goal. The German situation had become so desperate that Kesselring had finally committed his last reserve division, the Fallschirm-Panzerkorps Hermann Göring, who, like the more regular Fallschirmjäger units, were crack troops. Kesselring had ordered them to move south on the 22nd, having at long last accepted that an Allied seaborne invasion north of Rome was now unlikely and that, in any case, the more pressing need was south of the capital.

However, whether they would arrive in time to seriously influence the battle was another matter. They had been quite a long way north and had spent much of the month carrying out anti-partisan operations in northern Tuscany. The HG – Hermann Göring – Armoured Reconnaissance Battalion was the first unit to head south, but after two nights' march had only reached Lake Bolsena some fifty miles north of Rome. This was far too slow for Kesselring's urgent needs, and so they were ordered to throw caution to the wind and continue by daylight, a gamble that seemed to have paid off, as they were largely untouched by Allied aircraft. Even so, they still found themselves battling against the reams of refugees now fleeing northwards away from the fighting. Another night march took them to Artena, a few miles due south of Valmontone, via secondary roads and by weaving their way through numerous bomb craters and past battle damage. Meanwhile, HG Artillery, coming all the way from Pisa, had suffered far worse on the journey south, and had been 'reduced to a shell.'[82]

The HG Reconnaissance Battalion had meanwhile moved into position south of Artena, met by numerous disorientated German troops hopelessly lost and separated from their units, and hundreds of burnt-out vehicles and tanks that had recently been attacked from the air. Without having had a chance to reconnoitre the position or familiarise themselves in any way, they almost immediately came up against Howze Force advancing towards them. Both sides opened fire until the forward Sherman tanks of the Americans broke through and the newly arrived HG armoured reconnaissances troops were forced to pull back to Artena. When Colonel Howze himself reached the scene he gazed around. 'There was carnage indeed,' he noted, 'bodies and pieces of bodies strewn among the scores of wrecked and burning vehicles.'[83]

That same day, elements of US II Corps and VI Corps met up, and in so doing Fifth Army became whole again after 125 days of separation between the two fronts. By enormous good luck, the scoop was Eric Sevareid's. He had overslept, and when he awoke discovered the other correspondents had left without him to witness the meeting. By the time he got there and pieced together the story, most of the other journalists had long since written theirs up. Fortunately for Eric, however, Fifth Army had put a bulletin embargo in place until 2 p.m., precisely the time he had his wireless slot. From being the last to the scene, he was the first with the story, much to the delight of CBS.

Having completed his broadcast, Eric headed down the coast to Naples for an overnight visit. As he approached Terracina, he watched unsmiling Italian refugees trudging past. Eric soon understood why. 'Terracina,' he wrote, 'was an awesome shambles, its buildings spewn into the roadways, its whole skyline ripped away. There were still dead mules and bodies along the curbs, and a terrible stench issued from the ruins. So with Fondi; so with Formia.'[84] So with every village and town unfortunate enough to get in the way of the fighting.

For the most part, the appalling violence and level of destruction were impersonal, seen as an unavoidable side effect of fighting a war, a war in which, the Allies believed, they held the moral right. Occasionally, however, that argument was tested, especially when Allied troops committed the kind of crimes that were unacceptable no matter what the strained and difficult circumstances in which they found themselves.

Rather than being flung into the Pontecorvo–Pico gap, for example, the French Expeditionary Corps were now sweeping through the Ausoni Mountains, now almost entirely free of German resistance. On 25 May, Pasua Pisa's father and her son, Lorenzo, were being buried in Amaseno, the small market town in the valley below. Everyone from the tiny mountain-top community had gone to the funeral – everyone but Pasua and her mother. 'My mother and I stayed behind in the house,' she says. 'My grief was too great.'

Suddenly there were soldiers at the door – Goumiers, French colonial troops wearing striped woven burnouses over their uniforms, and with knives tucked into their belts. One of them grabbed Pasua and dragged her out of the house and in the courtyard brutally raped her. Then they left, sparing Pasua's mother. Other French colonial troops would not be so discerning. Before the battle was over, they would rape over and over again, bringing a new horror to the Italians, still reeling from the carnage brought to their homes. 'The Moroccans,' says Pasua, 'stole my life away.'

By the evening of 25 May, the situation in the Anzio bridgehead looked very promising. A large hole had been punched forward from the bridgehead, but although fighting had continued to be fierce to the north, Howze Force had clearly found a soft spot, and fortunately it was in precisely the direction of VI Corps' objective. Valmontone, Hamilton felt sure, would fall the following day and with it they would cut the Via Casilina. Sensing a great victory now within their grasp, Hamilton reported this to Brigadier-General Allen, commander of CCB, imploring him to try and get the whole of 1st Armored Division diverted into this gap as soon as possible. Allen agreed wholeheartedly with Hamilton's appreciation, and relayed this to division. The divisional commander, General Harmon, also agreed, and in turn urged General Truscott, the VI Corps commander, to order such a move. Truscott needed no convincing – it was, after all, the obvious course of action. 'By the following morning,' he wrote, 'we would be astride the German line of withdrawal through Valmontone.'[85]

Truscott returned to his headquarters late that evening, only to find General Brann, Clark's chief of operations, waiting for him with some stunning, and at first incomprehensible, news. There would be no all-out drive on Valmontone the following day, Brann told him. Instead, the main axis of the attack was to switch north, through the Alban Hills – and directly towards Rome.

FOURTEEN

General Clark and the Big Switch
26–30 May 1944

Life for Carla Capponi and her boyfriend, Paolo Bentivegna, had become almost unbearable since the end of April. Having survived the aftermath of their bomb attack on the Via Rasella, they had been betrayed by Guglielmo Blasi, a partisan with GAP Central whom Carla had had doubts about even before the bomb on 23 March. Struggling to keep himself and his family alive, Blasi had offered himself to the notorious Pietro Koch, Fascist commander of the vigilante Koch Gang. Remaining with the partisans but working as Koch's spy and informer, Blasi had since then almost single-handedly brought about the end of GAP Central.

Fortunately for Paolo and Carla, one of their fellow partisans managed to escape from Koch's new headquarters and so was able to warn them of the betrayal. Even so, Koch now knew all about Paolo's key role in the attack and declared him Public Enemy Number One. Now hunted like wolves, they were forced to change their place of refuge daily, and frequently went days without any food.

They had known the offensive was coming thanks to American agents in Rome working with the partisans, and it had been a relief to hear news that the battle had begun. But Carla seriously doubted whether they would still be alive when the Allies finally reached the Eternal City. Since the beginning of the Allied air offensive, Operation STRANGLE, food shortages had risen dramatically. Rome had begun to starve, and civilians were now dying as a consequence; and as the battle continued to rage, the situation only worsened. Top priority for the Germans now was supplying the front – with men, food, equipment and ammunition. With so many roads and bridges destroyed, with railway lines cut and marshalling yards wrecked, and with Allied fighter planes strafing and bombing anything that moved by day, that was hard enough. Feeding

Rome was nigh on impossible. The Vatican had protested to Britain, and the Foreign Secretary, Anthony Eden, passed on the letter to the Prime Minister. 'It is with pain that I write these words,' Churchill had replied. 'Rome must starve till freed.'[86]

But Carla was not only starving, she was also stricken with a lung infection, and coughing up blood. She was saved by the CLN, who helped her and Paolo to smuggle themselves out of Rome altogether, and to head for Palestrina in the hills to the east of Rome. There, protected by the local partisans, she lay low, happy to hear the guns getting closer and praying the Allies would reach them soon.

In the Liri Valley, the Germans had begun to fall back, even the Fallschirmjäger Division, who, until ordered to retreat, had continued to hold up the Poles at the village of Piedimonte. On the 24th, Hans Golda and his nebelwerfer battery had fought a valiant rearguard action while infantry streamed past, but had been stuck where they were waiting for their vehicles to arrive. Eventually, as tank shells had begun falling all around, they had appeared. After quickly loading up, they headed north through the night towards Arce on the Via Casilina and into new positions on the northern banks of the River Melfa, a tributary of the Liri that cut the road at right angles and which provided an obvious natural line of defence. 'Retreating along the Via Casilina at high speed under shellfire,' scribbled Hans. By the road was a pile of horses, torn to pieces, still in harness with the gunners lying next to them. 'Jabos all around,' he added. 'Charged through. An infantryman sitting in a motorcycle side car, burning. A horse shaking in the middle of the road. We drive straight over it.'

Despite such mayhem and carnage, however, Eighth Army was struggling to follow up with any kind of speed. The Poles, still unencumbered by their tanks and motorised transport, would have been a good option for continuing the chase to the Melfa, but Leese, recognising they were a spent force after battling through possibly the hardest fighting of the offensive to date, and having sustained horrendous casualties, withdrew them from the fight. Instead, it was left to XIII Corps on the right, and the Canadians on the left, to make their way through the now empty Senger Line, over the Forme d'Aquino – another Liri tributary – and then get across the Melfa.

The river had been reached by forward Canadian units on the 24th, but it had been impossible to get any further because of the hopeless congestion behind. 'The Canadian Corps are a bit rusty,' wrote Leese,

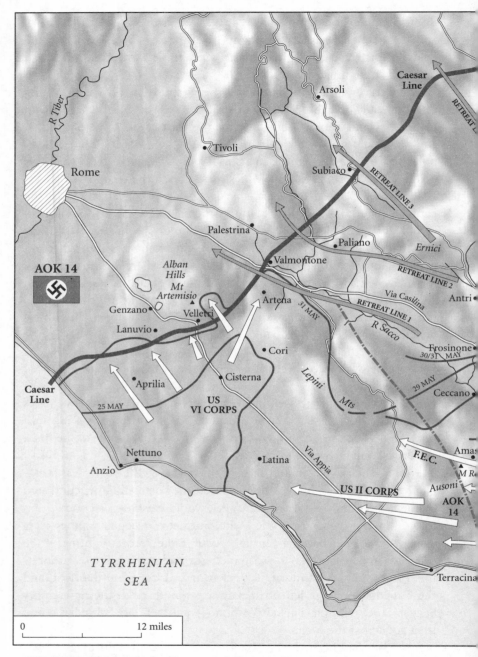

DIADEM: The battle for Rome and German lines of retreat for AOK 10

'in their staff work, inter-communication and traffic control.'[87] Certainly bridging equipment and bulldozers, so crucial for their advance, were not given the kind of priority they should have had. XIII Corps was unable to move at all that day because of the jams. It was also why the Perths, supposedly in the van of the Canadians' advance, did not clamber aboard their trucks for the ride to the start line of their advance until the evening of 24 May. 'The ride should have taken no more than twenty minutes,' noted Stan Scislowski, 'but ended up taking more like two hours.'[88]

Rather like the closing of two lanes of a motorway during rush hour, the rate at which vehicles arrived into a bottleneck was far greater than the speed with which they could pass through. An armoured division such as the 5th Canadian and 6th British, now vying for the few tracks, crossings and roads that would enable them to push forward, was made up of around 366 tanks and 3,048 other vehicles, while an infantry division would have as many as 3,375 vehicles. This made for an awful lot of traffic.*

Ted Wyke-Smith and his sappers were still busily building new bridges every night. In XIII Corps, priority was always given to his lorries and their bridging equipment, but this meant other vehicles in their way would have to pull off the road and let them pass, which, of course, caused further hold-ups. During the day, Ted would be travelling around in his jeep or in an armoured car, carrying out reconnaissance work for the next night's bridging. On the night of the 22nd, for example, he had driven to a conference with the CO at 11 p.m. It had been raining and was pitch black. No headlights could be used, so it was both hard and slow going. In such conditions, and with shell- and pot-holes dotting all the roads, accidents were common. On that occasion, he had helped to tow an ambulance out of a ditch. 'When a vehicle got wrecked,' he says, 'everyone had to gather around and get it off the road; get it out of the way as quickly as possible to keep the traffic moving'. But inevitably such incidents caused even more delays.

There were also the vast numbers of mines and intricate booby traps which the Germans were past masters at laying and preparing. This made the leading elements of any columns of vehicles, whether tanks or trucks, understandably nervous and cautious. In Russia, minefields

---

*These are only approximate figures, because they changed from time to time, especially during a battle when a number would be lost.

would be cleared by pouring massed Soviet forces across them; that was certainly not the Eighth way.

The Perth Regiment picked their way through the Senger Line early on the morning of 25 May. There was fog about but it did not stop them capturing a number of German troops, who, like Jupp Klein and his men before them, had been cut off during the retreat and had been trying to work their way back through enemy lines. Stan paused to look inside an abandoned German bunker, a somewhat reckless thing to do. He was fortunate – there were no booby traps. He was impressed by its strength. 'After seeing one of these dugouts,' he wrote, 'one could understand how and why the enemy were able to ride out a storm of shells and then come up fighting.'[89] Inevitably, he could not resist the urge to rummage about for loot. He was still inside, having taken a pack of undershorts, a razor and a couple of Mauser rifles, when some Canadian sappers turned up. As Stan emerged, the men accosted him. 'Man, are you ever lucky we had no grenades,' they told him, 'or you'd have been mincemeat by now!'

In the afternoon, the Perths advanced on foot towards the Melfa. Stan could hear small-arms fire getting louder and the steady crump of their tanks firing as they drew closer. Tension welled inside him. Soon they were passing through a field of wheat, five yards apart in an arrowhead formation, before emerging onto a cart track that led to the Melfa. There they discovered a couple of abandoned nebelwerfers. Wandering over to one of them, Stan suddenly noticed five grenades wired together next to one of the barrels. 'There was no mistaking it,' he noted, 'this baby was booby trapped.'[90]

They were across the river and within site of Ceprano by the following morning. For a brief moment, Stan realised he was the leading soldier in Eighth Army's advance. 'The only people ahead of me,' he wrote, 'were guys wearing field-grey.' Soon after, Dog Company paused as the tanks clanked past them. An old friend of Stan's from a different company, Pete McRorie, walked past. Stan called out and seconds later, Pete's foot landed heavily on a German anti-tank Teller mine, killing him and another infantryman. Stan had also been close enough to have been walloped flat by the blast. 'I looked around in a daze,' he noted, 'and saw the upper half of Pete's body lying in the middle of a road – a welter of blood, guts and bone.' He thought he might crack up at such a gruesome sight but instead found himself feeling thankful it was not him. 'Maybe without knowing it,' he wondered, 'I'd hardened myself to such terrible sights.'

Later that afternoon they took Ceprano but by the 27th, Dog Company were once again sitting still in shallow slit-trenches waiting for the order to advance once more. Stan could not understand it. As far as he was concerned there was nothing in front of them: no shelling, no mortar or machine-gun fire. He wasn't thirsting for action but found this inactivity frustrating all the same. 'When you've got the bastards on the run,' he noted, 'you stay right on top of them, not sit back and let them get away.'

But getting away they were. Von Vietinghoff and his senior commanders, von Senger included, had, since the collapse of the Senger Line, been doing their best to persuade Kesselring that a deep withdrawal was their only course of action, and had not only made plans but had begun to act on them in anticipation of approval. Kesselring's hands, however, were tied by Hitler and the German High Command, and so he initially forbade such a retreat. It was, of course, too late, but not until 28 May did Kesselring give official orders for AOK 10 to begin a fighting retreat using the kind of delaying tactics that had been employed to such good effect following the battle at Salerno the previous autumn. Nor was there any talk of giving up Rome. Rather, Kesselring's two armies were to eventually fall back behind the Caesar Line, the last major defensive position south of Rome. Like the Gustav Line, it ran across the width of Italy, beginning some fifteen miles south of Rome. It was far from complete, having only been begun in March, but was still another considerable defensive barrier, and which once again made the most of the high ground wherever possible.

The Allies had been aware of the Caesar Line, or 'C-Position', before the battle, and its existence was another reason why Alexander and Harding had favoured blocking off AOK 10 before they fell behind it with a strike from the Anzio bridgehead. Yet although this thrust towards Valmontone had been an integral part of Alex's battle plan, Clark had never been so convinced that this was the one and only course of action. Always the most assiduous planner, Clark was not prepared to leave anything to chance, and so had prepared three possible lines of attack from the bridgehead. One was towards Valmontone as Alex envisaged; the second was south-easterly towards Sezze in case the attack in the south had not gone as well as hoped; and the third was north to Rome via the Appian Way – or Route 7 – to the west of the Colli Laziali in the Alban Hills. Clark briefed his commanders on 5 May outlining all these plans, but later in the day, Alex visited him and told him to concentrate on only one line of attack. 'He said that the only attack he envisages is from the beachhead,' noted Clark, 'is the Cisterna-Cori-Valmontone attack.'

Three days later the two men had a further conference, where Alex directly expressed his concerns that Clark was not 'all-out' for the attack towards Valmontone and that he felt he was not in agreement with his plans. 'I told Alexander that I wanted to attack out of the beachhead with everything I had,' noted Clark, 'that if conditions were right I wanted to attack towards Cori [and Valmontone] but that what I was guarding against was preconceived ideas as to what exactly was to be done.' Clark agreed that potentially they had a big opportunity for a great victory but they should be wary of over-optimism. In light of his experiences up to now in Italy, this was understandable. 'He kept pulling on me the idea that we were to annihilate the entire German army,' continued Clark, 'and did it so many times that I told him that I did not believe that we had too many chances to do that; that the Boche was too smart.' Clark insisted that he wanted to maintain his flexibility, although his biggest concern had been that the main attack along the southern front might be stalled and that Alex would then order a premature break-out from Anzio. 'I told him that I had directed Truscott to give first priority to the Cori attack,' added Clark, 'but that he would continue plans for the attack to the west of Colli Laziali. I wanted to have plans prepared to meet any eventuality, keeping my mind free of any definite commitment before the battle started.'[91] With this, their meeting ended – unresolved.

Clark still expressed his desire for flexibility even once it was clear the main attack in the south was going well. During his meeting with Alex on 18 May, he raised the issue of the direction of VI Corps' attack from the bridgehead once more. Alexander was again adamant that an attack in the direction of Valmontone was the only course of action. When Clark pointed out the mountains he might have to fight through in order to take Valmontone, Alex 'brushed this aside'. The following day, during a meeting with Truscott, his VI Corps commander, Clark once again stressed that he wanted to maintain flexibility, regardless of Alex's orders. The plan to thrust towards Valmontone would be carried out as directed, but Truscott should be prepared to change the line of attack northwest towards Rome. 'Much depended,' added Clark, 'upon the German reaction to the attack on the main Allied front.'

What had concerned Alex was not so much a suspicion that Clark had other ulterior intentions, but more what he perceived as a lack of aggressiveness and over-caution. Yet Clark did have some reasons for caution. The attack towards Cori and then on to Valmontone meant funnelling VI Corps from the flat plain around Anzio into a comparatively narrow stretch of softly undulating low ground of about twenty miles. To their right were the Lepini Mountains, with Cori, and further on, Artena, lying on the lower slopes of the edge of this range. On their left, as they advanced, were the Alban Hills, in which the Caesar Line lay. Velletri, like Cori opposite, lay on the lower slopes overlooking the low ground. Before the battle, Clark would have been aware that, potentially, he could have had enemy troops in the high ground either side of him. He was also aware that making a flank march across two fronts of an undefeated force was a classic military sin. The threat to his southern flank had all but gone – although not entirely – by the evening of 25 May, but the threat to his flanks from the Alban Hills was very much still there. In fact, much of AOK 14 lay dug in along the Caesar Line, and from Clark's point of view, there was no guarantee that they would not counterattack and assault his vulnerable flank and rear. After the near failure at Salerno and the debacle of the Rapido, and following the disappointments of Anzio, and now the hard-fought-for success of the past two weeks, there was no way Clark was going to risk a major setback now. To his mind, AOK 14 had to be faced, and that meant continuing the pressure on Velletri.

Furthermore, Fifth Army intelligence reports suggested on 25 May that the German 362nd Division had withdrawn towards Valmontone to the east of Velletri. On the evidence of the way the Germans had fought the battle so far, Clark also suspected von Mackensen would shift units from the Alban Hills into the Valmontone gap, which would in turn thin out the German forces along the Caesar Line to the north. Moreover, he was not convinced that much could be achieved by pushing across to Valmontone. It would mean overextending his line of supply from the bridgehead, and, in any case, beyond the town lay more mountains, whose valleys cut across any potential line of advance.

As it happened, although Kesselring and his commanders were worried about such a threat to Valmontone, their concern was for the right wing of AOK 10 only, and they certainly did not envisage the whole of AOK 10 being destroyed there. In fact, the Via Casilina that passed through Valmontone was just one of five escape routes von Vietinghoff and his two corps commanders planned to use for their withdrawal. The other four all concertinaed northwards out from the narrow southern front, and hence further away from Valmontone with every mile. The next route to the east of Valmontone, for example, led through Genaz-zano, eight miles by a rough, track road across mountains; north of that lay another route, through Subiaco, fourteen miles as the crow flies, but barred from Valmontone by further mountains and only tracks, or *strade bianche*, as they are known in Italy. The fifth route was more than forty miles as the crow flies, and many more on the ground. VI Corps did not have trained mountain troops; some American paratroops dropped in to block these escape routes might have been put to good use, but Clark did not consider using the 509th Airborne Combat Team – who were out of the line but theoretically available – for this. Thus the chances of heavily motorised US troops being able to speed over mountains and across rivers – there were a minimum of five to reach Subiaco, for example – and cut off the retreating Germans, who were lightly motor-ised, and mostly passing down existing valley roads, were extremely slim.

At any rate, on the morning of 26 May, Clark issued orders that split his forces into two lines of attack rather than one. The 34th Red Bull and the 45th Divisions were now thrown north-west of Velletri through the Alban Hills, with almost all 1st Armored supporting them around Velletri, and with 36th Texas Division ready to attack northwards too. He preferred to deal with the threat to his flank by turning and attacking it face on; and it was also his judgement that this was the best and quickest way to take Rome, with the chance of destroying a large part of AOK 14 in the process. The other half of his forces – 3rd Infantry and 1st Special Force – were to carry on driving towards Valmontone, with the French Expeditionary Force continuing to push through the Lepini Mountains towards the Via Casilina, and II Corps also sweeping north.

On the other hand, there were also sound arguments for sticking with Alex and Harding's original plan. AOK 10 was on the run and, even if the Germans did reinforce Valmontone, the momentum was with the Americans and they would have surely won the day. By severing the Via Casilina, a number of German units would have been destroyed even if perhaps not the majority of AOK 10. Certainly, Truscott was dumb-founded by the decision, and protested vociferously. Even once he heard Clark's reasons for the switch he still believed the change of attack was mistaken, although he did his best to fall in line. General Harmon, commander of the 1st Armored, was also deeply gloomy about the change of plan, as was Colonel Hamilton Howze. 'It was a dreadfully bad decision,' noted Hamilton. 'It is a cardinal battle principle that in attack one should reinforce success.' The change around also caused organisational difficulties – Howze Force, for example, was now seconded to 3rd Division, with the accompanying change of command structure. Howze's main gripe, however – shared by Harmon – was not the missed opportunity to annihilate AOK 10, but rather that Clark was losing out on a golden opportunity to capture Rome quickly.

Equally horrified was Eric Sevareid, who attended Clark's press briefing on the morning of 26 May. He could not understand why the Allies were now apparently abandoning the officially stated strategy. 'It seemed to some of us,' he wrote, 'that in view of Alexander's declaration that the aim of the campaign was the destruction of the enemy in Italy, this was a serious mistake.' In his next broadcast script he wrote, 'There is a question whether the two aims [of getting Rome and of destroying the enemy] are compatible or mutually exclusive.' The censors cut this line and at a further briefing Clark referred directly to Eric's suggestion that they might no longer be able to capture the bulk of the Germans. 'That is sheer nonsense,' Clark told the assembled correspondents, pointing out the numerous lines of German escape to the north-east of Valmontone. 'Now the General spoke in a manner,' added Eric, 'that seemed to deny that the idea had ever entered his head.'[92]

What Clark was doing in front of the press, in the full knowledge that his words would be quoted around the world, was justifying his decision on military terms and making the point that he had never really approved of the Valmontone line of attack in the first place. This was seriously bad form. Clark expected complete loyalty from his subordinate commanders; Truscott, for example, strongly disagreed with Clark's change of attack, but dutifully supported his boss, and obeyed orders. Clark, on the other hand, regardless of the merits or otherwise of his reasoning, was flagrantly undermining *his* boss, Alexander, and, by changing the plan without full consultation with his superior, disobeying his orders. It was very much Alex's command style to get what he wanted by suggestion and gentle coercion, but when he gave specific and repeated orders, he meant them to be obeyed.

At the time, however, he accepted Clark's judgement, believing that VI Corps was attacking northwards in support of the main drive to Valmontone. Later that day, Alex even visited the VI Corps front, and although he did not see Clark he did spend time with General Al

Gruenther, Clark's much respected and widely liked Chief of Staff. Having been briefed by Gruenther, Alex told him, 'I am for any line of action which the Army Commander believes will offer a chance to continue his present success.' A few minutes later Alex added, 'I am sure that the Army Commander will continue to push towards Valmontone, won't he?'[93] Gruenther assured him he was continuing to do so. 'I am certain that he left with no mental reservations as to the wisdom of your attack,' Gruenther wrote later in a message to Clark. 'He stated that if you are able to capture the high ground north of Velletri it would put the enemy at a serious disadvantage, and would practically ensure the success of the bridgehead attack.'

To begin with it looked as though Clark's change of plan was going to bring a sweeping and rapid success, with the thrust towards Valmontone continuing to surge forward. As Colonel Howze's tanks rumbled onwards they saw plenty of still-burning German vehicles, but almost no resistance. Travelling in his armoured car, Hamilton saw only signs that the Germans had given up the fight. At one point he watched the tank ahead of him fire three rounds into a field of wheat. 'I thought this was imbecilic,' he noted, 'but went ahead to see an imploded 50mm German anti-tank gun with its crew strewn bloodily around. What had it been waiting for? It could have destroyed two or three of our tanks. The crew must have been exhausted – and asleep.'[94]

As the day progressed, they swept past Artena, where the 3rd Infantry had surrounded the town, and by late afternoon the leading tanks of Howze Force were just a tantalising mile from Valmontone and the Via Casilina. As Howze approached in his armoured car, he could see three of his tanks burning. When he eventually caught up with his leading tank commander, Lieutenant-Colonel Bogardus Cairns, he learned that they were now being engaged by large numbers of German infantry coming from the east, as well as a number of tanks from the north.

Howze ordered his tanks to fall back for the night. The following day Artena fell, and from the slopes above the town American artillery was now able to direct fire onto the Via Casilina. But the troops Howze Force had encountered were the men of the newly arrived 334th Division from the Adriatic, while the tanks were those of the Fallschirm-Panzerkorps Hermann Göring, more units of which had now reached the front. Also adding weight was the newly formed 92nd Division, and the remnants of the 715th Division who had joined them having retreated from the

French. Suddenly, from having faced almost no opposition at all, there was now a sizeable German force holding open the Via Casilina and offering a solid wall through which the exhausted Americans simply could not punch a hole.

On the northern front, Clark's forces had also had initial success before the Germans fell back behind the Caesar Line. At this point, the Americans were stopped dead, the enemy artillery from the high ground pinning them down and preventing them from even getting close to a breakthrough. For the moment, it looked as though Kesselring had at long last begun to stabilise his front.

Things were hardly going any better on the Eighth Army front. German rearguards, demolitions, mines, congestion, and far too many river cross- ings were grinding the massed armour of XIII Corps and the Canadian Corps almost to a halt, much to the frustration of everyone concerned, from Alexander and General Leese down to infantry privates like Stan Scislowski. In pushing through Ceprano, the Canadians were held up by a blown bridge across a wide section of the Liri. Stan ended up crossing the 120-foot stretch by rowing across in a flimsy wooden boat with seven other infantrymen, with German mortars firing into the mass of vehicles still stranded on the other side all the while.

That night the Canadian sappers worked hard to get a Bailey bridge across, only for it to buckle and collapse just as they were about to push the structure the last few yards to reach the far side. Stan heard that some of the sappers openly wept when the bridge tumbled into the water. Instead of building another one, the armour and vehicles still waiting to cross backtracked and inched their way across another bridge further back. By the time the Canadian 5th Armoured Division was ready to roll forward again, it was the early hours of 28 May, and the enemy had safely pulled back once more.

North of Ceprano, the Liri Valley narrows and is crisscrossed with numerous tributaries of the Liri. As such, it was no longer suitable country for armoured warfare. The Via Casilina was repeatedly blocked by mines and German demolitions, while the secondary roads and tracks were too narrow and often steep-sided, making it impossible to deploy off them at all, and ensuring that any advance could only be made with a line of tanks one behind the other. Setbacks such as the bridging failure at Ceprano ensured that units were forced to pass through one another. No less than five divisions – two of which were armoured – were vying for space in this maze of narrow tracks, streams, and gullies. As everyone involved could see, it was utter mayhem. 'In no way,' noted Stan, 'could it be described as an armoured juggernaut steamrolling its way through to Rome.'

Leese could have perhaps left some of his vehicles and armour behind and continued advancing more or less on foot, but he would need his motor transport once they emerged into the more open rolling country-side to the east and north of Rome. He wished he had been sent a division of mountain troops as he'd requested – troops trained in fighting in mountains and who were able to carry pack artillery and equipment by using mules and limited motor transport. But the best-trained mountain division, the 52nd, had been earmarked for Normandy, (even though there were no mountains there) and France was now the priority.

While units of von Senger's 14th Panzer Corps were holding the Allies at bay either side of the Via Casilina, the rest of AOK 10 was disappearing down the four other escape routes. Georg Zellner and his 3rd Battalion of the H and D Regiment, were ordered to pull back on 24 May, along with other units of the 44th Division. Carrying out a fighting retreat, they fell back down the fourth escape route in the direction of Sora. Following them hard were the New Zealanders of X Corps, who until then had not played an active part in the battle.

There were, however, some mountain troops that Alex could call on to help Eighth Army. Juin's French Expeditionary Corps was gradually being squeezed out between Eighth Army on their right and US II Corps on their left. General Juin therefore suggested his troops sweep out of the Lepini Mountains and cut across the Via Casilina towards the town of Ferentino, and then head up the Via Casilina towards Valmontone. Alex was keen for the French to thrust towards the Via Casilina, but not for them to actually use it; Eighth Army was having a hard enough time as it was with congestion, without clogging its main artery with even more traffic and troops. Juin was disappointed, but as it happened, Alex's decision proved to have been a sensible one because by the time the French were entering Ceccano, just south of Frosinone, on 30 May, the Canadians were finally reaching the town themselves.

The French colonial forces had done spectacularly well during the eighteen-day battle, capturing the crucially important Monte Maio on the 13th and then sweeping across the Aurunci and Ausoni Mountain ranges with astonishing speed and efficiency. All but one of the four divisions in the French Expeditionary Corps were colonial units, filled mostly with Moroccan and Algerian troops, while also in the Corps were three Groups of Tabors of Moroccan Goums.* Goums usually consisted of some 160 men, of whom fifty would be mounted. Individual Goumiers were irregular soldiers recruited mostly from the Berber tribes of the Atlas Mountains in Morocco. Raised in the martial and patriarchal society of these mountain tribes, the Goumiers were both respected and feared as ferocious soldiers, known for their bravery and savagery. Although they wore the basic French army uniform, it was not at all unusual, however, to see them wearing earrings, striped cloaks – or even necklesses made from their victims ears. They were, in effect, colonial mercenaries and while they were cheap to employ, they did consider that booty for doing well on the battlefield was an important quid pro quo for their services.

In Italy, however, 'booty' meant less the pickings off dead Germans and more the licence to rape and pillage. Their behaviour towards the local Italians was barbaric. Sporadic raping of Italians had been going on since they first arrived in Italy the previous winter. Now the Goums embarked on a frenzied spree of rape, murder and pillage that went largely unchecked by either the French officers or the Americans who witnessed it. Such actions, it seems, were considered by the Allied authorities as a fair price for having had the use of so many Goumiers. As one French officer explained, Moroccans were recruited, 'by way of a pact which granted them the right to sack and pillage'.[95] The reaction of the office of the Senior Civil Affairs Officer (SCAO) was certainly complacent in the extreme. 'If native African troops are to be used in Europe,' wrote one report, 'more of these outrages must be expected than would be expected from a similar number of British, American or white French troops; that it is impossible to suppress these outrages altogether; and that in any event the reports are greatly exaggerated.'[96]

But if anything, the number of rapes reported was far less than the reality, as many Italian women – and men – never told of such abuses – Pasua Pisa, for one. The shame was too great. Rather, the Allies chose to sweep the whole episode under the carpet largely because they feared it would cause awkwardness with the French and because it was far easier to brush it to one side when the victims were disempowered Italians.

---

*A Group of Tabors was the equivalent of a brigade of regular troops, while a *Goum* was the equivalent of a company, derived from the word *qum*, meaning a band or troop.

In Italy, however, the scars run deep. Hundreds have been brave enough to record what they witnessed. Anna of Frosinone (she has withheld her name) recalls seeing a number of Goumiers enter her house and slam the door behind them. Hearing her mother's cries from inside she banged on the door, but her grandmother, understanding what was going on, took her away from the house out of harm's way. When the soldiers had gone, she went back to the house. 'Mummy was on the bed crying,' she says, 'with her hair all messed up . . . her dress was torn and her shoes had gone and there was blood coming out of her ear. It was because they had torn her earrings out before they left.'[97] Later, Anna learned that her mother had been raped by five men.

Another girl, Angela, from Fondi, had fled with her family to the mountains and they were sheltering in a hut with a number of others. Twenty Goumiers arrived one night. 'We were so terrified,' she says. 'Me and my sister got away by some miracle. One of them stood by the door with his machine gun. They all came in and took the women who didn't manage to escape. These women were beaten too. They were like animals. Actually, worse than beasts – five or six pounding one woman, they did it one after the other.' A number of women died, others were left bleeding and infected. 'The valley was echoing with sobbing and wailing,' says Angela. 'They acted like devils. Their passage was like a wave of Hell. They didn't care about anything, not even age. They even took men and old women.'[98]

In Lenola, a village north of Fondi, fifty women were raped and children and old men also violated. The priest of Morolo, a village just south of the Via Casilina not far from Frosinone, claimed that there was not a single family in the parish who had not suffered some form of physical or psychological damage. 'All the women who were caught alone in the countryside or up the mountains were forced to undergo the shame of the feral instincts of those inhuman beings. As if this wasn't enough, the Moroccans finished what they had started by stealing money, precious objects, linen and even kitchen utensils.'[99]

The doctor to the mayor of Frosinone heard witness to, and saw with his own eyes, the evidence of countless such acts. Women of all ages were taken, from innocent peasant girls as young as twelve to elderly women. 'They forced them to submission with threats and gunshots – some wounding them; they dragged them into the cornfields or into sheds. Mothers were disgraced on their own beds before their crying children and their husbands held at bay by the butt of a rifle pointed at their chests. Old ladies of more than seventy were not spared. Some spouses were killed while defending their loved ones. Gold, linen and livestock which had been left by the Germans was taken away by the Moroccans.'[100] Another girl, Rosa, says, 'My mother was ashamed to tell us girls what the Moroccans did to our father, even though he was a man.'[101]

Norman Lewis, a British intelligence officer with the 312th Field Security Service based in Naples, wrote of the effects of this mass rape and pillage. He had heard reports that it was 'normal for two Moroccans to assault a woman simultaneously, one having normal intercourse while the other commits sodomy. In many cases severe damage to the genitals, rectum and uterus have been caused.' On 28 May, Norman visited Santa Maria a Vico, a village far south of the line, to see a girl who had reportedly gone insane as a result of an attack by a large party of colonial soldiers. He found her living alone with her mother – who had also been gang-raped – in abject poverty, and unable to walk because of her injuries. However, there was little sign of madness. Rather, it had been the local Carabinieri who had tried to commit her to an asylum. Only the lack of a bed had prevented them. As Norman observed, she would now be most unlikely ever to find a husband. 'At last one had faced flesh-and-blood reality of the kind of horror that drove the whole female population of Macedonian villages to throw themselves from cliffs rather than fall into the hands of the advancing Turks,' wrote Norman. 'A fate worse than death: it was in fact just that.'[102]

Official figures record that over 3,100 Italians were raped by these troops, and that does not include those who never came forward. Eventually, this whirlwind of terror passed as the Germans fell back and the Allies pushed forward. The scars, however, lasted a great deal longer.

FIFTEEN

The Fall of Rome
1–5 June 1944

Up until the beginning of May, combating guerrilla activity in Italy had been entirely the responsibility of the Highest SS and Police Führer, General Karl Wolff. Kesselring, however, felt strongly that the battle against enemy forces and terrorist bands was of equal importance and so had lobbied the German High Command that this task should come under his jurisdiction as Commander of Army Group C. Berlin agreed, with Himmler and Keitel, after consulting with Hitler, giving Kesselring strict and clear orders to combat the growing partisan problem in Italy. On 4 May, Kesselring repeated these orders to Wolff, instructing him specifically to concentrate on clearing the Apennines of guerrilla bands.

Wolff was able to call on a number of subordinate commanders and units, both German and Italian – to carry out this task. There were SS police regiments throughout occupied Italy, as well as a number of Waffen-SS units, including foreign units such as a battalion of the East Turkish Waffen-SS, and several Russian battalions of the Cossack and Caucasian Waffen-SS. In addition there were a number of Wehrmacht units, usually those resting in the rear and in the process of building up their strength, or those Kesselring did not consider sufficiently trained for front-line fighting.

This was the case of the East Grenadier Regiment, nominally part of the 334th Infantry Division. Largely made up of Russians – volunteers or otherwise – they were kept away from the front and instead given the task of helping to secure supply routes and battling partisans. Amongst this group of Russians, however, were a number of German officers and sergeants, including Unteroffizier Hans Sitka, a five-times wounded veteran of the Eastern Front.

Hans was from Brünn in the Sudetenland, and in September 1938 had found himself being forced to make a difficult decision. His call-up papers for the Czechoslovakian army had arrived, but with Hitler about to invade, he was worried he would have ended up on the opposite side to his two Austrian cousins. With a heavy heart, he had walked over the mountains and illegally crossed the border into Austria, where he had subsequently joined the German Sudeten Freecorps.

After a stint on the Western Front, he had been sent to Russia. Two years and four months later, in July 1943, he was back home, with a Gold Wound Award pinned on his chest, and a thousand terrible images forever imprinted on his mind. 'Could this be me?' he had asked himself as he looked in the mirror. 'This dirty, bearded, gaunt guy in a ripped uniform? It was hard to believe that I did not have to go back.'[103]

As he soon discovered on his arrival in Italy, however, there were plenty of dangers in fighting partisans. A typical operation would involve marching into unfamiliar territory, often in the mountains. He and his comrades would never know when someone might open fire on them, so he felt nervous and on edge most of the time. Often they would find nothing, but when they did they would become involved in a difficult fire-fight in which casualties were often high. And there were other worries too for the Germans in the East Regiment. 'For us Germans,' he noted, 'such operations were often suicide missions, and we didn't know whether we should be more afraid of the partisans or our own Russian troops.'[104] It must have been with similar feelings of trepidation that a mixed force of German and Italian troops had mounted an anti-partisan operation – or *rastrellamento* – against the Stella Rossa band on Monte Sole on 28 May.

May had been a good month for Lupo and his band of partisans. Thanks to the three arms drops, they had begun making raids into the valleys, attacking Fascists, blocking roads, and blowing up railway lines and bridges. They had also destroyed a German anti-aircraft battery at Vado, along the Setta Valley.

Spies had spotted the enemy forces preparing to attack, and so the partisans were ready and waiting, hidden in the thick scrub and trees of the mountain they knew so well. 'They came up in flanked positions,' recalls Carlo Venturi – or 'Ming' as he had become, 'on the Marzabotto side and the Vado side, carrying out a pincer movement. I was terrified. My legs were shaking.' As the mixed force drew near, the Stella Rossa opened fire, spraying them with Bren and Sten gun fire. They soon withdrew and, although they tried several further attacks throughout the day, were repeatedly driven back, and eventually called off the operation altogether.

'That was a good fight,' recalls Gianni Rossi. 'Really. We killed about 240 Germans – but only one of our men was wounded.' After that, they moved their headquarters, crossing the Reno and basing themselves in the mountains beyond instead. This, as Lupo recognised, was the way to fight: always on the move, hidden and making the enemy dance to their tune and not the other way round.

By the end of May, Lupo's position was stronger than ever. Confidence amongst his band was high. A few days before, the National Government of the south had declared all partisans to be soldiers of the regular Royal Army. This, Lupo argued, was not enough: they in the Stella Rossa had to prove themselves to be the finest troops in this new army. 'Now, more than ever,' wrote Lupo in a printed bulletin that bristled with stirring rhetoric, 'we must give tangible proof of our faith, our capabilities and our worth. We are about to enter a crucial phase in our fight!! Now that the hated Hun, beaten on every front by the glorious Allied troops, has been driven back to its den by our bayonets, awaiting extermination; now that the servile Fascists cling with criminal desperation to their sinking ship of despotism, our job is to shear off their blunted talons.' As Lupo correctly suspected, their fight against the 'Nazi-Fascists' had only just begun.[105]

Meanwhile, on the main battle front, the Allied attack was faltering. For four days, VI Corps could make no impression on the German defences of the Caesar Line, while Eighth Army continued to struggle slowly northwards at a rate of between three and four miles a day. In London, Churchill was beginning to fret. Looking at the arrows on his map, he could see that the advance appeared to have stalled, and that Clark was not bringing maximum pressure on Valmontone. 'I should feel myself wanting in comradeship,' he signalled to Alex, 'if I did not let you know that the glory of this battle, already great, will be measured, not by the capture of Rome or the juncture with the bridgehead, but by the number of German divisions cut off.'[106]

What the maps did not tell him, however, was that even by travelling mostly at night to avoid Allied air attacks, the retreating divisions of AOK 10 could walk down their escape routes faster than Eighth Army could follow in their motorised transport. Hans-Jürgen Kumberg had been amongst those of the 1st Fallschirmjäger Division holding XIII Corps at bay near Arce. They had more than fulfilled their task. By the time they fell back on the 29th, most of von Senger's 14th Panzer and the 51st Mountain Corps had escaped north-westwards. No part of AOK 10 was actually using the Via Casilina as a line of retreat.

Meanwhile, VI Corps was attacking against fortified positions in which the enemy had the advantage of height. Even at the main point of Clark's thrust, to the west of the village of Lanuvio, the ground was still hilly and running against the line of attack. Then, for some reason, the gods of fortune played into Clark's hands. For just as it seemed as though a bloody and bitter stalemate might grip the front once more, the Germans let down their guard.

It was largely thanks to the efforts of the 36th Texas Division – the division that had suffered so horrendously on the Rapido back in January, and the division which still held a grudge against their army commander, that a gap in the German line was spotted. The Texas men, shortly due to replace the 34th Red Bull Division to the west of Velletri, were holding the centre of the line. Ahead of them was the mass of Monte Artemisio, a forbidding ridge, steeply terraced and rising to some 3,000 feet, and over which there was nothing but a narrow and rough track. Aerial photographs, however, curiously showed no sign at all of it being occupied by the enemy. General Walker, the Texas Division commander, thought it would be worth patrolling the mountain vigorously to confirm or disprove this. Sure enough, by the morning of 28 May, he was able to report that it was indeed unguarded. Furthermore, his divisional chief engineer felt certain that it would be possible to bulldoze a way for tanks and other vehicles along the rough track that ran up to the summit. Truscott was initially dubious, but after cross-examining the divisional chief engineer, gave Walker the go-ahead to try and capture the ridge. Armed with an extra regiment of engineers and a number of powerful bulldozers, the Texas men began their assault on the night of 30 May.

Feldmarschall Kesselring, on one of his regular visits to the front, had also noticed this gap in the line between the 362nd Infantry Division – positioned between Velletri and Lanuvio – and the now almost complete Fallschirm-Panzerkorps Hermann Göring, positioned between the eastern side of Monte Artemisio and Valmontone. Immediately giving the order to fill the gap and to fill it fast, he was horrified when, a day later, the gap was still not closed. 'I personally spoke sharply to the Commander of Fourteenth Army,' noted Kesselring, 'and drew his attention to this inexcusable failure to take prompt action, pointing out to him that what could be accomplished easily with one battalion today might be impossible with a division tomorrow.'[107]

Von Mackensen had called for the gap to be closed but such was the shortage of men the only battalions available were two from the Hermann Göring division who had yet to reach the front; they did not arrive on Monte Artemisio in time to stop the Texas men's assault. Despite Kesselring's rebuke, von Mackensen had still not sufficiently closed the gap, and the Texas men were able to infiltrate first one then two regiments onto Monte Artemisio. A third regiment, using the new mountain route, slipped in behind Velletri, cutting off the German retreat in that part of the line. Suddenly, a massive hole had been blown in the Caesar defences.

Following hard on the heels of the Texas men was Eric Sevareid, who, along with a photographer from *Life* magazine, was hoping to witness this breach in the line. Travelling by jeep, they followed a trail rising sharply between high banks, until they were told by their driver they had to continue on foot. The two correspondents began hiking upwards under a blazing sun, machine-gun fire crackling nearby. Rounding a bend they were amazed to see tanks trundling up, toe-to-tail, their bulking breadth scraping stones and earth from the narrow channel that had been cut ahead of them. 'Scrambling around the tanks,' wrote Eric, 'we found the ubiquitous bulldozer simply carving the trail into a road, roaring and rearing its ponderous way at a forty-five degree angle upward. This was all madly impossible, and yet it was being done.'[108] This was the kind of American muscle the Germans in Italy could only dream of.

When Kesselring heard of the American infiltration, he wasted no time in recommending to Hitler that von Mackensen be sacked immediately. To his mind, his troublesome army commander had disobeyed two major orders: first, when he initially refused to move 29th Panzer Division south, and now with his failure to close a gap in the line that should never have existed in the first place. 'It was no longer possible,' noted Kesselring, 'after four years of war, to rely on the strict execution of an order.'[109] A counterattack by the Fallschirm-Panzerkorps Hermann Göring tried to unseat the Texas men, but failed; the Americans were, by then, too entrenched, and so Kesselring's worst fears had been realised.

Clark, on the other hand, now recognised that a great opportunity had suddenly and inadvertently arrived to smash the Caesar Line once and for all. He had also by now completely regrouped, with his two

British divisions brought up to the line in the west, and II Corps, with 3rd Division, Howze Force and 1st Special Force attached, also brought into line between the Texas men and Artena. Aware that VI Corps had suffered no small amount of casualties, the American general was nonetheless never afraid to throw men into the breach if he felt it was a risk worth taking. Moreover, all across AOK 14's front he now had both sustained and wide pressure – his favoured broad front policy. This kind of battering ram, with the full weight of the Allies' massed fire-power in support, was the type of assault Clark had dreamed of ever since arriving in Italy the previous September.

The night before the renewed assault, Clark gave another press conference, an 'off the record' briefing about the next phase of the battle. The Fifth Army commander also emphasised that this attack did not have the capture of Rome as its primary objective. Rather, he stressed, the main aim was 'to kill and annihilate as many of the Germans as possible' on Fifth Army's front, although he had not lost sight of the fact that Rome might be taken as a result. He spoke to the press men with confidence, but was hiding an anxiety he felt keenly. Back at his Anzio HQ, he sat down to dictate a letter to his wife, Renie – his pet dog, Pal, on his lap as he dictated. 'We are in as desperate a battle as Fifth Army has ever been in,' he wrote. 'If it were only the battle I had to worry about and not many other matters, it would be easy, but I am harassed at every turn on every conceivable subject – political, personal and many others.' He again reiterated his hope that they would annihilate much of AOK 14, and prayed for early results. 'I am on the go every minute,' he added, 'trying to visit my commanders to get the latest information and buoy them on to greater effort.'[110]

So now, as May gave way to June, the final act in the battle was about to be played out.

At headquarters of the Desert Air Force, Wing Commander Cocky Dundas was getting ready to return to operational flying once more. This had been on the cards since March, when the previous commander of the DAF, Harry Broadhurst, had told Cocky that he wanted him to command 239 Wing. Broadhurst had then been recalled to Britain as Montgomery had wanted him for the Normandy landings and when Air Vice-Marshal Dickson had taken over command of DAF, he had not wanted to lose one of his key staff officers immediately.

By the middle of April, however, Cocky had begun pressing Dickson to be allowed to go back on operations once more. Then, early in May, Brian Kingcombe, an old Battle of Britain friend who commanded 244 Wing, had mentioned that he needed a new wing leader, and asked Cocky whether he might like the job. Eventually, Dickson relented, and on 31 May Cocky bade farewell to DAF Headquarters and headed over to 244 Wing at Venafro.

His arrival proved to be timely, because that evening the Wing was holding a party to celebrate a successful time since the start of the battle – twenty-three confirmed enemy planes destroyed, as well as several more probables and a further twenty damaged. Held in an old barn, there were five different bars each presided over by one of the Wing's squadrons. 'Each vied to outdo the other in the potency of its drink,' ran the Wing's log, 'so that after a sip of some potions one felt the only thing to do was to call out the fire tender.'[111]

Back on the ground, Oberleutnant Hans Golda was also in better spirits, as for once he was not hungry. Surrounding his new farmhouse command post was an orchard of cherry trees, their branches heavy with blood-red ripe fruit. The farmhouse was comfortable too, with a deep cellar. After a tortuous three-day journey heading north towards Valmontone – in which they were harried by 'jabos' all the way – it was good to get his breath back and to have his first decent sleep in what felt like an age. His nebelwerfers were also well camouflaged by the trees. Ahead were fields of corn, the land sloping away until they rose once more into the Lepini Mountains. For one whole day he simply lay back on his bed in the farmhouse and idly plucked cherries. He felt consumed with joy.

The peace and beauty were shattered with the beginning of the American assault the following day, 1 June. Enemy artillery pounded their position. A direct hit obliterated the first floor of the farmhouse. Hans' men fired back for as long as they could, then, with evening arriving, and even heavier shelling from the enemy, they retreated into their cellar. They felt safe there until there was an enormous explosion and fire could be seen in the cellar entrance. 'There was screaming, groaning and pushing,' noted Hans. 'Finally the smoke cleared and I saw the entrance to the cellar had half caved in.' Hans tried to calm his men, but looking down at the tangle of bodies realised some would not survive. 'One of my radio operators was lying there with his left ear missing,' noted Hans. 'He looked at me without a word. I gave him solace then he slowly shut his eyes and lost consciousness.' Another radio operator was dead, his chest torn open. Someone else was ashen and groaning, his hip bleeding profusely. Those, like Hans, who were unharmed, did their best to tend the wounded. Later that evening, once it had become dark and the shelling had died down, they took the injured men out and loaded them onto one of their vehicles and took them to the dressing station. 'The cellar floor was covered in blood,' scribbled Hans, 'which stuck to our boots. We shovelled earth over it and slept on top, although the whole night I hardly shut my eyes.'[112]

Meanwhile, advancing towards Hans Golda and the German lines around Valmontone had been the tanks of Task Force Howze, and its commander, Colonel Howze, had been in a tank himself and glad to have had the chance for some shooting. 'We knocked out a few anti-tank guns,' he noted, 'killed a number of infantry, captured a fair bag of prisoners and received a lot of enemy artillery fire.' By nightfall, they were abreast the 3rd Infantry Division but to Hamilton's disappointment had been unable to penetrate further.

The next day, Hans Golda and his werfer team continued to fire from their now devastated position, but the German front was crumbling and in the afternoon they were ordered to withdraw north to Palestrina. In the light of this German withdrawal, Task Force Howze had a far easier day, and reached their original objective of Labico, astride the Via Casilina, while battered Valmontone, Alex's original goal for VI Corps, finally fell to the 3rd Infantry.

There was now no question of pushing on eastwards beyond the town, however. Catching the remnants of AOK 10 was left to Eighth Army, which was now in hot pursuit. Hans-Jürgen Kumberg was among those Fallschirmjäger troops still trying to stave off the British advance, and was part of yet another rearguard, now near Alatri, on the Subiaco escape road. In doing so he and his comrades had earned further respect from General Leese. 'The Para boys,' wrote the Eighth Army commander, 'even in hurried retreat are as tough as ever.'[113] Even so, as Hans freely admits, their numbers were now woefully few, and they were absolutely exhausted after fighting by day and walking by night almost continually since leaving Cassino.

Stan Scislowski and the other Canadians of the 5th Armored Division should have finally been able to catch and overwhelm them, as they were now about to enter the valleys north of Frosinone, and with the traffic congestion at last thinning out, the going would have been easier, and hence their advance swifter. General Burns, however, the Canadian Corps commander, chose this moment to pull them back and let the infantry division take over the lead. The change-over was supposed to be gradual – one brigade at a time – so as not to impede the advance, but it was still not the best time to risk momentum or lose fire power. At any rate, von Senger's rearguards certainly managed to keep them at bay while the rest of 14th Panzer Corps continued to slip away into the hills.

The Germans were now on the run across the front: the breakthrough at Valmontone had presaged the collapse of the whole of the Caesar Line along AOK 14's front. On 3 June, Colonel Hamilton Howze had the strange experience of receiving an order by air when General Keyes, the II Corps commander, buzzed over him in his Piper Cub and dropped a package with the words, 'Howze – get these tanks moving!' Now alongside the 88th Division, Hamilton and his Task Force Howze set off immediately. Initially, he felt his tanks were not progressing fast enough, cautiously approaching every new bit of terrain. So with the kind of ruthless determination of which Clark would have thoroughly approved, he ordered a platoon of tanks to rush on down the road at ten miles per hour. Inevitably, every so often the lead tank would hit a mine or be knocked out by enemy fire, but it ensured their rapid progress. Such an advance also meant they were not stopping to mop up any enemy troops, so that as the infantry followed more slowly behind, they often found themselves involved in heavy fire-fights. Even so, the Germans were in disarray. Hamilton's tanks made short work of several enemy columns, including a battery of horse-drawn artillery. At one point, Hamilton's jeep driver paused to relieve himself. Armed with only his pistol he disappeared into some scrub and returned with around twenty Germans, all with their hands up. Later in the day, a German colonel was captured and spent the rest of the day travelling with Hamilton in the jeep.

By the following morning, 4 June, they were closing in on the capital. Hamilton was now placed under the command of the 1st Special Force. It was agreed that the assault on the suburbs was an infantry job, so Hamilton and his tanks spent a frustrating morning waiting for the go-ahead to follow on behind. Eventually, at 3.30 p.m., Task Force Howze began its final drive for Rome. 'This attack made fine progress against considerable resistance,' noted Hamilton. 'We lost two tanks, but knocked out five, plus some guns, and killed and captured a good bag of Germans.'[114]

Following hard on Hamilton's heels was Eric Sevareid, who had begun to realise that the German defences had now collapsed so completely that the capital would surely fall that day. 'German vehicles were smouldering at every bend,' he noted, 'and dead Germans lay sprawled beside them, their faces thickening with the dust sprayed over them by the ceaseless wheels that passed within inches of their mortifying flesh.' He watched as an Italian child kicked at a dead German officer, until a woman pushed the boy aside and tugged off the dead man's boots. In the wrecked villages, he noticed threadbare Italians gathering in the rubble-strewn squares. 'And standing beside their ruined parents,' wrote Eric, 'the children, in their innocence of tragedy and death, were clapping their small and grimy hands as we passed them by.'[115]

In the city itself, the Germans had been leaving all day. Any remaining cars and vehicles had been requisitioned, but there were no detonations, no mass destruction of roads and buildings. Kesselring had, as promised, spared the Eternal City. Back in Rome and feeling largely recovered were Carla Capponi and her boyfriend, Paolo. They had returned a few days before to monitor the German retreat. By 4 June, they were even wearing partisan armbands: red, white and green with CLN spelled out. They were not alone – there were now hundreds of partisans, most armed, marking the German withdrawal.

Not that Hamilton Howze saw them. As dusk began to fall, he and his leading company were nearing the centre of Rome. In contrast, the streets were completely empty, with doors and windows shuttered tight. Hamilton called a halt with his company of tanks, waiting for the rest of his column to catch up. Some Italians clearly heard him and his driver talking, because suddenly a window opened and someone shouted 'Americano!' Soon, hundreds of Romans were emerging, throwing themselves upon Hamilton and his men, the women showering them with kisses. 'It was,' noted Hamilton, 'both gratifying and annoying.'[116]

Just to the south of the city, on the Via Casilina, Mark Clark and his small entourage of jeeps pulled off the side of the road while the Fifth Army commander conferred with his generals – Keyes of II Corps and Frederick of the 1st Special Service Force. They were standing at the foot of shallow hill on the top of which was a large sign inscribed 'ROMA'. For Clark this was a proud moment, and he was particularly keen to get a photograph of himself standing by this sign – a shot he knew would make for a great news picture. There had been some shooting going on nearby, but when it died down, Clark, Keyes and Frederick gingerly scrambled along a ditch and up towards the sign. When it seemed safe, they stood and no sooner had the camera shutters snapped than a bullet smacked into the sign next to them. 'I doubt that anybody ever saw so many generals duck so rapidly,' noted Clark. 'We crawled back down the ditch to safer ground, but later Frederick had someone get the sign and eventually brought it to me as a souvenir.'[117]

Rome had fallen, and the following day, 5 June, the city was awash with Americans, and the streets swarming with overjoyed Italians who believed that at last their salvation was at hand. Amongst them was Bucky Walters, who had been fighting with the 34th Division through Lanuvio and up through the west of the Alban Hills. 'It was very exciting,' admits Bucky. 'I guess that's one of the better parts of war.' They passed through the city in Bucky's jeep. 'We saw the Colosseum,' says Bucky, 'and this guy with me says, "Sarge", he says, "They wasn't supposed to bomb Rome were they? That place sure took a lot of hits!"'

Also there was Lieutenant Bob Wiggans of the 338th Infantry. 'We marched through Rome, strutting like peacocks,' he noted. 'The Italians were wild with joy.' He noticed that his aches and pains had completely disappeared. In the middle of the morning, Clark and his entourage of jeeps drove into the centre of the city too. The Fifth Army commander certainly wanted to savour the moment, but he also wanted to waste as little time as possible pursuing AOK 14 north of Rome, and so one of his staff officers suggested he meet his corps commanders for a quick conference at the Campidoglio on Capitoline Hill. Neither Clark nor any of the entourage had been to Rome before, and they lost their way; not that the Fifth Army commander minded too much – after all, it was good to see the sights and to bask in the adulation of the near-hysterical Roman crowd. When they eventually reached the Campidoglio they discovered the town hall was locked. After banging on the door several times, Clark pulled out his map, and laid it out on the balustrade. General Juin, especially, looked bewildered, but his corps commanders gathered by him, while around them all were pressing a mob of reporters and photographers. 'Well, gentlemen,' said Clark, glancing up at the assembled correspondents: 'I didn't really expect to have a press conference here – I just called a little meeting with my corps commanders to discuss the situation. However, I'll be happy to answer your questions.' Then he added, 'This is a great day for the Fifth Army.'

Watching this spectacle was Eric Sevareid. 'That was the immortal

remark of Rome's modern-day conqueror,' he noted. 'It was not, apparently, a great day for the world, for the Allies, for all the suffering people
who had desperately looked toward the time of peace.' Nor was he alone
in his disgust. Next to him, Eric heard one of his colleagues mutter, 'On
this historic occasion I feel like vomiting.'[118]

General Clark had, since his arrival in Italy, always prompted mixed
feelings. Like Montgomery before him, he was reluctant to compromise
and pursued what he believed to be right with ruthless determination.
And like Montgomery, he quite blatantly courted publicity. Earlier in
the campaign, Eric had followed Clark to the front. The Fifth Army
commander had worn his steel helmet all the way, but when it was time
for the photographers to take their pictures, he took it off and replaced
it with the cloth field cap that had become almost as much of a trademark
as Monty's tank beret. When the photographers had finished, the helmet
was put back on.

The trouble was that while blowing one's own trumpet was distasteful
Yes, Clark was vain, but he would argue that all he was doing was
making sure people back home knew about the valuable work the American Fifth Army was doing in Italy – and he was the figurehead of that
effort, so it was important that every suitable photo opportunity and
news story was exploited to the full. Clark recognised that they now
lived in a media age, and he also understood politics and the sentiments
back in Washington: he knew that his bosses were far less interested in
Italy than in northwest Europe; therefore any good publicity could only
help not only his own cause, but more importantly, that of the Allies in
Italy. A picture of him and his corps commanders leaning over a map
in the centre of Rome, the first European capital to fall to the Allies, *was*
good publicity. And, as Montgomery was well aware, the more famous
the general, the more famous the army. After all, even today, it is Montgomery of Alamein, not Alexander of Alamein; yet, Monty was the
subordinate general to Alex then, as was Clark the day Rome fell.

The trouble was that while blowing one's own trumpet was distasteful
to men like Eric Sevareid, it was absolute anathema to the majority of
British. Bragging, or 'shooting a line' was simply not the done thing;
Alex would never dream of claiming any form of personal glory for
himself. Captain Giles Lampson, the son of the British ambassador in
Cairo, and Clark's British ADC, or 'aide', found this difference in attitude
hard to swallow. 'One thing does rile me a lot here,' he wrote in a letter
to his fiancée, 'and that is the enormous amount of personal publicity

and boasting that goes on. One cannot move without fifteen press photographers in tow.' All the generals received fan mail and kept albums of photographs and scrapbooks of press cuttings as though it was the most normal thing in the world. 'However,' added Giles, 'if that is the way the American public wants its news and if it is going to stimulate interest in the war and help recruiting and so forth, then they are right to do it. But it strikes me as rather indecent and ostentatious.'

Most British soldiers in Italy, but especially the officers, shared this latter view. It also goes some way to explaining why, even more than sixty years on, nearly every Eighth Army veteran will claim that it was Mark Clark who prevented the Allies from destroying the German forces in Italy there and then. His arrogant desire to capture Rome, they argue, ensured that he placed personal ambition over the more pressing need to destroy the enemy. It is an argument that has developed into one of the main controversies to have emerged from the Italian campaign.

There is no question that Clark saw Rome as a great prize, not for the Allies but for Fifth Army – a force that he had nurtured since its formation in North Africa – and also for America. The glory that might be bestowed upon him would be welcome, but this should not cloud the fact that Clark recognised how important the capture of Rome, by Americans, would be back home in the US as far as future operations in Italy were concerned, and in giving Fifth Army the credit he believed they were due. Exacerbating this was his suspicion that the British – and Eighth Army in particular – were trying to steal his show whenever possible; and in the days before Montgomery left to take on the Normandy job, there was, in fact, some truth in this.

'Clark was always very sensitive about the taking of Rome,' said Alex. 'I assured Clark that neither I nor Leese wanted Eighth Army to participate in its capture; we felt it fell naturally into the Fifth Army's area.'[119] A few days before the battle began, one of Clark's periodic paranoias began to develop over the matter. 'I know factually that there are interests brewing for Eighth Army to take Rome,' he vented in his diary, 'and I might as well let Alexander know now that if he attempts any thing of the kind he will have another all-out battle on his hands; namely, with me.'[120] Strong words, but at that time he knew Fifth Army's role in the battle was due to be secondary – until the Anzio break-out at any rate – with Eighth Army's effort down the Liri Valley expected to be the main push. In other words, he could see that Eighth Army might storm ahead and reach Rome first despite reassurances to the contrary.

As the battle developed, however, and Fifth Army raced ahead of the Eighth, so his worries began to subside. Never one to hold back from ranting to his diary, his anger, when it surfaced, was directed at other matters once the battle began. Indeed, his concern about reaching Rome is barely mentioned again.

And if his motives for changing Alex's plan from the Anzio beachhead were to get to Rome quickly, then he was certainly taking an enormous risk, as events subsequently showed. It was good fortune on Monte Artemisio that enabled him to win the breakthrough, and prevented an embarrassing and costly stalemate. Had Fifth Army become unstuck, Eighth Army might have taken Rome after all, something that would never have occurred had he stuck to Alex's original plan and pressed his main effort up the Via Casilina. Certainly, by the beginning of June, Leese was rubbing his hands in glee at the prospect of stealing Clark's thunder. 'AL [Clark]* is making desperate efforts to get to Rome on his own,' he wrote to his wife on 1 June. 'I only hope he will do and can then go north on our own business, but I'm afraid he'll bungle it like Cassino and then we shall have to clear it up. I believe it would have been much better if he would wait for us to help but he was terrified we might get to Rome first.' Then, with mounting relish, he added, 'I only hope it does not warp his military decisions if he does fail now and we have to go. I shall race him to it all out and beat him.'

Interestingly, however, Leese never criticised Clark for the change of attack, even though he knew Alex's battle plan as well as anyone. On the contrary: 'The American effort from the bridgehead was extremely good,' he admitted in a letter to Montgomery, 'the troops fought magnificently with great dash.'[121] Nor did Kirkman, the XIII Corps commander, in his diary, complain about Clark's switch; and neither did Harold Macmillan, the British High Commissioner to the Advisory Council for Italy, despite being a very close friend of Alex's – and despite spending considerable time with the C-in-C throughout the battle. Yet all three were happy to complain about people and to gripe to their diaries whenever they felt the need. Nor even was there any criticism from Harding, the co-architect of DIADEM, in his diary. 'Battle has gone well,' he noted on 4 June, 'and as planned. Everyone very thrilled and pleased.'[122]

After the war, Clark was repeatedly grilled over his decision by inter-

---

*Leese used a number of code letters to represent people in his letters home. Clark was 'AL', while Montgomery was 'O'; why he chose these particular letters is not clear.

viewers, and always he gave much the same answers: that although he was concerned that Eighth Army might steal a march, his overriding reasons were of a military nature. Later, he claimed that on his brief return to the US in April, Roosevelt himself had told him he had to take Rome before D-Day. Yet by turning to face AOK 14 at the Caesar Line head on, it is reasonable to argue – as Hamilton Howze maintained – that the path to Rome took longer than it would have done had he exploited through Valmontone and headed up the Via Casilina. But it is also probable that in so doing, he destroyed more of AOK 14 than he would have done otherwise. Rather than annihilating one German army, as had been Alex's original plan, the Allies seriously mauled two. Indeed, AOK 14 had been routed, which had never been part of the brief.

Certainly it is unfair to suggest that the Allies failed to annihilate AOK 10 south of Rome because of Clark's decision to change his line of attack, and it is a myth that should be quashed. Because of Fifth Army's success in the south, the German axis had shifted; Eighth Army's progress in the Liri Valley had been slower than expected, which allowed much of AOK 10 to escape northeast; a golden opportunity to encircle them at the Senger Line had been missed. Nor should the brilliance of von Senger's delaying tactics as they retreated away from Eighth Army be discounted.

Yet neither should the Allied achievement be played down. Alex's battle plan had been brilliant. He had completely duped Kesselring, and had broken through three strong defensive lines – positions every bit as strong as those facing the Allies on the Western Front in the 1914–18 war. As Kesselring admitted, 'the Allies won a great victory'.[123] Kesselring lost between 50,000 to 60,000 men dead, wounded and captured. This was the equivalent of about four full-strength divisions, but since his divisions were mostly massively under strength, this loss was, in real terms, far worse.

The Allies suffered 43,746 killed, wounded and missing. But already, as they headed north, new divisions and fresh troops were being brought in; Alex had never lost his balance and nor did he intend to now. Incredibly, thanks to a smoothly operated replacement system, by 5 June, Fifth Army was at its highest ever complement – an effective strength of 369,356, despite the losses of the previous month. In contrast, Kesselring's forces were in disarray, horribly short of equipment and supplies, his men hungry and defeated, harried by enemy aircraft over their heads and by Italian partisans at their backs.

Nor was the Allied chance to finish the job over with the fall of Rome. As General John Harding noted in his diary on the day Rome fell, 'It now remains to be seen how quickly we can pursue and how far we can get before the Boche regains control of his forces.'[124] Complete victory in Italy for the Allies now seemed tantalisingly close. And Alexander, for one, was determined it would be achieved by his Armies.

PART II

The Brutal Summer

SIXTEEN

The North

Towards the end of May 1944, as part of General Wolff's rebel clearance operations, German planes dropped leaflets over the Val d'Orcia in southern Tuscany with a severe warning:

> Whoever knows the place where a band of rebels is in hiding and does not immediately inform the German Army, will be shot. Whoever gives food or shelter to a band or to individual rebels, will be shot. Every house in which rebels are found, or in which a rebel has stayed, will be blown up. So will every house from which anyone has fired on the German forces. In all such cases, all stores of food, wheat, and straw will be burned, the cattle will be taken away, and the inhabitants will be shot.

At the same time, Allied planes were dropping leaflets with precisely the opposite instructions, urging Italians not to report for army duty and to commit as many acts of sabotage as possible.

Iris Origo found that most Italians were both bewildered and frightened by these fliers. 'What will become of us?' was the phrase that was repeatedly put to her. Almost all were indifferent to the war. They simply wanted peace and for their sons to return home safely. 'All day a succession of young men come up, asking for advice,' noted Iris in her diary, 'including the Sicilian and Calabrian soldiers who are working on the place. In the evening, too, we have a visit from some of the women from Contignano, whose husbands and brothers have been taken as hostages by the Germans.'[125] These had been taken in retaliation for rebel activity, in which a mere two German troops had been forcibly disarmed and their equipment stolen. Her husband, Antonio, promised to do what he could, and assured them the hostages were probably taken only as a warning.

The following day, however, they discovered that seven of these nine hostages were indeed to be shot. Two days later, the hostages were reprieved but only because the two rebels responsible for disarming the German troops had been caught and executed in the meantime. A climate of fear had spread across the valley. Every day, Iris would find a small and pathetic group of people sitting in the courtyard. 'Haggard women, with babies in their arms and other children waiting for them at home; thin, ragged schoolboys, or old men, carrying sacks or suitcases – all begging for food to take back to Rome.'[126] The last day of the amnesty in which those who had so far failed to report for military service could still do so was 25 May; but the only one from the Val d'Orcia to hand himself in was suffering from pleurisy and was convinced he would immediately be sent back home again.

Allied aircraft now continuously bombed and machine-gunned the surrounding roads. One of the young refugee girls in Iris' care was so frightened she lost her ability to speak. 'She looks terrified,' noted Iris. Nor was the news of the Allied capture of Rome especially welcome as it meant they would likely be the next battleground. Iris feared that their personal crisis was only just beginning. Sure enough, by mid-morning on 5 June, German officers arrived at La Foce and requisitioned the Castelluccio, where the children lived, for a hospital. All that night, Iris could hear aircraft bombing and strafing the roads nearby; by morning, the courtyard was full of German Red Cross lorries. 'Their drivers, utterly exhausted, ask for coffee and food,' noted Iris. 'Many of them have had no sleep for three days – they look dazed and bewildered.'[127]

On 7 June, General Alexander issued a radio broadcast urging Italians to rise up. In his plans for the pursuit of the German forces north of Rome, Alex saw the partisans as a highly valuable third Allied army, who could do much to help, both by passing on important information and by acts of sabotage. Both the American OSS and the British SOE – Special Operations Executive – had set up bases in Italy, recognising that the partisans could, as in France, prove a powerful weapon. OSS operated in Italy under the Italian Secret Intelligence Section from Brindisi and Caserta, while the SOE operation was codenamed 'Maryland' and its agents went by the name 'No 1 Special Force', with its headquarters at Bari.

Certainly, thanks to the increased support given to the partisans by both SOE and OSS, their activities were becoming more effective.

Furthermore, with the recent Allied successes on the battlefield, confidence amongst the rebels was growing and with it their numbers. In the
Val d'Orcia, the partisans were indisputably in control of the surrounding
countryside. They were in the mountains of Romagna too, where the
8th Garibaldi Brigade, for example, had now completely re-formed and
was increasing its operations once more. And in the mountains south
of Bologna, Lupo was king.

Since their great victory against the 'Nazi-Fascists', the numbers of
the Stella Rossa had grown further and they were now operating over a
far wider area. On 4 June, twenty of Lupo's men had raided the Organisation Todt warehouses near the Futa Pass, some fifteen miles south of
Monte Sole. There they had emptied and destroyed the warehouses and
encouraged the Todt workers to go on strike. Two days later, Gianni
Rossi achieved a major coup in the mountains to the west of the River
Reno. He had been leading a small raiding party against the GNR Fascist
militia barracks in Tolé, but having successfully disarmed the militiamen
and stolen their weapons, he had decided to linger by the road that
ran beneath Monte Pastore, a couple of miles to the north. This road,
although winding through the mountains, ran roughly parallel to the
valley below and was an alternative route to Bologna, and one, Gianni
suspected, that the Germans and Fascists were increasingly using in their
efforts to avoid Allied air and partisan attacks.

Gianni had taken just four others with him on the raid to Tolé –
Carlo Venturi, and three of the former POWs, Jock, Hermann and
Steeve; they had learned that by operating with small groups they could
be more effective. Hiding behind a cemetery on the edge of the mountain
village of Montepastore, they sat and waited. Before long, a German staff
car appeared, grinding its way slowly along the mountain road. As it
drew near, the five partisans leapt out from their hiding position and
opened fire. The car, a *Kübelwagen*, crashed off the road, and Gianni
and the others cautiously approached. There had been just three in the
car, but Gianni could see all were dead. One had been an officer, another
a doctor; the third had been the driver. There was also a briefcase.
Opening it, they found a number of documents outlining the new
fortifications along the next major German defensive line between Pisa
and Rimini.

Clearly, the documents they had now captured would be of great use
to the Allies, but first they had to make sure they got rid of any evidence
of the attack – far better if the car and its contents simply disappeared,

spirited away somewhere in the mountains. After rounding up some local contadini, they dug a large pit in a field by the road, then rolled the car and the bodies into it and buried them. Then Gianni and the others hurried back to Lupo's headquarters, and from there, transmitted the details of the documents to OSS. Later, word reached Gianni and the others that the Germans had searched and searched for the missing men, and, presumably, those vital documents, but with no success: they had vanished into thin air. A week or so later, a British plane flew over Monte Sole and dropped leaflets, thanking them for capturing and delivering such vital information. 'Yes,' says Gianni, 'that was a real coup.'

That the Stella Rossa and other partisan bands were able to operate at all was largely due to the tacit support they received from the local population. Locals helped feed them, often housed them, gave them information, and helped warn them of approaching danger. In the mountains of Romagna, where Iader Miserocchi and the 8th Garibaldi Brigade were operating, the locals had devised a number of signals to help the partisans. 'One of the most important signals was to hang white sheets out of the windows,' says Iader. 'Even if it was raining! When we saw white sheets, we knew Germans and Fascist troops were on the move.' Another code was the words '*la Volpe*' – the fox – which was passed from house to house and then by messenger girls, or *staffette* as they were known. 'It was,' adds Iader, 'the mobile phone of the time.'

'The contadini all collaborated with us,' recalls Gianni Rossi, 'even though we all had money on our heads. They always helped willingly.' There were a number of reasons for this. Rural communities, because of their often-isolated locations, were traditionally more sceptical about national centralised government. With this came an inherent contempt for authority – authority that brought rules and taxation that ran counter to local custom and tradition. Also, a number of the partisans were the sons of local contadini or families in the valleys, so there was a personal interest in protecting them. There was also the question of being on the right side when it was all over, and most believed that eventually the Allies would prevail. Finally, most had little choice but to help. In the mountains, where partisans often ruled the roost, few dared defy them in any way.

It was a slightly different situation in the towns and valleys. Eighteen-year-old Cornelia Paselli lived in Gardelletta, in the Setta Valley, but had lived in the shadow of Monte Sole all her life. She knew a number of the partisans – Lupo, Gianni, and others – and most, if not all the mountain contadini, but while she was sympathetic to their cause, she and her family did their best to keep their heads down and avoid trouble. 'It was like this,' she says, 'if you saw something, you simply shut up, kept quiet.'

Cornelia's father, Virginio, held the Fascist tessera, but not out of conviction. As a railway worker, he felt he had no choice: his family came first and he needed to work to keep them all alive and as safe as possible. He was, however, a contadino by birth; the Paselli family had farmed on Monte Sole for generations. Indeed, Cornelia, the eldest of his four children, had been born in the family farmhouse near Casaglia, directly beneath the summit of Monte Sole. Virginio and his older brother, Giuseppe, had farmed the land together, but as their respective families began to grow, it had become increasingly hard to make ends meet. By the time Cornelia was three, she had been joined by a sister, Giuseppina, and so wanting a better life for his wife and two daughters, Virginio had taken a job with the railways and they moved down to Gardelletta.

Despite the move, they visited the family farm frequently, both on festival days and on numerous other occasions. Cornelia would often accompany her father on walks around the mountains, so that she knew the land and the mountain farms, hamlets and villages, like the back of her hand.

Like most children in Italy at that time, Cornelia had left school at fourteen. She had then become an apprentice to a seamstress in Bologna. By that time, Virginio had been promoted and they were now living at Ca' Veneziani, which was where she came to know Lupo and his family. Every morning, she cycled to nearby Vado, and then took the train into the city. It was hard work, and as an apprentice, she was not paid, but she loved it all the same and was distraught when the Allies began bombing Bologna and her father insisted she stay at home instead.

That had been in the spring that year, and soon after, a number of Bolognese had fled the city to avoid the bombs. Cornelia's dressmaking teacher had even asked her to take her eight-year-old son, Leandro, back with her to Ca' Veneziani. Cornelia's parents had been reluctant, but eventually she persuaded them. Leandro moved in with Maria and Luigi, ten-year-old twins. 'It was a big commitment,' admits Cornelia. '[Leandro] wasn't used to mountain life and we had to teach him how to be careful.' The boy was also another mouth to feed when food and other rations were becoming increasingly short.

By June 1944, rationing across the whole of northern Italy was severe, but was made worse by the fact that only 50–75 per cent of prescribed rations were being distributed. Principally, this was because of the problems of transport. Roads and railways had been damaged or destroyed by Allied attacks, and it was often too dangerous to travel. Each Fascist provincial head was allotted a number of vehicles and fuel with which to distribute foodstuffs, but in reality these figures were not being met, as the majority of vehicles and petrol were requisitioned by the Germans, whose own situation was so dire after the recent battles that confiscating Italian motor transport was a necessity for them. The demands of battle came before the needs of the Italians – an attitude shared by the Allies.

The partisans were hardly helping. Partisan raids on warehouses and grain depots had been so numerous that the government had been forced to decentralise supplies and place them in smaller, more dispersed stores. This, of course, only aggravated the distribution problems further. Yet the partisans, none of whom had ration cards or any legal status whatsoever, still had to be fed. This meant placing a strain on the contadini. On Monte Sole, for example, the Stella Rossa survived on ridiculously small amounts of food, but all of it came from raids on government stores or from the local farmers who protected them. What hidden reserves the contadini had were soon used up. Cornelia Paselli and her family had survived the winter on food given to them by their uncle and by keeping a few chickens and rabbits. These extras were now drying up, however.

In any case, the basic state-provided supplies were simply not enough. In Perugia, for example, the monthly oil ration was 225 grammes per person. The reality was that only 150g had been handed out, while by June this figure had fallen to just 92g. Butter and lard had dropped from 150g to 50g per month – in other words, one fifth of a small packet of butter that might be bought today. Hard cheese was supposed to be 100g, but by June it was not being distributed at all. Sugar rations had been given out just twice since December, and then only 250g rather than the agreed 500g. Milk was issued only to children and the sick and even then it was well below what was needed. The monthly meat ration was 120g, bone included, (to put this into perspective, a packet of eight rashers of bacon today weighs around 250g), but again, it was only infrequently distributed. Possibly the most disastrously rationed product was salt, which in pre-refrigeration Italy was essential for preserving food-stuffs. This had never risen above 200–300g per person per month.[128]

In other words, large portions of the population of northern Italy were starving or close to starving. The Repubblica Sociale Italiana was doing its best, but with its limited power there was not a lot it could do to solve the problem. The chronic food shortages were bad enough for Cornelia and her family, but even worse in the cities where the opportunities for supplementing rations were limited. A consequence was the rise of the black market, which in turn made the situation even worse, as most of it came from produce undeclared by farmers or from further raids on warehouses. Working hours in the north were long, inflation was high and salaries low, so the population became impoverished as well as starved. A kilo of black market butter in Genoa, for example, cost around 400 lire, or roughly £30 in today's prices. A kilo of salt was 250 lire, sugar 350 lire. A new pair of shoes would cost anything from 1,500 to 2,500 lire.

German authorities were little interested in civil strife or disobedience unless it directly affected them. Instead, law and order was, wherever possible, left to the Fascist authorities and the GNR. The Fascist militia was, in turn, struggling. Some were fervent Fascists, but most treated it simply as a job and a means of getting by. They, too, were regularly given far less than their agreed rations. Morale amongst the GNR was low due to shortages of equipment, weapons and clothing. They were also treated as inferior beings by their German partners. 'It is not possible to put German and Italian officers on the same level,' noted one German memo. 'Italian officers must execute orders that come from German liaison officers of lesser ranks.'[129] This hardly made them feel good about themselves. On top of that, many felt under constant threat from partisan action, and that they were, in any case, often largely ineffective; efforts to quash the growing black market invariably failed. GNR reports from the Bologna Province, for example, speak of an increase of 'pseudo rebels' – essentially criminals who, taking advantage of the anarchic situation, were mugging people at gunpoint and repeatedly breaking into homes and stealing all they could.[130]

This kind of lawlessness was causing problems in the low-lying Stura Valley south of Turin, where Cosimo Arrichiello was still stranded and pining for his home in the south. As far as he could tell, most of the partisans round about were nothing more than restless youths looking for trouble. A number of men posing as partisans had recently visited all the local farmers demanding goods, which, they later discovered, were sold on the black market. Another story came to light that shocked Cosimo further. Two young men, claiming to be partisans, visited an elderly farmer and his wife and daughter. Having accepted and eaten a meal, they then murdered them, ransacked the farmhouse, and set it on fire.

By the summer, Cosimo sensed that an alarming and tense atmosphere had settled over what should have been a comparatively peaceful area. 'A lot of the Carabinieri had left,' he says. 'Those who remained, like my friend Giacomo, were nervous of being seen to side with the Germans and Fascists and so they sat on the fence and did very little.' This, he believes, enabled the local partisans to run amok. 'They were quite useless,' he says of the partisans, 'just opportunists waiting for the Germans to lose and the Allies to arrive.'

At least within the Repubblica Sociale Italiana there was a pretence that Italy was still Italian. For those in the north that had been partitioned into the Third Reich, life was even more brutal. Living in Trieste, now part of the German Adriatic Coastland, was twenty-two-year-old Clara Duse. Her father had been a colonel in the army just before the armistice and on 8 September 1943, he and his wife and daughter had been in Parma, while he attended a staff course.

They had immediately caught a train and hurried back home to Trieste. Her father had intended to go on to Yugoslavia to rejoin his unit, but by the time they had reached Trieste, the army had already been disbanded. Instead, he had been told to report to the new German authorities, whereupon he and other senior Italian officers were told they had a clear choice: to fight with or against Germany. Clara's father had decided on the latter course, going underground instead. His brother had managed to secure him a job at the harbour, which exempted him from military service, and with false papers he had been able to survive in Trieste ever since.

The food shortages in the city were severe. Her father earned little, and had to be on his guard at all times, while her mother could do little but stay at home in their flat. Clara was still officially at university studying the history of art, but there were almost no classes left. She helped at a crèche at the hospital but that was purely voluntary. She was not paid a thing. 'We were more than hungry,' says Clara. 'We were malnourished. No fruit, no milk, no butter. We lived off little more than pea soup and beans.'

This miserable existence was compounded by the threatening presence of the SS. Military commander of the city was Higher SS and Police Führer,

Gruppenführer Odilo Globocnik, a native of Trieste but also one of the most sinister and brutal Nazis to have emerged from the Third Reich. As SS and Police Führer of the Lublin District in Poland, Globocnik had been responsible for carrying out Operation Reinhardt – the ethnic cleansing and systematic destruction of the Jewish people in Poland from 1942 – until moving to Trieste in the Adriatic Coastland in the far north-east of Italy. In this role he had overseen the liquidation of the Warsaw and Bialystok ghettos, and by the time he reached Trieste, had played a large part in the deaths of more than 1.5 million people in the three death camps of Treblinka, Sobibor and Belzec.

Back in the city of his birth, there were fewer Jews to deal with – although he was determined to exterminate any Jew that did live there – but increasing numbers of partisans, both Italian and Croat. He wasted no time in replicating the staff and operational system that had worked so well for him in Lublin. More than 150 of his old Operation Reinhardt gang moved with him to Trieste including Franz Stangl, Christian Wirth and Ernst Lerch, men who were all mass murderers many thousands of times over.

The centrepiece of his operations was the Risiera di San Saba, a disused former rice mill on the outskirts of the city, near to the football ground. Globocnik requisitioned it and turned it into a combined prison, police concentration camp, torture centre and crematorium. For this latter purpose, his former gassing expert in Lublin, Lorenz Hackenholt, was also brought to Trieste.

By the summer of 1944, more than ten thousand prisoners had already passed through this place of horrors; many thousands had also been executed there. Mass executions, usually more than a dozen at a time, took place two or three times a week, although in addition the SS carried out as many as ten individual executions per day. 'People round there used to hear the screaming,' says Clara. 'We knew about the ovens, that they were cremating people there.'

And yet there were areas of German-occupied Italy where the effects of war somehow managed to be kept in check. Not *everyone* was starving; nor was everyone harassed by German and Fascist troops or strafed and bombed by Allied aircraft. Where partisan activity was slight, far from the front line and away from the cities, it was possible to survive – not in comfort, but more easily than elsewhere. Along the Adriatic coast, for example, in the hill villages west of Rimini, Italian civilians had been having a comparatively 'good' war.

Living near the hill-top town of Gemmano, in the small village of Onferno, was the Quadrelli family. Although only around fifteen miles from Rimini, Onferno was, like so many parts of rural Italy, connected to the outside world by a small, unmetalled track. Theirs was another largely enclosed society. Eleven-year-old Italo, the middle child of three brothers, had barely left the village and the surrounding area all his life. His father had fought in the First World War but was too old for this latest one; his elder brother, Dino, was five years older and so was still too young to be conscripted.

The family were farmers, and, unusually, owned their own land. Following the First World War, Italo's father had headed out to Argentina in the hope of making some money. There he had met Italo's mother and had returned a few years later with enough money to buy three small farmsteads. Even so, it was a tough life, with the running of the farm dominating all their lives.

Every morning, Italo would help feed the animals, take the sheep out to pasture, then walk more than a mile to school. 'After school, we all played,' he says. 'We didn't have footballs; we didn't have bikes. We made up our own games.' He had plenty of friends, his family was close, and he always had enough to eat. There was cheese from the cows and sheep, and milk; honey from the bees his father kept; cured ham from the pigs; veal from the calves. They suffered from salt and sugar shortages like everyone else, but for the most part they managed to remain self-sufficient. Partisan activity in the area was slight, so the local GNR tended to leave them alone. Because they had no radio, they heard little news about what was happening the war. Thus the family had survived through four years of war unscathed. And they assumed it would stay that way too.

As both Mussolini and the Neo-Fascist leaders were aware, the Repubblica Sociale Italiana was not popular and nor was the war. This was hardly surprising. The majority of Italians had hoped their war would have been over with the armistice the previous September. More importantly, any population looks to its government for their welfare. Mussolini was all too aware of the importance of winning over hearts and minds, as was reflected in the rhetoric put out in the media. In the pro-government newspapers there were daily articles in which the efforts of the government to distribute food and improve rations were stressed.

Mussolini himself continued to use his journalistic skills to stir his people. 'Italians,' wrote the Duce on 6 June in the Bolognese newspaper, *Il Resto del Carlino,* 'the Anglo-American invaders, to whom the wicked monarchic treason opened the doors of the Fatherland in Sicily and Salerno, have entered Rome. The news will profoundly disturb you as it pains each of us.' He pointed out that the heroic Germans had not destroyed the city as they withdrew, whereas the Allies had already destroyed so many Italian cities. He urged the Italians of the south to rise up against the Anglo-American oppressors. 'To the Italians of the provinces of the RSI,' he continued, 'we give the supreme warning: let the fall of Rome not dull our energy and even less our will to fight back. Every measure will be taken to this end and we must all allow our consciences to be ruled by this duty, both in battle and in work.' And he underlined the difference between the Italy of the south and the north. 'The word of the Republic,' he told Italians, 'is very different from the word of the King, who is worried for his own safety and his crown and not for the Patria. SOLDIERS TO ARMS! WORKERS AND PEASANTS TO WORK! The Republic is threatened by plutocracy and its mercenaries of every race defend it! LONG LIVE ITALY! LONG LIVE THE RSI!'[131]

However transparent this kind of rhetoric may seem, it could still be effective. By portraying the oppressive, destructive nature of the Allies in contrast with the honour and glory of serving the *Patria* – the nation of Italy – Mussolini continued to win over people to the cause. Amongst the most fervent recruits were the young: William Cremonini and the Young Fascists had been swept along at the beginning of the war, but there was now a new generation answering the call to arms.

Amongst them was Carla Costa, a seventeen-year-old from Rome. Unusually in such cases, her parents were not supporters of fascism at all, yet since joining the *Onore e Combattimento* – a Neo-Fascist youth movement – in March, she had become an obsessive Fascist. At the beginning of June, Carla realised that she could not sit back and watch Rome fall to the Allies; she had to do something. Fortunately for Carla, her commander at Onore e Combattimento, Miranda Serra, had a suggestion. Serra knew of a man who was recruiting young women like herself for 'more strenuous duties in the Fascist cause'. Taking the address Serra had given her, Carla duly presented herself to a house in the Piazza Colonna in Rome on the afternoon of 2 June.

There were other girls from Onore e Combattimento waiting there too – all to see Lieutenant-Colonel Tommaso David, a former army officer who now ran a recruitment organisation for the Abwehr.* By the time Carla finally had her interview with David, it was nearing ten o'clock. 'When he learned that I had run away,' Carla admitted, 'he advised me in a fatherly way to reflect.'[132] She immediately replied that she already had done so and repeated her desire to make her contribution to the cause of Republican Fascist Italy. He told her he would sleep on the matter. In the meantime, however, he gave her a uniform and false identity card and sent her off with one of his agents to a nearby hotel for the night.

By now, Carla's mother had become frantic about her daughter's disappearance. Eventually, she rang one of Carla's school friends – also a Fascist – who told her about her daughter's plans. Through him, she was eventually given a number for Colonel David, whom she duly rang. It was by now 1 a.m., and so David suggested she collect her daughter the following morning.

But Carla was not having any of it. A violent argument ensued with Carla's mother eventually storming off and leaving her daughter. Even so, it still looked as though Carla would remain stranded in Rome. Colonel David had divided the recruits into two groups, and told them they would leave in turn the following morning. As the last to join, Carla was in the second section, but with the Americans now entering the city, it seemed unlikely David would be able to return. However, to her surprise and relief, he was true to his word, arriving at their rendez-vous in a lorry loaded with rations. Carla had little idea what to expect or what was going to be demanded of her, but as she clambered aboard the truck she passionately believed she was doing the right thing.

After a long and difficult journey they reached the GNR barracks in Via Carlo Ravissa in Milan on the morning of 9 June. Now codenamed 'Teresa', Carla began training for her new life – as a spy in the German Intelligence Service. She was still three weeks short of her seventeenth birthday.

Roberto Vivarelli was even younger, but although just fourteen years old he was determined to play his part in the struggle. The previous summer, the news of Mussolini's overthrow and the end of fascism had come like a blow to the head for this fiercely patriotic young boy. He had not given

---

*The official title of David's Abwehr recruiting organisation was the Gruppo Segreto Attentori Fascisti Repubblicani, or Gruppo SA for short.

up hope, however – convinced that it had been nothing more than a court conspiracy, and that fascism would once again prevail. The subsequent armistice had been an even more bitter pill to swallow. By this time, Roberto, then only thirteen, had become increasingly distraught from his intense feelings of betrayal and dishonour.

Perhaps the missing figure of his father had contributed to his strength of feelings. Roberto had adored him but he had been missing in action in Yugoslavia since 1942. Since April that year, the family had heard nothing of his fate. Vigorously honest and honourable, his father had been a successful lawyer in Milan, until, in 1935, he had closed the firm and gone to fight in the war in Abyssinia. Yet although he was a supporter of fascism, his political leanings had been shaped by tradition rather than any form of revolutionary fervour. 'For him,' wrote Roberto, 'fascism meant the Patria, and the Patria had a religious value. His political faith was fed by a spirit of service. One had to give one's all to the fatherland – if necessary even one's life. Fascism was his faith simply because in fascism my father saw the party of the Patria.'[133]

These were ideals that Roberto, in the absence of his father, had begun to adhere to as well, with increasing passion. His older brother had felt much the same way, and as soon as the armistice had been signed he had joined a German panzer grenadier unit. Extremely envious, Roberto had nonetheless been determined to do as much as he possibly could to help the new Republic and so had joined the *Movimento Giovanile Repubblicano*, a young Fascist organisation.

He had also been given permission from his mother to return to naval college, where he had been a student the previous year. The college had now been moved from Venice to Padova, and it was on his journey there that he had met a group of officers from the naval commando group Decima MAS. What had impressed Roberto had been their dedication not so much to fascism but rather to the side on which they had begun the war – ideals that had struck a deep chord within him.

Having discovered that the naval college now existed in name only, he had returned to his mother in Siena, but in the spring had been once again stirred by thoughts of joining the fight. His brother had since joined the Lupo battalion of Decima MAS, and when Roberto had subsequently watched a convoy of Decima MAS pass by on their way south, he had left a note for his mother, and with a friend, had headed to Rome, presenting themselves first at the headquarters of the Fascist Federation, and then to the Decima MAS. His trip had ended in disappointment, however. To enrol in the Decima MAS, he had been told to go to La Spezia, several hundred miles north on the Ligurian Coast. This had not been possible, and so he had gone home, defeated yet undeterred, and had instead formed a Fascist youth organisation in Siena known as the White Flames.

Everything changed with the fall of Cassino and the subsequent loss of Rome. To live in Allied-occupied Tuscany was inconceivable and so the fourteen-year-old persuaded his mother they should head north. By the middle of June, they were in Florence. Roberto felt as passionate and determined as ever that he must find a way to join the fight himself. 'I was just crazy about wanting to do something,' he says. 'The idea of staying home when others were fighting – I just couldn't bear it; I wanted to take part.'

For seventeen-year-old Antonio Cucciati, it was most definitely not a question of politics, but a matter of honour. 'When a gentleman starts a war,' he says, 'he fights on one side and should stay on that side. For us, 8 September [the armistice] was a dark day in history.' From the town of San Colombano, south-east of Milan, Antonio had been brought up to believe that loyalty and patriotism were important values. Further-more, his parents had welcomed Mussolini's reforms of the 1930s and had not turned their backs on the Duce since his return. 'Our feelings were this,' says Antonio, 'first the Patria, and then Mussolini.'

By trade a blacksmith, his father was nonetheless something of an entrepreneur, running an ironmonger's shop and a plumbing business, enabling him to send Antonio and his sister and younger brother to boarding school in Milan. 'We were educated by priests,' he says, 'and my sister by nuns. Our parents were very religious.'

Antonio had still been at school when the armistice had been declared but by the time the Allies renewed the battle, he was at technical college and itching to do his bit for his country. For him, however, there was only one possible unit he could join and that was the Decima MAS.

The X Flottiglia Mezzi d'Assalto – to give its full name – had, until the armistice, been just one of ten commando-style assault flotillas, and had found fame in December 1941 when frogmen on manned torpedoes managed to blow up two British battleships in Alexandria harbour, HMS *Valiant* and the *Queen Elizabeth*. At the armistice, the commander of the MAS flotillas, Admiral di Savoia, had left to join the King and Badoglio, leaving his deputy, Prince Valerio Borghese, to take command.

Having made a conscious decision to continue fighting on the side of Germany, Borghese submitted the Decima MAS to the German navy with a number of proposals for a certain degree of autonomy and reorganisation, and these were accepted.

Operationally, the unit was under the command of the German navy, but otherwise it was entirely Italian. A highly charismatic and dynamic man, Borghese quickly reformed and expanded the Decima MAS, evolving it into an elite marine formation with land as well as naval units. All members were volunteers, and unlike for the New Army divisions, training was in Italy, not Germany. Since then they had proved themselves in battle as one of the few Italian units to fight alongside the Germans at Anzio.

Despite their semi-autonomous nature, the RSI recognised the Decima MAS's propaganda value, ensuring its ongoing exploits and dashing commander continued to feature heavily in the newspapers. 'For us boys,' says Antonio, 'the Decima MAS was the *non plus ultra*.' The tops. And so, at the end of June, he and a friend decided to head to Milan and volunteer, both leaving home in secret without telling their parents.

His friend decided to turn back after they had hitchhiked thirty miles or so, but Antonio continued all the way to Milan and duly signed on the dotted line. The Decima MAS had a number of different units within its make-up, and Antonio was asked which he would like to join. 'If I'd joined a *mezzi d'assalto* battalion I would have had to go on to do six months of study,' he says. 'So I joined the *Nuotatori e Paracadutisti* instead. There was still a lot of training, of course, but I liked the idea of being a paratrooper and being thrown out of an aeroplane.'

Initially posted to Turin, after two weeks' initial induction he was sent to San Fedele Intelvi in the Alps for his training. Meanwhile, his mother and younger brother had gone to Milan to look for him. Antonio had departed without leaving even a note, but they had guessed where he had gone to – for some time he had talked about wanting to join the Decima MAS. In Milan they found Antonio's signature on the register of volunteers, but when his mother demanded he be sent home, she was given short shrift. 'They said I'd signed up and that was that,' says Antonio. 'They needed me.'

SEVENTEEN

The Problems of Generalship
June 1944

If the major Allied raison d'être for the Italian campaign was to draw German divisions away from Normandy and the Eastern Front, Alexander had admirably fulfilled that task. More German divisions were on their way. Since the beginning of the battle, five divisions and three further battalions had been moved to the front from the Adriatic coast and northern Italy, and in addition to the 16th Waffen-SS Division from Hungary, two Luftwaffe field divisions had been moved from the Western Front, a further division from Croatia and ten more battalions from Germany itself. Added to these was a large amount of war materiel: weapons, motor transport, ammunition, and tanks. And men: four divisions had been completely withdrawn to be re-formed, while even those still in good shape required replacements. Manpower was not limitless. 'The Wehrmacht High Command,' admitted Kesselring, 'provided Army Group with replacements to a hitherto unusual extent.'[134] One of the Luftwaffe field divisions was ordered from Belgium on 2 June, just four days before the Allies landed in Normandy. From the moment of the D-Day landings, Hitler was actively fighting on three fronts – in France, in Italy, and in the Soviet Union.

Now that Rome had fallen, Kesselring's problems were numerous. Although the rout of AOK 14 had not been part of Alexander's specific battle plan, that was what had happened, largely thanks to the mismanagement by von Mackensen and more specifically because of the punishment they had received at the hands of the Fifth Army. 'The first of June,' wrote Kesselring, 'marked the beginning of an appalling deterioration of the Fourteenth Army's plight. The fighting strength of the divisional combat groups retiring behind the Tiber and the Aniene had ebbed to a bare minimum.'[135] Morale was very low and Kesselring was aware that a prevailing shroud of pessimism had descended upon the remaining units – made up of just a handful of threadbare battalions within just one corps. 'On the face it,' admitted Kesselring, 'these figures spelled doom for Fourteenth Army.'

AOK 10 was in slightly better shape, and had stolen the march on Eighth Army, but the German C-in-C was all too aware that the mountains through which it was retreating offered few roads and that they were still being relentlessly harried from the air. Moreover, von Vietinghoff's men were absolutely exhausted and their numbers massively reduced. Hans-Jürgen Kumberg's 4th Fallschirmjäger Regiment, for example, now had a fighting strength of just 151 men – less than a normal company. 'A bad night march,' scrawled Major Georg Zellner on 8 June, as his battalion continued to retreat back through Avezzano and north towards Rieti. 'At our destination at 4 a.m. Billet in a monastery (destroyed). No food. We shoot the pigeons.' The heat was oppressive; he and his men felt weak, physically and mentally. Some of his men were wearing civilian clothes because their uniforms had fallen to pieces. Their feet were raw after marching for so long, and they keenly felt the resentment of the majority of the civilian population as they passed through one impoverished village after another, and pillaged what they could to survive. 'Reached our destination after another night march through difficult land,' he noted two days later. 'We crept through the night like ghosts. This is how it has been since 24 May. We fight by day, or wait in our positions for the enemy. As soon as darkness comes, we set off . . . Usually another enormous mountain has to be conquered. We pull ourselves up with our last strength. Hardly have we arrived and the enemy planes are already overhead. One can't really speak of a battalion any more. Lumps and tatters – we pull ourselves along.' His thoughts were, as ever, with his family. 'My only wish,' he added, 'is that my children are spared this sort of madness.'[136]

The retreat was far harder for those on foot who had to cope with endless night marches and pitifully small amounts of sleep during the day. The 4th Fallschirmjäger Regiment were falling back through winding mountain roads to the east of the Tiber. Whenever they stopped they frequently found themselves coming under shellfire once more. 'We didn't have time to dig any foxholes,' says Hans, 'because we were always on the move.' One time, Hans had been squatting down to relieve himself when a shell screamed over and landed nearby. Hans was knocked to the ground and pasted with dirt and grit and hit in the buttock by a tiny shell splinter. 'It didn't bleed heavily,' says Hans, 'and since we

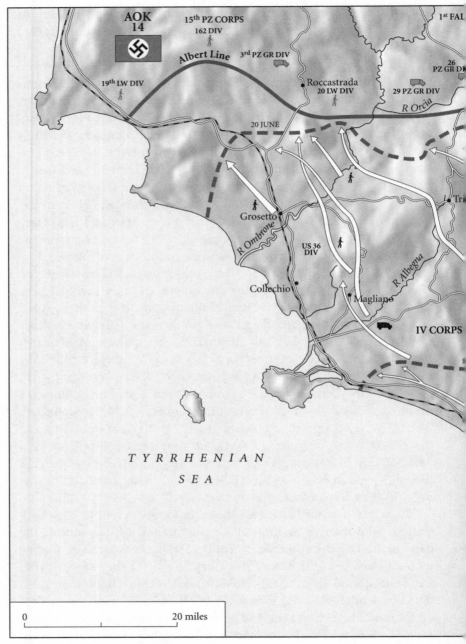

The Allied pursuit from Rome to the Albert Line, 5–20 June 1944

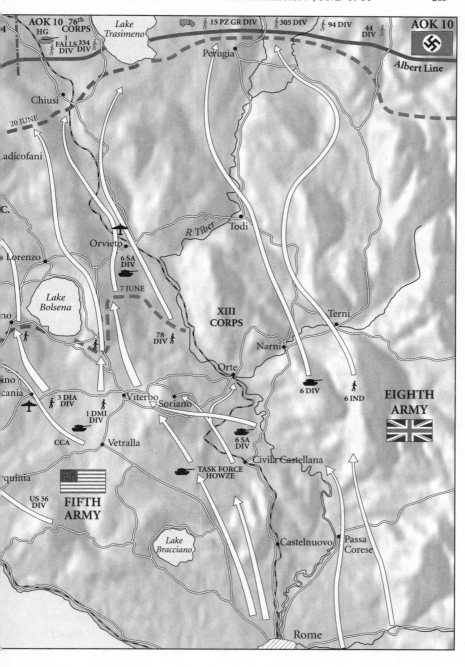

were retreating there wasn't time to look at it properly, so it's still there.'

The retreat was less traumatic for Hans Golda and his werfer battery, however, who had to have vehicles in order to move their rocket firers, and so were able to avoid trudging back on foot like the vast majority of German troops. The defeat and the hardships of such a retreat affected different people in different ways, but generally it was easier for the younger ones, especially those without the ties of wives and children back home. This was certainly true of Hans-Jürgen Kumberg, although there were exceptions such as the naturally positive and cheery Hans Golda, who was older than most of his men, and married with a young son.

After fighting against the Americans north of Rome, Werfer Regiment 71 had been transferred back into AOK 10 and having crossed the Tiber was attached to the 334th Infantry Division. 'We would take up our positions,' noted Hans, 'wait until the Tommy arrived, fire our werfers until the pressure was too strong, and then we'd go back in an enormous jump and the same thing started all over again.' The countryside north-east of Rome was far less ravaged than it had been in the south and Hans and his men found there were rich pickings to be had – in terms of both food and clothing. In Rieti, they helped themselves to new clothes from the market, and at their next stop, at San Gemini north of Terni, they found themselves based next to a shoe factory. 'Everyone,' noted Hans, 'got themselves a good supply of shoes.'[137]

Despite the parlous state of his forces, Kesselring knew that fresh divisions were on their way and that logistical difficulties would inevitably slow the Allies down. He also recognised that the US Fifth Army had the easier country in which to advance. Another conundrum was caused by the River Tiber. This extremely long river ran down the middle of the country – and thence into Rome – and proved an obvious army boundary for both his own forces and those of the Allies. Yet the river's course increasingly ran north-eastwards, which meant that AOK 14's front became wider and wider with every step it retreated.

Clearly, Kesselring had to reinforce AOK 14 and quickly, and inject it with new energy and resolve. As was so often the case, it was von Senger who was expected to come to the immediate rescue, passing three of his best and most complete divisions over to join AOK 14. Meanwhile, in place of the sacked von Mackensen, a new army commander had arrived as well. General Joachim Lemelsen was a cavalryman with the kind of fresh, energetic personality Kesselring was looking for; and someone who accepted orders from his commander-in-chief and obeyed them immediately. A lifelong soldier and bachelor, Lemelsen was a former corps commander who had served under Generaloberst Guderian on the Eastern Front. He had also impressed Kesselring during a brief tenureship of AOK 10 the previous autumn when von Vietinghoff had been away on sick leave.

With these decisions made, Kesselring was able to develop a more purposeful plan of retreat. Badly mauled divisions were to be sent back with all haste to the next major defensive line, the Pisa–Rimini Line – or the Gothic Line as it had been named.* Those units that were still fit and in some kind of order, along with the new divisions as they arrived, would then stop and make a stand south of the Gothic Line, across the peninsula with Lake Trasimeno as its centre point. Everything, he decreed, had to be done to impede the Allied advance and that meant an even greater amount of demolition: every bridge, every road, every tunnel, every power station, every port – all had to be blown to smithereens. In addition, his engineers were to lay as many mines and booby traps as were humanly possible. This, Kesselring hoped, would give him a chance to consolidate his front once more into a continuous line across the peninsula, and would also enable him to complete his fortifications further north. With a bit of luck, he might be able to hold the Allies at bay throughout the summer, and then grind them down to another bitter stalemate with the onset of the Italian winter.

With his usual optimism, Kesselring felt there was a chance his plan might just work. Hitler also urged Kesselring to make a stand south of the Gothic Line, ordering him to give up as little territory as possible, and 'to reconstitute the front north of Rome as far to the south as possible'.[138] Not that there was any carefully thought-out military reasoning behind the Führer's demands; rather he was driven by a fanatical urge to cling to every inch of territory, no matter the cost.

Those of more rational mind within the German High Command, however, along with Kesselring's two army commanders, von Vietinghoff and Lemelsen, did not seriously believe they had a hope in hell of saving Italy. As was perfectly plain to see, all the momentum was with the

---

*Hitler had decided the name 'Gothic Line' was too pretentious and so insisted on it being renamed the 'Green Line'. However, the Allies still referred to it as the Gothic Line, and since I have referred to the Senger Line in its German form, it is only fair to continue to refer to the Green Line as the Gothic Line.

Allies. After all, they were rich in men and materiel and flushed with the success of a great victory.

Unbeknownst to either Kesselring or the German High Command, however, Alexander had his difficulties too – or rather, one very specific problem that had been hanging over him for some time, but which had been crystallised by his superior in the Mediterranean, the Supreme Allied Commander, General 'Jumbo' Maitland Wilson, on 22 May: namely the loss of seven divisions for an amphibious operation in the south of France in support of OVERLORD.

Operation ANVIL, as it was called, had been bubbling under the surface ever since the decision had been made to invade Italy, and had been the cause of a major strategic rift between Britain and the United States. Back in August 1943, when ANVIL had first been suggested, no one had thought that the campaign in Italy and a landing in southern France around the same time as those in Normandy would ever compete with one another. This was because it was believed that by the summer of 1944, the goals set out for the Italian campaign – namely reaching the Pisa–Rimini Line and the containment of significant amounts of German troops – would have been achieved long before then.

Since that time, however, much had changed. Hitler had chosen to fight south of Rome after all, and the Allied advance had stalled. Furthermore, the subsequent operation at Anzio had required a large number of landing craft to keep the beachhead supplied. Meanwhile, Eisenhower and Montgomery, preparing for D-Day in England, had also demanded more landing craft. These, it seemed, could only come from the Mediterranean, which was already saddled with the demands from Anzio and the future ANVIL operation. Suddenly, Italy and ANVIL had been competing with each other after all. With this in mind, the British Chiefs of Staff had suggested ANVIL be cancelled. The American chiefs had refused to do this, instead insisting that a number of plans for amphibious operations that might help OVERLORD should be prepared; their concession had been that these plans should not, at that time, take precedence over the needs of the Italian campaign.

But this had not settled the matter and inevitably the ANVIL debate had soon reared its head once more. On 21 March, General Wilson had sent an appreciation of operations in the Mediterranean to both the American and British Chiefs of Staff. At that time, final dates for Alex's renewed drive for Rome had not been agreed, but General Wilson had written that he hoped the city would be in Allied hands by the middle of June at the latest. The effect of this on the Normandy landings would, he had suggested, be considerable, and he had strongly opposed withdrawing either troops or aircraft for any other operation until Rome had fallen. He had then outlined four plans for operations once Rome had been captured. The first was ANVIL; the second a further big offensive in Italy, with a minor supporting amphibious operation; the third idea had been to make a landing in the Gulf of Genoa behind the German line; and the fourth had been a landing in Istria in the north-easternmost corner of Italy. Of the four plans, Wilson had favoured the second, because it enabled him to concentrate all his forces on one battlefield and because he already had enough landing craft for the supporting amphibious operation.

By a strange coincidence, Eisenhower had suggested cancelling ANVIL on the same day, and had instead proposed making a far smaller landing on the southern coast of France or along the Ligurian coast in north-west Italy five days before D-Day. This, he argued, would keep German troops in southern France away from Normandy and would release an important amount of Mediterranean shipping for D-Day.

The British chiefs concurred with both these views entirely. The American chiefs, however, had agreed only to postpone ANVIL, not cancel it. Yes, they had argued, there was sense in ensuring the two fronts in Italy were joined, but afterwards they should continue to put pressure on the Germans without necessarily advancing from their new front line. Instead, ANVIL should then be launched in full force around the middle of July. The flaw in this argument was that the original purpose of an invasion of southern France had been to pin down German troops *before* the Normandy landings – it had been designed to draw German forces away from northern France at a vital moment. To land six weeks or more after the D-Day landings would scarcely help at all.

However, the American chiefs were now digging in their heels. In what amounted to bargaining equipment against strategy, they promised sixty-six landing craft from the Pacific. This was nonetheless a considerable offer because this shipping was urgently needed for future operations in that theatre, and because within the US there was massive public demand for greater American efforts in the Pacific. 'They are prepared to make a great sacrifice in the Pacific to make a delayed Anvil possible,' Field Marshal Sir John Dill told the British chiefs from Washington, 'but they are *not* prepared to make the sacrifice for operations in Italy.' Unfortunately, before Dill's detailed letter had arrived, setting out the condition of the offer, the British chiefs had already responded, telling the Americans that they would refuse to be drawn into favouring ANVIL over Italy, and suggesting the issue be further postponed. 'We may, indeed, find when the time comes that Anvil is the best card to play,' wrote the British chiefs. 'Alternatively, it may pay us better to press the battle in Italy to the limit.'[139]

The effect of this airily scripted note was to put up the backs of the Americans even more. To make matters worse, the same day a further message had arrived from Jumbo Wilson telling them that Alexander had postponed the launch of DIADEM from April to 11 May, which would, in turn push any southern France operation back as well.

The nub of the problem was that Britain and America continued to hold very different approaches to strategy. The Americans had a clear and defined goal: to defeat Germany as quickly and decisively as possible, and that meant by concentrating the Allied effort in France. Gnawing away at Marshall and the US Chiefs was the belief that the British-led involvement in the Mediterranean would hinder this aim. They believed that a decisive offensive in Italy would inevitably drag Allied forces into south-east Europe, which would suck up even more troops and equipment that could be better used more directly in support of the offensive in the west.

In the weeks that followed, countless telegrams flew back and forth across the Atlantic and the Mediterranean, but both the American and British chiefs refused to budge on the matter. By April, Churchill had waded in as well. 'What I cannot bear,' he told Marshall, 'is to agree beforehand to starve a battle or have to break it off just at the moment when success, after long efforts and heavy losses, may be in view.'[140]

Another impasse had been reached, but with both sides recognising the need to make some kind of a decision, General Wilson had been issued a renewed directive on 19 April, drafted by the British and agreed by the Americans, in which ANVIL had been postponed indefinitely. Italy had been given the priority, but as a sop to the Americans Wilson had also been asked to prepare a number of plans for a post-D-Day amphibious operation using available resources in the Mediterranean.

After much consultation, General Wilson – a keen believer in impartiality – delivered his appreciation on 17 May, outlining a number of options but highlighting a large-scale landing in southern France à la ANVIL as the most practicable. The Americans were so delighted with

Willi Holtfreter (*left*), one of the few remaining German fighter pilots in Italy by May 1944. He and his colleagues from III/JG53 were so outnumbered every time they took to the sky, there was very little they could do to help the battle on the ground; it took all their skill just to get back in one piece.

ABOVE: Ion Calvocoressi (*left*) with other ADCs from Eighth Army Tactical HQ.

RIGHT: The men who made up the Allied Armies in Italy were drawn from many corners of the globe and included a staggering number of different nationalities, races and creeds, from Nepal to Brazil and from Morocco to the Maldives. Here Indian Sikhs greet British troops in the Liri Valley.

Life in the South. Italian boys in Naples show quite visibly the affects of the chronic shortage of food. Too many Italians in the south starved to death, something that was far more common in the north.

LEFT: And everywhere there was destruction. This elderly Italian lady sits on the steps of a church amid the ruins.

Southern Italy's women suffered particularly. Almost half the women aged 18–45 were involved in prostitution, a horrifying statistic that was brought upon them by the threat of starvation. Here a woman suffers the indignity of being publicly deloused.

RIGHT: Harold Macmillan with Alexander. The two were great friends, and supported each other in their extremely difficult political and military roles. Macmillan worked tirelessly to try to restructure the appallingly cumbersome Allied Military Government and Control Commission, and believed strongly in Italian political independence in the south.

BELOW: Italian troops of the CIL, who fought alongside the Allies. This picture was taken in April 1944, when the CIL was still poorly trained and equipped. Although they played an important part in the battle for Rimini in July 1944, fighting alongside II Polish Corps, the Allies were often reluctant to use them.

Mark Clark. Arrogant maybe, but a far better general than many give him credit for. Whatever the rights and wrongs of his decision to attack Rome through the Alban Hills, his actions ensured that many more German troops were captured or killed than would have been the case had he sent VI Corps all-out to Valmontone.

RIGHT: Marquesa Iris Origo – seated centre – with some of the evacuees and orphans taken into her care at La Foce. Most of these children had come to the Val d'Orcia to avoid the Allied bombing of the cities, but by June 1944 they found themselves terrifyingly caught on the front line as the war rolled north.

Fighter-bomber over German lines. For front-line German troops, there were two particular aspects of the Italian campaign that made their lives a misery. The first were the 'Jabos' – the fighter-bombers who bombed and strafed the Germans both at the front and anywhere else they dared to show their heads.

he second was the threat of
artisan actions against them.
he partisans' guerrilla
tivities wore away at German
orale and tied down troops
at could have been better
sed against the Allies. It says
uch about the effectiveness of
is type of warfare that the
ermans felt the 'partisan
enace' so keenly, especially
hen most were young,
readbare and poorly
quipped, like the boys here.

LEFT: Gianni Rossi, second in
command of the partisan
brigade, the Stella Rossa.
Despite the name, Gianni and
the brigade's commander,
Mario Musolesi, were
determinedly non-political and
certainly not Communist. Their
only political doctrine was to
rid Italy of both Germans and
Fascism.

LEFT: Men of the Bir el Gobi Company in Milan William Cremonini is second from left.

RIGHT: The young Fascist and German spy, Carla Costa. Just seventeen when she began working for the Abwehr, she became one of the most dedicated agents to operate behind Allied lines.

BELOW: The 8th Garibaldi Brigade of partisans, who operated in the mountains of Romagna south of Forlì. Almost completely decimated in April 1944, they reformed stronger and better equipped and were one of the many bands of resistors to become a major thorn in the sides of both the Germans and the Fascist government in the north.

RIGHT: GNR militia carry out an execution of the Romagnan partisan, Aldo Palareti. Minutes after this photograph was taken, he was dead...

...half his head blown away by the Neo-Fascist firing squad.

Kendall Brooke, a young South African officer with the Royal Natal Carbineers. Like all South Africans, Kendall volunteered for service, and was one of many in the 6th South African Armoured Division who fought tirelessly and with considerable skill during the long slog from Rome to the Apennines.

North of Rome there were still plenty of hills but at least there was a break from the mountains. In this more open country, a convoy of trucks from Eighth Army take a brief break. After a month of hard-fought and bitter fighting, and with the loss of key divisions hanging over them, the Allies found it hard to maintain momentum as they pursued the retreating Germans north.

Men of the 16th Waffen-SS Division at Cecina on the Tuscan coast. A comparatively newly formed division, they were to prove formidable opponents to both the US and South African forces they came up against and also to the partisans in whose zone of operations they were deployed.

Reg Harris, a farmer's son from Wiltshire, and a section leader in the 3rd Coldstream Guards. Reg fought his way up the leg of Italy from Rome to Monte Sole.

this apparent *volte face* by the British, they once again offered to bring landing craft from the Pacific for use in the operation. It looked as though ANVIL was back on after all. Five days later, General Wilson had warned Alex that he might well have to hand over seven divisions some time from the middle of June.

Alex took the news on the chin, but was all too aware that exactly the same thing had occurred the previous autumn just as Kesselring had been forced to fall back. Back then, the seven to be withdrawn had all been highly competent and extremely experienced divisions. So they would be again; more galling for Alex was the fact that four of the seven would be the French divisions – his only troops trained in mountain warfare and who would have been more than useful as he launched his assault across the Apennines. 'I hope our tap will not be turned off too soon,' he had signalled to Churchill on 30 May, 'and prevent us from gaining the full fruits of our present advantageous decision.'[141]

Yet Alex had not pressed the point too hard before the fall of Rome, hoping that with that significant victory and the Germans on the run, the decision to invade southern France might yet be overturned in his favour. All too aware that it was the Americans who favoured ANVIL, Alex was careful to lay on very thickly the magnitude of the US Fifth Army's triumphant capture of Rome. Quite apart from the fact that Clark's forces had routed AOK 14, the tense strategical situation goes some way to explaining why Alex never censured the Fifth Army commander for quite blatantly disobeying his order to thrust all-out towards Valmontone. Clark, he knew, felt as strongly about exploiting their success in Italy as he did. Now was not the time for any sign of disunity.

On 7 June, with Clark's forces thundering north of Rome in pursuit of the Germans, Alex signalled to Jumbo Wilson his future intentions, which were to complete the destruction of the German forces in Italy, and in the process force the enemy to draw on the maximum of his reserves. In so doing, he argued, he would be giving the greatest possible help to Eisenhower's Normandy invasion. 'I now have two highly organised and skilful armies,' he told Wilson, 'capable of carrying out large scale attacks and mobile operations in the closest co-operation. Morale is irresistibly high as a result of recent successes and the whole forms one closely articulated machine, capable of carrying out assaults and rapid exploitation in the most difficult terrain. Neither the Apennines nor even the Alps should prove a serious obstacle.'

With this in mind, he proposed to give the enemy no breathing space and to pursue the Germans up the peninsula. If the enemy were able to reach the Gothic Line then he hoped to launch a full-scale attack towards Bologna no later than 15 August. From Bologna, he would establish a firm base and then thrust either over the Alps into France or northeastwards to Austria through the Ljubljana Gap. It was essentially the development of a plan he had first envisaged as far back as the previous October. 'As I explained,' wrote Alex later, 'this plan was only possible on the assumption that I retained the forces I then had in Italy.'[142] And that meant both ground and air forces.

He had good cause for optimism. Regardless of how showy Clark's corps commander conference had been in Rome on 5 June, the Fifth Army commander had held it primarily out of necessity and had not been slow in pursuit: the Americans had taken Civitavecchia, an important port north of the city on the 7th, which would ease potential logistical problems. Meanwhile, Alex assured Wilson, the major railway lines from the southern ports as far as Rome were expected to be fully repaired by early July. Although Alex's appreciation was widely circulated, he still underlined his concern in a signal to General Brooke the following day. 'It seems to me,' Alex warned him, 'that it would be criminal to throw away such a wonderful opportunity of bringing off a really great coup.'[143]

After a period of brief but welcome harmony between the Combined Chiefs of Staff, this new appreciation from Alex blasted wide open the debate over Allied strategy once more. This time, however, the argument *had* to be resolved, and quickly, and began on 10 June with a series of talks in London between the Combined Chiefs. From Alex's point of view, the decision to continue all-out in Italy was unquestionably the right one. First, it would make the best use of momentum and morale and the excellent teamwork achieved between the air forces and the army. Second, he correctly guessed that Hitler would insist on fighting for every inch and so would be forced to reinforce Kesselring during the next few weeks, precisely the time when success or failure in Normandy hung in the balance. Moreover, by pushing on into northern Italy the Allies would be able to deny Hitler the use of Italy's industrial cities and would open up airfields even closer to the Third Reich. In contrast, he could find little to favour the ANVIL plan at all.

Jumbo Wilson was personally prepared to be swayed by Alex's arguments, although his largely American staff was not. In any case, he could not suddenly change the views he had given the Combined Chiefs

overnight, and so, until the debates over the decision had been concluded, had to insist Alex begin the withdrawal of the divisions earmarked for ANVIL.

In this, Alex acquiesced, although this sudden need for reorganisation
hardly helped the speed of the Allied pursuit. Until 11 June, however,
the Fifth Army advance had made great strides. After a week they had
reached Lake Bolsena, over thirty miles north of Rome. With far gentler,
more rolling countryside than much of Eighth Army's more mountainous sector, they once again outpaced Leese's divisions, and were
presented, briefly, with another opportunity to turn east and drive a
permanent wedge between the two retreating German armies.

This was Kesselring's major worry during the first few days of the
German retreat. It needn't have been. Alex was unaware just how separated the two German armies were, and was more concerned about
having his own two armies at peak strength and fighting fit for when he
made his assault on the Gothic Line. Moreover, the difficulties for Fifth
Army were much the same as they had been advancing north-east of
Valmontone. Lying in their way was the wide River Tiber, and then the
central Apennines.

Furthermore, Alex was conscious that his supply lines could not
support a huge advance using the full strength of his forces. He was also
keenly aware that some of those units had been fighting almost non-stop
since the beginning of the battle and needed a rest. US II Corps, for
example, although not earmarked for southern France, had been in
action almost continually since the opening night of the battle. He and
Clark would need them again, regardless of the ANVIL decision. For
II Corps' two rookie divisions, it had been a baptism of fire, but they
had reason to feel proud of their performance. 'Since 11 May,' noted
Lieutenant Bob Wiggans, the farmer from New York, 'we had advanced
135 miles, smashed the Gustav Line, relieved the Anzio beachhead,
helped capture Rome, and utterly annihilated two of Germany's finest
divisions.'[144]

General Mark Clark was lucky still to be alive. Flying over Civitavecchia
on 10 June, his pilot failed to see the cable of a barrage balloon. The
wing could easily have been ripped off, but instead the cable wrapped
itself around the wing so that the Piper Cub began spiralling around it
and rapidly losing height. After the third spiral, the plane broke free but
not before a large section of the wing was torn off, ripping open a fuel

tank and covering the plane in petrol. Miraculously, they then managed to get down safely and land in a cornfield. 'I never had a worse experience,' wrote Clark to his wife.[145]

Having cheated death, however, Clark was determined to argue Alex's case with his American superiors. He had, like Alex, been aware of the shadow of ANVIL hanging over future operations in Italy, and had accepted that he would lose both VI Corps and the French Expeditionary Corps – but he didn't like it one bit. 'To prepare for the eventuality of ANVIL they are sacrificing a great victory here,' he wrote in his diary. 'It just doesn't make sense.'[146] He was also worried about General Juin, a man he could not praise highly enough, but whom, it seemed, General de Gaulle, the Free French leader, was prepared to cast aside before the ANVIL operation. He knew Juin was deeply depressed about the whole matter. 'In my opinion, it is all a great pity,' Juin told him. 'History will judge this decision severely.'[147]

Clark urged him not to lose heart: General Marshall, he told him in strict confidence, was about to arrive in Italy, and he was planning to talk to him about it then, man to man. On 18 June, Clark met both Marshall and the Chief of the Air Staff, General 'Hap' Arnold, at Rome then drove them to his new command post at Tuscania. Wasting no time to paint the broader American view, Marshall stressed that the invasion of southern France was essential to Eisenhower. There were over forty divisions in America waiting to be thrown into the theatre. The ports of southern France were essential for them to get those troops into France with all speed. ANVIL, it seemed, had become a logistical necessity, rather than an operation of strategic importance.

After a couple of hours with the American Chief of Staff, Clark rolled over, his fighting talk gone. He pointed out that by withdrawing divisions for southern France, they would be throwing away the chance for a great victory, but this made no impression at all on Marshall. In that case, Clark told him, if the decision was final, it would have his full support.

Clark had known Marshall a long time. He could see that the Chief was not to be budged. And nothing he or Alexander, or anyone else said would make the slightest difference.

EIGHTEEN

The Typhoon Rolls North

On 5 June, General Sir Oliver Leese had taken a plane ride over Rome and had seen all the bridges still intact across the River Tiber. 'A wonderful sight,' Leese told his wife later. They had then flown south-east over the battlefield, and the now desolate towns of Valmontone and Velletri. 'All utterly destroyed,' he scribbled, 'and one saw the continuous shell holes of the American artillery programmes.'[148]

The sixty-mile stretch between Rome and Cassino now lay devastated. The peoples of the towns and villages within the Anzio beachhead had all been forcibly evacuated soon after the landing – some 80,000 in all. Immediately beyond the front line the civilian population had been left to fend for themselves. In the small town of Genzano in the Alban Hills, for example, the population had soon found themselves within range of the American guns and so gradually people had begun moving to the banks of the nearby Lake Nemi. The Alban Hills were volcanic and the townspeople discovered that once the top layer of rock at the lake's edge was dug away there were softer layers of solidified lava beneath that could be quite easily excavated into caves – caves in which more and more people began to live a troglodyte existence. One cave was destroyed when a large Allied bomb scored a direct hit. Once the front passed and they were able to dig out the rubble, the townspeople discovered more than thirty bodies, many of whom had been trapped alive when rubble had blocked the entrance.

By the time the front line had finally passed, many of the people of Genzano had been living in those caves for almost six months. 'To live in little caverns dug by us,' says Leonardo Bocale, one of the Genzano cave-dwellers, 'without any facilities for hygiene, without a life, without knowing what our future could be, tossed like animals ... we were abandoned: culturally, materially, spiritually.'[149]

The people of the towns and villages further south had mostly taken to the mountains once the first Cassino battles had begun. For Tommaso Pelle and his wife, from Esperia, it had been an especially difficult time, as they had been expecting a child any moment. The baby was eventually born on the bare earth, without a doctor or any kind of medicine. 'We slept on the ground,' says Tommaso, 'in the middle of the woods, hidden in caves, without a bed, without blankets.' Eventually, the Germans rounded them up and put them in a refugee camp at Ferentino, where they remained until the Americans arrived and they began to head back to Esperia. 'There was nothing left,' says Tommaso. 'No police, no work, bombs in the middle of the fields. I had a family to keep and so I took up selling black-market tobacco.' This he did by travelling around the area, breaking into abandoned homes and stealing what tobacco he could find. He would roll this into a ball of around 4–5kg and sell it bit by bit. 'If they had money, I would take money,' he says. 'If not, anything would do: flour, oil, vegetables, dried figs. Anything.' Until he had sufficiently repaired his own home, they lived wherever they found themselves, eating dandelions and boiled herbs and whatever scraps of food they could lay their hands on.[150]

Responsibility for civilians in the immediate aftermath of the battle was left to the armed forces – or rather the Allied Military Government, or 'AMG' as it was known. Usually, AMG officials would reach a town or village to find the place almost entirely destroyed and with no more than a handful of people living there and no form of government whatsoever. During the ensuing days, those who had been hiding in mountains or caves began to traipse back to their shattered homes. Most were lice-ridden, on the point of starvation, and lacked even basic items such as shoes and half-decent clothes.

In Fifth Army's sector, for example, a refugee camp was set up at Ausonia on 22 May. By the evening, some 850 civilians were already housed there, lured by the prospect of food. The same day, a trail of several thousand refugees had been seen heading towards Minturno, near where II Corps had begun the battle; a Civil Affairs Officer (CAO) had immediately been sent to see whether a further camp should be set up there.

Camps were set up as quickly and efficiently as possible. At Ausonia, a baker was quickly found and his own ovens repaired immediately. Two days after opening the camp bread was being produced and handed out. Ration tickets marked with an 'AMG' stamp were distributed, a soup kitchen established, and plenty of latrines dug. Medicals were given. A register of all able-bodied men was also made, with the idea that a job should be found within the army for all of them. Proclamations and rules were also posted, but when it was realised that a great many civilians were illiterate, a *bandolier* – rather like a town crier – was appointed to read out the salient points. 'An unbelievable disregard of all rules was promptly noted,' observed a Fifth Army report. 'Each person tried to cheat on the obtaining of rations. Curfew was completely unobserved. Cleanliness rules were broken right in front of the officers. People wandered out of the settlement. A priest asked permission to go to Esperia, was refused same, and promptly went anyway.'[151] Clearly AMG Civil Affairs Officers had to establish some kind of order to perform the tasks required, but what they failed to appreciate was that these people were hungry, had been living rough for weeks if not months, and were desperate to get home, not be treated like prisoners and herded about as though they were cattle.

As Leese had taken his aerial tour, he had seen the 6th South African Armoured Division moving up the Via Casilina to take over the spearhead of XIII Corps and indeed, Eighth Army, on the western side of the Tiber.

Although the South African 12th Infantry Brigade had been involved in a holding role alongside the New Zealanders in the initial stages of the DIADEM offensive, this was now the first time South African troops were going into action since the Battle of Alamein over a year and a half before. And it was the first time ever for the 6th Armoured Division, a new fighting unit that had only been formed in February the previous year; and while the division had a nucleus of seasoned campaigners from North Africa, most of its troops were new to war.

One of those was twenty-one-year-old Kendall Brooke, a subaltern in the Royal Natal Carbineers. The son of an Englishman who had emigrated to South Africa to farm, Kendall was the middle of three brothers brought up in the Eastern Cape. And like all his fellows, he was a volunteer. Conscription had been tried by the fledgling Union of South Africa during the First World War and had caused uproar – hardly surprising considering the Boer War had ended only thirteen years before. Even by 1939, Britain had been the enemy within the lifetime of many Afrikaners. Indeed, Kendall's own mother, an Afrikaner of Danish-Dutch extraction, had been, along with the rest of her family, rounded up by the British and placed in a concentration camp during the Anglo-Boer War. One of her sisters had died there.

But although there had been no conscription this time around, huge numbers had still volunteered. 'It was just your duty and that was the way things were,' says Kendall. 'I had been taught history at boarding school and elsewhere and one was inculcated with the idea that anything that was done in the name of the King was right. The fact that Britain was going to war meant they were right and the enemy was totally wrong and away you went.'

In actual fact, Kendall had not volunteered right away, because when he finished school his parents had encouraged him to go to university. He did not, however, complete his studies and after two years – and by now aged nineteen – he had joined the Tank Corps, and then, shortly after being commissioned, he was transferred to the Royal Natal Carbineers.

The regiment had left to join the 6th Armoured Division in September 1943. Kendall and the other new subalterns in the regiment had assembled outside Pietermaritzburg just before embarkation where they had been addressed by the Commanding Officer, Colonel Murray Comrie. A man with two Military Crosses to his name, Comrie was a veteran of the North African campaign. Although only in his mid-thirties, he looked like an old man to Kendall. 'Gentlemen,' Comrie said, eyeing the young men before him, 'I expect two things of you: you will know your job and you will look after your men. Any dereliction or diminished performance in either of those two areas and you will leave the regiment the following day.' He also warned them that they were heading to war and some would most likely never return. 'If that's a prospect you're not prepared to live with,' he added, 'then you say so now and you can leave immediately no questions asked.' No one did. 'The man next to me was muttering, "Oh my God", under his breath,' says Kendall. 'It rather brought home the reality.'

Since then they had trained in Egypt and Palestine and had finally reached Italy in April 1944, a country that was enormously different from the dry, desert scrub in which they had been training. And now, at long last, they were moving to the front. Although the Royal Natal Carbineers had been part of 12th Brigade holding the line north-east of Cassino, for Kendall and the other young officers of the regiment the time had finally come to test their worth. Only in the days, weeks, and months to come would their promise to Colonel Comrie be properly put to the test.

By darkness on 5 June they had reached Valmontone. It was still dark as they continued along the Via Casilina, around the jutting butte of rock on which the town had been built. Jagged ruins loomed over them, silhouetted darkly against the moonlit sky. Kendall was struck by the overpowering stench of death that hung heavy in the air. 'It has a very peculiar, distinctive taste,' he says, 'rather sweet, slightly sickly.'

Since the fall of Rome on 4 June, rumours had abounded about American heavy-handedness. Lone British jeeps had reportedly been turned away at gunpoint after Clark's orders that Eighth Army troops were not allowed inside the city. This, of course, did not include the men of the two British divisions who had been part of VI Corps and who had entered the city along with the rest of Fifth Army. Thankfully, the embargo had been lifted by 6 June when XIII Corps passed through on its way north. Indeed, their procession through the capital was every bit as much of a triumphal march as that of the Americans the day before. Kendall Brooke was certainly thrilled to see so many Italians cheering and throwing flowers. 'It was difficult not to feel a bit of a lad,' he says. 'It was a place that had been a military target going back to Hannibal and to find myself in the vanguard of a conquering army going through the city was an intoxicating experience.' Not everyone was so affected by the moment, however. Kendall noticed that in the truck in front, the infantrymen had their heads down, either sleeping or playing cards. 'It had no impact on them at all,' he says.

In the Val d'Orcia, Antonio and Iris Origo were bracing themselves for the moment the front line passed through their small corner of Italy. On 12 June, Iris took a horse and trap to Montepulciano to try and buy much-needed medicine for one of the babies being sheltered at La Foce. On the way, she and her companion had to leap for cover twice as Allied fighter planes swooped over their heads. At Montepulciano they discovered a German anti-aircraft battery at the gates of the town. The townspeople were nervous and rumours abounded. German troops appeared to be everywhere, and on her return home she discovered that German troops were about to set up an artillery emplacement on their land.

Two days later, German Pioneers arrived at La Foce itself and billeted themselves in and around the house. More had arrived by the following day. By 16 June, the Allies had broken through at Orvieto, some twenty miles to the south, and were now half way to Chiusi, barely ten miles away. 'The cannon fire is louder now,' scribbled Iris, 'and our first shell has fallen beside one of our farms.' Later that evening, the German sappers moved out. The captain in charge told Iris, 'I'd give a lot to be in your place, to be able to talk in a few days to some British officers and find out what they really think about the war.' Iris had heard such talk from other German officers, who, like Georg Zellner, were sick of the war, depressed about the bombing of Germany's cities and desperate to get back home. 'But there is not one of them,' she added, 'who does not still express his blind conviction that Germany *cannot* be beaten, and their equally blind belief in a terrible *Vergeltung* [retaliation] against England.'

It was going to take more than a few days, however, before the war passed through La Foce. Little did Iris realise it, but the new front line – the Albert Line as it had now been named – passed directly through the Val d'Orcia.* It was along this line that Kesselring had ordered his men to make their next stand. In a taste of things to come, on 18 June, paratroopers of the 1st Fallschirmjäger Corps arrived – 'the most complete set of ruffians that I have ever set eyes upon' – and took over the house. Warned to remove everything of value, Iris and Antonio did their best to lock up what they could. This had little effect, however, whilst on the farms and in the surrounding countryside, the arrival of the paratroopers had much the same effect as a swarm of locusts. All that day a stream of terrified contadini appeared at La Foce looking to Iris and Antonio for help. 'All have had their food stores stolen,' noted Iris, 'most have lost at least a pig, or some geese or fowls, some have been turned out of their house altogether, and three have had their daughters raped.'[152]

Compounding the difficulties of the frightened civilians of the Val d'Orcia were the increased activities of the partisans. A few days after the fall of Rome, the local Carabinieri in Montepulciano had deserted and joined the partisans, taking with them all their arms and ammunition. With the local Fascists melting away with every day that passed, and fired by Alexander's call to arms, the local partisans were making life increasingly troublesome for the arriving Germans. Troops, equip-

---

*Somewhat confusingly, several of the German defensive lines have different names, depending on which side one was on. The Albert Line, as the Germans called it, was always referred to as the Trasimene Line by the Allies.

ment, and precious vehicles were captured. In every case, the Germans acted swiftly, taking hostages and razing farmhouses to the ground. A further nine hostages, including the town mayor, were taken from Montepulciano in response to the shooting of a German soldier. These were later released, but the following day ten hostages were taken from nearby Chianciano instead. Locals urged the partisans to hold fire until the Germans had passed, but the request was ignored and further attacks were made. Eventually, on 23 June, a partisan was captured by the Germans and publicly hanged from a lamp post in the centre of Montepulciano, and there he was left to swing in the summer heat as a warning to others.

The partisans of the Val d'Orcia were getting off lightly, however. The partisan problem was becoming an increasingly big headache for Kesselring, and one that he was hearing about constantly on his visits to the front and reading in reports from his commanders. What concerned him was that partisan activity was only going to get worse and lead to 'uncontrollable chaos'.[153] General Lemelsen, newly in command of AOK 14, was also surprised by the 'startling suddenness' with which partisan activity had increased. 'From now on not a night passed in which despatch riders, single lorries and soldiers were not ambushed, robbed or dragged away and their lorries burnt,' he said. Even the commander of the newly arrived 20th Luftwaffe Field Division had been attacked in his car and shot. 'It is understandable,' Lemelsen continued, 'that the troops, heavily tried by the moral hardships of the continuous hard struggles at the front, now seeing themselves threatened in the rear by the guerrillas on their supply routes, became more disquieted and irritated from day to day.'[154]

Hans Golda would have agreed with this comment wholeheartedly. The partisans were a pain. 'We would often discover partisans were in the area,' he noted. 'I wanted to give them a good hiding.'[155] So too did Kesselring, who decided that drastic measures needed to be taken to stop the rot. 'The fight against the partisans must be carried on with the utmost severity,' he told his commanders on 17 June. 'I will protect any commander who exceeds our usual restraint in the choice and severity of the methods he adopts against the partisans.'

Not surprisingly, certain commanders took this as carte blanche to act with unrestrained brutality. In the weeks that followed, the mass killings began: eighty-three men executed at Niccioleta in west Tuscany on 13 June; forty in Gubbio on 21 June; more than thirty men, women and children murdered at the tiny village of Bettola in Emilia Romagna on 23–24 June; in Civitella, 212 people, including women, children and infants, massacred on 29 June by men of the Fallschirm-Panzerkorps Hermann Göring. There were others: ten people here, twenty there. Like the young partisan in Montepulciano, others were strung up on lamp posts for all to see. But this was only the beginning.

Meanwhile, the Allies were closing in on the Albert Line. Eighth Army had done well to catch up with Fifth Army, but after advancing over a hundred miles in two weeks, both forces were struggling with the inevitable over-extended supply lines; the Allied railhead was now 200 miles to the south. Another continued hindrance was the many rivers that had to be crossed. 'We are having a big problem with bridging,' Leese told Montgomery, 'as some of the rivers are formidable obstacles.'[156] Ted Wyke-Smith and the sappers of 78th Division continued to work tirelessly. 'In the advance from Cassino to Lake Trasimeno,' he says, 'my sappers built twenty-six bridges in twenty-eight days. All by night.' It was a quite phenomenal feat, and at the end of it Ted and his men were absolutely exhausted. So too was the rest of 78th Division, who had been in the thick of the fighting since the beginning, and who were now sent, en masse, to the Middle East for refitting and retraining.

On 13 June, the Royal Natal Carbineers had been near Lake Bolsena. Overlooking the village of Bagnoregio, the Support Company's mortar teams and 6-pounder anti-tanks guns began pounding a series of caves just below the village. 'Knocked hell out of them,' noted Corporal Dick Frost in his diary with satisfaction. Like Kendall Brooke, Dick had also been swept along by the popular response to South Africa's call to arms, although he was beginning to wish he hadn't – several of his mates had already been killed in the short time they had been in action. Now, however, they appeared to have the upper hand, and by midday B Company had taken the village successfully. Only then did they discover there had not been any Germans in the caves after all. Rather, the inhabitants had been Italians sheltering as the war blasted their homes on the ridge above. 'Heard later,' noted Dick, 'that we had only shot a few Ites and a pig.'[157]

Nor did Eighth Army troops have too many qualms about stealing food from the locals; the Germans were not the only guilty ones. 'Scrounged a bucket of fresh spuds,' noted Dick on 11 June, 'much to Ites' annoyance.' A few days later he managed to find a goose and another bird and a cellar filled with 'vino'.[158] The men of the 24th Guards Brigade, attached to the 6th South African Armoured Division, were no better. Corporal Reg Harris, a section leader with 2 Company, 3rd Coldstream Guards, admits they lived partly off the land as they pushed north. 'What it must have been like for the local population to have two armies ravaging its land can only be imagined,' he says, 'but in war, when there is a good chance that you may be killed the next day, moral consider-ations don't carry much weight.' One time an Italian lady asked them in good English to be careful of her potatoes. 'We were,' says Reg. 'We dug, peeled and ate them very carefully.'

By 18 June, the South Africans and their Guards Brigade comrades were only about six miles south-east of La Foce, having occupied the village of Cetona. In command of a troop of 6-pounders, Kendall Brooke was peering across the valley immediately north-west of the village towards the ridge opposite, when he suddenly spotted a long, black horizontal shadow thrown onto the wall of a building by the early morning sun. Straining his eyes closer, he realised he had spotted a Tiger tank, one of the most powerful and destructive tanks ever used in the war. Realising it was out of range of their 6-pounder guns, Kendall called for their Priest self-propelled gun. This was a 3-inch naval gun mounted on a tank chassis, but the Tiger was still in an untouchable position. Moreover, such was the thickness of the Tiger's armour, it was almost impervious to anything in the Allied armament.

Then Kendall had a stroke of luck. He noticed the tell-tale puff of smoke that meant it had just started its engines, then watched it begin to move off. 'Why it didn't fire at us, I'll never know,' he says. 'Perhaps there was something wrong with it. At any rate, it turned away and made to go over a rise, and we managed to get a shot up its arse and it went up in flames.'

It was, as Kendall admits, a lucky shot but not long after he was not so fortunate, as the Germans began to shell the ridge where his anti-tank guns were still emplaced. Most of the shells landed harmlessly in a ploughed field but one crashed near to a stone wall. 'Two of my men were fatally wounded,' says Kendall, 'and I received shrapnel in my chest and shoulder.' Kendall was operated on in a field hospital tent later that night and soon patched up. But for a few weeks the war would go on without him.

Kendall was just one of increasing numbers of casualties. All the way from Rome they had found themselves repeatedly coming under harassing fire and engaged in small fire-fights, but the further north they went, the stiffer the resistance had become. And it was about to get even stronger, because by now the Germans had successfully fallen back behind their main delaying position. The battle for the Albert Line was about to begin.

NINETEEN

Breaking the Albert Line
20–30 June 1944

Although it was not until 20 June that the Corpo Italiano di Liberazione (CIL) became fully assembled, Lieutenant Eugenio Corti and the men of the 184th Artillery had been carrying out a holding role in the British V Corps sector for some weeks. The experience had hardly done much to improve Eugenio's spirits. Too many of the men were horribly under-trained, and they were missing even basic equipment. With the fall of Rome the Germans had fallen back in the east of the peninsula too, and as the Nembo Division slowly followed, Eugenio was further depressed by the sight of towns and villages that had been reduced to dust.

As elsewhere, the Germans had left a web of mines and booby traps as they fell back, an even bigger problem for the Italian royalist troops than it might have been because of the lack of mine detectors.

'Before the armistice we fought with gasoline bottles against tanks,' Eugenio's sergeant complained. 'Now that we're with the most equipped army in the world, we're missing the few magnetic mine detectors that we had before.'

'Mine detectors?' retorted another artilleryman. 'We're even missing clothes to wear.'[159]

Nonetheless, they had continued heading north in pursuit of the retreating Germans only to be halted for almost a week in the small village of Cerratina, near Pescara. Eugenio couldn't understand. With every day that passed, the Germans were getting further away, leaving in their wake more minefields and blown roads and bridges than ever. Little did Eugenio realise that General Alexander had quite deliberately slowed the Allied advance on the Adriatic for a few days, in order to save on bridging equipment and transport that was now desperately needed by the main bulk of Eighth Army and Fifth Army to the west of the Tiber.

Even so, Alex had his eye on the east coast, because he knew that capturing the large port of Ancona as soon as possible would ease his logistical difficulties enormously. With this in mind, he sent General Anders and his Polish Corps across the peninsula, and with a few British artillery units, the 7th Queen's Hussars, and the entire CIL, ordered him to 'pursue the enemy at the highest possible speed and capture Ancona'.[160]

Anders' advance began on 17 June, by which time most of the German forces along the Adriatic had fallen back behind the Albert Line along a commanding ridge that ran to the sea a dozen miles to the south of Ancona. Thus when the Corpo Italiano di Liberazione resumed its advance it did so with only mines and blown roads to contend with. Ahead of them were the partisans of the Majella Brigade who had come down from the mountains as the Germans had retreated. Eugenio had been on reconnaissance when he reached the town of Teramo, some fifty miles south of Ancona on 20 June, and quickly noticed threatening Communist graffiti on the walls of the town. Partisans, complete with trademark red scarves around their necks and weapons on their shoulders, wandered about the town. 'After the Fascists,' noted Eugenio, 'we now had the Communists, at a time when the nation was exhausted; this was the harsh reality.'

As was so often the case, the red scarves and vehement anti-fascism led men like Eugenio to assume that these were Communist partisans, when in fact, the Majella Brigade was not a specifically Communist band at all, although they were certainly left wing and had Communists among their number. Formed shortly after the armistice from a core of former Italian Army officers, they had fought doggedly in the Abruzzi Mountains with the help of British supplies. Like all partisan bands, however, many of their numbers came from young, frightened, men hoping to avoid being rounded up and drafted into the New Republican Army or as workers for the Germans.

Over the next few days, however, as the rest of the CIL caught up, tensions between the royalist – and predominantly right-wing – Italian troops and the partisans began to mount. One of the Nembo officers caught a partisan raping the wife of a Fascist who was being held in prison. When the partisan fired at him, the officer smoked him out with a grenade. A handful of Nembo paratroopers got into a brawl with some partisans, and having got the upper hand, made the partisans drop to their knees and kiss a Fascist identity card. Eugenio found himself face to face with a young partisan in a house where he had been hoping to find some friends from home. The young man was happy to boast to Eugenio about the men he had killed. 'We didn't do anything to the Germans who surrendered,' he told Eugenio; 'but we killed all the Fascists, those dogs.' Eugenio asked him why they had different rules for Italians. 'Because the Fascists are Fascists,' the boy replied. Eugenio was appalled.[161]

A few days later, the Nembo Division moved north again, this time to the war zone along the Albert Line. Their deployment had not come a moment too soon.

Now based at a runway near Lake Bracciano, north of Rome, 244 Wing had finally been equipped as fighter-bombers. Since the fall of Rome, they had had a frustrating time. The air fighting that had briefly flared up during the battle was over; there were simply no enemy aircraft to engage – since the beginning of June, Kesselring's forces at the front had no fighter air cover whatsoever. Even III/JG53 had moved north, heading to Maniago in the Adriatic Coastland on 2 June, and far out of reach of Allied fighters. Three weeks later, III/JG53 left Italy altogether. Willi Holtfreter had survived to fight another day.

The alternative to air combat was to attack ground targets, but this was not a particularly efficient use of a wing of Spitfires armed only with machine guns and cannons. And so, on 20 June, 244 Wing were given a load of bomb racks to fit to the underside of their Spitfires and a week in which to teach themselves the art of dive-bombing.

With no bomb ranges available, they practised by dropping fluorescent markers into the sea and aiming their bombs at these. Achieving a successful technique was simply a case of trial and error. Cocky Dundas discovered that if he flew towards the target, then watched it disappear under his wing and reappear behind and slightly away, then he would be in roughly the right position to begin his dive. He would then turn the Spitfire onto its back and dive down through the vertical from around 8,000 feet. This gave him an angle of dive of about twenty degrees off the vertical, and when he was under 2,000 feet, he would pull out of the dive, count 'one-and-two-and-three' then drop his bomb. 'No doubt the whole procedure sounds thoroughly Heath Robinson,' he admitted, 'but it worked.'[162] Soon he was able to regularly hit within fifty yards of the target.

Even so, their first fighter-bomber mission was hardly the roaring success they had hoped for. 'We dropped our bombs with indifferent accuracy,' noted Cocky, 'and returned to base feeling rather let down.'[163]

Back down on the ground, Kesselring's forces, still badly mauled, had nonetheless regrouped and, with new troops arriving daily, had managed to regain some kind of balance. Hans Golda and Werfer Regiment 71 had been dug in around the village of Gioiella for the best part of a week. Only a couple of miles to the west of the tranquil Lake Trasimeno, the chance to stop and pause had been most welcome. To his delight, Hans had been billeted in 'a beautiful room in a beautiful house with beautiful furniture'. The bed was comfortable and he had managed to get plenty of rest. 'The German leadership had really achieved something good here,' he noted, 'because out of a load of fleeing soldiers they'd made a strong defensive front which could cause the enemy some problems.'

To his right were the remnants of the 1st Fallschirmjäger Division, where Hans-Jürgen Kumberg was dug in. Despite once more showing an extremely courageous defence, however, both the paratroopers and the 334th Infantry were eventually forced back, overcome by sheer weight of fire. 'We'd been at Cassino such a long time that we knew every inch of our surroundings,' says Hans; 'but now we were constantly faced with something new. We were on the go all the time.' He noticed the British always followed the same form of attack: an artillery barrage, followed by infantry and usually tanks. The shelling, although uncomfortable, at least gave them warning of what was to come. 'Usually the infantry came forward walking,' says Hans. 'They always thought no one could be alive any more after the barrage. We would open fire and then they would fall back.' Another barrage would follow, and usually the dreaded jabos would soon appear with bombs and machine-gun and cannon fire. Only when their positions appeared to be in danger of being overrun, would they retreat.

To the right of Hans-Jürgen Kumberg in the Val d'Orcia were the men of the Fallschirm-Panzerkorps Hermann Göring, and it was against them that the South Africans and Guardsmen were now fighting. The objective for the Guards Brigade was Montepulciano, and would involve hard fighting to take it. As ever, night-time patrol work was an integral part of the British approach to battle.

They were near Chianciano when Corporal Reg Harris and his section of 2 Company, 3rd Coldstream Guards were detailed to go on a night patrol with their platoon commander, Lieutenant Geoffrey 'Wacky' Jones. Although the lieutenant was only twenty-one, Reg rated him as the best platoon officer he had served with so far during the war – and after four years in the army and nearly two years' overseas fighting through Tunisia and southern Italy, Reg had known a fair few.

They studied the map carefully and memorised the key features during the afternoon, before setting off once darkness had fallen. Reg had grown up in Fonthill in south Wiltshire, the son of a farm worker, and was used to an outdoors life. As a boy he shot rabbits and rats and game, both day and night. As a result he was a crack shot and prided himself on having excellent eyesight, even in the dark. But to his mind, Wacky Jones' night sight was even better. 'He led us,' says Reg, 'without the slightest hesitation.' When Reg heard a click from a hundred yards or so away, he tapped Jones on the shoulder and asked him whether he'd heard it. 'Yes,' the lieutenant whispered back, 'a German patrol, one man cocked his weapon. They'll be waiting for us, so we'll go back another way.'

They had moved forward another half mile when the lieutenant ordered his men to stop, lie down and wait for him. He was, he told them, going to go on into the village and would be about twenty minutes. Soon enough they could hear the sound of engines revving and hammering and clanging, and Reg began to wonder whether Jones had run into serious trouble. Then suddenly he reappeared and silently they moved off once more, heading back to their lines. The noise they'd heard, the lieutenant told Reg, was coming from a German vehicle repair depot. As soon as they were back, Jones told the artillery about the depot, giving them careful coordinates. Soon after the gunners opened fire. 'When we passed that way as we advanced,' says Reg, 'we found the depot had been blown to pieces.'

Further east, Major Georg Zellner and his bedraggled battalion of the H und D Regiment reached the village of Ramazzano, a few miles northeast of Perugia after a long and difficult night march through the rain. His men were exhausted and wet and so was he, but he soon found an old fortified farmstead. 'A hundred civilians are living in the cellars,' he scrawled in his diary. 'Women and children – a wild swarm, shouts and yells. In between the shells crash down.'

Orders arrived: he was now in reserve, but the division was to hold the line at any cost. Georg thought it was madness. 'And we should hold out against a force twenty times superior,' he noted, 'against tanks, (we haven't had any of those for a long time), against planes, (I haven't seen any of our own for a quarter of a year).' He felt beyond despair, his thoughts only on his wife and children back home. Nor did he think much of the talk about secret weapons that were going to be directed against England. 'This won't stop a catastrophe from happening,' he added. 'There's not a single soldier who still believes in it. Instead, we laugh.'[164]

At least his men were no longer hungry. Around them, the countryside was bursting with fruit. 'Now the chickens, doves, calves and pigs are left in peace,' wrote Georg. 'The farmers are amazed that we are so restrained.' On 22 June, however, his 3rd Battalion was duly sent forward a couple of miles. Having put his men in position, he looked for a command post and eventually found one: a white farmhouse. It seemed far too conspicuous for his liking but one his staff officers persuaded him.

Early the following morning, he was woken by a deafening crash as a shell landed directly in front of the house. He sprang out of bed and had just put on his left boot when another crash exploded around him. Furniture was destroyed, walls collapsed and the air filled with dust and screams. Grabbing his right boot, he tried to get out, but could see nothing. A table blocked his way. Throwing it over, he desperately looked for a way out. Where was the exit? He couldn't see anything – the dust hurt his eyes. But then ahead of him was a faint glow – it had to be the door. Charging over, he discovered the stairs had gone. Jumping into the yard, and with his right boot still in his hand, he then ran over to a shed, which seemed a little more protected. Suddenly the firing eased off, and Georg began to take stock. 'I had more than luck,' he scribbled. 'A direct hit on the kitchen. I was only in the next door room.'[165]

Back in the Val d'Orcia, the inhabitants of La Foce were discovering what it was like to be in the middle of a war zone. Antonio and Iris Origo had decamped to the cellar, along with the refugee children who had come to her all those months before to escape the bombing. Above, the Hermann Göring men were busy with the battle. They looked, thought Iris, 'unspeakably worn out and dirty'.[166] The sound of guns, both the Germans' and those of the Guards Brigade, was thundering around the estate, while shells were beginning to land terrifyingly close, one bursting through the garden just below them, another in the stables.

The civilians on the estate were increasingly turning to Iris and

Antonio for help. By 22 June, there were about sixty people in the cellar with them. 'An old grandmother from a neighbouring farm is among them,' wrote Iris, 'half paralysed, with a weak heart, she has been dragged along by her son and daughter and now collapses, utterly exhausted.' Infants were whimpering from hunger. During lulls, Iris went upstairs to the kitchen to prepare hot ersatz coffee and to try and find something for them all to eat. In the past few days, she had seen two nearby villages, Radicofani and Contignano, destroyed; the countryside had become pitted with shell holes; girls had been raped, and both people and cattle killed. 'Otherwise,' she wrote, 'the events of the last week have had little enough effect upon either side: it is the civilians who have suffered.'[167]

West of the Val d'Orcia, Fifth Army was also making its assault on the Albert Line. Juin's Frenchmen had not yet been withdrawn and were attacking along the western half of the River Orcia, while the 1st Armored Division, refreshed after a much-needed period of rest and maintenance, were further west again on the left flank of the French.

Colonel Hamilton Howze's Task Force was in reserve for the attack, but one man who was now back with the 1st Armored Regiment in Combat Command A was Private First Class Ray Saidel. His radio school had been moved from Naples at the beginning of the month, near to Lake Bracciano, north of Rome. Whilst there, Ray discovered his regiment were not far away and managed to get permission to go and find his company.

He found the familiar Company G markings on the tanks and vehicles, but the names on the tanks and the people around them did not look familiar. Further up the hill he saw a poker game going on. 'I thought that for sure there'd be someone I knew around the poker game,' says Ray. Sure enough, he found his old friend Sergeant Jerome Lowrey, his closest friend in the regiment and a man with whom he had shared many experiences both in Tunisia and Italy. 'He told me they'd had a lot of losses while I'd been gone,' says Ray. 'I said, "Get me back here – I'm sick of radio school. I've just about completed it; only a couple of weeks to go."' They jumped into a jeep and at the school Lowrey explained that Ray was one of the few originals of the company left and that it was essential he leave the school and be transferred back right away. Ray was duly sent back to the company – although not before taking five days' leave in Rome – his first leave since being deployed to North Africa eighteen months before.

From Manchester, New Hampshire, and the son of a Lithuanian parents, Ray had been something of a precocious child. Jewish and with a deeply left-wing uncle, Ray had grown up politically motivated and nurturing an intense loathing of fascism and Nazism. At high school he had organised political demonstrations and had continued to be politically active when he had begun university. While at university he had joined the ROTC – the Reserve Officer Training Corps – and had subsequently volunteered for the Army as soon as he was old enough – one of very people to do so for moral and political reasons. 'I just felt we had to beat these people,' he explains. 'I had no doubts at all.'

He should have become an officer, and easily passed the board. When he was given a security check, however, his school and university politics showed up on his file and he was refused entry to the Officer Candidates School and sent to the ranks. More than two years on, he was still Private First Class Saidel.

Now he was back with Company G and, having joined a tank recovery crew, was part of a column attacking through rolling southern Tuscan countryside towards the hill town of Roccastrada.

This was a part of the line held by von Senger's almost entirely reconstituted 14th Panzer Corps and specifically the 3rd Panzer Grenadier Division and the newly arrived 20th Luftwaffe Field Division. Also there to help were the Pioneer companies of the 16th Waffen-SS 'Reichsführer' Panzer-Grenadier Division. A comparatively new outfit formed the previous October, it had been on peace-keeping duties in Hungary and in May had been posted to Italy during Kesselring's crisis at the height of the battle for Rome. The division was still officially in reserve, with its headquarters near Pisa, but their Pioneer units had been ordered south to help lay mines along the Albert Line. They had initially been sent to Radicofani, just south of La Foce, but having completed their task discovered they were needed in the Roccastrada sector as well.

The SS had been formed by Hermann Göring in 1923, as a bodyguard for Hitler following his release from prison. Just eight chosen men had formed the original *Schutz Staffel*, or Protection Squad, and not until Heinrich Himmler took over as Reichsführer-SS in 1928 did the SS begin to grow and evolve into the massive organisation it would become. The Waffen-SS – or SS-Verfügungstruppe as it had originally been called – had begun development in 1934, a year after Hitler's rise to power, and was designed by Himmler to be an independent SS army, and an elite body of troops. Police duties or guarding concentration camps were not part of their remit: Waffen-SS units were to be placed in the front line of combat; and so they had been, winning a reputation for their fine standard of training and superior fighting qualities.

Standards had inevitably fallen as the war progressed but it was the Waffen-SS's elite status that had attracted nineteen-year-old Rudi Schreiber.* He had been born and brought up on a country estate in Posen on the German–Polish border. His father had been chauffeur and valet to Count von der Schulenburg. Both his father and the Count had survived the First World War and believed in traditional German imperialist military values; neither were enormous fans of Hitler. Nonetheless, the teenage Rudi had been happy enough to join the Hitler Youth and had risen to become the leader of his local troop. Various military units would visit them as part of a recruitment drive and it was after the visit of the Waffen-SS that Rudi was determined to volunteer for them. 'They were the best,' he says, 'and I wanted to be a part of that.'

Having volunteered when still only seventeen, he was not then called upon for training until after his eighteenth birthday in January 1943. 'My mother was very upset about me going off to war,' he says. 'She had prayed that it would have been over by the time I was of age.' Rudi, however, was excited, happy to be doing his bit for his country and to be joining such a prestigious unit.

Having joined the 2nd Company of the SS-Pioneer Battalion 16, Rudi's tasks were those of any sapper – mine laying, building defences and so on – but like Jupp Klein in the Fallschirmjäger, Rudi and his comrades were also expected to play a role as front-line troops when necessary, and it was while they were around Roccastrada that they came under fire from the Americans for the first time. Rudi had been impressed by the beautiful Italian countryside and the fireflies that shone in the dark at night, but as he readied himself for the night on 21 June, they suddenly heard an enemy patrol ahead of them. The Pioneers opened fire and the patrol disappeared, but two hours they later came under attack again, this time with tanks opening fire upon them. Packing up as quickly as they could, they fell back, but as they did so, Rudi was wounded in his right arm. 'It was only a flesh wound,' he says, 'but it was still bad enough for me to have to go to hospital.'

The next day the Americans pressed forward once more. But at Roccastrada, the tanks of the 1st Armored Regiment found themselves being

*Rudi Schreiber is not his real name; he has requested that his true identity be protected.

held up by what appeared to be one lone anti-tank gun. 'He's on this little ridge,' recalls Ray Saidel, 'in a tiny cemetery. We were coming over another ridge across the valley and he knocked out three of our tanks.' They were held up for quite some time, but when they eventually managed to go forward again, Ray went over to the cemetery and found the German gun still there. Beside the gun was a solitary German gunner, the top of his head completely shot away and surrounded by a pool of dark, congealed blood. 'I don't know if he had anyone else there with him when he was firing,' says Ray, 'but what impressed me was what a brave, brave soldier this guy was.'

Later, on that same day, 22 June, heavier shells began crashing around La Foce. A lull followed and a German sergeant came down to the cellar where Iris and other civilians were sheltering. 'You must get out,' he told them, 'and get the children away. You can't keep them here. And we need the cellar.' If they got going, he added, they might be able to get out of range during the current lull.

Confusion followed, with both Antonio and Iris besieged by terrified people asking them what they should do. There was only one answer: to get to Chianciano or Montepulciano, where they could hopefully find shelter. Hastily packing a basket of baby food and grabbing a pram filled with nappies and children's clothes, Iris also took a tiny case of underclothes and other small belongings. 'Each of the children carried his own coat and jersey,' she noted. 'The grown-ups each carried a baby, or a sack of bread. And so, in a long, straggling line, with the children clutching at our skirts, half walking, half running, we started off down the Chianciano road.'[168]

Before they had left, the Germans had warned them to keep well spread out so as not to make too obvious a target for Allied fighter planes, and to stick to the middle of the road to avoid mines, but the dangers seemed so numerous, Iris did not believe they would get all the children to safety. Shellfire had begun again, some nearby, some further off. Corpses lay uncovered by the roadside. Overhead, the sun blazed down upon them; but apart from the babies, not a child was crying.

At the top of the hill before Chianciano, they divided into two parties. Those who had friends or family in Chianciano headed on towards the town, while Antonio and Iris, leading the children and others, set off across country towards Montepulciano. There were now sixty of them in all, and with the mined road behind them, they made good progress until collapsing, exhausted, on a ridge behind La Foce. Iris began to worry once more. So much had been left behind: the unburied body of one of their tenants; their dogs; the house. After resting for as long as they dared, they set off again, Antonio taking a more dangerous road on which the pram could be pushed, and Iris leading the rest along a rough track that led up and down a series of steep gullies. Twice planes roared over and they crouched off the track until they had passed, but then they reached open wheat fields. The shellfire had begun again and just a few hundred yards below them they could see them exploding on the Montepulciano road. More planes came over and they once more crouched down, hiding themselves in the corn. 'I remember thinking at that moment,' noted Iris, 'with Benedetta lying beside me and two other children clutching at my skirts: This can't be real – this isn't really happening.'

They pushed on and eventually reached the Montepulciano road where they found a farm occupied by a German Red Cross unit. The Germans warned them not to go on to Montepulciano; by the following day, they said, it would be too dangerous. For a moment, Iris wavered, but with no food and no shelter, they had no choice but to continue towards the town.

Four hours later they were below Montepulciano, the town staring down at them from the hill above. Iris' doubts over what they were doing had begun to grow once more but then suddenly people began to appear. Having seen them from the ramparts, they were now coming down the hill to meet them and help them finish the final stretch of their journey. 'Never,' wrote Iris, 'was there a more touching welcome.' Many were partisans, others were refugees themselves, but they lifted the children onto their shoulders and in a triumphant procession they all climbed up into the walled town.

With Antonio and Iris acting as billeting officers, they managed to find homes for everyone. Every man, woman and child had made it. 'We have left behind everything that we possess,' wrote Iris, 'but never in my life have I felt so rich and so thankful as looking down on all the children as they lay asleep. Whatever may happen tomorrow, tonight they are safe and sound!'[169]

All along the front, the Allies were continuing to throw their massive superiority in fire power against the Germans. Covering the westernmost stretch of the line up to the Tyrrhenian coast was the rest of the 16th

Waffen-SS Division, brought out of reserve and now part of von Senger's 14th Panzer Corps.

At just after midnight on the morning of 26 June, Obersturmführer Willfried Segebrecht, commander of the 1st Company of the 16th Panzer Reconnaissance Battalion, was given his orders at the battalion command post. At long last they were going into action. 'Now it's finally happening,' he scribbled, 'but not as we armoured scout men had imagined, but like infantry.' He couldn't understand why his company, so highly trained, had to go into battle on foot. 'The troublesome driving, radio, and scouting training,' he noted, 'was for nothing.'[170] He couldn't help feeling rather depressed about it.

The trouble was that even new divisions to the theatre were struggling with the shortage of equipment. What Kesselring needed from all his men now battling along the Albert Line was for them to hold the Allies for as long as possible. So far, they had held out for five days – and for making a stand, gas-guzzling tanks, self-propelled guns, and half-tracks were not considered essential.

Along a twisting road between low-lying mountains, Willfried and his company wound their way south until they reached the tiny village of Belvedere and, at about four in the morning, began to organise themselves and move into position. Above, Allied reconnaissance planes swirled about – aircraft that would soon be directing fire onto Willfried and his men. The battalion was holding the front along a six-mile stretch to the coast, with Willfried's 1st Company in the middle holding Monte Calvi, an 1,800-foot mountain overlooking the Tyrrhenian Sea to the west.

With the US 36th Texas Division recently withdrawn, the rested 34th Red Bulls had now taken over the sector belonging to what had become the US IV Corps. Sergeant Bucky Walters and the 135th Infantry were in reserve, but assaulting up along the coast were two regimental combat teams, the 133rd and the 442nd, and despite the tenacity of the SS men, the American weight of fire soon proved too much.

From his command post on Monte Calvi, Willfried could hear heavy fighting going on in the 3rd Company's sector, which covered the Via Aurelia coast road. Immediately sending out a reconnaissance patrol to find out what was going on, they soon returned with two prisoners. 'These two were strong, good-looking soldiers, who didn't reveal anything except their names,' noted Willfried. 'They were well fed, had chewing gum in their mouths and didn't seem to be at all concerned about being taken prisoner.' For a while they sat with him, sharing their cigarettes until suddenly Willfried began to hear fighting to his rear. A call through to 3rd Company told him the worst: the Americans had broken through along the coast road and were threatening to overrun 3rd Company's position. 'The enemy is only 50 metres–20 metres from us,' the 3rd Company telephonist told him. 'Send us some help.' But Willfried couldn't help. If he pulled out with his company the whole of the front section would break up. 'Once again, on the telephone,' scribbled Willfried, 'the staff calls for Leader Wonderland One. That's us. Then, I only hear the noise of fighting, then silence. The telephonist had held the connection with me until the last moment and fell at his post.'[171]

By this time the Americans were attacking his own positions, both infantry and tanks swarming in front of him in the flat ground to the south of Monte Calvi. In the meantime, his first platoon was now being shot at from behind. To the left of the 2nd Company, the SS-Panzer Grenadier Regiment 35 had also been overrun, which had in turn forced back the 2nd Company. With both his fellow company commanders already dead, Willfried now faced the prospect of becoming completely encircled. After agreeing to cover the 2nd Company as they fell back, Willfried then began to make plans to lead his own company out. 'We are going to need luck to get out of this encirclement,' he scribbled. 'I order the few remaining vehicles to be blown. The tanks are getting closer but we have no possibility of fighting them because we have not got any anti-tank weapons.'

At around half-past four in the afternoon Willfried and his men began to fall back, heading straight across the mountainous and hilly terrain to the north. The two American prisoners were left behind, but flocking to his side were remnants of the 2nd and 3rd Companies and two companies of the 35th Regiment. He now had around two hundred men, hurriedly escaping through a gap between the two pincers of the Red Bull Division. The walking wounded did their best to keep up. One man, with a bullet through a lung, only reluctantly accepted a stretcher. Their route was extremely difficult – with no path and continually taking them over stony heights and then through deep gullies. And to make matters worse, the sun was beating down upon them viciously.

Despite this, Willfried refused to let heads sag, and by discarding everything but their weapons and ammunition, they finally reached the safety of battalion headquarters at around eight that evening. His commander, Sturmbannführer Walter Reder, was 'overcome with joy' to see them, having given them all up for lost. Willfried felt absolutely exhausted. Finding a small hollow, he and Untersturmführer Neuner, his deputy, set themselves down, and covering themselves with a towel and some straw, tried to sleep. 'We don't sleep well,' noted Willfried. 'Our nerves had been overstretched that day.'[172]

Meanwhile, in the east, II Polish Corps had finally caught up with the Germans, who were now defending the northern bank of the River Chienti, which flowed east to the sea some twenty miles south of Ancona.

The 27th of June was Wladek Rubnikowicz's Saint's Day, a personal date more important to Poles than their birthdays. Wladek was with his platoon on the south banks of the Chienti, when suddenly a despatch rider appeared with a parcel for him from the regiment CO, Major Bittner. 'To you on your Saint's Day,' read the note; 'I wish you and other officers best greetings and safe continuance in your future battles,' and with it was a bottle of whisky. Wladek was thrilled and immediately gathered his platoon around his armoured car and opened the whisky for them all to enjoy. At that same moment, enemy shells started screaming in. 'Lieutenant, lieutenant,' shouted Iwo Michalski, the youngest lad in his platoon, 'the whisky will be spilled!' Wladek grabbed the bottle. 'Fortunately,' he says, 'the whisky wasn't spilled. The bombardment stopped as suddenly as it started and we could continue to enjoy our drink.'

The following night, they were spread out along the southern bank of the Chienti. Wladek spent much time walking up and down between his men, checking everything was all right, and at one moment paused by the young Iwo Michalski, who was manning a Bren gun. Suddenly they both heard the distinct sound of breaking twigs. Both listened carefully and as the sound of movement grew nearer and nearer Wladek whispered to Iwo to load the machine gun. With the noise continuing to get closer, Wladek was about to give the order to open fire – and so reveal their position – when both men saw a cow making its way towards them from the direction of the river. 'Our mood lightened,' says Wladek, 'and we began to laugh.'

On 24 June, reports had reached Montepulciano that Allied troops were now at La Foce. That night Iris Origo slept well for the first time in ages. Three days later, more concrete news of their home reached her and Antonio, and it was better than they had dared hope: a few shells had landed around the house and in the garden but the villa itself was untouched. The same day, the South Africans took Chiusi. Dick Frost thought the town 'looked very battered'. The Royal Natal Carbineers did not stop, however, instead pushing on northwards, where Dick and the mortar platoon were soon busy again. 'We did a good deal of firing that evening,' he noted. Two of his mates were killed that night in ugly circumstances. Having put his hands up, a captured German then shot and killed them both. 'Andy Savage shot the Jerry,' added Dick, 'as well as two others with him.'[173]

'The Germans have gone at last!' noted Iris Origo on the morning of the 29th.[174] By the afternoon, the Scots Guards had arrived and the following morning the Coldstreamers took over, moving their HQ to a villa near the town gates. Reg Harris and his section were dug in 300 yards away along a terraced cherry orchard. His men were just helping themselves to some of the cherries when German artillery opened fire, their shells screaming over and falling around the new battalion head-quarters.

Reg thought little about it at the time as it was a substantial villa and the shellfire had not been heavy, but an hour later Major Crichton, the company CO, hurried up to him. 'Corporal Harris, I've got some bad news for you,' he said. 'Lieutenant Jones has just been killed.'

'Oh my God, no,' Reg replied.

'I'm afraid so,' said the CO. 'I knew you'd be upset, that's why I came round to tell you myself.'

Later, Reg found out what had happened. When the shelling had begun, 'Wacky' Jones had called a corporal away from the doorway, but then, inexplicably, had stood there himself. A moment later, a shell landed in front of him, killing him instantly. 'What a quite avoidable waste of life,' says Reg. 'I never got an officer of his calibre again.'

That same day, Feldmarschall Kesselring gave the order to withdraw completely from along the Albert Line. It says much for the tenacity of the Germans that with insufficient troops, guns and equipment, they were able to hold on for as long as ten days. Yet equally, the determination of the Allied troops, battering away at the German positions, was every bit as impressive. Despite having so many divisions out of the line, they had still forced Kesselring to pull back. All they needed now was the blessing of the Combined Chiefs of Staff: to be able to keep their forces intact and to go on and finish the job.

At his advance HQ, Alexander would not have to wait much longer for their verdict, for just two days later, on 2 July, the ANVIL debate finally came to a close.

TWENTY

The Politics of War

British intelligence officer Norman Lewis had been in Naples just over a fortnight when an extremely pretty, yet clearly malnourished, young girl had arrived at the offices of the British Field Security Service. He had seen her a few days before when he had gone to Aversa, a town a few miles north of Naples, to investigate reports by Italians that Allied deserters had assaulted them. As she had stood before him in the office, he had noticed she was shaking, her eyes downcast. Silently, she had handed him a letter – supposedly from her father, but, Norman guessed, almost certainly written on her father's behalf by the local priest. 'Sir,' it had read, 'I noticed when your honour was good enough to call that from the way you looked at my daughter she made a good impression on you. This girl, as you know, has no mother, and she hasn't eaten for four days. Being out of work, I can't feed my family. If you could arrange to give her a good square meal once a day, I'd be quite happy for her to stay, and perhaps we could come to some mutually satisfactory understanding in due course.'[175] The man was effectively offering to prostitute his own daughter; for her to become Norman's slave.

Norman had turned thirty-six on 28 June and was thus one of the older members of the 312th Field Security Service. Even so, in a comparatively short life he had already owned a chain of eight photography shops in London and the south of England, been a car dealer for Bugatti, had written several travel books, and had been sent to the Yemen as a spy for the Foreign Office. Married to a Sicilian wife, he spoke French, German, Russian, Italian and even Arabic, but despite these gifts had been denied a commission and sent to Field Security instead. Eventually posted to North Africa – where he had had the bizarre task of arresting his commanding officer for lunacy – he had eventually been posted to

Italy, arriving ashore at Salerno with the 312th Field Security Service attached to Fifth Army.

Despite this obviously colourful and eventful life, Norman had seen nothing to compare with what he had witnessed in southern Italy – the mad, messy tragedy of so many ruined lives like that of the shaking girl. That had been back in October the previous autumn, when Naples had returned to almost medieval conditions: large parts of it had been reduced to rubble by Allied bombs and then German air attacks and demolitions. There had been no water because the drains had been destroyed; no electricity because the power station had also been blown up; no food; no jobs, and disease had been rife.

Some of the debris had since been cleared and the water supply restarted, but after nine months of Allied occupation, Naples, a city that had been battered, browbeaten and abused, remained a truly grim place to be – that is, if you were Italian. Eric Sevareid noticed that along the waterfront, most of the buildings were windowless. The majority of Italians were dressed in little more than rags, unnoticed by the mass of Allied troops that filled the town. 'Even the children,' he noted, 'appeared grimed and ageing.'[176]

Allied food planners had aimed to distribute an average level of food of around 2,000 calories per person per day. In fact, had the March supplies of sugar and cheese arrived in Naples, civilians would have received just 615 calories a day. But they hadn't, and so the vast majority of people were forced to survive on even less. If most Neapolitans had the equivalent of a large chocolate bar a day – around 500 calories – they were doing well.

Since the Allies' arrival, the cost of living had rocketed by 321 per cent. The highest salary for an Italian civil servant in Naples was 5,496 lire a month, the equivalent of a little under £14. A postman, on the other hand, earned just 450 lire. This was an entirely normal, average, working-class salary – and equated to little more than £1 a month, or £30 by early twenty-first-century standards. With that, he was expected to feed his family – a wife, possibly five or more children and two or more grandparents. It simply could not be done.

If the black market was thriving in the north, it was positively rampant in the south, largely because Allied stockpiles of food were greater than those of the Germans or the Repubblica Sociale Italiana. On average, around 75 per cent of the available food in the south could only be found on the black market. According to the AAI's Psychological Warfare

Executive, 65 per cent of the per capita income of Neapolitans was derived from transactions in stolen Allied supplies, while an estimated one-third of all Allied supplies and equipment reaching Italy were stolen and resold on the black market.

Scavenging had become an art form. Neapolitans would head out of the city every day and comb the hedgerows looking for edible plants. In Naples, the city's aquarium had long since lost its fish, most of them eaten no matter how inedible. Stray dogs were liable to be knocked over the head and turned into stew, while rabbits hanging up in butcher's shops were always skinned and headless: Neapolitan butchers had discovered the casual observer could hardly tell the difference between a skinned and decapitated rabbit and cat.

With salaries so far below the cost of living, families were forced to go to greater lengths to survive. With a shortage of jobs but with southern Italy pullulating with Allied troops, there was one horrible yet obvious solution: prostitution. Soon after reaching Naples for the first time, Norman Lewis had stopped by a disused public building. Outside stood a truck full of Army supplies, and around it GIs were helping themselves to tins of food then hurrying inside. Norman followed them to discover a vast room 'with jostling soldiery' and a row of Italian ladies, about a yard apart, leaning against the walls. 'By the side of each woman stood a small pile of tins,' noted Norman, 'and it soon became clear that it was possible to make love to any one of them in this very public place by adding another tin to the pile.' Norman was amazed. 'The women kept absolutely still,' he added, 'they said nothing, their faces were as empty of expression as graven images. They might have been selling fish, except that this place lacked the excitement of a fish market.'[177]

Prostitutes were to be found in almost every street of almost every town in the south. There were plenty of AMG-approved brothels, but the numbers of 'official' prostitutes accounted for a small proportion of the total number who sold their bodies for sex. A report by the US Fifth Army Surgeon General revealed that Italian doctors claimed that by 1944 half the 'available' women in Italy had some form of venereal disease.[178] It was a staggering statistic.

The destruction of Italian transportation systems and power facilities, first by Allied bombers and then by the Germans during their retreat, contributed enormously to the south's woes: what food was still being produced was almost impossible to distribute. In the south, 75 per cent of Allied-occupied Italy's pre-war trains, 85 per cent of its coaches, 90 per cent of its trucks and lorries, and 87.5 per cent of its merchant fleet had been destroyed by the war.

There is no doubt, however, that politics and the system of government and administration imposed by the Allies also had much to do with the persistent problems that still dogged southern Italy by the summer of 1944.

It did not help that the plans for the administration of Italy had been drawn up by a number of 'desk wallahs' at Allied Forces Headquarters (AFHQ) in Algiers, away across the Mediterranean in northwest Africa – people who had no practical experience of military government, no understanding of Italy or what the administrative needs would be of a nation devastated by war and its accompanying destruction. Yet these bureaucrats had drawn up the structure of not only Allied Military Government of Occupied Territories (AMGOT), but also of the Allied Control Commission (ACC), the body that had been created to ensure that Marshal Badoglio's government conformed with Allied wishes.

The structure they had devised was as follows: Allied-held Italy was divided between that part directly run by military authorities – AMGOT, or AMG – and that transferred to the authority of the Italian government, known as the King's Italy. All forward areas were run by AMG, and then, as the front advanced up the leg of Italy, so territory was passed back to the Italian government. There was one exception – a small enclave around Naples remained exclusively under the control of AMG.

Always looking over the Italian government's shoulder, however, was the Allied Control Commission. This body had complete control over all Italian armed forces and war materiel and was authorised to exploit all southern Italy's resources to the full, and ensure the complete eradication of fascism. In other words, the Italian government had much the same power as the Repubblica Sociale Italiana in the north. Yes, they were free to govern as they wished, but just as long as they conformed precisely with Allied wishes. The Badoglio government had also been obliged to provide 180,000 men to be employed by the Allies in various services such as manual labour, and a further 45,000 for use in military rear areas. The Italians had furthermore been ordered to make available any Italian currency that the Allies might require, and to honour Allied military-issued lire; to hand over control of banking and business; and also any foreign exchange and overseas trade. As had been the case before the Risorgimento of 1870, it seemed that Italy had once more become a geographical concept only.

Overseeing all this was Allied Forces Headquarters and the office of General Jumbo Maitland Wilson, the Supreme Allied Commander. Not until 24 May had Wilson moved an advance HQ to the Reggio in Caserta; even at the beginning of July, AFHQ was, incredibly, still based well over a thousand miles away in Algiers, even though Italy was, by some margin, the largest theatre in the Mediterranean.

As C-in-C of Allied Armies in Italy, Alexander had been appointed Military Governor and thus head of the AMG. President of the Allied Control Commission, on the other hand, was General Jumbo Wilson, although the Deputy President, the British Lieutenant-General Sir Noel Mason-MacFarlane, was effectively in charge as Wilson was already busy being Supreme Commander. The former Governor of Gibraltar, Mason-MacFarlane was necessarily expected to work hand-in-hand with the AMG because there was, inevitably, a huge amount of crossover, such as over who ran port operations, railways, roads, civilian needs and food distribution.

As if there weren't already enough administrative bodies in Italy, there was a further organisation added to this already unwieldy apparatus: the Advisory Council for Italy, comprising representatives from the USA, Britain, Russia and Free France, and whose job it was to advise – though not dictate to – the Italian government.

No one was more critical of this confused behemoth of an administration than Britain's member of the Advisory Council (until the end of March at any rate) and Resident Minister at AFHQ, Harold Macmillan, who thought it 'ill-conceived, ill-staffed, and ill-equipped for purpose ... It is also overstaffed throughout.' He was not wrong. As early as October 1943, the Allied Control Commission alone numbered some 1,500 officers and a further 4,000 other staff. To make matters worse, those with any experience had also soon after been whisked off to Britain to plan for OVERLORD, leaving new and inexperienced staff in control.

One of the many by-products of this huge and confusing administration was the scandalous level to which the black market was soon operating. King of this racket in the Naples area and soon much of southern Italy was Vito Genovese, a mobster from New York who had in the 1920s and '30s worked for the notorious American gangster Lucky Luciano. In 1937, he had fled to his native Italy to avoid facing murder charges, and had subsequently declared himself a hard-line Fascist, become a friend of Mussolini, and Count Ciano's drug supplier. With the Allied landings, however, he had changed sides and ingratiated himself as a translator and guide to AMG officials.

This had given him precisely the kind of access he needed and in no time he had cornered the black market in the Naples area, tipping off officials about other black marketeers so he could get them shut down and take over their business. Norman Lewis was all too aware of Genovese and his illegal enterprise, and that the gangster was being protected by senior AMG officials. 'One soon finds that however many underlings are arrested,' he noted, 'those who employ them are beyond the reach of the law.'[179]

This was the problem with such a top-heavy organisation as AMG: it made life easier for corrupt officials to hide things – goods, documents, guilty parties – in a labyrinth of subsections and paperwork. It was why Colonel Charles Poletti, sometime Lieutenant Governor of New York, could get away with being a senior player in the black market whilst continuing to reassure his superiors that he was doing all he could to beat the racket. Previously the Senior Civil Affairs Officer in Palermo, he had then been appointed the Control Commission's Regional Commissioner for Campania, a remit that included Naples. Despite writing a report about black-market practices in the area and his efforts to clean it up, Poletti was up to his eyeballs in dodgy dealing, 'employing' as his number one guide and translator none other than Vito Genovese.

And while Italians were starving, thousands of men in uniform – the much-scorned 'base-wallahs' – were getting suntans and living very comfortably indeed. Eric Sevareid was appalled by the vast numbers of uniformed men who appeared to be doing little except waste public funds. 'PBS (Peninsular Base Section),' he wrote, 'became a hateful expression to the combat men. Sometimes they came back exhausted from the fronts to Naples on leave only to be arrested for failing to salute some officer on the crowded Via Roma.' On the island of Capri there was even a PBS Officers' Rest Camp. 'In Naples,' continued Eric, 'the base institutions seemed to expand without limits and to exist merely for their own existence. With each new batch of Red Cross girls, for example, more offices had to be found, more apartments, more cars and drivers, more cooks and servants.'[180] Italians should have been making good money with all this potential trade. But they weren't. Instead they were being tossed a tin of food for selling their souls.

*   *   *

It was much to the frustration of Harold Macmillan that not more was being done about the cumbersome administrative system in Italy, but despite being one of the most influential people in Allied-occupied Italy he had no official administrative role; rather, as Resident Minister at AFHQ and political *adviser,* he had no actual authority to make changes unless specifically instructed to so.

Like Churchill, Macmillan had an American mother and British father. Educated at Eton and Oxford, he later served with the Grenadier Guards with distinction on the Western Front, where he was wounded no less than five times. After the First World War, he married Lady Dorothy Cavendish, the daughter of the Duke of Devonshire, and initially joined the family publishing firm before entering politics and becoming a Conservative MP. His family by marriage might have opened many doors, but such was his consistent hatred of military appeasement and outspoken support for the unemployed that he remained consigned to the back benches for much of the 1930s.

Macmillan finally gained ministerial office in Churchill's wartime government, but it was not until he was posted to North Africa as second-choice Resident Minister at AFHQ that he began to make a name for himself with his obvious intelligence, deft diplomatic skills and apparent unflappability. A tall man with a slight frame and sloping shoulders, he wore flimsy round spectacles and ill-fitting suits, while a slightly untidy moustache did little to hide misshapen front teeth.

As such, Macmillan hardly cut much of a dash; and yet, in tandem with Robert Murphy, his counterpart at AFHQ, the two men had nonetheless brokered the armistice deal with Italy and had since become two of the most influential people in Allied–Italian politics. It had helped that the two were friends and worked well together; yet despite their growing expertise and experience, they had found their efforts were repeatedly hampered by what Macmillan considered unnecessary interference from outside and by differences in approach between America and Britain in particular.

One especially divisive issue was over the future of King Vittorio Emanuele III. At the time of the armistice, Churchill had pushed strongly for leaving the monarchy issue alone until after the fall of Rome. This had been accepted at the time, but as the months had dragged on and Rome had seemed as out of grasp as ever, this policy had been harder to justify, especially as a number of leading Italian politicians, exiled throughout the Fascist era, had now returned. One of these had been

Count Carlo Sforza, the former Italian Foreign Minister, and a man who had been a notable figure among Italians in America and a key player in the anti-monarchist Italian-American vote. With elections approaching in the US, Roosevelt had been anxious that Sforza should be handled with care.

Unfortunately, however, Sforza had made it blatantly clear that he wanted not only to force the King's abdication but also to take over from Badoglio as prime minister. Sure enough, the Americans had also begun calling for the King to fall on his sword. On the face of it, this might have been a sensible idea. After all, the King had behaved poorly during the armistice, fleeing Rome and lacking moral courage. He had also supported Mussolini for far too long and therefore was perceived to have been tarnished by fascism. On the other hand, the Italian navy and merchant navy, not to say the Corpo Italiano di Liberazione, had continued to fight under the banner of the King. 'We are not sure what would be the effect on all these people,' wrote Macmillan, 'of an abdication which was *not* voluntary, but enforced.'[181]

Also muscling in on the Italian political scene had been the Russians. Stalin had sent none other than Andrei Vyshinsky, the prosecutor of the Great Purges of the 1930s, to be the Soviet representative on the Advisory Council. Vyshinsky and his Russian colleagues wasted no time. Macmillan had noticed that most of Vyshinsky's vast Russian team had 'disappeared' soon after arrival, clearly to make contact with Italian Communists. Then, at the end of March, they had pulled out their trump card, returning to Italy the hugely influential Palmiro Togliatti, the exiled leader of the Italian Communist Party. Effortlessly, it seemed, they had turned the Italian Communists into a major political force.

Furthermore, they had contrived to drive a greater wedge between Britain and America's differences over policy in Italy. Churchill had still been clinging to his 'no change until Rome' policy, but the Russians were pressing for both the abdication of the King and a return to party politics, especially now that they had considerably strengthened the Communist Party in Italy. With none of the paranoia about communism that would later blight US policy, Roosevelt had instead been concerned to act decisively before the American elections, and so joined in with Russian demands.

It had been clear to Macmillan that the six parties of the clandestine CLN would soon have to be brought into formal government. His concerns, along with those of Churchill, had been that first, any change of government should still adhere to the conditions laid out by the armistice terms, and second, that any new government must agree to keep clear of the monarchy question until the whole Italian people could be consulted – in other words, until after the war.

Although the Advisory Council had approved Churchill and Macmillan's conditions, the path to a change in government had been made far smoother by Togliatti's sudden and unexpected announcement that the Italian Communist Party would also willingly enter the government without raising the issue of the King and the monarchy. It had been a smart move – albeit under orders from Moscow – because it had appeared magnanimous and had forced the hands of the other, less left-wing, parties of the CLN to follow suit. 'This Communist position makes the liberal and moderate parties very uncomfortable,' Macmillan had noted in his diary. 'On the one hand, they long to enter the government and would hate to see the Communists and socialists collar all the best jobs and all the best power; on the other hand, they have made so many speeches and uttered such brave words, that a lot of the latter would need to be eaten if they were to come along and join Badoglio.'[182]

Macmillan had begun to realise that a concession such as the promise of abdication would enable the other parties to enter government without too much loss of face. Macmillan had always advocated giving the Italians as much opportunity to govern themselves as possible, so that the Allies could get on with the job of winning the war, and also because he believed it was best for Italy's post-war future. 'If we can obtain a "broad-based democratic government" by a comparatively modest move by the King,' he had added, 'we are not entitled to demand a drastic one merely to please American voters. On the other hand, I should much like to get something which will please our allies and help the President to be re-elected.'[183]

In a nutshell, this was what had happened. On 10 April, he and Robert Murphy had duly gone to visit the King in Brindisi and had told him it would best if he were to announce his abdication there and then. The King had taken some persuading, but had eventually agreed to abdicate power but not his title: his son, Umberto, Prince of Piemonte, would become Lieutenant General of the Realm upon the Allied entry into Rome. With this agreed, Badoglio had duly formed a new six-party government, in which he had remained prime minister, but which included Togliatti, Count Sforza and other ministers from across the parties.

The abdication of power had taken place as agreed. A few days later, against Macmillan's advice, Badoglio and his Cabinet had been flown to Rome, where they had met with General Mason-Macfarlane, the nominal head of the Control Commission, and Ivanoe Bonomi and other party leaders within the Roman CLN. In the course of the meeting, Badoglio had been forced to step down, and backed by the majority of the CLN party leaders, it had been agreed that Bonomi – the last prime minister of the pre-Fascist era – should take over and form a new six-party government.

All had been well until Mason-Macfarlane declared that the appointment of Count Sforza as Foreign Minister would not be acceptable to the Allies. This was patently Churchill's own view on the matter, not that of Roosevelt or the Americans and prompted an outcry in the American press.

It had not been the first time Mason-Macfarlane had put his foot in it, and it was one of the prime reasons why Macmillan favoured placing politicians and diplomats in the senior administrative posts in Italy rather than military men. The upshot had been that Mason-Macfarlane had been forced to express to Bonomi that his views on Sforza's appointment were not those of the Americans. Much to Churchill's annoyance, Sforza had consequently remained in that post. 'Actually,' noted Macmillan, 'although the management of the Italian affair was certainly fumbling, the result was quite good.'[184] Bonomi was no radical, while his new cabinet introduced a younger generation of political leaders that added weight and depth to the new administration.

At the time of the armistice, the King's Italy had been consigned to a small corner of the heel of Italy. Now, a new broad-based party political government was in power, and controlling half the country. There was still precious little the new government could do without the approval of the over-staffed Allied Control Commission, and in that regard their authority remained undermined in similar ways to that of the RSI in the north. There were, however, two fundamental differences. In the south, Italy was now moving closer towards democracy. After all the intrigue and machinations of the past nine months, a consensus had been agreed which could provide the basis for Italy's future.

Perhaps more importantly, in the south, Italians enjoyed free speech. And however appalling the conditions were for the majority of Italians living there, they did, in theory, enjoy common rights denied to those living in the north. Eugenio Corti had realised this when, the previous

September, he had finally crossed over into Allied lines. 'I wondered if the British and Americans realised that behind their lines one could feel a respect for men,' he wrote. 'It felt like this whenever one saw notices where occupation troops threatened fines and at most jail sentences that on the other side were invariably punished with death. We would no longer hear talk of executions and more executions, and this fear – which makes man nothing more than a beast – would no longer hang over us.' And that was something at least.

TWENTY-ONE

Differences of Opinion

Having crossed the Chienti River on 20 June, II Polish Corps took the town of Macerata. Wladek Rubnikowicz, standing half out of the top of his armoured car as they processed through the town, had never seen such a welcome before. People lined the streets cheering and waving. 'The wine flowed,' says Wladek, 'they were so pleased the Germans had departed.'

Now accompanying the 12th Lancers was the American war correspondent, Martha Gellhorn. Eric Sevareid had left Italy for the Normandy front, but Martha was pleased to have reached this now secondary theatre, where she believed that because of its reduced status she might get more freedom to move around and better access to interesting stories. Fascinated by the strange polyglot nature of the Allied forces in Italy, she decided to attach herself to the Poles for a couple of weeks, an experience, she hoped, that would form the basis of a piece for *Collier's* magazine.

Martha was thirty-five, and already something of a name, known not only for her brilliant despatches and articles on the American Depression and the Spanish Civil War, but also for her marriage to the writer Ernest Hemingway. They had met in Spain, but her determination to pursue her career and so leave Hemingway for protracted periods had been the cause of bitter arguments and much resentment, and the marriage had begun to flounder.

Nor was she an accredited war reporter and, despite her work for *Collier's*, she had to use her wits to get herself into the firing line. Smuggling herself onto the first hospital ship to go to France, she had witnessed the D-Day landings and had even gone ashore onto Easy Red on Omaha Beach to help the field ambulance teams. This time, she had reached Italy by chatting up an RAF pilot in London who was about to fly back to Naples and agreed to give her passage.

'Blonde, tall, dashing,' *Collier's* wrote of her, 'she comes pretty close to living up to Hollywood's idea of what a big-league woman reporter should be.'[185] Certainly good looks and charm combined with her fierce determination and intelligence had helped her reach some of the world's most dangerous spots but, as with Eric Sevareid, it was her ability to express war in terms of the individuals who were taking part – and her evident compassion for these people – that made her such a popular and gifted writer.

Now with the Poles as they advanced ever nearer to Ancona, Martha attached herself to the men of Wladek Rubnikowicz's 2nd Squadron. Conversing in a scrambled pidgin form of English, French and German, she found she could understand them perfectly, and, it seemed, they her. Russia, and whether they would ever have a home to which they could return, was, she discovered, a primary topic of conversation, and she noticed they repeatedly tuned in on their radios to news of the Russians' offensive against Germany in Byelorussia on the Eastern Front, launched on 22 June, with avid, yet agonised, interest. Martha tried to reassure them that all would be well when the war was over. 'I tried to say I could not believe that this war which is fought to maintain the rights of man will end by ignoring the rights of Poles,' she wrote, then added: 'but I am not a Pole; I belong to a large free country and I speak with the optimism of those who are forever safe.'[186]

She listened to their stories, most as terrible and tragic as that of Wladek Rubnikowicz. There was the major who had been reprieved from a death sentence and had been made to act first as a servant to German NCOs and then as a slave labourer. He had escaped but had not heard anything from or about his wife in nearly five years. Another told her how his father had died in prison camp, and his mother and sister were still, as far as he knew, in a gulag in Russia. Another man, Chrostek, had just been given leave to marry a Polish nurse; his first fiancée had been killed by the Gestapo, having been tortured in an effort to get her to talk about the Polish resistance. 'It seemed to me,' wrote Martha, 'that no American had the right to talk to the Poles, since we had never even brushed such suffering ourselves.'[187] Her piece was never published by *Collier's*, its tone considered too critical of America's Russian allies.

General Mark Clark might have been convinced that Marshall had already won the ANVIL debate, but Alexander, for one, was not prepared to roll over quite so easily. And, as it happened, following the Combined Chiefs of Staff's talks in London, he had reason to believe there was still a sliver of hope, for although they had agreed the Italian campaign should be halted once Alex's forces reached the Gothic Line, still nothing concrete had been decided over the question of ANVIL. Rather, four possible amphibious landings were still being considered – two along the west coast of France, one at the head of the Adriatic along the Istrian coast, and finally one in southern France. On balance, when the talks finished on 14 June, the Combined Chiefs had favoured the west coast of France, which would not have required troops and materiel from Italy after all.

General Marshall, however, had no such doubts. At no point had the Combined Chiefs ever considered pushing further north than the Pisa–Rimini Line and he saw no reason for them to change their minds: once Alex's forces reached the Gothic Line, they would have achieved what they had originally set out to do and from then on, a holding position would be sufficient. More importantly, however, Eisenhower still needed a big port such as Marseille, and preferably Toulon as well, through which to feed troops and equipment waiting in America. Since Allied forces in France were currently being supplied by only one temporary floating harbour on the Normandy coast, there was some logic to this argument. Furthermore, there was every chance the French – or rather, De Gaulle – would refuse to allow his troops to continue fighting in Italy in any case. Nor was Marshall interested in becoming embroiled in the Balkans. At a dinner during his visit to Italy following the London talks, he said to Macmillan, 'Say, where is this Ljubljana? If it's in the Balkans, we can't go there.'[188]

Following this dinner, however, Alex took Macmillan aside and asked him to go to London immediately to press his case to the Prime Minister for continuing the all-out offensive in Italy. The two had become great friends: Alex trusted Macmillan implicitly, while Macmillan's respect for Alex as a commander knew no bounds. 'We talked the whole thing over for an hour,' noted Macmillan, 'he explaining the strategical and tactical aspects with his usual simplicity but with quite a new vigour.'[189]

Alex knew that Kesselring's armies were a beaten force. This was self-evident from the way in which even new divisions like the 16th Waffen-SS were being knocked back by the severe lack of essential equipment with which to fight a modern war. Alex also had copies of intercepts that revealed the degree of German losses since 11 May. With this information, he realised that Kesselring was going to try and hold a 180-mile line with a fighting force equating to merely ten to twelve divisions. In contrast, and providing his present forces were left intact, he would be able to amass such a powerful force of men and overwhelming fire power that there was little to stop him splitting Kesselring's forces in half and annihilating them once and for all. Nothing, he believed, could then prevent him from marching on Vienna, unless Hitler chose to send at least ten or more fresh divisions to Kesselring's aid. 'If this should be the German course of action,' he wrote to Churchill, 'I understand it is just what is required to help OVERLORD. I believe we have here and now an opportunity of delivering such a defeat on the German Army as will have unpredictable results and such a change must not be missed at this stage of the war.'[190]

Macmillan, accompanied by Jumbo Wilson's British Chief of Staff, General Gammell, arrived in London on the afternoon of 21 June, and that evening they went to see Churchill. The PM was in bed in his annexe to the war rooms in Whitehall, and although Macmillan reiterated all that Alex had told him, it was clear that Churchill needed little convincing. At meetings with the Chiefs of Staff over the next couple of days, however, the Chief of the Imperial General Staff was less won over. Brooke, with his usual clear-headedness, pointed out that even on Alex's most optimistic reckoning, the advance towards Trieste would not start until some time in September, which would mean fighting through the Alps in the autumn. No matter how slight German opposition might be by then, to attack through the mountains in winter was, Brooke felt, a recipe for disaster.

He had a point. In many ways, Alex's talk of reaching Vienna was something of a red herring – and possibly an unfortunate one at that, because rather than opening the eyes of the Combined Chiefs to the far-reaching opportunities that might be achieved, talk of the Ljubljana Gap merely exacerbated American suspicions about British designs on the Balkans. Nor was anyone at this stage thinking about the post-war implications with regard to the Soviet Union and its influence in Eastern Europe.

Far more convincing was his argument of drawing yet more German troops to Italy and of benefiting from the capture of the industrial cities of the north and airfields even closer to Germany. It was another intercept, this time of Hitler's earlier orders to Kesselring to make a stand to the south of the Gothic Line, which persuaded Brooke that the war in

Italy was worth continuing. Despite American claims that German forces would probably simply cut and run in the face of a further sustained Allied attack – which would do little to help Eisenhower – there was now no doubt that, on the contrary, they intended to stand and fight.

The decision that faced the Combined Chiefs came down to this: what course of action would give the best chance of helping the Allies in Normandy? Was it a potentially problematic amphibious landing in southern France? Or continuing an all-out attack in Italy? The former would open up key ports and allow a direct flow of troops and equipment into France. It could not, however, be launched until mid-August, more than six weeks away, and troops would not be able to build up in any strength until some weeks after that. Alex's campaign, on the other hand, was already in full flow, with morale, as he had stressed, high amongst his forces. A renewed, massed, offensive would undoubtedly draw more German troops away from both Russia and northern France with more immediate effect than any future landing in the south of France. It is hard to see how anything less than a major German reinforcement of Italy could possibly prevent the Allies from completing their victory in Italy. They had both fire power and momentum in their favour; and with that being the case, there would be little to stop them from crossing into France instead, which, unlike the northeast, could not be so easily reinforced from Austria. Nor would an assault through the French Alps have the same emotional or material effect on Hitler. After all, France was not Austria; and nor did southern France contain the oil reserves of the Balkans, which were so crucial to Hitler's war effort.

The British were convinced that the latter course was the right one, but as far as the Americans were concerned, the matter was now closed. The American chiefs had effectively passed the casting vote to Eisenhower, who made his decision based largely on an appreciation by Jumbo Wilson, his opposite number in the Mediterranean. Wilson, through loyalty to both Alex and the British chiefs, had publicly come round to favouring a continuation of the Italian campaign, but privately he supported ANVIL. This came across all too obviously in his letter to Eisenhower, in which he failed to make any comment about Hitler's determination to continue the fight in Italy and the implications that this had for the battle in Normandy. Instead, he talked of the opportunities that could be gained from an advance towards 'southern Hungary'.[191] Unsurprisingly, Eisenhower gave his wholehearted support to the invasion of southern France.

On 26 June, the British outlined their arguments in a telegram to the Americans – which were flatly rebutted. So too were Churchill's pleas to Roosevelt. Fear of becoming embroiled in the Balkans continued to prey on the President's mind. 'Finally,' wrote Roosevelt to Churchill, 'for purely political considerations over here, I would never survive even a slight setback in Overlord if it were known that fairly large forces had been diverted to the Balkans.'[192]

Distraught, the Prime Minister sent off one further telegram, an impassioned argument begging the President to reconsider. But Roosevelt was not to be swayed, and returned to the old American argument that once the Allies smashed the Gothic Line, the Germans would be sure to simply retreat further north and beyond reach. Nor did he want to further dissipate Allied forces into a new theatre in the Balkans. 'I always think of my early geometry,' he concluded. 'A straight line is the shortest distance between two points.'[193]

Having got the better of the Americans so often over matters of strategy, the British now had to concede defeat. On 2 July, the Combined Chiefs issued a new directive to Jumbo Wilson, ordering him to launch ANVIL by 15 August at the latest.

On 1 July, Harold Macmillan, newly arrived back from London, went to see Alex at the C-in-C's advance HQ on the banks of Lake Bolsena and found him in his usual imperturbable good humour. The final verdict from the Combined Chiefs had not reached Alex's camp, and so on the afternoon of 2 July the two of them took a brief break from the war to have a look around Orvieto cathedral, fortunately undamaged by the fighting when it had passed through the town a couple of weeks before. Back at advance HQ, they had taken an American DUKW amphibious vehicle out for a turn around the lake, enjoying the quiet summer evening air. Only on their return did Alex find a telegram informing him that ANVIL was on and that he was to return to London at once.

Immediately, the C-in-C began thinking whether he could possibly scrape together more forces. The situation was actually worse than it had been the previous autumn, because not only had he now lost seven divisions – the heart of Clark's Fifth Army – but also a significant number of additional armoured and engineer battalions, eleven artillery batteries, and a large number of anti-aircraft units. Furthermore, he was to lose 70 per cent of the Mediterranean Allied Tactical Air Force. Perhaps, though, more aircraft could be gleaned from Coastal Command; one or maybe two divisions from the Middle East; maybe even another two Italian divisions could be used. Surely on Gibraltar and Malta there were troops that could now be spared?

He knew he could no longer expect too many divisions from America, although news soon arrived that both a Brazilian division and the first American all-black infantry division, the 92nd, were on their way. Hoping for large-scale economic aid from the US, Brazil had declared war on Germany back in August 1942 after a U-boat had sunk five Brazilian merchantmen. The country's contribution thus far had been negligible and Clark doubted how good its troops would be. The 92nd Division was similarly untested in combat. Britain, he knew, would have been more willing to send fresh divisions to join Fifth Army, but as he was well aware, its manpower resources had pretty much dried up. As early as the previous autumn, all the men and women of Britain had been fully absorbed into the war effort. More young men – and women – would come of age, but essentially there were no longer any untapped sources of additional supply. The demands for manpower, however, were still increasing, which meant that other areas – such as industry – had to be reduced. This in turn meant a lowering of British production levels, which then led to an even greater dependency on American industrial muscle. The price for this was loss of influence, as the ANVIL debate had proved.

Mark Clark was conscious of Britain's manpower problems and repeatedly grumbled to his diary that Eighth Army was for ever trying to make Fifth Army take the brunt of the casualties so as to preserve its own. Even after news of the withdrawal of VI Corps and French divisions, he was still chuntering about what he believed was Eighth Army's unwillingness to take casualties. 'I must tell Alexander,' he noted on 19 June, 'that in the light of these withdrawals, he must have the Eighth Army carry the ball from now on.' This was obviously a grossly unfair comment since for the first two weeks of the battle, Eighth Army had faced the brunt of Kesselring's forces. Furthermore, since following Fifth Army in the easier, open countryside north of Rome, XIII Corps had quickly caught up.

Yet casualties and the shortage of manpower certainly preyed on the minds of the British commanders. Alexander admitted as much to Clark at the height of the battle when he confessed his need to reduce losses. Leese, too, made repeated references to casualties, and his hopes of keeping figures down in his diary and letters. 'I think,' wrote Leese to

Montgomery in July, 'that the American outlook towards casualties is different to ours. They have an inexhaustible supply of manpower, and it seems to me that they treat their man-power as a mass-production commodity in the same way as they do their vehicles and guns.'[194]

Regardless of manpower difficulties, Alex would now have to continue the campaign in Italy with what resources were left to him. His new directive was drawn up by Jumbo Wilson on 3 July, instructing him to advance through the Apennines and reach the River Po in the northern plains. From there he was directed to continue his advance north of the Po. In other words, his brief was much the same as he himself had outlined to General Wilson et al. on 7 June: the destruction of the German forces was thus to continue. The only difference was that now he had a far smaller force and a drastic cut in air forces with which to complete the task. And with those losses, the momentum, soaring confidence, and drive that had empowered the Allied forces in Italy, had drifted away on the hot summer air.

And yet, in a way, the ANVIL decision had come as something of a relief. Clark had expressed his concern over the debilitating effect on morale the ongoing uncertainty had been causing his troops, something that Alex had felt keenly too. 'Now that we knew finally where we stood,' he noted, 'and what our resources would be, we were at least free from the doubts and indecisions of the past month and could develop our strategy to suit our strength.'[195]

It was now of urgent importance to reach the Gothic Line as quickly as possible in order to give themselves enough time before the end of the summer to crack the now formidable Gothic Line defences. Kesselring had fallen back from the Albert Line, but had halted again precisely in order to delay reaching the Gothic Line for as long as possible. As Alex was losing his balance, Kesselring was slowly but surely regaining his.

Although still concerned about AOK 14 – despite having Lemelsen in command and von Senger as his senior corps commander – Kesselring was nonetheless pleased with the way his front was stiffening. A weight had also been lifted from his shoulders following a visit to see Hitler. Orders had been repeatedly arriving from the German High Command ordering him to stand firm and not give an inch of ground, and so with Beelitz, now his Chief of Staff, he had flown to the Führer's headquarters in an effort to explain the situation in Italy to them in person. After

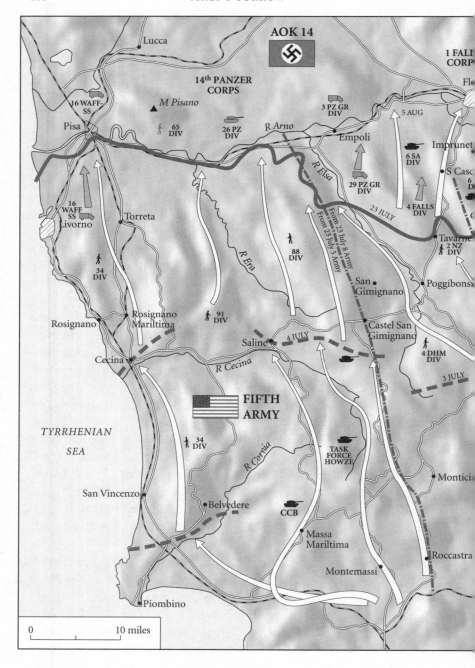

From the Albert Line to the River Arno, July/Aug. 1944

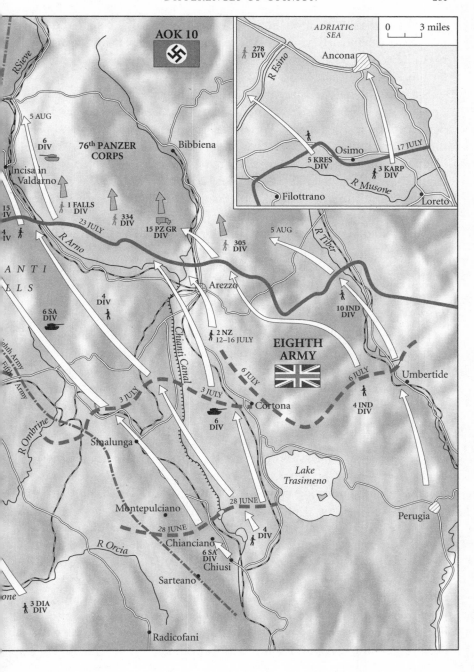

speaking for more than an hour he ended by insisting he should be given a free hand. Hitler replied in equal length, repeatedly trying to make Kesselring accept principles of strategy that were possibly applicable to Russia, but not Italy.

'The point is not whether my armies are fighting or running away,' Kesselring told him, his frustration rising. 'I can assure you they will fight and die if I ask them. We are talking about something entirely different, a question much more vital: whether after Stalingrad and Tunis you can afford the loss of yet two more armies.' This would surely happen, Kesselring assured him, if Hitler continued to insist he give up not an inch of ground, with the consequence of opening the way for the Allies into Germany. On the other hand, if he was left to his own devices, Kesselring told him that he was prepared to guarantee delaying the Allied advance appreciably, to halt it for as long as possible in the Apennines and thereby maintain the campaign through the winter and into 1945. 'Hitler said no more,' noted Kesselring, 'or rather, he muttered a few words which, according to Beelitz, were not uncomplimentary. Anyhow, I had won my point.'[196]

Following his withdrawal from the Albert Line, Kesselring planned to continue his delaying tactics. His plan was simple: to stand and fight, then fall back a few miles, then stand and fight again. The key was to make a stand long enough to force the Allies to deploy and make a prepared assault, and then to withdraw just at the point when the enemy weight of fire became too much.

It was a tactic that would certainly buy him time, but was costly too, and says much about Kesselring's ruthless determination and ability to hold his nerve that he never once wavered. Still poorly equipped and fragile after the punishing fighting of May and June, Kesselring's forces were far from being out of the woods: they had lost well over 80,000 men since the beginning of May. And with casualties mounting once more, both Lemelsen and von Vietinghoff repeatedly expressed their concerns to Kesselring about the strain it was placing on their forces. Certainly for junior commanders – men like Willfried Segebrecht or Georg Zellner – these tactics seemed inexplicably foolhardy. 'If only we would retreat 60kms,' wrote a despairing Georg Zellner, 'we'd be sitting in the mountains and we could defend ourselves properly. But no. It's prestige, and the divisions are the victims of this.'[197]

Georg did not appreciate, however, that the Gothic Line was not yet finished – at least, it was not yet as strong as Kesselring wanted. Nor had he realised that however difficult and exhausting these delaying tactics were to perform, they were quite definitely the best way to slow down the Allies' advance. And in Italy in the summer of 1944, time was of the essence.

TWENTY-TWO

Summer Heat
July 1944

As the summer progressed and supplies, agents and liaison officers from both SOE and OSS continued to help the partisans, so armed resistance against the Germans and Neo-Fascists became noticeably more effective. In the mountains of Romagna, south of Forlì, the 8th Garibaldi Brigade had learned much since their near-annihilation back in April. Now well organised and with good supplies of weapons and equipment, they were an altogether different outfit from the idealistic yet ill-disciplined band that had been so nearly destroyed three months before.

Commanding the 2nd Battalion was Iader Miserocchi who, with his men, was operating in a zone along the River Savio between the small towns of Sarsina and Bagno di Romagna. It was a stretch of about fourteen miles, but a key one because along the river ran an important road that offered a significant German supply line south to the front. Barely a truck or car could pass down the road without Iader and his men knowing about it, and with their new weapons they had been able to attack and snipe at any enemy columns that appeared and make raids on GNR barracks and any small units of militia which dared risk entering their territory. Meanwhile the other Garibaldi battalions, operating in the Bibente Valley to the west and elsewhere in the mountains, were carrying out much the same kind of operations.

Gone too were the Communist red scarves. 'By around June,' says Iader, 'we were conscious that red was visible from far off.' Instead, many now wore bits of British army uniforms – trousers, shirts, and battle blouses. 'And boots,' adds Iader. 'Boots were the scarcest and most important thing.' As 2nd Battalion commander, Iader would be in regular contact with the brigade commander, Pietro Mauri, meeting once or perhaps twice a week. Otherwise contact between the brigades was maintained by *staffette* – female messengers – or even by letter. The Garibaldi

Brigade headquarters was based at the tiny mountain hamlet of Pieve di Rivoschio, but no one slept in the same place for more than one night at a time. It was an incredibly tough life, with few creature comforts, pitiful amounts of food, and the threat of death hanging over every individual. It was even worse for Iader, who, since April, had been suffering from pleurisy and struggling with daily fevers.

Yet the fact that the 8th Garibaldi Brigade was now some 1,400 strong and operating in an organised and well-structured manner was largely due to Bruno Vailati (or Italo Morandi, his real name), their military instructor. A former student in Bologna, 'Bruno' had been staying with friends in Santa Sofia when the armistice had been signed. Rather than facing the draft, he had joined some escaped British POWs and made his way south and across Allied lines. From there he had gone to Bari, the headquarters of SOE Italy, to be trained as an agent for No 1 Special Force. After the April rastrellamento, Bruno had been dropped into the Romagna Mountains along with a radio-telegraphist and had begun the task of turning around the fortunes of the 8th Brigade, organising supply drops and imparting to the partisans the basics of guerrilla warfare.

On 17 July, however, a large-scale rastrellamento involving more than a 3,500 German and Italian troops was launched against them, part of Kesselring's operation to clear the Apennines of partisans before he fell back to the Gothic Line. Attacking down the two main roads through the mountains, one in Iader Miserocchi's zone along the Savio, and one down the Bidente Valley towards Santa Sofia, the mixed force of German and Republican troops soon came under fire from partisans. However, since April, they had learned not to engage an enemy in force and so having taken a few pot-shots, they disappeared into the mountains. Despite remaining in the area for several days, the mixed German-Fascist force was unable to flush out the guerrillas.

But although the partisans had survived virtually unscathed, the Germans and Italians had reacted strongly against the local civilian population, burning buildings and executing civilians. In the Colle del Carnaio, in Iader's zone, twenty houses were burned and twenty-six men and one boy were strung up and hanged. In Santa Sofia, at the heart of the 8th Brigade's territory, thirty men were subsequently taken hostage and the population warned that for every German killed from then on, twelve hostages would be executed. In the village of Tavolicci, GNR troops had swept in and massacred sixty-four people, of whom nineteen had been under the age of ten.

If this had been designed to frighten the civilian population from helping the partisans, it was working. 'Our aim,' pointed out Bruno Vailati shortly after the rastrellamento, 'is to inflict on the enemy the maximum possible damage.' What bothered him was that their actions were not causing too many problems for the Germans. As he pointed out, over the past month, the entire Brigade had killed only thirty-odd Germans and Italian Fascists and destroyed as many vehicles. 'You will agree with me,' he added, 'that all of this does not represent serious damage for a military organisation such as the German one.'[198] By the end of July, the local population, upon whom they relied so heavily for survival, was reeling from the severe measures carried out by the German and Italian Fascist forces in retaliation for the partisans' activities.

With this in mind, Bruno now proposed a series of measures. For the time being, he suggested, they should avoid the kind of guerrilla action that would most likely provoke a reprisal. It was the Germans, not the Italian Fascists, they had the most to worry about. With that in mind, he recommended they stop actions against small isolated columns of German vehicles. Instead, they should concentrate on acts of sabotage: blowing bridges and roads, making it impossible for traffic to pass – all of which made life very hard for the Germans but did not need to involve killing any of their troops. To perform such actions effectively, he proposed further training.

Attacks on Italian Fascists, on the other hand, should be actively stepped up. 'You will see,' he wrote, 'that the Germans will not be troubled by the killing of a Fascist or a spy by one or two partisans. Without the support of the Germans, the Fascists will do little.' The key was to make Fascists live in fear of their lives anywhere within the partisans' operational area. 'I think that this psychological aspect of our activity can continue with a minimum of actions on our part,' he continued. 'Such actions do not occupy the majority of our manpower, and, being aimed exclusively towards Fascists, they are less likely to provoke German reprisals.'[199] While the 8th Garibaldi Brigade were fortunate to have someone like Vailati to train them in the use of explosions and detonation and other guerrilla tactics, most partisans further south at this time were less well organised and had to rely on former soldiers – both Italian and former POWs – to provide them with rudimentary training. Mark Clark had come across a number of partisans within a couple of miles of German rearguards during a trip to the front. Pausing to talk to them, Clark was told that they been harassing the enemy retreat and had killed a number of Germans. What, Clark asked, could he do to help them? 'There are many things we need,' the leader of the band replied. 'We are trying to bury the dead and to police the area. We need medical supplies and food.'[200] The American commander told them he would do what he could. Clark recognised that the partisans had already proved a great help. With the sudden cut in Allied troops, they could soon become invaluable.

The Stella Rossa had certainly been playing its part, and by July it was causing serious havoc along German supply lines down the Setta and Reno Valleys. Nonetheless, it was in July that Lupo and the band faced a major crisis, and it was one entirely of their own making. For some time, the local branch of the CLNAI in Bologna, the Comando Unico Militare Emilia-Romagna (CUMER), had been urging Lupo to move the Stella Rossa away from Monte Sole entirely, so as to avoid the risk of reprisals against the civilians living there. Lupo, however, had refused: Monte Sole was his home, it was a place he knew intimately, and furthermore, he resented the interference of CUMER.

One evening, in direct defiance of CUMER, he ordered the entire brigade to head to Monte Sole itself, but one group, led by Sugano, one of the original founders of the Stella Rossa, refused. A heated discussion broke out and even shots were fired; one bullet narrowly missed hitting Lupo. Eventually, a resolution of sorts was agreed, and Sugano, along with quite a large number of men, decided to break away from the Stella Rossa and join the Modena Division of partisans instead.

Carlo Venturi was tempted to go with Sugano, but after much soul-searching decided to stay with the Stella Rossa. He, too, felt a sentimental attachment to Monte Sole and in any case, his family at Casalecchio were nearby; should the worst come to the worst, he wanted to be able to reach them easily. Even so, Carlo was far from happy. Life as a partisan was beginning to get to him. It was hardly surprising. Still a teenager, he missed his family, felt intimidated by the constant danger and atmosphere of suspicion, and like many in his situation, wished he could spend a night in a proper bed rather than sleeping rough. Being an outlaw was tough indeed.

For the most part, Allied front-line troops had little to do with partisans. Unfortunately, it was often only the unburied dead that they did see, as Reg Harris discovered. The 3rd Coldstream Guards were pushing north into Chianti in July, the men often advancing and digging in as many as three times a day. One morning, however, Reg was told that they would most likely be in their current position for at least twenty-four hours, as ahead was a steep hill, terraced to the summit and held by German troops. Support would be needed before they tackled it.

Reg had just finished digging his slit trenches when he became conscious of a terrible smell. Looking around, he discovered the bodies of four civilians. Soon after an Italian approached him and told him the dead men were all partisans, and that the one nearest Reg's trench had been his brother. Reg offered to dig a shallow grave and the Italian helped him, telling him he would move his brother and bury him properly once the front had moved forward.

Having dug an eighteen-inch deep hole in the ground, Reg gathered two bits of wood and slipped them under the dead partisan's body and with the help of the brother, lifted him up. No sooner had they done so, however, than the body split in half. 'The result can be imagined,' says Reg, 'and with thousands of maggots rolling out my helper let out a scream that I'll always remember, and dropping his end of the sticks he took to his heels and was off like a greyhound.' There was nothing for it but to finish the job on his own. Much to his annoyance, no sooner had he completed his grisly task than the company was told they would be attacking the hill right away after all.

While the 12th Tactical Air Command was moving to Corsica in preparation for the invasion of southern France, the Desert Air Force continued to operate from Italy. Now based at Perugia, 244 Wing were as busy as ever, and in their new role as fighter-bombers were realising that flak was often a greater threat than the most talented enemy fighter pilots.

On 10 July, Cocky Dundas was leading a formation of Spitfires on an interdiction mission near Arezzo. Suddenly he felt a massive thud as a burst of 88mm flak exploded beside him and several pieces of shrapnel hit his aircraft. One piece had punctured his glycol tank, the radiator coolant, and not for the first time in this war he found his cockpit rapidly filling with white smoke.

Immediately jettisoning his bomb, he pulled the plane into a diving turn and at the same time, reached up to open his canopy. Unfortunately, the force of a 240mph wind behind it slammed it back again just as Cocky was looking up, so that the metal strip at the front slashed him across the face. The smoke was now chokingly thick, so although not a little dazed, he pushed his elbow with all his might against the canopy and this time, forced it up and away.

Cocky was frightened. There was plenty of time to contemplate all manner of terrible ends, but not much time in which to get himself to safety, especially with his engine temperature rising rapidly. Below, the rugged Tuscan countryside looked like a disastrous place in which to try and force land. However, with luck, he might just be able to reach Castiglione airfield on Lake Trasimeno.

Setting his course, he nonetheless feared his chances of making it were slim. The alternative was to bail out, a prospect he dreaded. The miles slid by. His temperature gauge continued to rise towards the danger mark. Then, away in the distance, he spotted through the haze the silvery waters of Lake Trasimeno. Clinging to every foot of height he could, he chugged on, the needle now rising over and above the danger mark.

Then, with a wave of relief, he knew he would be all right, as he had the height to glide the last few miles. Lowering the undercarriage, he cut the engine, switched off the petrol and glided through the Italian sky, landing calmly on the Castiglione runway. 'I sat still and listened to the lovely silence,' noted Cocky. 'Then I put up my hand to unclip my oxygen mask and found that my face was sticky with blood.'[201] An ambulance came over to his stricken plane, but instead of going straight to the medical officer, Cocky first headed to the officers' mess tent for a large brandy. With that inside him, and his face stitched up, he was fine. Once again, fortune had smiled upon him.

Throughout July, the Allies continued to push steadily north, the Germans continuing their delayed retreat in accordance with Kesselring's instructions: fall back, stand, fight; fall back, stand, fight. Retreating through the Tiber Valley was Georg Zellner and his 3rd Battalion of the H und D Regiment. By 6 July, they had reached the hamlet of Trevine. By the afternoon of the 8th, the enemy had caught up and had begun shelling Georg's position. On the 9th, the shelling grew heavier; there were signs that the enemy were preparing to attack. 'One gets nervous,' he admitted. 'We talk about the progress of the war. The whole thing is excessively sad and what will be the end of it? We don't dare to think about that. Our own aerial fire is shooting like mad. We have to hold out.'

Sure enough, the following day the 10th Indian Division attacked, breaking through on Georg's left. In the evening, Georg's men retreated

again, this time a couple of miles to Monte Santa Maria Tibernia.
Throughout 11 July, Georg and his men dug in; the Indians attacked
again on the 12th. 'The enemy continues to advance and at 1600 hours
is standing on my neck,' wrote Georg. 'On the right hand side, scattered
soldiers are retreating.' By evening, Santa Maria was surrounded; hiding
with his command post until darkness, Georg and his staff then slipped
back a further mile to another farming hamlet, Cagnano. Until 5 a.m.,
he was busy checking his battalion into their new positions. During the
day, two Indian reconnaissance patrols were forced back, but the following day, the 14th, the enemy attacked again. 'Once again,' scribbled
Georg, 'we have to hold our position and it's a bad one . . . Enemy
troops come ever and again. Towards 0200 hours, there's a great mass
of troops in front of our hollow. We shoot through every peep hole.
This carries on the whole night. In the few pauses we play poker in
order to take our minds off things.'

Somehow, they managed to hold their attackers off. Plagued by mosquitoes and eaten alive by lice, he had at least finally received three
letters from his wife and one from his daughter, causing him 'great
happiness'; even in such hectic fighting, letters *could* reach the front.
Then came a glimmer of hope. Word reached him that he had been
recommended for the German Cross, a high award for valour, and also
that he had been selected to take part in a regimental leadership training
course. This meant that in a few days he would be gone. His excitement
was mixed with worried pessimism: the news was probably a mistake,
he told himself; and anyway, he knew too many people who had been
killed just before they'd been due to leave the front; the same was bound
to happen to him.

As the enemy attacks continued at Cagnano, Georg knew they could
not hold out much longer. 'Nerves are at breaking point,' he scrawled.
A bet was made with the adjutant – two crates of *sekt* that his transfer
would not work out. By the following morning, he was still alive, but
enemy air attacks were increasing, and the shelling heavier. He now had
just twenty-four hours to survive. The hours ticked by, the Indians
continuing to attack and paste the German positions with shell and
mortar fire.

Then at 6 p.m., the unbelievable finally happened: after saying his
farewells, Georg left his command post and the front line. His ordeal,
for the time being, was over.[202]

*   *   *

General Alexander had returned from London on 11 July, and Ion Calvocoressi had been sent down from Leese's Tactical HQ to collect him and General Harding from the airfield at Castiglione on the edge of Lake Trasimeno. Both men, Ion thought, seemed to be in good spirits, despite the drastic changes that were about to take effect thanks to the invasion of southern France. 'We now have to take over the whole French Corps sector,' noted Ion, 'which means that our front stretches over 4/5 of Italy.'

The French were due to come out of the line for good on 22 July, but before that fateful day, General Juin held a grand parade in Siena – which his troops had taken on the 3rd – to mark the 14 July Bastille Day celebrations. General Leese, accompanied by Ion, had arrived on time and had been ushered to a makeshift stand at the bottom of the Piazza del Campo. Clark, however, was half an hour late and when he did eventually arrive, pulled into the square in a long cavalcade of jeeps before stepping from an immaculate looking limousine adorned with the American flag on one wing and three stars on the other. It was the kind of ostentation Clark took as a given, but which to Leese seemed unnecessarily vulgar. Since protocol dictated that neither Alex nor Juin arrive before Clark, they then followed after the Fifth Army commander, and took their place on a rostrum in the centre of the piazza to watch the parade.

To Leese's great indignation, he was not asked to join them on the rostrum, and for this perceived slight, blamed Clark entirely. In a state of high dudgeon, Leese and his ADCs left before the ceremony was over. 'Mark Clark behaved with his normal rudeness,' noted Ion, leaping to his boss' defence. 'He has no manners and is so jealous of the 8th Army that he always tries to humiliate it.'

In fact, the parade had been Juin's show, not Clark's, and in many ways it was perfectly reasonable to have only his Army Group and Army Commander with him on the rostrum. Some explanation to Leese, however, might have been a good idea. Unfortunately, Leese was already feeling particularly ill-disposed towards the Fifth Army commander after Clark's ungracious behaviour in the immediate aftermath of the fall of Rome. The rumours of British troops being threatened on pain of death if they attempted to enter the city on 4 and 5 June had spread like wildfire around Eighth Army. Leese also had felt slighted by Clark's unwillingness to mention Eighth Army in any communiqué about the capture of Rome. Clark, however, had believed that he was behaving in

just the same way Eighth Army had done during the first six months of
the campaign: they were getting their just deserts. It was, of course,
rather petty, and derived from Clark's misguided inferiority complex
about his own and American status in the theatre. The irony that was
lost on Clark was that he had more than proved himself in Italy. A
greater show of magnanimity and graciousness would have done so much
to improve his reputation and standing – the very things he craved. As
it was, discord between the two army commanders helped no one.

Even so, the two armies, in their changing forms, continued to batter
away at every new German line of resistance. General Anders' Poles –
helped by the Corpo Italiano di Liberazione – were continuing their
attack towards Ancona, while the main thrust by Eighth Army was
XIII Corps' drive towards Florence. With the 1st Armored Division
now withdrawn for rest and reorganisation, Fifth Army was pushing
northwards with three divisions along a thirty-mile stretch to the coast.

It had been the 135th Infantry that had led the 34th Red Bull Division's
charge along the Tyrrhenian Coast, taking Cecina on 1 July, and then
finding themselves involved in an even tougher battle at Rosignano. 'The
Germans would usually withdraw from a town as we got near,' says
Bucky Walters, who was now back in action as recon' sergeant with the
135th's Cannon Company, 'and I don't know why the heck they didn't
with Rosignano.' Instead, the Americans were forced to fight for every
street. The battle for the town grew heavier as the 16th Waffen-SS
reinforced their positions and counterattacked. They were thrown back
but it made progress slow. Heavy American shelling of the town was
followed by house-to-house fighting. Unfortunately, most of the civilian
population had remained in the town, caught unawares by the sudden
advance of the front and not suspecting that their homes would become
the scene of bitter fighting. The 16th SS eventually pulled out on 11 July.
Still as poorly equipped as when Willfried Segebrecht had been fighting
two weeks before, they had been forced to use oxen and carts to take
away their guns and equipment.

'I got into town after the infantry had done street-to-street,' says
Bucky. 'There were a lot of Italian dead. I felt awful about that.' With
the sizzling summer heat, and fearing disease might soon spread, the
Americans cleared the bodies as quickly as they could and cremated
the lot.

In his job as recon' sergeant, Bucky was often probing ahead of the
forward troops. Accompanying Captain Paul Blommen, Bucky would

drive forward in their jeep looking for suitable places to deploy their guns. A few miles north of Rosignano was Gabbro and as the two men reached the edge of the village, ahead of the infantry, rifle and machine gun fire started to ping all around them. Taking immediate but well protected cover, they could tell the SS men were pulling out. After a while, all seemed quiet, and civilians began emerging into the streets. Bucky radioed back and told the men of Cannon Company that the village was now empty and told the pack Howitzers to move up. No sooner had the guns arrived and begun setting up position than they came under an intense German bombardment. One of the 135th's batteries was all but destroyed, and one of Bucky's best friends, Troop Sergeant Lester Mazelin, was severely wounded. Earlier, Bucky had noticed the church steeple in the village and he and Captain Blommen had agreed that it would make a good observation post. What they hadn't realised was that German observers were still up there, quietly biding their time until the bulk of Cannon Company had moved in.

The next day, Bucky and Captain Blommen were once again probing forward looking for places to deploy their guns. They were now not far from Livorno and came across a blown bridge over a river. Nearby were a few houses, but not a soul stirred. The remains of the bridge had clearly been mined, but by now they were pretty familiar with German mine-laying techniques and so carefully picked their way across by foot, avoiding the obvious places where mines and booby traps would have been laid.

On the other side they clambered up a track to a farmhouse. Gingerly stepping inside, they discovered an Italian family crouching with fright. In broken Italian, Bucky reassured them and soon discovered from them that the farm was heavily mined. Outside, the Italians showed Bucky and Captain Blommen the newly dug areas where the mines had been laid, then scuttled back inside. Through the olive groves, however, Blommen had noticed an ideal place to set up the guns. As they made their way towards the defilade, they spotted a short away below them four German self-propelled guns pulling out.

'Sergeant, get back to the jeep and get the radio man,' Blommen told Bucky.

'Yes, Captain,' Bucky replied, 'but stay here. Don't forget what the Ites told us about the mines.' Bucky left him, picking his back the way he'd come. Having collected the radio man, he retraced his steps once more. 'We were just coming back up the hill when we heard this explosion,' says Bucky, 'and when we got to the olive grove, there he was, fifty-sixty feet into the orchard, dead. He must have been looking for a better vantage point, but I don't know what made him do it because he knew it was mined.'

Two days later, 15 July, his wounded friend, Sergeant Mazelin, also died. 'That sort of shakes you up,' reflects Bucky, 'it really shakes you up.'

The Red Bulls eventually took Livorno on 19 July, the day after the Poles captured Ancona. Livorno was deserted, the civilians having either fled or been evacuated. When Bucky arrived there he found a ghost town, lying in ruins, pulverised by Allied bombing. The all-important port was a wreck as well. Ships had been deliberately sunk at the harbour entrance and the port facilities blown. Rudi Schreiber's comrades in the 16th Waffen-SS Pioneers had done their task well. It would be weeks before the Allies could use the port properly.

Meanwhile, Eighth Army now had to make good the loss of the French Corps. Brought in alongside the 6th South African Armoured Division were General Freyberg's New Zealanders, who had been having a comparatively quiet time over the past few months. Tini Glover, a Maori in the 28th Battalion, was relieved to be finally getting into action, because ever since leaving New Zealand almost a year before, he had been waiting to fulfil a pledge he'd made himself to kill three Germans. It had been the night before he had been due to embark from Wellington on the *New Amsterdam* and he'd been drinking in the Masonic Hotel with his cousin.

'Tini, don't go killing all those Germans by yourself,' his cousin had said to him.

'If I kill three before they kill me,' Tini had drunkenly replied, 'I don't mind.'

'Why three?' his cousin had asked.

Tini told him: one for his uncle who'd just been killed at Takrouna in Tunisia, one for himself, and one for luck.

A long sea voyage had been followed by training in the desert in Egypt, so Tini hadn't reached Italy until Christmas 1943. Then when he did finally go into the line at Cassino in March, he was badly wounded in his arm by a chance piece of flying shrapnel before he'd even so much as seen a German. His mates told him he would be going back home with that kind of wound, a line that had been repeated at the field dressing station where he was operated on. 'It was beginning to prey on my mind,' admits Tini, 'because of my boast about getting these three Germans.' Luck was with him, however. On reaching hospital he was given the new wonder drug, penicillin, and the wound – and his broken arm – soon began to heal. Convalescence camp followed and by the beginning of May he was back with the 28th Battalion. In fact, the Maori Battalion had been almost directly opposite Georg Zellner and the H und D Regiment during the May battles and it was during this time that Tini managed to shoot one German during a patrol. But they had been merely holding the line and there had been few opportunities for the infantry to see much action. After that, they were taken out of the line again, and so Tini had still not fulfilled his pledge.

Tini was from Tolaga Bay in the East Cape of New Zealand's North Island. As the oldest son, he was raised by his grandparents – an old Maori custom – which was just as well, because he didn't have much time for his father. 'My father worshipped my sister and he wasn't so hard on my younger brother,' says Tini, 'but he used to get drunk and knock the hell out of me.'

When war came, a lot of Maori volunteered to fight, even though unlike white New Zealanders – or *pakehas* as the Maori call them – they did not face conscription. Tini joined up in part because all his mates were doing so and he didn't want to be left out; but there was more to it than that. 'We were second-class citizens,' he says. 'We went to fight to show them we could do our stuff.'

Initially placed in a reinforcement battalion based in New Zealand, Tini had missed out on 28th (Maori) Battalion's exploits in North Africa, where they had repeatedly distinguished themselves and gained a reputation as fearsome soldiers. He was not quite twenty by the time he was eventually posted overseas, although he was already married. 'I went on final leave and found out my girlfriend was up the family way,' explains Tini. His mother thought it would be best if he did the decent thing and so they got married before he left. 'By the time I got to the Middle East,' he says, 'I heard that she'd had a miscarriage and the sad thing was she couldn't then have any more.'

The battalion was divided on a tribal basis. Like most Maori from his corner of North Island, Tini was part of the Ngati Porou tribe, and so joined C Company – known as Nga Kaupoi – the Cowboys. Consequently, there were a number of familiar faces when Tini joined them. 'I had a lot of mates in the company,' says Tini. 'Mates from Tolaga Bay.'

He was with some of those friends from home when, on the night of 21/22 July, trucks took the battalion through Siena and along the winding, dusty roads of the Chianti Hills and up to the front line, taking over positions previously held by the French. They stopped at Castellina in Chianti and the following day pushed forward north-west towards Tavarnelle, reaching the edge of the town by about 3 o'clock in the afternoon. A recce patrol was sent forward and enemy tanks were spotted, and so 28th Battalion was ordered to attack straight away. 'The enemy got away,' says Tini, 'but we captured the town.'

The local inhabitants did not receive these dark-faced soldiers very enthusiastically. The town was quiet, and the few shops were shut. Tini and a few others in the company spotted a piano accordion factory and store, and using a captured land mine, hand grenade, and a piece of string, blew the entire front of the shop out. 'So everyone in our company had a piano accordion,' says Tini. 'But after a while they got too heavy to carry and so we threw them away.'

The next morning the Maori renewed their advance. Tini's section was passing through a copse: ahead of them was a wheat field rising up towards a ridge. They spread out and began wading through the wheat when Corporal Nepia, the section leader, suddenly told to them to hurry back to the copse. No sooner had they turned back and run than mortar shells began to paste the field where they had just been. 'Hey, Nep,' asked Tini, 'what made you tell us to get back to the trees?'

'I was imagining myself early in the morning in Rotorua,' Nepia told him, 'taking the cows across the fields and the birds would be in the trees singing. Then I realised there wasn't a single bird singing and I knew they must have been disturbed.'

It was a couple of days later that Tini finally came face to face with some German soldiers. C Company were cautiously advancing down a long, straight track when they saw a number of D Company men lying dead in the road. It looked as though a machine-gunner had got them, so Tini, along with the platoon commander and two other men, very carefully crept forward to see what enemy rearguards lay up ahead.

Having safely reached a haystack and hidden underneath it, the rest of the section followed them. It was then that the enemy machine guns opened fire. Tini's section leader was hit, and another man killed. Suddenly Tini spotted the German who was doing the firing. 'I've got him in my sights,' Tini told the platoon commander. 'What the f*** are you waiting for then?' the officer replied. Tini fired and saw he'd shot the soldier straight in the head. 'I thought, that's two now,' says Tini.

Moments later, he spotted another German, limping away, so he killed him too. That was three.

Some of the section then crossed the road, towards a small barn, Tini giving them covering fire on the Bren. A German suddenly sprang up and was about to shoot but Tini hit him first. Moments later he looked up the road and saw several oxen and behind them German boots. Opening fire, he killed the oxen and shot the men hiding behind them. 'They managed to pull one joker away while I was changing mags,' says Tini, 'and the next thing we know rifle grenades are coming down on us in this barn.' Tini was hit by another piece of shrapnel – in the crotch. 'It bled like hell,' he says. They couldn't escape out of the front of the barn, but there was a narrow window at the back. Smashing it out, they clambered through. There was only one thing for it: to run like hell back to safety. Bren guns, however, are extremely heavy – some 25 lbs – and so Tini ditched his, flinging it down a well behind the barn. He couldn't decide whether to head back down the road, which would have been quicker but offered a better target, or through the vines to the side. 'I thought, bugger it, I'll go down the road,' says Tini. 'A champion runner couldn't have caught me I was pumping so hard.' He could hear bees buzzing about his ears then realised it was machine-gun bullets. Leaping over a bank he dived for safety. Moments later the others followed. His platoon commander had been nicked in the face, but otherwise they were all in one piece. Tini, however, would be out of the line for a while again with his second wound. This time, though, he no longer had the burden of his pledge hanging over him. His honour had been more than satisfied.

Oberleutnant Hans Golda, meanwhile, had been having a comparatively quiet few weeks. Following the fierce battle around Lake Trasimeno, the Werfer Regiment 71 had fallen back to a peaceful valley north-west of Arezzo, where suddenly the war had seemed a thousand miles away. Having prepared their positions they then discovered the war was ignoring them for the time being. From the local Italians they bought chickens and geese to eat; and in the warm summer evenings, they stayed outside drinking local wine and watching the fireflies twinkle in the fields.

After ten days of living idly in this secret valley, they began to hear the sounds of war once more: shelling getting ever closer and reconnaissance planes overhead. A few days later they were ordered to move out, and with heavy hearts were about to leave when shells began falling on their adopted house. 'Our quiet valley was like a cauldron,' noted Hans. 'A thick cloud of smoke stopped us from seeing anything. There was a stench of sulphur.' But his men were all right and once the shelling quietened down they hurriedly moved out. 'We rolled on further, our fourteen-day holiday was over,' added Hans. 'We had to drink to its health.' Arezzo had fallen and Hans and his men now retreated several miles to Figline Valdarno on the banks of the River Arno, some fifteen miles south-east of Florence.

Yet again, they found themselves sleeping rough in an old barn. On 24 July, Hans settled down for the night feeling unusually depressed. His bed was a corner of a cowshed, which was empty of cattle but teeming with rats. He found it hard to sleep. Looking at his watch, he realised it had gone midnight – it was now his birthday and he was lying on a hard floor with rodents scurrying around him.

Suddenly a noise disturbed him and he rolled over and rubbed his eyes. Standing in front of him was the whole battery, their faces freshly washed and their hair combed, and all clutching a freshly lit candle. In front of them stood a large, carefully decorated basket filled with bottles and packages. One of the men was clutching an enormous bunch of flowers and holding up a notice for Hans to see. They then began to sing him 'Happy Birthday'. 'I just stand there in my underwear,' wrote Hans. 'My lads, who are normally such rugged types, are singing with such dedication.'

Their efforts touched his heart. Wine was poured and cigarettes handed out. A bottle of Schnapps was uncorked and passed around. 'Who's turned us into drunkards?' they shouted. 'The Old Guy, the Boss!' came the refrain.

The party continued until morning and then Hans held a lunch for his entire battery. The cowshed was smartened up and scrubbed. Rough tables were laid out. One of the men sprayed the barn with some perfume he had found. Chickens and fowl were bought, plucked and prepared, while for pudding they found some tins of peaches. 'That was a birthday party,' noted Hans, 'the most beautiful day of my life. The location was a stinking cowshed but for us it was beautiful and better than the best salon. Those who organised it were hard soldiers in heavy action who honoured and respected their boss. You can't get a higher compliment than this!'[203]

The next day, they were on the move again, crossing the Arno into new positions. They had now reached Kesselring's last line of defence before the Gothic Line.

TWENTY-THREE

Crossing the Arno
July–August 1944

From the beginning of July, the US 12th Tactical Air Command began moving its units to Corsica in preparation for the invasion of southern France – now renamed Operation DRAGOON. However, the French island was also an ideal base for operations over central and northern Italy, and so the 12th TAC was able to continue to support Alexander's drive northwards.

As Alex was all too aware, Allied air power still had a huge role to play in Italy despite the recent cuts in his forces, and he knew that he needed to make the most of the maximum amount of aircraft at his disposal while he could. Earlier a plan had been made to destroy all the bridges across the River Po, seen as the last barrier before the Alps. In the flush of success after the fall of Rome, this plan had been cancelled as it was feared it might be counter-productive and hinder the speed of the Allies' advance. Although still hopeful of breaking the Gothic Line before the summer was out, Alex recognised, however, that he no longer had the forces for a long pursuit north of the River Po and so now decided to resurrect the idea. The destruction of the Po's bridges, he hoped, would not only seriously hinder Kesselring's supply lines, but also force the Germans to stand and fight before the Po, should a breakthrough in the Gothic Line be achieved.

Operation MALLORY MAJOR was to be carried out by the medium bombers and fighter planes of the Mediterranean Allied Tactical Air Force. All rail and road bridges across the Po were to be destroyed as well as across its tributaries, while further railway targets north and south of the river were also to be blasted.

The 27th Fighter Bomber Group had been amongst those transferred to Corsica and was based at Serraggia in the south of the island, but they were in the thick of the action over the Po just a day after the operation orders were issued. On 12 July, Lieutenant Charles Dills took part in a bombing mission on the railway bridge at Ostiglia, to the east of Mantova, and two further attacks on railway lines over the next few days.

Their job would have been a lot easier, Charles believed, had they still been flying their old P-40 Warhawks. They may have been battered and old – and inherited from the 33rd Fighter Group who had flown them during the North African campaign – but they were good planes to operate at low altitudes. But in June, his squadron had been re-equipped with the P-47 Thunderbolt. One of the biggest fighter aircraft of the war, it had proved itself to be an excellent aircraft at high altitudes, but less effective closer to earth. For a start, at nearly seven tons, it was not the best aircraft for any form of dive bombing. 'When you pulled out of a dive,' says Charles, 'it mushed terribly. That is, it kept going down before it would start coming up.' Charles noticed that to begin with a number of pilots came back with telephone wires and bits of foliage still stuck to the undercarriage. Nor could they cruise around at 200 feet, darting in and around mountains and valleys which gave them the element of surprise. In their Thunderbolts, they had to fly much higher to counter the lack of low-level manoeuvrability. 'The P-47 always had altitude,' says Charles, 'and was brazenly visible to anyone holding even a peashooter.'

On 18 July, he was sent on a trip to Bari to pick up some new maps. It was a long way, and he became aware that he was occasionally dozing off as he flew. This was not the first time this had happened. Over the past week, he knew he'd been doing it in combat missions as well. One of his fellow pilots had even mentioned to him that his left wing appeared to drop occasionally. Although he was not prepared to admit this to himself, he was utterly burned out, exhausted physically and mentally, and should not have been flying.

The reason for this extreme fatigue was that for the past six weeks, he had regularly worked twenty-hour days as Acting Group Operations Officer. In any fighter group there were always four operations officers: the Group Operations Officer, who was normally at least a lieutenant-colonel; under him the Assistant Operations Officer, the Weather Officer, and finally the Radar Officer. Charles had been made Group Radar Officer by his former squadron commander, who was now at Group HQ, but unfortunately his appointment coincided with the departure of the Group's Ops Officer for leave back in the States. The Deputy Ops Officer had been made a squadron commander, while the Weather

Officer had been shot down. This had left Charles in charge. 'I was trying to do a four-man job by myself,' says Charles.

At one point, he had lost his temper. He'd been told the Group needed to fly over and 'buzz' Cecina. Charles had pointed out there was very heavy flak around Cecina and if there was no specific target it would be better not to fly there. No, he had been told: they had to buzz Cecina – that was an order. The pilots had duly taken off and buzzed Cecina, losing one pilot dead, two planes destroyed and three seriously damaged. On learning this, Charles rang up the Wing HQ and blasted the major there. 'What the hell are you running up there?' he'd shouted. 'A circus?' The major apologised. The orders, he explained, had come from the top. 'A couple of days later,' says Charles, 'I read in *Stars & Stripes* that Secretary of War Stimpson had been visiting Cecina that day. I reckon someone thought up that show to impress him. He probably wouldn't have noticed, but it cost some kid his life.'

While carrying out this Group role Charles had continued flying. Despite falling asleep at the controls on his way to Bari, he kept his exhaustion to himself, and three days later, on 21 July, was bombing a road over the Po just north of Parma – his eighty-sixth combat mission.

Experienced pilots like Charles Dills might have been feeling the strain, but his contributions helped to make MALLORY MAJOR an outstanding success. Most bridges on the broad River Po were by necessity long, with spans of 250 feet or more. The Allies had suspected that to repair such massive constructions would be beyond the Germans' capabilities, and so it was to prove. By the beginning of August, every bridge across the Po had been destroyed, and not a single train could cross the river. The only way Kesselring could get his troops and supplies to the Gothic Line was by using ferries and hastily built pontoons by night.

Further west, Genoa, on the coast, had been effectively isolated by widespread rail and road destruction. All routes from France were closed, while the Brenner Pass through the Alps between Italy and Austria was also blocked. With almost all railways cut in numerous places, with roads badly disrupted, and with German motor transport shot to pieces, German efforts to supply the front were once again causing major headaches. That they also faced repeated attacks and further acts of sabotage from partisan bands was making the task even harder. German patience with these troublesome guerrillas was beginning to wear very thin indeed.

*   *   *

The man responsible for overseeing Kesselring's anti-partisan war had returned to Italy at the beginning of July after a six-week period of sick leave in Karlsbad, and he now had another title to his name: Plenipotentiary General of the German Wehrmacht in Italy. There was now very little limit to General Wolff's power in northern Italy.

The situation in Italy had changed drastically while he had been away, not least with regard to the partisans, who, Wolff realised, had now got badly out of hand. He was also taken aback to learn that in the battle against the partisans, Kesselring had issued orders for especially harsh treatment of such rebels. Yet as he soon discovered, these had been urged upon Kesselring by the German High Command, after the Army Group Commander had warned Berlin about the escalating partisan problem in Italy. In fact, a copy of orders from Feldmarschall Keitel instructing Kesselring to make sure German troops used whatever means, 'without restriction (even against women and children)' to destroy the partisan menace, was waiting for Wolff in his in-tray.[204] 'If I had been there,' Wolff reflected, 'I would have acted as a brake, and I would have urged him to be more cautious in applying extreme measures.'[205]

Kesselring was the first to admit that Wolff preferred a more lenient approach to the partisan threat, as he had shown on several occasions, not least back in March when he had dealt with the general strike of workers in the north without resorting to mass roundups and executions. But while the SS general could influence the way in which counter-terrorism measures were handled in the north, the Feldmarschall was determined, for the time being at any rate, to continue his uncompromising approach near the front, where experienced and battle-hardened troops could carry out sweeping rastrellamenti with a swift and ruthless efficiency that was often missing in the less well-trained SS police and especially the GNR.

In any case, Wolff was soon off again. Part of his job was to ensure the safety and security of Mussolini, so when the Duce travelled with Marshal Graziani to Germany to inspect his four new divisions and see how their training was progressing, Wolff accompanied him.

Mussolini had been gratified by the cheering crowds that had lined the streets as his motorcade had passed through the towns of northern Italy and his rousing speeches to his new divisions had prompted a spontaneous and enthusiastic response from the young recruits, some of whom had been reduced to tears. With his spirits high, Mussolini had travelled to Poland to see Hitler at the Wolf's Lair, determined to get his divisions back in Italy as soon as possible.

Waiting for Mussolini at the Wolf's Lair platform was the Führer himself. It was around 3 p.m. on 20 July, and as Hitler greeted Mussolini, he extended only one hand in welcome, rather than two as was his usual way, his right hand remaining hidden by a cape. It was only as they walked from the platform, with Wolff hovering behind, that Hitler explained that a few hours earlier an attempted assassination had been made and his right arm had been injured in the bomb blast. Once in the Wolf's Lair, the Duce was shown the bomb-damaged room, and the jacket Hitler had been wearing, now torn and shredded. 'We no longer have a monopoly of treachery,' Mussolini later told Graziani.[206]

Despite the bomb attack, the meeting to discuss the future of the new Italian divisions went ahead as planned. Keitel immediately demanded that three of the four divisions were needed on the Eastern Front, prompting a fierce argument with Graziani. Whether the bomb attack led Hitler to feel more generous towards his old friend is unclear, but he overruled Keitel and agreed that not only should all four divisions be sent back to Italy, but that the 600,000 Italian troops still languishing as POWs in Germany should be given the status of civilian workers. The Führer would soon renege completely on this latter concession, but at the time Mussolini was able to return to his hermit existence in the Villa Feltrinelli on Lake Garda in better spirits than he had been for a long time. Indeed, as Mussolini had left the Wolf's Lair, Hitler had told him, 'I consider you as my best, and perhaps only, friend I have in the world.'[207] It was the last time the two would ever meet.

Although General Wolff had a substantial force of SS, Wehrmacht and GNR troops among his security forces in northern Italy, he and Ambassador Rahn gave permission for Mussolini to form a new, armed militia, the Brigate Nere – or the Black Brigades. These were the brainchild of Alessandro Pavolini, the Fascist Party leader, who wanted to militarise the Party by creating Action Squads rather like the Fascist hit squads – squadristi – of the 1920s. As such, the Black Brigades were to be Fascist Party rather than state troops – rather like the SS.

Even stuck away on Lake Garda, Mussolini had become aware that the intensification of the partisan war, not just at the front but throughout the north of Italy, was creating open civil war in many places. In June, Pavolini had put before him his plans for the militarisation of the

Fascist Party, but the Duce had delayed authorising it and had instead turned to Marshal Graziani to lead what he dramatically called 'The March of the Social Republic against the Partisans'. But Graziani, shorn of both troops and power by the Germans, told Mussolini that this would be impossible until a large number of grievances had been rectified. Why, he asked, were so many people joining the partisans? It was because no Italians wanted to be despatched to Germany as workers; because of the distrust of fascism, which he believed was finished as a movement in Italy; because 'everyone is convinced that the Government counts for nothing, and that the Germans are the real masters'; because the majority believed Germany, and thus Republican Italy, were going to lose the war; because the reconstruction of the Republican Army, with just four divisions still in Germany, seemed to be little more than a pipe dream. 'Is this Army,' he asked, 'a reality or an illusion?'[208]

Pavolini, meanwhile, argued that it was pointless to try and fight an anti-partisan war with Italian Army troops. 'Wherever the army exists on national soil,' he pointed out to Mussolini, 'it is directly represented by a nuclei of officers and men ready to desert and pass to the other side.'[209] This was why, he argued, the Black Brigade 'Action Squads' were needed – men who would be loyal to Italy and to fascism and who could be depended upon to see the job done.

And so Mussolini relented and authorised the formation of the Black Brigades on 26 July. The HQ of this corps became the newly militarised headquarters of the Fascist Party in Maderno on Lake Garda. Provincial Fascist Federal Commissioners now became commanders of the Black Brigades. Each brigade would be numbered but would take as its title the name of someone who had died in the name of fascism. Their task was to include the maintenance of order, the defence of the Repubblica Sociale Italiana, and counter-terrorism and anti-partisan actions. Their uniform, however, was hardly a triumph of marketing. Looking very like early SS troops of the 1930s, members of the Black Brigades wore high boots, baggy trousers, black German-style field caps and helmets. Their shirts, were, of course, also black. Considering the vast majority of civilians in northern Italy were no longer interested in fascism, and that the squadristi had hardly been loved by the Italian people, this intimidating look was not altogether sensible. In fact, the very formation of the Black Brigades and the militarisation of the Party was a high-risk strategy indeed.

*   *   *

Pavolini's personal bodyguard, the Bir el Gobi Company, seamlessly became part of the Black Brigades. Since their formation, they had been based in Maderno, accompanying Pavolini wherever he went, and fulfilling their role as protectors of the Fascist Party leader. Like most Italian troops and militia, they lacked funds and equipment. Several of the officers, however, realised that Florence might offer an opportunity for them to get their hands on a good supply of weapons, ammunition and other materiel. With the Allies only a few miles south of the city, there were now few Republican forces left there; a raid on the Carabinieri barracks might prove extremely worth their while – after all, if the barracks were about to be overrun, there was no point leaving everything there for the Allies.

The man given the task of stealing this booty from their own side was Lieutenant Barnini and his platoon, which included his senior NCO, Sergeant William Cremonini. The first obstacle to be overcome was the lack of transport, but fortunately the father of one of the officers managed to get hold of a Fiat 626 truck and enough petrol, and so the platoon of twenty-six men began the long, 160-mile journey to Florence.

They reached the city without mishap, and Barnini reported to Pavolini, who, in his newly militarised role, had set up a tactical headquarters at the Excelsior Hotel. 'I introduced myself to Pavolini,' noted Barnini, 'and told him I would do whatever was needed to protect the Party. He was very encouraging about my plans.'[210] The atmosphere in Florence was tense. As with Rome, Kesselring had, on Hitler's express orders, declared Florence to be an open city, so there were almost no German troops at all within the city. From the south, the guns boomed incessantly.

At the Excelsior, Barnini attended a meeting with Pavolini and the Florentine GNR and SS police commanders. As he and William had now discovered, the Carabiniere Barracks were indeed bursting with trucks, petrol, weapons and ammunition. 'In short,' wrote Barnini, 'it was exactly what we wanted for our Company to become completely autonomous.' A plan was agreed between them and the GNR commanders that they would raid the barracks at nine the following morning. Lieutenant Barnini, however, had other ideas. Realising the GNR commander would take the lion's share of the booty, he led his Bir el Gobi platoon to raid the barracks three hours earlier than planned, at 6 a.m. There, they disarmed the Carabinieri who still remained, set them free, including the officers, and by 8 a.m. had already sent their lorry to Maderno stuffed with all the best weapons they had found – hundreds of rifles, but also machine guns, mortars, pistols, and masses of ammunition. They then hid the rest so that the GNR would not take it and over the next four days sent back several more truck loads of equipment – so much, in fact, that back at Maderno they hardly had room enough to store it all.

Meanwhile, both Reg Harris with the Coldstream Guards and Dick Frost in the Royal Natal Carbineers had been involved in stiff fighting directly to the south of the city as Kesselring's forces had made another of their stands. The New Zealanders on their left had also been having a tough time as they battled their way through the Chianti Hills. At Impruneta, the South Africans faced the heaviest resistance they had yet encountered as they came up against the doggedly determined men of the 1st Fall-schirmjäger Division. 'Florence so near yet so far,' scribbled Dick on 1 August. 'Air Force very active as well as our artillery. We must be building for a big push.'[211]

By the 3rd, however, the South Africans were finally pushing into the southern outskirts of the city, and at the same time, Kesselring ordered all his troops to fall back behind the Arno, so that the only German troops left on the south of the river were a few rearguards of the 4th Fallschirmjäger Regiment. Despite mutual concern to spare the city, both Allied artillery and aircraft did stray their fire into the city centre, hitting, amongst others, the Piazza Museo Istituto dell'Arte.

At 6 p.m., having been given Hitler's direct permission, Kesselring gave the order for the German engineers to blow the bridges across the Arno. A mighty explosion erupted, masonry tumbled into the water, and a great cloud of dust temporarily shrouded the river. When it settled, five of the six bridges had been destroyed. The only survivor was the fourteenth-century Ponte Vecchio, which in any case was not wide enough for vehicles and was blocked at either end with a mountain of rubble from buildings blown up for the purpose.

In the early hours, the Allies, accompanied by increasingly visible numbers of partisans, reached the river, only to discover that there was no way over. Throughout the day they were then stalled and harassed by snipers and rearguards and the usual web of mines and booby traps. Although the Germans retreated from the city later on the 4th, one Fall-schirmjäger regiment remained on the north of the river to garrison the city centre and to cover any efforts by the Allies to try and cross the Arno.

All this time, William Cremonini and the platoon of Bir el Gobi men remained behind, helping Pavolini to establish a number of Fascist volunteers to continue the fight in the city once it had been entirely overrun. 'There wasn't really that much we could do,' says William, although they had also been using the time to scavenge more supplies. This included striking gold with the discovery of 2,000 litres of petrol at a dump in Firenzuola, a small Apennine town some twenty-five miles to the north of Florence.

Nor had they had much contact with their allies, the Germans. There had been no linking of arms, or fighting shoulder to shoulder with their Axis partners. In fact, the only time William had anything to do with them at all was when some Fallschirmjäger men tried to take one of his trucks, something that he quickly managed to stop.

The last German troops left on the night of 10/11 August, and the Bir el Gobi men later on the 11th. 'All round the city,' recalls William, 'people spoke of 20,000 Florentine partisans, but in truth, we didn't see any of them.'[212] As he points out, had such a number emerged in the city centre, they could have easily overwhelmed the Germans and perhaps saved the bridges from being blown. As it was, despite the Allies being a stone's throw away on the other side of the Arno, William and his comrades left Florence without any interference whatsoever. By good fortune they managed to avoid heavy air attacks as they drove back towards Lake Garda. Only once did they come under attack, and although one of their truck drivers was killed, everyone else in his platoon reached Maderno unscathed.

Other members of the Bir el Gobi Company, however, had not fared so well while Barnini's platoon had been away. Posted to Piemonte to begin counter-partisan actions in the mountains around Turin, they had been travelling on the main Milan–Turin highway when their coach was ambushed by partisans lying in wait on a bridge across the road.

Accompanying the troops had been Mussolini's daughter, Elena Curti. Still based in Maderno, she had come to know most of the Bir el Gobi men well – so much so that they had awarded her the honorific position of 'Godmother of the Company', a title she was proud and delighted to have been given. Because of her attachment to the company and because she was still acting as 'The Eyes of Mussolini Within the Party' she had decided to join them on their trip to Piemonte.

It happened very fast. Bullets peppered the coach. The windscreen was shattered; the driver, Quintavalle, although badly hit, managed to drive on to safety. Elena had been sitting next to her friend, Nello Carducci, at the moment machine-gun fire ripped through into the coach. He immediately hurled her to the floor, saving her life: a bullet tore through her seat and hit Vittorio Ricciarelli, the man sitting behind her, in the stomach. 'He was only eighteen,' says Elena, 'with red hair and green eyes. He stared incredulously at the blood pouring out of him, lifted his questioning eyes, and died.'

She now heard others calling her. Enzo Bartocci, another good friend and an officer with the Company, had also been hit. A bullet had struck his cheek and exited under his chin. Blood was pouring from his mouth and his throat and he was beginning to suffocate. Elena managed to staunch his wound in his throat and slowly his breathing became more regular. Meanwhile, the wounded Quintavalle was still managing to drive on, stopping only once they had reached the Sanità tollgate. 'He was the true hero,' says Elena, 'he was our saviour. Without his courage we would all have been massacred.'

William Cremonini heard the news of the attack as soon as he arrived back in Maderno from his trip to Florence. He could only assume a spy at Maderno had warned the partisans of the rest of the Company's movements. 'Otherwise,' he says, 'it is hard to explain the fact that other troops passed untroubled and yet the ambush struck us.' At any rate, Lieutenant Barnini was not going to take unnecessary risks with his men. Due to follow the others, the platoon spent two days reassembling and getting ready and then set off quietly without telling anyone at general headquarters.

While the battle for Florence had been raging, Martha Gellhorn had left the Poles and headed to Rome. On 3 August, she went to the Ardeatine Caves to see for herself the scene of the massacre of 335 in March that had shocked so many.

The caves had been opened up back in June. Colonel Charles Poletti, despite his links to the mobster, Vito Genovese, had continued his rise within the Allied Military Government and had been appointed Regional Commissioner for Rome. One of his first tasks had been to set up a commission of Allied and Italian officials to conduct an inquest into the massacre. The first job was to exhume the bodies – a horrendous task carried out by a team of highly-qualified forensic scientists.

They were still digging out the bodies – or what remained of them –

at the beginning of August. 'Yesterday I saw the worst thing I have ever seen in my life,' wrote Martha in a letter to one of her friends. 'It was so horrible that it passed the point where the mind or spirit can comprehend it.' The stench was appalling. 'A great pit full of decomposing bodies which had melted into each other, and shrunken,' she continued, 'and outside the people of Rome had made a sort of shrine and there were pictures pinned up, of real people, imagined to be somewhere in that pit where nothing was real and nothing was people.'[213]

Martha had been hearing about other massacres. Her friend Virginia Cowles, another war correspondent, had also been staying in Rome, newly returned from a tour of the front. She told Martha about villages in the north where piles of executed dead lay unburied.

And a few days later, an even worse massacre than that at the Ardeatine Caves would take place. With the Germans now withdrawn behind the River Arno, work on the Gothic Line was speeding up, and in the Apuan Mountains to the north of Lucca, the Germans had begun clearing the valleys and mountains of civilians. Working on the principle that partisans could only operate with the help and support of the local civilians, mass evacuations seemed to be a good way of making the partisans' task a great deal more difficult and ensuring that when the Gothic Line battles began, partisan interference would be kept to a minimum.

There was also a practical aspect to the decision to evacuate the area. As with towns like Cassino and the villages along the Gustav Line earlier in the year, the area around the Gothic Line would be no place for civilians once the full fire power of the Germans, and more especially the Allies, was unleashed in the forthcoming battle. Even so, a delegation of local parish priests from the area appealed against the evacuation order. Received by the Germans, they were nonetheless given short shrift; the evacuation order stood. Be warned then, the priests replied: the mountain communities were made up of proud and tenacious people, capable of resisting and who would not be easily budged. This was brave talk but foolhardy. German irritation was then further raised by an announcement by the local Apuan Patriots, ordering the Germans to evacuate instead. 'Those not fulfilling these requirements will dig their own grave,' ran the proclamation. 'Forewarned is forearmed.'[214]

Perhaps they did not know who they were up against, because they had just picked a fight with the 16th Waffen-SS Division, who were already deeply frustrated by a difficult and costly retreat since first going into action against the US Red Bull Division. It was also the case that

although the 16th Waffen-SS was a comparatively new division, amongst
its commanders were some of the most experienced in dealing with
Italian partisans – men who had dealt with the Russian partisans with
equal brutality.

The Waffen-SS men were further enraged when the 10th Garibaldi
Brigade, who operated in the Apuans, held off a sweeping rastrellamento
on 30 and 31 July. The German troops were having a hard enough
time combating the Americans without having to deal with large-scale
partisan formations to their rear. The partisans then followed their
success by printing notices instructing the locals to disobey the German
evacuation orders and to remain where they were, which they pasted all
over Sant' Anna and the surrounding villages. Their overconfidence was
getting the better of them.

By 12 August, the 10th Garibaldi Brigade had moved away, but Sant'
Anna and neighbouring Stazzema were swollen with refugees from
nearby Farnocchia, who had mostly adhered to the evacuation order. As
far as the Germans were concerned, however, Sant' Anna had become
the centre of partisan – and civilian – resistance, and so a regiment of
front-line, battle-hardened troops, the 35th Panzer Grenadier Regiment,
was sent to carry out an extreme rastrellamento. The area was to be
cleared, and that was exactly what they did. Houses were burned; civilians were rounded up and herded into barns. Grenades were hurled at
them, machine-gunners opened fire, and then the sheds set on fire.
Those not dead by bullets or shrapnel died in the flames. In all, 560
men, women and children of all ages were killed in one of the most
horrific bloodbaths Italy had ever seen. The civilians of the Apuans had
paid a terrible price for the partisans' bravado.

TWENTY-FOUR

A Change of Plan
August 1944

On 24 July, King George VI flew into Italy using the alias of General Lyon, landing at 244 Wing's base at Perugia. There to meet him was Air Vice-Marshal Dickson and Wing Commander Cocky Dundas, who was temporarily in command of the Wing. It was a timely visit, much appreciated by Eighth Army, and reminded the men fighting there that they had not been forgotten – at least, not by their King.

The arrival of the monarch at Leese's Tactical HQ meant a lot of extra work and a few anxious moments for Ion Calvocoressi, whose task it was, as senior ADC, to make sure suitable arrangements were made and that everything went swimmingly. The King had to be given a comfortable and perfectly sited caravan in which to stay, and a sumptuous dinner for twenty people – including General Alex – had to be laid on.

Ion need not have worried. He had found the perfect spot for the King's caravan – under a fine oak tree with a view of Arezzo and the Apennines beyond. The 10th Indian Division were attacking at the time, so the King had the unique experience of watching the battle from his bath with the Grenadier Guards band playing just behind his caravan. 'He was thrilled,' wrote Oliver Leese. The dinner proved equally successful. 'The King was in great form throughout,' noted Ion, 'joking with the General and pulling Alex's leg.' Earlier, Ion had been presented to the King, who, thought Ion, 'seemed awfully well and didn't stammer at all.'

As well as making a tour of the troops, the King found time to hand out several VCs and to knight both John Harding, Alexander's Chief of Staff, and Leese. 'It was wonderful to be knighted in the field,' wrote Leese to his wife, 'and I was very proud.'[215]

It was a busy time for Ion Calvocoressi. The day after the King left Italy, they had to make another long and difficult move, this time north

of Siena to Tavarnelle, where the soldiers of the Maori Battalion had
raided the accordion factory. The moving of Leese's Tactical HQ happened all too regularly while the army was advancing. The general
insisted it should always be sited on a hill, with commanding views. The
difficulty for Ion and Major Bruce, whose task it was to organise the
moves, was finding somewhere that fulfilled those criteria but which was
not overly exposed to enemy shelling. It was also extremely important
to get the layout and camouflage of the site right as well.

By now, however, Ion and Major Bruce had finely honed such moves.
Sites were found the day before a move. Packing up the existing camp
would take place straight after breakfast and they would aim to be on
the road by 10 a.m. By mid-afternoon, setting up the new camp would
normally have been completed, with any visitor thinking it had been
there for ages. Caravans would have been sited, tents erected, and slit-
trenches dug. Telephone lines and electric cables would have been laid
and connected, and camouflage netting draped. Each move involved no
less than 250 men in all, seventy-three vehicles and fifteen caravans.
Logistically, it was quite a feat.

On 3 August, Leese went out to see Kirkman, who took him to a
forward observation post. Kirkman was very concerned about Alex and
Harding's plan for the assault on the Gothic Line, which had been to
bludgeon their way through the central Apennines from Florence to
Bologna, using Eighth and Fifth Armies side by side, but with the Poles
carrying out a feint up the Adriatic coast first – a deception plan to
make Kesselring believe that was the direction of the main attack. From
the observation post, Kirkman hoped to show Leese the endless peaks
of the Apennines, but it was a misty day of low cloud and they could
see little. Instead, Kirkman had to depend on his own rhetoric to get his
point across. Since the loss of the seven divisions, he argued, 15th Army
Group were now without any trained mountain divisions. The loss also
meant that Eighth Army would have to take the brunt of the fighting to
come. But, he added forcibly, Eighth Army's modus operandi was to
attack in a great concentration of tanks and fire power. These two arms,
however, would be less effective in the high and jagged peaks of the
Apennines than they would be closer to the Adriatic.

Kirkman, who was a gunner by trade, felt it would be better to make
the main assault where Eighth Army's great advantage in tanks and guns
could be best exploited. There was no part of the Gothic Line that
favoured the attacker, but the hills along the Adriatic coast were certainly

far lower than the lofty heights of the central Apennines. Furthermore, the distance through the mountains between the Gothic Line and Bologna was about forty miles, but half that between the start of the Gothic Line and Rimini, after which the plains of the north began. Leese needed little persuading, since he had already had much the same concerns. He thus agreed to suggest a dramatic change of plan to Alexander.

Leese met Alex and Harding at Orvieto airfield the next day, 4 August. It was sizzlingly hot, and so they sheltered from the sun under the wing of a Dakota. Back in June, when Alex had still hoped to win the ANVIL argument, he had envisaged the assault on the Gothic Line would be nothing – 'merely an incident' – in the Allies' pursuit.[216] This had changed since the withdrawal of the divisions for southern France, but Alex had been inclined to stick to his original plan, largely because of the time factor; to change the plan now would involve moving the bulk of Eighth Army, already massed in the centre of the peninsula, to the Adriatic, a massive logistical headache that would take several weeks to carry out. Time was the all-consuming factor: they *had* to get their breakthrough before the summer was out.

Furthermore, Leese's support of Kirkman was based on two false premises. First, he believed that the bulk of Kesselring's forces were expecting an Allied attack north of Florence and so had concentrated most of his forces there. This was, in fact, not the case; rather, they been massed in that area for the defence of Florence and had not yet been redeployed. Second, his maps and aerial photographs of the Adriatic sector were deceiving him. Certainly, the hills there were lower, and along the coast there was the flat coastal road, but the line of the hills ran at ninety degrees to any proposed advance. To fight through along the Adriatic coast would involve crossing over ridge after ridge after ridge. And beneath every ridge was a valley, and in those valleys were rivers – rivers that would have to be crossed; and the difficulties of getting over these had not improved since their days in the Liri Valley.

For Leese, however, there was a further advantage of moving Eighth Army to the Adriatic. He never mentioned that the issues he had with Clark were a factor, but Harding, for one, certainly believed they played their part in his thought processes. 'Gen. Leese,' noted Harding, 'was still very jealous of Gen. Clark over the capture of Rome when the two armies had fought more or less on the same axis.'[217] As both Alex and Harding recognised, close co-operation between Fifth and Eighth Armies would be essential in their existing plan. Ill-feeling between the army commanders was not helpful. Nor were they eager to make Eighth Army carry out a plan in which they had little confidence; far better that Leese fight to a plan in which he both believed and had confidence.

And, it had to be admitted, fighting through the central Apennines would not be easy. Yes, there were serious difficulties to be overcome along the Adriatic, but in the mountains between Florence and Bologna there were only man-made routes, roads blasted by the skill of Italian engineering. These, with their sheer ledges and endless tunnels, would, of course, be easy for the Germans to destroy and would take time to repair. It did not take much imagination to picture how all those Allied trucks, tanks and vehicles might fare.

Leese's suggestion also made Alex realise he could instead return to his favoured two-punch strategy, which would split the reserves Kesselring had available for defence. Fifth Army could attack through the centre of the Apennines, while Eighth Army could assault along the Adriatic. If time was the only reason not to change the plan, they should take a deep breath and accept the loss of time the change would incur. Better to have a plan, Alex reasoned, that enabled him to maintain his balance, rather than one his commanders disliked for want of a couple of weeks. Thus he and Harding agreed in principle to Leese's suggestion.

With Clark also having agreed to the idea, a commanders' conference was held at Leese's Tactical HQ on 10 August. Leese had already been to visit Clark three days before. The two had got on well, sipping Coca-Cola together, the supposed slight at Siena seemingly forgotten. Clark, Leese noted, was 'rather nicer than usual' and cheerfully showed the Eighth Army commander around his luxury caravan, replete with large sofa, set-in radio, and vast cocktail cabinet.[218] Leese had been most impressed, especially by the mahogany finish, and basin and shower that provided both cold *and* hot water.

At any rate, both army commanders were in a co-operative mood by the time they next met at Leese's HQ. The sun was shining and Leese, in his usual informal way, suggested they hold the conference outside in a glade of olive trees, and proceeded to conduct the entire discussion whilst lying under a tree with his hands behind his head. Perhaps the surroundings and lack of formality encouraged a benevolent atmosphere; perhaps the knowledge that the two army commanders would be separated for the forthcoming battle helped produce a conciliatory feeling amongst them; whatever the reasons, Alex and his senior commanders agreed on almost everything that August afternoon. Eighth Army would attack first on 25 August – a fortnight away – in what was now called Operation OLIVE, while Fifth Army's assault would follow around 1 September. By this time, it was hoped, Kesselring would have moved a number of his forces to the Adriatic and weakened the centre for when Fifth Army launched its own attack. The only thorny issue was over who would have command over Kirkman's XIII Corps, which was to be deployed in the centre, in Fifth Army's sector. The obvious and sensible solution was to pass command over to Clark, and although Leese must have been loath to lose his senior corps to Fifth Army, he magnanimously agreed. As the meeting broke up, Clark warmly thanked Leese for 'his unselfish approach to the problem'. 'From this conference,' Clark's Chief of Staff, Al Gruenther, noted, 'there developed a plan which is far more effective than the one which had previously been decided upon. The big disadvantage in the new plan is the delay. It is too early,' he added, 'to evaluate the advantage which the German will be able to take of that delay.'[219]

That was true enough. Despite the declared satisfaction of the commanders, the change to the Adriatic was a huge gamble.

Alex was still desperately searching for extra troops. He wanted to be able to attack with eighteen divisions and with six held in reserve, but he had only twenty in total. One solution was to turn to the Italians. Badoglio had been demanding a greater role for the Royal Army, and since taking over as prime minister, so too had Bonomi and his government. Indeed, he and his ministers had been becoming ever more vocal in their frustration. In July, Benedetto Croce, the highly regarded philosopher and Minister Without Portfolio, had been especially outspoken in his criticism of the Allies, claiming there was a 'profound contradiction' between official encouragement to Italy and actual Allied restrictions, which made 'many Italians think the Allies plan to keep Italy in an inferior status in the war'.[220]

Quite apart from the fact that the Italians had only ever been given the status of 'co-belligerents' rather than thick-as-thieves allies, there was the problem of both arming them and training them. All Italy's armament factories were in the north, so if the Allies wanted these troops, they would have to equip them. When Alex suggested, in mid-July, that they make greater efforts to use Italian troops, the Americans flatly refused to get involved; Roosevelt may have had a broad-minded view of future Italian democracy, but this did not mean he was prepared to

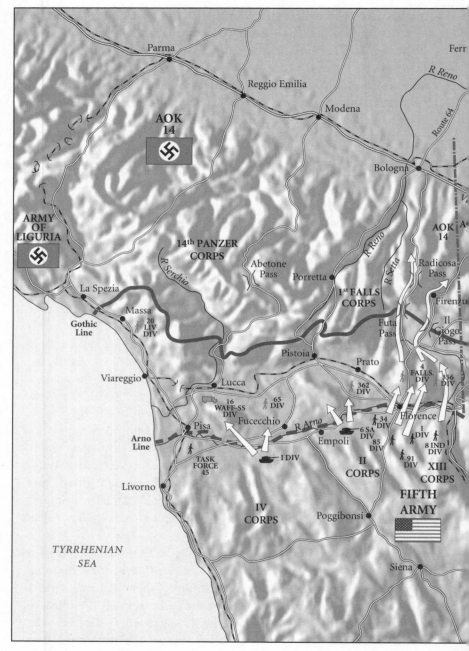

Alexander's battle plan for the Gothic Line, August 1944

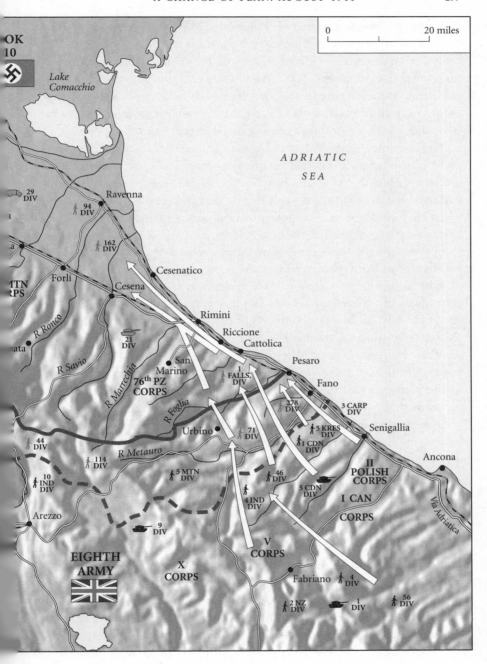

0   20 miles

OK
10

Lake
Comacchio

ADRIATIC

SEA

29
DIV

Ravenna

94
DIV

162
DIV

Cesenatico

MTN
RPS

Forli

Cesena

Rimini

R Ronco

Riccione

21
DIV

Cattolica

R Savio

San
Marino

Pesaro

ata

76th PZ
CORPS

R Marecchia

1
FALLS.
DIV

Fano

R Foglia

278
DIV

3 CARP
DIV

Urbino

71
DIV

5 KRES
DIV

Senigallia

44
DIV

R Metauro

1 CDN
DIV

114
DIV

5 MTN
DIV

46
DIV

II
POLISH
CORPS

Ancona

10
IND
DIV

4 IND
DIV

5 CDN
DIV

I CAN

Arezzo

CORPS

9
DIV

V
CORPS

Via Adriatica

EIGHTH
ARMY

X
CORPS

Fabriano

4
DIV

2 NZ
DIV

1
DIV

56
DIV

waste American war materiel on Italian troops. Churchill, however, did agree to allow the release of enough British kit to equip four new – or rather, reconstituted – Italian divisions of 12,000 men each. There was no shortage of volunteers. The difficulty was going to be getting them fit for battle. 'We are trying in a matter of weeks,' declared an Eighth Army report, 'to train, convert and raise to British standards Italian formations of an army which has always been weak on officers and discipline.'[221]

This weakness, inherent because the structure, training and equipment of the Italian army had for many years fallen some way short of modern standards, lay at the heart of the matter. It was why Germany preferred not to waste any time or resources training young Italian males when they could be put to more practical use as manual workers; and it was why the Allies had been so reluctant to use them as front-line troops. But Alex's needs now outweighed such reservations. He had to get his troops from wherever he could.

And so he did. A Greek brigade trained in mountain warfare had arrived and had been placed in Eighth Army Reserve, while in Fifth Army the first all-black infantry regiment had reached Italy and been temporarily attached to the 1st Armored until the rest of the 92nd 'Buffalo' Division arrived. The Brazilian division was also on its way. For the most part, these welcome additions could play little or no part in the battle about to be resumed, but at least he could call on seven divisions that had been rested and refreshed.

One of these was the 46th Division, which had left Italy in March to be retrained and refitted in the Middle East. Known as the 'Midlands' division, the 46th had evolved somewhat since first arriving in Northwest Africa with the First Army in January 1943; now only the 5th Sherwood Foresters and the 2/5th Leicestershire Regiment could truly be said to come from the heart of England.

Peter Moore was a twenty-two-year-old lieutenant with the Leicesters and already something of a seasoned campaigner: having survived some particularly intense fighting in Tunisia and the invasion of the Mediterranean island of Pantelleria – a precursor to the invasion of Sicily – he was subsequently wounded at Salerno, where he was struck in the leg by a piece of shrapnel. At the time, Peter had thought little of it, but within a week his leg had become infected, swelling to an unhealthy size and giving him a violent fever. It was a full seven months before he could return to his battalion, which by that time had returned from Italy and was retraining in Palestine.

There had been considerable changes during the period he had been away. The Leicesters, like a lot of regional British regiments, were filled with a number of local men. Peter himself was from an old Leicestershire family, and had put his name down for the same regiment in which his father had served in the First World War. Something of a reluctant soldier – he had hated cadet corps at school – he had nonetheless been pleased to discover several familiar faces and like-minded people when he was eventually posted to 2/5th Battalion. One of those had been Wilf Bray, who had been a young subaltern at the time Peter had joined. They had become great friends, but back in January Peter had heard that Wilf had been killed on the Volturno. Around the same time, Peter Everard, another close friend, had been wounded by a mine. These had been hard blows, but Peter had rejoined the battalion happy in the knowledge that Colin Stockdale, an old and trusted friend from boyhood, had survived the winter battles. In fact, a recent letter from Colin had done much to renew Peter's determination to get himself declared fit and back with his battalion once more.

Only once he had arrived in Palestine did Peter learn that Colin, too, had been killed – his letter had reached Peter a whole five weeks after his death. Peter was stunned, and desolate with grief. They had been friends since spending summer holidays on Anglesey as teenagers; they had even courted two sisters together.

There had been other changes too. 'It is rather depressing,' he wrote in a letter home, 'to serve under captains whom I last knew as 2/Lts.' Even more galling was the fact that he had been told he was to become a captain the day he was invalided out; he never had received that extra pip and was now back as a lieutenant once more. 'I suppose,' he added, 'that is the price of absence.'[222]

The Leicesters had reached Naples in early July and had then been sent to Bastardo in Umbria to carry out intense training for the battle ahead. During this time, the officers of B Company became friends with a local Italian wine producer and his family. Peter even developed a deep crush on the farmer's pretty seventeen-year-old daughter, Luigia, although nothing came of it. 'She was my great, hopeless, lost love of the war, all very chaste and innocent,' he noted, 'and I adored her.' That month of summer training in Umbria confirmed Peter's innate Italophilia. 'If I had been asked,' wrote Peter, 'I would have said that I could envisage no post-war future more satisfying and agreeable than settling down in Umbria.'[223]

Sadly for Peter, however – and all concerned – there was a battle to
be fought first. On 18 August, he saw Luigia for the last time at a party
held at the farmer's house. Two days later, his battalion began the move
from their Umbrian idyll up to the front.

Kesselring had lost three veteran divisions too, including the Hermann
Göring, but had gained the equivalent of eight new ones – which
although of lesser experience and quality, now gave him twenty-six
divisions in Italy, of which all but four were within shouting distance of
the front. This was six more than Alexander could call upon; for the
first time in the campaign, the Allies had fewer divisions at the front
than the Germans. Even so, a large number of Kesselring's units remained
under-strength. For example, of the eighty-one infantry battalions now
available to AOK 10, only twenty-three were considered by von Vietinghoff's staff to be 'strong' – that is, of more than 400 men; and 400 men
was still less than half most Allied equivalents. Nine were classified as
'weak' – that is, less than 200 strong. The now promoted Leutnant Jupp
Klein, recovered from his wounds and back in charge of his company of
engineers in the 1st Fallschirmjäger Division, had also at last been given
some replacements. 'They were new soldiers from paratroop school,' says
Jupp, 'and that made up the company to around eighty or ninety men.'
It was still a lot less than in those Allied companies they were about to
face on the Adriatic Front.

Kesselring was still uncertain about Allied intentions, however. The
limited intelligence available to him had suggested that an Allied attack
along the Adriatic was likely, but then further intelligence indicated the
Allies were massing forces east of Florence. He was given further anxiety
by prospects of an Allied landing either side of the Alps, either in
southern France or the Gulf of Genoa, which he viewed as the most
sensible place for them to make an amphibious assault. In the Gulf of
Genoa, particularly, the mountains were comparatively low, which he
felt would have given the Allies a straightforward opportunity to debouch
into the northern plains and also to make the most of the partisan effort,
which he felt was especially strong in that area.

Even after the invasion of southern France, he continued to believe
the Allied effort would be directed towards Italy and an attempt to
outflank the Gothic Line; indeed, rumours continued to persist about
an additional landing in the Gulf of Genoa. With this in mind, Marshal
Graziani had been given responsibility for the coastal area around Genoa,

and took command of the new 'Army of Liguria'. This was a mixed force made up of the new Italian divisions fresh from Germany, but also the German 90th Panzer Grenadier Division, which had been poised in reserve near Bologna until sent westwards.

Meanwhile, from the German High Command came orders to be mindful of an Allied landing in the northern Adriatic. In fact, Kesselring had even been ordered to prepare contingency plans to fall back north of the River Po, with von Vietinghoff authorising reconnaissance for a new defensive line north of the River Adige between Venice and the Alps. This operation was codenamed AUTUMN FOG – or *Herbstnebel* – and detailed plans had been sent to the High Command for approval.

In the meantime, however, Kesselring was pleased with the way the Gothic Line was progressing, and although incomplete and underdeveloped in parts, it still presented a formidable defensive barrier. It was not, like the Great Wall of China or Hadrian's Wall, a single, continuous barrier. Rather, it was a series of defences, woven into the beautiful hills and mountains of the Apennines, 180 miles long and several miles deep. The Adriatic sector was made up of two principal lines of defences, Green I and Green II, also known as A and B.

The hills of the Adriatic coast might not have offered the kind of natural defences of the dominatingly jagged and imposing mountains further inland, but there had been no lack of sweat and toil by the engineers and Todt workers in AOK 10's sector of the line. Mines had been laid across roads, over fields, along river beds – more than 100,000 in all; a continuous anti-tank ditch almost six miles long had been dug; trees had been felled and 80 miles of tangled barbed wire laid in front of any possible advance. Over 2,500 concealed concrete machine-gun posts littered every hill and dominated every approach. Panther tank turrets, with their high-velocity 75mm guns, had been sunk into yet more concrete with bunkers for the ammunition. As if that was not enough, there were also 500 anti-tank and Nebelwerfer positions, and some 2,500 dugouts of various depth and strength. Large concrete bunkers had also been built to house coastal artillery. Allied aerial reconnaissance photographs showed a dense network of machine-gun posts, gun positions and ditches, each providing covering fire.

Formidable though this was, the majority of these defences had been built by press-ganged and deeply unmotivated Italians. In places, some had even sabotaged the work, and progress had suffered at the hands of repeated air attacks and the Allies' continuing efforts to disrupt supply lines, which inevitably had a knock-on effect on the amount of materials reaching the Todt workers. Not only that, the numerous deaths and injuries inflicted by Allied air attacks only caused more misery for the Italians and further hamstrung their work.

At any rate, Oberleutnant Hans Golda was far from impressed by the defences. His battery had reached the Adriatic in the middle of the month, and it seemed to him that there was still a great deal to do. The Werfer Regiment 71 took up positions close to the coast, just a couple of miles south-west of Cattolica at Monteluro. Here, Hans discovered that while mines and wire had been laid, the wire was rusty and 'useless'. Nor had their own bunkers and positions been completed, and so Hans and his men had to work flat out to get them finished. Hans could only speak from the experience of his own stretch of the line, but as far as he was concerned it was poorly prepared.

Certainly there was a lack of urgency about Kesselring's preparations, and as a consequence, he and his commanders were about to make some of the same mistakes they had made back in May. Once again, none of the senior German commanders expected another major offensive by the Allies in the near future, despite the piecemeal intelligence warnings. Rather, they were anticipating a more muted attack, a continuation of the broad pressure the Allies had been applying in recent weeks. The August lull had duped them into a false sense of security – so much so that on 20 August von Vietinghoff issued a new training directive for troops installed behind the Gothic Line, and then, incredibly, he went off on leave. Heidrich, commander of the 1st Fallschirmjäger Division, was also away. As in May, Kesselring's forces were about to get a rude awakening.

The Germans had been caught short in May, but Kesselring had at least had time to build up his strength in the months before. This time, however, his supply situation was more serious despite the brief lull. The loss of the bridges across the Po had much to do with it, as had the continued harrying of his lines of supply before the bulk of the of Allies' Tactical Air Command had been switched to operations over southern France.

But the partisans had also more than played their part. In the strategically critical mountains of the Monte Sole massif, between the Setta and Reno Valleys, the Stella Rossa were undisputed masters. Flush with arms and equipment, they had deftly seen off any German or Fascist attempts at a rastrellamento, so that the massif had become almost completely off-limits to anyone who was not either in or supportive of the band. And not just the Monte Sole massif: the Stella Rossa were operating over a wide area, and pushing far further south than they had before. On 19 August, the Stella Rossa was involved in another large-scale fire-fight some fifteen miles south across the border into Tuscany. The fight began as a detachment of partisans – mostly Russian deserters – saw off several German patrols. A charismatic Russian nicknamed Karoton even managed to kill the German commander, before the detachment fell back and rejoined the main body of the brigade. Rather than wait for a further rastrellamento, however, Lupo then ordered a counterattack using the entire Stella Rossa in a classic envelopment. As the German troops fell back from the initial onslaught, other partisans attacked the retreating Germans from along the wooded slopes of Monte Oggioli, killing and wounding large numbers and destroying a battery of enemy artillery.

Such battles greatly increased their confidence, but despite this success, Lupo insisted that most of their operations be hit-and-run guerrilla actions. In this manner they continued to cause havoc with the German lines of supply: telephone lines were cut; trucks attacked and shoved down mountainsides; roads were blown; lone patrols and passing troops attacked and disarmed. In the big scheme of things, these attacks were small scale, but they were being repeated all across northern Italy – and accumulatively, they were beginning to grind down the German war effort, undermining morale and ensuring that no German soldier could ever completely relax. Between June and August, Kesselring's intelligence officer told him that the partisans had accounted for as many as 5,000 killed and up to 30,000 wounded or kidnapped, the equivalent of more than two complete divisions. The Feldmarschall believed this figure had to be too high, but accepted it was not too far off the mark. 'In any case,' he noted, 'the proportion of casualties on the German side alone greatly exceeded the total partisan losses.'[224]

In the hills overlooking the azure blue Adriatic, not a single Italian could have known what momentous events had been taking place at Orvieto airfield earlier in the month. Nor would either Alexander or Leese have given much consideration to how their fateful decision would affect the lives of tens of thousands of Italians who now stood in the way of the proposed Allied attack.

Indeed, in Onferno, the summer was rolling by fairly peacefully. As elsewhere, the farmers were anticipating a good harvest, and for Italo Quadrelli, the closest he had got to the war was when one of the very few German reconnaissance planes had been shot down nearby. 'It fell right by Onferno,' says Italo, 'and we boys all ran to the wreck.'

And so for the moment, Italo Quadrelli and his family continued their day-to-day existence, ignorant of the hurricane that was about to tear through their quiet corner of southern Romagna.

TWENTY-FIVE

Despair
August 1944

After the fall of Florence, Martha Gellhorn had made her way to the city. Billeted with an elderly American in his house in the hills south of the Arno, she had the surreal experience of watching the Germans firing their guns from Fiesole, whilst outgoing Allied shells, fired from a British battery in the villa's garden, screamed over like freight trains. Meanwhile, the British artillery captain played Chopin on the piano as the American's Italian wife sang seventeenth-century Italian songs.

Florence itself was in a terrible way, even though much of the city had indeed been spared. Water was scarce, while the Germans had taken every available means of transport, from hearses to hand carts. The whole place, she thought, looked drab and soiled. At the Boboli Gardens she discovered open mass graves had been dug and the corpses left there. In the streets, teenage partisans wearing armbands and brandishing rifles loitered excitedly, while the Pitti Palace had become a refugee centre in which the Civilian Affairs Officers, with the help of the Red Cross, were once again trying to sort out the humanitarian crisis that followed in the wake of the front line.

Later, once the Americans had taken over the city, she made her way across the rubble at either end of the Ponte Vecchio and wandered about the shuttered streets. She also befriended a young American major. They went to the Excelsior Hotel, Pavolini's headquarters just a week before, and spent the night together in one of the many deserted rooms.

Also in Florence was the teenage German spy, Carla Costa. At the beginning of July, she and another agent, Anna Spata, had been visited at Colonel David's base in Milan by two German Abwehr agents and told they would soon be sent on a mission into enemy territory. Passport photographs were taken of both of them for their false papers and identity cards, fake ration books were issued, and they were given lessons in identification of Allied aircraft and military insignia and markings.

Then on 6 August, the day after the Allies reached Florence, Carla
and Anna were summoned to Abwehr offices in Milan and briefed for
their forthcoming missions. Anna was to head to Salerno, Carla to
Florence and then on to Rome. Their tasks were twofold: to deliver
messages and money; and to gather as much information as possible
about the location of military headquarters and any troop movements.
They were to make a note of the markings and insignia of any vehicles
or troops they saw, and anything else they could discover about civilian
morale, relations between Allied troops and Italians, food supplies and
so on. Each of the girls was then given 15,000 lire and a silk handkerchief
which bore a secret message. This was to be used should any doubt
about them arise on the part of the Germans.

Escorted through the front line by German troops on the night of
11 August, Carla then made her way on her own to Florence, and to a
pre-arranged address in the north of the city, where she spent the night.
The following day, she went to the Archbishopric of Florence, posing as
a refugee, and was immediately directed to a convent in the south of the
city. Armed with a note from the Archbishopric, she easily crossed the
Arno and began circulating through the southern half of the city, going
into hotels where Allied army personnel were already stationed and
picking up what information she could. Having told people she was
trying to get back to Rome, two civilians even asked her to take letters
with her on their behalf.

Pleased with her first efforts at snooping, she passed back across the
Arno, as ordered, and made her way successfully back to the German
lines and reported her findings at the nearest German regimental headquarters. The first part of her mission now completed, she was escorted
back across the lines once more.

This time she crossed the Arno and went straight to the refugee centre
at the Pitti Palace, hoping to get herself a ride to Rome. Securing a pass
was no easy matter, however, and after two fruitless days, she gave up in
despair, and without the necessary paperwork made her way to the
refugee embarkation point. Almost immediately, she was able to sweet-
talk her way onto a truck heading south.

Although it was a step in the right direction, the lorry was not,
however, going to Rome, but to another refugee camp, and so she spent
another frustrating day stuck where she was until she was given passage
to a further camp. From there she eventually got a ride to Rome, arriving

in the city on 27 August. It had been ten days since reaching Florence for the second time, but at least she had made it. Indeed, difficult though her journey had been, she had shown just the kind of courage and initiative her German masters had hoped from her. Now, however, it was time for the real work to begin. With the Germans' lack of reconnaissance aircraft and limited intelligence resources, this work of hers, she knew, was of vital importance. Carla was determined she was not going to let anyone down – not her bosses in the Abwehr, not Colonel David, not her fellow agents, and most definitely not herself.

As the Abwehr had correctly realised, young teenage girls were unlikely suspects as spies. To the Allied military police, nurses, Red Cross workers and Civil Affairs Officers, this rather plain-looking seventeen-year-old probably looked much the same as the thousands of other Italian girls, displaced and impoverished, who filled the camps and cities of Allied Occupied Italy.

Despite the installation of the new government, and despite the ongoing efforts of the Allied Military Government and Allied Control Commission, southern Italy remained, in the summer of 1944, a generally miserable place to be. Promises of an increase in rations had not been honoured, and unless increases in shipping were made and the black-market racketeers like Vito Genovese firmly stamped on, there was no prospect of the situation improving. In Rome food shortages were exacerbated by a massive shortage of power. The large hydroelectric plants at Tivoli and Terni had been seriously damaged by German sabotage, and despite the best efforts of the Allied engineers, the combined plants were only able to provide around 12 per cent of their former output. To make matters worse, the Tiber was so low there was insufficient water to supply the two steam power plants that offered an alternative power source. The one cause for cheer was that it had been a bumper year for the harvest. Yet even here there was a sting in the tail, as many farmers between Rome and Florence were too worried about mines to harvest their crop, while others were reluctant to deliver their grain to government pools. Finally, food distribution continued to be affected by the severely weakened transportation system.

In the second week of August, Norman Lewis was posted to the city of Benevento, some forty miles inland from Naples. A town of around fifty thousand, it had been largely destroyed the previous year by Allied bombers, and fifteen months on showed little sign of any kind of resurrection. The city was like a post-apocalyptic ruin. On his way into the town, he passed a row of young girls – *scugnizzi* – 'masturbating on the rim of a broken fountain'. His new office was in the old police station and was also severely bomb damaged, with collapsed ceilings and piles of plaster and debris swept into the corners. The water supply for the town was switched on for only a few minutes every day. Despair filled the air. The eleventh-century cathedral had been destroyed, along with, Norman had been told, one in five houses in the city. 'The custom here is to wear mourning for seven years for a close relative,' noted Norman, 'so the whole population is dressed in black. The poverty of these people is beyond belief.'[225]

The head man in Benevento, Norman discovered, was Francesco Alta-mura, of the pro-Allied SIM – or Italian secret police. Altamura had been told to place himself at Norman's disposal, and duly presented himself. He then took Norman to meet the other city dignitaries. These included a wealthy coffin maker, much in demand in recent times, and also the owner of the best-kept brothel in the area. Within minutes he had offered Norman a bribe, explaining that he had another brothel in Naples, but it had lost its official endorsement thanks to AMG officials in the pay of rivals. It would be worth 100,000 lire were Norman to help him get its official sanction once more.

Norman later asked Altamura whether there was a car he could use. In the entire city, there were only five registered, but eventually they found a Bianchi standing on wooden blocks in a garage, and which was also missing some engine parts. Despite this, Altamura assured him that the car could be made workable once more – for a friend. The implica-tion was crystal clear: it would be best if Norman played ball.

On his second day in Benevento, a grimy waif called Giuseppina appeared at Norman's office. Just twelve years old, she told him that her parents had been killed in the 'great bombing' and that she lived under a house down by the river. She had, she explained, come for her blanket as usual. Norman was taken aback. Blankets were much sought after and not easily obtained, but when he told her this, she replied that the Canadian who had been in charge before him had given her a new blanket once a week. 'Only at this point,' wrote Norman, 'did I realise the tragic significance of the request, and that this skinny, undeveloped little girl was a child prostitute.'[226]

*   *   *

In the German-occupied north, radio bulletins and newspapers continued to cajole and intimidate in equal measure. There were warnings to farmers not to hoard – on pain of death; warnings not to spread any information that might aid the enemy – on pain of death; warnings not to aid or assist bandits – on pain of death. Meanwhile, day in, day out, German advertisements encouraged Italian workers to head to Germany for a new life of honest labour and decent pay. They were always the same: same design, same lettering, same images. The only difference was the skills that were required: drivers were needed one day, cooks the next, hotel staff the day after that. A facsimile of a postcard sent by a contented Italian worker in Germany was printed in *Il Resto del Carlino*. 'Now I'm in Berlin where I am working as a mechanic in a big workshop and I am enjoying it,' it ran. 'If only you could see what a beautiful city this is. We work twelve hours a day and we don't drink wine but only beer, which costs very little – 1 lira per flask and I drink two flasks a day. If I knew I was going to be so happy I would have come sooner.'[227] Whoever wrote this piece of flagrant propaganda presumably assumed that most Italians knew little about the ruined and bomb-blasted city Berlin had become.

Next to the adverts for workers were those for SS recruits. 'A Call from the Italian SS for the Defence of the Country: Volunteers!' one ran, 'The proud battalions of the voluntary Italian SS legions, who are heroically fighting elbow to elbow with the bold troops of our friend Germany in the defence of the holy ground of our Patria, we call on you.'[228]

Inevitably, some people did opt to go to Germany, the majority out of desperation more than anything else. Most manpower, however, came from forcible deportations. In Turin, for example, as many as 3,000 workers from the Fiat factory were deported for resisting German attempts to dismantle machinery to be sent to Germany. Raids carried out in public places were also on the increase, the victims given a physical examination and then shipped off to the Reich. Rumours abounded that once the harvest was over, even farmers would be rounded up and deported. Regardless of the truth of this, an atmosphere of fear and repression hung heavy over northern Italy.

Nor had the militarisation of the government done much to ease the fears of the majority. The public response to Pavolini's formation of the Black Brigades had been quite good – around 40,000 by the beginning of September – although the reasons for joining were varied, just as they were for those who had chosen to become partisans: for every passionate

Fascist, there was a young man desperate for a job and a chance to earn a regular wage. Like many partisans, others joined in an effort to avoid deportation.

In Forlì, the 25th 'A. Capanni' Black Brigade had done little since its formation to make the majority of the population feel safer. In the view of Dr Silvio Zavatti, a middle-aged civilian who lived in the city, the brigade was made up of little more than 'spoilt youngsters' who liked throwing their weight around, bullying any men who did not join them and 'requisitioning' animals and other goods in the name of the Republican government. Within a few weeks of their formation, they had proved their strong-arm tactics by arresting and then summarily executing five deserters from the New Army.[229]

A few days later, the Brigade achieved a significant coup, when, on the tip-off of an informer, they surrounded and attacked a safehouse in which a local partisan leader, Silvio Corbari, and three of his followers were sheltering. One of those was twenty-one-year-old Iris Versari, who had been helping Corbari as a courier the previous autumn, but who had since become an active guerrilla. A German soldier accompanying the Black Brigade kicked down the door and shot Iris Versari in the leg. She shot him in turn, then realising she could not escape, took her own life. Another of the partisans, Arturo Spazzoli, was cut down, while Corbari and a fourth partisan, Adriano Casadei, were taken prisoner.

The two captured men were taken to the town square of Castrocaro, a small town south-west of Forlì. After kissing and hugging his friend Casadei, Corbari was publicly hanged. The rope was then placed around Casadei's neck. Turning to the crowd Casadei said, 'We are the real Italians.' One of the Black Brigade men punched him in the face, and then hanged him. They then produced the corpses of Spazzoli and Iris Versari and hanged them in the square as well, their bodies still dripping blood onto the ground below. Later in the day, all four were cut down and taken to the Piazza Saffi in Forlì, where they were hanged again, from lamp posts in the square. Dr Zavatti had watched this spectacle with mounting disgust. 'The Fascists of the Black Brigade,' he said, 'were flogging the bodies of the deceased like animals, and acts of impudence were performed on the body of Versari, which was nearly naked.'[230] Unsurprisingly, this kind of public show of vindictive brutality did little to win hearts and minds. Rather, it suggested that something close to anarchy had descended.

Nor was there much sign that the formation of the Black Brigades was deterring partisan activity in any way, as Commander Pavolini – as he now was – soon discovered for himself. Along with his Bir el Gobi Company, Pavolini had gone to Savigliano, a town in Piemonte only a few miles from where Cosimo Arrichiello was still keeping his head down on the Bolti family farm. Had Cosimo known that the Fascist Party leader and several bands of Black Brigades and units of Decima MAS were in the area he might have been more worried, but as it was, Commander Pavolini and his men were concerned only with combating the many thousands of partisans now operating from the Piemonte Mountains.

It was on a trip to inspect a mobile company of the Black Brigades detached to the Decima MAS that Pavolini came under fire. The Republicans immediately found themselves pinned down, with Pavolini and several other Fascist dignitaries suffering wounds and unable to move for more than four hours until the partisans were eventually forced to fall back. Pavolini's wound was not serious, but as he was discovering, the partisan menace was getting worse, not better.

Part of the reason for increased partisan activity was the prospect of the imminent arrival of the Allies. This belief that the Germans and Fascists would soon be kicked out of Italy had undoubtedly led to the over-confidence of the partisans in the Apuan Mountains around Sant' Anna, but it was a widely shared belief, and one that had been encouraged by SOE and OSS agents in an effort to get the maximum advantage from the partisans before and during the big offensive against the Gothic Line.

But the partisans were also better organised by the late summer of 1944, again, in part due to help from Allied agents, and in part due to the efforts of the Comitato di Liberazione Nazionale per l'Alta Italia (CLNAI), which had been working hard to bring a level of efficiency and unity to the rising numbers of partisan bands.

In June 1944, the CLNAI had tried to co-ordinate the resistance movement by forming the Corps of Volunteers of Freedom (CVL) under the direction of the CLNAI leaders, Ferruccio Parri, of the Action Party, and the Communist, Luigi Longo. Parri and Longo recognised, however, that their leadership of the CVL was causing political tensions between them and the other three parties within the CLNAI. Nor were they military men, and so on 25 June, via an agent in the north, they contacted the Italian General Staff in Rome, asking for General Rafaele Cadorna to be sent to Milan to act as Military Adviser to the CVL/CLNAI.

This was a shrewd move on the part of Parri and Longo. Cadorna had won fame for his stand against the Germans in Rome following the armistice, but was also known as a no-nonsense conservative and vehement anti-fascist. The Allies and the Rome government duly obliged: Cadorna parachuted into northern Italy on 12 August, along with an Italian-speaking British major, Oliver Churchill.

Unfortunately, Cadorna soon discovered there was little he could do, and that he had been brought to the north as a neutral figurehead and little more. Nor had he been given much of a brief by the Allies. This reflected their own confused attitude towards the partisans and more specifically the CLNAI, for while Alexander certainly recognised the partisans' value in the military campaign, he also knew that the more organised the resistance became, so it would become more politicised. This would not have been a problem were it not for the increasing authority of the Communists, towards whom the British remained deeply suspicious. With this in mind, Alexander was permitted by London to assist any partisans so long as they were not Communist-backed. At the same time, SOE in Bari had set up a radio station for the partisans called *Italia Combatte*, which they used by for relaying messages of encouragement and propaganda, and which was also run hand-in-hand with the Psychological Warfare Executive (PWE) at AFHQ. The Americans, on the other hand, had a more laid-back attitude and continued to send in OSS agents and supplies to help the Communist-backed Garibaldi Brigades. Despite this, rivalries broke out between the various bands with the Communists frequently stealing arms drops from their non-Communist comrades, or trying to coerce them to become Garibaldis too. Many Italians resented this, and a large number of those who were against the Fascists and the German occupation were equally against the Communists, and were fearful of them ever coming into power once the war was over.

One band that had remained determinedly non-political was the Stella Rossa, despite the best efforts of CUMER, the local branch of the CVL/CLNAI. Repeated letters were sent from the CUMER headquarters warning Lupo to toe the line, and arguing that only by presenting a united front would victory be secured. Lupo, however, dismissed such notions. After all, the Stella Rossa was the only partisan band to have been formed following the armistice and to have survived the winter intact and with the same command; their independent approach had worked so far and neither Lupo nor Gianni Rossi saw any reason why they should suddenly start kowtowing to CUMER and the CVL.

Rather, Lupo preferred to regard the Allies as his superiors, and insisted on only taking instructions through OSS. Moreover, when the Allies did finally come, Lupo fully expected to be embraced heartily by the conquering armies, and to be given a continuing role within the Allied ranks rather than have anything further to do with the CVL.

This was a false hope. What to do with partisans once the front passed through their territory had been a conundrum that had been dealt with fairly easily during the early advance north. However, as the Allies reached areas of greater numbers and better-organised partisans, it had become more of a problem.

While the Allies were extremely happy for partisans to risk their lives fighting on their behalf *behind* the front line, they had no interest in having them fighting shoulder to shoulder with Allied troops in front of it. As an OSS report on the partisan contribution put it, guerrillas did 'not always meet the standards of discipline maintained in regular military forces'. Nor were they trained in any sense for front-line combat. Moreover, the report continued, those of a political nature 'frequently show a tendency to demand that the political ideologies for which they have fought be translated into administrative practice by the victorious Allies'.[231] Lupo and the Stella Rossa may have been a case apart, but as far as the Allies were concerned, there was only one way partisans could fight alongside the Allies and that was if they volunteered as individuals for the Italian Royal Army – rather than as bands – and swore allegiance to the monarchy. Unsurprisingly, few were prepared to do this.

While General Wolff's troops and the Decima MAS and Black Brigades continued their efforts to tame the partisans in the north, along the front line the massacres continued. Sixteen men of the 2nd Company of the 16th Waffen-SS Armoured Battalion were killed by partisans in the Apuans when they had gone to the village of Ceserano in search of food. News of the deaths duly reached the division and Rudi Schreiber, now recovered from his wound and back with the division's Pioneers, was among those sent to investigate. 'We found the first of the bodies by the road as we reached the village,' says Rudi. 'Their faces had been beaten. Others had been killed with single shots. In a battle, you can be hit anywhere, but it was not possible for those men to have been beaten like that in a fire-fight.' Rudi was convinced these men had been captured and deliberately beaten to death.

Retribution was not long in coming. The men had been from the same battalion as Willfried Segebrecht, commanded by Sturmbannführer Walter Reder, and so on 19 August Reder led his men to Monte San Terenzo. At Bardine, they rounded up the inhabitants and shot the lot – 107 in all. A further 53 men were bound by their necks and hands to fence posts and then executed with single pistol shots. Over the following days, most of the villages around Monte San Terenzo were also overrun and by 24 August 342 men, women and children from the area lay dead.

Even Mussolini was appalled by the news of these and other massacres – so much so that he wrote formally to Ambassador Rahn complaining about German brutality and indiscriminate executions of innocent people. Such things excited popular feeling, he warned, and 'furnished the enemy with excellent propaganda material'.[232] Furthermore, he pointed out, they only encouraged retaliatory attacks.

On the whole, Mussolini was right. And as the killing of Walter Reder's men ably demonstrated, partisan attacks could be every bit as brutal as German and Fascist assaults. Lupo may have tried to avoid killing whenever possible, but even the Stella Rossa had their fair share of blood on their hands.

Just beyond La Quercia, below Monte Sole in the Setta Valley, there was a GNR barracks. In early June, about thirty militia from the barracks deserted and joined the Stella Rossa. The same evening, a number of partisans, including Gianni and Lupo, raided the barracks and disarmed the remaining GNR men, who had been in the middle of supper when the rebels attacked. The militia men were interrogated. 'Join us,' the partisans told them, 'or you will be shot.' Most agreed to come, but a small group refused. Lupo gave them some more time to think it over, but still they refused. And so they were duly murdered, with knives in order to save ammunition.

On another occasion, two German soldiers were captured by a group of partisans in Gabbiano di Monzuno, to the south of the Monte Sole massif. Both men put their hands in the air in surrender, but one was shot anyway. The other was taken to a partisan encampment where he pleaded for his life, producing photographs of his wife and children. His cries for mercy fell on deaf ears. Rather, he was pinned to the ground with knives through his hands and left in the sun to die.

Other people, suspected of being Fascists, were found and murdered. Others who refused to toe the partisan line were also treated brutally. A terrible cycle of violence developed whereby one or more deaths would be avenged by another. For example, the Germans caught Francesco Calzolari, a member of the Stella Rossa. After torturing him, he was eventually strung up to be hanged, but the rope broke. It was an Italian Fascist who went to find a thicker cord. The Stella Rossa found this out and the next Fascist to be caught was killed in the same way.

And yet there were also cases of humanity winning through. At another barracks, the Stella Rossa disarmed the GNR, made them walk around the town square and then sent them home. During an attack on the barracks at Tolé, one of the partisans, Oder Volelli, discovered that the GNR officer in charge was the father of one of his best friends from school. 'Where's your son?' Oder asked him. 'In hiding, evading the draft,' the commander replied. But when the partisans searched the barracks for weapons, they found the son hidden in a cupboard. Oder embraced his friend and asked him to join them. 'No,' his friend replied, 'it's not for me.' Oder shook his hand and let him go.

In Trieste, there was little compassion on the part of the German occupiers, even though the SS Commander, General Odilo Globocnik was, in fact, a Trieste native. On 24 July, Clara Duse was woken at around four in the morning by a loud banging on the door of the family flat. It was the SS and they had come to arrest her father. As he was taken away, Clara's mother collapsed with shock and grief.

The next morning, Clara went to the local prison – rather than the Risiera di San Saba – where she had learned that he had been taken. There she joined a long queue of relatives of inmates, all hoping to learn word of the men inside. But no visitors were allowed, although Clara learned that they could bring a little food for the prisoners. She also discovered that her father had been rounded up along with a number of former officers now working in the resistance.

For several days she spent her time going from office to office, trying her best to learn news of her father, and standing in queues in the hot summer sun trying to get some food passed to him in prison. Her mother, meanwhile, had become virtually bed-ridden with worry. Others tried to help – even Trieste's bishop – but Clara could find out nothing. 'No question was answered,' says Clara. 'The uncertainty was the worst thing.'

Then one night, news. It was late when the phone rang – an old school friend of Clara's was on the line; he'd heard that the political prisoners were going to be deported to Germany, and were due to leave at 5 the next morning from the station. Clara and her mother gathered some food and warm clothing, hid some gold coins in the lining of a jacket, and despite the strict curfew, headed through the night to the station, hiding in doorways if they heard anyone coming.

At the station, an Italian pointed to the furthest platform. 'There was a long line of cattle trucks,' says Clara, 'with the doors nailed, but through a little opening we finally saw my father's face, and we were able to hand him the little parcel.' No sooner had they done so, than a very young German soldier saw them and pushed them away with the butt of his rifle.

Clara never saw her father again.

TWENTY-SIX

The Gothic Line
25 August–1 September 1944

Eighth Army had given much thought to the way the DIADEM battles had gone. Papers had been produced, analysing their performance, and detailing with admirable clarity where they could have done better. Traffic congestion was one notable area, speed of exploitation another. 'According to enemy prisoners,' noted General Kirkman in his post-Rome notes for XIII Corps, '[exploitation] is where the British Army often fails.' Enemy demolitions, Kirkman reckoned, were the biggest cause of slow exploitation, but one factor for future success was beyond dispute: 'When a deliberate attack is being staged,' he noted, 'there must always be one or more specifically organised pursuit forces containing infantry in motor transport and a large proportion of armour ready to go through the moment the opportunity arises.'[233]

It was with these factors in mind that Leese and his commanders had prepared their battle plan for Operation OLIVE. One way of easing congestion and confusion over inter-corps boundaries was to attack on a much broader front. This time, no less than three corps were to attack along an eighteen-mile stretch from the coast, and rapid exploitation was recognised as being key to their success. Despite the numerous ridges that had to be overcome, everyone was fully aware how tantalisingly close the northern plains were and of the need to get there quickly before the summer was out.

And yet despite this, there was a sense that Leese's battle plan had not been entirely properly thought through. Nearest the coast, the Poles were to continue their drive up the coast, but once Pesaro had been taken they were then to fall into reserve. Next to them, it had originally been V Corps, now revitalised with experienced and fresh divisions like the 46th, with the two divisions of the Canadian Corps further inland on their left.

This seemed like a sensible deployment. V Corps' central position was the best part of the line from which to exploit any pursuit, because the hills were lower here than further inland, and because as they drove northwards they would be able to cut in towards the coastal road where the Via Adriatica offered the best chance of a rapid pursuit of armour and motorised infantry. And V Corps was the best formation to do this because it was the largest by far – with five divisions and now bolstered by units of the Corpo Italiano di Liberazione. As a result, it had the strength in depth needed for a strong assault followed by a quick and equally strong exploitation.

However, the Poles then pointed out that in their experience of fighting along the Adriatic, progress along the Via Adriatica had often been slower than further inland, thanks to heavy enemy demolitions. This was hardly anything new: the Germans always made a point of sabotaging key routes when retreating. Yet, the Via Adriatica still remained the key to any hopes of a rapid pursuit. Nonetheless, it seems to have prompted Leese to make a radical and potentially far-reaching decision. Almost casually, and without any proper explanation, he decided to switch the Canadians and V Corps, but bizarrely, made no modifications regarding the pursuit. In other words, the Canadians were still to perform the task originally given to V Corps – of cutting the Via Adriatica and heading down the coast road with all haste – but with less than half the amount of forces. Since both Canadian divisions would be involved in the initial assault on the Gothic Line, this meant there would be no fresh armoured troops to carry out the subsequent pursuit along the coast.

This disparity of forces was because Leese absolutely refused to bolster the Canadians with any other units. Although there can be no doubting Leese's faith in the Canadian divisions, he still had little confidence in the Canadian Corps Commander, General Burns, and so refused to place any more troops under his command. 'Before DIADEM, Leese had caught Burns telling a great lie,' says Ion Calvocoressi. 'When Leese confronted him about it, Burns had looked very shifty.' At any rate, this incident was one of the main reasons Leese felt he could not trust the Canadian commander. It was unfortunate, because a consequence was that V Corps, with all its armour and trucks, would be operating in the steeper, hillier country inland, where it would be forced to make use of horribly narrow roads and tracks hardly suited to vehicles of any kind, let alone hulking lorries and tanks.

*   *   *

That Leese could begin his battle with three corps at all was little short of a miracle. Eighth Army had its strengths and weaknesses, but its logistical team was superlative. Somehow, despite the mountains, despite the narrow roads and endless winding tracks, and despite the massive amounts of vehicles and equipment that had needed to be moved, Leese's forces had made the switch across to the Adriatic in time. A staggering 400,000 gallons of petrol a day had been guzzled by 60,000 vehicles; at one point on 21 August, more than 10,000 vehicles had passed a single point on Highway 6 within twenty-four hours. Thanks to this logistical feat, everyone in Eighth Army was where they were supposed to be by 25 August, including 1,122 guns in position and seventy-one full-strength infantry battalions – around 59,000 men.

A self-assured air of confidence exuded from General Leese, and in the days before the battle he toured the line giving rousing pre-battle pep talks to his troops. They were so nearly there, he told them – just one last effort and the campaign would be theirs. 'Gentlemen,' he finished with a flourish, 'we march on Vienna!'[234]

The Eighth Army commander was given a further fillip by the arrival of the British Prime Minister on the eve of battle, who had come to Italy to see 'the commanders and the troops from whom so much was being demanded, after so much had been taken'.[235] Once again, Ion Calvocoressi and the other ADCs had been busy in preparation. Tactical HQ was now on the Adriatic coast, and in the afternoon, Ion accompanied Leese to Jesi airfield to collect Alexander and Churchill, pausing en route to allow the general a brief swim in the sea.

The drive back to 'Tac HQ' was long and dusty, but the PM was thrilled to be so close to the front. Just as the party sat down to dinner, a Bren gun was heard not far away. 'Hark!' said Churchill, turning to Ion, 'I hear the sound of musketry.'

Ion thought the Prime Minister was on 'terrific form'. Always happy to be amongst such men, Churchill regaled them with anecdotes about Stalin and admitted his loathing of De Gaulle, gossip that was lapped up by Leese and the ADCs alike. The PM was happy to grumble about the Allied invasion of southern France as well. 'Winston was all on our side re: the absurd S of France invasion,' wrote Ion, 'and said Marshall was very stubborn.' They then stayed up to watch the opening barrage of the offensive. Churchill, smoking his enormous cigars, was delighted to hear the colossal boom of more than a thousand guns, and to see the flashes flickering along the horizon. 'The rapid, ceaseless thudding of the cannonade,' wrote the PM, 'reminded me of the First World War. Artillery was certainly being used on a great scale.'[236]

Away to the north, Hans Golda and his fellow officers had spent the past ten days billeted with some Italians – 'three families of three brothers who lived together like one big family'. They had all got along together famously, sharing supper every night and entertaining the children whenever they could. Always a gregarious fellow, Hans had enjoyed befriending these civilians. Now, though, it was time to bid them farewell and get back to the war. 'We said goodbye to our families sadly,' he wrote. 'The women and children cried, and we went into our bunkers ready to carry out our hard duty.'[237]

Hans and the Werfer Regiment 71 were among those on the receiving end of Eighth Army's opening barrage. The regiment's preparations of their positions were still incomplete and enemy artillery fire once more disrupted their efforts. This, however, was nothing like as bad as the pummelling they had been receiving from the dreaded jabos. 'The bombers attacked without a break,' noted Hans, 'systematically on the infantry positions and on the B positions. They cut roads through the barbed wire and tried to blow up the minefields by chucking out a whole load of small bombs.' The fighter-bombers even scored a direct hit on 9th Battery, killing a number of men and wounding many more.

Throughout the campaign, both sides had fought with differing advantages and disadvantages. The Allies had the equipment and the overwhelming fire power, but the Germans had the advantage of a country perfectly suited for defence; the Allies had more men – most of the time – but the Germans could choose where they fought and generally had the benefit of height. Yet the Allies had one decisive advantage above all, and that was mastery of the skies. Even in August, when so many of the air forces were in southern France, the Desert Air Force made a crucial difference, both before and during the battle.

The new Allied offensive once again caught the Germans off guard. Twenty-five thousand Allied artillery shells had been fired towards Pesaro and the Gothic Line defences. At dawn, medium bombers of the Desert Air Force then flew over, carpet bombing the same areas. These included the B-26 Marauders of the 24th South African Air Force. Flight Sergeant Ernest Wall was a wireless operator/air gunner (WOP/AG) with 24th SAAF. A Scot from Edinburgh, he had joined the RAF and had been trained as a wireless operator before being posted overseas to the Middle

East to finish his training and eventually to join an operational unit.

It was whilst recovering from a bout of heatstroke in hospital in Palestine that he saw a notice asking for volunteers for the SAAF. Having missed his RAF operational training unit due to his hospitalisation, he signed up and at Gambut in Egypt joined 24 Squadron, a bomber unit that had already won a considerable reputation during the North African campaign. Immediately sent to join a B-26 crew, he had begun to wonder whether he had made a huge mistake: not only had he never seen a Marauder before, he had never fired the .5 inch Browning machine guns either. To make matters worse, he learned that replacement crew, like himself, had been desperately needed because of very high losses suffered by the squadron.

That had been in May. Raids across the Aegean had given him a baptism of fire, but recognising that experience is the best form of training, Ernest had learned fast. By the time the squadron had moved to Italy in July, he had become something of an old hand, despite still being only nineteen years old.

Now, on this opening day of the battle, Ernest and his crew were, for the first time, flying in direct support of the Poles and Canadians below. Everyone in the squadron flew three operational flights that day and on subsequent days, and instead of the 1,000lb heavy bomb load, each Marauder was fitted with 500lb anti-personnel canisters, and six 20lb fragmentation bomb clusters. The aim was to carpet bomb the enemy positions, to detonate the mines and shred the barbed wire – and, of course, destroy any fixed positions. In fact, the aim was much the same as the barrages that had preceded attacks along the Western Front twenty-five years before. The difference was that aerial attacks like these were considerably more effective.

However terrifying it may have been to be on the receiving end of such attacks, it was certainly no picnic for the air crew involved. Indeed 24 SAAF had been very badly mauled back in March when eight out of twelve aircraft had been shot down during a low-level attack on Crete. 'Marauders weren't designed for low-level flying,' explains Ernest. 'At under a thousand feet and travelling at only 250 mph you feel pretty exposed, I can tell you.' Aerial attacks might no longer have been a worry, but light flak and small-arms fire would shake the plane and rattle across the underside constantly. 'You could hear bullets pinging along the fuselage,' says Ernest, 'and you just prayed they wouldn't hit anything vital. It was a bit hairy.'

*   *   *

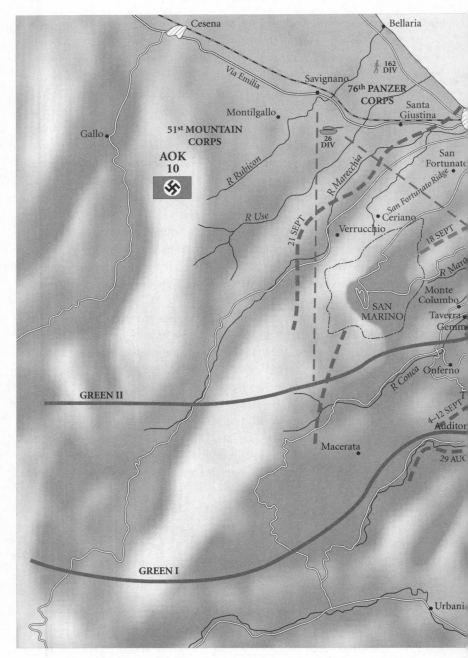

Eighth Army's attack on the Gothic Line, Aug.–Sept. 1944

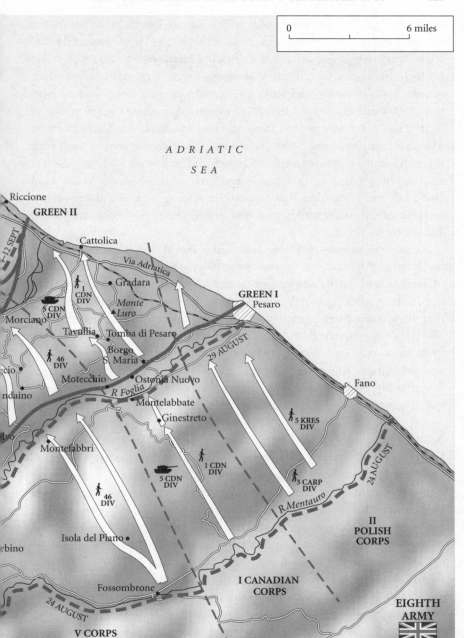

0   6 miles

ADRIATIC

SEA

Riccione

GREEN II

Cattolica

Via Adriatica

Gradara

1 CDN DIV

Monte Luro

5 CDN DIV

Morciano

Tavullia

Tomba di Pesaro

GREEN I

Pesaro

Borgo S. Maria

29 AUGUST

46 DIV

cio

Motecchio

R Foglia

Ostonia Nuovo

Fano

ndaino

Montelabbate

Ginestreto

5 KRES DIV

lvo

Montefabbri

1 CDN DIV

24 AUGUST

5 CDN DIV

3 CARP DIV

46 DIV

R Mentauro

II POLISH CORPS

Isola del Piano

bino

I CANADIAN CORPS

Fossombrone

24 AUGUST

EIGHTH ARMY

V CORPS

Only three German divisions of the 76th Panzer Corps stood before the Gothic Line and they were soon pushed back. The 2/5th Leicesters had found themselves opposite the German 71st Division, and their first obstacle had been to cross the Metauro River. The night before their attack, 26/27 August, Lieutenant Peter Moore had been sent out on patrol and had discovered that their proposed crossing area was free of mines, the water was not too deep and low enough for vehicles to cross. The following morning, they made a surprise two-company attack with no preliminary bombardment. Although they came under heavy mortar and machine-gun fire, they made good use of the hollows in the land and with the remaining two companies adding support along with a number of Churchill tanks, they had forced the enemy back off Mount Tomba by nightfall.

At first, Kesselring had been sceptical about Allied intentions despite the weight of fire power. By this time, however, von Vietinghoff's Chief of Staff, acting in his commander's absence, had managed to persuade the Feldmarschall that AOK 10 was now facing a major offensive and that they needed reinforcing along the Adriatic with serious urgency. The following day, the 28th, von Vietinghoff was back; the three divisions in front of the Gothic Line had been hurriedly pulled back behind it, and three more divisions had been released to join 76th Panzer Corps. Whether they would arrive in time to save the Gothic Line, however, was going to be a very close call.

Between the coast and the German 71st Division had been the veteran 1st Fallschirmjäger Division. Hans-Jürgen Kumberg was back in Germany, finishing his parachute training, but Jupp Klein and his company of Pioneers fought every inch of the way. 'It was vicious fighting,' admits Jupp, and a sharp reality check for his new men. 'These young soldiers had been so anxious to get to the front and to fight man against man,' he says, 'but they had no experience. Once again, the older men were left and the younger men died.'

Any soldier can be killed or maimed by an unlucky shell or a chance bullet, but it was unquestionably the case that the greater the combat experience, the more one learned how to survive. Although, as Jupp says, 'It's more than experience. It's a kind of sixth sense. When there was danger, I could smell it. The older ones were all the same.'

Sergeant Sam Bradshaw had been fighting for even longer than Jupp. From Crosby on Merseyside, Sam had fought in Eritrea, throughout much of the North African campaign, had been seriously wounded twice, and was now one of the most experienced and battle-hardened men in the 6th Royal Tank Regiment. He was still only twenty-three.

Although a tank man, when the regiment was retraining in Iraq before being shipped over to Italy, Sam had been persuaded to join the regiment's Reconnaissance Unit. In the open desert warfare of the North African campaign, the regiment had had recce tanks within each squadron, but it was recognised that in Italy, where the fighting was far closer, a separate recce unit was needed. As both an experienced trooper and a radio man, Sam soon became a key member of the unit.

During the battle for Rome, 6 Royal Tank Regiment had been in a quiet sector of the line but had now joined the 4th Indian Division in V Corps, on the left of 46th Division, and the regiment's recce unit was leading their advance towards the Gothic Line, pushing ahead in their turret-less light Stuart tanks and Dingo armoured car. Until their new CO arrived, Sam was effectively in charge of the unit and with three Stuart tanks under his command had been the first to reach the ancient town of Urbino on 26 August. No sooner had he got there, however, than a message arrived to 'press on regardless'. On they rumbled, into more mountainous country once more. Darkness was falling and so Sam called a halt by a shallow cave next to the track.

He had been looking back at Urbino, worried that the 4th Indians' trucks were all now pulling into the main square in the town and so making themselves an easy target for German artillery, when a jeep pulled up alongside him and their new recce commander, Lieutenant Macdonald, introduced himself. Sam had seen plenty of fresh new officers in his time, and had no qualms about putting him in the picture right away. 'You're the commander and we have to obey your orders,' Sam told him, 'but you have to share the work. We can't afford to have passengers.'

'That's OK with me,' Macdonald assured him. 'You tell me, I'll do it.'

The following morning, however, they were soon in disagreement. Sam was certain that across the valley there were German rearguard anti-tank guns waiting for them. Macdonald wanted to press on, as were their orders. 'You've got to interpret those orders according to the situation,' Sam explained. 'You're told to press on but that doesn't mean you go and get yourself killed; there's no point.' Furthermore, Sam added, if they pushed forward and were hit, they would only block the road and halt the advance anyway.

'Well, if you're afraid to go forward . . .' Macdonald retorted.

'Don't you say that to me,' said Sam angrily. 'I've been in this war a long time. I'm trying to give you the benefit of my advice and experience.'

But Macdonald would not listen. Sam pleaded with him. 'What about your crew? If you want to go, go on foot, but don't take them too.' Again, Macdonald ignored him. 'What you're doing is crazy,' Sam insisted.

'Don't you talk to me like that,' Macdonald snapped, then got into his Stuart and went forward. Sure enough, a hundred yards further on, the tank was hit. One man got out but was promptly machine-gunned to death. Macdonald and the others were broiled in their tank. 'I thought, Christ, they were my friends,' says Sam. 'I felt it was my fault. I should have stopped him – I should have belted him, knocked him out or something. Those fellows had trusted me, and I felt terrible.'

In the Leicesters' sector of the line, the men were already exhausted. By the afternoon of the 30th, they had reached the River Foglia, the last crossing before the Gothic Line on the far side. It had been twelve miles as the crow flies between the Metauro and the Foglia, but more like thirty by foot. During their march, Peter Moore began to realise what an enormous task faced them. 'The lines of communication were appalling,' he noted. 'There were only two inadequate narrow mountain roads on the whole of the divisional front running in the direction of our line of attack, going up and down from valley to valley.'[238] And, as a consequence of V Corps' switch with the Canadians, the hills they were crossing were rapidly turning into mountains. They had only been in the battle four days, but the fighting followed by the hard march with almost no sleep in between would have taken its toll on any fighting men.

There was to be no pausing, however. On the 31st, C and D Companies were sent in to attack across the Foglia against 'Green I' of the Gothic Line, with A and Peter's B Company in reserve. The two leading companies headed off into battle, while Peter and his men kept their heads down on the reverse slopes behind them. Suddenly, the 46th Division commander, General 'Ginger' Hawkesworth, appeared on the ridge of the hill in his jeep shouting encouragement. Just behind him came another jeep with a sapper captain. Peter and the Captain looked at each other with mutual recognition. 'Waterfield!' shouted Peter, 'What a place to meet!' They had both been at school together, and promised themselves a drink together once the war was over. 'A day or two later,' wrote Peter, 'I learned that he and his driver were killed minutes after when their jeep hit a mine.'[239]

Meanwhile, C and D Companies had crossed the Foglia but were now being pinned down as they climbed the slopes on the other side. Peter could only watch, and listen to the talk between the two companies on the wireless. It made for sobering listening. Peter's friend Bill Preece, whom he had known from home, had been killed. Ever since rejoining the battalion, Peter had noticed Bill becoming increasingly fatalistic, convinced his luck could not last. And now he was dead – yet another good friend gone. Another friend, Captain John Ellis, was alive and, it seemed, safe, but had a bullet through his head.

The tanks were firing smoke canisters to cover the infantry but the firing continued through the smoke. More and more artillery shells kept whistling over, while Peter, along with the rest of B and C Companies, waited until darkness fell when they would launch their own attack.

They used the time sensibly, however, noting where the most intense machine-gun fire was coming from. Through his binoculars, Peter studied a particularly steep part of the hillside, a point where the Germans would be unlikely to expect an attack. Peter's task would be to lead his platoon round the cliff from the right-hand side; if they were successful, they would be able to outflank the position that was still pinning C and D Companies down.

Peter outlined the plan to his section leaders while it was still light and urged the men to snatch some sleep while they could, despite the racket all around them. At 11 p.m., they moved out, along with the rest of A and B Companies. Peter's task was to open a gap and pass through a minefield in front of the Germans and seize the enemy positions above the steep slope. Using mine detectors, they marked out a passage through the mines without a hitch. Then Peter went forward with one section to reconnoitre a line of attack. Ahead was a cliff of about thirty feet, but to the right, as he'd hoped, there was a possible way up.

Peter had just sent a runner back to get the others when suddenly a number of German soldiers came down the hill straight towards them. Grabbing a grenade from his belt, he pulled out the pin and hurled it at them. It landed right between them, but then failed to explode. There was, however, no turning back. Urging his men forward, Peter and his men rushed at the Germans, shouting and firing. With the first burst of his Tommy gun, he killed two and wounded three more, but then his gun jammed. Despite this, Peter continued rushing up the slope, shouting encouragement, pursuing the retreating enemy.

Bursts of German machine-gun fire continued to spit around them, but after one burst Peter and his men paused, quickly set up the 2-inch mortar in the direction of the enemy machine-gun nest, and then pressed on, firing as they went and making as much noise as possible to try and give the impression there were more than just two dozen of them.

By the time the faint strip of dawn broke across the horizon, they had reached their objective – a hill called La Cantina, or the 'NAAFI' as the men rechristened it. It was a wide plateau and the Germans had gone. Peter felt absolutely exhausted, his mind dwelling on one German he had killed. 'I was haunted by the cries of the young German,' he wrote, 'who called for his mother when I hit him.' The first breach in the Gothic Line, however, had been made.

To the right of the Leicesters, the Canadians had also been busy. Now back at the front after nearly three months out of the line was the Perth Regiment. Like the Leicesters, they had reached the Foglia on the 29th, pausing on the Ginestreto Ridge overlooking the river. There they remained all that day and on into the 30th, waiting for the order to advance.

'Waiting to go into battle sure plays hell with an infantryman's nerves,' noted Stan Scislowski. 'No sooner did word come down the pike that we were on one hour's notice to move than every organ in our bodies switches into high gear, especially the bowel and the kidney.'[240] Stan relieved the tension by his favoured pastime – scrounging. As long as he was kept busy nosing through empty houses or picking his way through discarded equipment, he reckoned he could keep any morbid thoughts at bay.

At mid-morning on the 30th, he watched a wave of medium bombers fly over and bomb the enemy positions of the Gothic Line in front of them. Stan had never been so close to an aerial bombardment of that kind and was amazed by the shuddering of the ground and the massive columns of smoke and dust. 'It was as though a colossal pair of hands seized the ridge on which we stood,' he noted, 'and shook it like someone sifting ashes. Now we had a fair idea of what an earthquake had to feel like.'[241] Before the dust had settled, another wave of bombers arrived, and more bombs rained down on the ground ahead of them. 'I found myself feeling sorry for the poor bastards across the flats,' wrote Stan, 'hunched up in their slit-trenches and dugouts, hands clamped to their ears, terrified out of their wits as the world exploded around them.'[242]

Nonetheless, when the roar of aero engines had long disappeared and the dust had settled, Stan had felt rather deflated to see the view in front of him look much the same as before the attack. To him, the Gothic Line appeared quiet, almost untouched. Yet it was this very quietness that had caught the attention of the Canadian 5th Armoured Division commander, General Bert Hoffmeister, the previous afternoon. Crawling forward on his belly to observe the line, Hoffmeister could not see a single a soul. The road across the anti-tank ditch had not been blown; no enemy shells were hurtling their way. Hoffmeister was flummoxed; it all seemed wrong to him. Yet patrols confirmed the lack of fire coming from the enemy positions, and reported sounds that suggested that the Germans were in the process of changing hands with new units taking over the positions of troops being rested.

Hoffmeister had originally planned to attack on the night of 1/2 September – allowing them the traditional Eighth Army pause to gather strength; but following the carpet bombing of the minefields Burns was now persuaded to launch the assault right away. It was a risk, but it appeared as though they might just catch the Germans off guard.

By 4.30 p.m., both Canadian divisions, the 1st and the 5th Armoured, were ready to advance on the Gothic Line. Theirs was a three-mile front towards the German defences from the village of Borgo Santa Maria to just beyond Montecchio. The Perths' objective was a ridge, listed on their military maps as Point 111, which ran slightly to the east of Montecchio.

The advance soon began to falter. With no artillery barrage preceding it, the infantry, advancing in broad daylight, soon began to realise what it had been like attacking across no-man's-land in Flanders during the First World War. The reports had been right: units of the newly arrived 26th Panzer Division were only just reaching the front; such was the paucity of German troops along the forward positions of the Gothic Line that only some 50 per cent of the prepared positions were manned. Yet as the Canadians had discovered at Vimy Ridge in 1917, it took only a handful of machine-gun teams to cut down swathes of advancing Canadian infantry. More than twenty years on, however, German machine guns – still known by Allied troops, in a throwback to the last war, as 'Spandaus' – were far superior weapons to the Maxims of old.

In fact, they were in many ways the most lethal machine guns of the war: the MG 42 had a velocity of around 755 metres per second and a firing rate of more than 800 rounds per minute; that is, about 12 bullets per second.*

Baker Company had led the Perths' attack but after crossing the river had funnelled themselves through an intact road across the anti-tank ditch and had been cut to pieces. Dog Company, meanwhile, had been waiting to follow them in a torn-up vineyard just short of the river until a breathless runner arrived to tell them about the fate of Baker Company and that they were now to take over the advance. 'A hard knot of fear hit the pit of my stomach,' noted Stan. 'But in a way I was glad to get moving.'

As they came to the river, they saw a mass of transport, tanks, dust and smoke. Crossing over through this chaos they reached the remnants of Baker Company, now huddled against a shallow embankment. Beyond, however, there was only one alternative to advancing down the same road where Baker Company had been mowed down, and that was to cross a flat field marked out with mine warnings that looked horribly untouched by the carpet bombers. This was the route Dog Company's CO preferred to try. And Stan's 18 Platoon was to lead the way.

Stan was terrified. He knew he had no choice in the matter but as he climbed over the fence he felt sure they were all as good as dead. The prospect of stepping on a mine had been his greatest fear since arriving in Italy, and he now needed every last shred of courage to make himself take each step. He had accepted that with every action he went into his chances of survival were lessening, but the thought of being blown into so many tiny pieces there wouldn't even be enough of him left to bury was hard to come to terms with. And sure enough, after a few paces, there came the first explosion – thankfully not a big one, only a *schu*-mine, one that would rip off a foot or leg but would not obliterate its victim. A moment later, two more went off, at which point Stan and the others froze. Blackie Rowe, the platoon sergeant, yelled at them to keep going, and on they went again. Stan turned to his friend Gord, next to him. 'I can't see us getting out of here alive,' he said, then bang, Gord was down as well.

---

*There was, however, a fatal flaw in both the MG 42 and MG 34: the recoil system was not very efficient which meant the barrels very quickly overheated. Since in the heat of battle it was often inappropriate to change barrels, they soon lost their accuracy and their effectiveness diminished rapidly.

Before they had gone another thirty yards, three more had been felled. Stan felt a mixture of emotions: fear of dying; anger at being made to do something so pointless; and pride for being brave enough to keep going anyway. He desperately wanted to turn around and get out of there but so long as his buddies moved forward, so would he. 'To walk through that frightful garden,' commented Stan, 'took steely nerves far beyond that we thought we had.' Yet after progressing more than 200 yards, the company CO recalled them. Stan was so relieved to get back alive that he no longer felt any anger about the folly of the order in the first place.

They were now back to square one, and faced with crossing the road over the anti-tank ditch. If they could just get across that, then they would be well placed to attack Point 111. Fortunately, it was by now quite dark, and although a lone machine gunner repeatedly fired a three-second spurt across the road, the Perth men soon noticed that it fired as regular as clockwork at twenty-second intervals. So long as pairs of them sprinted across the moment the three-second burst finished, they should make it all right.

In this way, the whole of Dog Company safely got across the anti-tank ditch in less than quarter of an hour. Pausing while they gathered their wits, Stan listened to the battle going on either side of them. Mortar bombs crunched as they exploded, artillery shells screamed overhead, machine guns clattered. Finally, with everyone ready, and with a tank now alongside them to help, they were given the command to fix bayonets. They were about to bayonet charge the enemy for the first time in their army careers.

To begin with they advanced silently and then about fifty yards from the German positions a Spandau opened fire and they all fell to the decks. Stan lay face down on the dusty grass. He knew it needed just one man to get up and urge them all forward, and while a part of him would have liked to have won a medal, he knew he simply didn't have the nerve. After a few moments, one of the lieutenants eventually urged them forward: 'Come on Dog Company, up and at 'em, what the hell are you waiting for?' Suddenly the whole company was on its feet, Stan included, charging and firing and yelling at the top of their voices. And when they reached the German positions, the enemy were standing there, their arms in the air pleading, '*Kameraden! Kameraden!*'[243]

Dog Company had now broken the crust of the Gothic Line, and this gave the Canadians the lever with which to make the most of the limited number of German defenders. As more troops moved into the gap, so they were able to fire onto the German positions either side of them from behind.

Stan felt pretty proud of himself, but having survived the minefield and the bayonet charge he was then concussed the following morning when one of their own artillery shells landed close by. Disorientated and groggy and with his ears ringing, he was taken back to the field dressing station, where for a while he had a crisis of conscience. Only after a pep talk from the regiment's padre did he find the strength to rejoin Dog Company, as he knew he should.

That day, 31 August, Martha Gellhorn reached the Gothic Line and stepped out of a command car close to where Dog Company had breached the line. She had been with the Canadians for the past few days, watching the fight unfurl; it all seemed impossible to follow. 'Suddenly,' she wrote, 'you will see antlike figures of infantry outlined against the sky; probably they are going in to attack that cluster of farmhouses. Then they disappear, and you do not know what became of them. Tanks roll serenely across the crest of a hill, then the formation breaks.' Then other tanks might appear firing from behind trees. Hoffmeister had not flinched and had boldly poured armour into the gap on the 31st. The Fallschirmjäger to the east of Point 111 had fought back with typical tenacity, and it was this stage of the mêlée that Martha had witnessed. 'A battle is a jigsaw puzzle,' she wrote 'of fighting men, bewildered terrified civilians, noise, smells, jokes, pain, fear, unfinished conversations and high explosives.'[244] She might also have added that it was a mixture of chaos, moments of extreme bravery, bitter misfortune, and colossal luck.

The battle raged all day and into the night. Stan Scislowski and the Perths fought off a German counterattack on Point 204, more than a mile beyond the first breach of the Gothic Line and were then ordered back while the artillery pasted the area. As the infantry moved forward to reoccupy the ridge, Stan and four others were hit by two grenades. One man was killed, the others wounded. Stan was struck by a fragment in the head, an injury that would see him out of action for a fortnight.

Casualties on both sides had been high, but by dawn on 1 September the forward positions of the Gothic Line had been overrun all along the line. Allied confidence was beginning to look justified after all.

TWENTY-SEVEN

The Tragedy of Gemmano
1–12 September 1944

Oberleutnant Hans Golda and the 8th Werfer Battery had been firing from their brand new bunkers throughout the last day of August, but in their positions to the east of Monte Luro, between the railway and the road, they had had a relatively peaceful day.

As September dawned, however, the sound of battle drew ever closer, and throughout the morning the artillery duel became increasingly intense, with Hans and his men firing salvo after salvo of mortar rockets, while enemy shells continued to scream across the sky. By the afternoon, a number of infantry had arrived, hot and covered in the dust and grime of battle as they fell back from the continuing Canadian drive, and took shelter in Hans' bunker.

Despite radio contact with the other batteries, Hans had little idea of what was going on, except that the enemy was getting nearer. Above, circling like vultures, were the cab ranks of the Desert Air Force's fighter-bombers. Ahead, clouds of smoke and dust occasionally billowed and drifted away on the sultry late summer air. Throughout the afternoon, the werfers continued firing towards the Canadian advance to their right. In the evening, they could see the jabos dive over Monte Luro itself and watched the bombs fall and explode followed by more clouds of dust and debris. Then, as darkness fell, news reached them that the mountain had fallen. Around 11 p.m., Hans was given the order to move back. After nearly two weeks of hard toil helping to build their bunkers, they were now forced to leave them after just one day of heavy fighting. It was galling to say the least.

They fell back only a couple of miles to Gradara, near to where they had been billeted before the battle began. Fairly certain they would soon be told to retreat again, Hans took the opportunity to say a proper farewell to their Italian friends. Despite promises of returning, he did not expect ever to see them again.

At seven the following morning Hans was woken from a few hours' sleep with the news that enemy tanks were just a few hundred yards away and that Gradara was being pasted by heavy artillery and tank fire and about to be overrun. His battery positions were out of the firing line, however, and so he sent one of the new officers, Leutnant Phoenix, to have a quick recce. Both young and extremely nervous, Phoenix headed off only to come back a few minutes later, sheepishly explaining that he'd forgotten his binoculars. 'Despite the critical situation,' Hans noted, 'we couldn't help laughing at him.'[245]

When he eventually returned, Phoenix was able to add little to what they already knew. Once again, the werfers began firing, but the tanks were now so close their rocket mortars were going over them. But still they received no return fire until suddenly the tanks began to clank and creak towards them. Hans felt his blood freeze. Any moment, he was certain they would be obliterated. Ordering everyone to pack up and get out of there as quickly as possible, he joined in with his men, helping them to hitch up the werfers and load the ammunition, but never once taking his eye off the tanks as their squeaking and rumbling grew louder and louder. When everything was ready, he quickly gathered his men about him. They were to meet up again on the south side of Cattolica, on the coast, a mile or so further back. The gunners were to hurry away on foot, the drivers to get going straight away. Jumping into the cab of the last truck, the vehicle in front promptly broke down. The men jumped out and pushed and the engine caught only to cut out again. Beginning to panic, Hans was waiting for the tank shells to fall any second. Then the driver, calm as anything, produced a can of oil, poured it into the troublesome engine, and as if by magic, the truck roared back into life. In moments they were off, leaving only a cloud of dust and engine smoke behind them.

By nightfall on the 2nd, all along the Canadians' front, AOK 10 was falling back in some disorder to the far side of the River Conca and to the second line of Gothic Line defences, Green II. Visiting AOK 10 headquarters, Kesselring admitted that he had once again been too late in recognising the scale of Eighth Army's attack. The Desert Air Force had also made life particularly difficult, so that despite Stan Scislowski's concerns about the ineffectiveness of the bombing, newly arriving units of the 26th Panzer Division had reached the front on 29 August only to discover many of the positions they had been supposed to occupy had already been obliterated. Compounding the situation was the severe shortage of fuel and the chaos of the railways, which ensured reinforcements had been severely hindered on their route to the front. Finally, the decisive and bold leadership of the Canadian commanders, combined with the dogged determination of their men, had not conformed to normal Eighth Army practice; the lessons of the Liri Valley, it seemed, had been learned, and their relentless drive forward, eschewing any pause for breath, had taken the Germans by surprise.

With Pesaro – or what was left of it – now in Polish hands and with the Canadians cutting across them to the north of the city on the Via Adriatica, Anders' men went into reserve as planned. The last month had been particularly difficult for the Poles. At the beginning of August, with the Russian advance within sight of Warsaw, the Polish Home Army had staged a massive insurrection. But rather than clearing the city before the arrival of the Red Army, as had been their aim, they had been left high and dry as the Russians checked their advance and refused to give the Poles any help. The German response had been swift and typically ruthless, with reinforcements brought in to crush the rebels. Meanwhile, despite pleas from Churchill and Roosevelt, Stalin refused to allow British or American aircraft to use any of their forward airfields as a base from which to aid the insurrectionists. Allied air drops were organised from Italy and the Mediterranean, but these were far too few to make much difference.

The fact that the Polish Home Army had been given such scant support sent a clear warning to the men of II Polish Corps that the chances of a favourable post-war settlement were slim. From Cassino through to the capture of Ancona and Pesaro, the Poles had fought with extraordinary bravery and determination, and at a considerable cost. Proportionally, they had suffered more casualties than any other unit on the Allied side. Now, there was barely a man among them – Wladek Rubnikowicz included – who did not wonder what their enormous sacrifice had been for. Once again, Poland had been abandoned. 'We all,' wrote General Anders, 'felt very bitter.'[246]

But it was at this critical moment in the battle, with the Gothic Line smashed open by the Allied blitzkrieg and the northern plains within tantalisingly easy reach, that Leese's failure to give extra support to the

Canadian Corps came back to haunt him. On the night of 2/3 September, the Canadians secured a further bridgehead over the Conca, but exhausted and weakened, were stopped at the coastal town of Riccione, where Green II of the Gothic Line began. This left 1st Armoured Division of V Corps to lead the pursuit.

The plan was for 1st Armoured to pass through 46th Division, but their tanks and trucks had to complete their approach march first – again, not far as the crow flies, but quite a distance when travelling up and down over narrow, winding tracks barely wide or sturdy enough for 30-ton tanks. And in any case, before they could attack, 46th Division had to pave the way to the River Conca, and they had not progressed as fast as the Canadians.

Operating even a few miles further inland than the Canadians, they found the ridges had become steeper and more pronounced. Furthermore, perched on top of these mountains and ridges were numerous walled villages and small towns, obvious strong points from which the Germans could defend themselves. Each had to be captured before anyone in V Corps could move forward again. On the night of 31 August, the Leicesters had assaulted Mondaino, just such a village. The attack had been led by A and C Companies, and with B and D following behind, so Peter Moore had been groping his way through the steep vineyards leading up to the village as the attack had begun. Defending Mondaino had been men of the recently arrived 98th Division, of a different calibre to the 71st. Moreover, the defenders had been better armed with a number of tanks and self-propelled guns to help them. Peter had been only able to listen to the deafening din of shellfire, mortars, machine-gun fire and hand grenades, as A and D Companies fought their way through the village.

By dawn, Mondaino had been taken, but once again Peter was having to come to terms with the loss of two more fellow officers and friends, Ian Rawson and Eric Capron. Like Bill Preece before him, Eric had had a foreboding that he would be killed, but the same could not be said about Ian Rawson, whose death particularly affected Peter. A bright, cynical, highly amusing man, Ian had become a close friend since he had rejoined the battalion and he would miss him greatly. 'Life,' Peter had noted, 'was never dull when Ian was around.'[247]

The 56th and 4th Indian Divisions had been finding the advance to Green II even harder as they battled across terrain that was even more mountainous, and were now lagging some way behind 46th Division. In

the town of Montecalvo, Sam Bradshaw and his recce unit found themselves getting out of their Stuarts and becoming involved in street fighting, clearing houses one by one with Tommy guns and hand grenades.
And as well as battling through such difficult terrain, they were also
contending with the endless mines and booby traps the Germans left in
their wake. A couple of days later, he was with the Gurkhas, advancing
through Tavoletto. It was getting dark as they trundled on beyond the
town, and so Sam began to look for a place to stop. Out on the road
ahead was a farmhouse, and after checking it was unoccupied, Sam
moved his team of tanks into the courtyard. Sam's driver was another
like Stan Scislowski who was always on the lookout for loot to scrounge,
and immediately headed for one of the barns. 'Don't go in,' Sam yelled
at him, 'it could be booby trapped.' He stopped dead and then Sam
walked with him to the door of the barn. On the ground was a thick
spread of inviting-looking straw. 'Ah, lovely!' said Sam's driver. 'He was
just about to throw himself down but I pulled him back,' says Sam.
'Underneath were twenty-four *schu*-mines. We would have both been
killed just like that.'

Sam nearly was a couple of days later. His recce tanks were again far
ahead of the rest of the regiment, this time advancing with the 4/11th
Sikhs, and Sam was acting as liaison officer to the Indian infantry. They
had pushed through the town of Auditore and had emerged into a long
valley, with a shallow river running along the bottom and with rising
ground to fields and farmhouses beyond. Looking towards the enemy
positions on the far side, Sam counted three haystacks, but the following
morning, when the attack was due to begin, there were eleven haystacks.
'I thought, that's bloody strange,' says Sam. 'And when you're tired that's
when you begin to doubt and wonder whether you're imagining things.'

The attack was about to go in with just one company, but Sam insisted
on seeing the colonel of the Sikhs and reporting that he believed the
enemy positions had been considerably strengthened overnight. On
hearing this, the colonel postponed the attack, and ordered patrols to
be sent forward. Meanwhile Sam was ordered to try and find a fording
point across the river. Believing his tank would attract enemy fire and
be shot to pieces, he went off on foot on his own, found a suitable place
to ford the river, took a bearing, then headed back towards the tank.
But then he saw a large number of German troops in the trees on the
Sikhs' side of the river, a little further away. Sam began to run for his
life. As he neared his tank he yelled at the crew to start it up and get

ready to reverse and to warn the infantry. He was now being fired upon and as he was about to clamber onto the tank, he felt a sting in his throat. 'I went over the side of the tank,' says Sam, 'and lay down and there was blood running all over the place and I thought, Christ, I've been shot in the throat.' His wireless operator began panicking, but Sam tried to calm him down and told him to get the field dressings. There was only one and the lad dropped it in some oil. Sam had one of his own, but it did little to stem the bleeding. It hurt like hell, he could hardly talk, and he worried he would bleed to death. Despite this, Sam still managed to get the river fording point bearings sent out by codex over the radio. 'By then,' he says, 'I was feeling bloody bad. I thought I was dying.'

Once the tank was safe, Sam told his crew he would be all right and somehow managed to get himself out of the machine and start staggering back towards the rear. He did not get far, however, and soon collapsed in a ditch by the side of the road, until rescued by two Sikhs, who took him back to a Red Cross post. There he was given morphine and put in a Red Cross jeep. The driver was an American volunteer and as they set off shells began screaming over. 'This driver was panicking,' says Sam, 'driving all over the road and I was more worried about going over a sheer drop than I was about being hit by a shell.' For the second time that morning, Sam, who was still only twenty-three years old, found himself trying to calm a frightened young man, reassuring him that the chances of them being hit were small and to drive straight with his eyes on the road. Eventually, they reached a small village where the school had been turned into a dressing station. It was Sam's third serious wound in what had been for him a very long, hard war.

Over the next three days, the Leicesters continued to push forward, taking Saludecio and reaching the River Conca at Morciano on the 4th. Ahead of them, on the far side of the river, lay the Coriano Ridge, but a few miles to their left, on the southern side of the river, stood the village of Gemmano, perched on top of a 1200-foot high hill.

Quickly recognising the potential importance of Gemmano, General Herr of the 76th Panzer Corps had, on 1 September, ordered the German 100th Mountain Regiment to move into the Conca Valley between Gemmano and Onferno. Italo Quadrelli and his family had heard the battle raging to the south and getting ever closer but it was only with the arrival of the German mountain troops in Onferno on the 3rd that they suddenly found themselves thrown out of their home and in the centre of a battle zone.

The first German troops arrived on horses into the Quadrelli yard, firing shots. While the family hurried inside out of harm's way, the soldiers stole their pigs. Not long after, the troops returned, and requisitioned their family home, which they said they now needed for a command post. 'My father took us to Olare, a hamlet nearby where some friends had dug a big shelter,' says Italo. 'We needed to hide my older brother from the Germans so they would not take him away to work.' His grandparents, however, had insisted on staying on at the farm, Germans or no Germans, hoping that by doing so they would be able to keep an eye on things and to save as much of the farm and their animals as possible. Although an old man, Italo's grandfather was still ordered to help the Germans. 'They used to take the old men and their mules and order them to transport loads for them,' says Italo. 'But my grandfather refused by pretending to be ill and so he was beaten.'

Just a few miles away, however, the Germans had still not yet taken up positions in Gemmano. In fact, many of the civilians, sheltering in caves beneath the village, had seen British troops of the 56th Division coming down the slopes of Montefiore, to the south, and had cheered, believing they were about to be liberated.

Tragically, this golden opportunity to capture Gemmano quickly and easily was not taken. Instead, believing it to be occupied, the British sent over bombers and trained their artillery in a combined bombardment that utterly destroyed this beautiful hill-top village. When the German mountain troops finally reached Gemmano the following day, they found, as they had at Monte Cassino, that the ruins and rubble made the place into a formidable hilltop fortress.

By this time, Italo Quadrelli and his family had been moved out of their first refuge by the Germans, and were now sheltering in a large rock cave in the hills nearby, along with most of the population of Onferno. Fortunately a local man, Walter Casadei, had, on his own initiative, built this shelter some time before. Here, the tufa rock was fairly soft and easily excavated, and as more refugees arrived, so the shelter had grown into three sizeable chambers. There were now around four hundred of them crammed into this dark, dank, hole in the hillside. Conditions were appalling. There was no sanitation, very few creature comforts and a severe shortage of food and water. 'We had to eat pig fat,' says Italo. 'Can you imagine? My God, we were hungry.'

But at least they were safe – which was more than could be said for their homes. Gemmano – and the surrounding villages – could and should have been spared, but by one of the quirks of war, this village, with its high, commanding position over the front all the way to Rimini, had been gifted to the German defenders. And now that they had it, they were not going to easily give it up.

Now based in a large house in the spa town of Bagno di Lucca, in the mountains north of Lucca, was the 14th Panzer Corps Commander, General Frido von Senger und Etterlin. Still commanding the western sector of the German front line from Pistoia all the way to the coast, he had been given the additional responsibility of guarding the coast all the way to Genoa as well.

Despite his far-reaching authority, he could not help feeling depressed. His son, a soldier like himself, had recently been wounded for the eighth time and had lost an arm, while news of the failure of the July plot against Hitler had dampened his spirits further. Although he had known about the assassination plan, he had not been involved, and while he had always doubted its chances of success, he was sad that friends who had taken part in the plot had been executed as a result. But he also knew that its failure meant the war would drag on. 'Each further day,' he wrote, 'would make the war more meaningless than it already was, claiming the blood of thousands of people, of fathers and of adolescent sons.'[248]

In France, the Allies had broken out of Normandy and Paris had fallen; in southern France, DRAGOON had been almost unopposed and German resistance crushed; on the Eastern Front, the Soviets had pushed German forces back into Poland; Romania had capitulated; and in the past few days, so too had Bulgaria. August had not been a good month for Germany. Yet incredibly, its fighting forces still seemed in good heart. Not that von Senger believed it was down to stoicism; rather, he blamed eleven years of Nazi propaganda for having progressively undermined the capacity of the German people – young and old – for independent political thought and discrimination.

His task now was to gradually withdraw his troops behind the Gothic Line. Just a few miles in front of his headquarters, the line was strongest in his sector, consisting of not only a network of defensive positions, but also, in the wide stretch of land between the Arno and the forward part of the line, hundreds of thousands of mines and booby traps designed to cause as much mayhem to the advancing Americans as possible.

Among those who had been busy laying them, both inland and along the coast as part of ongoing anti-invasion measures, was Rudi Schreiber of the 16th Waffen-SS Pioneer Battalion. He had also been involved in building bunkers along the Gothic Line itself, but at the beginning of September was back in Pisa, a city that was about to be evacuated. The task of the Pioneers was to build a series of underwater bridges known as forders across the River Arno to enable the division's forward units to withdraw safely. It was whilst there that Rudi came across a watch shop in the city. Bomb damage had shattered the glass at the front of the shop, and Rudi looked down at a number of wrist-watches sitting there amidst the glass. He stretched out his arm to take one but then stopped himself. Looting was not allowed – that had been drummed into him during his training; Rudi was not going to risk a court martial and disgrace over a wrist-watch.

General Lemelsen, the AOK 14 commander, had been fully expecting an attack on his front, and on 29 August Kesselring gave him permission to begin pulling his troops back behind the Gothic Line. Clark's steady advance began two days later as Lemelsen's forces started their withdrawal. Crossing the Arno near Pisa was Combat Command A, of the 1st Armored Division, now commanded by Colonel Hamilton Howze, who had been promoted to CCA commander during the recent divisional reshuffle. Helping the engineers ford the river was Private First Class Ray Saidel and his crew, who were using the crane of their T-2 Sherman tank recoverer to pull a bulldozer across and so enable it to lower and shape the far bank. On either side, however, were the minefields that had been laid by German engineers like Rudi Schreiber. Ray had been working there on the river for several hours when men of the 370th Regimental Combat Team began to cross over. These were the first troops of the all-black 92nd Infantry Division to have reached the theatre, temporarily attached to the 1st Armored.

Although the minefields were marked, and a sunken road cleared, the infantrymen began crossing into the mined area, either side of the road, setting off *schu*-mines one after the other. The men started retracing their steps. All of a sudden Ray saw a lone soldier out on his own, to the left of the road, and the young man was beginning to panic. Ray yelled at him to stand still, and then hurried along the road parallel to where the man was standing. 'My head is level with your feet,' Ray told him calmly, 'and if you step on a mine, you'll lose a foot but I'll lose my head.' This seemed to convince the soldier to keep still, so Ray then told him to turn around, and put his feet exactly where his footprints were and walk slowly out of there. 'He got out of there OK,' says Ray.

Pisa fell to the Americans on 2 September, and a couple of days later Colonel Howze's infantry had reached the outskirts of Lucca. Ray's company were camped some fifteen miles back, but five of their tanks were up at the front and needed water, so Ray, along with his old friend Jerome Lowrey and four others, drove up with the water. Ever since Tunisia, Ray and Jerome had done some pretty crazy things, but now, having made contact with their tanks, they decided to walk forward and see if they could get into Lucca where there was talk of partisans fighting the retreating Germans. Just short of the city, the 370th Regimental Combat Team were digging in, and occasional shells were whistling over, but otherwise it seemed fairly quiet. Once past the 370th's outposts, they met a partisan on a bicycle, who agreed to guide them into the town itself.

Ray and his buddies saw neither partisans nor Germans, but there were plenty of Italian civilians who mobbed and cheered them and peppered them with questions about when the rest of the Americans would be coming. 'They fed us and wined us,' says Ray, 'but we had to get back. We weren't supposed to be there.'

The city fell the following day, as the last of the 16th Waffen-SS fell back to the Gothic Line. Elsewhere along the Fifth Army front, resistance was now negligible. From his advance HQ in Tavarnelle, south of Florence, General Clark had made his plans and was waiting for Alexander to tell him to launch his own attack on the Gothic Line defences. 'We are all set for the thrust over the mountains toward Bologna,' he wrote to General Marshall. 'It is hard to wait for we are quite ready and eager to go.'[249]

'A lovely day once more, but with a nip in the air,' noted Ion Calvocoressi, as he drove through the flattened villages beyond the River Foglia. 'The first day of autumn, I would say.' On the high ground in front of the Conca, he could see Rimini in the distance and the wide open Adriatic beyond.

It was 4 September, and with the hint of the changing seasons there was an even greater urgency for Eighth Army to wrap up the battle with no more ado. Already, however, some of the momentum brought by the Canadians had gone. First Armoured had suffered endless difficulties crossing the countless ridges and valleys to reach the river, and were then held up by 46th Division who had only just reached the River Conca that same day. Ahead of them lay the Coriano Ridge. It was not especially high, and nor was it the last ridge before the plains – there were still some soft folds, several river crossings, and the San Fortunata Ridge beyond to tackle, but it was certainly the most significant feature that still barred Eighth Army's way, for at its end it gradually dropped into Rimini. The approach was a long, gentle, several-mile-long climb from the Conca Valley to the top, up through a patchwork of fields and vineyards, and dotted with largely deserted farmhouses. Along the top, ran the numerous fortified positions of Green II.

First Armoured's attack did not go in until mid-afternoon, by which time the sun was already beginning to set and was streaming into the eyes of the tank men. Meanwhile, from their prepared positions, the Germans poured shells and mortar fire onto the attackers. Among those firing was Hans Golda and the batteries of Werfer Regiment 71, who were now dug in at Coriano town itself. Large numbers of tanks were knocked out by enemy fire, but as many again broke down after the stresses and strains of the long approach march. Compounding the difficulties was the blinding sun, which caused the tank crews to manoeuvre erratically. By dusk, German resistance was stiffening rather than weakening, as the 29th Panzer and 356th Infantry Divisions began reaching Green II while the assault was being played out. As night came, the British attack had to be withdrawn.

Hans Golda's positions had received little enemy fire, but the ridge as a whole was not only being hit by the British armour but also by reams of bombers and jabos, as well as by British naval guns off the Rimini coast. During the ten days of fighting German casualties had been high and they had lost more than 4,000 as POWs, but by the 5th, with two fresh divisions now at the front, the British tanks could not get their breakthrough. Nor could 56th Division, who were trying to outflank and isolate Gemmano by attacking along the western end of the ridge towards the village of Croce. Then it began to rain – and heavily too. 'The battle is a bit stuck on the left,' scribbled Ion Calvocoressi on the 6th, 'and it looks as though we shall have a big fight.' Leese's hopes of smashing his way through and out into the plains without pause were being dashed with just a few miles to go. And as his forces continued to batter away at the Coriano Ridge, so the situation at Gemmano was also becoming increasingly desperate. Not until the 10th were Gemmano and the surrounding hill finally cleared, by which time an entire British infantry brigade had been flung against the German defenders with severe casualties: one company of the 2/5th Queen's had been reduced to just thirty men.

With dark clouds now rolling across the battlefield, Leese was painfully reminded about the preciousness of time, that so vital commodity. But a pause was now needed. Eighth Army took a deep breath and prepared yet another set-piece attack.

TWENTY-EIGHT

Mountain Passes and Bloody Ridges
12–21 September 1944

While the tactical air forces had been flying flat out in support of the men on the ground, the heavy bombers of 205 Group RAF and the USAAF 15th Air Force had continued operating from their bases around Foggia, flying day in, day out, over targets in northern Italy, the Balkans and even Germany itself. For the most part, their targets were marshalling yards, ports, munitions factories and industrial centres, pasted with bombs in the hope of further disabling Hitler's war machine.

On 10 September, however, their target was the harbour facilities of Trieste. The civilian population was now very used to the sound of the air-raid siren droning out, although more often than not the hundreds of bombers that droned over the sky had continued on their way to attack targets in Romania or Hungary.

Life had already become even harder for Clara Duse. Since her father's arrest and deportation, the family had been publicly listed as 'Enemies of the Reich', and so all bank accounts had been closed, ration cards confiscated and any legal rights stripped from them. Her mother was ill, suffering from a grief- and stress-induced breakdown. They were surviving thanks to the few pieces of gold her mother still possessed and the kindness of friends, but it was difficult.

That day, 10 September, the siren began to wail and Clara quickly got her mother out of bed and led her down the staircase. Theirs was the top-floor flat and they had not quite reached the bottom when there was a huge explosion, shaking the building and covering them with dust. Coughing and spluttering, Clara tightly clutched her mother's hand and led her outside. Looking up she saw drifting down, ever so slowly, some bits of paper. 'It was wallpaper from my bedroom,' says Clara. 'Our flat was completely destroyed.' Now, in addition to their woes, their home had gone.

*   *   *

Lieutenant Eugenio Corti was now on his way south, heading for a British training school where he and a number of others were to be taught how to use British artillery equipment that would soon be assigned to Italian units. In due course, they would then pass this infor- mation on to their own men. It was all part of Alexander's efforts to train six Italian 'combat groups' – the equivalent of three divisions – to a standard whereby they could be brought into the fight at the front line.

After the fall of Rimini, most of the CIL had been withdrawn from the line and had returned to Le Marche. There, after one disagreement too many with his immediate superior, Eugenio and his good friend, 2nd Lieutenant Canèr, had been 'banished' from the 2nd Artillery Group. Eugenio had instead been posted to an anti-aircraft unit.

It had been a crushing blow – he had been sad to leave his men, his friends, and his pride had been hurt, and he now trundled south with little enthusiasm for a course that all of them viewed as something of a nuisance. Pausing in Rome, they had watched with mounting resentment Italian women walking on the arms of Allied troops. No one paid them the slightest bit of attention, because very few Italians in the south were aware that Italian troops had been fighting at the front on the side of the Allies. 'It's only Radio Bari who remembers us sometimes,' said one, 'because the King still has some influence in Bari. These here, though, are waging war on the King: you know they want to take his place.' Eugenio, who was keen to see Italy become a democratic republic, kept quiet.[250]

The British training school was in Cerreto, a short way north of Benevento, and on the way they passed through the ruins of Cassino. Nearly six months on, it was a desolate place, and, infested with malaria and still full of mines and unexploded ordnance, it remained uninhabi- ted. Eugenio had been shocked – he'd seen plenty of destruction in Italy but nothing compared to Cassino. 'Not only had all the buildings been reduced to debris,' he wrote, 'but also every living creature, vegetation too, had been killed. Motionless water stagnated on the enclosed flat land between the mountains where the city once rose and flooded the large expanse of ruins; there wasn't a single tree or shrub as far as the eye could see.'[251]

Fifth Army, meanwhile, had enjoyed a quiet month throughout much of August, which had provided a welcome opportunity for rest and reorganisation of Clark's depleted forces. New troops had arrived in the theatre, such as the 370th Regimental Combat Team and the Brazilian Expeditionary Force, while others had left Italy – men like Sergeant Bucky Walters, who had been sent home on rotation after two-and-a-half years overseas. And others, like Lieutenant Kendall Brooke, had recovered from wounds suffered in earlier fighting and had rejoined their units.

Dick Frost of the Royal Natal Carbineers had certainly been glad of the pause, but on 3 September – Britain and South Africa's fifth anniversary of the war – the 6th South African Armoured Division was on the move again, heading north on the approach to battle. That day they passed through the smashed and desolate town of Empoli, crossed over the Arno and rumbled on towards Pistoia, which they reached on 12 September. 'Parked in a dirty square,' scribbled Dick Frost, 'swarming with flies and practically deserted.' Ahead were the Apennines, rising imperiously and dominating the town below.

The South Africans and a British Guards Brigade were now part of the US IV Corps, along with the 1st Armored, but would not be leading Clark's assault of the central Gothic Line. With his now limited resources, the Fifth Army commander knew he had to handle his forces very carefully indeed, and so had decided on using II Corps as his spearhead, with the British XIII Corps in support.

With no natural route through the mountains, Clark recognised that the main thrust of his advance would have to be made down existing roads, and specifically over the two major passes – the Futa and the Giogo. Both stood on the Gothic Line, but the Futa was the pass over which Route 65, the main road from Florence to Bologna, ran. Guessing this was likely to be the more heavily defended of the two, he decided to send the 34th Red Bull and 91st Divisions astride Route 65 in an attempt to mask the main thrust of his attack, which was to be towards the Giogo Pass. This would be led by the 85th 'Custer' Division; 91st Division would then swing across the mountains from Route 65 to join them, with the 88th in reserve ready to exploit any success. Meanwhile, Kirkman's XIII Corps would help them by attacking along the Faenza and Forlì roads into Romagna to the east of the Giogo Pass.

Clark might have been worried about his much-reduced forces, but so too was General Lemelsen. Precisely as Alexander had hoped, Kesselring had moved a number of his troops away from the centre of the line to help fill the breach on the Adriatic. Although only one of those divisions had been taken directly from AOK 14, Lemelsen was keenly aware that the mobile reserves of 26th and 29th Panzer Grenadier Divisions would have been of enormous help to him when Fifth Army attacked his positions. Massively overstretched, it left him with only one division – the 4th Fallschirmjäger – covering both the Futa and Giogo Passes, and one – the 715th Infantry – in XIII Corps' sector. To make matters worse, partisans to the rear – the Stella Rossa included – along with the continued efforts of the Allied air forces, were making supply of the front very difficult indeed.

Yet despite the overwhelming superiority of manpower, the task ahead for Fifth Army was a daunting one. Steep mountains rose over 3,000 feet. The Giogo pass itself was dominated by Monte Altuzzo on one side and the high ridge of Monticelli on the other. Blasted into the rock facing the attackers were reinforced machine-gun and mortar positions, while in front were swamps of barbed wire a foot high and twenty-five feet deep. On the reverse side of these peaks were larger, deeper bunkers dug so deep that they would be impervious to almost anything the Allies could hurl at them. And then there was the terrain itself. Plunging cliffs and thick vegetation of shrub and small trees made it impossible for the Americans to mount any large-scale co-ordinated attack.

Lieutenant Bob Wiggans was all too aware of just how tough the forthcoming fight for the pass would be. On the 12th, General Coulter, the commanding officer of the Custermen, addressed his officers for a pre-battle pep talk. 'I don't know what it did for the other officers,' wrote Bob, 'but for me it didn't have the desired effect. I knew only that the lucky would get through this battle.'[252]

That night, Bob's company moved out in a sober mood, tramping up a narrow mountain trail in single file with bulging webbing and heavy packs on their backs. Accompanying them were not trucks and other vehicles but mules and mule skinners, loaded with ammunition and equipment. As the trail became steeper and narrower, Bob was aware that a quietness had settled over his men. He himself could not help thinking about his wife and family and his home, and imagined them tucked up in bed, warm and safe and free of fear. 'Having stood on the brink of death so many times already,' he noted, 'everything in the world seemed of greater value and beauty.'

They attacked the Gothic Line at 6 a.m., following a heavy artillery barrage. As the summit disappeared under a huge amount of smoke, dust and blasted rock, Bob and his men set off, conscious of the fact that however heavy the shelling, the Fallschirmjäger dug in above them would still emerge unscathed when it was over. And so they did. All day long, the mountains thundered with the sound of battle. Bob found himself caught up in a continuous fire-fight as shells and mortars whistled over in both directions, bullets cut through the air and kicked up dirt and chips of stone. Progress was measured in yards. By nightfall, they had achieved little except they now knew precisely where the main German positions were. 'It became apparent,' noted Bob, 'this battle could be won only by the tactics General Grant used in our terrible Civil War: hammer and pound until the sheer weight of our combined fire eventually overcame the enemy.'[253]

Not until the fifth day of fighting, with the Americans having resisted counterattack after counterattack, but with the paratroopers every bit as stubborn, did the German positions begin to crack. In the morning, Bob was on the mountain, linked to the artillery behind by field telephone, and directing fire from the large 155mm howitzers onto an enemy pillbox. At one point, he watched amazed as a shell from a direct hit merely bounced off and over the mountain. He then called on the Corps artillery for support from the 240mm guns, the biggest they had. 'They smashed that pillbox with the third round,' says Bob. 'We then rushed forward and captured the pillbox and fifty men inside.' While the men of the 91st finally forced their way over Monticelli, the Custermen prepared for their own knock-out blow. Throughout the rest of the day and into the night they fought, but by that time, Lemelsen had ordered the whole of 1st Fallschirmjäger Corps to fall back to the next line of defences in the heights north of Firenzuola, some six miles to the north. By morning on the 18th, Monte Altuzzo was in the hands of the battered 338th Infantry, a hole had been punched through the Gothic Line, and the Giogo Pass was open. By that time, however, both sides had suffered appalling losses: the Americans had 2,731 casualties, the Germans even more, and the dead littered the mountains. 'We were dirty, unshaven, hungry, dead tired,' noted Bob, 'and pretty well decimated.' The battles along the Gothic Line were proving to be among the most brutal and costly of the entire campaign.

As part of Lemelsen's efforts to readjust the front line, the 16th Waffen-SS were brought east to hold a large stretch of the line to the west of 1st Fallschirmjäger Division. Sturmbannführer Reder's 16th Reconnaissance Battalion was to take over positions south of San Marcello Pistoiese, some

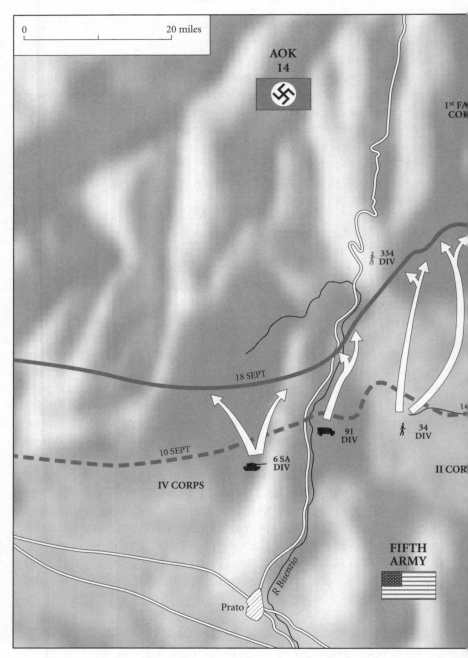

Fifth Army's assault on the Gothic Line, 10–18 Sept. 1944

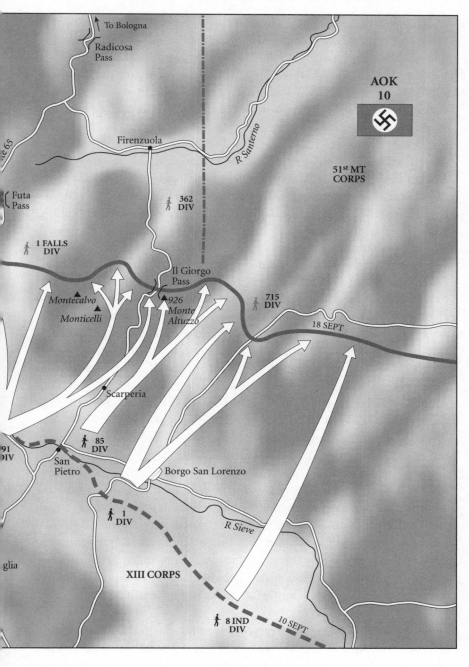

To Bologna

Radicosa
Pass

AOK
10

Firenzuola

R Santerno

51ST MT
CORPS

Futa
Pass

362
DIV

1 FALLS
DIV

Il Giorgo
Pass

Montecalvo

926

715
DIV

Monticelli

*Monte
Altuzzo*

18 SEPT

Scarperia

85
DIV

91
DIV

San
Pietro

Borgo San Lorenzo

1
DIV

R Sieve

glia

XIII CORPS

8 IND
DIV

10 SEPT

fifteen miles north-east of Pistoia. Willfried Segebrecht, commander of
the 1st Company, was sorry to leave the coastal area behind. 'Until now,'
he noted, 'we'd seen Italy as a land of peaches and sunshine, but now it
was different. We couldn't see into the distance; the mountains were
somehow oppressive.' Nor had his spirits been improved by the usual
supply problems. For one whole day during the move, they had been
stuck, stranded without any petrol.

Now opposite the South Africans, their part of the front was quiet
apart from shellfire hurtling over in both directions. However, Willfried
had noticed the effects of such artillery exchanges were different in the
mountains than in the open rolling countryside further south. Now, due
to the long echoes and rolling repeats, the din seemed to be never-ending.
His men were also realising that up there, in the mountains, the shards
and splinters of rock that were sprayed over them as the shells exploded
were far more lethal than when detonating in ground of deeper soil.
'There were,' noted Willfried, 'terrible wounds.'[254] And they were discovering that life in the mountains was frugal and harsh and short on
creature comforts. All the machines and vehicles had been left behind;
now they had just the infantryman's basic kit: rifle, mortar, machine
gun and hand-grenade – and hob-nailed boots; boots that scraped loudly
on the stony mountain paths. Willfried envied the Americans – for
their apparently inexhaustible supplies of everything, but also for their
rubber-soled boots, which, he believed, enabled them to creep through
the terrain soundlessly.

On his first morning in the mountains, Willfried clambered out of
his dugout and stretched himself in the sunshine. Hardly thirty yards
away, Unterscharführer Bühler appeared from his own dugout and
stretched as well. Willfried called out to him, then a moment later the
express train of a shell resounded through the mountains and a moment
later Bühler had disappeared, blown into a thousand pieces. Willfried
was distraught. He had known and fought alongside Bühler since the
days of the blitzkrieg in the west; they had been together in Holland,
France, Russia and the Balkans. 'I couldn't believe it,' noted Willfried,
'and I crept back into my bunker and was not ashamed of my tears.'[255]

Allied air activity had also increased once more, with the dreaded jabos
bombing and strafing German positions and columns with what felt like
the persistence of angry wasps. A number of units of the Mediterranean
Allied Tactical Air Force had remained in France, but the majority were

still based on Corsica, returned to fighting over Italy. One pilot not returning, however, was Charles Dills, who had flown his last combat mission on 17 August over southern France. His fatigue had worsened and he was now regularly nodding off whilst flying. Finally it dawned on him that sooner or later someone was going to get killed as a result, and not necessarily himself. 'They should have grounded me at least twenty missions earlier, in my opinion,' says Charles. 'I was absolutely spent.' Sent to Naples, by the middle of September Charles was sailing back to the US, his time as a combat fighter pilot over.

Despite the return of many of MATAF's units, however, the Desert Air Force was still flying at full stretch. Wing Commander Cocky Dundas had never known such an exhausting or frightening period of air combat, despite having flown throughout the Battle of Britain. Each and every day, morning, noon and evening, he and his pilots in 244 Wing were clambering into their Spitfires and climbing high into the sky before plunging down into the thick of the battle raging below. However frightening it might have been on the receiving end of the jabos' attacks, it was every bit as stressful and terrifying for those flying the machines. The flak was always intense as they flew over those ridges, mountains and valleys, and could not be evaded. 'It poured up at us in every known form,' wrote Cocky, 'big black puffs powdering the sky around us as we ran in to the target, thousands of little white puffs lower down as we dived, streaks of tracer hissing across the valleys as we dropped our bombs and clawed upwards again.'[256]

In the briefing tent at Perugia, Cocky would watch the faces of the pilots as the army liaison officers and operations officers talked them through the next sortie. Cocky found that when he said 'good luck' to his men, he meant it, literally, because it really was a matter of pure chance whether one was hit by flak or not, and if hit, whether one was able to make it back, bale out, crash land or be killed. 'It was not surprising,' he noted, 'that I often saw fear in the eyes of those young men as they listened to the briefings. It is not surprising that from time to time someone would find it almost impossible to control his fear.'[257]

A particularly hated target was a road bridge north of Rimini, around which were especially large numbers of anti-aircraft batteries. When a whole squadron was ordered to attack it, Cocky felt it only fair that he should take the lead. Taking off from Perugia, they headed out to sea through clear skies, then north of Rimini turned back towards land.

Black puffs of flak appeared before they had even crossed the coast, their Spitfires bucking and rocking from the blasts. The target was still four or five miles away, and Cocky found the urge to swerve away and fly out of the fray almost overwhelming. 'I felt naked and exposed,' he noted, 'and was sure that I was going to be hit.' The target passed under his wing and he flipped the Spitfire on its back and dived, down through greater bursts of flak until streams of tracer began pouring towards him. Dropping his bomb load, he continued diving almost to the deck and over the R/T told the others to do the same. Suddenly there was an explosion and his plane juddered violently. Quickly glancing around him, he saw a large hole halfway along his port side wing.

Despite this, he managed to fly back to base without too much difficulty, but when he landed, he discovered one of his tyres had also been punctured and so, as he touched down, the aircraft slewed and the undercarriage leg collapsed. Cocky was fine, and when he returned to his quarters, the others treated his misadventure as a great joke. 'But for once I was not feeling jokey,' wrote Cocky. 'I told them to go to hell and lay down on my bunk and thought, "Oh Christ, Oh Christ, I can't go on like this." '258

On Monte Sole, the partisans of the Stella Rossa were still struggling in the daily fight for survival. For some, the constant danger and hardships had become too much. Carlo Venturi, for one, had left the brigade. One day, following an argument with one of his friends, he had wandered northwards and, spurred by an urgent desire to see his family, had walked to Casalecchio. Fascist and German troops in the town, however, prevented him from getting close to his old family home, and rather than finding his family, he was forced to hide instead.

Unsure what he should do, he sadly headed back to the mountains, where he came across several former Stella Rossa partisans who had split with Sugano and were now with the 62nd Garibaldi Brigade. These men were keen for him to join them, and conscious that he faced recriminations if he went back to Monte Sole, Carlo agreed. His life as a partisan was not over yet.

Meanwhile, Lupo and his vice-commander, Gianni Rossi, heard the distant guns twenty miles to the south with mounting excitement. The sound of battle had been a much-needed fillip after a frustrating few weeks. Not only had Gianni's younger brother, Leone, been killed, they had also been pushed into something of a corner and forced to play

ABOVE: The Guards Brigade in Montepulciano. It was not far from here that Reg Harris's hugely popular platoon commander was killed.

RIGHT: 'Germany is truly your friend,' runs the caption on this German propaganda poster. Nothing could have been further from the truth; in fact, it was German policy to bleed Italy dry of money and both man- and manufacturing power.

LA GERMANIA È VERAMENTE VOSTRA AMICA

LEFT: Walter Reder, commander of the 16th Waffen-SS Reconnaissance Battalion. A veteran of the Eastern Front – and of fighting Russian partisans – he was a highly capable commander and a man who had no qualms about carrying out Kesselring's orders to the letter.

RIGHT: Feldmarschall Kesselring – or 'Smiling Albert' as he was known. A genial and popular commander, in June 1944 he nonetheless authorised brutal reprisals against partisan activities. The mass shootings, hangings and burning of villages would soon escalate out of control, bringing untold suffering, and mark an ugly stain on an otherwise distinguished military career.

LEFT: It did not pay to anger the 16th Waffen-SS Division. When partisans ambushed and killed some of their number, Reder and his Reconnaissance Battalion were ordered to destroy the local guerrillas. The result was the San Terenzo massacre, a horrific form of shock and awe tactics.

BELOW: Karl Wolff, the Highest SS and Police Führer in Italy, who with Kesselring and Ambassador Rudolf Rahn was one of three men who ran Italy from the time of the Italian armistice until the end of the war. One of the leading Nazis – and not without dirt on his hands – he nonetheless worked hard to temper the brutality of Kesselring's anti-partisan measures and to bring about an early end to the war in Italy.

LEFT: These men were partisans from the 29th GAP Brigade in Ravenna and were publicly strung up for their resistance activities. Sights such as this were common in German-occupied northern Italy and many of those hanged for all to see were civilians, guilty of nothing, executed in retaliation for partisan activities. It was an extreme policy and did not work.

RIGHT: Iris Versari, shot during a fire-fight with GNR troops and then strung up on a lamppost in the centre of Forlì. Neo-Fascists jeered and tore most of her clothes from her dead body.

LEFT: Victims of the Sant' Anna massacre. After Kesselring's June announcement, the summer of 1944 became one of appalling terror in which there were hundreds of massacres. Some of the victims were partisans but the majority were the innocent – the elderly, women and children.

LEFT: By the beginning of August, the Allies were closing in on Florence. He[re] tanks from the 6th South African Armoured Divisio[n] push on through Impruner[ta].

RIGHT: Fallschirmjä[ger] defending the northe[rn] half of Florence on [the] banks of the Ri[ver] Arno. Only the Po[nte] Vecchio of Floren[ce's] bridges was sav[ed].

BELOW: Florentine partisa[ns] firing on the Via de Serrag[li], one of the many narrow streets on the southern banks of the Arno that saw vicious fighting.

ABOVE: General Oliver Leese. It was during a meeting with Alexander at Orvieto airfield on 4 August that Leese persuaded the C-in-C to switch Eighth Army's attack on the Gothic Line from the centre to the Adriatic Coast.

RIGHT: Ken Neill, a New Zealander who had flown with 225 Squadron throughout the Tunisian campaign and then rejoined them in Italy.

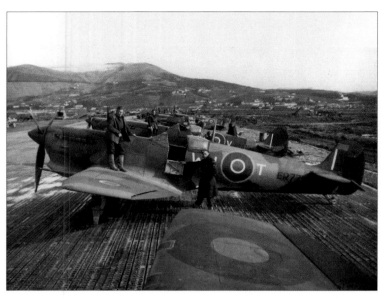

LEFT: Spitfires of 22[?] Squadron lined up a[t] Florence airfield. These were Mk V, clipped-wing models suited to low altitude flying where the shortened wings ma[de] them more manoeuvrable. They are standing on American-made PSP matting, a fine invention that enable[d] aircraft to fly in otherwise impossible conditions.

ABOVE: The infantryman's lot. 'Digging in' was a habitual task for men at the front. All too often, the ground was rocky and the soil shallow. The key, however, was to dig deep enough to be able to li[e] below ground level, which, it was hoped, would offer enough protection from anything but a direct shell or mortar blast.

The only known photograph of Mario Musolesi, better known as 'Lupo', commander of the Stella Rossa. Revered by his men, he was, during the summer of 1944, the undisputed King of Monte Sole.

ABOVE: The Monte Sole Massif from the ...tta Valley. Monte Sole itself is No.7, ...hile No.9 is the church at Casaglia. The ...metery is just to the right.

RIGHT: The number of bridges built by the Allies was truly astonishing. The sappers – not to mention Mr Bailey – were among the unsung heroes of the Allies' campaign.

An anti-tank ditch along the Gothic Line, just one of the fine pieces of engineering along this formidable defensive position.

British troops walk through the shattered remains of Gemmano, September 1944.

ABOVE: Sam Bradshaw. Another veteran of North Africa, Sam had already been seriously wounded twice before being badly hit a third time during Eighth Army's attack on the Gothic Line. Tank men with Sam's experience were hard to replace.

LEFT: Peter Moore (*left*) with a friend whilst on leave in Rome. Rome and Florence became popular places for Allied soldiers to unwind briefly after long, difficult times at the front, and Peter had certainly earned his time off after enduring Eighth Army's bitter battle for the Gothic Line.

ball by the Comando Unico Militare Emilia-Romagna (CUMER), the Bologna headquarters of the CLN.

In August, several arms drops had been thwarted by the Germans, and CUMER had made it clear that henceforth the only way to the Allies was through them. It was both contact with and recognition from the Allies that Lupo wanted most for his band and so he gave in to pressure from CUMER to allow them to send two more political commissars: 'Giacomo' and 'Sergio' (a representative of the Italian Communist Party) were now to work alongside Lupo and Gianni's old friend and fellow Stella Rossa founder, il Vecchio.*

A new initiative started by the political commissars was to hold regular sessions called 'Hours of Politics' for the partisans. These hour-long meetings were divided into two halves. In the first half hour, they would talk about the brigade operations, but in the second, they discussed the possible post-war situation, and urged the men to think about a new, Communist future for Italy.

It was this politicisation of the brigade that really annoyed Lupo. Although he had nothing against the Bologna commissars per se, and recognised that they were helping to keep discipline and instil a sense of spirit amongst the men, he disliked the way Communist Party doctrine was being foisted upon his men. For example, he had noticed that some of the men had started giving him the Communist salute. He didn't like any kind of salute, but if there had to be one he felt it should be of a military rather than political kind. On the whole, it was the younger ones who seemed most impressionable to such indoctrination, but others found it unsettling, and had complained to Lupo. He began to worry that politics would end up dividing the Stella Rossa, and complained to il Vecchio that if they were to have commissars, they should be from different political parties, and not just the Communists.

On 11 September, Lupo called a meeting of his battalion commanders. Most felt the Commissars were of little help, but did think they should maintain their links with CUMER and the CLN. Without their support and help, they argued, they would soon struggle to keep going. This meant they had to keep the commissars, but a compromise was agreed. The commissars would remain at brigade command, but partisans with

---

*The political commissar chain of command within the Stella Rossa was as follows: political commissar, Umberto Crisaldi (il Vecchio); vice-commissar, Ferruccio Magnani (Giacomo); representative of the Italian Communist Party, Agostino Ottani (Sergio).

different political leanings would from now on act as political commissars within each of the four battalions.

While this undoubtedly helped create a new-found sense of cohesion
and vigour within the Stella Rossa, the lack of arms drops was not so
easily solved, and was, in fact, less to do with CUMER and more to do
with a change of Allied policy. Since the reduction of the theatre in July,
cutbacks had been made on all aspects of the Allied war effort in Italy,
and that meant resources for clandestine warfare too. The priority was
once again France, to help the resistance groups there, and also to
support the partisans in Yugoslavia and the Balkans, where it was felt
that with the help of the SOE and OSS, Tito's largely Communist partisans could draw off a number of German divisions without any further
Allied involvement on the ground.

Someone had to pay the price for this new pecking order, and it was
the Italian partisans, who, having been encouraged to take up arms were
now suddenly being left high and dry, to fend for themselves. As a result,
after their run of successes, the Stella Rossa were now critically low on
arms and ammunition.

On 17 September, Kesselring issued a final warning to the Stella Rossa
and other partisans and civilians in the area, printed in the Bologna
newspaper, *Il Resto del Carlino*. The actions of partisans, he announced,
could simply no longer be tolerated; from now on they would be acted
upon immediately and in the most severe manner possible. 'This battle
without quarter for the destruction of banditry and delinquency,' he
warned, 'must therefore be carried out by the entire Italian population.'

The partisans took no heed, however. The Allies would surely reach
them soon; and so they couldn't throw down their arms now – not when
they were just on the point of victory.

Meanwhile, high in the Alpine valleys north-west of Turin, units of the
Decima MAS, GNR and Black Brigades were continuing their war against
the Piemonte partisans. Up in the Alps there were few Germans, and in
Piemonte, no key supply routes leading into the Reich, and so the
fighting was a purely Italian matter – a private civil war in which Republican forces tried to impose the will of the RSI and the partisans did their
best to resist. And apart from killing and capturing one another, not a
great deal was being achieved.

William Cremonini and the Bir el Gobi Company were now operating
in the mountains near Vallo Torinese, and down valleys such as the Val

di Viu, and it was here that luck was running out for Emilio Sacerdote and his wife and daughter. Known simply as 'Dote', Emilio had played an important part in the resistance movement in the Torinese Alps. He had had an opportunity to flee to Switzerland back in January, but had turned down the chance, instead feeling it was his duty to stay and help the young and frightened boys who had fled to the mountains. As a veteran of the First World War – and a decorated veteran as well – he had been able to teach them something about handling weapons. He'd taught them, too, not to waver in their refusal ever to serve the Nazi-fascists.

Since then he had been with the autonomous partisan band of the Lanzo Torinese Valley, then in April had joined the 19th Giambone Brigade. By September, he was acting as liaison officer between the Susa Alpine Battalion and the partisans still in the Val di Viu.

At fifty-one Emilio was much older than the majority of partisans and as well as being a former war hero, had also been a highly regarded lawyer and magistrate. Although based in Turin, as the 'King's Substitute Procurator' he had presided over cases across the north of Italy through-out much of the Fascist era.

And yet Emilio had had greater reason than most to turn his back on the Fascists and especially the German occupiers – for he was a Jew. Mussolini had never been instinctively anti-Semitic, and until the Race Manifesto of July 1938, anti-Semitism had never previously featured in Italian fascist doctrine. Indeed, the new race laws were seen as a sop to Mussolini's Nazi ally. Even then, there were many who opposed the race laws, and they were not pursued with particular zeal. However, the Race Laws had meant that Emilio had been publicly declared a Jew, and as a consequence he had voluntarily resigned his post and then been struck off the register of lawyers.

The rastrellamenti of September, carried out by the Bir el Gobi Company amongst others, had hit the partisans of the Val di Viù hard. Another exodus of men had fled to Switzerland but with their almost non-existent resources, Emilio and his family had been forced to hide in a basement flat in the small town of Lemie. And in any case, he still felt a profound duty to help his 'boys', most of whom were now struggling to find enough food to survive, let alone offer much active resistance.

On 30 September, Emilio and his wife were warned of another Fascist search party. Hiding behind a stack of wood in the basement, and praying the stray dog that had befriended them would not give the game away, they crouched, terrified, while Fascists stomped around the flat above them. Once they were gone, however, Emilio and his wife decided that they now had no choice but to head back to Turin where they had friends who might help and hide them. Putting all their belongings into two suitcases, they gave them to their landlady to hide, then put on two layers of clothes so that they did not have to carry anything, and set out on foot towards Lanzo.

They had not gone far, however, when a car stopped beside them and two Fascists told them to get in. Emilio knew they were now in serious trouble but tried to reassure his wife and daughter and to get rid of incriminating papers by surreptitiously throwing them out of the window. Taken to Lanzo, they were thrown into a cell. 'We look at each other,' wrote his wife, 'silenced by grief, knowing that a terrible fatality is pursuing us. We are ground down by passing time; night falls yet no one comes to us.'[259]

Eventually they were called for. Interrogations followed – long interrogations – and then they were taken to a hotel, the Albergo Torino, under guard. Here husband and wife spent a last night together. At first light, eight German SS policemen knocked on the door and told them to dress, while another took away all their other possessions. 'I see my beloved,' wrote his wife, 'I will always see him thus – with his hands trembling, unable to button up his jacket and his belt.'[260] Minutes later, the Germans took him away.

Back on the Adriatic Front, bewildered and distraught villagers had been emerging from their caves beneath Gemmano, only to discover the world they had known all their lives was now very different. When the 4th Indian Division finally wrested Onferno from German hands a few days later, Italo Quadrelli discovered his home, like so many others, had not survived the battle. Having been bombed, it had then caught fire and burned to the ground. Italo and his family had gone back and looked at the ruins. In the yard, the bodies of dead pigs and Germans had been piled on top of each other. 'There were corpses everywhere,' says Italo. 'Everything had been destroyed. Everything.'

There were also now plenty of perfectly alive troops as well – men of the 4th Indian Division. These included Gurkhas and bearded Sikhs, wearing turbans rather than tin helmets. Italo found them terrifying. 'I was nine,' says Italo. 'I had never seen a coloured man before.' With no home left, they began to trudge south to the town of Levola, where they had family. It was a difficult journey, and one that Italo had to make barefoot; he had neither shoes nor any other clothes. Given some food and cigarettes by the arriving troops, his father, desolate at the family's losses, smoked continually, one after the other, as they walked south. Italo could not get over the scale of the Allied army they were now walking through. 'I'd barely seen a car before either,' he says, 'but filing out across the countryside were thousands of vehicles and thousands of troops.'

There was still much to be done by Leese's troops before Operation OLIVE was over and the mountains finally behind them for good. Eighth Army's renewed attempt to smash through Green II began on the evening of 12 September, with the usual barrage and aerial bombardment that preceded operations on the ground. The Canadians and V Corps were now to attack side by side and not only take the Coriano Ridge but also cross the next series of rivers, capture the San Fortunato Ridge and then break through into the plains beyond.

Although Gemmano had now been taken, the western end of the Coriano Ridge, the far side of the Conca, had not, and it was here that 46th Division attacked. Such had been the losses, the Leicesters were now reduced to just three companies, a reduction that had been repeated throughout the 139th Infantry Brigade. During the lull, the newly promoted Captain Peter Moore had been re-reading Siegfried Sassoon's *Memoirs Of An Infantry Officer* to remind himself that no matter how bad things were, it had been worse for the previous generation in the last war. Sadly, however, he was mistaken. The chances of survival for front-line troops in the Gothic Line battles were about the same as those on the Western Front, and had Peter then sat down and compared notes with a veteran of the 1914–18 war they would have had an uncomfortably large amount in common.

Furthermore, the casualty rates among the junior officers were the highest, as Peter was discovering with the never-ending loss of one friend and fellow officer after another. Bitter fighting took place around Croce on the 14th, and the following day Peter was advancing with the battalion through that ruined village, stepping over the evidence of considerable slaughter. Bodies lay everywhere, and although Peter had developed a strong stomach after nearly two years of fighting, he couldn't help feeling sickened by the sight of men with skulls crushed and flattened by tank tracks and the overpowering stench of putrefying flesh.

Their objective that day was the village of Monte Colombo, which rose above them. Shells were pouring down towards them, and the ground over which they were to advance looked horribly exposed. To make matters worse, Peter then lost his trusted sergeant, who was badly wounded in the leg by a shell fragment.

The loss of their sergeant seemed somehow to stiffen B Company's resolve, however, and as they began their assault they discovered there were more stone walls and trees offering cover than Peter had first appreciated. Accompanied by three tanks, they crept forward until they reached the edge of the village then dashed in, prepared for bitter house-to-house fighting. The defenders, however, had finally had enough and began surrendering in droves. Peter walked down a cobbled street on his own and, at an open-fronted workshop, came face-to-face with a German machine-gun crew. 'I am not sure who was more surprised,' he noted, 'they or I, but I got in first with a sharp "*Hände hoch!*" and pointed my Tommy gun at them.' One of the Germans had a Luger, much sought after by Allied troops, so Peter took it from him, as well as some Zeiss binoculars, and marched them back to company headquarters. Although Monte Colombo was then heavily shelled, the German counterattack never came. The Leicesters' part in Operation OLIVE had now come to an end.

This first phase of the renewed battle had gone well for Eighth Army with the whole of Coriano Ridge captured in the first few days' fighting. Thereafter, however, resistance stiffened once more, with tenacious defence by the Germans followed by the arrival of two more divisions on 17 September. Von Vietinghoff now had the elements of ten divisions in the line, more than the attackers.

Hans Golda and the Werfer Regiment 71 had fallen back to the San Fortunato Ridge before Eighth Army's renewed offensive, and were dug in on the reverse slopes. Even making that move had been problematic, and Hans had prepared Italian ox teams to take the nebelwerfers before getting his hands on some black market petrol at the last moment. The new positions were among vineyards, heavy with ripe juicy grapes, which he and the men ate hungrily. Hans was also grateful to discover several Italian army officer uniforms in the empty house he had taken for his headquarters – his own uniform had become threadbare, and the trousers, boots and shoes were appropriated with relish.

As the Eighth Army assault was renewed, the air attacks intensified once more. From their positions, Hans and his men had watched wave after wave of bombers drop their bomb loads on Rimini. From morning until late in the evening, they could see bombs detonating. Among those pasting Rimini that day was Flight Sergeant Eric Wall and his B-26 Marauder crew; the Desert Air Force's bombers had been operating flat-out throughout the battle, and 24 SAAF Squadron had been no exception.

By 14 September, Hans' battery was firing constantly, their rounds of six rockets ideal for pouring onto massed advancing forces. It was typical of German efficiency that no matter how bad the shortages of food, fuel and other supplies, they made sure ammunition reached the front. But while Hans' men never ran out of rockets, the quality of the missiles was increasingly poor, with fatal consequences. Hans had spread his battery out, using two farmhouses and a number of straw ricks as cover and camouflage. One of the werfers was between the two houses, and suddenly a rocket misfired, sending out splinters of missile casing. One of these hit one of his men, Adam Jäger, tearing open his chest. Hans hurried over, but the lad died in his arms moments later. Meanwhile, another splinter had hit one of the straw ricks, and in no time at all, another rick had caught fire as well as both of the houses. Soon reconnaissance planes were circling overhead. The men hurriedly took cover away from the inferno. 'In spite of this,' wrote Hans bitterly, 'the pigs were soon shooting smoke grenades on our position and then we were carpet-bombed. The chance of us getting our arses out of there seemed like one in a million.'[261] They crouched as low as they could, their hands over their heads, and the bombs continued falling all about them. But a miracle occurred – the bombing stopped, the planes disappeared, and when they emerged once more, not one more of his men had been killed or even wounded.

As Eighth Army pushed forward yet again, so the Werfer Regiment fell back, in order to keep their nebelwerfers in range of the attackers. That night, 16 September, Hans heard the night bombers rumble over Rimini and the battle area. 'From our house,' he wrote, 'we could see the detonating bombs, the flames and the burning haystacks and houses. We saw the yellow and red flames of burning supplies and heard the heavy detonations of the big bombs and the light crack of the splinter bombs.'[262] For a long while after, the fires continued to glow in the night. By morning, the countryside around them looked as though it had been raked over – the houses were blackened wrecks, orchards had been ripped apart and animals lay strewn in the fields. And after firing their first salvo of the day, one of his officers was killed by a further misfiring rocket. They had survived enemy artillery fire and aerial bombardments, but had lost two men due to their own faulty ammunition – missiles that may have been sabotaged by forced labour back in the Reich. Hans was distraught. 'I couldn't eat,' he noted, 'and I couldn't sleep. We were having bad luck and we couldn't shake it off.'[263]

By the 19th, the Canadians were fighting on the outskirts of Rimini itself, now a shell of a city after repeated bombardment by the Allies and about to become even more of a wreck as German troops prepared demolitions of the all-important port facilities. Among those strapping on the dynamite was Jupp Klein and his band of Pioneers. Since the start of the fighting his company had been reduced to almost its original post-Cassino size; virtually all the new recruits he had received during the summer had been either killed or wounded.

Meanwhile, 56th Division and 1st Armoured were now attacking the San Fortunato spur. Yet again, rivers were getting in the way, and with only one ford over the River Ausa below the ridge, 1st Armoured's advance was not only slowed but also made their armour an easy target. Moreover, the infantry leading the assault were now strongly counterattacked by the 90th Panzer Grenadier Division, fresh into the line after their stint on the west coast with Graziani's Army of Liguria. When 1st Armoured finally emerged across the Ausa to help, they were blasted by a hail of anti-tank fire dug in on the reverse slope. However, they gallantly pressed onwards and with the Canadians continuing to push the Germans back at San Fortunato itself, the Germans finally abandoned their positions, blowing up the installations in Rimini as they went and falling back across the River Rubicon, the scene of Caesar's army's crossing some two thousand years before. Now moving through the Canadians on the edge of Rimini were the New Zealanders, including the 28th (Maori) Battalion. Passing a secondary road from San Marino, they then crossed over the railway line, the carnage of the previous few days' fighting evident for all to see. 'There was shell smoke and the smell of bloody cordite and bodies,' recalls Tini Glover. 'And there were bodies everywhere. Seemed like thousands.' Operation OLIVE was over, but the Battle of the Rivers was about to begin.

Losses in the battle had been appalling – more than a thousand a day in Eighth Army alone since the assault had been renewed on 12 September, and around 14,000 since Operation OLIVE had opened.

German losses had been even worse – around 16,000. First Armoured Division had virtually ceased to exist, as had one brigade in 56th Division. Quite apart from the tragedy of those losses, Alexander now faced the problem of how to replace them. Leese's men were exhausted, and no doubt both commanders were wishing things might have been different; that they might have had just a bit more summertime, and been allowed to have kept some of those divisions sent to southern France – divisions that had found almost no opposition at all and which could have achieved the same result with half the number.

But an army commander has to look forward, not back. Clark's men had done well in the central Apennines, breaching the Gothic Line and pushing Lemelsen's forces back to within thirty miles of that mecca, Bologna, and Eighth Army was now at long last in the plains of the north. Somehow, some way, they needed one last almighty effort and a truly astonishing victory would be theirs.

But it was raining, and raining hard, and the promised land where the Allies' vast superiority in armour and fire power was supposed to make hay had already become a nightmare of rivers, dykes and soggy meadows. The low ground had become every bit as difficult to fight on as the mountains and ridges behind them.

As September drew to a close, things were beginning to look pretty bleak in the Apennines too, despite Fifth Army's early successes. On 20 September, the Royal Natal Carbineers passed through Prato and reached a village heaving with refugees. 'The winter is going to be hell if we don't get through the mountains,' Dick Frost noted in his diary. The rain barely let up over the next few days. 'Terrific wind at night and much rain,' Dick recorded on the 28th. The following day, the Carbineers were all issued with winter kit. 'War news not too good,' he recorded, 'and looks as if we will be in the mountains all winter.'[264] As was so often the case with troops on the ground, Dick had an uncanny sixth sense about future prospects.

PART III

The Winter of Discontent

TWENTY-NINE

Death in the Mountains
22–29 September 1944

It was not only the partisans of the Stella Rossa who sensed the front might soon pass through Monte Sole – the people in the valleys either side thought it too. At Ca' Veneziani, next to the River Setta, Cornelia Paselli had heard the guns fifteen miles to the south and seen more and more Allied aircraft overhead. No longer were they targeting just Bologna, but the German lines of communications and anti-aircraft positions around Vado and elsewhere along the valley. Every night, Cornelia's father, Virginio, took his family to sleep in the tunnel under the railway station at Vado.

In the mountains above them, Lupo's men were gathered on the Monte Sole massif once more. In part this was because the movement of the front line had restricted their movement to the south. It was also, however, be- cause of the believed imminent liberation of Bologna. Assuming the Allies would reach the city by the beginning of October, CUMER in Bologna had begun making plans and had asked Lupo to take command of all partisans in the area and lead them in an assault to liberate the city ahead of the Allies. Lupo had refused. It was, he felt, too much responsibility, and in any case he wanted the Stella Rossa to fight shoulder to shoulder with the Allies, and to enter the city together as brothers in arms. With this in mind, he insisted they all keep close together for easy and quick deployment, rather than spread far and wide across the mountains. But while there was logic in this, it was nonetheless an extremely high-risk strategy. They had still not received any more arms drops, and their ammunition shortage was as critical as ever. Should the Germans plan a rastrellamento now, they would be sitting ducks, massed as they were on Monte Sole.

In Milan, Carla Costa was glowing from the success of her first two missions as a spy for the German Intelligence Service. Her German superiors in the Abwehr were very pleased with her. She had shown great courage and initiative on her twin missions to Florence and Rome, had held her nerve during several potentially dangerous situations, and had managed to cross back over German lines having carried out the tasks given her and armed with a wealth of information and a large number of pro-Allied and left-wing newspapers. Her immediate superior, Colonel Tommaso David, was just as delighted with her efforts, and glad she had persuaded him to take her into his fold back in June.

In fact, so pleased was David with the way some of his girls had performed, he invited three of them to accompany him on a visit to the government headquarters of the Repubblica Sociale Italiana in Maderno – and Carla was one of those chosen. Not only that, once at Lake Garda, she was singled out by Colonel David and told she was to be given the signal honour of presenting her mission reports and the newspapers she had brought back from Rome to none other than the Duce himself.

For an ardent Fascist like Carla, this was indeed a great honour. On the morning of 23 September, a car arrived at the Albergo Milano where the three girls were staying, sent to bring her to Mussolini. Wearing her Blackshirt uniform, she was taken to see the Duce's private secretary at Gargnano, who gave her a special pass that would enable her to get through the roadblock protecting Mussolini's villa. SS sentries manned the roadblock, and from there she was escorted on foot to the front door of the Villa Feltrinelli by a Blackshirt bodyguard. Once inside, Carla was led to an anteroom, where her papers were again inspected and then she was taken up the main staircase and into a large room on the second floor, where, sitting behind the desk, was Mussolini.

The Duce began by congratulating her on passing through enemy lines four times, which, he said, was all the more commendable because of her very young age. He told her that he wished there were more people like her and fewer *vigliacchi* – cowards – who had deserted the Fascist cause. After giving her report, she asked whether she might have a signed photograph. Mussolini duly obliged, then clasped her hand, gave her the Fascist salute and bid her farewell.

It had been a thrilling day, but there were further rewards awaiting her return in Milan, where she was given a written commendation from the German High Command and told she had been recommended for the German Iron Cross, Second Class. Carla could not have been more proud.

*   *   *

Yet despite the efforts of Carla and other German secret agents, for much of the time Kesselring's most important intelligence came from what he could see with his own two eyes, and from what his commanders at the front told him. And what he could see now was that German fortunes in Italy were on a knife edge: if Eighth Army succeeded in forcing its way along Route 9 to link up with Fifth Army at Bologna, the game would be all but over in Italy. Even so, as ever, he intended to fight every step of the way – through the mountains south of Bologna, and behind the numerous rivers that flowed down from the Apennines and out across Eighth Army's advance to the sea. And even if the Allied armies did link up once more, his forces would fall back to yet more defensive lines both north and south of the River Po, positions his Todt workers had been toiling over since the summer months.

Despite his imperturbable optimism and determination to keep fighting, even Kesselring recognised the situation was critical. Nonetheless, he had been gifted a colossal lucky break by the rain that September. As all troops in Italy had discovered the previous winter, Italy was not always a place of golden sunshine during the darkest months, and yet it could frequently be dry, sunny and mild until well into autumn. Not in 1944, however. Eighth Army had reached the Rubicon, but four days' heavy rain then brought them to a mud-splattered halt. They could barely move forward and it was difficult to bring up supplies or new troops because the torrents now gushing along the normally trickling river courses had washed away many of the hastily erected Bailey bridges behind them.

With all momentum gone, a brief lull ensued along the Adriatic Front, giving von Vietinghoff's men the chance to catch their breath. It was into this situation that Unteroffizier Franz Maassen arrived to join the battered 278th Infantry Division. The son of a baker from Düsseldorf, Franz came from a traditional Catholic family. His had been a perfectly contented childhood: he was close to his parents and particularly close to his older brother, Willy, despite the seven-year age gap between them. Nor were the family ever particularly ardent supporters of the Nazis. Once, when the Brownshirts sacked a synagogue in Düsseldorf, they came into the family bakery, bragging and celebrating about what they had done. Franz's mother had been furious, and threw them out of the shop. 'My Father really told her off,' says Franz. 'If you talk to them like that, he said, you'll get in real trouble.'

His brother joined the army in 1936, but Franz never joined the Hitler

Youth – he was always too busy. 'I told them, I've got to be up at four in the morning and then I have to work in the evenings and at weekends. So when have I got time to go to Hitler Youth?' Like most boys his age, however, he found the sweeping victories at the beginning of the war exciting, and in 1940, aged eighteen, he too joined the army. 'I was young and I was gung-ho,' he admits. 'We had won great victories in Poland, in Belgium, in Holland, in France. Next was Britain. I really wanted to be a part of that. I wanted to be one of those invading Britain.'

However, although he was still training for amphibious landings as late as the spring of 1941, he never did cross the Channel. Rather, in the autumn of 1942, having married Liesel, his childhood sweetheart, he was posted to Russia. He survived the Eastern Front, but only just. A bout of dysentery saved him from Stalingrad, where only six men out of his division of more than 12,000 got out again unscathed. After recovering, he was posted back to Russia and fought through the Battle of Kursk in the summer of 1943, until he was wounded – shot in the hip as he was trying to carry a wounded comrade to safety. Having recovered, he was then put forward for officer training by a man whose life he had saved in Russia. 'I was recommended for a commission,' he says, 'but I was just a baker's son with no academic qualifications, so I was made a sergeant and posted to Italy instead.'

His journey to the front had not been without incident. His train through the Brenner Pass had come under air attack. The rail was also cut, so they had to get out and join another train further on. Once in Verona, he witnessed an attack on a café by partisans. To make matters worse, the barracks he was put in had only straw on the concrete floor and no beds, and were infested with hundreds of rats. It was with some relief that Franz was finally sent to the registration centre in Forlì, and then on to the headquarters of the 278th Division at Cesena.

Franz was one of a dozen men joining the division as replacements. Temporarily commanding them en route to the front had been a former Luftwaffe fighter pilot, who, due to the shortage of fuel, had been sent to the front as an infantryman, even though he had had no infantry training whatsoever; such were the shortages facing Germany now. A few weeks later Franz heard he'd been killed. Before being sent to their battalions, however, the new arrivals were presented to the divisional commander, Generalleutnant Harry Hoppe, another veteran of the Eastern Front and a highly decorated and respected soldier. Hoppe had asked Franz whether he had a wife and children back home. Yes, Franz told him, a wife and one son. 'And what are you fighting for?' the General asked him. 'I gave the standard nonsense,' says Franz. 'For Führer and for Fatherland.'

'Rubbish,' Hoppe replied – it was, he told Franz, for family and home that they fought. And they must continue to fight. 'And when you've got no more ammunition,' Hoppe added, 'then you jump at the Tommies' throats!'

Franz was impressed, recognising Hoppe as the kind of tough, no-nonsense soldier he liked. 'My thoughts,' he says, 'were that I'd landed amongst a good heap.' His presentation to Hoppe over, Franz reported along with ten other replacements to the headquarters of the 994th Infantry Regiment. Now at Cesena, they were some way from the 2nd Battalion lines. It was dark and raining, and although the jabos had gone home, enemy shells were still screaming over at regular intervals. Someone from the battalion arrived to guide them through the night to their lines. The first obstacle was the bridge at Cesena, which had been destroyed, leaving rubble and blocks of stone sticking out of the water. 'Just as we reach the bridge,' noted Franz in his diary, 'it lies under a barrage of fire. Tommy knows that all the reinforcements have got to go over here and so attacks it constantly.' Despite this, Franz managed to get his *gruppe** across by leaping from one block of stone to the other. From there they were led through a complicated labyrinth – through hedges and empty houses, over hills, through valleys and sodden meadows, and eventually to a shuttered hut in which the battalion commander, Hauptmann Hans Kurz, had his headquarters. Franz's long journey to the front was over.

The rain might have played into Kesselring's hands along the Adriatic, but it was slower to take effect on Fifth Army's front. The 88th Division had passed through the exhausted Custermen, and was making great strides towards Imola, bisecting Lemelsen's battered 4th Fallschirmjäger and 715th Divisions, and, by directing its advance in a more north-easterly direction, hoping to help out Eighth Army. Buckling from the sustained weight of Fifth Army's attack, AOK 14's situation was now so

---

*A German gruppe was the equivalent of a British infantry section or US squad, and nominally consisted of ten men: the NCO gruppe leader, his deputy, a three-man light machine-gun team and five other riflemen.

serious that Lemelsen persuaded Kesselring to transfer two divisions
back from AOK 10 and into the breach. These had not arrived in time
to stop the Americans taking the crucial peak of Monte Battaglia and
getting within twelve miles of Imola; but with the aid of heavy rain and
thick fog, they had stopped the 88th 'Blue Devils' Division from getting
any further. As with Eighth Army, Clark's forces had come frustratingly
close to pulling off a complete breakthrough, only to be stopped at the
final hurdle.

Casualties amongst the 88th were high and steadily increased as they
fought off one counterattack after another on Monte Battaglia – or Battle
Mountain, as the Blue Devils now called it. As the rain continued to
beat down, so supply routes and tracks through the mountains towards
Imola worsened. In the east, Eighth Army remained completely bogged
down. With this in mind, Clark sensibly decided to switch the direction
of his main attack back towards Bologna, and, since the Futa Pass was
now in Fifth Army's hands, down Route 65.

In any case, Clark had been continuing the pressure south of Bologna
whilst making his all-out thrust towards Imola. The South Africans, for
example, had now reached the town of Castiglione dei Pepoli, high in
the mountains between the Reno and Setta Valleys, and a mere twenty-
five miles as the crow flies from Bologna. Lemelsen, also appreciating
the threat towards Bologna, felt it was safe to shift some of his troops
in the western half of the line, and so took the 16th Waffen-SS away
from von Senger's 14th Panzer Corps and moved them into the Setta
and Reno Valleys under the 1st Fallschirmjäger Division.

Hauptsturmführer Willfried Segebrecht and his 1st Company had
reached the line near Castellaro, some ten miles west of the Reno Valley,
on the night of 21 September. It was reasonably quiet, although jabos
regularly flew over them, and artillery of both sides ensured the men
kept alert. Every night Willfried walked up and down the length of their
line, visiting his men in their foxholes. One man he always paused to
have a few words with was Rottenführer Schelasin. Willfried would pass
him his hip flask and give the corporal a swig; he in turn would wish
his commander good health.

Willfried, like all the troops at the front, was keenly aware of the
partisan menace, but a few days later, on the night of Tuesday the 26th,
they were brought out of the line once more and moved to Rioveggio,
just a couple of miles south of Monte Sole. They were now the divisional
reserve, ready to be thrown into the line along the Reno and Setta Valleys

where it was felt the weight of the Allied thrust in their sector would most obviously come.

It was especially uncomfortable being in Rioveggio with a known band of these bandits directly behind them in the mountains. Willfried had been told there were some two thousand men in the Stella Rossa, who for some time had made life along the valleys almost impossible for the German troops. Apparently, they were well armed too, equipped with grenade launchers, machine pistols, machine guns, grenades, and explosives. 'For us, the fighting troops on the Gothic Line,' he noted, 'the question of supplies was a question of life. Without regular supplies of munitions and food, and without the possibility of moving the wounded back, our positions against the Allies could not be held.' It was bad enough the partisans operating in these mountains when the front had been further south. Now that they were almost on top of one another, it was intolerable.

The arrival of the 16th Waffen-SS in the area and the general movement of troops had confused both the civilians in the valleys and Lupo's men still concentrated in the Monte Sole massif. As the division's two infantry regiments, the 35th and 36th Panzer Grenadier Regiments, had moved down to the front, so the 362nd Infantry had moved out. They had been in the line for several weeks, were tired, and so had come back down the Setta and Reno Valleys in what looked like a disorganised mass, and with the guns still booming only a dozen miles away, many partisans and civilians had concluded their war was almost over. A captured sack of German mail added fuel to this theory. Studying the letters, Lupo and Gianni Rossi discovered that many of the troops who had written them were suffering from low morale: they complained about the nightmare of incessant jabo attacks and the weight of Allied fire power, and wrote of their desire to get home. Then, five days later, Sturmbannführer Reder's 16th Reconnaissance Battalion had also travelled along the Setta to Rioveggio. To the untrained eye, it seemed like a lot of German troops had been falling back over the past few days.

This apparent retreat also persuaded Virginio Paselli that it was time to move his family somewhere safer. Having survived the First World War, he knew a little about fighting and soldiering, and felt certain that when the front moved forward, it would do so through the valleys. They would, he told his wife and children, be safer in the mountains, and so he took them all to Cerpiano, a small village perched on a spur directly beneath Monte Sole itself. There, Sister Antonietta Benni, a lay nun who had taught Cornelia and the other children at school, had arranged a kind of refuge in a large church house known as 'Il Palazzo' belonging to the Diocese of Bologna. There were already others there, and each family was given a room of their own in which they could stay. 'Everyone was calm,' says Cornelia. 'We all knew each other. I had with me a dress and coat to sew; I thought I could use my time sewing while we waited for the front to pass.'

The 16th Waffen-SS had taken over positions north of Castiglione just as the line had moved back to within the Stella Rossa's area of operations. Not only was Feldmarschall Kesselring fully aware of the partisan brigade's existence, so too was General Schlemm, the commander of 1st Fallschirmjäger Corps, to whom the 16th Waffen-SS was now attached. Clearly, something had to be done about them: Schlemm's troops simply could not fight one battle at the front and another at their backs. Consequently, Schlemm asked Generalleutnant Max Simon,* commander of the 16th Waffen-SS, if he had any troops he could spare to carry out an action against the Stella Rossa. Simon told him that Reder's 16th Reconnaissance Battalion might be used in such a capacity; furthermore, they already had experience of such operations from their time in the Massa-Carrara area where they had been involved in a number of anti-partisan actions including that at Bardine-San Terenzo. But as Simon pointed out, troops of all types of arms were needed in such operations, and so in addition to Reder's men, a platoon from the Panzer Regiment 36, and a flak unit from the 16th Artillery were also to be drawn from the division. On top of that, a battalion of the East Regiment, with which Hans Sitka was still serving, from the 334th Infantry Division was also to take part, as was the Wehrmacht Flak-Regiment 105.

Co-ordination and planning of the attack had been left to Obersturm-bannführer Loos, of the 16th Waffen-SS divisional staff. The brief was to clear the mountains from Grizzana Morandi to Sasso Marconi – that is, the entire Monte Sole massif – of all partisans. Thanks to the Fascist, Lorenzo Mingardi, and his network of spies and informers, Loos knew the Stella Rossa were now concentrated around Monte Sole. Nothing was to be left to chance, with the troops attacking in a wide encirclement that would then trap Lupo's men, although it was Reder's recce battalion who were expected to carry out the main thrust of the attack. As one of

---

*Max Simon's full title was SS-Gruppenführer und Generalleutnant Waffen-SS.

the company commanders taking part, Willfried Segebrecht was fully briefed about the Stella Rossa and what they could expect. 'This brigade is known as one of the most radical and fanatical,' he recorded, 'with strong Communist tendencies.' Its men would be wearing a mixture of Italian, American, British and even German uniforms, and amongst their number were German Russian deserters. 'Hard and desperate battles,' noted Willfried, 'which could be supported and strengthened by the resident population are to be expected.'[265] The operation was to begin at dawn on Friday, 29 September.

Despite the news that Waffen-SS troops were now camped at Rioveggio, Lupo's confidence remained high. Cornelia Paselli saw Lupo, Gianni and others at Caprara on the 27th. She had gone to look for food and had been able to buy some apples from a contadino there. 'They were all sitting there,' says Cornelia, 'as though everything was normal.' Lupo looked at her and said, 'So you're here. You're safe up in the mountains.'

The following day, word reached the Stella Rossa that the Allies had reached Lagaro, only a few miles south of Grizzana. In a few days, if not sooner, they would surely reach them on Monte Sole. So, late on the afternoon of Thursday the 28th, when Lupo and Gianni decided to walk with Leone down to the farmstead of Cadotto, they brushed aside Vecchio's concerns.

'You're better off staying where you are,' insisted il Vecchio.

'What's your problem?' Lupo replied. 'Let the Germans come. Lagaro has already been freed.'

'I think you're wrong this time,' il Vecchio told him.[266]

But Lupo and Gianni had girlfriends at Cadotto, and Leone – one of the 1st Battalion's company commanders – had his wife staying there too, and so the three headed off, promising il Vecchio they would be back right away.

However, Lupo did partially heed il Vecchio's warnings, for on reaching Cadotto, he spent time making sure the squad of men there were suitably positioned and that patrols would be sent out and that guards were on duty. On the other hand, neither he nor Gianni went back to headquarters that night; it had begun to rain, and hard, and a night with their girlfriends seemed a more attractive proposition.

A few miles to the south, in the early hours of the morning of Friday, 29 September, the men of Reder's recce battalion moved out of their billets. On the other side of the mountains, in the Reno Valley, Hans

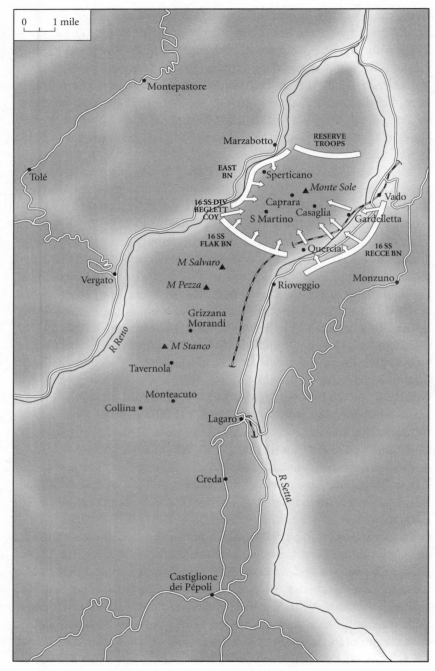

0   1 mile

Montepastore

Marzabotto

RESERVE
TROOPS

EAST
BN

Sperticano

Tolé

Monte Sole

16 SS DIV
BEGLETT
COY

Caprara

Vado

S Martino

Casaglia

Gardelletta

16 SS
FLAK BN

Quercia

16 SS
RECCE BN

M Salvaro

Monzuno

M Pezza

Rioveggio

Vergato

R Reno

Grizzana
Morandi

M Stanco

Tavernola

Monteacuto

Collina

Lagaro

Creda

R Setta

Castiglione
dei Pépoli

The German attack on Monte Sole

Sitka and the East Regiment were also moving into position south of Marzabotto. It was still pouring with rain as Willfried's men set off along with the 5th Company, crossing over the Setta and the railway and moving into their attack positions between La Quercia and Le Murazze by 5 a.m. Further along the valley, and coming from Vado, were the 3rd and 2nd Companies. Each had been given very precise areas of the mountain to attack, and each was in radio contact with Reder, who remained at battalion headquarters in Rioveggio. Willfried's 1st Company was to assault up the slopes towards San Martino in a wide arc, clearing any farmsteads on the way where partisans were found.

By 6 a.m., the men of Willfried's company were approaching Cadotto, which loomed through the heavy rain and the dark of the early dawn. A lone guard had been keeping watch on the track leading to the farmstead, but the patrols Lupo had ordered were nowhere to be seen. Huddled up against a hedge, the cold had ensured the guard had not fallen asleep. As he moved silently through the mist and rain, he suddenly saw figures in front of him, then too late realised they were German troops. He managed to fire two shots of his rifle and shout out a warning before being killed by a volley of fire. The fighting had begun.

It was the partisans in the stable who reacted first. Just awake, and confused by the firing, two men, Rino and Colonello, forced open the stable door with the butts of their guns, and charged out only to be fired on by German troops now twenty or so yards away. Rino was hit, but Colonello managed to empty the magazine of his Sten, and with the rest of the partisans in the barn opening fire too, the 1st Company men fell back.

By now Lupo and Gianni and the others in the house were awake. Gianni went to the door, but as he opened it bullets ripped past, almost slicing Leone's wife in half. The firing stopped for a moment, and so Gianni took the opportunity to call out to Colonello. There was now one dead, and one seriously wounded, Colonello told him, and as far as he could tell, they were completely surrounded.

'Do what you can,' Gianni told him, 'and we will try and get to the command post.'

'We're surrounded on all sides,' Colonello replied. 'You won't make it.'

In the farmhouse, Lupo was raging about the lack of patrols – they should have been out there, he shouted; should have warned them. By now, the Germans had set up a machine gun and were firing with tracer bullets towards the barn. In moments it had caught fire. Hurrying up to the first floor of the house, Lupo and Gianni looked out from a window and could see German troops moving forward above Cadotto towards Steccola and brigade headquarters at Prunaro di Sopra, and yet more troops arriving from the track. It was true: they were surrounded. Even so, Gianni still felt they should try and make a run for it and head across the dense scrub and woods to Ca' Termine. The three men – Gianni, Lupo and Leone – went from a door in the house into the hayloft and jumped down into the stable. They then climbed down the wall behind and jumped into a ditch that faced towards Ca' Termine, and then ran for their lives. Gianni was ahead of the other two when three Germans spotted them and opened fire, hitting him in the elbow. Despite this, Gianni fired back, as did Lupo and Leone, and the three Germans dropped to the ground. It was not far to the trees, but the ground was muddy and wet after all the rain. More Germans began firing at them and Gianni was hit again, in the other arm, and fell over in the mud. The other two collapsed beside him, bullets whistling over their heads. 'I can't go on,' said Gianni. He knew he was losing consciousness. '*Stai tranquillo*,' Lupo reassured him – keep calm. Somehow, Gianni managed to get himself to his feet again, running blindly. Enemy fire was still following him, but he was no longer aware of what had happened to Lupo or Leone.

Then suddenly the firing stopped. Ahead of him was a partisan patrol. By now he was in a bad way, but for the moment he was safe. The partisans helped him to Ca' Termine, where his wounds were dressed and he was able to rest for a short while.

One of Willfried Segebrecht's sergeants had been badly wounded in the chest and had been brought back to him at his command post below Cadotto. 'Binding the wound didn't help,' noted Willfried, 'and with every heartbeat blood streamed out. He begged me with barely a voice to send his parents his greetings.'[267] Fire-fights were continuing at Cadotto against Colonello and the remaining partisans there, and at another farmhouse further up the mountain at Ca' di Durino, where, amongst others, il Vecchio was now trying to escape. More of Willfried's men were being killed and wounded, including a young lieutenant who had joined his company only a few days before. One of his troop leaders, an opera singer from Dresden, had also been badly wounded. Progress was frustratingly slow. With only machine guns and small arms, it was difficult to prise the partisans at Cadotto out of their stone buildings.

Had Willfried known how poorly armed Colonello and the others were, he might have stormed it earlier. As the attacker, however, and lacking the kind of heavy fire power he would have liked, it was not a risk he was prepared to take.

At the village of Cerpiano, Cornelia Paselli and the rest of the family had been woken early by her father. 'Wake up! Wake up!' he told them urgently. 'The Germans are burning houses. It's not safe here. Go and take refuge in the church.' Assuming it would be the men the Germans were after, he told them he was going to head up onto Monte Sole and hide in the dense wood and scrub there.

Cornelia, her mother, sister, and the twins, hurried along the track leading to the church at Casaglia. An aunt and some cousins were also with them and most of the people of Cerpiano now frantically made their way to the church and other places of refuge. Through the rain along the slopes below, they could hear shooting – machine-gun and rifle fire, the explosions of grenades. Houses were burning, thick black smoke billowing into the heavy sky. It was just before 8 a.m. by the time they reached the church. 'We prayed,' says Cornelia. 'We were waiting . . . we were afraid.'

At around nine o'clock, there was a loud banging at the door, and German troops shouted at them to open the doors and get out. Frightened, but doing as they were told, the nearly two hundred people who had been taking refuge in the church shuffled out to the small courtyard outside, where the rain had finally stopped. There were just seven or eight Germans, men of Hauptsturmführer Schmidkuntz's 3rd Company. Cornelia watched them talking with the priest, Don Ubaldo, and tried to listen. She couldn't speak German but understood the gist. The Germans had found a number of arms at Ca' Dizzola, a farmstead a short distance away between Casaglia and Cerpiano. This was where the 4th Battalion had been based, but they had slipped away before the Germans had reached there. Cornelia sensed the men believed she and others in the church were somehow guilty of stashing arms, of being partisans themselves. Beginning to fear the worst, she started to think about making a getaway. The Germans seemed to be in a hurry, barking orders at the group of frightened civilians, and ushering them down the track towards Ca' Dizzola and Cerpiano.

The column was halted at the cemetery, by a fork in the track. Don Ubaldo went towards the Germans, talked with them, and then explained to the civilians that they had to stay where they were for the moment. One of the soldiers smashed the lock on the iron cemetery gate with the butt of his rifle, while another stood guard with a sub-machine gun.

It began to rain again. Two guards were left watching them while the other troops, along with the priest, went back towards the church. Twenty minutes passed, the civilians just standing there, on the fork in the road outside the cemetery. Cornelia kept thinking about escape – of jumping off the road and down into the scrub below, but the guards never took their eyes off them. Her mother was crying. 'There was only one reason to open the gate,' says Cornelia. 'I said to myself, this is the end. There was no reason otherwise for them to have opened the gate. I kept thinking, if only I could move a few metres, I could jump and hide myself.'

When the other Germans returned they were without the priest. One of them gave an order. '*Raus! Raus!*' he shouted, ushering them through the gate into the cemetery. 'There was an old lady with an umbrella,' says Cornelia, 'they even gave her an arm to help her inside.' The cemetery was not a large place – only a little bigger than a tennis court – but it was walled all the way round with a small stone chapel. With far-reaching views, and watched over by Monte Sole itself, it was a pretty spot – a typical small country graveyard.

A number of the women were now starting to shout and cry, wanting to get themselves to the back of the throng. Cornelia also felt a deep desire for survival but although frightened, remained calm. 'Everybody was pushing,' she says, 'forwards, backwards – like a waving mass'. She wanted to be in the centre but ended up on the extreme left, close to one of the walls. 'I only wanted to be safe, to jump, to hide myself,' she says, 'but there was no way out.'

A German came in with a machine gun, and set it up in the left hand corner in front of them, and began loading cylinders of ammunition onto and beside the weapon. Suddenly one of the women began to panic. 'I want to go to my daughter!' she shouted, running forward, 'I must go to my daughter!' She was shot dead immediately. 'Then there was a kind of jolt,' says Cornelia, 'an explosion so intense that I was thrown into the air and landed in the middle of the crowd.' People were shouting and crying, calling out names, others screaming for help. But Cornelia couldn't say anything; she felt mute, still thinking that somehow she must do something, but now she was on the ground in the middle of the mass of people and the machine gun had started firing. Bodies started falling on top of her and all around her. Blood spread all over her body. 'I immediately thought: This is other people's blood – but what if they have shot me and I haven't felt it? And then I fainted.'

When she came to again, more bodies were piled around her. She could hear voices, then her mother calling out to her. 'Cornelia, Cornelia, are you still alive?'

'Mama, be quiet, please!' she whispered back. 'Don't talk otherwise they will kill you.'

'The twins are dead, the twins are dead,' her mother called out.

'Please, mama,' Cornelia implored, 'don't talk.'

But her mother called out to her other daughter, and then another shot rang out and her sister Giuseppina started to shout, 'My head, my head! I'm hurt!'

'Shush!' Cornelia told her. 'Be quiet, I'm coming.' Cornelia could not easily move, however, but then her sister suddenly calmed down; the bullet had just grazed her; it had been another's blood that had covered her head and frightened her.

They waited there a long time. Gradually, however, it became clear that the soldiers had gone and by about four that afternoon, Cornelia finally felt it was safe to try and get away. She had by then been lying under the corpses for more than six hours.

'Dead bodies are really heavy,' she says, 'but eventually I managed to free myself.' Miraculously she was largely unharmed, but completely drenched in blood. Cornelia didn't know what she should do. Gigi and Maria were dead; and her mother's legs had been almost severed off by the bullets. There was no one about, except the dead and a few wounded. Cornelia cleared some of them away and lifted her mother and sat her against the wall by the chapel. She still had the fabric with her for sewing her coat, and so she used the sleeves to tie her mother's legs and stem the flow of blood. 'Mama, stay here and try and keep calm,' Cornelia told her, 'I'm going to go and look for help.' She had thought to go back to Cerpiano, but outside the cemetery she could still see troops and heard shouting coming from the village, and so instead, ran down to the valley toward Gardelletta, barefoot and through the brambles and scrub.

Further down the slopes to the south, Willfried Segebrecht's men had destroyed all the farmhouses around Cadotto, killing a number of partisans and even more civilians in the process, but they had been unable to destroy Cadotto itself. The thick stone walls of the farmhouse and the concrete roof of the barn had been impervious to the small arms they possessed. Willfried had wished they had had some anti-tank guns with them or heavy mortars, but it was not to be, and so late in the afternoon he had ordered his men to fall back for the day. This had given the surviving partisans, Colonello included, the chance they needed to make good their escape.

Meanwhile, Cornelia had reached Gardelletta, only to spot a German soldier in the village square. She then ran along to their home in Ca' Veneziani, but it was locked, and, she knew, empty, and so instead she went on to the farm a few hundred yards above from where they used to get milk and where they had left their pet lamb before taking refuge in Cerpiano. 'I entered the house and the wife was dead on the floor,' says Cornelia, 'and then I found her husband dead as well.' And then she saw the lamb, also killed, and at this point the great strength she had shown all day finally snapped, and she began to cry and cry.

On Monte Sole, Cornelia's father, Virginio, was now wandering through the scrub in a state of deranged grief. From the summit, he had seen it all. He had tried to get the partisans he had been with at the time to do something, to distract the soldiers in the cemetery below, but they had told him it was impossible, and so instead he had stayed where he was, watching the troops massacring his family, and seeing the villages of the mountains that he loved so much being razed to the ground. Finally, at around midnight, he scrambled down the mountain and went to the cemetery, but by then the gate had been locked once more. Only yards away, shrouded in the inky darkness, his twins lay among the near two hundred dead; his daughter Giuseppina sat tending Angelina, his wife, as she slipped in and out of consciousness, slowly dying. But Virginio had not seen them. Believing his entire family had been murdered, and rapidly losing his mind, he slipped away again into the night.

Darkness had fallen on the Mountain of the Sun, and would remain there even when dawn arrived once more. A mountain community had been destroyed with ruthless brutality, and the shadow of death would be felt over that place for a long, long time to come.

THIRTY

The Reason Why

As Angelina Paselli lay dying in the cemetery, she told her daughter Giuseppina that she had dreamed her husband had been there. Whether it had been her dream or whether she had actually seen him pressing his face against the iron gate was unclear, but she was now increasingly fretful during her conscious moments, repeatedly calling for Giuseppina and convinced that Cornelia must also have been killed.

In fact, her eldest daughter was very much alive. After finding the dead lamb, Cornelia had wandered aimlessly, sobbing and thinking of her mother, sister, the twins, and all those who had been slaughtered. Reaching the river, she had begun wading across until shots had rung out and bullets hissed into the water around her. Raising her arms, she had shouted, 'Mama, help me!' and then the shooting had stopped. Able to reach the far bank, she had then remembered there was a house nearby and that she knew the people who lived there. Calling out their name, one of her father's colleagues had then appeared, telling her to be quiet and ushering her to a hut in the woods nearby where a few others had been sheltering.

Cornelia begged them to help her. She told them of the massacre, and that her mother was gravely injured. 'She hasn't even had a drink,' she told them. But they refused either to move or let her go; the man had also lost his family in the shootings, and they feared that if they went back up on to the mountains they would only get themselves killed. 'Stay here the night,' they told her, 'and we'll go in the morning.' Although safe, Cornelia was distraught. The others were stopping her leaving, from getting help. Exhausted, she lay down on some straw, but was unable to sleep. Her mother and sister needed her, and now she was trapped in the hut.

*   *   *

The massacre at the cemetery had been far from an isolated incident. All over the mountains, the villages, hamlets and farmsteads had been 'cleared' of people by the troops – Waffen-SS and Wehrmacht alike – with men, women and children herded into barns and shot. The barns had then been set on fire, along with all other buildings. Nor was the operation considered over.

The next morning, Saturday the 30th, Willfried Segebrecht returned to Cadotto, and finding it deserted, his men blew the farmstead up using a stack of grenades they found stored there. Elsewhere, soldiers were combing through the mountains, setting fire to more buildings and finishing off what they had begun the day before. Gianni Rossi and a number of other partisans were by now hiding in the dense woods that covered the summit of Monte Salvaro. His wounds were serious, but at present, not life threatening. No one knew what had happened to Lupo; Gianni hadn't seen him since their escape from Cadotto the previous morning, but felt sure he was still alive.

The troops also returned to Cerpiano. Hiding in a wood next to the village was seventeen-year-old Francesco Pirini. His family had lived in the same house in Gardelletta since 1770, but like other families in the valley, they had headed to the mountains once the aerial bombardments had begun, back in August. Francesco had seen the fires on the slopes below early the previous morning and as the troops approached the village had attempted to escape and head to the top of Monte Sole with a number of partisans. The Germans had begun shooting after them, however, and so he had hid in the woods, hoping to get back to the house where he knew his family were staying. He had then watched in horror as troops had spread through the village, getting everyone still there out of the houses – including nine members of his own family – and leading them to Cerpiano's tiny chapel. Then he had watched one soldier lob a grenade in through the window, and had heard the screams of those inside.

Most of those in the chapel had still been alive, however, including Sister Antonietta Benni, but troops had remained guarding them, and when an old man had tried to free them he had been shot. Francesco had remained rooted to the spot in the wood, frozen with fear and overcome with a sense of helplessness. All through the night and on into Saturday morning, his family and others from Cerpiano – forty-nine in all – remained trapped in the chapel. Francesco, still quivering in his hiding place, then watched more troops arrive, open the door of the chapel and shoot everyone inside. Then the men went to the school house and began playing the piano there. 'I was absolutely terrified,' says Francesco. 'I had just seen them kill my family.'

It was not until the following Tuesday, that Cornelia was allowed to leave the hut, by which time Reder's battalion were back in the line to the south and the operation finally over. She scrambled up to Cerpiano where she saw a woman looking for food. 'Cornelia, is that you?' she said, looking at the bedraggled girl, still caked with dried blood. Cornelia hurried over to her and learned that Giuseppina was still alive, and resting in a refuge in the village, but that her mother had died two days before. Soon after, the two sisters were reunited and together went to a refuge at San Mamante, a farmstead a few miles to the north, and there a week later their father found them. 'When he saw us,' says Cornelia, 'he laughed and cried – of pain, of happiness.' He had thought they were dead too. Cornelia was shocked to see him unshaven and thin, and with the lustre gone from his eyes. 'He seemed a different person,' she says. 'It was painful – I really suffered seeing him like that.'

Virginio told them he was going to go and find some food and that he would then come back. He didn't, however. As if his woes had not already been enough, he was then picked up by German troops and taken away to be an Organisation Todt worker. A few months later, he too was dead, killed by exhaustion and a broken heart.

Seven hundred and seventy-two people were killed over three days on Monte Sole, and, as with the slaughter of 191 in the cemetery at Casaglia, most were civilians, making it the single worst massacre in Western Europe during the entire war. Two hundred and sixteen partisans now lay dead, around two-thirds of their number. Of the rest, Lupo had disappeared and the others had been scattered by the rastrellamento. Many, like Gianni Rossi, had managed to sneak through the front line and reach the safety of the Allies – and a hospital – but the Stella Rossa was finished.

As such, the operation had been a great success for the Germans. One hundred and seventy-four buildings had been burned to the ground, seven ammunition dumps containing mines, rifles, and hand grenades had been destroyed, and ammunition exploded. Papers and reports, passwords, typewriters and a printing press had been discovered and taken for examination, whilst 315 cows and fourteen horses were a

welcome bonus to have been gained from their victory. Willfried
Segebrecht admitted that civilians had been killed in the fighting, but
laid the blame squarely with the partisans. 'The battles were made more
difficult,' he noted, 'due to the malicious battle methods used by the
partisans, such as shooting from ambush positions, from holes in cellars,
haystacks, dugouts and caves. Some of these places were partly occupied
by women and civilians, even by children, in order to trick us into
believing they were harmless.'[268]

Certainly there was some confusion over who was a partisan and who
was not, but the mass executions cannot be so explained. Rather, it
had been part of a deliberate strategy. The German commanders, from
Kesselring to General Schlemm, and from Generalleutnant Max Simon
to Sturmbannführer Reder to Willfried Segebrecht, were all seasoned
practitioners in combating guerrilla warfare: Max Simon, for example,
had fought two years of continuous combat in Russia and later even
wrote a pamphlet about fighting techniques against the Soviets. Once
the decision for a clear-up operation had been made, they believed
there was only one way to carry it out, and that was with swift and
comprehensive brutality. They knew perfectly well that partisan bands
like the Stella Rossa only existed because of the tacit support of the local
civilian population. Consequently, as experience had shown, the only
way to be certain of eradicating a major problem like the Stella Rossa,
was to burn down and destroy all the houses, and shoot everyone in
sight. No people, no problem. The policy had a brutal logic and quickly
and emphatically achieved all its aims. As Willfried noted, 'The Stella
Rossa had been destroyed and once again, supplies and reinforcements
could reach us.'[269]

Despite the logic of the policy, why German commanders felt able to
order such atrocities be carried out, and why ordinary soldiers were able
to commit them, is harder to explain.

Some, it seems, may have been conditioned by their experiences
on the Eastern Front. The ferocity and scale of the fighting in Russia
undoubtedly had a brutalising and dehumanising effect on many
German troops who fought there. 'In Italy,' Jupp Klein says, 'the British
would attack and you would see tanks coming towards you, and infantry
here and there. In Russia there would be thousands of men coming at
you all at once and you had to shoot them, cut them all down. It was a
deep shock to me.' In his first action, he and his men took over a Russian

trench full of corpses. A Russian mortar came over and killed the two men either side of him. 'It was just terrible,' he says. 'Out of our whole company, only twenty were left.' Nor, he says, did Russians ever take any prisoners. POWs were shot; that was just the way it was.

Franz Maassen felt much the same way. 'The Russians were terrible,' he says. 'Although we were retreating, whenever we were in a fight we'd end up with say, fifty dead, and they'd have a thousand killed. I used to see Russians with no weapons at all – no rifles or anything – just linking arms and advancing towards us. We'd just mow them down. It was awful.'

In Russia, German troops also had the added difficulty of trying to deal with Russian partisans. Franz Maassen says this was a constant problem for them while he was fighting on the Eastern Front: an officer was killed by them, as were a number of men in his company. He also lost a close friend at the hands of these guerrillas.

Peter Rogge had been a theology student, but in Russia had been Franz's Number 2 in a machine-gun section. One time, during the battle of Kursk, they had been in a foxhole together, Franz firing and Peter feeding the ammunition belts; just as they'd swapped over roles, Peter had been shot in the face. Badly wounded, he had been hurriedly sent back to a field dressing station.

Soon after, Franz's company had been falling back once more and as they had retreated, so they had come across a burnt-out ambulance. 'The driver had had his hands tied to the steering wheel with wire,' says Franz, 'and had then been set on fire. And by the side of the road were the wounded men and one of them was Peter. All four had been stripped, had had their heads smashed in and their penises cut off. That's what the partisans did.'

Franz and Jupp Klein had not fought in Russia because they had been fanatical Nazis. Like most German servicemen, they had done so for the same reasons Allied troops fought: out of a sense of duty to their families, friends and country; out of pride, expectation, or because they had to. They were not alone, however, in believing the invasion of Russia was entirely justified, largely because years of Nazi propaganda had persuaded them and the majority of their fellow countrymen that the threat of the westward spread of communism had to be stopped – an evil that was painted in much the same way in Germany as Nazism was in Britain and America. 'One thing is clear,' says Jupp Klein more than sixty years on, 'if Hitler had not come, and not another one like him, then Germany would have become Communist. The Russians would have taken over Europe, and no one would have been spared.'

No sooner had Franz Maassen arrived in Italy, than he witnessed an attack by partisans as he was sitting in a café. He'd already had enough of them in Russia, and now here they were again. 'I hated the partisans,' he says. 'I wasn't personally involved in any of the round-ups, but I wouldn't have minded if I was.' Rudi Schreiber was of the same sentiment after seeing his dead comrades, their faces beaten, at Monte San Terenzo. He claims that his time with the division in the Massa-Carrara area was the worst period of his active service, entirely because of the partisan actions in the area. 'We were furious that these people who were civilians were getting involved in the war,' he says. 'But the thing that really got to us was the gruesomeness that they showed towards prisoners. We were permanently in danger.' Often used as a messenger courier, he had done his fair share of driving around the surrounding countryside on a motorbike, and had found the experience deeply nerve-racking. 'We were on edge all the time,' he says, 'waiting for a shot to come.'

General Frido von Senger was also keenly aware of the partisan menace. 'Raids were a daily occurrence,' he wrote, 'and it was difficult to capture the guerrillas, who roamed about the high mountains.'[270] He believed that partisan hit-and-run actions prompted justifiable anger among his men, 'especially when the situation was critical'. Indeed, between 17 and 30 September, partisans in Italy carried out 280 separate attacks on German troops, caused 129 deaths and wounded 3,633, as well as taking 8,241 prisoners. In nuisance terms – delays, destroyed vehicles and so on – their impact was even greater.

Rumours of partisan atrocities also spread through German units like wildfire – Chinese whispers often exaggerating their barbarity. And it is also true that partisans often spoke with the same wrathful rhetoric the Germans adopted in their own anti-partisan warnings. Even the Stella Rossa printed notices threatening counter-reprisals. 'We warn you that our counter-measures shall be *terrible and uncompromising*,' claimed a poster directed at the 'Republican Fascists of Monzuno' – notices that would have been seen by German troops too. 'Your possessions,' it continued, 'destroyed by us, will sanction the hour of justice with the light of their flames. Your relations will be killed without distinction of age or sex, and their deaths will justly satisfy the anger of those who, through your fault, cry and die today.'[271]

Such language hardly appeased the attitudes of German forces in the area, but to cap it all, as if to confirm the degeneracy of these lowlifes, they were apparently all Communist too! 'The techniques and actions of the partisans,' announced Kesselring in his warning of 17 September, 'have assumed a Bolshevik character. These low criminals of Moscow use their criminal methods to fight the authorities who have the responsibility of maintaining order and security in Italy.' In other words, Communists were an affront to civil stability and order; Communists wanted anarchy and chaos. This stance, regardless of its validity, served the German commanders' purpose well: by projecting the image and encouraging the myth that all partisans in Italy were little better than those in Russia, then in fighting them, German troops would be ridding the world of a rapidly spreading scourge of evil. And then there was the Stella Rossa – the 'Red Star'; as far as the Germans were concerned, this band of brigands was even openly flaunting its devotion to Bolshevism. That they had been determined to remain politically autonomous was an irony lost on both the partisans and their attackers alike.

Even though many German troops had never served in Russia, a substantial proportion had, especially the commanders and NCOs, and so the experience of the Eastern Front, and the perceived evil of communism, spread through the ranks to become endemic throughout the German divisions in Italy.

Of course, men exposed to sustained and often brutal combat in the front line soon become different people to those they were before the war. Seeing good friends obliterated, or losing limbs, or having chunks of their face removed and their guts spilled doubtless takes its toll psychologically on any soldier. But while death and violence in battle can be reasoned with – even understood – it is harder to accept when coming from an unseen enemy at a soldier's back. When soldiers stormed through a 'known partisan area' – an area where they believed, or had been told, that almost every single person they encountered was aiding and abetting the bandits in some way – they had neither the time nor inclination to discriminate. As far as they were concerned, these people had made their lives hell. These scum had been responsible for the deaths of their friends; and if shooting them and burning their houses meant the problem would go away and improve their chances of getting home, that was a price many were prepared to pay.

Anger and contempt; the resolution of a problem that was making their lives a misery; revenge for the loss of friends and comrades; the dehumanisation caused by bitter warfare. All these factors perhaps help explain why perfectly ordinary young men were able to line up women and children and calmly machine-gun them to death on Monte Sole. It is a terrible tragedy of war that here again it was the civilians who suffered the most as a result.

The brutalising effects of war could, on occasion, be seen in the behaviour of Allied troops, and certainly there were instances where individuals demonstrated an appalling casualness towards prisoners and Italians civilians. Soon after landing at Salerno, Norman Lewis recalled watching a British officer interrogating an Italian civilian, and repeatedly hitting him about the head with a chair. At the end of the interrogation, the officer called in a private and asked him in a conversational manner, 'Would you like to take this man away and shoot him?' The private spat on his hands and replied, 'I don't mind if I do, sir.' 'The most revolting episode,' noted Norman, 'I have seen since joining the forces.'[272]

A few days later he heard that American troops had been ordered by certain officers to beat to death any Germans who tried to surrender to them. Norman could not believe this was true, but it was confirmed to him by several American soldiers he met in hospital whilst suffering with malaria.

The war correspondent Eric Sevareid was also shocked by American treatment of POWs. Shortly after the launch of the DIADEM offensive, he met some GIs in a house in the battered village of Santa Maria Infante. They were resting and smoking cigarettes, with a dead German sprawled at their feet. Eric asked them what had happened to this man. 'Oh him?' one of them replied. 'Son of a bitch kept lagging behind the others when we brought them in. We got tired of hurrying him up all the time.'

'Thus casually was deliberate murder announced,' wrote Eric, 'by boys who a year before had taken no lives but those of squirrel or pheasant.'[273] Just a few days later he was talking with a young lieutenant when a private rushed in, wondering what to do with a number of Italian civilians still in a village they were trying to clear. 'If you can spare a guard send them back,' the lieutenant replied. 'If you can't, why, shoot 'em in the back.'[274] A couple of weeks later, he met some Texans who had captured a sniper, then ordered him to turn and run. As the German did so, they shot him dead. And then, of course, there is the behaviour of the French colonial forces' Goums, who committed more than three thousand rapes in the Frosinone area south of Rome, causing so many lives to be ruined – a truly awful legacy of the Allied occupation of southern Italy.

This specific atrocity aside, there also seemed to be, among certain Allied troops, the attitude that Italian girls and women were somehow fair game; and there is evidence to suggest that the raping of civilians was more prevalent among Allied forces than Axis. This may have been in part a bi-product of the vast amount of prostitution in the south. But it was also because the punishment for being caught rarely fitted the severity of the crime – even though a life sentence could be given for rape, this was rare and in any case would probably be commuted once the war was over, if not before: the Allies could not afford to lose frontline troops by keeping them in prison. One of Sam Bradshaw's men was accused of, and punished for, raping an Italian woman. 'He was a good bloke,' says Sam, 'but he was women mad.' One day, they had stopped at a village and Sam had sent him off to go and find some eggs. Soon after, however, he heard a woman screaming, and running over, saw an old man lying on the floor with a bleeding face. The old man told him that an English soldier had beaten him up and taken his daughter. Sam's officer ordered him to go and find the culprit, but first he found the woman, with her dress torn and face cut. Through her tears she told Sam it had been an Englishman in a black beret who had done this to her.

Sam duly found the man in a barn. 'She was willing,' the trooper told him; 'I didn't do it.'

'What about the old man?' Sam asked him.

'He was being awkward about me,' the trooper replied, 'and saying I was no good.'

Sam told him he was a liar and placed him under arrest. He was given three years.

German troops caught raping anyone could expect to be shot if found guilty, and it seems this was quite an effective deterrent. Clara Duse knew a Jewish girl from Trieste who was raped by German troops but other such reports of rape were not common. Paradoxically, despite German massacres of civilians in Italy, soldiers were given strict codes of behaviour and that included not stealing or pillaging. Hans Golda and his men paid for all the geese and chickens they cooked along the way. And although in times of desperation, such as during the long retreat after the DIADEM battles, theft of food was common, in static positions German soldiers were generally far more respectful in their interactions with Italian civilians than the Allies. It was why Rudi Schreiber, for example, said that he had felt unable to take a watch from the smashed shopfront in Pisa. German troops also tended to pillage less wantonly, whereas the Allies, on the whole, regarded the fat of the land as the spoils of war, and the right of conquering liberators.

One of the other big complaints about the Allies from the Italians was the apparently indiscriminate strafing of civilians by fighters and fighter-bombers. In April, the fourteen-year-old Fascist, Roberto Vivar-elli, had been in a truck with a number of other Italians travelling from Rome back to his home in Siena when it was attacked by an American fighter plane. Everyone had jumped out of the vehicle and dived for the side of the road, but Roberto had been the only survivor. 'I was absolutely shocked to see these people killed,' he says, 'and I was traumatised and burst into tears and walked away.'

Once, when Charles Dills was group operations officer for the 27th Fighter-Bomber Group, a pilot reported having hit a target that then exploded. He wasn't sure what it had been, but had looked like a pile of hay. 'The intelligence officer,' says Charles, 'wrote down, "Destroyed – one fast moving haystack."' Charles freely admits they often had little idea of what they were shooting at. 'But you didn't worry about it too much either,' he says. 'If some guy's out near the front line driving his truck, what the hell does he expect?' Charles points out that a hay cart might well have been protecting a machine gun or some other weapons; he, for one, was not prepared to take that risk.

It was unquestionably true that more Italians were being killed by Allied bombing, shellfire and strafing than were being slaughtered by the Germans; but impersonal deaths as a result of inaccurate fire or mistaken identity should never be viewed in the same light as lining people up against a wall and shooting them in cold blood. In war, however, the majority of commanders, from the general to the section leader, put the lives of their men before those of the civilians unfortunate to be caught up in the maelstrom, and in that regard, both the Allies and Germans in Italy shared something in common.

THIRTY-ONE

Rain, Mud and Misery, Part I
1–14 October 1944

As September gave way to October, the rain seemed to fall even harder. Stan Scislowski, back with the Perths and now wearing winter battledress, trudged along a road near the Adriatic coast, getting closer to the rattle of small-arms fire up ahead with every step. He was miserable, his head down, eyes staring at the road, the rain clattering against his helmet and running off in front of his nose. They were not yet under direct fire, but already he could feel his resolve weakening. He couldn't understand how on earth they were expected to win a battle when they felt so wretched.

Suddenly there was a low moan, and the column instantly disintegrated as the men dived for the side of the road. Seconds later, six rocket mortars – 'moaning minnies' – landed around them. Another salvo followed, then they picked themselves up and continued trudging on their way, the rain beating against their faces harder than ever, and seeping through their capes and clothes until it ran down their bodies.

Soon they were within range of the mortars, which began coming over with greater frequency. Stan's column continued heading forwards along a drainage ditch, walking in water that was shin deep. He was in the lead section, fifth down the line and spaced about five yards from the men either side of him when a mortar shell landed right between the next two men in front of him, Norm Diamond and Don Neal. Stan and the man behind were knocked off their feet by the blast, but when he got up again he saw Norm lying on his back in the water, blooding running from a gaping wound in his head and flowing back past Stan's boots. Five yards on was the grotesquely mangled body of Don Neal.

And then something inside him snapped. Stan dropped his rifle and ran, heading for a house off the road, pushing his way inside and hiding under a bed, where, to his amazement, he found two other quivering Canadians. Within a few minutes he had calmed down again; but he

was in turmoil about having suffered an uncontrollable battlefield breakdown. He wasn't sure how he was ever going to be able to look his mates
in the face again.

A sergeant and two other men stomped into the room and ordered
Stan and the other men to get out from under the bed immediately.
Stan did so, but the other two remained rooted where they were until
finally emerging on pain of death. Despite Stan's shame, his sergeant
allowed him to be accompanied back to the regimental aid post. Once
there, and whilst sitting on a wooden crate waiting to be seen by a
doctor, he suddenly felt his mind clearing and the 'shell shock' clear.
From that moment he knew he'd be alright, and before the day was over,
he was back with Dog Company once more. Many others were not so
lucky.

Franz Maassen was not exactly in the best of spirits just a few miles
away. His gruppe were at the very end of the divisional positions, with
the 114th Jäger Division on their right. There were just ten of them, in
five two-man foxholes spread out fifty–sixty yards apart at the foot of a
shallow hill amidst a hedge of blackberries and vines. In front of the
hedge was a muddy track, while behind, in the direction of the British,
were open fields for a hundred yards or so and then a number of bushes
with a few largely hidden houses. It was not the kind of position Franz
would have chosen, as it gave the British plenty of opportunity for cover
for whenever they tried to advance. Between them, they had one machine
gun, three machine pistols, one grenade thrower, four carbines, one
pistol, eight hand grenades, very limited amounts of ammunition and
no anti-tank weapons of any kind.

Furthermore, they were soaked, utterly wet through so that it was
almost impossible to recognise their uniforms under all the mud. All
they could do was sit in their water-logged holes in the ground, waiting
for the enemy. 'Yesterday was really shit,' he wrote in a letter to his wife
and small son. 'I began to feel as if I was in a canoe. The water in our
foxhole stood up to our knees and we bailed it out with our cooking
pots; it was like liquid manure. These are the joys of the infantryman, and
there I was dreaming about being at home in a nice warm sitting-room, a
warm bath or a bed – nice dreams!'

Mice and rats were also a problem, and the enemy shelling was
significantly more intense than it had been in Russia. 'As I've been
writing these lines,' he added, 'I must have thrown myself down at least

twenty times and one has to do this because the Tommy is not a bad shot with his artillery and what loads he sends straight over to us!'

While the rain continued to bring further misery to the troops along the front, in the south, Italians were still suffering appalling hardships; and there were precious few signs of improvement. It was obvious that the cumbersome Allied Control Commission was of little help. There seemed to be a lack of a clear plan for Italy, while in London and Washington it was undoubtedly the case that the Bonomi government was perceived not as a government at all, but rather an instrument of administering Allied control.

This, of course, was frustrating for Bonomi and his mixture of cross-party politicians, who not only wanted to be free of Allied political shackles, but also believed, with certain justification, that they were best equipped to deal with a country whose people, customs and history the AMG officials could not hope to understand properly.

Harold Macmillan, however, was one Allied politician who, as Resident Minister at AFHQ, had long been a critic of the top-heavy Allied administration, and had been a firm advocate of giving the Bonomi government greater autonomy. One way to do this, he believed, was to conclude a peace treaty with southern Italy, giving them recognition as an independent nation and making them an Allied partner rather than a 'co-belligerent' that had surrendered to the Allies.

This was a step too far for London and Washington, but Macmillan did at least have the personal support of Churchill, who agreed that a politician, rather than a military man like General Mason-Macfarlane, should head up the Allied Control Commission. This was sensible because Mason-Macfarlane, whilst perfectly effective as Governor of the tiny colony of Gibraltar, was completely out of his depth in Italy. Indeed, the Prime Minister suggested to Roosevelt that Macmillan should be the man to replace him, and although the appointment had yet to be confirmed, the President agreed in principle. In addition, Macmillan was to remain as British Minister Resident at Allied Headquarters in Caserta, and also British Political Adviser to the Supreme Allied Commander.

Furthermore, on 26 September Churchill and Roosevelt made a declaration regarding the future of Italy, recognising that during the past twelve months, the Italians of the liberated areas had shown their desire to be free and to fight on the side of the United Nations against the Axis powers. With this in mind, they proposed a 'New Deal' for Italy. Greater responsibility *would* be given to the Bonomi government; the word 'Control' would be henceforth dropped from the name of the Allied Control Commission; the British High Commissioner would become a full ambassador; and the Italians would be asked to send representatives to Washington and London. They also accepted that greater efforts were needed on the part of Britain and America to help them restore the Italian economy. To this end, they would assist the Italians in repairing electric power systems, the railways and roads, and certain trading restrictions would be modified. Finally, Roosevelt and Churchill stated that they looked forward to the day when all Italy would be free and free elections could be held.

This went down well in Italy, although parts of the 'New Deal' proved to be little more than hot air. Ever since their arrival in southern Italy, the Allies had been working hard to get public services up and running again. Some 300,000 workers were already employed in machine shops, cement and brick factories and steel mills. However, in October, the Allied Commission's weekly bulletin was already warning that 'it will take six to nine months before production could benefit the civilian economy; and only if the military had no further use for it'.[275] In other words, the civilian population came second behind the Allies' war effort, and so no improvement could be expected until after the fighting had finished.

It was thus two steps forward and one step back for the Bonomi government, which had also been concerned by what had *not* been said in the declaration. There had been no mention, for example, of half a million Italian POWs still in American and British hands. Nor did they say how exactly Italian rehabilitation was going to be financed.

In part, this was because Britain and America had different views – not to say agendas – with regard to Italy's economic crisis. Not only that, British and American policies had contributed towards the disaster: it hadn't been just because of the destruction of industry, transport networks, shipping and power stations in southern Italy. Britain, for example, had set the exchange rate at £1 sterling to 400 lire, based on their occupation of Italian East Africa in 1941 – a clearly absurd basis for such an important decision, and even more unforgivable when there were better informed men such as Harold Macmillan urging 200 lire to the pound as a more realistic and appropriate level. His pleas, however, had fallen on deaf ears. British vindictiveness towards the Italians in the aftermath of the armistice was undoubtedly partly to blame for such a decision, and while this was perhaps understandable considering Italy's involvement against Britain earlier in the war, a policy that punished the entire civilian population in the south was an ugly form of retribution.

America, on the other hand, had refused to grant Italy any Lend-Lease deals, despite having the capacity to do so, and furthermore, had done little to curb American troop spending. Disparity between American and British pay had always been a cause of British resentment, but the disparity between American and Italian pay was verging on the ridiculous. Armed with specially printed AMG lire, American troops, especially, drove up prices and contributed their fair share to the inflation problems.

There was also a perception problem. Italians were starving, but surrounded by strapping young men eating candy bars and smoking Lucky Strikes. There were apparently not enough vehicles to deliver food to Rome and other cities, but plenty of jeeps to take GIs and Tommies on sightseeing tours around the Colosseum and St Peter's. Italians had to queue for hour upon hour every day for their meagre rations, but Allied soldiers in Rome could go to the 'British Shop' or one of many officers' clubs, or, for other ranks, the Valiani Restaurant, and enjoy slap-up meals, plenty of beer and wine and, if they wanted it, 'a bit of skirt' afterwards. For many, this was seen as essential R & R for troops who had been fighting in appalling conditions at the front, their just desert; but it was also understandable that it caused resentment among impoverished Italians.

Macmillan and the Control Commission had recognised that inflation needed to be reined in fast, but this was far easier said than done. An Anti-Inflation Committee had been appointed, and one of its first moves had been to try and raise the bread ration from 200 to 300 grammes per person. By giving everyone enough food on which to survive, it had been hoped, the need to resort to the black market would be less, which in turn would help break it. This, however, had been another pipe dream – a policy that had looked good on paper, but which in practice was hard to achieve: the appalling transport system, corrupt officials, and the dominance of black-market racketeers would see to that.

Such decisions had been made by Control Commission officials only, but on 4 October, and with the American presidential election a matter of weeks away, Roosevelt announced publicly that he would be sending more wheat to Italy to make the 300 grammes a day bread ration a reality. He had not, however, consulted with anyone in Italy or explained how this extra wheat was going to get there, and so AMG officers were flooded with demands from Italians wanting to know how soon the new ration would be put into effect – for which they had no answer. On 10 October, and again without any prior consultation, the President magnanimously declared that the US would give the Italian government the dollar equivalent of the Allied paper money issued to American troops in Italy, an offer, embarrassingly, that neither Britain, nor France for that matter, could afford to match. In any case, by this time, inflation was spiralling out of control and southern Italy was on the point of complete social collapse. Just over a week later, the US declared that Italian representatives in Washington should be accorded full diplomatic status, even though there had been no change to the armistice terms, which meant that Italy remained officially a 'non-friendly' nation. Again, the British government had not been consulted beforehand and it refused to comply. A little more thought and consultation beforehand might have made life easier for everyone.

For far too many Italians, moral and political considerations were nothing compared with the need simply to survive. Violence, lawlessness and civil unrest were growing alarmingly. With the exhilaration of libera-tion quickly replaced by disillusionment, bands of former partisans roamed the countryside pillaging farms and often disposing of their booty through central criminal organisations. Black-market racketeers and gangsters continued to rule the roost, and even political violence was breaking out. In September, Alcide De Gasperi, the Christian Democrat leader, accused the Communists – with apparent justification – of break-ing up Christian Democrat meetings in the provinces. Meanwhile in Sicily, five hand grenades were thrown into the midst of a Communist Party meeting. In Rome, at the trial of Pietro Caruso, a mob broke through police lines and tried to lynch the former Fascist chief of police. Unable to find him, they seized Signor Carretta instead, a former Fascist prison governor and a witness in the case. Dragging him to the middle of the Ponte Umberto, they beat him to a pulp and flung him in the Tiber.

As the Allies were discovering, reconstruction of a country was not easy when no properly thought-out plan had been prepared. The focus had always been to force Italy out of the war, then force the Germans out of Italy – and worry about the peace afterwards. At the end of September, Norman Lewis was posted away from Italy, depressed by his inability to make even a small improvement in the lives of the Italians in Benevento under his jurisdiction. 'In their hearts, these people must be thoroughly sick and tired of us,' he wrote. 'A year ago we liberated them from the Fascist Monster, and they still sit doing their best to smile politely at us, as hungry as ever, more disease-ridden than ever before, in the ruins of their beautiful city where law and order have ceased to exist.' And what, he asked, was to be their prize? 'The rebirth of democracy. The glorious prospect of being able one day to choose their rulers from a list of powerful men, most of whose corruptions are generally known and accepted with weary resignation. The days of Benito Mussolini must seem like a lost paradise compared with this.'[276]

Macmillan may have become the most powerful Allied politician in Italy, but it did not help matters in Italy that his remit as adviser to the Supreme Allied Commander, Mediterranean, meant his attentions were spread far and wide. In Greece there was now the problem of an escalating civil war between Communist and royalist factions as the Germans began to withdraw rapidly, while relations with Tito and the Yugoslav partisans were becoming more strained as Soviet influence grew and that of the British fell away.

Indeed, Greece was proving a headache for Alexander too, as he was now forced to order the 4th Indian Division across the Adriatic to help suppress the civil war there. At the same time he had to manage expectations in London and Washington, where it was widely believed that with the Allies so close to victory, one more push would see them home.

Looking at the map and totting up the vast superiority in aircraft, artillery and armour, they could be forgiven for seeing the situation differently to those on the ground. Alex, however, was all too aware that the decisive victory they so craved – while geographically within touching distance – was in all other respects still tantalisingly out of reach. As Bob Wiggans and the 85th 'Custer' Division had discovered at Monte Altuzzo, massed fire power did not count for a whole load; it was the dogged determination of the infantryman that had really won the day. The same was increasingly the case in the Battle for the Rivers now going on along the Adriatic. Aerial bombardment and shelling could only achieve so much; manpower was what was needed to secure victory – overwhelming manpower.

And this was what the Allies lacked. 'We are inflicting very heavy losses on the enemy and are making slow but steady progress,' Alex signalled to Brooke, 'but our losses are also heavy and we are fighting in country where, it is generally agreed, a superiority of at least 3–1 [in manpower] is required for successful offensive operations. It will be small wonder, therefore, if we fail to score a really decisive success when the opposing forces are so equally matched.'[277]

As one of Alex's closest confidants and friends, Macmillan had been a regular visitor to the C-in-C's headquarters, which were now to be found in a clearing in some woods near Siena. Always impressed by the air of calm efficiency that pervaded Alex's HQ, Macmillan felt that outwardly his friend seemed as charming and even-tempered as ever. 'But these continuous five years of command,' he noted, 'almost always in conditions of great anxiety and usually with insufficient forces, have left their mark on him.'[278] Everyone, it seemed, even the imperturbable Alexander, was beginning to feel the strain.

Back in the Apennines, Bob Wiggans and the 338th Infantry had swept into the town of Firenzuola on 21 September having fought attritional skirmishes all the way up from Monte Altuzzo. 'The town was a shambles,' noted Bob. 'American planes had bombed it. Our artillery had hammered it, and now German artillery was having a go at it. Buildings were smashed to bits; debris was everywhere.'[279] Most of the Custermen were absolutely shattered, and in their weakened state scores of men succumbed to a virulent outbreak of hepatitis. Bob was one of them. He knew something was seriously wrong when, just north of Firenzuola, he felt so weak he had to have one of his men carry his rifle and pack. By the following morning, he had a raging fever and, in a semi-conscious state, had to be evacuated by jeep and taken to a field hospital in the rear. From there he was flown to a military hospital near Naples. 'My yellow eyes and tired body had lost over sixty pounds,' he wrote. 'I had lost my fighting desire to live.'[280] In six weeks of fighting from the launch of the attack on Monte Altuzzo, the division had lost 168 officers and 4,899 men, more than a third of their fighting force.

Despite the losses, Clark launched his renewed offensive down Route 65 on 2 October. Kirkman's XIII Corps took over the drive along the Imola axis, using 78th Division, now returned from recuperation and retraining in the Middle East. This meant he could use all four divisions of II Corps in the main attack. Each division was to rotate their regiments at five-day intervals so that one regiment was always in reserve. This was in part because the roads and tracks were so bad it was impossible to pass divisions through one another, and also a means of counteracting the troop shortage. Once again, similarities with the Western Front in the previous war were creeping in, but with the South Africans – now attached to IV Corps – also joining in to the left of the 34th Red Bull Division, it meant Clark could attack with his favoured broad-front approach.

With the Guards Brigade pushing on down the Setta Valley itself, and Combat Command B of the US 1st Armored Division heading down Route 64 in the Reno Valley, the South Africans were in the middle, heading along a mountain track that followed a ridge all the way to Monte Sole and which was dominated by a series of imposing peaks. Needless to say, all of these needed to be taken, and once again, it was the lot of the infantrymen to take the lead in their capture.

On 2 October, the Royal Natal Carbineers moved into position in the rain and mist to the village of Camugnano. By the following morning, the mist had cleared and as dawn broke, Lieutenant Kendall Brooke looked out from his foxhole and saw the towering mass of Monte Vigese directly in front of them. 'It looked like the Matterhorn,' says Kendall, 'a bloody great soaring mountain that was clearly to be our next objective.'

And so it was, although not before the Imperial Light Horse had attacked and captured the small villages and settlements lying immediately around its base. On the 6th, the Carbineers passed through the Imperial Light Horse and prepared to take Vigese. A Company was to lead the attack, and the CO, Major Peter Francis, ordered them to advance in three platoons, each taking a different route – one through the village of Vigo, one straight up to the summit, and the third, commanded by Kendall, heading halfway up the mountain, and over a series of cliff tops, with a promontory on which German troops were dug in as their objective.

Kendall and his men moved forward in absolute silence, with anything that could clang together or make a noise either tied or removed. Within a hundred yards of the German positions Kendall could hear the men of the 16th Waffen-SS's 36th Panzer Regiment talking to each other. There they waited until the darkness of the night had thinned and the very first hint of dawn gave them enough light to be able to see what was in front of them. As the rain continued to pour down, Kendall led them up a narrow winding track. Ahead of them was a machine-gun nest, based around a cave dug into the side of the mountain. Spotting a groundsheet hanging down from the front of the cave, Kendall opened

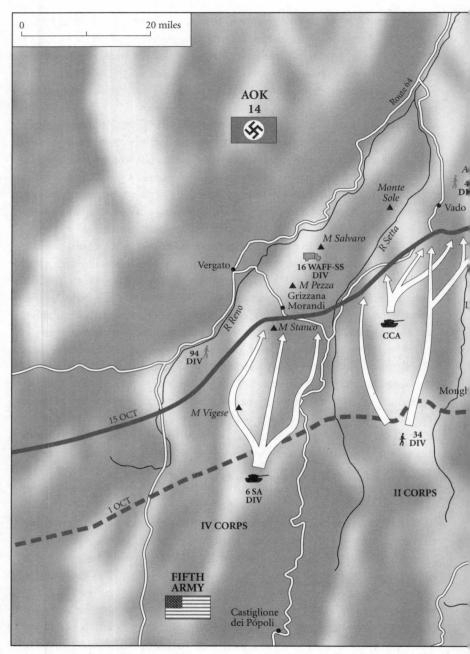

Fifth Army's attempt to break through the Apennines, 1–15 Oct. 1944

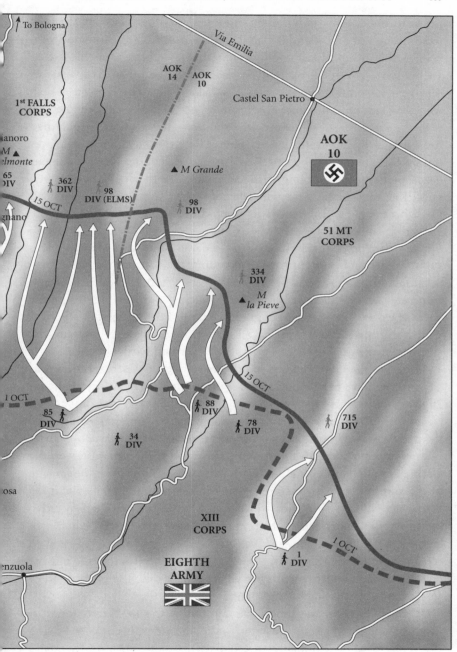

fire with his Tommy gun, killing one man. Another German emerged looking startled and with his hands up, but a third also came out from behind the groundsheet fiddling with the safety catch on his Luger. To his horror, Kendall realised he had already emptied his magazine. 'I had the uncomfortable experience,' says Kendall, 'of grabbing this chap who was surrendering and holding him between myself and the guy with the Luger.' It all happened in a moment, but by now Kendall had been joined by a number of his men. His sergeant, Stan Austin, was urging the man with the Luger to surrender, but the German, in his dazed panic, kept fumbling with the pistol. Another of Kendall's men said, 'Kill him, Stan.' 'And the next moment,' says Kendall, 'Stan had fired three shots and the guy was stone dead before he hit the ground. He was a youngster.'

They then took their objective, as did the other two platoons, and captured a number of prisoners including the German captain commanding all the positions on Monte Vigese. The operation had been a complete success. 'It was all over pretty quickly,' says Kendall, 'primarily because we were creeping through the misery of the heavy rain and mist with no artillery preparation at all. The key was taking these guys by surprise in the grey of dawn before their eyes had hardly opened.'

Just a few days later, he was in action again as the Carbineers tried to capture the next peak along the ridge, Monte Stanco. At first light on 10 October, two companies, B and D, attacked, with A Company in reserve. The D Company men took the summit, but suffered high casualties and so Kendall's platoon was ordered forward to the village of Stanco, nestling directly beneath the summit, as support. By now, however, the Germans were hammering the South African positions from the far side of the summit, and shells were landing in the mountain valley that lay below the village – and over which Kendall and his men had to cross. However, he soon realised that the shells were arriving in batches of eight with a pause in between. Waiting for the last of a salvo of eight to scream over, Kendall shouted, 'Now!' and they all ran across the narrow valley and had almost reached the village by the time the next round of shells started exploding behind them.

Meanwhile, German troops had reinforced the northern slopes of Monte Stanco and begun pushing round the sides, eventually forcing the remains of D Company to fall back by mid-morning. Kendall's platoon were given the task of acting as a rearguard for the withdrawal. 'I was told to stay where I was for fifteen minutes,' he says. 'It was one of the longest fifteen minutes of my life, and at about fourteen-and-three-quarter minutes, I said, "Let's go."' Hurrying across the open valley, they took cover in a ravine, and worked their way up the stream until they reached the safety of their defensive positions, once more on the high ground overlooking Stanco village.

Not until three days later, after continued hard fighting, did the South Africans finally prise the 16th Waffen-SS men from the summit for good, when the 12th Brigade mounted a successful two-battalion attack. In much the same way, Clark's renewed offensive progressed along the Fifth Army: bit by bit in the rain and mist, two steps forward and one step back, chipping away until the Germans were finally forced to fall back to the next mountain. They were making progress, but all the time they were losing more and more men. High casualties were a side effect of the broad front strategy, but Clark could no longer afford the kind of losses Fifth Army had been able to take on the chin back in May and June. The question was, would they be able to make enough progress to break out of the mountains, or would they fall short, exhausted and depleted, before they reached their goal?

Eighth Army now had a new commander. General Leese had been promoted to take over 11th Army Group in India. Naturally flattered, he was nonetheless sorry to be leaving Eighth Army, with whom he had served – except for two brief months – since September 1942. Ion Calvocoressi had been on leave in Cairo when the announcement was made, and had been shocked on his return to learn of this completely unexpected news. General Leese had also asked him to follow him. 'My feelings are very mixed and the main one is extreme depression,' he noted on 30 September, 'but I must think. Pouring with rain and filthy weather.' Like Leese, he was loath to leave Eighth Army, but his loyalty to Leese combined with his interest to return to India – the place of his birth – helped sway his decision.

Leese visited as many of his commanders as possible to say goodbye in person, although there was no opportunity to see his old rival, General Clark. They exchanged friendly messages, however, and in truth, since Leese's perceived slight at Siena, they had got along very much better. Leese did, however, go to see Anders. 'I was sorry to leave the Polish Corps,' he noted. 'I had been very proud of my association with them and I was particularly sad to leave General Anders, with whom I had become great friends.' One of Anders' ADCs pointed out that it was probably a good thing, all the same. 'They felt,' wrote Leese, 'that if I didn't go soon, their General's French would be irretrievably ruined!'[281] With Leese at the helm, Eighth Army French had continued to prosper at the expense of the more purer form.

While there is nothing to suggest that Leese was pushed from Eighth Army, a change at the top and some new ideas were needed. Despite the overall success of OLIVE and the misfortune of the weather, Leese had made some odd tactical decisions – such as the switch of V Corps and the Canadians before the battle, and in the end, with a complete breakthrough only just halted by the skin of the Germans' teeth, this lack of judgement could have proved decisive.

The new Eighth Army commander was Lieutenant-General Sir Richard McCreery, who had, in the distant days of 1940, served alongside Alexander at Dunkirk. Later, he had become Alex's Chief of Staff in North Africa, and more recently had been X Corps commander. Tall, lean, bright and highly experienced, Dick McCreery was a man Alex liked, trusted, and believed was the right person for the job. He had the kind of phlegm and cool-headedness that Alex liked to see in his commanders.

He was also prepared to be more experimental than Leese. Having commanded X Corps in the comparatively quiet mountains between the main fighting, he felt that Eighth Army's axis of attack should now shift inland, with a series of left hooks through the Romagna Mountains, in the mode of Juin's French troops. The immediate goal was Route 9, the Via Emilia, the old Roman road that ran in a straight line from Rimini to Bologna and on, hugging the edge where the plains met the Apennines. However, it was felt that the deeper inland they bisected Route 9, the better the ground was likely to be underfoot, as it was further away from the coast and not dominated by quite so many rivers. Furthermore, the closer they were to Fifth Army, the better they could concentrate their forces.

McCreery gave this task to the 10th Indian Division of his old X Corps, and further west, to Anders' II Polish Corps, which had been out of the line since the capture of Pesaro a month before. The Poles' first objectives were Monte Grosso and the town of Predappio, in the heart of the 8th Garibaldi Brigade's zone of influence, and then the prize of Forlì itself. It was a long march for them, however, and would take a couple of weeks before they were ready to attack.

In the meantime, McCreery had hoped to get Eighth Army across the

Rubicon* on the night of 6/7 October, weather allowing, in support of Clark's latest Fifth Army drive. Unfortunately, it had not allowed, and rain continued to pour down relentlessly. Tenth Indian Division had shown signs of progress through the hills, however, and despite the weather, the Canadians and the rest of V Corps began to move forward once again on 9 October.

Hans Golda and his 8th Battery had been dug in around a farmstead near Savignano on the Rubicon, but that evening, as the Canadians and New Zealanders pushed forward once more, they were ordered to move back. There was a lot of ammunition to take with them – twenty-five rounds of 21cm werfer rockets, and as they finished loading one of the trucks, Hans felt a strong premonition of impending disaster, and so ordered his driver to get going quickly and ordered everyone else to take cover within the farmhouse. No sooner had he said this than a shell whooshed over and hit the house. A moment later, another arrived, scoring a direct hit on the ammunition lorry.

Foxholes had been dug in the kitchen in the farmhouse, and in one of the cowsheds sacks of wheat had been used to create a makeshift bunker, but they now needed every bit of protection they could find as rockets exploded and whistled off in all directions from the burning truck. The whole house shook from the detonations. At one moment there was a loud crash, followed by screaming. Five men from the shed ran into the house where Hans was taking cover, mouths open and eyes wide with fright. Smoke was everywhere, and more rockets exploded into the cowshed where the rough bunker had been destroyed. Hans sprang out of his foxhole in the kitchen, only to find the farmer's wife slumped down on the stairs. 'Her hair glimmered black and hung like a curtain in front of her face,' wrote Hans. 'Her hands were yellow and white. A lake of blood was slowly spreading on the floor; she was dead. A splinter had torn her chest and lower body to pieces.'[282] Suddenly the farmer appeared, took his wife in his arms, and ran out into the yard where ammunition was continuing to detonate in all directions. Hans never saw him again.

Hurrying to the cowshed, Hans found several of his men wounded – one had splinters all over his body, another had severe burns to his legs.

*The River Rubicon is referred to in the British official history as the Fiumicino, while the River Uso is called the Rubicon. I have used the names as they exist today in Italy and as listed on all maps, including those of the period.

Explosions were continuing incessantly. Another man had a large hole in his head above his right eye, while around them the haystacks and sheds were on fire, thick, choking smoke billowing across the entire farm.

Hans then remembered the men who had been hiding under the stove. Rushing back to the kitchen he was relieved to find they were all okay. Suddenly the explosions stopped, but the beautiful farmhouse where they had enjoyed several days' respite was burning ferociously and its owners probably now both dead. Flames rose from the destroyed walls. Those still fit helped the wounded and through the smoke and flames they loaded up into their remaining vehicles. When the last of his men was safely out, Hans jumped into the remaining vehicle and left the scene of desolation, although for several miles he continued to look back at the flames as they rose into the darkening sky.

The 2/5 Leicesters were on the Rubicon, near Montilgallo. Peter Moore had been away on leave in Rome and had returned to the front feeling much better and was now in command of 12 Platoon. The beneficial effects of his break soon began to wear off, however, when he realised he was now the oldest officer in the battalion apart from the CO and the quartermaster, and despite being only twenty-three. Nor were hardly any of his original platoon left; nearly all had been either killed or wounded or had become sick. Another section had been drafted, and they were dug in only a couple of hundred yards from the German positions. As Peter had crept round the platoon foxholes his first night back, the corporal from the new section told him his men wanted to move further back. As he spoke, some of the men started getting out of their trenches. Pointing his Tommy gun at them, Peter hissed, 'Get back in that slit trench or I will shoot you.' He had no intention of doing any such thing, but he seemed to convince the men otherwise. 'It was the one and only time that I felt the need to use such force,' he noted. 'Like all officers I felt a bond of respect and affection for the men we were privileged to command.'[283]

Directly opposite the Leicesters was the 114th Jäger Division, but less than half a mile from Peter was Franz Maassen and his ten-man gruppe. They had been eating too many of the grapes dangling down in front of them and now they all had diarrhoea. 'But it's suicide to leave the foxholes during the day because of the arri [artillery] fire and the jabos,' noted Franz, 'so we shit in a tin can and throw this out of the foxhole.' One day, however, Franz's most trusted and experienced soldier, Walter

Surk had had enough. 'He stands up and just walks out of the foxhole,' says Franz, 'goes a few metres out into no man's land and takes a crap, making sure his arse is facing Tommy. Amazingly, nothing happens to him, as normally you only need to put your little finger out of the foxhole and a marksman would shoot it off.'

On 9 October, a heavy British artillery barrage opened up once more, far worse than anything Franz had ever experienced in Russia. With every impact, the ground trembled. Franz and his men shook helplessly, and he thought of all their relatives crouching with fear in cellars as Allied bombers flew over the cities; his sister-in-law had been killed during a bombing raid on Düsseldorf the previous summer. All around him, the earth was ploughed up by the shells. Trees, bushes, shrubs and mountains of earth were flung into the air. 'One doesn't know whether one will be hit,' noted Franz, 'and you fear not only for your own wretched life, but also for your own men. You can't even hear the screaming under the thunder and the racket. I crouched in my foxhole with Walter Surk. Tommy keeps drumming. We crawl as far as we can into our foxhole, hugging our legs close to our bodies, our knees tightly together, our elbows on our knees, our hands in front of our faces looking down.'

Fragmentation bombs now rained over, embedding themselves into the ground and then hurling more thousands of fragments into the air again. 'The force of the impact,' added Franz, 'throws our bodies with a thump against the wall. We are aware of the explosion as the earth rises violently around us. My shoulder thumps against the mud wall. With a loud ring, our steel helmets knock together.'

As the barrage eventually lifted, not one man had been so much as wounded. Word arrived that they were to fall back. Franz gathered everyone around him; they checked their weapons, and then he ordered them to retreat one by one, and at least a hundred yards apart so as to minimise the impact of any shell that might land around them. His orders: to meet behind the hill at the back of them, then right at the church to the company command post. A couple of the men Franz had to grab by the belt and hold until it was their turn. In the meantime, Walter was firing the machine gun, keeping the enemy pinned down. Then Franz took over, sending Walter on his way. By this time, the Tommies of the 46th Division had pulled back, not wanting to be scythed down by Franz's Spandau fire. As the jabos appeared and the artillery opened fire again, Franz packed up and headed back himself.

Everyone made it safely to the command post, but they then had further to go. Franz ordered them to get going again, once more spaced well apart. And as before, he was last, covering their backs with the machine gun and checking that no enemy troops were driving through. The men in front of him stopped by a hut and only then did he realise that another platoon had come between him and his own men – from the back, in the rain, and a hundred yards apart, one soldier looked much like another.

Franz was exhausted, not least because the machine gun and a box of ammunition were extremely heavy to carry. Confident that his men were now out of harm's way, he paused to get a light for his cigarette before pushing on again. Trudging up a shallow hill, he reached the top only for enemy shells to start screaming over once more. Taking cover in a haystack, he waited for about half an hour until there was a pause in the shelling, then ran down a muddy path into a narrow gully. 'And there I saw all my men and many more besides,' he says. 'Shells had landed in amongst them. The gully had meant they'd all been caught in there.' He found Walter Surk without an apparent scratch on him, but quite dead all the same. Franz was distraught; in just a few short weeks, Walter had become his trusted friend. 'I wish he'd reach his hand out to me,' noted Franz. 'I press his hands and cross them on his chest. There you go my boy. I could shake your hand. I'll never forget you. May you live forever.'

Not one of his men had survived. 'That evening we buried them,' wrote Franz, 'my good comrades.'

THIRTY-TWO

Rain, Mud and Misery, Part II
15–31 October 1944

While his colleagues in the Royal Natal Carbineers (RNC) had been involved in bitter fighting for Monte Vigese and Monte Stanco, Dick Frost had been left behind with the mortar carriers. On 10 October, he had moved to the RNC's forward base in the hamlet of Collina, a collection of stone houses straddled along a curved ridge a mile south of Stanco. Although out of the thick of the action, Collina had soon come under German shellfire, and one shell hit the house Dick was billeted in and set a dump of a hundred mortar bombs on fire. 'Collina is a hell of a mess,' he scribbled. 'Spent the rest of the evening trying to put out the fire by forming a chain and passing buckets of water to and fro.'[284]

A few days later, with Stanco safely in Allied hands, the South Africans reached the Monte Sole massif – two weeks too late for the Stella Rossa and the civilians who had been living there. Next on their list of peaks to capture was Monte Pezze. On the night of 16/17 October, Kendall Brooke and his platoon were patrolling the mountain. The north slope was still occupied, but the southern was not, and Kendall and his men climbed up easily, finding a couple of ledges on the lee side just below the summit. 'It was the perfect place to be,' says Kendall, 'because any enemy fire either landed on the high ground behind you, or went over you into the valley below. So we were fine until a couple of 5.5-inch shells fell short from our own guns.' One of these shells passed over Kendall's head and killed an officer of the Witwatersrand Rifles/De la Rey Regiment who had been on the same cadet course as him back in South Africa.

Kendall's patrol and others confirmed that the reverse side was heavily occupied, and so the following morning a two-battalion attack was launched. Once again, A Company of the Carbineers was in reserve.

Kendall was relieved not to be first into the attack because the infantry were to advance behind a creeping barrage, a tactic in which he no longer had much confidence. As the guns began to boom and echo around the mountains, Kendall noticed a young officer from the First City/Cape Town Highlanders who was about to go in, looking terribly agitated. Turning to Kendall he asked him the time. He was nervous about missing the start of the attack and did not want to be accused of ducking his responsibilities. 'I'm terribly worried about today,' he suddenly said to Kendall, 'because I think it's going to be bloody rough. I've never slept with a woman and I don't want to end my life without knowing what it was like.'

Such were the kind of fears that gripped young men as they faced battle and the prospect of an early death. Kendall never did find out whether the young man made it through.

Eastwards across the mountains, in the Romagna, the 8th Garibaldi Brigade had been doing well since the July rastrellamento, with the military training by Bruno Vailati paying off. In August, another rastrellamento had been launched in the 2nd Battalion's zone, but under Bruno's instructions, Iader Miserocchi and his men had mined the roads and set up a number of other obstructions, holding up a battalion of German troops for three days. 'Bruno then sent word to the Allies to bomb them,' says Iader, 'so we were firing at them and obstructing them and the RAF bombed them as well.'

By the end of September, as to the south X Corps pressed forward, the 8th Garibaldi found itself in the front line. By the fourth week in September, troops of the 8th Indian Division had reached Bagno di Romagna, at the southern end of Iader's zone of operations. German troops were now falling back in line with the rest of the front while the 8th Garibaldi remained an ever-present menace, making their withdrawal as difficult as possible. On 25 September, as Todt workers were repairing a road near Linaro that the Germans intended to use in their retreat, Iader's men arrived shooting over the heads of the labourers and forcing the German guards to run for their lives. The workers were then freed and dispersed.

In the days that followed, the 2nd Battalion – indeed the whole brigade – had numerous clashes with German forces. On the 27th, Iader and his men moved into the town of Sarsina, occupying it and liberating it from Fascist control. All of Iader's zone of operations was now in partisan hands. Unlike the Stella Rossa, it looked as though the 8th Garibaldi Brigade would survive.

Iader's men were still holding Sarsina and the Savio Valley as far as Mercato Saraceno by the time the Poles arrived in the middle of October. The main thrust of Anders' two divisions was up through the heart of the 8th Garibaldi's area, to Santa Sofia and into the Bidente Valley to the west of Iader's men, but troops of the 3rd Carpathian Division did reach Sarsina as well.

Feelings were still running high within the Polish Corps. The Warsaw Uprising had finally ended on 2 October and there was a great deal of bitterness, directed at the Western Allies and especially towards the Soviets, whom they blamed for refusing to come to the aid of the Polish resistance. In the middle of September, Anders had flown to Britain for talks with the Polish government-in-exile and with the British. He had returned feeling more despondent than ever about Poland's future. General Sosabowski, the Polish Commander-in-Chief and an outspoken critic of the Soviet Union, had been forced to resign and it was clear to Anders that Britain was now powerless to stop post-war control of Poland by the Soviet Union, and naïve in her appreciation of Soviet intentions. 'In my great anxiety and concern to maintain the morale and unity of the Army Corps,' Anders wrote on his return to Italy to the Polish President in London, 'I have to report that the soldiers reject every thought of a possible organisation of a Polish Government under Russian occupation, with the participation of traitors and Soviet agents.' After all, this was not what he or any of his men had been fighting this long and bitter struggle for. His men still had faith in Britain and America, he added, 'but they do not trust the Soviets, and reject any idea of penetration by the agents of the Soviet Government whose schemes and final aim are obvious.'[285]

It was in this depressed and bitter mood that Polish troops arrived in Sarsina to be confronted by Communist partisans. It was like a red rag to a bull. 'The Poles burned down four or five houses we had been staying in,' says Iader, 'as a protest because we were Communist.' Wladek Rubnikowicz was not aware of the incident and was fighting further west at the time, but does not deny such things happened. 'We weren't very keen on Communists,' he says. 'For us, the Russians were as bad, if not worse, than the Nazis.'

*   *   *

The weather was getting to everyone. Twenty-fourth SAAF Squadron had not flown a single operational sortie so far in October. Pescara airfield had become a quagmire, as had the tented camp where the aircrew and ground staff lived. The airfield ran alongside the River Pescara, and the men had watched the rising waters with a certain degree of concern – local Italians had told them that many years before Italian troops had camped along the same spot, the river had flooded, and hundreds had been drowned. 'It was absolutely miserable,' says Ernest Wall. 'We were soaked in our tents, there was mud and water everywhere, but most of all it was just so frustrating.' Not until the 9th did the first few members of the squadron begin the move north to Jesi, where facilities were better, and although the move was complete by the 16th, even then there was no flying. Engineers valiantly tried to build a 1,000-yard pierced-steel plating runway, but no sooner did they get a section ready than the weather deteriorated once more and much of their work was consequently undone.

Life was marginally better, however, at Peretola airfield, near Florence, where 225 Squadron were now operating. One of the first RAF armed reconnaissance squadrons, they had served throughout the Tunisian campaign, and in Italy had been part of the 12th Tactical Air Command. Moving to Corsica for the invasion of southern France, they had returned to Italy at the beginning of September. Twelfth TAC was a much smaller force now, as many of its units had been sent to northwest Europe – and indeed before the month was out, it would be renamed 22nd Tactical Air Command – but 225 Squadron, equipped with Spitfires, had become a true-blooded Mediterranean theatre outfit and was to remain that way.

Commanding 'A' Flight was Flight Lieutenant Ken Neill, a New Zealander who had left Scotland with the squadron back in 1942 for the invasion of north-west Africa and who had stayed with 225 until becoming tour expired a little over a year later in October 1943. He had remained in the Mediterranean, however, becoming an instructor in Egypt and Palestine. Then in August, having had ten months out of a front-line squadron, he had been posted back to Italy, and on to Corsica to rejoin 225 Squadron once more. 'I was pleased to have been sent back to 225,' he says. 'I would much rather have gone back to my old squadron than any other.'

Ken was a farmer's son, brought up on a large farm on the South Island in the 1920s and '30s, but a world away from the turbulent events brewing in Europe and elsewhere. However, the war, when it came, caught up even with people like Ken, living as he was in a degree of isolation in the open farmland of rural New Zealand. 'I wasn't one of those people dying to get into the fray,' he admits, 'but I could see that I was going to have to get involved.' With the support of his father, a veteran of the First World War, he decided to wait until he was nineteen and then join the Royal New Zealand Air Force, despite having never even seen an aircraft airborne before.

Training in New Zealand had been followed by a long sea voyage to England, where, after completing his operational training, he had been finally posted to 225 Squadron. At that time they had been flying already obsolete Hurricanes, but now, back in Italy, they were flying Spitfire Mk IXs, an aircraft that could operate at nearly 400 mph. They were also clipped-wing versions, with the famous elliptical wing stunted at the ends to allow for improved manoeuvrability at lower levels. Every bit of agility was needed when flying at sometimes hair-raisingly low altitudes, for although they tended to operate at around 6,000 feet, they would frequently have to drop far lower in order to carry out the quite specific reconnaissance work that was required of them. On 14 October, for example, Ken and his wing man were hunting for hostile artillery batteries in the Massa-La Spezia area, but because of the weather, visibility was so poor they flew down to just 500 feet off the deck.

It was, as ever, dangerous work flying over Italy and being subjected to all manner of flak, but unlike the Poor Bloody Infantry, Ken and his fellow pilots were able to return to the safety of their airfields after every sortie, and in the case of the 225 pilots at Peretola, to their decidedly smart billets at the end of every day. Not that it had always been that way. During the Salerno landings, their airfield had been almost on top of the battlefield, and throughout the past two winters, first in Tunisia and then in southern Italy, the squadron had been forced to live under canvas amidst the mud and rain. 'It was certainly not very pleasant,' admits Ken.

Consequently, he had been only too happy to be given the task – along with his fellow flight commander – of finding new accommodation on the squadron's move back to Italy. 'We found the Villa Cora,' says Ken. 'It was really very luxurious.' A magnificent neo-classical palazzo perched high above the Boboli Gardens, the Villa Cora had an ornate formal garden and far-reaching views overlooking the Arno, Duomo and the heart of Florence. And when they were not holding parties of their own in the lavish ballroom, the pilots could head into the city and enjoy the benefits of the Majestic Hotel. 'It was known as the DAF Club,' says Ken, 'and we would go there most Saturday nights to eat and dance, which we all enjoyed.' At least some people were able to make the most of what Italy had to offer.

Not so the men on the ground, Allied or German. With no reserve units available at all, Feldmarschall Kesselring and his commanders could only replace their exhausted divisions with those slightly less exhausted. There was simply no opportunity for fatigued and depleted units to rest behind the lines. Once in new positions, these battle-worn, barely regrouped, under-manned divisions were usually given a certain amount of replacement troops and new equipment, but it was never enough. Even in quiet areas, such as in von Senger's western half of the line, troops were spread so thinly that any kind of training was impossible. Often a depleted division of barely three thousand troops would hold as much as twenty miles of the front.

Yet as ever, Kesselring was not allowed the freedom of action he needed. Both he and his commanders were tearing their hair out in frustration because their hands were once again being tied by Hitler and the High Command. Consequently, he was limited to making short-term decisions concerning the immediate situation. Von Vietinghoff, for example, had been making repeated requests for permission to shorten the line by carrying out a delaying action back towards what was to become the position of the Genghis Khan Line, but when Kesselring referred this back to the High Command he was given short shrift, and Hitler's desire for them to fight for every yard was reiterated.

And all the time, Fifth Army was continuing to batter its way forward, clawing as much as a mile one day, a hundred yards the next. Getting equipment and basics such as food and ammunition to the front was becoming increasingly difficult, with blown roads and tracks that had turned to mud stifling every move. Ted Wyke-Smith and his band of bridging engineers now had to contend with gaping ravines and gushing mountain rivers as they tried desperately to open up new ways of reaching the front-line troops. 'We had to put up these enormous, high-level bridges,' he says, 'which were very difficult under normal circumstances but nigh on impossible with that amount of rain and mud.' At Castel del Rio, they had to build an entirely new road down steep slopes of the ravine, then built a Bailey bridge across the river. The problem was that no sooner had they started building the bridge than the river level suddenly rose dramatically. 'Our bridge was all washed away,' says Ted. 'What had been a trickle in the valley was now a raging chocolate brown torrent sweeping everything before it.'

Despite these appalling conditions in which to press an attack, on 20 October the 88th Blue Devils scaled and captured the Monte Grande massif, just five miles as the crow flies from the Via Emilia. Three days later, the 34th Red Bulls took Monte Belmonte, just nine miles from the centre of Bologna, while on the Red Bulls' left, the South Africans had reached Monte Salvaro, where only three weeks before a seriously injured Gianni Rossi had sheltered following the German rastrellamento.

These had been important and hard-fought gains, each peak an epic of grit and determination, and Kesselring was fully aware that his forces now stood a whisker away from a decisive defeat; should Bologna fall – and by the third week of October that was looking ever more likely – he would not be able to stop the Allies from breaking out into the central plains. That would spell potential disaster. With this in mind, he realised it was essential to rapidly reinforce AOK 14 and ensure Fifth Army did not make the decisive breakthrough they were now so close to achieving.

A gamble was needed. Lemelsen was away sick and so von Senger was given temporary command of AOK 14. He was quick to respond to the rapidly escalating crisis. Three divisions from 14th Panzer Corps – the 16th Waffen-SS included – had already been shifted into the centre of the line since the beginning of the month; but von Senger also now hastily moved all his artillery too – all but one battery that remained standing sentinel north of Lucca.

In addition to these moves, Kesselring ordered 29th Panzer from AOK 10 to bolster the fight against the Americans; the 90th Panzer Grenadier were brought in from the Alpine frontier, and then, finally, on 23 October, the 1st Fallschirmjäger Division was moved west, south of Castel San Pietro to the Monte Grande area. It was a decision von Vietinghoff magnanimously agreed to, and which his 76th Corps commander, General Herr, accepted grudgingly, but it was a judicious move and one that helped stiffen German resolve in the mountains. The German paratroopers had a formidable reputation among both German and Allied forces alike, and the news that they would soon be adding weight in the crucial battle raging south of Bologna gave heart to the tired German troops desperately trying to hold the Americans at bay around Monte Grande. Indeed, by the time Hans-Jürgen Kumberg and the 4th Fallschirmjäger Regiment moved into their new positions in the pouring rain on the 25th, the US Blue Devils had already been halted.

This drastic weakening of von Vietinghoff's line, and the thrust south of Forlì by the Poles also finally persuaded Hitler to relent over the shortening of AOK 10's line. On 19 October, Kesselring accordingly told von Vietinghoff that he could fall back to the River Savio. A few days later, with the 1st Fallschirmjäger Division now shifted west, there was a further need to close the gap made by their loss. Hitler's response to the request for another withdrawal along the Adriatic Front had not been as emphatic as usual, and more open to interpretation. Taking advantage of this, on 25 October, Kesselring authorised a withdrawal that von Vietinghoff had already begun – this time some twelve miles to the River Ronco.

These dramatic and swiftly carried-out moves affected most of the German troops along the front. Hans Golda and the Werfer Regiment 71 had been taken out of the line after the fall of Cesena on 19 October, and moved to Medicina, just twelve miles due east of Bologna. After an exhausting and stressful few weeks, Hans had been glad for the rest. 'Once again,' he wrote, 'I could sleep in peace without the feeling that a shell would land on the house in the next moment.'[286]

Not for long, however. A few days later, the regiment was moved south to the Monte Grande area alongside the Fallschirmjäger boys. Hans' 8th Battery was one of three centred on the village of Liano. Before the front line reached there, Liano had been a quiet, peaceful place of a dozen houses, a small school – which was also a convent – and a castle. Hans was impressed by the stunning views. He could see Bologna in the distance, the beautiful town of Castel San Pietro behind him and ahead, Monte Calderaro, with its ruined church where the Americans were dug in, and to the side, Monte Cerere rising over them, and the further mass of peaks beyond.

Hans set up his command post in the sacristy of the church, and the first morning was woken by the village schoolchildren singing as they celebrated mass in the church. 'Röffner jumped up in his shirt and pants, and pulled the door open and stood for a second in the church before quickly taking cover,' noted Hans. 'The priest and a lot of girls had seen him and laughed a lot about his shocked face and funny clothes.'[287]

Unteroffizier Franz Maassen, meanwhile, was now in position along the Ronco, a mile or two south-east of Forlì. Since the loss of his men, he had been placed in charge of a new gruppe and given a more roving, reconnaissance role within the Headquarters Company of 994th Infantry

Regiment: men as experienced as him were thin on the ground by the autumn of 1944 and Hauptmann Kurz was determined to make the most of him.

For once the weather was clear, but that had meant more jabos about, and crossing over the Ronco at Meldola, a few miles to the south, had been a hairy experience. Franz had been glad to reach the edge of Forlì safely. 'The quarters not bad,' he scribbled in his diary, 'but from my experience, one doesn't stay in these sort of quarters nearly as long as in the most desperate sheds that we have to lie in for weeks on end.' His lugubrious infantry's nous was to prove him right. That night they moved into a cellar of a house, and it promptly began to rain again. Soon the cellar floor was under water.

Meanwhile, Eighth Army had been moving forward once more as the Germans fell back. On 24 October, Stan Scislowski and the Perth Regiment had moved up to the River Savio. He was struck by how quiet it was – no sound of shelling or mortars, no small-arms chatter. His platoon requisitioned a house for the night, and inside they found a family of terrified Italians. The children shied away, afraid to speak or take the chocolate bars Stan and his mates offered them. Even the adults cowered when they tried to offer them cigarettes. Eventually, after much cajoling they seemed to relax a bit. 'From what we could make of it,' noted Stan, 'the Jerries had really been scaring the daylights out of them, telling all kinds of horror stories about us.'[288]

Unlike the 1st Canadian Division, who had faced strong rearguards in the south half of the Canadian sector, the 5th Armoured Division had had no such problems, and on 25 October, Stan and his mates in Dog Company crossed the river unopposed. They moved down the Cesena–Ravenna road, ten miles short of Forlì, setting up new positions around a group of solidly built houses. And there they remained, for after ten weeks of heavy fighting, the Canadian Corps was about to go into army reserve.

In his cellar, Franz Maassen was soaked to the skin once more. Since his matches became damp he had been smoking almost non-stop, alternating with one of his men so that they always had a light. Franz was never short of cigarettes, because although the daily cigarette ration was not especially generous, he always waited a few days to report any deaths or casualties. This way, casualties' rations kept coming up to the front. 'It made no difference to them,' says Franz. 'I used to smoke about seventy a day that way.'

On the morning of 28 October, Maassen's gruppe was suddenly ordered to stand by. The enemy had crossed the Ronco, and they were to prepare to counterattack. Franz and his men headed out into the pouring rain and ran down the 400 yard slope towards the river, through vines and bushes. There in front of them they saw a small group of British troops. These were, in fact, engineers of the 1st King's Royal Rifles. With no time to load and aim his machine pistol, he lifted the bazooka he was carrying and fired, killing every one of them.

Apart from these few men, there was no obvious sign of a massed British crossing, however, so Franz set up an observation post in some bushes at the corner of a field and awaited instructions. Soon after, Leutnant Münker arrived, and together he and Franz crept into the meadow beyond to recce the area and try and find out where exactly the British were. There were numerous bushes and a wood beyond and Franz was pretty sure the enemy were not far in front of them. Sure enough, as they dashed forward, enemy fire started pinging around them. Taking cover in a shell hole, Franz peered out over the brim, and began to laugh. From the woods and bushes ahead, the British were pushing a helmet up on a stick. It was an old trick to try and tempt the enemy to fire and so reveal his position. 'But they were so stupid,' noted Franz 'and pushed the stick so far out we could see it easily.' And now he knew exactly where *they* were.

First, however, they needed to get back to the rest of Franz's group. This was no easy matter, but they managed to crawl away and were making good progress when they suddenly saw several British troops away to their right. 'Okay, let's fire on the count of three,' Münker told him. Franz had duly stood up only for his sub-machine gun to jam. Cursing wildly, he flung himself back on the ground as return shots whistled over their heads.

Hugging the ground so that the smell of soil and wet grass filled their nostrils, they inched their way backwards across the meadow, Franz doing his best to make the most of every dip in the ground and each clump of thick grass. They were making good but slow progress when Franz suddenly discovered Egon Genz, his machine-gunner had crept forward to join him and Münker. 'What are you doing here?' Franz hissed at him.

'*Unteroffizier*, I wanted to help,' Genz replied. It was a brave gesture, but a foolhardy one as Genz was struggling with the heavy machine gun, and now there were three, rather than two of them who had to get back to the cover of their positions.

Even so, they were managing it, seemingly undetected, when, with 150 yards to go, Münker lost patience, and jumped up. As he did so, a shot took off his cap, but sprinting as fast as he could, Franz saw that he appeared to make the dash unscathed. It was not a chance Franz was prepared to take, however, and so together with Genz, he continued his crawl. But then, in a moment of madness, Genz also suddenly stood up to run. As he bent over to pick up the machine gun, he was hit in the stomach. Franz watched aghast as the young man calmly stuffed his guts into his stomach with both hands and stumbled back. 'The Tommies,' noted Franz, 'decently, let him walk.'

By the time Franz had safely reached the rest of his men, their own artillery had opened up, but although shells were whistling over towards the British, they were also falling on their positions too. With neither a radio nor flares with which to signal to the artillery, it was left to Franz to rush back across 400 yards of mostly exposed ground behind them to warn the gunners to lift their fire.

He made it and reported to Kurz. Could he hold out? Kurz wanted to know. Franz thought they could although he explained about the loss of Genz, who had died of his wound, and the machine gun. Kurz's orders were to the point. 'Maassen, make a counterattack,' he told him, 'and tell me when you've got the machine gun to safety.'

Franz cursed. He could scarcely believe it. With just his ten men, he was expected to attack the British across largely open ground. First, however, he had to somehow recover the machine gun; it was a task he knew he must do himself. Once safely back at the observation post, he told his men to give him covering fire while he tried to snatch the gun. Crouching and running at the same time, he reached the machine gun and fell flat on the ground. He had not been fired upon at all, and while he lay there catching his breath, he realised the Tommies must have fallen back. Looking ahead, he could see no sign of any enemy at all and so called his men over to join him. Once they reached him, he told them they would charge across the meadow to the edge of the wood ahead.

Making their way to the trees safely without a further shot being fired, they discovered the British had withdrawn through the wood completely. Soon after, Franz was joined by another gruppe from a different company. Their leader, Unteroffizier Neureither, suggested to Franz that they make a joint frontal attack on the British through the wood. Franz thought this was crazy, and suggested an alternative plan – that they creep round the edge of the trees along the river bank, and come in behind where the British now were, and so cut them off from getting back across the Ronco. 'I let him know that if we attack the enemy with a frontal assault,' noted Franz, 'we'll just push him back across the Ronco, where he'll gather his forces, re-form and firing heavily on us, attack again.'

Neureither disagreed. Franz decided to take his men on his own, and managed to successfully infiltrate behind a company of the 1st King's Royal Rifles. Opening fire and hurling grenades, they caught the British by surprise and with Neureither's men attacking from the right, the British quickly surrendered. Less than twenty Germans had captured ninety-three of the enemy, and during the entire day, Franz had lost just two men – Genz and another who had been killed by shrapnel from their own artillery.

Having rounded up the prisoners, Franz then spotted a badly wounded British sergeant lying on the ground, awaiting attention. Going over to give him some water, Franz lifted his canteen to the man's lips, but the sergeant just turned his face away so that the water trickled down his tightly closed mouth. 'The sergeant looked at me with pure hatred in his eyes,' says Franz. 'He died later in the night. I've never forgotten that expression.'

Generally speaking, however, soldiers of either side had little hatred for one another. Most men, whether German or Allied, recognised that the misery of their situation was something they shared in common. Indeed, there was even grudging respect. But on occasion, a line was crossed, and with it, all compassion dissolved, as Willfried Segebrecht's men of the 16th Waffen-SS Reconnaissance Battalion discovered during clashes with their American opponents.

The 16th Waffen-SS still held most of the Monte Sole massif from the South Africans, but down below in the Setta Valley, the 34th Red Bulls had pushed them back as far as Vado. It was here that the 16th Reconnaissance Battalion had been fighting during the second half of the month. On 17 October, as thick fog engulfed their positions, one of Willfried's platoons had been decimated by a surprise attack by the Americans using flamethrowers, a weapon they personally had not seen before. Willfried and his men had been horrified by what the flames had done to their comrades. Eighteen men had been burned alive, the remains charred beyond recognition and shrunken to the size of children. 'A great rage' possessed Willfried and his men.[289]

Soon after, they counterattacked, using Panzerfausts on the American infantrymen, and overrunning one of the Red Bulls' positions. Four prisoners were taken, and Willfried's men made them carry one of their mortars and ammunition with them. They then turned this weapon on the prisoners and blew them to pieces.

Back at the Ronco, Eighth Army's progress had been stalled once more. Elsewhere along the river, the German 278th Division had seen off efforts by the British 4th Division to cross the river, but the deluge of rain now falling swept away large amounts of British bridging gear. Muddy torrents made even normally shallow stretches unfordable.

On the 27th, the Fifth Army offensive was also called off. Although a great driver of his men, even Clark realised his troops had been pushed to the limit and that German opposition had become too strong. It was a great disappointment to him and as always when his temper became short, he began pointing fingers. Amongst his own troops, the 34th Red Bulls' performance, he believed, had been lacklustre. Despite heavy casualties, Clark felt they had not had the will to 'slug it out' and had become 'diseased'.

Not that his wrath was directed solely at the 34th Division. As far as he was concerned, Eighth Army had a lot to answer for too. Unaware of the extreme difficulties facing McCreery's men, Clark could not understand why they were sitting idly in the mud while his Fifth Army fought on through the driving rain in the mountains. 'It is perfectly disgraceful, the inactivity of Eighth Army,' he riled in his diary. 'There is no will to fight.' Why, he wanted to know, couldn't some of Eighth Army's troops be sent over to reinforce his Army in the same way that Kesselring had done with his forces?

The difference was that Kesselring's men were defending not attacking, and in any case, Eighth Army had been fighting continuously since 24 August. Some units, like 1st Armoured Division had been disbanded entirely because they had lost so many men. Alexander, and then McCreery, patiently explained this to him, but he dismissed their reasonings. Once again, he began to suspect Eighth Army of underhand tactics, and of deliberately making life harder for Fifth Army. 'If anyone is to advance into the Po Valley, they much prefer that the British Eighth Army get the credit.'[290] This was nonsense, and reflected Clark's personal frustrations in the Apennines rather than any reasoned analysis of the situation.

Meanwhile General Kirkman, who had never been a fan of Clark's broad front approach to warfare, was pointing the finger at the Fifth Army commander for what he perceived had been mistaken tactics all along, and General Harding was depressed by Kirkman's griping and constant complaining about conditions and lack of support.

Tempers were increasingly short amongst the troops as well. In the mountains south-east of Bologna, Ted Wyke-Smith was still doing his best to improve mountain roads and establish bridges over mountain rivers. At the beginning of November, he had been ordered up to Sasso-leone with a column of bridging gear to help the American 88th Division, who, despite considerable losses, were still holding the line in the wet and the mud a few miles to the north at Monte Grande.

Built into the hillside like so many Apennine towns, the streets were narrow and the only place to park vehicles was in the town square. Bringing in his column of vehicles he realised too late that it was already full of trucks and jeeps. An American major hurried over and said to him, 'Hey, soldier, get your goddam trucks out of here.' When Ted explained that he was trying to, the major pulled out his pistol, pressed the muzzle against his face, and told him to get the hell out of there right away. 'I thought, for Christ's sake,' recalls Ted, 'it's not cowboys and Indians.'

It was understandable that spirits were sagging and tempers fraying amongst the Allies. So much had been given since the opening of the Gothic Line battles ten weeks before, and for want of a few days, a few more men, and a bit of decent weather the victory they believed was rightly theirs had been denied them. Their goal was so, so close – a few more miles, that was all; but that short step still seemed so tantalisingly out of reach. The rain beating down, the mud that got everywhere and the misery of fighting in such conditions in such a god-awful place had started to get everyone down. So too had the lack of support from London and Washington. And now, instead of victory, they faced the prospect of failure and criticism.

THIRTY-THREE

The Infantryman's Lot
November 1944

For one so young, Carla Costa had once again shown an extraordinary cool-headedness on this, her third mission. The first morning across enemy lines she had been stopped by a partisan who was suspicious about seeing a strange face in the village. Thinking on her feet, she had given the perfect answer, explaining that she was a refugee escaping from the north and providing him with convincing yet completely inconsequential information about German positions.

Set free, she had then made her way to Rome, had carried out all that had been asked of her, delivering funds and messages, and collecting a number of further newspapers. By 22 October she was nearly home and dry, having reached Pistoia, and the following morning she began walking on the main road up into the mountains, towards San Marcello Pistoiese. At one point she took a short cut and when she rejoined the main road, hailed down two cyclists and asked them for a ride on the back of their bicycles. The two young men agreed, but they had only gone a few hundred yards when they were stopped by American military police.

Little did Carla realise it, but one of her fellow agents had squealed. Mario Martinelli had been a serial criminal before being recruited by the Abwehr, but had proved an effective spy. However, he had been picked up by Carabinieri officers just outside Florence for not having the correct travel permit, and had then been taken to Fifth Army headquarters in Tavarnelle, where he had been interrogated by the 306th Counter Intelligence Corps Detachment. For several days he had refused to talk. In the meantime, American counterintelligence agents had followed up leads and were able to confront Martinelli with overwhelming evidence of his Abwehr operations. This finally broke him, and out came a full and detailed confession, which included furnishing them with details about Carla.

Armed with a full description and details of her most likely route, Special Agent Gordon Mason had not had a particularly hard job catching her, and he now arrested her and took her back to Tavarnelle. Getting any information out of her, however, would be considerably more difficult.

Like all good commanders, Feldmarschall Kesselring liked to get up to the front and on the 22nd, the day of Carla Costa's arrest, he had set out at 5 a.m. driving from one division to another, beginning in the Apennines. What he saw gave him confidence – his men in apparent good heart and fighting tenaciously. He sensed the crisis of a few days before had passed, and that they would now be able to hold the line into the winter after all.

Driving through daylight hours was still an extremely hazardous business, especially when the skies were as clear as they were that day, and jabos harassed them all the way. Late in the day, whilst driving between Bologna and Forlì on his way to visit his last two divisions, his car passed a column and, as it did so, collided with a long-barrelled gun that was being turned out of a side road. The crash caused the car to veer off the road and overturn, and in the process Kesselring received a bad gash on the side of the head and severe concussion. 'Soon after my accident,' he noted later, 'the story got about that the Feldmarschall was doing well, but that the gun had had to be scrapped.'[291]

Smiling Albert was making light of the episode, but in fact he had been seriously injured. He was still unconscious the following morning and his head was a mess; even once he finally came round, it was unclear whether he had sustained brain damage. For several days it was touch and go whether he would pull through. So concerned was Hitler that he demanded daily bulletins on his progress. Kesselring did gradually recover, but it was clear he would not be back at the front for some time. Fortunately for the German forces in Italy, his absence came at a time when the acute danger of the late summer was over. Command of Army Group C passed to von Vietinghoff, Lemelsen took over the reins of AOK 10, and General Heinz Ziegler – rather than von Senger – took over AOK 14.

Alexander may have been fit and well compared with his opposite number, but he was certainly suffering from headaches of his own. The first was a strategy for the winter. Whether he could ever have broken through the central Apennines with both armies side by side and starting their offensive two or even three weeks earlier will never be known. Had he not lost key divisions, air power and supplies to southern France, however, it is hard to see how he could have failed. But there was no point looking back. As he was well aware, the Italian campaign, from its inception, had been designed merely to support the main offensive in the west – a campaign that was, for the most part, going well. Normandy had been won, Paris and Brussels liberated, and Allied troops were now fighting on German soil for the first time. Whatever Alex now planned for the future, his task of supporting the campaign in northwest Europe remained unchanged.

One option was to halt the offensive in Italy and transfer troops to north-west Europe. Eisenhower rejected this offer, however. Another option was to transfer part of his troops across the Adriatic, and continue a two-fisted approach, with one arm continuing in Italy and the other along the Yugoslav coast, where German resistance would be slight. This, Alex believed, would have certain advantages if they could push the Germans back to the River Adige in north-east Italy first, and he began to plan seriously for such an operation for the following spring, with the hope that it might enable them to reach Austria before the Russians did.

But it was how to help Eisenhower in the short term that really mattered, and on 29 October, at a conference at his encampment near Siena, Alexander met with his commanders to outline his plans for the next few months. He had recognised that hopes of forcing the Germans back across the Po and up to the Adige in the short term were now unrealistic. Instead, he proposed the more limited goal of capturing Bologna and Ravenna. Eighth Army should continue their offensive with all available resources until 15 December, with Ravenna their objective. This, he hoped, would draw off the enemy from Clark's troops. Fifth Army would withdraw troops from the front line for rest in preparation for one more offensive effort to capture Bologna, which would begin around 30 November. Alex did include a caveat, however. If the weather was so bad that the chances of success looked slim, these offensives would be cancelled, in which case they would simply have to accept the best winter position and, if the war was not over beforehand, wait until the spring.

Another headache was the shortage of ammunition. 'To a force which relied so much on artillery,' noted Alex, 'the only effective superiority we possessed for a campaign in an Italian winter, this was a most serious matter.'[292] The problem had surfaced back in the summer by a major production miscalculation towards the end of 1943 when stocks of shells and ammunition had been high. As a result, and on the assumption that the war in Europe would continue for another year, production of both in the United States and of shells in Britain had been reduced, and in Britain, the spare labour as a result of this cut-back had been transferred to aircraft factories instead. By the autumn, however, it had become clear that the war against Germany would continue into 1945 and this realisation coincided with a sharp rise in expenditure due to heavy fighting in northwest Europe and along the Gothic Line in Italy.

Both Fifth and Eighth Armies depended massively on fire power, but the Americans especially. Alex now had enough ammunition for his current Eighth Army operations and for an all-out offensive in December lasting about fifteen days. American ammunition, on the other hand, was sufficient for only about ten days of intensive fighting. The ammunition crisis was also why Alex was already, at the end of October, beginning to think almost entirely in terms of a spring offensive. 'Deliveries in the first quarter of the 1945 are so limited,' signalled Alex, 'that it will be necessary to exercise the strictest economy for several months to build up large enough stocks to sustain a full-scale offensive.'[293]

His other major problem was the critical shortage of manpower. Churchill had visited him in Italy in October, and had been predictably enthused by Alex's cross-Adriatic plan. On the back of their talks, the Prime Minister had asked Roosevelt for a further three US divisions; this, however, had been turned down flat. Alex now faced the prospect of losing yet more divisions to Greece, but by disbanding a number of light anti-aircraft and Royal Armoured Corps units he had managed to scrape together a further 17,000 troops. In August, he had converted 5,000 gunners into infantry as well. Clark had also been doing his best to get desperately needed troops. His four US divisions had been taking average losses of 550 a day in October, a staggeringly high figure, and so he had turned to General Devers, commanding Seventh Army in southern France, and whose forces were still cruising in comparison. Devers refused to help, so Alex turned directly to his old friend Eisenhower. 'My last chance is to appeal to you personally,' he wrote. 'Anything you can do to help Clark will be to our mutual advantage.'[294] Eisenhower immediately agreed to divert 3,000 troops from US Seventh Army in France.

It was still not enough, and now, to make matters worse, desertions were beginning to become a massive problem. The death sentence for desertion had been lifted back in 1930, and so for many, surviving the war with the risk of penal servitude was better than risking their lives stranded in the mountains fighting for a cause that seemed increasingly senseless: since Italy was so obviously now a sideshow, it was felt by some that the Russians and those fighting in northwest Europe could carry the can from now on. Fear of letting down one's mates tended to be a powerful prevention for desertion, but it only needed a few to break the mould and the rot soon set in.

Sergeant Reg Harris had a taste of this in his section back in August. After an attack, one of his men went missing, yet they never found his body: he hadn't been reported as wounded and they never received word from the Germans that he had been taken prisoner. 'So either he had crawled into a hole without his body being found,' noted Reg, 'or he had gone native, as some soldiers did, especially if they had an Italian girlfriend whose family were willing to hide him.' Later, as they were crossing the Arno, another new member of his section, Guardsman Law, actually told Reg he was going to desert the following day when they were due to make an attack. Reg was furious and told him that if he tried to leave them in the middle of a fight, he would shoot him first. Far better, Reg told him, if he deserted now, at night, then they could get a better chap in his place. 'Telling him I would shoot him was not a bluff,' says Reg. 'By that time we had become very hard, and I'm quite certain if he had let us down I would have shot him, terrible as it seems thinking about it today.'

In the German forces, non-German troops often deserted in droves. One of the Stella Rossa's battalions had been almost entirely made up of Russian deserters, while numerous Polish troops fighting for the Germans crept over the lines, gave themselves up and then continued fighting for II Polish Corps instead. Desertion amongst German troops, on the other hand, was rare due to a number of factors including pride, fear of severe punishment, and differences of culture between German and Allied troops, although hoping for or indeed inflicting a wound that would get them home was common enough, especially now that they could all sense the war was drawing to a close. In Franz Maassen's first gruppe, getting such a wound had become something of a joke amongst them. 'Alfred Glander, for example,' noted Franz, 'discovered a new trick for getting a self-inflicted wound. He lies on his back in the foxhole, stretches out his foot with the tip of his boot and shouts, "Shrapnel over here!" Naturally, we all laugh at his discovery and every single one of us wishes for a splinter like this.' A couple of days later, as Franz noted, one of his men was lucky enough to be wounded by a piece of shrapnel. "Boss, it got me!" the man shouted with glee. 'I bind up his thigh,' added Franz, 'where he has got a big flesh wound and he's so happy that he can leave. The lad is nineteen years old.'

Stan Scislowski and most of his mates in Dog Company found themselves hoping for what they called a 'holiday wound' – 'a wound just serious enough to get us out of action for a couple of weeks,' wrote Stan, 'or better still, a couple of months. It got so I'd even settle for a wound serious enough to give me a trip back to Blighty.'[295] He'd arrived in Italy with vague ideas of winning a VC, but those ambitions had long gone. Now he would have been only too happy to finish the war in an unheroic rear-echelon job; anything that would get him away from the front and the likelihood of getting himself killed.

Humour – black or otherwise – was an important part of the infantryman's life. In the 3rd Coldstream Guards there was a man called Guardsman Arthur Quiney. 'In every platoon,' says Reg Harris, 'there were men with pet ailments – some had bad backs, some bad stomachs, but Quiney was a martyr to his feet.' During one attack, Quiney had been badly hit in the arms and chest, and afterwards, as he waited to be taken back to the field dressing station, he looked terrible – covered in blood and bandages, and missing chunks of flesh. Major Crichton then came over to him and asked him how he was. 'Not too bad, Sir,' Quiney replied. Crichton assured him all would be well as an ambulance was on his way. 'Thank God for that, Sir,' said Quiney, brightening. 'My bloody feet are killing me!'

Kendall Brooke had two inveterate gamblers in his platoon, Andrew Savage and David Quinan. 'They never drew a cent out of their pay books,' says Kendall, 'they lived on everybody else's.' On Monte Pezze, when his patrol had been perched on a ledge near the summit, Kendall watched some of his men playing poker. One of them, Private Futter, picked a straight flush, and he was clearly delighted that at long last he now had a chance to settle old scores with Quinan and Savage. 'And that was the moment this bloody shell came over our heads,' says Kendall. 'Everyone dived and he threw away his straight flush. It took him an hour before he stopped cursing everyone from Field Marshal Smuts to the gunner who'd fired the shell.'

Humour helped ease tension, while the intense camaraderie that developed between the men of a section, group or platoon played a huge part in ensuring men continued to battle on day after day, night after night, while facing constant life-threatening danger. Men also of course became hardened – both physically to the conditions in which they found themselves and also to the appalling sights they witnessed.

The Gothic Line battles had seen some of the fiercest fighting and worst conditions of the entire campaign. In October, Kendall Brooke spent twenty-five days with only one night under cover. 'That was tough,' he says, particularly as it had rained almost every day, and often torrentially so. Almost constantly wet through, living off monotonous rations and confronted by thick, glutinous mud whenever they weren't on hard rock – this was the soldier's lot, repeated all across the front line. Casualties in September and October had been higher than at any point during the whole campaign – worse even than those suffered during the battles at Cassino. Fifth Army's four US divisions in the line – and not including the 6th South African Armoured Division or XIII Corps – had lost 25,758 men since 10 September, well over half their strength. The 88th Division had lost an appalling 9,167, of which over 5,000 were battle casualties and the rest due to illness and combat fatigue. Considering the number of infantrymen in a full-strength US infantry division was around 9,250 men in 1944, this represented almost 100 per cent losses.* It was brutal. 'You had to deal with problems like food and other supplies not always coming through,' says Kendall, 'and simply make the best of it in terms of your own personal comfort. You became tremendously hard; you had your pack on your back and your Tommy gun and your gear, and you could slog your way up and down mountains with the Italian mud on your boots. You could keep going and you were very hardy.'

But most men could only keep going for so long. Almost everyone who served in Italy for any length of time became a casualty at one time or other. And at some point, as Stan Scislowski had discovered, the deprivations and violence, the loss of friends and comrades, and the strain of wondering whether the next minute would be your last, became too much. Something would snap. 'It takes a special kind of courage to

---

*Figures for 1943 suggest that a full-strength US Infantry Division consisted of 14,253 men, of which 9,354 were infantry. The rest were artillery and auxiliary units, medical staff, chaplains and divisional headquarters staff.

keep on going when all hell's flying about every which way,' noted Stan, 'and men are dying brutally all around you.'[296] He reckoned there was not a single moment when under shell or mortar fire that he was not scared almost witless. Yet some people found being in combat less frightening. Reg Harris, for one, was never unduly troubled by nerves or gripped by terror. He was, however, a rarity. As a battle-hardened NCO, Franz Maassen was the kind of soldier who provided the bedrock of any infantry battalion, yet fear certainly played tricks with him. 'One's got experience of what wounds and pain mean and this memory is always in one's head,' he noted. 'Every time I was under attack and I thought back to my old wounds, I always felt the burning and the hot shell splinter in my hip. And to keep going with this in one's head, one really does need courage.'

Back in July, Reg Harris had recognised that one of their toughest section leaders had reached a point where his nerves were now in tatters. They were to take a ridge beyond a village, and it was the turn of Corporal Sessford's section to lead the attack. As Sessford came up, Reg could see he was trembling uncontrollably. 'Are you all right, Sess?' Reg asked.

'Of course I am,' Sessford snapped back.

'But he wasn't,' says Reg, 'and he knew it.' Worse, he knew that Reg could tell. For a man of Sessford's experience and pride this was too much to bear.

Sessford had led the attack, and Reg's platoon had followed soon after. It had been a tough fight, but the ridge had been taken. Only afterwards did Reg learn that Sessford had been killed whilst making a suicidal leap directly in front of the German positions. Machine-gun fire had cut him down immediately. 'I believe it was his fear of being seen to be afraid that made him do it,' says Reg, 'and yet I would say he was one of the bravest men I've met, because it's easy for someone who feels no fear to do brave deeds, but Sess was scared stiff.'

Fifth Army may have ceased offensive operations for the time being, but along Eighth Army's front, the battle for Forlì was about to begin, and leading the charge were the partisans of the 8th Garibaldi Brigade, and more specifically, Iader Miserocchi's 2nd Battalion. Leaving Meldola on the night of 31 October, Iader and his men, accompanied by the brigade commander, Italo Morandi, were involved in two heavy engagements around the airfield and pushed on to successfully reach the village of

Carpena barely a mile outside the city. Remaining in the village through-out 1 November, they were joined that evening at Carpena by the men of the other three battalions. Having now linked up with the partisans within the city, they planned that night to enter the city and take control.

Just as they were about to launch their attack, however, word arrived from one of their *staffette* that the Allies had ordered them to fall back to Meldola, eight miles to the south. 'This order surprised us,' they recorded in their military bulletin, 'since each of us was preparing worth-ily to fulfil his duty, prepared to do anything to swiftly liberate our brothers who were still under the yoke of Nazifascism, whilst at the same time helping the advance of the Allied troops, saving their time and their men.'[297] Iader was furious. 'We were very disillusioned,' he says. 'We fought believing we truly were Allies. Instead the English, partly because we were Communists and partly because Forlì was the Duce's city, wanted to liberate it themselves.'

The partisans had reckoned there were only around two thousand German troops around Forlì, but that was before both the 356th and 278th Divisions had been pulled back nearer to the city, and before Lemelsen had ordered up reinforcements of artillery. Anxious though the 8th Garibaldi men had been to take the city, they might have soon found themselves facing far stiffer resistance than they had initially expected.

That Lemelsen had been able to reinforce Forlì had been because V Corps' advance had once again been confounded by particularly heavy rain; however, by the beginning of the month units of the British 4th Division had begun arriving opposite the German positions. Among the defenders was Franz Maassen, who now found himself being ordered to his battalion commander's headquarters to be briefed for an un-usual and extremely dangerous mission. 'It's lucky you're not blonde and you've got dark hair like me,' Hauptmann Kurz told him conver-sationally. 'We both look like Ites.' Franz was confused, but then his commander came to the point. 'This evening, you're coming with me behind enemy lines, across to the Tommy in civilian clothes. I've got no air reconnaissance and I need to know how strong the Tommy is – whether he's got tanks, whether he's about to attack and so on.' He then told Franz to get rid of any personal identification, including his dog tags. Nor were they to take any weapons. 'Are you ready to do this?' Kurz asked him.

'Yes, Herr Hauptman,' Franz replied.

'And another thing,' Kurz added, 'if anyone catches us, we'll be up against a wall.'

It was raining and pitch black as they went across no-man's-land, but as they neared the enemy lines they had to work their way around spotlights that had been set up to protect the British against night attacks. Reaching a village safely, they noted four tanks, then pressed on. Franz was soaked to the skin and with his heart still racing, was desperate for a cigarette to calm his nerves. Kurz could speak fluent Italian, but Franz knew barely a word, and when they met an Italian man, he looked at them with surprise. For a second, Franz froze, but Kurz said something and the man passed by.

By the time they had counted various artillery batteries and several columns of infantry, it was beginning to get light, and so they lay up all day in a wood. Franz was amazed how easily Kurz was able to sleep. 'Has the guy got no nerves?' he noted, unable to sleep himself when Kurz took his turn to keep watch. 'Is it excitement? Fear? Are my nerves overstretched?' he wrote. 'To be sure I must be tired enough.'

Once night came again, they set off back, crawling past the British spotlights and safely through their own lines. Franz had already won an Iron Cross 2nd Class for his work on the River Ronco, but now Kurz took him back to his battalion HQ and, patting him on the shoulder, said, 'Maassen, today you have earned the Iron Cross 1st Class'. 'I hadn't really got that impression,' Franz noted modestly.

Meanwhile, in her cell at Tavarnelle, Carla Costa was confounding Special Agent Mason and the team of the 306th Counter Intelligence Corps Detachment. Although she was found to be alert, intelligent, and mature for her seventeen years, they also discovered she was a young woman with more fervent Fascist beliefs than anyone they had ever encountered during their thirteen months in Italy. 'She is,' wrote Mason, 'utterly unafraid of death.'

Although she was kept in a locked cell, the trio of special agents trying to break her had army nurses stay by her side at all times, hoping that if they showed her special care and kindness she might respond positively. It did nothing. They gave her writing material, but with these she simply wrote endless reams of Fascist propaganda, Fascist songs and epitaphs to herself. 'Here lies Carla Costa, perverse Fascist,' she scribbled. 'Do not pray for him [sic], because it is time wasted.' On another sheet, she scribbled, 'Fascist Carla Costa was born and died a sinner.'[298]

It had taken two days to get her to confess to even the information they indisputably already knew, and over a week until she began to let slip anything that might be useful. Graphic details of Fascist atrocities did not affect her in the slightest. Nor did hour upon hour of questioning. Only on 4 November, having been grilled intensively for nearly two weeks, and having been confronted by a mass of specially collated evidence against her, did she finally give a complete and full confession. 'Despite her youth and sex,' it was written in her report, '[the] subject has proven herself the most stubborn and tenacious enemy agent or suspect whom CIC, 5th Army, has encountered in the course of its work in Italy, during which period Agents of this Detachment have handled and interrogated thousands of espionage and other types of suspects, ranging from Italian Fascist generals, German Army officers and every shade and pattern of Fascist *gerarchi*, to peasants, farmers, peddlers, pimps and prostitutes.'[299]

Despite this, despite her avowed allegiance to the Fascist cause, and despite hers being an entirely open-and-shut case, the American counter-intelligence team suggested she be locked up until the end of the war and then set free. Carla had been preparing herself to face the firing squad, but instead found leniency and, perhaps, even the grudging respect of her interrogators.

Although Fifth Army had ceased offensive operations, the front was never entirely inactive. Periodic barrages – or 'stonks' to use the soldier's parlance – of mortar- and shell-fire kept the men alert, while every night troops on both sides would be sent out on patrol, both to observe the enemy and to try and capture a few prisoners.

On 6 November, Kendall Brooke was in charge of a standing patrol along a mountain path that actually ran into the Monte Sole massif, half way between Monte Salvaro and Monte Sole itself. 'It was a path that ran along a ridge,' he says, 'and if the enemy was going to make any move against us up there, it would have had to have been down that track.' The path ran through a narrow cutting; above was a knoll called simply 'Point 512'. Kendall and his men had taken over from a British Guards patrol the previous night and during the day, using the knoll as cover, they had clambered down to a farmhouse some four hundred yards beneath them. 'I went inside this farm,' says Kendall, 'and there was a sight that has stayed with me ever since.' Lined up on the grass outside the house were the bodies of twelve women who had obviously been lined up and shot. 'One had a child in her arms,' he says. 'They'd mainly fallen over face down, but the one with the child was lying face up. They'd obviously been there for a while and were getting a bit high. The house had been ransacked and there wasn't a man in sight.'

In fact, they'd been there more than five weeks, ever since the rastrellamento on Monte Sole. Kendall and his men had unwittingly stumbled upon some of the victims at an outlying barn of the village of San Martino.

Kendall never had a chance to tell anyone about his gruesome discovery. Later that night, he and his men were due to be relieved, but just as the relief had arrived, Kendall was called up to the command post by the two men manning the machine gun. They thought they had heard something, but then they had thought they'd heard something the night before; despite crawling all over the place, they had found nothing. 'It's peculiar in the mountains,' says Kendall, 'you're never quite sure where the sounds are coming from.' They listened for a while, but heard nothing more, and then Kendall met up with the relief officer and took him forward to show him where the booby traps were. Somehow, Kendall was ahead of him, however, and suddenly realised there *were* other men up there. 'I literally bumped into these Germans,' he says. 'It was very dark. One was very highly trained and reactions were completely instinctive, so I just dived at these guys.' He was grappling with one of them, who, it turned out, was an officer, and was much smaller than him. One of the others hit Kendall over the head with the butt of his machine pistol and then fired at almost point-blank range.

Fortunately, the machine pistol jammed after firing one round, but that one bullet went straight through the side of Kendall's face and out the other side. 'I really did see stars,' he says, 'and there was an immediate rush of blood down my throat and I felt as though the whole of the front of my face had been blown off.' There was no sense of panic, however. 'I thought I'd be dead, but I was quite calm about it,' he admits. 'It's a profoundly interesting experience – although not one I'd recommend. I thought of my parents and regretted how sad they were going to be and I wished I could have said something to them. But there was no sense of fear. None at all.' Nor was he in pain; rather he felt stunned. Blood was 'pissing everywhere' and he thought they would leave him, but instead they dragged him off.

It had all happened so quickly. For a brief moment there had been utter confusion. The Germans had scurried away before Kendall's men had had a chance to properly react. Taken to the battalion headquarters just beneath Monte Sole, incredibly, he never, at any point, lost consciousness. Once there, he was given a mirror and in the flickering light of a fire saw the appalling mess that his face had become. 'I had a grotesquely swollen head,' he says, 'and of course there was blood everywhere. I hardly recognised myself.' He was then bundled into a kübelwagen with the officer who had captured him sitting up front, a guard next to him, and a blanket thrown over his head. Strangely, although they took the binoculars around his neck, they never searched him – had they done so they would have found a number of maps in the inside pocket of his leather jerkin. Instead, he had the extraordinary presence of mind to tear off bits of his maps and notations and surreptitiously throw them out of the side of the car. By the time he reached the hospital, he had destroyed the lot.

After ten days he had miraculously recovered enough to be interrogated by the SS. Playing dumb, they soon gave up on him. 'They thought I was just a rather unintelligent, ill-informed junior officer,' says Kendall, 'which was fortunate because actually I knew that our offensive had been called off.' His interrogations over, he was sent as a POW to Germany.

At Liano, Hans Golda had been enjoying a few quiet days. The rain was pouring down but this at least kept the jabos at bay, and allowed him and his men the chance to get to know the locals and, over a few glasses of wine in the evening, try and forget about the war for a few precious moments.

However, the moment the skies cleared the jabos were over again – this time silver American fighter-bombers. The 9th Battery on the left of Hans' position were badly hit, and their cellar command post blown in, trapping a number of their men. Hans and his men hurried over to help, frantically digging away the rubble as quickly as they could. 'The head of the battery officer was seen,' noted Hans. 'He was still alive and yelled, "Get me out!", then he went white; he was dead.' As they dug they could hear the screams of the men buried below, but gradually, one by one, the shouting stopped. 'We were standing at the grave of twenty-four young German soldiers,' wrote Hans, 'buried alive.' As darkness fell, they managed to bring out the first of the bodies, but the job took three days to complete. By that time, those killed had begun to rot. 'The smell of the bodies was unimaginable,' scribbled Hans. 'People were throwing up as they worked.'

Then their own position was hit – a bomb landing by the window of the church crypt. One of his men had his legs crushed and was trapped with one of the nuns lying on top of him. Another sister was pulled out alive, as was the half-naked and badly wounded village school teacher; her mother, however, had been killed, and so had the Mother Superior. Clearly, it was too dangerous for the remaining civilians to stay in Liano any longer. 'All the civilians were then transported away in the VW,' noted Hans. Then he added wistfully, 'They had become our friends.'

Back at Forlì, the British were finally preparing to attack on the night of 7 November. In the meantime, however, Franz Maassen and his men were ordered to creep forward towards an isolated house where they were to act as observers and look-outs for when the British attack came. 'At what point should we fall back?' Franz asked the new and inexperienced officer.

'When you see an overwhelming amount of enemy,' the officer told him.

'What do you consider overwhelming?' Franz asked.

'Thirty or so,' came the reply.

Franz had barely set up his machine-gun teams in the upstairs of the house when he saw many more than thirty men pushing forward and so he gave the order to fall back. On his return to the battalion, however, he was severely reprimanded by Hauptman Kurz, who immediately ordered them to go back to the house, but this time with the officer as well. Struggling forward, they got to the house once more with the British having almost reached the other side. Franz's gruppe were now completely outnumbered and after firing a few rounds and pushing the British front troops back, they once more scurried to the safety of their lines. 'The officer in charge was roasted by Kurz,' says Franz. 'I always made sure I had my orders very precisely and although I was given hell, Kurz knew it wasn't my decision.' But Kurz did accuse the officer of cowardice, and later that night, the young *leutnant* slipped over to the British lines and gave himself up. 'I suppose he thought he might be court-martialled,' says Franz. 'Anyway, he told the British about our positions.'

That same night, without the usual artillery barrage preceding them,

4th Division crept across the airfield. Having almost reached the German lines undetected they were then involved in confused and heavy fighting, but by morning the battle was all but over. Whether the German officer's treachery made matters worse for Franz or not, he and his men found themselves surrounded and forced to surrender. It was a bitter blow, and despite the stealth and weight of the British attack, Franz was convinced that had they not been betrayed, they would have been able to pull out successfully. Like Kendall Brooke, he would spend the rest of the war as a POW. At least, however, they were both alive.

So too was the recently promoted Captain Peter Moore, despite the enormously high casualties amongst his fellow officers. The 46th Division had taken over from 10th Indian south of Forlì, and after the city finally fell on 9 November, pushed on towards Faenza, nine miles further on towards Bologna along the Via Emilia.

Not only was he now a captain, he also had a Military Cross to his name, awarded for his part in the night assault across the River Foglia at the beginning of the Gothic Line battles. 'I felt the same sensation of pleasurable surprise,' he wrote, 'that I had in the summer term at Oundle when I was awarded my first XI cricket colours.' Nonetheless, there were feelings of guilt too – that he should have been awarded one when other men who he felt were equally deserving had received no recognition at all.

And he felt further pangs of guilt too after stopping at a large wine co-operative store on their approach to Faenza. Discovering ample vats of wine in a deserted barn, the temptation was too great, even though he had no clear idea of what he would do with it. Arranging for one of their sizeable 15-hundredweight water wagons to drive over to the vats, they then filled the tanker with the stuff and drove off. 'This appalling practice, of which I had just been guilty,' he noted, 'was not known as looting, but as liberating and was regarded as a legitimate form of war reparation.'[300] It was not something Peter had taken much part in before, however, and a sense of shame and regret began preying on his mind.

Around the same time, four young Italian girls were blown up and killed when they detonated a German mine near where the Leicesters were dug in some three miles short of Faenza, a tragedy that Peter felt keenly. He was feeling increasingly sorry for the Italians, and believed they had now more than paid for Mussolini's mistakes. 'It is a strange sight,' he wrote in a letter to his parents, 'a country where every station,

every powerhouse and all its services are completely ruined. Italy will
have to start again from very scratch after the war.'[301] Peter could not
have been more right.

THIRTY-FOUR

The Partisan Crisis
November–December 1944

On the night of 3 November, an RAF Liberator of 148 Squadron, containing three agents and a number of supply canisters, left Brindisi and flew north towards the Apennines. Two of the agents were Italians recruited by No 1 Special Force, SOE, but the third was a young but already highly decorated soldier and SOE operative, twenty-four-year-old Major John Barton, DSO, MC.

John Barton's task – codenamed 'Cisco/Red' – was either to capture or assassinate a senior German general,* whose headquarters was reportedly near Mirandola, a town in the central plains a few miles south of the River Po. As arranged, fires had been lit for them at the drop zone. Parachuting from 3,000 feet, all three landed safely at around 10 p.m., as did all but one of the canisters. On the ground, John was met by Major Wilcockson, a fellow SOE agent, and a number of partisans, and taken to a safe house in the tiny mountain village of Gova, some forty miles west of Bologna.

Once there, the two Italians left on their mission to Bologna, while Wilcockson and the partisan commanders examined the contents of the supply drop. Although pleased with the weapons and ammunition, Wilcockson was exasperated by the absence of boots and clothing, especially since the equipment had been padded by hundreds of useless sandbags. Most of the partisans in his area had few clothes other than those they had left home with. Some had items of British uniforms, but with a long month of heavy rain and rapidly falling temperatures, they were all desperately short of heavy clothing, boots and great coats. Living rough in barns and caves in the freezing cold mountains was an utterly miserable and sometimes life-threatening existence.

---

*Barton never mentions his target's name in his report, referring to him only as 'General X'. However, it was most likely to have been either von Vietinghoff or Lemelsen.

The following day, John was led to a neighbouring mission, that of another agent, Major Johnstone. There he waited several days for a guide, but since he could speak neither German nor Italian, he also took the opportunity to form a small squad of men to accompany him on his mission – an ex-POW as an interpreter, a former Italian paratrooper, and a German-Italian who assured him he could pass as a German.

The day they left, an Allied drop was made over Johnstone's area. 'It was pathetic!' wrote John. The containers had been dropped from too great a height, had been spread over a vast area – some falling into German hands – and half the parachutes had not opened, so that much of the ammunition was ruined. 'Wilcockson said he received some ancient Italian rifles from this drop,' wrote John, 'and that they were far more dangerous to the firers than to the person fired at.'[302]

After three days' walk, John Barton and his squad reached the edge of the mountains overlooking Reggio Emilia. They were now in a German-Fascist controlled area and had to continue at night. The others wanted John to ditch his uniform, but incredibly, he had been ordered to keep it on throughout his mission and so refused to change into civvies. This, it seems, was too much for the German-Italian, who promptly left them.

Using borrowed bicycles, they headed down from the mountains towards the centre of Reggio. John had noticed there was hardly any traffic on the road, and what there was had been very old and very noisy and easy to avoid, particularly as it was night-time. Once in Reggio itself, they were stopped by a German bicycle patrol, but they simply pedalled away and down a side road before the soldiers could unsling their rifles and open fire.

Earlier in the day, the Allies had attempted to bomb the railway station, missed completely and had destroyed a number of houses round about. In the ruins of one of these John and his squad found an ideal hide-out for a few days. From there, John was also able to observe the station. A train that was unloading goods, he learned, could travel no more than ten miles due to destroyed bridges on the route. He also made contact with the local GAP commandant, and arranged for a guide to take them to Modena, the next port of call on their journey.

They left on bicycles during the evening three days later, although now without the Italian paratrooper. Having changed into civvies, he had gone to see a friend and had been stopped by a patrol. His papers had been in order but he had been caught carrying a pistol. 'Foolish man!' noted John. 'We did not see him again.'

Once more travelling by the half light of the moon, they cycled to Modena, passing a long two-mile horse-drawn German column. No one paid them the slightest attention. Nor did they in Modena. Rather, the biggest danger they had so far faced came from Allied bombing and strafing of both the towns and roads on which they travelled. A few days later, and still on their bicycles, John, along with the former POW and their latest guide, headed north towards Mandola. 'Unfortunately,' reported John, 'the partisans had ambushed a small party of Germans on the road we had hoped to use and the Germans were very busy burning houses, searching everywhere and shooting people. Seventy-five houses were burned to the ground.'[303]

Taking a detour, they followed the route of the River Secchio until they reached Concordia, a few miles from Mirandola. There, local partisans advised them to head east, towards Ferrara. After several rides through the night, they reached the Ferrara area and made contact with the partisan commandant. Eager to help, he produced a number of German prisoners and Russian deserters, whom John interrogated in turn. None, however, could tell him where the elusive general was based.

Despite this, John was determined not to give up, even though he had now spent nearly a month in the field, and despite the extremely tense and dangerous situation in which he found himself. 'The whole district was being continually searched and pillaged,' he wrote, 'and the few partisans had a very thin time living in their holes. Many were captured and shot immediately.' He had noticed that everywhere there was an atmosphere of fear and distrust. Fascist militia and Black-shirts were, he reported, quite ruthless, burning houses and shooting suspects without blinking. Torture was also 'quite normal'. On the other hand, as Bruno Vailati had observed in the Romagna Mountains, Germans took no notice of these practices unless one of their own troops was killed, at which point they would respond with frightening and ruthless efficiency. Nor, as far as he could tell, was being a Fascist a safeguard against German pillaging. 'As yet,' he noted, 'the Germans have not completely stripped the countryside, but are doing it slowly and systematically.' Most Italians, he observed, were desperately short of food and basic goods, and pathetically poor. 'Everywhere,' he added, 'the question is, "When are the Allies coming? We cannot hold out much longer!"'[304]

*   *   *

John Barton's mission had coincided with a time of crisis for the partisans. Throughout the summer, when the days had been long, hot and dry, their strength had risen and supplies from the Allies had been plentiful. Victory, it was widely expected, was just around the corner. It was why the partisans in the Apuans had acted with such defiant arrogance towards the 16th Waffen-SS before the massacre at Sant' Anna; it was why Lupo had remained so confident on Monte Sole.

But that victory had not come, and now they faced a long, bitter winter. Living in caves and barns was tough but bearable when the nights were warm and dry, and when there was fruit on the trees and a good harvest being collected. Surviving in freezing temperatures, in the rain and snow, and with food more scarce than ever, was a different matter altogether. It was a gloomy prospect and one that was made worse by the lessening of supplies, which had suffered as a result of the pinch imposed on the Mediterranean Command, and also because of the weather. Six hundred tons of supplies had been due to be dropped during October, but only seventy-three tons had actually been delivered. It was why partisan commanders and their SOE and OSS liaison officers were so upset when drops were inaccurate or half empty and filled with sand bags rather than something useful.

The onset of winter and the shortage of supplies had also come at a time of increased anti-partisan measures by General Wolff. Kesselring had been alarmed by even greater increases of partisan activity throughout September. 'Supply traffic severely handicapped,' he wrote, 'and acts of sabotage become more and more frequent. This pest must be countered.' In the Alps, several partisan bands had even experimented in local self-government by declaring whole areas to be independent republics, such as the Republic of Domdossola in the Val d'Ossola, which was declared on 26 September.

This was intolerable to Kesselring and four days later he instructed Wolff to carry out an 'Anti-partisan Week' using not only all SS police available but also any tactical reserves, supply and rear-echelon troops, Italian militia and any other forces he could lay his hands on. 'The Anti-partisan Week,' Kesselring told Wolff, 'must make finally clear to the partisan bands the extent of our power, and the fight against these bands must be carried out with the utmost severity.'[305]

Wolff's operations lasted until the end of the month, and by the end of them the short-lived Republic of Domdossola had been crushed, 1,539 partisans were dead, 1,248 had been taken prisoner, a further 1,973 suspects had been captured, and 2,012 had been rounded up for Organisation Todt. For the Alpine partisans, these operations had been a major setback.

The CLNAI were also keenly aware of the potential dangers that now faced them, and strongly believed that even greater unity was the key to survival. The problem was that the struggle between the political factions was threatening to undermine this goal. General Cadorna, for example, having been given no firm remit from the Allies and little authority from the CLNAI, had found his hands horribly tied in his role as military advisor to the Corps of Volunteers of Freedom and consequently he achieved little. Conscious of this, Ferruccio Parri and Leo Valiani of the CLNAI had met the head of SOE Italy, Colonel Roseberry, in Lugano in Switzerland at the end of October. Roseberry pressed for the Italians to define more clearly Cadorna's role and to place him in charge of a unified military command in the north – one that included command of all the Garibaldi brigades as well as the Green Flame and non-political bands. The CLNAI, in turn, demanded political recognition from the Allies. The result of the meeting was SOE's recommendation to the Allies that a meeting be held between them and the CLNAI in Rome.

Before the CLNAI delegation could reach Rome, however, a further blow befell the partisans, and ironically, it came from none other than Alexander, one of their champions. Deeply concerned about the potential plight of the resistance movement, he now saw no point in them wasting their lives until the next major offensive was launched, when he hoped they would once more be able to give direct help to the Allied forces.

With this in mind, on 13 November, he made a radio proclamation on *Italia Combatte* to all the partisans of the north, asking them to lay down their arms, to conserve ammunition, and to wait for further instructions. However well intentioned Alexander's proclamation may have been, it was greeted with utter despair by the partisans. Outrage filled the columns of southern newspapers. The Action Party paper, *Italia Libera,* charged that a return to underground resistance was not only 'morally wrong but practically impossible', and made the point that the fight against the Nazi-Fascists was not 'a summer sport that can be called off at a moment's notice'.[306]

The announcement coincided with a more placatory approach from General Wolff, who had always been cautious about applying 'extreme measures'. Indeed, despite 'Anti-partisan Week', Wolff had urged Mussolini to declare an amnesty to partisans, and in October claimed to have brought as many as 80,000 partisans back to the cities and into regular occupations. 'I had obtained the assurances of the fanatical Fascist police of Pavolini,' he said, 'that these people, if they returned to their homes and took up normal lives again, would not be bothered by members of the Fascist Police.'[307] Indeed, while battles continued against the partisans, there were noticeably fewer mass executions of the kind that had blighted the summer, and as part of his efforts not to antagonise the majority of the pro-partisan population further, the misguided reports of Black Brigade actions in the Republican press were also dropped. On the other hand, the Fascist press was quick to report the 'callousness' of the Allies for 'cynically leaving the partisans to their fate'.[308]

Wolff's figures were a gross exaggeration, but his approach, with the winter weather on his side, was definitely paying off. Alex's statement had undoubtedly been a terrible own-goal. In truth, it had not been properly thought through, as General Harding later admitted. Nor had they referred the matter to SOE or OSS, or even the Italian government, before making the statement. It was uncharacteristic of Alexander who was normally so assured in matters of diplomacy, and in fact, came at a time when he and others in Italy were doing as much as they possibly could to safeguard the partisan movement in Italy.

Indeed, after Colonel Roseberry's encounter with Parri and Valiani in Lugano, Alex had written a detailed report outlining the urgent need to give increased support to the partisans and to give greater recognition to the CLNAI. This forced a major and long overdue re-evaluation at AFHQ of their attitudes towards the Italian resistance and its part in the future of the north. At the same time, back in London, Lord Selborne, the Minister for Economic Welfare, had also taken up the cause of the Italian resistance, based on information received from both Alexander and No 1 Special Force. Writing to Churchill, he pointed out that public opinion was behind them – as Kesselring was also keenly aware – and that future Allied relations with the Italians in the north would be affected by the support they gave the partisans now. Winter would be hard for them. Without urgent supplies, the partisans and their existing SOE and OSS missions would face collapse and be exposed to terrible reprisals. At the same time, the Allies in Italy would be depriving themselves of a valuable weapon. 'When you have called a Maquis out into open warfare,' he told the Prime Minister, 'it is not fair to let it drop like a hot potato. These men have burned their boats and have no retreat.'[309]

Churchill agreed and demanded the situation be rectified. So too did General McNarney, Jumbo Wilson's American deputy, so that despite Air Marshal Slessor's belief that supply dropping in Italy was a wasted effort, an increase in supply was agreed upon. The US 51st Troop Carrier Wing was even diverted from operations in the Balkans, and as a result there was an increase in the amount of supplies airlifted.

Unwittingly, however, Alexander's proclamation of 13 November helped the Allies' negotiating hand when the CLNAI delegation arrived clandestinely in the south in the third week of November. Short of funds and supplies, having suffered from recent rastrellamenti, and with morale wavering, the CLNAI were desperate to improve their lot and so were now ready to make concessions to the Allies – concessions that several months before, during the height of their summer successes, they would never have considered. And as Alfredo Pizzoni, the chairman of the CLNAI, admitted to General Wilson, there were, they believed, at the end of November, only around 90,000 partisans, of whom just over half were in the towns and cities. Of these, about 40 per cent were armed, whilst in the mountains, they reckoned only a meagre 8 per cent carried weapons.

In addition to Pizzoni – a Milanese banker and one of the few non-party members of the movement – the delegation consisted of Ferruccio Parri of the Action Party, and Gian Carlo Pajetta, a veteran of the Spanish Civil War and the second most senior Communist within the CLNAI after Luigi Longo. What they wanted was official recognition as the agent of the Italian government in the occupied north, and to gain the acceptance of the CVL as a regular armed force to be integrated into the Italian Army, which would then avoid the demobilisation of partisan bands once the Allies arrived.

Both Macmillan and Alexander were now anxious to create a tripartite agreement between the CLNAI, the Supreme Allied Commander and the Bonomi government. The main concern for the Allies was the establishment of the Allied Military Government in liberated areas as the war was finally drawing to a close. The final stages of the campaign might move so fast that there would be 'empty spaces' occupied by local CLNs before the AMG could get there. How could the Allies be sure these partisan-led and politically varying committees would lay down arms and hand over power to AMG? The experience of the civil war that had so quickly evolved in Greece had burnt Allied – or rather, British – fingers. Even Alex, who was also keen to draw up an agreement with the CLNAI as soon as possible, had concerns about a repetition of the Greek situation. 'The operations of SOE [and OSS] in arming nearly 100,000 so-called patriots,' he wrote, 'will produce the same revolutionary situation unless we devise a system for, immediately on the liberation of the territory, taking them in to either our or the Italian Army.'[310]

There was a major difference, however, between Italy and Greece and that was that the Communists in Italy, unlike EAM/ELAS* in Greece, had made it their policy to do everything in their power to avoid civil war once the Nazis and Fascists had been driven out of Italy. The post-Fascist revolution in Italy was to be achieved by the creation of a parliamentary democratic republic, which, they hoped, would be led by the Communists as supported by a majority of the voting population. Their task, during these months of resistance, was to build up a consensus of support. Thus it was that despite being the most radical of the major non-Fascist political parties, they were also the most willing to compromise, just as they had been back in the spring over the monarchy issue.

It was at this moment that a different kind of crisis struck the Italian government in the south. For several months, the parties forming the CLN – which made up the cabinet – had been beginning to split apart. Led by the socialists, the left was demanding social change, which included industrial and agrarian reform, the establishment of a socialist republic, and the purge of all former Fascists from public life. This latter change was already in hand, but it was the manner and degree in which this was being carried out that was causing a divergence of views; after all, every civil servant had had to hold a Fascist Party tessera to keep his job, but this did not mean they had been die-hard Fascists. Bonomi and the conservatives felt some leeway was needed and that the elimination of almost the entire governing class would not serve Italy well. Nor were they keen to prosecute Marshal Badoglio. Count Sforza, as High Commissioner for Sanctions Against Fascism, strongly disagreed, however, and demanded a complete purge, as did the other leftist members of the cabinet.

The second major point of conflict was over the position of the CLN. The six-party coalition had been formed by the Central CLN in Rome,

*EAM/ELAS – Ethnikón Apeleftherotikón Métopon-ethnikós Laïkós Apeleftherotikós Strátos, the Greek Communist-backed National Liberation Front/National Popular Liberation Army.

but Bonomi now believed that since the government, rather than AMG, ran most of the liberated country, he, as prime minister, represented the state, and was therefore responsible to the head of state – that is, the King and Prince Umberto – not the CLN. In this, he had the support of the Liberals but not the Actionists, Socialists or Communists, who believed it was the CLN, not the King, who represented the people, and were increasingly suspicious that Bonomi wanted to restore a pre-Fascist constitutional monarchy to which they had no intention of returning.

These issues festered and the split in differences widened, until on 25 November Bonomi tendered his resignation to Prince Umberto, having become exasperated with what he saw as repeated efforts of the extreme left to interfere and gain greater influence. The CLN were then forced to find a way of re-establishing a new cabinet. The Liberals conceded that it should have the authority of the CLN, and so Bonomi acquiesced on the matter, but over other matters compromises clearly needed to be made. With Count Sforza as the new chairman of the CLN, they began to try and form a new cabinet. Bonomi, it was hoped, would continue as prime minister, with Sforza as Minister for Foreign Affairs. Once again, however, the British objected to such an appointment, and although not a veto, it was couched in such a way that it could be interpreted as such, not only by the Italians, but also by the Americans.

An international storm followed. The British insisted they had merely been expressing an opinion, but the damage was done. With Britain's reserves of manpower falling sharply and with America's growth accelerating, this episode, on the surface so unimportant, demonstrated how much British influence was on the decline. America was now even more the senior partner. If Britain appeared to step out of line, it could no longer expect any closing of the ranks. In America there was stinging criticism, not just of the British stance in Italy, but also about its intervention in Greece. 'The Greek news is very bad,' noted Harold Macmillan wistfully in his diary at the beginning of 7 December, 'and so is the Italian. Greece has a revolution, and Italy is without a government. And in both cases we have drifted apart from our American ally.'[311] As luck would have it, both he and Alexander were in London at the time. Had Macmillan, especially, been in Italy, the whole matter might well have been resolved more easily.

And yet the whole debacle had, in many ways, a positive outcome. Bonomi agreed to accept the CLN's de facto position, but insisted on pledging allegiance to Prince Umberto as the 'Lieutenant General of the

Realm'. The purge issue also ended in victory for Bonomi and the conservatives. Sforza was offered the job of ambassador in Washington but turned it down; since he was affiliated to the Actionists, however, he remained, like the party, outside the cabinet, as did the Socialists. Bonomi's new four-party cabinet, sworn in on 12 December, strengthened Bonomi's position but also that of the Communists and the Christian Democrats. The crisis was over.

While this fiasco was carrying on, a bi-partite agreement had been drawn up between the Allies and the CLNAI, with Macmillan hoping the Italian government could be brought in at a later date once the dust had settled. On the Allies' part, they agreed to provide 160 million lire a month during the German occupation. Supplies would also be increased, and the CLNAI would be consulted on 'all matters relating to armed resistance, anti-scorch, and the maintenance of order'.[312] The Allies also agreed to recognise the CVL as the military arm of the CLNAI, and although Cadorna was to be appointed the official military commander of the Italian resistance, the partisans were to come under overall command of General Alexander and were to obey his instructions without question. When the war finally came to an end, the CLNAI was to maintain law and order *only* until the Allied Military Government could be established. Power would then be passed in turn to the established Italian government.

For the CLNAI – and especially the Action and Communist parties – these were harsh terms, but bruised and depleted as they were, and desperately short of cash, they were in no position to haggle. Alexander had them over a barrel and was determined to exert as much control as possible. The agreement was signed on 7 December, and on 26 December was reaffirmed by Bonomi's government. However humiliating this may have been for the leadership of the CLNAI, it was undoubtedly in the best interests of the future of the Allied campaign and of post-war Italy – and consequently in the best interests of the majority of Italians.

Meanwhile, Major John Barton was continuing his efforts to locate his elusive German general. 'We stayed at the house of a Fascist Captain of Militia,' he reported, 'who was a good Fascist by day and an even better partisan by night.' Running trucks of supplies between Bordeno and Verona, he carried arms one way for the partisans and for the Germans the other.

It was the captain who told John that his target was most likely in the Verona-Brescia area, much further to the north of the Po, and he offered to go to Verona to try and find out. The day after he left, John and his translator spotted three trucks of Fascist troops rumbling down the road. Deciding to play safe, they jumped out of windows at the back of the house and hid amongst the sugar beet in the field outside. It was as well that they did, because the Fascists stopped and searched the house. 'There was obviously a spy at work,' noted John, 'for the Fascists went to all the partisans' houses, found weapons, explosives etc, and took them all prisoner.' For some reason, however, the now disappeared GNR captain did not appear to be at the top of his list of suspects.

The rastrellamento went on for several days, during which time John and his translator lived in fields and begged for food from women and children. This experience clearly proved too much for his former POW side-kick, who one day walked out on him. 'When things cooled down again,' noted John, 'I found that all my partisan contacts had been taken or shot.' He hung around the area for a further ten days, but there was no sign of the captain, most of the civilians in the area had begun to suspect him, rather than the GNR captain, of being a German spy, and since he was now lousy and troubled by scabies, he decided to head back to base.

Having made his way back to the Modena area, he made contact with the partisans there, and asked them to send messages to Milan, Verona, and Venice asking for information on the whereabouts of the German general. Accompanied by an American air gunner who had bailed out a few days before, he headed back to the mountains, where he found Major Wilcockson still cursing the lack of clothing and medical supplies. After waiting a few days at Gova, John was guided south across Allied lines and back to safety. He had been away two months, and in that time had achieved nothing, but had learned much about both sides in German-occupied Italy, and about the conditions and fears in which the partisans and civilians alike lived. 'Everyone is terribly frightened of the Air Force,' he noted, 'the civilian population most of all.' He had spent Christmas Day with a man whose wife and child had been killed by a bomb falling in his back yard. 'To me it was just wanton jettisoning of bombs from aircraft returning home,' he wrote; 'to the civilians it is a very real terror.'[313]

He had also discovered a population torn apart by hunger, fear and mistrust. John had found the experience testing enough – both physically and mentally – yet he was a professional soldier, and despite the dangers, was able to return to a safer world at his mission's end – a world in which he would find clean clothes, a decent bed, food, drink and friends whom he trusted implicitly.

But in the towns and cities of the plains, and up in the mountains to the south, partisans were weakening by the day through lack of food and clothing, freezing in the appalling winter conditions and hunted down like dogs. Morale was low, disillusionment great, and the future very uncertain indeed.

THIRTY-FIVE

White Christmas
December 1944

After his arrest, the Jewish lawyer and partisan Emilio Sacerdote had been sent to Bolzano concentration camp in the Dolomites, run by the SS security forces. This was where all Italian Jews were sent before being moved on to camps within the Reich. As a Jew and a partisan, Emilio was put in Block L, the wing reserved for particularly dangerous inmates and where especially rough treatment could be expected. Hard manual labour was the order of the day, and his age – fifty-one – counted for nothing. 'Dearests,' he wrote to his wife and daughter, 'I haven't heard from you for a month. I am becoming more and more miserable, working along the road with shovels and pickaxes, snow or no snow. Please write to me.' Of course, they had been writing to him, but although he was permitted just two letters a month, these rarely reached him inside the camp.

Just three days later, on 14 December, he wrote to them again. As per instructions, it was brief. 'I am leaving for my new residence,' he told them.[314] Residence was hardly the word; he was in fact being shoved onto a cattle track along with 150 others, of whom eighty were also Jewish. Through the monochrome winter landscape a train took him to Flossenbürg, a concentration camp in Germany where more than 50,000 prisoners had already died.

The cycle of men flowing in and out of Italy continued amongst the armed forces too. At the end of November, Peter Moore had been resigned to facing a testing winter in Italy, but then suddenly the Leicesters had been taken out of the line and transported by truck all the way south to Bari. On arrival, the men debussed and the cooks quickly began preparing food and tea. Local water was never drunk, so the men ambled over to the water wagons to fill up their water bottles – water that had to be used for drinking but also shaving. Peter was having a mug of tea when a runner from another company came up and handed over a note from Major Fisher. 'A bold little wine,' ran the note, 'perhaps rather coarse. Does not travel well. Recommended for shaving but not drinking.' Peter's wine-filled water wagon had finally been discovered. It was an episode that would take him a long time to live down.

The Leicesters were on their way to Greece to combat EAM/ELAS, and soon the rest of the division would follow. Thus Alexander would soon lose yet another of his seasoned divisions.

Von Vietinghoff was losing men too, however – the 16th Waffen-SS were about to leave Italy for Hungary. And there were other changes, in the areas of command. Lemelsen's replacement at AOK 14, General Ziegler, had been wounded in a partisan ambush, so General Herr of 76th Corps, had taken over the reins until the arrival of General Kurt von Tippelskirch in December. Even more significant, however, were the changes in the Allied command. On 4 November, Field Marshal Sir John Dill, Head of the British Military Mission in Washington, had died, and the Prime Minister had no hesitation in appointing General Jumbo Wilson as his successor, and suggesting to Roosevelt that Alexander be made Supreme Commander in his place. In fact, Dill had been due to retire in any case, and several months before, Alex had been told by Churchill that he would get the top job and be promoted to Field Marshal. So it proved, with his promotion backdated to 4 June, the day of the fall of Rome.

Alex was determined not to become the political desk-man General Wilson had been and so asked to remain as Commander-in-Chief of Allied Armies in Italy and to combine the roles. He also suggested that Clark should take over as commander of 15th Army Group, 'from a comparatively small tactical and integrated operational headquarters on the same lines as I had in Tunisia'.[315] Finally, he requested that Major-General Lucian Truscott be brought back from France and made Fifth Army commander. Both Churchill and Roosevelt were entirely happy with these suggestions and Eisenhower graciously agreed to release Truscott. At the same time, Alexander took the opportunity to cut back the massive Supreme Headquarters staff, keeping most of his A.A.I. team for his new role. This was more his style, but it also reflected the influence of his friend, Harold Macmillan.

Despite Clark's occasional outbursts of histrionics, Alex was glad to have Wayne – as he always called him – as commander of 15th Army Group. He had long recognised that Clark was both vain and ambitious, but they had been together a long time, and he liked him as a man and respected him as a commander, despite differences of opinion – differences that inevitably occur in any army command in any theatre in any war. The feeling was mutual. 'I thought Alex was a fine soldier,' said Clark. 'I thought he was the best of the lot. And we got on remarkably well . . . I couldn't pay him too high a tribute.'[316] But Alex had also noticed a change in Clark over the long summer and autumn months. 'He learned a lot as time went on,' said Alex. 'Clark would always listen to me, even if he didn't like what I said.' And he recognised that Clark was a good army commander. Certainly he pushed his men hard, but he was tough, resolute, had a cool head and never shirked from making difficult decisions. And in the crucial and difficult final months of the war, their working relationship improved. 'I recommended him for Army Group Commander,' said Alex, 'and he appreciated that.'[317]

Nor were just the senior commanders earning promotions. On 11 November, Brian Kingcombe, the group captain at 244 Wing, was posted home. A couple of days later, Air Vice-Marshal Dickson, CO of the Desert Air Force, called Cocky Dundas over to his headquarters. He, too, was leaving Italy, he told Cocky, having been recalled to the Air Ministry. However, he went on, there had been one thing he had been determined to do before leaving and that was secure Cocky's appointment as commanding officer of 244 Wing in Kingcombe's place. What was more, approval had finally come through that day. Cocky was now a group captain, despite being only a few months past his twenty-fourth birthday.

Cocky was rightly very proud, but deeply shaken too. The responsibility was huge. He now had to answer for the operational efficiency and administration of five fighter-bomber squadrons. That meant around a hundred aircraft and about two thousand men. 'My doubts and fears,' he wrote, 'were sharpened by the knowledge, in my heart of hearts, that I was just about played out so far as fighting was concerned.' Yet he also knew that as CO he could not sit behind a desk for the rest of the war. Somehow, he would simply have to stick it out to the end. 'In a haze of happiness and uncertainty,' he noted, 'I drove back to the airfield and told my astonished batman to get going with a needle and thread and turn me into a group captain.'[318]

A never-ending problem for the army commanders of both sides was the juggling of their troops. As the Fallschirmjäger had proved time and

time again, much could be achieved with comparatively few crack soldiers. The converse was also true. The temptation was to overexpose the
better units at the expense of the weaker, but of course this was ultimately
counter-productive. Nonetheless, on both sides, the weakest divisions
were placed in the quietest sectors. Von Vietinghoff now had three
German-trained Italian divisions within Graziani's Army of Liguria. Not
one German in Army Group C thought these units were anything other
than hopeless cases. This was partly because of an endemic attitude
towards the Italians as soldiers that had become deep-rooted since the
beginning of the war, and in part because a great many of their number
were extremely reluctant soldiers who had no interest in sacrificing their
lives for a cause in which they had little or no belief whatsoever. Finally,
and perhaps most importantly, because they were entirely new divisions,
they had no combat experience and there were precious few NCOs and
officers from the old army. Without them, the New Army had little
chance of success.

Much the same problems faced the troops of the Brazilian Expeditionary Force and the 92nd 'Buffalo' Infantry Division, which now also
occupied positions in the quiet western end of the line. Beggars could
not be choosers, and Clark had been grateful for the Brazilian troops,
but it was clear their training had been inadequate. Indeed, during their
first attack on Monte Castello in the Reno Valley, they had been thrown
back with enormous ease. General Mascarenhas, the Brazilian commander, made it clear that he did not think his troops were capable of
much in the way of offensive actions, and warned Clark that if the
division was annihilated, 'it would be a disaster not only for Brazil but
for the United States'. 'You know,' Mascarenhas added, 'we came over
here for victory and prestige, not to be cut to pieces.'[319]

The 92nd Division was also struggling. Clark had been keen to get
the division into action and had recommended generosity with regard
to the handing out of medals in an effort to build up morale; after all,
it was in everyone's interest to see the first all-black combat division do
well. But after the 370th Infantry Regiment's reasonable performance in
the crossing of the Arno and the capture of Pisa, the division had begun
to stumble and had failed to complete its comparatively straightforward
objectives in the Apuans and the Serchio Valley south of Massa.

Again, lack of experience, especially amongst the NCOs and officers,
had been at the root of the problem, although other factors had compounded the situation. It was crazy to have established a segregated

division in the first place; worse, all but the most junior officer positions had been given to white southerners, where, even eighty years after the abolition of slavery, there remained chronic and institutionalised racism.

Twenty-four-year-old Albert Burke was master sergeant at Divisional Headquarters. From the small town of Marietta, Ohio, Albert's northern upbringing had been happy enough and thankfully free of the kind of difficulties faced by blacks in the south. At school he had had a white girlfriend for a time, something that was not considered especially unusual.

A bright young man, he had won a state scholarship to Wilberforce College, and after a year there moved to Ohio University. Despite the scholarship, however, university proved too expensive and so he had been forced to quit and get a job instead, working for Yeller's Drug Company. Drafted in June 1942, he had then been sent south for training. 'I was a little naïve when I went into the Service,' he admits, 'because I didn't know much about segregation.' He found out about it fast, however. The white officers were frequently deeply racist, while the vast majority of the recruits were from desperately poor backgrounds and extremely poorly educated, if at all. In this environment, Albert shone. It also helped that he was possessed of an almost photographic memory. 'I could remember things,' he says. 'They called me a walking encyclopaedia. I could get orders, read them a couple of times and remember the lot.' Made a private first class right away, he rapidly rose up the NCO ranks, so that by the time they left to head overseas, he was the most senior sergeant in the entire division.

He was based in part at divisional HQ in Viareggio and in part at command posts at the front, and a large part of his job was the administration and allocation of replacement troops. The all-black 366th Regiment, initially sent overseas independently from the rest of the 'Buffalo' Division, had been in Italy since earlier in the year and had been used as support troops, mainly guarding airfields. In November, they had arrived at the front, and the various companies had been split up and attached to the existing front-line battalions. First, however, they had received a welcome speech from 92nd Infantry Division's commanding officer, Major-General Ned Almond, a career soldier from Virginia. 'Your Negro newspapers have seen fit to cause you to be brought over here', he told them. 'Now I'm going to see that you suffer your share of the casualties.'[320] 'Almond didn't like black officers at all,' says Albert, who saw more of their CO than most of the troops. 'Didn't like blacks at all. To be honest, I always thought he was kind of evil.'

It was, of course, the desperate shortage of troops that had brought the 366th into the division and to the front line, but although in a quiet sector it was hardly surprising that they struggled against even light opposition. 'Here's a rifle company they're sending into combat,' says Albert. 'They've had very little training, they haven't been in combat before, they don't know anything about where they are or anything. It's like taking these guys off the street and putting them up there and saying, you hold this place.'

Clark, on information received by Almond, made a report to Alexander on the performance of the 92nd Division on 14 December. In it, he cited the efforts of a 411-man strong infantry battalion that had attacked over 'moderately difficult terrain' one day at the end of November. Twenty-four hours after first entering the fray there had been just seventy men left, yet casualty figures were one killed, fifty-nine wounded and four cases of exhaustion. Under artillery and mortar fire, the rest had apparently turned and run. Clark was careful to add that this was just a preliminary report, and that the division was still new to combat and impressions were far from conclusive. 'It is my intention,' he concluded, 'to give the division increasing opportunity to learn combat responsibility and to demonstrate its ability to carry a full lead in offensive operations.'[321] In fact, they would be given that opportunity sooner than they could know.

Meanwhile, along the eastern half of the line, the war ground on in the mud and rain and carnage. On 30 November, the 8th Garibaldi Brigade was formally disbanded at a ceremony in Forlì. Most of their number had been resentful and angry at being denied the right to liberate their city, and furious that the Allies were now demanding they lay down their arms, although there was a festive mood that day. For them, the war was over although there was much reconstruction to be done: over two thousand houses had been flattened, and 130 bridges destroyed. There was also almost no food and no firewood.

Iader Miserocchi had not been part of the celebrations, however. Having gathered a number of partisans together, they had then headed across no-man's-land, where they had joined Allied forces in the advance on Ravenna. Iader had then slipped into his home city itself and joined the 28th Garibaldi Brigade. This time, with the help of the Allied freelance special force, Popski's Private Army,* and with the Canadians advancing to the south and west of the city, they had liberated Ravenna on 4 December. 'I had the great honour,' says Iader, 'of commanding the first platoon which crossed the river and entered the city.'

Eighth Army was now advancing in an arc between Ravenna and south of the Via Emilia. Alexander and Clark had originally agreed that Fifth Army's renewed offensive would begin on 1 December; this had then been postponed until 7 December, by which time it had been hoped that Eighth Army would have reached Imola and the River Santerno. As ever in these winter months, however, everything would depend on the weather.

Von Vietinghoff, meanwhile, had sensed Fifth Army must surely attack again at any moment, and was beginning to feel at a loss as to how he could stop them. He was also beginning to understand the difficulties Kesselring had faced for so long as army group commander. His battalions facing Eighth Army had now been reduced to around two hundred men each, and when, on 4 December, he asked the High Command if he could withdraw his forces to the Genghis Khan Line in an effort to concentrate his forces around Bologna, the reply, three days later, was an emphatic 'no'.

As a result he believed he had little choice but to try and halt the current and most pressing threat from Eighth Army and so reluctantly ordered his mobile reserve division, the 90th Panzer Grenadier, towards Faenza.

Amongst those hurrying down the Via Emilia on the night of 8 December was Hans Golda and the Werfer Regiment 71. 'The artillery was rolling forward, going into positions,' noted Hans. 'It was raining without ceasing and the night was very dark.' It was obvious to him that the infantry was not going to be ready by 7 a.m. the following day, when the counterattack was due to begin, but it went ahead anyway. 'At 7 a.m. all hell broke loose,' he wrote. 'The werfers shot, the artillery started, the concert began.'

Although the counterattack had begun well enough and had taken the British by surprise, it lacked sufficient force of weight, and soon faltered. British artillery responded heavily, firing some 50,000 rounds.

*One of several irregular special forces that emerged during the campaign in North Africa. Founded by Vladimir Peniakoff, a Belgian of Russian parentage, who was an officer in the British Army, Popski's Private Army carried out numerous and many highly valuable operations behind enemy lines in both North Africa and Italy.

And accompanying them, as ever, were the jabos, hurtling over the German positions dropping bombs, and following up with their machine guns and cannons. 'On top of all this,' scribbled Hans, 'came the bombers. They laid carpet after carpet of mixed bombs.' Among the bombers were the Marauders of 24 SAAF Squadron, who on the 10th were specifically targeting gun positions around Castel Bolognese. Sheltering in a school building in the town, Hans and his men were crouched down, frozen with fear. 'The screams of the civilians were lost in the noise,' he noted, 'and then the music was over and heavy smoke lay over the whole area. We counted sixty bomb impacts within a circle of fifty metres around the school. We were so tired.'[322]

There would be no respite for them, however, and the following day the bombers were back again, this time with Flight Sergeant Ernest Wall amongst them. Unaware of the terror they were causing on the ground below, Ernest had in many ways been relieved to have finally got back in the air again after six weeks grounded due to the weather.

A short distance to the north, the Canadian 5th Armoured Division was once again on the move. They had not been involved in the capture of Ravenna, but on the night of 10 December the Perths crossed the River Lamone. It was a hairy experience for Stan Scislowski, who had paddled across the river in their collapsible canvas assault boat with a speed he hadn't realised he possessed. The countryside in which they were now fighting was proving every bit as inhospitable as the mountains, however – flat as a board, with almost no cover. Ahead of them were a series of irrigation canals, each with high dykes either side. A couple of days later a large patrol had crossed the first of these dykes, the Fosso Vecchio, prompting heavy retaliatory mortar and artillery fire. Stan and three others had been asked to carry an injured mortar man back to safety.

With enemy mortars zeroing in on the one available cart track, they had decided to take him cross-country, a decision they soon regretted. 'The brown gumbo we had to slog through damn near killed me,' admitted Stan. 'With each step, great gobs of the stuff stuck to our boots. We stumbled. We fell to our knees. We cursed each other. Fingers went numb. Wrists ached, arms felt like they were being pulled out of their sockets.' Suddenly German mortar shells began falling all around them. 'With bombs going off we literally flew across the field,' admits Stan. 'Never till that moment had I known that fear and the overpowering need to save someone's life, including our own, could give us the strength and stamina and sense of purpose to carry on.'[323] And with this surge of adrenalin and a dose of luck, they made it back to safety.

At 8.55 a.m. on 13 December, Flight Lieutenant Ken Neill and his wingman, Flying Officer Den Bray, took off from Florence on another tactical reconnaissance flight, this time over the German positions opposite the 92nd 'Buffalo' Division, along the coast in the mountains around Massa. The squadron always operated in pairs of aircraft – one man to carry out the task assigned to them, the other to protect his back. They saw little until Ken spotted a farm below them with a lot of mud tracks around it. Telling Den that he was going to fly down and take a closer look, he suddenly heard a ping and immediately his engine began to run rough. Oil pressure started to drop dramatically, and although he still had enough power to climb back up and gain some height, he soon realised he was not going to be able to make it back to base.

Radioing to Den that he was going to bail out, he then discovered to his horror that the canopy would not jettison, despite repeated tugging on the release knob. The only alternative was to slide the canopy back, as he normally did when getting in and out, but to do that he needed to be flying less than 150 mph – and at that speed it was impossible to turn the aircraft over and keep it level long enough to fall cleanly out.

With 88mm flak beginning to burst around them, Den headed back to base on his own. 'With the flak I couldn't really hang around,' he says, 'and besides, I didn't want to identify his position too much.' In any case, there was nothing Den could have done, although Ken had tried to flip over his Spitfire and was now in the middle of a terrifying out of control dive. Half in and half out of his cockpit, and unable to reach the control column, he was hurtling towards the ground and instant death. 'I thought I was going to come to a sticky end,' he says, 'but I kicked a bit and eventually I came free and pulled the parachute rip cord. I was jerked around and looking downwards, and at that second, my aircraft hit the ground and exploded. Another few seconds and I would have been down there with it.'

Moments later, he was crashing through some trees on the edge of a small clearing. Releasing his harness, he landed on the ground with a thump, only to see an Italian youth of about sixteen standing a short distance away. '*Tedesco?*' the boy asked him. 'No,' Ken replied, '*Inglese.*' A few minutes later a number of others appeared, armed with Sten guns and rifles. One man who was clearly in charge told the others to grab the parachute quickly and then they led Ken to a farmhouse nearby and into a hayloft. For the next few hours, men kept reappearing with news on the German reaction to the crash, until eventually it became clear the Germans, having not seen his parachute, had decided he must have been killed in his aircraft.

Ken was then asked whether he wanted to join their partisan band or whether he would like to rejoin his unit. 'I didn't have any wish to be a partisan,' says Ken, 'and actually our instructions were to try and get back over Allied lines.' The partisans seemed to accept his decision and the following morning a guide called Enrico arrived to lead him back. Ken had landed in the Apuans, east of La Spezia. He now faced a long trek through the mountains – harsh peaks that had recently become covered in freezing snow.

Back at Faenza, the 90th Panzer Grenadier Division's assault had failed to push 46th Division back across the River Lamone, so the British bridgehead south of the town still stood. It had also been costly and casualties had quickly mounted. Nonetheless, it had been a bold move by von Vietinghoff and succeeded in stalling Eighth Army's advance along the Via Emilia, and as a result, Fifth Army's offensive had not begun; Bologna, von Vietinghoff hoped, might yet be saved. Also playing into his hands was the weather, which had worsened once again.

After more than three months of near-continual fighting, 46th Division was on its knees, with some of its battalions reduced to just 150 men. Certainly it was in no fit state to continue the drive to Imola, and so McCreery ordered the 10th Indian and New Zealand Divisions to sidestep into the bridgehead instead and to take over the role of V Corps' strike force.

Their plan of attack was to push forward to the next river, the Senio, cut the Via Emilia and isolate Faenza, which still remained, a week after it had first been approached, in German hands. Yet the lack of equipment and armour once again hampered efforts. The Kiwi sappers had managed to build a bridge over the Lamone, and a jeep track to approach it, but it soon became almost impassable and had to be closed for twelve hours in every twenty-four, just for repairs.

They were finally ready to attack on the night of 14/15 December. The Maoris' task was to drive up towards the Via Emilia and capture a number of key houses and positions about a mile south of the road, with the railway line running south out of Faenza as its right-hand boundary. Supporting them would be a squadron of tanks. In C Company, Tini Glover was now leading 14th Platoon's reserve section, who were to follow behind the two lead sections. 'We had a lot of new fellows,' says Tini, 'and I had this bloody joker with a machine gun who'd never been in action.' Tini was also nursing a black eye; it had been his birthday a few days before, and he'd got drunk and then had a fight. His opponent had been so laid out he'd not even been able to take part in the attack.

They headed out across muddy fields towards the first farmhouse objectives, with artificial moonlight from special lights to mark their way. To begin with, everything went according to plan. They took the first farmhouse and captured eighteen Germans whom they disarmed and then locked in a room in the house. There was no sign of the support tanks, however, but 14 and 13 Platoons pressed on to their next objective and there discovered two Tiger tanks and increasing numbers of German infantry. Despite radioing back for artillery support, none arrived, and they now found themselves under fire from the Tigers. Fourteen Platoon fell back to another farmhouse. 'It was scary,' says Tini, 'very scary. It was a shambles.' Lieutenant Mahuika was wounded so Lieutenant Paniora took over. By first light, however, two more Tigers had arrived, while there was still no sign of their own armour. The Germans then counterattacked, and Lieutenant Paniora was killed. This left Sergeant-Major Wanoa in charge. Realising their situation was now hopeless, he called for a smoke screen to cover their escape from the house. 'It was a bastard fight,' says Tini. 'Our tanks really let us down.' Tini did not know it, but once again it was the mud and conditions that had done for the armour; they had been unable to get forward. The remains of 14 Platoon fell back. Tini was carrying a lad he knew from home who had been wounded badly in the chest. As Stan Scislowski had discovered a few days before, carrying wounded men through thick mud was no easy task and Tini, having been up all night, was exhausted. 'When I got him back to the RAP [regimental aid post] they said, Tini, you've been carrying a stiff, mate. And I cried. It was f***ing horrible.'

Little had been achieved, and too many men had been pointlessly killed. The futility was underlined when the following night, having taken a road that allowed the armour forward at long last, and supported by anti-tanks guns, they were far more successful. By morning on the 17th, the Germans had left Faenza and the Allies had reached the River Senio.

*   *   *

The 15th of December was Hans-Jürgen Kumberg's last at the front for
a while. Having so far survived the campaign with no more than a cut
wrist and a splinter in his backside, his luck finally ran out. Still based
at Montecalderado in the Monte Grande area, he and the rest of the
Fallschirmjäger troops were waiting for the launch of the next Fifth
Army offensive. It was thus ironic that having survived plenty of
extremely bitter and heavy fighting that he should be wounded during
a lull.

Company headquarters was a farmhouse beneath Monte Castellaro.
In the evening Hans had just finished his rations of plums and rice,
when he stepped outside the farmhouse to relieve himself. 'We had
candlelight inside, but it was blacked out,' he says. 'The enemy had been
shelling us for some days, and I suppose as I opened the door, they must
have seen the brief shaft of light.' At any rate, as he returned and closed
the door once more, a mortar shell came over and exploded right outside
sending shrapnel splinters through the wood and into his stomach. As
Hans points out, stomach wounds were usually fatal. 'We didn't have
any penicillin,' he says, 'and the stomach cavity would get inflamed and
you'd die.' But his meal saved him. With a stomach full of rice, the
shrapnel got no further, becoming embedded in his just-eaten supper.

Put on a stretcher – on his back, which prevented too much loss of
fluid and blood – he was carried under heavy artillery fire some three
miles to the nearest field dressing station, where he was quickly operated
on. 'The next morning,' says Hans, 'the doctor showed me the shell
fragment and told me just how lucky I'd been.'

Flight Lieutenant Ken Neill had been trudging through the snow for two
days, conversing with his guide in French. On the first day they had
passed through a partially ruined mountain village. Apparently, the
villagers had been helping the partisans and so had suffered a rastrellamento by the Fascists. 'They had mown down one house in ten,' says
Ken, 'and had taken out the children and executed them and smashed
their heads on the rocks and you could see evidence of that.'

The first night they had stayed in a mountain village, sitting in a
room before a blazing fire but which had no chimney. Ken was also
keenly aware that all these people were risking their lives helping him.
Enrico had even said as much. You're lucky, he'd said, if we get caught
you'll go to a POW camp, but I'll go to a torture chamber in La Spezia.
The next day they set off again. Eventually they came to a saddle in the

mountain chain where they met up with a number of people huddled together waiting to be guided south across the lines. A one-armed guide appeared, but wanted to be paid. Ken delved into his escape kit and handed over some money. 'It was getting dark,' he says, 'and I still had my revolver and I could see that there were some pretty shady looking characters. I saw they were eyeing my revolver and I didn't want a knife in my back, so I gave it away.'

Since it was too risky to try and cross in large groups, the one-armed guide took Ken, Enrico and two others. Going round the face of a mountain in the gathering dark on an icy track was a precarious business, but after an hour or so they realised the guide had given them the slip. Despite this setback, they decided to press on. At one point, Ken lost his footing and slipped over the edge of a sharp drop; he could even hear Germans talking in a machine-gun nest below, but managed to clasp hold of a rock. Grabbing him by the wrists, one of the others helped pull him up again. Ken feared they had been heard. To his relief, however, they managed to continue on their way apparently undetected.

At first light, they dropped down into a valley towards the 92nd 'Buffalo' Division's lines, but the Germans on the other side of the valley spotted them. 'We had to run from one house to another,' says Ken, 'as they shot at us.' Eventually, however, they reached the safety of the American lines. After a hot meal and a sleep, Ken bid Enrico goodbye, then got a lift on a lorry back to Florence. 'I asked the driver if he could drop me off at the DAF Club,' he says, 'and funnily enough there was a big South African major there who I'd met a few times and become quite friendly with, and he looked at me as though I was back from the dead.'

In the Setta Valley, Sergeant Reg Harris and the 3rd Coldstream Guards were now based at La Quercia, the tiny village nestling under the railway viaduct on the river banks, and only a short distance from where both Cornelia Paselli and Francesco Pirini and their families had lived. The Germans now occupied Monte Sole itself. The slopes were heavily mined and well-sighted guns and machine-gun nests overlooked the approaches.

On 14 December, the Royal Natal Carbineers moved up the Setta Valley taking over positions at Gardelletta. 'Very eerie,' noted Dick of the night-time journey to their new positions. 'Passed houses where Guards had had their bombs blown up. Terrible track, ankle deep in

mud in places. Mules collapsed and wouldn't get up.' In the cold light
of day, Dick emerged from their new company headquarters and gazed
up at the imposing sight of Monte Sole itself. 'Worst thing about this
position,' he noted at the end of their first day there, 'is that one cannot
move in daylight and Monte Sole looks right at one all the time. Hope
against hope that Jerry won't find us.'[324] The Germans were only too
aware of just how formidable a position Monte Sole was. They were not
going to give it up easily.

Dick Frost simply wanted to keep his head down and survive the war.
He wasn't interested in heroics and was dreading the moment when they
would have to assault Monte Sole. Soldiers along the front were rarely
given the kind of explicit briefings handed out before the DIADEM
offensive in May, but the bush telegraph ensured that most knew when
something was brewing.

Fifth Army had been poised to attack all month. The original conditions – Eighth Army's reaching of the River Santerno – had now
been adjusted, and Truscott's forces were due to jump off the moment
Eighth Army crossed the Senio instead. Even this, however, was proving
no easy matter. The Canadians had been struggling to get across the
three lines of dykes that barred their path before reaching the Senio.
Lemelsen had also rushed reinforcements up – the 98th Division, along
with various units from the 90th Panzer Grenadier and 278th Infantry,
and just under twenty tanks, had been formed into an ad hoc battle
group which blocked the Canadian 5th Armoured Division's attempt to
break through.

On the night of the 19/20th, the Perths crossed over the thirty-foot
wide Fosso Munio dyke, in silence and without mishap. But Stan Scislowski was about to endure one of the most terrifying battles since arriving
in Italy. Beyond the dyke lay 600 yards of open muddy flats, and the
Germans had the area covered with a clear field of fire. Baker Company,
leading the attack, was cut to pieces, and as the follow-up companies
also made their way across the dyke, they found themselves coming
under heavy artillery and mortar fire. Stan spent most of the night
cowering in a house that was slowly but surely disintegrating around
him. Only once the Canadian armour arrived in force were they finally
able to make progress. It was not until the 21st, however, that they
reached the Senio.

Despite such stiff resistance on Eighth Army's front, Alex and Clark
were poised to launch their joint offensive at forty-eight hours' notice

from 22 December, with Fifth Army driving towards Bologna from the south and Eighth Army from the south-east. They believed that despite the month's setbacks, there was at last the opportunity for a fairly concentrated and co-ordinated punch on German defences, especially as it had at last stopped raining – northern Italy now lay sheathed in snow.

No sooner had these plans been agreed than intelligence reached the Allies of an enemy plan for a counter-offensive on the quiet west coast sector. Mussolini had been suggesting for some time that his new divisions should lead a counter-offensive on the west coast. Since the formation of his New Army, the Germans had barely considered them worthy of front-line duty. However, the Germans could see the advantages of a limited offensive down the Serchio Valley; what they termed 'a reconnaissance in force' meant to disrupt the front and reduce the pressure on Bologna. Despite Mussolini's pleas, the final assault force was entirely German, with the Italian Monte Rosa Division acting only in a supporting role.

The US 92nd Division were swept aside with consummate ease when the Germans attacked on 26 December. The Allies, however, having learnt of the Axis plans, had already sent the battle-hardened 8th Indian Division, with two further divisions waiting in reserve if necessary. Once the 92nd Division troops had streamed past them, the Indians were able to hold the line. With their limited objectives achieved, the Germans fell back, their 'reconnaissance in force' over.

The Serchio offensive may have been a minor sideshow in the big scheme of things, but it had wider knock-on effects. The Monte Rosa Division had hardly showered itself in glory and to the German command it confirmed, once and for all, the inadequacy of the new Italian divisions; while amongst the Allies accusing fingers were being pointed at the 92nd 'Buffalo' Division.

In war, experience is everything. The 92nd's problems, however, were compounded by the fact that its replacements had to be black. 'There were not enough people of colour being trained as infantry,' points out Albert Burke. 'Most coloured people were being trained as a quartermaster, or truck drivers, cooks and that sort of thing. Maintenance. We was running out of personnel.' Consequently, the men who did arrive as replacements were even worse trained and more inexperienced than those before them.

The fighting in the Serchio also killed dead Alex and Clark's hopes of

reaching Bologna before Christmas. The problem was that they could
not afford to allow the fighting to grind on until the middle of January.
'In that event,' wrote Alex, 'if the fighting was as severe as it had been
so far in December, all the artillery ammunition accumulated by past
economies would have been used up and there would remain only one
January allotment, insufficient even for a fortnight's operations at current rates.' They had already overrun the date that he had previously set
for the cessation of active operations and now had increasingly poor
chances of taking Bologna with the resources still available. 'I accordingly
decided,' noted the Field Marshal, 'on 30th December, to abandon my
existing plan, to go on the defensive for the present and to concentrate
on making a real success of our spring offensive.'[325]

German snipers on the Senio dyke ensured the men of Dog Company,
Perth Regiment had been keeping their heads down in their requisitioned
villa not far from the river – a house that supposedly belonged to the
local land baron, a well-known Fascist. On Christmas morning, however,
the Canadians discovered the snipers had taken a day off. Stan Scislowski
had woken early to learn that a hunting party had gone out in the night
and killed a cow, dragging the beast back to the house where it had been
butchered. No great cook, Stan and a few others had been left to prepare
a table, and to find plates and suitable cutlery.

While these preparations were going on, the Dog Company men were
distracted by shouting coming from the German lines. Suddenly, there
on the top of the far side of the dyke was a German soldier riding a grey
horse bareback and brandishing a bottle of wine, while other Germans
cheered. Soon after, singing could be heard from the German lines,
drifting out into that ice-cold white Christmas air. 'It was really heart-
warming to hear them sing Silent Night,' wrote Stan. 'How could you
hate them, even after what they'd done to us only four nights before?'[326]

Some twenty-five miles away as the crow flies, Hans Golda was also
helping to prepare a feast for what would be the last Christmas of the
war. To his great relief they were back at Liano, a place he had come to
cherish deeply, and that day they also sang carols; each man was given
a Christmas package, and then they sat down in the castle to a supper
they would never forget. 'Tommy remained quiet,' noted Hans. 'There
wasn't a shot on the whole front. We went to bed relatively early and I
lay for a long time with my eyes open, under my covers, and thought of
home. At this time at home, the Christ child would be coming to my

boy and I could see the picture in front of me – a picture of my wife carrying him to the Christmas tree, and him looking at the lights with big shining eyes. My lips were smiling even though, at the same time, my heart was missing them and I was homesick. Then I slept and in my dreams, I was with my family. This was a soldier's Christmas near the enemy.'[327]

PART IV

Endgame

THIRTY-SIX

Stalemate
January–February 1945

On the Monte Sole massif, Dick Frost spent New Year's Eve at Veggio, just below Monte Pezze, eating a 'very good dinner'. Unfortunately, he then rather spoiled things for himself by drinking too much and making himself ill, so that by midnight he was already fast asleep. A treat was in store on 1 January 1945, however, as he was given a ride through the snow back to Divisional Headquarters at Castiglione, and there he had his first bath in almost a month. 'My clothes were filthy,' he noted, 'and it really is a great relief to get a change.'[328]

Hans Golda was never one to miss the opportunity for a party and although he had had a bad cold the past few days, was feeling much better by New Year's Eve. The men still had to remain alert and at their firing positions, but they brought out food and plenty of drink and even managed to drag along some local women. 'Most of the men were pretty drunk,' wrote Hans, 'and Klaus let the girls go home so that the hot-heads didn't try anything.'

The young women might have gone before midnight, but the men were still in a mood for mischief-making, and a number of them headed for the church tower and at midnight began ringing the bells. 'This was going to cause trouble,' wrote Hans, and sure enough they did not have to wait long for a reply. 'Bang! Bang! The enemy answered with artillery but by then we were all under cover.'[329]

Stan Scislowski and the Perths had been spending a few days' rest in Ravenna, but on New Year's Day they were ordered back to the front. Offensive operations may have ceased, but this did not mean the front was entirely inactive, and the Canadians were now ordered to press northwards to clear the coastal area between the large salt lake of the Valli di Comacchio and Ravenna.

Stan was depressed. Everyone sensed the war was coming to an end, but just when that might be was anyone's guess. 'Knowing the Germans' remarkable capacity to recover from catastrophic defeats,' wrote Stan, 'some of us felt that the war might even go on for another year.' It was also freezing cold. Stan was dressed in longjohns, battledress, a leather jerkin, and two pairs of socks, but as they rumbled along to the front in open-backed Dodge trucks to the drop-off point, he still felt icy cold. 'We damn near froze our butts and balls off,' he noted.

The troops along the front line might have been able to celebrate Christmas, but not so Clara Duse and her family, for whom the struggle for survival was becoming ever more hard. Thanks to her cousin, Giulio, who was in hiding in the country, she and her mother had had the use of his small flat in the centre of Trieste, but apart from the few gold coins they had saved from better days, they had nothing. Nor was Clara's mother any better; rather, her depression had worsened, and she was now almost entirely bed-bound. Clara had tried to find some work, but most of what was available involved working for the Germans. She did go for an interview as a personal assistant to a German officer, but she quickly realised that he was after a mistress not a secretary.

With no fuel and no hot water, she and her mother would often go to see her Great-Uncle Giovanni who also lived in the city and who had a wood stove, and there they would find other members of the family, all huddled around in the semi-darkness. In the city, kitchens were set up to feed the poorest of the population. For a few coins, they offered a small meal of, say, dried bean soup, or dried pea soup, and a roll of grey and gritty bread. 'We lived on that for several months,' says Clara. 'My gums started bleeding, probably through lack of vitamins.'

On New Year's Eve she heard the Germans celebrating in the city, even letting off fireworks, but for her and her family the New Year brought worse news. When trying to renew her father's ration book, she was told it would not be possible as he was now listed as dead. It was a terrible way to learn the news. Soon after, they received confirmation that he had indeed perished, at Mauthausen concentration camp. 'It would have been better a bullet,' she says, 'rather than starvation and hard labour.' In January, one of her cousins, to whom she was very close, also died, of leukaemia, leaving behind two small children. Soon after that, another of her friends died of tuberculosis. Her mother's depression deepened. 'She would not talk or eat,' says Clara, 'or go to the air shelter. She said she just wanted to die, so I sat with her.'

The bad news seemed never-ending. A Jewish friend was arrested and sent to Auschwitz; another cousin was arrested for being a suspected partisan. Through all this, Clara merely tried to stay alive, and prayed that the war would soon be over.

It would, in the spring, if Alexander had anything to do with it. The previous winter, Alex had been forced to face the wave of disappointment that had spread across the Western Allies, when all eyes, it seemed, had been turned to Italy and their failure to capture Rome. Now, however, the disappointments could be shared: Montgomery's airborne assault at Arnhem had failed; the Americans had been strongly counterattacked in the Ardennes; and the Russian advance had slowed in the East. The war had not finished in 1944 after all.

The ripples of these disappointments had still touched Italy, however, and Alex had faced yet further setbacks since his recent elevation. His plans for sending Eighth Army across the Adriatic had been scrapped, and, at the beginning of December, a new directive had instructed him to confine his efforts to Italy with the goal of taking Bologna and then concentrating on purely containing German forces.

But then the shock of the German counter-offensive in the Ardennes – launched on 16 December – began to take hold and made the Western Allies realise they still faced a formidable task in defeating Germany. Compounding this concern was the shortage of manpower and ammunition, in which case, the question was being asked, were two fronts in Europe really necessary? Planners in London and Washington now estimated that by April 1945, there would be ninety-one Allied divisions against ninety German on the Western Front and twenty-four Allied against twenty-seven German divisions in Italy. In other words, in neither theatre would the Allies have a decisive superiority in manpower. The obvious solution for the Joint Chiefs of Staff was to recommend transferring divisions from the Mediterranean to help Eisenhower's spring offensive. At meetings between the Western Allies on Malta at the end of January, Alex argued his case for Italy and a compromise was agreed. General Marshall suggested Alex keep Fifth Army intact, but that he provide three British divisions from Italy as soon as possible, and two more as soon as they could be released from Greece. Marshall also wanted part of the US Twelfth Air Force for northwest Europe – and so Alex lost two fighter groups as well. This was conveyed in a new directive, which reduced his role further to that of simply containing the German forces at their present line – unless, of course, Army Group C should withdraw of its own accord or show any sign of weakening, in which case he should be prepared 'to take immediate advantage'.[330]

On top of this, the Canadian government decided they wanted all their troops in one theatre. In a way, however, this solved one of Alex's problems: sorry though he was to lose them, the two Canadian divisions would be quietly withdrawn – hopefully without the Germans realising it – while the third to be handed over to Eisenhower would be the British 5th Division, which, although it had been due to return to Italy, had been retraining in the Middle East since shortly after the fall of Rome.

Nor was it all bad news: incredibly, General Marshall had also agreed to send the brand-new US 10th Mountain Division to Italy. This division had been trained in the Rocky Mountains in Colorado, had amongst its number some of America's finest skiers, and was led by the First World War winner of the Medal of Honor, Major General George P. Hays. The division certainly viewed itself as highly trained, even elite, troops, yet it seems that Clark was offered them because they had been rejected for the Pacific and northwest Europe theatres. 'I was happy to get any division at that time,' noted Clark, 'and, of course, the 10th Mountain was ideally suited for the high Apennines.'[331]

At least Alex and his commanders now knew where they stood, and they could get on with the job in hand – and that, despite directives that spoke of containment and consolidation, meant defeating the German armed forces in Italy completely and utterly once and for all. And in this, Alex had the total support of not only Clark, but also Truscott and McCreery. January, February and March were to be months of planning. Like DIADEM the year before, once the weather improved and the ground dried out, Alex meant to strike the decisive blow no matter what obstacles lay in his path.

Feldmarschall Kesselring returned to retake the reins of Army Group C in January, having made a full recovery from his head wound. As with the Allied Chiefs of Staff, Italy was hardly preying on the minds of Hitler and the High Command, who now had their hands more than full with the resumed Russian advance. Even so, back in December, von Vietinghoff had been told emphatically that no voluntary withdrawals were allowed, and that policy had not changed once Kesselring returned – as he discovered in February when he asked Jodl for advice from Hitler and the High Command on future plans.

Nonetheless, the Feldmarschall started making preparations for the spring as well, based on the assumption that once the Allied offensive began he would be able to handle the pressures from above and gain the necessary permission to act as he saw fit. Work had been continuing on the Genghis Khan Line, and it was here that he intended to fall back to first, confident that he could hold the Allies there before withdrawing across the River Adige. In essence, it was a repeat of his plan for retreating to the Gothic Line the previous summer, albeit over a shorter distance.

Hampering him, as ever, was his truly terrible supply situation, while the lack of anything other than a handful of aircraft ensured his intelligence was still woefully poor. He had suffered losses of manpower too. In addition to the withdrawal of the 16th Waffen-SS, two further divisions were taken from him, which rather offset Alexander's losses.

However, Kesselring still found some reasons for optimism. Travelling around the front he found the morale of his men as good as ever, while he was also satisfied with the strength of his units, which meant he had a crucial superiority in manpower. 'The stage was set,' he wrote, 'for the decisive battle.'[332]

In January, Lieutenant Eugenio Corti left Cerreto with the new Folgore Combat Group, and headed north back towards Le Marche, where they were to complete a further month's training before going into the line. Now completely equipped with British uniforms and machinery – they even travelled in Bedford trucks – their badges were the only things that remained from their Italian Army uniforms. 'But even without looking at these,' wrote Eugenio, 'the Italians were immediately distinguishable from the others.'[333]

Stan Scislowski agreed, although for not quite the same reasons. The Cremona Combat Group had arrived to take over their positions on 13 January. 'My immediate impression of these big, sturdy-looking fellows was that they were seriously lacking in field discipline,' noted Stan. 'What an unholy racket they made!' Stan and his mates were appalled at the shouting going on, and the way the Italians lit up cigarettes in the open – a serious taboo for combat infantry at the front. 'With all the commotion around us,' he wrote, 'I naturally expected Jerry to open up full bore at any moment.'[334] He had only just returned from a dangerous night patrol in which one of their men had been seriously wounded, and now couldn't wait to get the changeover completed and to be on the road and out of further danger.

With freezing rain and icy roads, however, their journey south, when it began, was slow and tortuous, and it was over fifty miles to Cattolica, south of Rimini, where they were due to pause. By that time, Stan was in serious trouble. During the night patrol, he had jarred his knee trying to help carry his wounded mate back across frozen mud furrows, and now discovered his entire leg had swollen to the same width as his thigh. Sent to the medical officer, he was given a cursory examination and then packed off to hospital, first in Jesi, and then to the 104th British General Hospital in Rome. Stan would not be going to northwest Europe with the rest of the division. Miracle though it was, he had somehow survived more than a year of bitter fighting. Ironically, it was an injured knee that had finally brought his time at the front to an end.

Stan was not the only one to have left the fighting behind. By the beginning of 1945, a number of old-timers had been taken out of front-line duties. Wladek Rubnikowicz was now training cadets in Casarano in southern Italy. Rudi Schreiber had preceded the 16th Waffen-SS Division's departure by being posted to officer training school. So too had Hans-Jürgen Kumberg. Having recovered from his life-threatening stomach wound, he had briefly rejoined his battalion, before being posted to the Oberst Rudolf Böhmler's 1st Fallschirmjäger Officers' School at Bosco Chiese Nova north of Verona. Leutnant Jupp Klein had also been at Böhmler's School carrying out mountain training but was now in charge of a company of fifty Pioneers constructing defences along the River Adige near Bolzano. Ken Neill, having returned safely to 225 Squadron, was taken off ops and posted back to Britain. Ted Wyke-Smith had also been moved to take command of an Army Troops Company, whose job was to build more durable, heavy-duty bridges behind the advancing army. It was a promotion and with it came a captaincy, but he was disappointed to leave his old bridging team and the men with whom he had forged an intense camaraderie and deep trust. 'I thought, bugger the captaincy,' he says, 'I want to stay with my lads.'

There were further changes at the top as well. General Sidney Kirkman had become ill – physically drained after battling his way through North Africa and Italy – and had been sent home, while von Vietinghoff was given command of the Army Group Kurland in East Prussia. The atmosphere in Italy had changed; everyone was waiting, aware that soon there would be one last mighty clash, but at the same time conscious that this might well prove to be the endgame of the war. No one wanted to die, but for most men at the front, the prospect of being killed when the end appeared to be so near seemed somehow worse. Very few were relishing what was to come.

On the other hand, there were others still at the front who had come through years of being in the firing line. Ray Saidel of the US 1st Armored Division had survived North Africa, Anzio, all the fighting on the long road north, and was still in one piece by the start of 1945. He'd had some close calls; recently he'd even trodden on a mine that had been planted in a stream he had tried to cross, but for some reason it hadn't exploded. Now, in January, with the snow all around and the fighting country as poorly designed for tanks as ever, he and a number of others from A Company, 1st Tank Battalion, were taken out of the line and retrained as infantry. 'What do you want to be?' Ray's old friend Sergeant Lowrey had asked him. 'Radio man? Machine gunner?'

'Let me be a rifleman,' Ray replied, 'because it's less to carry in the mountains.' And so, at the beginning of February, Ray went back up to the front as a rifleman with 1st Squad, 2nd Platoon of the 1st Provisional Rifle Company, a severely under-strength unit of just sixty-five men. His platoon found itself camping out in a largely destroyed house over-looking the Reno River near the town of Vergato, and beneath Monte Salvaro. Conditions were pretty miserable. A succession of troops had used the place and empty cans of food and excrement had been tossed into one of the rooms. Mice and rats abounded. 'It was pretty stinky,' admits Ray. 'When you wanted to go to the bathroom, you had to do it in a box and then throw it out.' To then communicate with troops in a different part of the house, they had to go outside and crawl across the ground that was consequently increasingly covered with their own excrement. 'It wasn't a nice thing to climb through,' says Ray. Nor was there any way for them to wash themselves properly. They were soon filthy and bearded. On a clear night they could hear the Germans in Vergato, but the enemy never seemed to have spotted the Americans. 'If they had,' says Ray, 'they'd have blown us away.'

Also now back at the front was Lieutenant Bob Wiggans of the 85th 'Custer' Division. Still weak and underweight, he was, in truth, not really fit for front-line action. But he was anxious to be back amongst his men, and the division needed him, so he was put on a ship from Naples to Livorno and sent back north. 'There were two kinds of soldiers on that

ship and they were easily distinguishable,' he says. 'The lean veteran
soldiers returning from hospitals, and a large contingent of young, well-
conditioned, warmly clothed, eager soldiers.' Although the latter wore
no insignia and insisted on keeping their unit details a secret, Bob and
the other veterans knew these were all men of the much-heralded 10th
Mountain Division. Rivalry between these young bucks and the old-
timers would be intense in the months to come.

Bob reached his old battalion whilst they were still out of the line
retraining and practising river crossings over the Arno for when – and
if – they drove the Germans north towards the Po. They began moving
back into the Apennines on 8 January, having removed all divisional
insignia themselves in an effort to confuse the Germans over which units
were where. The conditions were once again appalling. 'The snow was
about a foot deep on the level,' noted Bob, 'but where we lived on the
reverse slopes and in the ravines, it was waist deep.' Between snowfalls
there was frequently hail and rain. Occasionally, the temperature would
rise enough to melt the snow briefly, but then it would turn to ice. The
fog, ice and narrow trails made it incredibly difficult for the mules and
mule skinners to reach them so they were often short of supplies – and,
crucially, food.

Nor was Bob a well man anyway. He had found the climb up to their
positions exhausting and had once more had a high fever by the
time they reached there. 'I wasn't in as good shape as I thought,' he
admitted.[335]

Now finally in uniform was the teenage Fascist, Roberto Vivarelli, who,
back in November, had joined Commander Pavolini's personal bodyguard of Blackshirts, the Bir el Gobi Company, when still a few weeks
shy of his fifteenth birthday. His mother had had much to do with it, as
she was now herself head of a group of women auxiliaries based at the
Party Leader's residence in Milan, the Villa Necchi. Soon after joining
the Bir el Gobi, Roberto had been sent to company headquarters in
Maderno to be given his kit and on the return journey had been forced
to ride on the footplate of the truck keeping a watch out for enemy
planes. On his return, he had promptly come down with bronchitis.

Whilst recovering in his mother's flat, he saw Pavolini a number of
times, and observed someone he believed was a determined but rather
sad man. 'To me,' says Roberto, 'he was an enigma. Ideologically he was
steadier and more rigid than Mussolini himself. Personally, however, in

the contact I had with him, he was a perfectly nice human being.' He may have been, but Pavolini remained a fanatical Fascist, and the leader of a militarised party whose government was crumbling apart at the seams, their hands tied by their German masters and now deeply unpopular with the majority of the population who, more than ever, could sense that fascism was about to fall once and for all. Nowhere in northern Italy was now safe; civil war was beginning to take root, and with it, the rule of law was collapsing into anarchy. The only exception was over matters that directly affected the Germans, in which case German martial law remained as ruthless as ever.

As the Bir el Gobi Company were discovering during their time in Milan, attacks by Gappist and SAP partisans were common. William Cremonini's platoon commander, Lieutenant Barnini, had been accosted by two partisans who then lobbed hand grenades at him. He had managed to put some distance between himself and the grenades before they had exploded and so had been unhurt. Another of their fellows was not so lucky, however, and was shot dead by Gappists at a theatre in the city. William had been sitting near the man at the time. 'It was dangerous,' says William. 'The partisans killed indiscriminately. The lad killed at the theatre was only a boy.'

In mid-January, the Bir el Gobi Company were sent back to the Alps, this time further north to the Biella region, to continue the civil war with yet more anti-partisan operations. For Roberto Vivarelli, this was a disappointing introduction to life as a soldier. He had hoped to be sent to the front; instead they were spending their time traipsing around in the snow, dressed in white capes, hunting for seemingly non-existent partisans. For over a month Roberto did not see a single partisan, partly because there were by now comparatively few of them left, and partly because as soon as they saw the Bir el Gobi men coming, the partisans hid.

Transport for the Bir el Gobi men was either on foot or in a single camouflaged Fiat truck which usually had to tow another vehicle due to the lack of fuel. Desperately short of food, some of the men once even dressed up as partisans and went to a contadino's house to beg for something to eat. And Roberto was constantly plagued by lice; as he was discovering, there was little glamour in being a soldier.

On 18 February, Lieutenant Barnini had led part of his platoon on a rastrellamento on the Castel di Masino, about eight miles away from their base at Cavaglia, where they had heard the partisans had stored a cache of arms. When the platoon arrived there, they were fired upon, and although they managed to get inside the castle, a long fire-fight ensued. Realising they were heavily outnumbered, Barnini sent one of his men hurrying back to Cavaglia to fetch help.

The rescue party consisted of just four men, led by William Cremonini, and one boy-soldier, Roberto. They immediately lost valuable time when their only truck would not start. They eventually got going, but by the time they neared the castle it was already dusk. They could smell cordite on the air, and they approached cautiously on foot. Roberto felt excited, and safe, thanks to the calm steadfastness exuded by William. The place was quiet; there was no sound of gun-fire, no shouting – nothing. William then grabbed one of the villagers and put his sub-machine gun to the man's head. 'There's no one left here', the man told him.

'OK then,' said William, 'you prove it. You guide me and then you'll be the first to know if we find someone.' The man led them to the castle and there William and his men found two dead volunteers from Barnini's platoon but no one else. Letting the man go, he was then approached by a lady who, she told him tearfully, was the owner of the castle. 'We were wearing white snow camouflage and she thought I was a German,' he says. 'She was crying and crying and so I stopped her and said, "*Signora*, please explain to me in Italian". She stopped crying instantly and explained that the partisans had occupied the castle – which I already knew – but otherwise she could tell me nothing except that they had gone.'

William decided to see the village priest, and asked him to make contact with the partisans on their behalf. The priest tried to make excuses, telling William there was a curfew on and that it was really not possible, but William insisted. 'Look, here is a pass,' he told the priest. 'Go and find them or else at midnight we will set fire to your buildings.'

At around 11.30 p.m., the priest returned with a note from Lieutenant Barnini. They had been taken hostage by men of the 76th Garibaldi Brigade, but would be freed for the same number of their partisans. 'From that moment,' says William, 'we began a process of exchange.' This was not easy as some of the partisan prisoners were being held by the Germans in Milan, but eventually they managed it and all the captured men were freed. Not only that, they had been well treated and had been fed as much as the other partisans; the 76th Brigade Commander, Ghandi, had kept to his word with an admirable sense of

: It was harder for Germans to ever get away from the war, thanks to the twin threats of Allied air forces and partisans, but letters from home were considered essential in maintaining morale. Incredibly, despite the difficulties, German post did tend to get through, reaching recipients in the most extreme corners of the battlefield.

LEFT: Ernest Wall (*bottom right*) and his crew from 24 SAAF Squadron. Whenever they could, bomber crews would tirelessly take to the skies but all too often, in the autumn of 1944, their efforts were frustrated by the weather.

And their aircraft, a B-26 Marauder, W-E6.

LEFT: By October, the Allies found themselves grinding to a halt, largely thanks to the weather, or more specifically the rain, which poured down in torrents almost every day, flooding rivers, washing away roads and turning dust to thick, glutinous mud.

ABOVE: As if the mountains and the mud were not bad enough, there were also the never-ending rivers to cross. These offered ideal positions for the defenders and enormous practical difficulties for the attackers. Here, Eighth Army tanks cross the Savio, some more successfully than others.

LEFT: Franz Maassen, a highly capable and courageous unteroffizier in the 274th Infantry Division. He was also a twice-wounded veteran of the war in Russia.

RIGHT: The rain wore everyone down. In this sketch by Ted Wyke-Smith, he perfectly captures the world-weariness of Allied infantry at the front.

BELOW: Members of the 8th Garibaldi Brigade in Forlì, shortly after its fall to the Allies in November 1944. Iader Miserocchi is beneath the arrow.

RIGHT: For other partisans, however, the winter of 1944–45 was a grim and desperate time. Emilio Sacerdote was both a partisan and a Jew and when captured was interned first at the concentration camp in Bolzano then sent to the death camp of Flossemburg in Germany.

Mussolini in Milan in December 1944. It was Il Duce's last public appearance and went surprisingly well. Even so four months later the Milanese would be mocking his bloodied corpse. Behind him stands Alessandro Pavolini, in his Black Shirt paramilitary uniform.

Major Stephen Hastings (*second from left*), a British Liaison Officer with No.1 Special Force, SOE, with men from the XIII Piacenza Partisans. When he parachuted in to help them in February 1945, Stephen found morale low after the harsh winter and the endless rastrellamenti by the Fascist and German forces.

Wrecked German vehicles and war materiel along the banks of the River Po. Most of this was destroyed by the Germans themselves before they attempted to cross Italy's widest river. The rest was shot up by Allied planes.

RIGHT: The rain wore everyone down. In this sketch by Ted Wyke-Smith, he perfectly captures the world-weariness of Allied infantry at the front.

BELOW: Members of the 8th Garibaldi Brigade in Forlì, shortly after its fall to the Allies in November 1944. Iader Miserocchi is beneath the arrow.

RIGHT: For other partisans, however, the winter of 1944–45 was a grim and desperate time. Emilio Sacerdote was both a partisan and a Jew and when captured was interned first at the concentration camp in Bolzano then sent to the death camp of Flossemburg in Germany.

ABOVE: After the rain came the snow. US troops walk back down the mountain.

LEFT: Albert Burke, Master Sergeant of the 92nd 'Buffalo' Division, the first all-black combat division in the US Army.

RIGHT: Hans Kumberg. In December, Hans was lucky to survive when a shell fragment hit him in the stomach.

Fresh, spirited American troops, flushed with victory, are bringing in thousands of hungry, ragged, battle-weary prisoners. (News item)

Mussolini in Milan in December 1944. It was Il Duce's last public appearance and went surprisingly well. Even so, four months later the Milanese would be mocking his bloodied corpse. Behind him stands Alessandro Pavolini, in his Black Shirt paramilitary uniform.

Major Stephen Hastings (*second from left*), a British Liaison Officer with No.1 Special Force, SOE, with men from the XIII Piacenza Partisans. When he parachuted in to help them in February 1945, Stephen found morale low after the harsh winter and the endless rastrellamenti by the Fascist and German forces.

Wrecked German vehicles and war materiel along the banks of the River Po. Most of this was destroyed by the Germans themselves before they attempted to cross Italy's widest river. The rest was shot up by Allied planes.

ABOVE: A long column of German prisoners at the war's end. Far too many tragedies were played out in these final days, and for most of the men here, the future looked grim: a year, maybe more, in prison camps followed by the uncertain return home to a country both ruined and divided.

BELOW: The cemetery at Casaglia as it is today. Bullet holes still pockmark the wall and iron grave markers show the indentation where bullets struck. It is a beautiful, haunting place, one still shrouded in a veil of melancholy.

honour. Indeed, as the exchange finally took place thirteen days later, partisans and Bir el Gobi men raised a toast together: 'Long live Italy!'[336]

For the men of the Bir el Gobi Company, and especially those who had spent nearly two weeks in the mountains with the partisans, this episode marked a turning point. Perceptions had changed. Most of them were trained soldiers and they wanted to fight for Italy at the front and against the Allies, not trudge around the mountains trying to kill their fellow countrymen. As was becoming increasingly obvious to them, this small, private war in the mountains was achieving precious little, and leaving behind nothing but bitterness and ruined lives.

At this time, the partisans had yet to emerge from the crisis of the winter months. The weather and conditions played a large part, although the continued shortage of supplies was another factor. There are some large discrepancies between the official figures for the amounts of equipment dropped to the partisans at this time and those listed by 334 Wing, who played the biggest role in carrying out special operations drops at this time.

Certainly the weather continued to limit the number of missions. The number of aborted missions was high, while the appalling winter conditions meant many never took off in the first place. The other reason was that the major part of their effort was still being directed towards the Balkans and specifically Yugoslavia. In February, 334 Wing dropped 1,869.42 tons of supplies to Tito's partisans, from 942 sorties. The Italian partisans, in contrast, received just 32 tons of supplies from fourteen sorties made by 334 Wing and nothing from the 51st Troop Carrier Wing; twenty-three missions were aborted or cancelled. In January, Italian partisans had been delivered just 45 tons of supplies by the Wing.[337] In contrast, official records claim that 363.76 tons were dropped in January and 950.69 in February; who was delivering this considerable extra tonnage is not clear.

Supply packages varied in size, but were delivered in 'cells' made from quarter-inch thick cardboard and light metal. A typical cell that weighed just over 140lbs could contain six Sten guns, 2,700 rounds of ammunition, plus various bits of gun-cleaning gear. A 250lb cell would equate to nine Sten guns and ammunition, or one Bren machine gun with fourteen magazines and 2,000 rounds of ammunition. In other words, one ton of supplies might mean four Brens and thirty-six Stens. Even if 900 tons of supplies really were dropped during February, it was still not

very much for in excess of 100,000 partisans – a figure that would swell
to possibly double that by April, and it was why Allied agents in the
field repeatedly claimed they were not receiving anything like the amount
of supplies they needed.[338]

If figures have been somewhat manipulated, it would not really be all
that surprising. Fears of a 'second Greece' had not subsided. The thought
of thousands of highly armed partisans streaming through the cities
of northern Italy declaring that the revolution was nigh was a prospect
the AFHQ and AMG had absolutely no stomach for, and, whatever the
likelihood, not a risk they were prepared to take. Thoughts of having to
quell an armed insurrection after a long and bloody campaign against
Germany and republican Fascist Italy did not sit well.

The partisans had played an invaluable part in the campaign so far
and the Allies hoped they would help with the final offensive too. But
with the war drawing to a close, they wanted this help to be carefully
controlled. The number of Allied missions in support of the partisans
was greatly increased during the first months of 1945. OSS tended to
use mostly Italian or American-Italian agents to help individual partisan
bands, irrespective of political leaning. SOE, on the other hand, preferred
to send what they called 'British Liaison Officers' (BLO) into areas where
several bands operated under the control of one command, rather like
CUMER had been trying to get Lupo to do before the destruction of
the Stella Rossa. The task of the liaison officers was not only to provide
training and encouragement to the partisans, but also to manipulate
them into behaving and performing in a way that would support the
Allies' offensive, yet which would not end in armed, Communist,
revolution.

One of these new 'BLOs' was Captain Stephen Hastings, formerly of
the Scots Guards and the SAS. Having seen considerable action in North
Africa, he was a highly competent soldier, but also had experience of
operating deep behind enemy lines. However, working with irregular
guerrillas in the cold and still snow-covered mountains was an entirely
new experience. Nonetheless, Stephen was anxious to get going. Since
falling ill after a summer of intense SAS operations in the Western
Desert, he had spent more than six months in a staff post in Cairo
before joining SOE in Algiers. He had then been sent in with the invasion
of southern France in August with a brief to link up with the resistance
there and report on their needs. It had been a 'pretty farcical interlude'[339]
and with his old regiment having suffered badly in Italy, he had begun

to feel guilty that he was sitting pretty while others far less experienced than he were being killed. On the point of throwing in the towel and returning to orthodox front-line duties, he then saw a signal from Bari asking for volunteers to go 'into the field' in northern Italy. He leapt at the chance.

Stephen parachuted into the mountains south of Piacenza on 2 February, along with a radio operator, 'Chalky' White, and an interpreter and right-hand man, Giorgio Insom, a half Italian-half Russian with whom Stephen had gelled immediately. Their mission was called 'Clover II' and their task was to make their way towards the Nure Valley in what had recently been designated the 13th Partisan Zone. This area, Stephen had been warned, had been particularly hard hit by the Black Brigades' rastrellamenti.

Stephen and his two companions eventually managed to meet up with the commander of the 13th Zone, Colonel Marziolo, in the small mountain village of Groppallo, overlooking the Nure Valley some twenty-five miles south of Piacenza. Marziolo had under his rather shaky command three partisan bands. Around Groppallo was the Justice and Liberty Division. To the north, towards the town of Morfasso, in the Val d'Arda, was the Prati Division, affiliated to the Christian Democrats; and to the west, in the Val Trebbia, was the Communist Garibaldi Brigade, the First Division Piacenza. Such had been the rastrellamenti over the winter that none of these brigades had more than 100–200 men at most. Morale was low. Colonel Marziolo, a fifty-year-old former army officer, told Stephen about the hardships they had endured that winter. They had lacked arms, ammunition and food, and this situation had not improved. Clothes were threadbare, boots worn through. Numerous villages had been burned and left in ruins. He was shown a photograph of more than twenty grinning Germans grouped around the body of a woman they held naked and spread-eagled between them. An NCO posed with a dagger ready to cut her open. Another picture showed a girl, hands tied behind her back, hanging on a meat hook. They had been killed during one of the many rastrellamenti. 'I was shocked by this,' admits Stephen. 'I was used to the Western Desert where there was no feeling of hatred at all.'

He also soon discovered that their lives had been made harder by the continued presence of 'Franchi', Marziolo's predecessor, who had become more bandit than freedom fighter. Franchi (his real name Sogno) had formerly been a lieutenant in the Italian army and he had, since the previous August, been supported heavily by SOE and by the regional CLNAI/CVL headquarters, the Comitato di Liberazione Nord Emilia (CLNE). Notorious for bullying the mountain people, he was also rumoured to have made a pact with the Fascists. 'But as I quickly discovered,' says Stephen, 'it was impossible to establish any facts.' Stephen's task was now to weld these disparate groups together, re-inject a healthy dose of morale, and prepare them for the spring offensive. This, he quickly realised, was going to be no easy matter, although the arrival of a few supply drops would certainly do much to win him respect. Whether they would appear, however, was another matter. There was much for him – and the partisans – to do in the weeks to come.

THIRTY-SEVEN

Getting Ready
February–April 1945

By the beginning of February, General Karl Wolff, Plenipotentiary General and Highest SS and Police Führer in Italy, had realised that Germany could no longer win the war. Until that point, he, like millions of others, had accepted Hitler's promises of all-powerful secret weapons, of the arrival of a new air force of jet aircraft, and of the renewal of the U-boat war. 'It was only at the end of January,' he said, 'that I realised the rottenness of our position.'[340] He had been speaking to friends serving on the Western Front who had taken part in the Ardennes offensive and had not liked what he had heard. They had told him that not one of the promised 3,000 aircraft had materialised; indeed, the Ardennes offensive had failed, in no small part due to the Allies' continued massive air superiority.

Frustrated and angry, he went to visit Himmler to ask him about German plans. The Reichsführer was evasive, but offered to arrange a meeting with Hitler. Two days later, at Hitler's headquarters in Berlin, and with von Ribbentrop and several other leading Nazis present, Wolff spoke openly with the Führer. The previous October, with Kesselring's blessing, he had made tentative contact with Allen Dulles, the American chargé d'affaires and senior OSS officer in Berne, Switzerland, proposing that he and Kesselring would sign a document confirming that the Germans would not destroy any non-military sites in return for an understanding that the partisans were to stop all sabotage activities. This had been flatly rejected, but in December, through Cardinal Schuster of Milan, contact had been made once more with Dulles. 'I told the Führer everything,' said Wolff, and suggested they should continue these feelers with the Allies with urgent vigour. It was true, the Western Allies and the Soviets were held together by a thread, but Wolff told Hitler that he thought the chances of them turning on one another in the near future were slight. 'Before that happens,' he told him, 'we shall be dead or beaten to the ground, and that must not happen – we must do something first.'[341]

This was astonishingly frank, and a hugely high-risk strategy – either very brave or extremely foolhardy. Coming from other men, on a day when Hitler was in a less equable mood, this would have been considered tantamount to treason, and there was only one punishment for that. However, Wolff was an old favourite, and on that day the Führer was calm and polite and seemed to agree with much that had been said. At any rate, he did not specifically order Wolff to stop these feelers, and so, on his return to Italy, the Plenipotentiary General began setting in motion approaches to the Allies that he hoped would lead to a shortening of the war and which would save many lives – German, Italian and Allied.

Hitler's old friend Mussolini was now almost as reclusive as the Führer, although back in December there had been an appearance that had proved that some of the Duce's old magnetism had not entirely deserted him. Spurred on by the insistence of Pavolini and other leading Fascists, he had given a speech in Milan, and despite only last-minute publicity, the Teatro Lirico had been packed. He blamed Italy's plight on the King and defeatist generals, as well as the middle classes, then turned to the threat from the Soviet Union and the plight of Britain, which, he said, was politically 'finished'. He had also returned to his favourite theme of socializzazione, and his hopes for a united Italy once more. The applause he received was enormous and afterwards large crowds followed him wherever he went. Even then, with the Axis partners on the brink of collapse, the Duce still commanded a considerable following.

On his return from Milan, however, he had retreated into his closeted existence once more. Elena Curti still visited him every other week. 'He had changed,' she admits. 'He was much more withdrawn. The fire had dimmed, I suppose.' Nonetheless, he was still writing prodigiously and gave a large number of interviews to journalists in which he repeatedly referred to his legacy and the future of Europe. He also talked of Britain's failure, pointing out that it had gone to war to save Poland, but that Poland was now in the hands of the Russians.

Tragically for the Poles, the events of the Yalta Conference had only served to darken Poland's future. 'February 12,' wrote General Anders, 'remains deeply impressed on my memory.' Anders had been in Florence, at Clark's new headquarters, where General Marshall was visiting on his way back from Yalta. At a dinner held by Clark, he talked at length with Marshall, although the American chief was somewhat evasive over Polish matters. This gave Anders a gut feeling that all was not well, but nothing had prepared him for the bombshell that was communicated late that night. A statement by the Big Three had been released about the future of Poland, which, while it accepted the desire to see a democratic independent Poland emerge from the wreckage of war, also announced the establishment of the Polish Provisional Government of National Unity. This, as all were aware, was made up of pro-Soviet lackeys. Worse, it announced that Britain and America had accepted Russian demands to partition much of Eastern Poland into the Soviet Union. 'There followed a few days,' wrote Anders, 'in which we Poles were numbed and bewildered. This was followed by a violent reaction in the Army as the men realised the great injustice that had been done them.'[342] Still in southern Italy, Wladek Rubnikowicz was heartbroken. 'You cannot imagine what it was like to hear that,' he says. 'We all felt betrayed, that we'd been sold out by the very Allies in whom we had placed so much trust. I loved my country. To know that all we had fought for had been for nothing was completely devastating.'

Anders' reaction was to inform McCreery that he could no longer expect his men to continue the fight. The Eighth Army commander tried to talk him out of it, as did Clark. Anders, who had great respect for Clark and whom he considered a friend, listened to his arguments, so that by the time he then met with Alexander, he had already decided there was no option but to ask his men to continue fighting. It was very fortunate for the Allies that Anders was a man with such a deep sense of honour and dignity – and that he was so beloved by his men.

The front line might have been largely static at this time, but for the men dug in along it, front-line duty could still be a gruelling experience. Nightly patrol work, especially, was part and parcel of the infantryman's lot. The objective for the Allies was to learn as much about the enemy as possible before the launch of the spring offensive. Much could be learned by creeping towards enemy positions and observing, but the greatest prize of all was the capture of prisoners. 'Patrolling,' noted Bob Wiggans, now entrenched in the Monte Grande area opposite the Fallschirmjäger Pioneers, 'is about the most nerve-racking assignment a doughboy gets'. He had noticed that after several weeks on Monte

Grande, his men were beginning to get 'jittery'. It was not surprising. The weather remained awful, artillery and mortar duels continued intermittently all day, and the suspense and nervous attention this placed on the men stretched nerves to breaking point. Newspaper reports back home in the States reported activity in Italy with lines like, 'Artillery duels and patrol clashes were reported on the Fifth Army front in Italy,' but as Bob points out, 'for the doughboy participating in the patrol clash, it was another D-Day for him.'[343]

By the middle of February, Bob and his men had made so many patrols they knew the German positions as well as their own, but prisoners seemed to be eluding them. Bob sensed what was coming and sure enough an order arrived for the battalion to mount a raid in force to capture some prisoners. The 3rd Battalion duly got down to preparing for such an operation, which they planned to carry out on 22 February. They were told it *had* to succeed, and that it was to be a no-holds-barred raid for which even ammunition restrictions would be lifted.

A German listening outpost, known as the Casa Raggi, was decided upon as the target, as patrols had discovered that in front of it were occupied enemy foxholes. These – or rather, the men in them – were to be the target. Thirty-four men were to be used in the raid, divided into a ten-man attacking group led by Bob, and a second twenty-four-man support group. Secrecy and surprise went hand-in-hand. Timing had to be perfect. Every man had to know his role precisely.

By the time of the raid, everyone was keyed up. At 1 a.m. on the 23rd, each man had to be in position and ready. At 01.10 precisely, the firing would begin. And so it did, ripping the night apart and catching the enemy completely off guard. Artillery shells screamed overhead, explosions echoed around the mountains, mortars exploded, machine guns chattered and tracer criss-crossed over the mountain. Under this cover, a startled German paratrooper was grabbed from his foxhole and pulled back to the Custermen's lines. By the time Bob made it safely back again, he was gasping for breath and utterly exhausted. Not yet fully recovered from his illness, the raid had taken more out of him than he had expected.

There was a twist, however. Their prized prisoner, it seemed, knew less than the Americans. As Colonel Jackson, the battalion CO, told it, 'as luck would have it, he was about the dumbest of the wooden-headed Krauts. Had only been back from hospital three days and had no idea of where he himself was at the time of capture.' To add insult to injury, the following night another German voluntarily crossed over to their lines and gave himself up. 'This boy had all the dope,' added Colonel Jackson, 'he talked freely and spilled the beans on lots of important plans which he had overheard.'[344] Such were the ironies of war.

Meanwhile, along the western half of the front, Truscott ordered several limited attacks to be carried out during February to improve their positions before the offensive. Along the coast, the 92nd 'Buffalo' Division were given a chance to show their mettle, and were ordered to advance forward down the Serchio Valley and also to win ground across the flat coastal corridor between the mountains and the sea. In the Serchio, the Americans pushed back the Italian forces opposite them with ease but were then counterattacked successfully by German reserves brought up to fill the breach. In the coastal section, the Americans faltered almost from the start, running into minefields and struggling against heavy enemy artillery and mortar fire; one battalion fell back as another advanced, and in the confusion the assault broke down entirely. Three days after it was begun, General Almond was forced to call off the attack entirely. This limited thrust had cost forty-seven officers and 659 men – a heavy price for 145 prisoners and almost no ground.

Further inland, the 10th Mountain Division, together with the Brazilians, had more success. Now positioned in the mountains to the west of the Reno Valley, their task was to clear two ridges that would enable the front line to draw level with the South Africans and the 1st Armored who remained dug in along the Reno Valley and across the Monte Sole massif. Although snow still covered the mountains, the 10th Mountain had been training for just such operations; moreover, opposite them was the 232nd Infantry Division, a German unit made up of mostly older or convalescing troops who had originally been intended for rear-area duty only. Attacking without artillery, the 10th Mountain men took the enemy by surprise and their initial objectives with ease. In fighting that lasted between 19 February and 5 March, the 10th Mountain Division managed to gain a six-mile front between the commanding Monte Grande d'Aiano and Highway 64 in the Reno Valley – a highly favourable starting point for when the spring offensive was finally launched.

Much to the annoyance of the other US divisions who had been slogging it out in Italy for over a year, the dashing 10th Mountain soon became darlings of the press for this first flush of success. For the beleaguered 92nd Division, however, there were further recriminations.

They had already just recently suffered a humiliating enquiry into 'the loss of combat efficiency' amongst the 2nd Battalion, 370th Infantry, back in November. Now confidence in their fighting capabilities had reached rock bottom.

At divisional headquarters, Master Sergeant Albert Burke found this a dispiriting time. He knew the men were under-trained and under-supported. 'That's where the problems existed,' he says. 'Almond damned us all the time. He never did give us any credit for even the good things we did.' Negativity had spread through the division. There were numerous aspects that undermined confidence and morale, such as the widely held belief that the white officers were considered superior to the black officers by the division's commanders and were accordingly given better treatment. Failure in battle and rising losses were also hard habits to break and traumatic for the men. 'I had one young man come up to me,' says Albert, 'and he asked me whether I was ever afraid. I said, "Don't let anybody tell you they're never afraid. But you do get used to it. It doesn't bother me any more and one day you'll feel the same. You keep your faith in the man upstairs. You'll be all right."' The young recruit had come to see him because he had known Albert's sister back in the States. 'He wanted to tell me all about himself,' says Albert, 'but I said I didn't want to know ... I didn't want to know their names. I tried not to because I knew the chances were they'd get themselves killed.'

Nor was there much incentive for risking their necks. For most black soldiers, America was a land of racial discrimination and never-ending poverty, something that Clark recognised. 'The Negro soldier,' he noted, 'needed greater incentive; a feeling that he was fighting as an equal. Only the proper environment in his own country can provide such an incentive.'[345] He was quite right. Albert certainly felt little sense of national pride – and his upbringing had been better than that of the vast majority of blacks in the division. 'It was bullshit,' he says. 'We were just interested in getting home. That was the way I felt, really.'

At any rate, a reorganisation of the division followed their February failures. Despite all the problems, significant numbers of officers and soldiers had more than proved themselves since arriving in Italy, and these were now all transferred into the 370th Infantry, while those considered less competent were sifted out into the other regiments. In addition, General Marshall released the highly regarded Japanese-American 442nd 'Nisei' Infantry Regiment from southern France to join the 92nd Division. This meant that the other all-black regiments were now no longer considered suitable for major front-line operations; on the other hand, by the end of March, the 'Buffalo' Division had two high calibre infantry regiments with which to play a key part in the spring offensive.

Reorganisation was being carried out all along the Allied front. Troops were withdrawn in rotation, retrained, and in some cases, as in the 92nd Division, consolidated. The 3rd Coldstream Guards, for example, were finally taken out of the line from beneath Monte Sole and sent back to Spoleto in Umbria, where, due to the number of casualties both battalions had suffered and because of the shortage of reinforcements, they were amalgamated. With the new battalion now fully up to strength, Reg Harris was given a month of home leave – his first time back in Wiltshire for two-and-a-half years. 'Imagine it,' he wrote, 'I had come out in 1942, it was now 1945, and in the meantime my son Toby had been born and was now old enough to run around and talk – well, I was overjoyed to say the least.'

Despite sending veterans like Reg home for well-earned leave, the quest for extra troops continued as staffs drew on every single available source of manpower they could to make good the recent losses. More Brazilians arrived; so did the Jewish Brigade from the Middle East. Two new Polish brigades were formed – and most of the men for these were Poles who had been forced to fight for the Germans, but who had then either been captured or had escaped across the lines. All five Italian combat groups were brought up to the front; even partisan bands were brought into the line – Iader Miserocchi's new band, the 28th Garibaldi, were positioned south of Lake Comacchio, and the 36th Garibaldi Brigade in XIII Corps' mountain sector. Both armies were also recruiting, clothing and equipping former partisans into reconnaissance units each comprising about 500 men. It was into one of these units that Gianni Rossi, now recovered from his wounds, was recruited.

Even those used to being in the rear services were called to the front. Twenty-one-year-old Tom Finney from Preston, Lancashire, had been an English football star in the making as war had broken out, but in 1942 he had received his call-up papers just like everyone else his age – playing football was not a reserved occupation. He had joined the Royal Armoured Corps in 1942, but had in fact then spent most of the war playing football, touring the Middle East and Italy and entertaining the troops. But in February, he too was told that he was finally going to be needed at the front. 'I was suddenly called in to be interviewed by one of the base officers at Foggia,' Tom recalls, 'and he said to me, "Have you seen any action yet?" I said, "No." And he said, "Well, you bloody soon will." The following day I was off to join the 9th Queen's Royal Lancers.'

New equipment was also arriving – equipment that would make their lives much easier in the flat, watery countryside of the north-east: types of tracked amphibious vehicles called 'Fantails' and 'Kangaroos'; and also flame-throwing tanks, particularly vicious pieces of kit. The armoured regiments were given tanks with better guns, as well as bridge-laying tanks. Training was thorough and intensive. As with Operation DIADEM a year before, Alexander and his commanders were determined to leave nothing to chance in their preparation. They meant to show that, despite being in a secondary theatre, they could still play an important part in hastening the end of the war.

While preparations progressed on the ground, the air forces never let up with their invaluable contribution to the Allied effort. Despite losses to the Western Front, the Mediterranean air forces were still formidable. Weather continued to hinder operations but now that the Allies were that much further north and no longer being called upon directly to support operations on the ground, the tactical air forces were able to concentrate on hitting targets all the way north to Innsbruck. The Brenner Battle, as it was known, had begun in November and was still going on into March, and was directed at the strategically crucial rail and road link through the Alps between Verona and Austria.

For the aircrews involved the Brenner route was a horror. There were more than 3,000 anti-aircraft guns in Italy, but by the end of March some 952 were dotted along this narrow mountain corridor, making it the most heavily defended complex in the world. Needless to say, losses of Allied aircraft were high.

The Marauders of the 24 SAAF Squadron were now taking part in the Brenner Battles. On 23 March, Ernest Wall took part in his 68th and penultimate mission, a daylight raid to bomb railway marshalling yards near Innsbruck. They were accompanied by P51 Mustangs, but the danger came less from possible enemy aircraft than from the extremely heavy concentrations of flak. 'It was pretty intense,' he says, 'but you could hardly turn round and go home. You simply had to get on with it.' After dropping their bombs, his pilot, Lieutenant Talbot, decided to shoot up one of the main streets in Innsbruck itself, only narrowly to miss crashing into a large hill as they climbed away once more. There was, however, one small benefit of flying over the Brenner Pass. 'With snow-covered mountains and frozen lakes,' says Ernest, 'the views were really spectacular.'

Meanwhile the fighter-bombers of the Desert Air Force, most of which had shorter ranges, concentrated on interdicting targets either side of the River Po, pasting bridges, railways, roads and anything that moved. In December, 244 Wing had moved to Bellaria, just north of Rimini, and were now operating from pierced-steel plating runways. Group Captain Cocky Dundas had instigated new variations on the 'Rover David' tactics designed to help them hit targets even when there was low cloud. Cocky even suggested to the army that at a predetermined moment they should lay down a line of white smoke shells directly in front of the area they wanted hit. Cocky and his aircraft would then swoop in low and strafe everything in front. Results so far had been good: in December, the pilots of 244 Wing had managed almost single-handedly to clear a section of the German front line ahead of the advancing infantry.

Allied tactical planning had now been passed to Clark and his army commanders, Truscott and McCreery. Alexander had hoped to maintain his overall control of operations, but by February this had become impossible – such were the demands of his position, he spent just five days at his headquarters during the entire month. The rest of the time he was in Malta, Yalta, Greece, Belgrade and even at the Russian front.

By the beginning of March, Clark had pretty much crystallised his plans. Following the Alexander style, he devised another two-fisted approach. He had noticed that the vast bulk of German forces and defences were concentrated to the east and south of the River Reno, which ran in a northerly direction to Bologna and twenty miles beyond, then swung more than ninety degrees towards the Adriatic coast. He had realised, however, that if Fifth Army's main thrust remained to the west of the River Reno, then once out of the mountains they would be able to sweep north to the Po without any further obstacles of note in their way. A feint attack would be carried out by II Corps, in the Apennines to the east of the Reno Valley, while thanks to 10th Mountain Division's efforts in February, he now had the perfect start line for his principal assault.

For Eighth Army, he planned a daring outflanking manoeuvre through the eastern edge of AOK 10. Until offensive operations had ceased, Eighth Army had been driving in a north-westerly direction towards Bologna. Instead, Clark decided they should make their main attack through the western edge of Lake Comacchio towards Argenta. The problem was that the Germans, helped by the winter's rain, had flooded large parts of the plains to the south-west of Argenta, leaving only a narrow gap between the flood waters and Lake Comacchio. This was now known as the Argenta Gap, was sure to be mined and, if the Germans got wind of the plan, could be easily defended. The solution was two-fold. First, new Fantail tanks could enable a certain number of troops to get across Lake Comacchio and the flood waters to the south-west of the lake and outflank the Argenta Gap. Second, Eighth Army's attack could be split, with a second thrust directed north of the Via Emilia, but to the south of the flooding. This, McCreery and Clark hoped, would give Eighth Army the kind of balance and flexibility to deal with a number of eventualities.

As ever with a two-fisted attack, one punch had to be delivered before the other. There were two reasons for this. The first was that by staggering the dates of attack, both armies were able to have the benefit of the maximum support from the air. In this, Alexander, as Supreme Commander, insisted his air commanders should contribute fully – he was convinced that the air forces held the key to blasting open breaches in the German lines.

Second, the first punch should draw off enemy troops from the area of the next attack. This meant that whichever Army attacked second became the primary assault force. McCreery, worried about the untested performance of the Fantails and the narrowness of the Argenta Gap, wanted Fifth Army to go first. However, key to the entire scheme was, as ever, the deception plans. These once again focused on continued German paranoia about being outflanked by an amphibious assault, and the most obvious place to do this was north of the Po on the Adriatic coast, close to Eighth Army's sector. Landing craft and increased shipping were thus built up at Ravenna, suggesting a major two-pronged attack by Eighth Army, one by land and one by sea. If Fifth Army attacked first, this deception would collapse. Furthermore, Clark's plan for Fifth Army was not only less dependent on variables, but also quite clearly offered the most likely route for a decisive breakthrough.

McCreery, however, did not see it this way, believing Clark was belittling Eighth Army and showing bias towards the American Fifth. This was simply not the case; rather Clark and McCreery simply had differences of approach and character. After long and costly years of fighting, Eighth Army's commanders had developed an understandable caution – a caution that most of the troops would not have recognised. Clark, on the other hand, was more bullish, and had the kind of forthright manner that did not always sit well with the more measured, calm, and even reserved nature of men like McCreery. The Eighth Army commander also wanted to delay the attack until May. 'The feeling in Eighth Army is: Let's wait and the job may be easier,' noted Clark in his diary. 'My feeling is that when the Boche crumble on all sides we must hit him soon with everything we have.'[346]

He had a point. Eisenhower's forces had just crossed the Rhine at Remagen, while the Red Army was now knocking on the door of Berlin. Both Alexander and Clark believed their forces in Italy should play their part in closing the ring. Consequently, Clark insisted the launch date would be 10 April – which was later brought forward to the 9th – with Fifth Army starting four or five days later. It was a risk, admittedly, but a calculated one: by then he hoped the weather would have sufficiently improved, and the ground hardened. This date also allowed him enough ammunition and replacements for a two-month battle, which, he hoped, would be ample. 'My infantry superiority,' he noted, 'will be approximately 1.4, hardly sufficient for a breakthrough, particularly in the mountain terrain.' Still, he added, 'with a little bit of luck, we may have a great victory south of the River Po'.[347]

German preparations for the spring offensive were once again hampered by their lack of intelligence and by the continued Allied destruction of their supply lines. Three new Arada 234 jet aircraft had miraculously been sent to Italy, but these fast twin-engine reconnaissance planes were too few in number and too late arriving to be of any serious benefit. On the back of 10th Mountain's success, 29th Panzer Grenadier Division had been moved hurriedly across from Eighth Army's front, but, as ever, Kesselring was responding to Allied actions rather than benefiting from actual knowledge. At the end of March, on the basis of the Allied deception plans, the division was moved back again, but this time posted north to the Adriatic coast south of Venice.

The Brenner Battles had seriously hampered German preparations. Back in October, an average of thirty-eight trains had passed daily between Verona and Bolzano. By March, this figure was just eight. In April it would drop to five.[348] Either side of the Po, the situation was just as bad. Further civilian buses, trucks and remaining cars were commandeered. Oxen were also now widely used, while one truck was used to tow two others. Such was the petrol shortage that substitute fuels were used, such as methane gas, and mixtures of alcohol and benzol. A few small oil wells in northern Italy managed to eke out an extra 1,000 litres of fuel a day. Up until the end of 1944, German forces in Italy had still received around 50,000 tons of coal per month. By January, this tap had been completely cut off. Nonetheless, they had been working hard preparing their defensive positions, and so long as they could hold the Allies along these lines, the Germans still had a chance of keeping the enemy at bay. After all, they had achieved great things already with very little.

Kesselring, however, would not be in Italy to defend this latest Allied offensive when it finally came. He had at long last been given an audience with Hitler on 9 March, only to learn he was now to take over from von Runstedt as commander of the entire Western Front, a daunting promotion at any time, but especially so in the circumstances. Stepping into the breach in Italy once again was von Vietinghoff, who, much to his relief, was recalled from East Prussia. But although Italy might have been a more comfortable posting than the Eastern Front, he soon found his hands were as tied as ever by Hitler and the High Command, who continued to dismiss out of hand any suggestions of withdrawal.

Entering into the increasingly fragile German line were more replacement troops, although numbers were now far less than either Kesselring or von Vietinghoff would have liked. One of those was eighteen-year-old Friedrich Büchner, the son of a slate factory owner from the small Thüringen town of Ludwigsstadt in south-east Germany.

As everywhere in the Third Reich, the long years of war had been keenly felt in Ludwigsstadt. The young men had all gone, and for people like Friedrich's father, trying to run a business had been tough. Times were hard; there was little labour and not much slate. The factory began manufacturing wooden ammunition boxes instead. During school holidays and at weekends, Friedrich had done what he could to help his father, but all too soon it was his turn to head off to war.

Friedrich had been just thirteen when the war had begun – a mere boy who had understood little about what was going on or why. Of course, like most lads his age, he had followed events as they had unfolded, but never had it occurred to him that it would still be going on by the time he was old enough to fight. At seventeen, he volunteered for the army, not because he was in any hurry to go off to war but because he knew he would be called up at eighteen and had the wherewithal to realise that by volunteering he would be given more choice of regiments and even the chance for training as a reserve officer.

Three months' basic training had begun on 31 May 1944, and was then followed by a reserve officers' course, and then a stint as an instructor – partly because there was now a shortage of instructors and partly because it was considered good experience for future officers. Then in March, he was suddenly given a field posting in Verona. 'It was a big surprise when I found out I was going to Italy,' he says. 'There were forty people on my course and only three of us went to Italy. The rest went to the Eastern and Western Fronts.'

Having reached Verona without being bombed or strafed on the way, he was posted to join the veteran 98th Infantry Division. As a Fahnenjunker – an aspiring officer – he reached Italy as an Unteroffizier, and was attached to the 3rd Company of the division's anti-tank battalion. Despite his youth and inexperience, Friedrich was then placed in charge of a 20mm anti-tank gun a few miles north of Faenza, not far from the forward positions along the River Senio.

Despite Germany's now desperate situation, Friedrich noticed that morale amongst the men was surprisingly good. 'The war wasn't over yet,' he says. 'There was still a job to be done.' All of them were waiting for the inevitable Allied offensive to begin. Considerable preparations had been made. Friedrich's battery of anti-tank guns was dug in outside a village, directly in front of a railway embankment. The gun positions and foxholes had been prepared, and ahead of them, along the Senio itself, there were more elaborate bunkers, minefields and gun emplacements, as well as anti-tank ditches.

He and the rest of his five-man gun crew lived in the barn of a nearby farm. The Italians remained living in the farmhouse itself, and continued with their day-to-day lives, despite finding themselves part of the front line. Relations between troops and civilians were good. 'We treated them well,' says Friedrich. 'I didn't get any feeling of resentment from them at all.' If they wanted washing doing, they paid the Italian *signora* and provided the soap; they also bought wine from them too. 'There was no looting,' he insists. 'You could be shot if you were caught, so no one did it. It was too dangerous.'

Not so very far from Friedrich was seventeen-year-old Antonio Cucciati, now finally getting his first taste of life at the front. The NP (Nuotatori e Paracadutisti) Battalion of the Decima MAS had been sent to Alfonsine, on the banks of the River Senio near Ravenna, opposite the Canadians' old sector. 'Don't cock it up because you always do,' the German troops had told them as the Italians had taken over their positions. Antonio quickly realised what a polyglot force lay on the other side of the river. 'There were Poles, Indians, New Zealanders,' he says, 'but there was no feeling of hatred between us. We were like two boxers.' No-man's-land was literally the width of the river. By day, the two sides would often shout greetings to one another. 'As long as there were no orders to fire,' says Antonio, 'we were the best of friends.'

Also heading to the front was the Bir el Gobi Company. Following the episode at the Castel di Masino, the company had spent another demoralising couple of weeks in the mountains, attached to a German anti-partisan unit. They had never once seen a single partisan. Eventually summoned back to Maderno by Pavolini, they were then told that they would be heading back to the mountains, this time to Valtellina. It was here that Pavolini and the other leading Fascists hoped to make their final stand. Before becoming the last bulwark of the Repubblica Sociale Italiana, however, the area first needed to be cleared of partisans.

Few of the men were happy about this, and Lieutenant Barnini, supported by the other officers, told Pavolini frankly that they wanted to finish the war on the front and, if need be, die there too. They did not believe in the Valtellina attack, and even less the Black Brigades and their rastrellamento operations. It was an astonishing outburst, but reflected their growing disillusionment. Yet it also says much about Pavolini's own state of mind that with tears in his eyes he gave them his blessing and waved them on their way to Bologna.

While the Neo-Fascists were planning their last stand, General Wolff was progressing with his peace feelers. In this he was being helped by Baron Parilli, an Italian industrialist who had taken up a mediating role between the SS and the OSS in Switzerland due to his fears of a possible German scorched-earth policy in the north; a peace settlement, he hoped, would prevent such action from the retreating Germans. At any rate, Parilli had reported back to Wolff on 27 February having made tentative contact with Dulles and his advisor Gero von Gävernitz. Wolff had then asked Parilli to return to Switzerland to make arrangements for two of his SS officers to make contact with the Americans. This had also proved successful, with the result that the next step was a meeting between Dulles and Wolff himself. As a show of good faith, Wolff had even arranged for the release of two senior figures from the CLNAI who had recently been captured – one of whom was none other than the Action Party leader, Ferruccio Parri.

Much to Dulles' surprise, Wolff arrived in person at their agreed rendezvous in Switzerland on 8 March, having first discussed matters with Ambassador Rahn. He was now determined that German troops in Italy should lay down their arms as soon as possible, and although he acknowledged to Dulles that the surrender of German forces in Italy required Kesselring's – and subsequently von Vietinghoff's – authority, he stressed that he was certain they could be won over.

Dulles was impressed and reported back favourably to Alexander, who felt the contact made with Wolff was worth pursuing. Accordingly, a second meeting was held on 19 March, with Alexander's blessing, and with his American Chief of Staff, General Lemnitzer, leading the discussions. Allied terms, however, were clear and non-negotiable: unconditional surrender and nothing else.

Despite this, Wolff did not balk at the Allies' hard line, although he recognised he now faced a tough challenge to win the authority for the surrender. Taking another huge risk, his next move was to return to Germany and to report to Himmler, to whom he confessed only a fraction of the discussions he had had with Dulles; certainly no mention was made of any Allied generals having been at the talks in Switzerland. As it was, he was severely reprimanded by Himmler for having acted alone. Even so, the Reichsführer told him to keep the negotiation doors open, although for the moment, however, he was to proceed no further and certainly not without higher authority.

It was hardly the reaction Wolff had been hoping for, and to make matters worse, the Allies had caught wind of his trip to Berlin. Alexander, his suspicions aroused, now told Dulles to close the door to any further approaches from the SS commander. Wolff, of course, was unaware of this. Back in Italy by the end of March, he was frustrated but determined there was still a way in which he could help bring the war to a close.

In the mountains south of Piacenza, SOE liaison officer Stephen Hastings and his team had worked hard and fast to bring some cohesion to the disparate partisan bands of the 13th Zone. Welding them together was no easy matter. 'They were scattered throughout the mountains,' says Stephen, 'and at each other's throats most of the time, chattering politics non-stop'. Meeting and talking with the leaders of these divisions was a time-consuming process involving long and arduous hikes across the mountains. Slowly but surely, however, having won their trust and side-lined the bandit, Franchi, he was able to cajole them together. 'My principal bargaining chip,' he recalls, 'was promising deliveries of arms, boots, blankets, food and other equipment only to those who were prepared to answer to a central command.'

Mercifully, supply drops did arrive – fewer than he would have liked, but enough to provide him with the credibility he needed and for him to achieve his aims. Consequently, on 1 April he was able to signal that all three divisions had agreed to co-operate with one another under a unified command. Moreover, the system of intelligence gathering was now running smoothly. 'If local Fascists coughed we knew about it,' says Stephen. 'We had the names of German officers, details of troop numbers – everything.'

Stephen struggled to get to grips with the politics of these mountain fighters, however. One day, his two bodyguards came to talk to him. Both were Communists, and somewhat shamefacedly, they told him they could no longer work for him. When Stephen asked why not, they explained that it was because he and his two fellow officers always ate separately from the rest of the partisans. This, they said, was not good communism. Stephen explained that he did so for a good reason: he wanted to keep his distance, important for maintaining his authority. Agreeing to disagree, Stephen bade them farewell.

Despite such incidents, and his inability to stifle the politicisation of the partisans, he felt the men of the 13th Zone were now ready to begin offensive operations once more. On 5 April, he received an order from the Allies to get ready for an all-out effort. At the same time, word reached him in his mountain HQ at Grappallo that a mixed Italian and German force was advancing to Castell'Arquato, where there was a key bridge over the River Arda. A couple of months before, the news of advancing troops would have sent the partisans hurrying back to their mountain hide-outs, but now, led by the Prati Division, the partisans went to meet the Fascist-German force and drove them off. It was just the confidence-boost the Piacentino partisans needed.

While such skirmishes were going on in the mountains south of Piacenza, the opening moves of the Allied offensive were being carried out. Along the Adriatic, Eighth Army's preliminary feints were going entirely according to plan. The Royal Marine Commandos had captured the narrow spit that ran between Lake Comacchio and the sea, and took 900 prisoners of 162nd Turkoman Division in the process. This attack was made mainly to pave the way for the Commandos and Fantails to mount the flanking move across the lake, but was also part of the deception plan – and von Vietinghoff fell for it hook, line and sinker, believing, as intended, that an Allied parachute and amphibious assault north of Lake Comacchio was imminent.

At the same time, the 92nd 'Buffalo' Division redeemed themselves by launching a successful diversion on the west coast and capturing a further 500 prisoners. Furthermore, the Buffalo Division's operation convinced Lemelsen, now back in charge of AOK 14, that his western flank needed reinforcing, and so he ordered a regimental group of the 90th Panzer Grenadier to the Tyrrhenian coast. Consequently, when Eighth Army opened their main attack, von Vietinghoff had no completely intact reserve division to call upon whatsoever.

By dawn on 9 April, the Allies were ready. The goal was the complete annihilation of the German forces in Italy, and with it, the end of the war.

THIRTY-EIGHT

The Last Offensive
9–20 April 1945

Group Captain Cocky Dundas had learned at the beginning of April that the Allied offensive was soon to begin, and it was made very clear to him that the army was relying heavily on massive air support. On Alexander's direct orders, a maximum air effort was needed, and that included not only the Desert Air Force and 22nd Tactical Air Command,* but also the heavy bombers of the Mediterranean Allied Strategic Air Force too. 'The intention,' noted Cocky, 'was that we should dish out to the German ground forces treatment similar to that experienced by British and French troops during the fall of France and the Low Countries five years earlier.'[349] There was a big difference, however, for the Allied air forces assembled in Italy were, despite recent cuts, considerably stronger than anything the Luftwaffe had been able to muster back in May 1940.

Until April, Italy had been given the lowest priority for the heavy bombers of MASAF as they continued to target Germany, Austria and the Balkans, but they now added considerable muscle, blitzing targets along the Brenner route, and joining in over the battlefield at the start of the offensive. Indeed, the air plan for the battle was methodical and systematic, and in direct support of V Corps and Polish Corps as they led Eighth Army's attack across the Senio. Just after midday on 9 April, the heavies droned north from Foggia, out over the Adriatic then turned in towards the battlefield. Eight hundred and twenty-five Liberators and Flying Fortresses were on their way, the first arriving at 1.50 p.m. and pasting German positions along the Senio with 175,000 fragmentation and general purpose bombs. An hour later came the mediums, attacking

*The remnants of the 12th Tactical Air Command had been renamed the 22nd Tactical Air Command on 19 October 1944.

in front of the Poles first and then ahead of V Corps. In between the fighter-bombers continued their work of interdiction, bombing and strafing specific targets and enemy communications. Cocky Dundas' 244 Wing flew 121 sorties that day, most of which were targets along the Senio.

For young Friedrich Büchner, this was a fearsome introduction to battle. 'It was absolutely terrifying,' he says. He and his comrades took cover in old wine cellars built under the railway embankment. So too did a number of local Italians. 'They began shouting and screaming with fear,' says Friedrich. 'The noise of the exploding bombs was completely deafening.'

Late in the afternoon, 1,500 guns began two forty-two-minute barrages. Then, as dusk fell, fighter-bombers flew over again, and flame-throwing tanks spat their fire at the flood banks. Last, but not least, stepping towards the smoke and mayhem, came the infantry. It was too much for the defenders and, as Alex had hoped, the German line buckled almost immediately.

'That was day one,' says Friedrich Büchner, 'and that night we packed up and started to move back.' They went about eight miles, then stopped and dug new gun positions. 'We were under fire nearly all the time,' he admits, 'although we were firing back too.' They even let off a few shells at the jabos, 'but I don't think we ever hit one.' By the morning of the 11th, the Germans had fallen back to the River Santerno and had suffered more than 3,000 casualties.

One of those was Antonio Cucciati, who had also had an horrendous baptism of fire in his first major battle. The Decima MAS had been close to Lake Comacchio and as soon as they had realised they were in danger of being attacked from behind, had retreated. 'Otherwise,' says Antonio, 'we would have been cut off.' Like Friedrich Büchner, Antonio found no respite from the constant aerial and artillery attacks. 'You had to keep listening all the time,' he says. The man he was with suddenly said, 'On the floor, guys – a shell's going to hit us.' As Antonio flung himself onto the ground he could feel a warm sensation in his shoulder. Moments later he lost consciousness.

When he awoke, he was in hospital in Argenta. He'd been hit in the shoulder by shrapnel, but because he had knocked his nose as he'd hit the ground, blood had been coming out of his mouth. His comrades had assumed the blood had come from his lungs, and that he'd been critically wounded. Fortunately, however, he was not as critically hit as

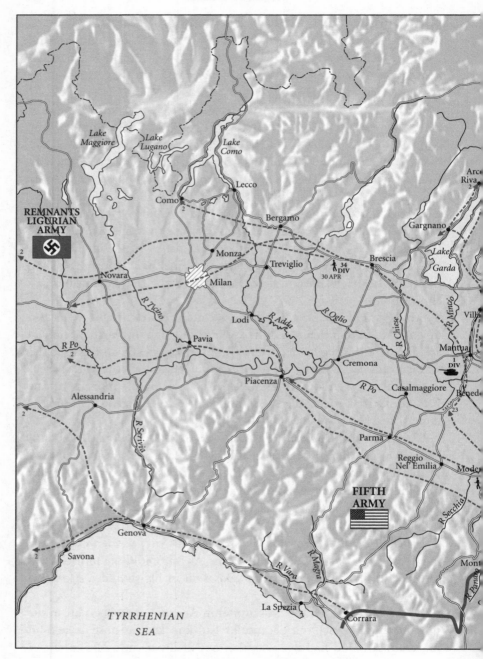

The final offensive, April–May 1945

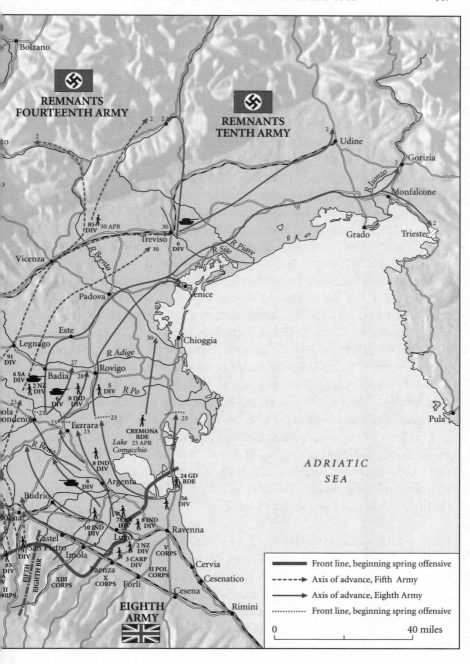

REMNANTS
FOURTEENTH ARMY

REMNANTS
TENTH ARMY

Bolzano

Udine

Gorizia

R. Isonzo

Monfalcone

2

85 30 APR
DIV

30

Treviso

6
DIV

R Sile

R Piave

Grado

Trieste

Vicenza

R. Brenta

30

Padova

Venice

Este

30

Chioggia

Legnago

91
DIV

R Adige

27

6 SA
DIV

Badia

28

Rovigo

2 NZ
DIV

6
DIV

8 IND
DIV

5
DIV

R Po

ola
ondeno

23

23

Ferrara

23

Pula

CREMONA
BDE

Lake
Comacchio

23 APR

23

8 IND
DIV

ADRIATIC
SEA

R Reno

6
DIV

Argenta

24 GD
BDE

Budrio

56
DIV

ena

85
DIV

V
II
RPS

FIFTH

EIGHTH BR

Castel
San Pietro

78
DIV

10 IND
DIV

Imola

Faenza

XIII
CORPS

2 NZ
DIV

3 CARP
DIV

II POL
CORPS

8 IND
DIV

Lugo

V
CORPS

Ravenna

Cervia

X CORPS

Forlí

Cesenatico

Cesena

Rimini

EIGHTH
ARMY

▬▬▬	Front line, beginning spring offensive
– – –▶	Axis of advance, Fifth Army
——▶	Axis of advance, Eighth Army
··········	Front line, beginning spring offensive

0   40 miles

it had at first seemed, and after two blood transfusions, he was moved to the safety of a hospital in Padova.

That same night, Hans Golda and his 8th Werfer Battery had been ordered from their old positions in Liano and told to cross the Via Emilia towards Lugo. 'It was a dangerous journey,' noted Hans. 'In front of us the sky was full of dazzling light. An unknown number of spotlights lit up the battlefield. Every red flash of light was followed by a deep roll of thunder; that was the artillery.' Taking up their positions, by first light they were already firing their nebelwerfers. Jabos swirled overhead, smoke and the boom of battle filled the sky. Soon, they were running out of ammunition. The moment the jabos seemed to disappear, they sped as fast as they could to get more stocks, praying they wouldn't be attacked. Hans was aware, however, that their infantry was being pushed back. The distance to their targets became smaller and smaller: 3,000 metres, then 2,500; then 2,000. By the time the enemy was 1,500 metres away, they were too close for the werfers' range. That night they crossed the ford over the River Sillaro, amidst traffic jams and the chaos of retreat. Burning vehicles and dead horses and oxen lay strewn across the river. The air was thick with the stench of burning. Clouds of smoke and dust hung heavily over the ground. Hans felt his nerves tightening. 'Every moment,' he noted, 'was full of tension and fear.'[350]

It was on 11 April that a brigade of 56th Division, using Fantails, successfully crossed the floods at the south-west of Lake Comacchio and emerged three miles behind the enemy's forward positions. General Herr and his 76th Corps commander, General von Schwerin, had been relying on the floods to prove impassable, and 56th Division's appearance caught them completely by surprise. Although in typical fashion the startled Germans rallied strongly, the next day they were forced to withdraw through the Argenta Gap.

On the 12th, Cocky Dundas faced one of those terrible decisions that occasionally confront commanders in times of war. A couple of days before the battle opened, Cocky had been leading a dive-bombing sortie and had just dropped his bombs and was climbing out of the fray, but at the same time watching the planes behind him still diving down. His eyes had been on one aircraft in particular, some five hundred yards behind him, when, in a split second, the Spitfire had been obliterated completely in an explosion of flames and debris. 'I had never before seen anything like it,' noted Cocky. 'At one moment there was the familiar, solid shape of a Spitfire; at the next, a flash, as though the aircraft had vaporised and turned into a million pieces of confetti.'

He had assumed that a freak shot had hit the aircraft's bomb detonator, but then on the 12th one of his trusted squadron commanders had been killed in much the same way. A few hours later, Cocky was informed that a batch of suspect bombs and been delivered to 244 Wing. A sample taken back at the supply depot had shown that a small number had been issued with faulty fuses. A number of these lethal explosives were now amongst 244 Wing's arsenal. There was no way of identifying them, so the only way to prevent any more fatal explosions was to clear out the lot and suspend operations until a new batch arrived.

Cocky called his squadron commanders to his house to talk over the matter, and the decision was made. It would be impossible to cancel the operations of five squadrons at that critical moment. They would carry on. Fortunately, there were no more deaths in this manner. 'But for two or three days,' noted Cocky, 'those of us who had sat in my house and had decided to carry on felt that a new dimension had been added to the always chancy business of dive bombing.'[351]

In the meantime, 78th Division had burst across the Santerno, and on the morning of the 14th, captured an important bridge across the River Reno at Bastia, at the mouth of the Gap. It was at this moment that Trooper Tom Finney was finally blooded as 78th Division swung north towards Argenta. The 9th Lancers were in the thick of it, part of a mobile armoured unit known as 'Kangaroo Force'. Tom was made a tank driver in 'C' Squadron, replacing a boy who had been killed the day before. 'C' Squadron was the reconnaissance squadron, and used light, fast, Stuart tanks. But despite the advantage of speed, these tanks were lightly armoured and lightly armed, and their crews were particularly vulnerable.

South of the Gap, meanwhile, the Poles and New Zealanders were also continuing to push the German forces back. General Herr, now that he was in the middle of a desperate battle, was ignoring directives from Berlin and had ordered his divisions to fall back along a wide front between Lake Comacchio and the hinge south of Bologna in an effort to keep his line intact. With this in mind McCreery decided to keep up the pressure along both of Eighth Army's thrusts, with XIII Corps taking over control of the north-west thrust, and leaving V Corps to concentrate on pushing north towards Argenta. Eighth Army's effort had now split into two separate but equally successful operations. McCreery had every reason to be extremely pleased.

So too had Clark. His decision to launch the offensive in April appeared to be paying off; Eighth Army, he believed, was clearly 'rested, revitalised and ready for the kill', and he now knew that the biggest obstacle – successfully breaking into the Argenta Gap – had been overcome. Rome had been a big prize, but so too was Bologna. Its capture, he sensed, was at long last just around the corner.

The only sombre news came from America, where it was announced that President Roosevelt had died on 12 April, aged sixty-three. He had been ill for a long time and his health had begun to decline rapidly, but the news still came as a great shock. Roosevelt had nurtured the United States through the war, so that by the time of his death the outcome was no longer in any doubt, particularly in the West, where Hitler's thousand-year Reich was rapidly imploding.

In Italy, it was time for Fifth Army to launch the second punch against the German lines. Early on the morning of the 14th, Fifth Army's front was blanketed in fog, so thick that air operations, and thus the launch of their attack, were impossible. By 7 a.m. there was still no change, but by eight, the mist was beginning to break up, and at 8.30, the roar of aero engines thundered overhead. Wave after wave appeared, while up ahead, over the German lines, their bombs hammered the enemy positions. At 9.10 a.m., the artillery opened up as well. At 9.45 the infantry of the 10th Mountain Division set off, while directly in front of them fighter-bombers continued to swirl and swoop, dropping bombs and spitting bullets, rockets and cannon on specific machine-gun nests and other enemy outposts. It was a hard slog for the troops, but by the afternoon of 15 April, 10th Mountain had seized the high ground overlooking the Reno Valley and Highway 64, while in the valley itself, Combat Command B of the 1st Armored had taken Vergato and the Brazilians had reached Montese in the mountains on the west flank of 10th Mountain Division.

That same day, US II Corps was getting ready to attack. On the Monte Sole massif to the east of the Reno Valley, the South Africans were hoping to capture Monte Sole, that stubborn pinnacle that had witnessed so much hardship, misery and death. First, however, the air forces had their part to play. On that day, the bombers dropped a staggering 1,500 tons

of bombs on German positions in front of Fifth Army – three times
more than the Luftwaffe had used to destroy Coventry back in November
1940. At noon on 15 April, Dick Frost of the Royal Natal Carbineers
watched 'hundreds' of bombers fly over and plaster the enemy positions.
'Said to be using petrol bombs,' he noted, 'and it certainly seems so.
Huge clouds of black smoke drift up and there is no enemy opposition.'
Later that afternoon, fighter-bombers appeared, firing rockets, dropping
bombs and machine-gunning the unfortunate Germans below. 'Really a
terrific sight,' he wrote. 'The rockets must be terrifying and petrol bombs
almost as bad.'[352] At 10 p.m., the guns began a thunderous artillery
barrage, and then, at midnight, Dick and his mates began their own
assault. By the following morning, the Cape Town Highlanders had
claimed Monte Sole. At long last, the war in the Monte Sole massif was
over.

There was also a third punch to be aimed at the Germans, in the form
of the Corps of Volunteers of Freedom and the disparate bands of
partisans poised to launch a general strike and insurrection in the north.
'Patriots!' Clark had broadcast to them on 11 April. 'The final great
battles for the liberation of Italy and the destruction of the German
invader have started. You are prepared and ready to fight.'[353] 'However,'
he told them, 'the time for your concerted action in aiding the Allied
armies has not yet come.' For the moment, he needed them to be patient
and to wait for the signal.

In fact, partisan bands, especially in the mountains, had already begun
to go on the offensive. In the mountains south of Piacenza, Stephen
Hastings and the men of the 13th Zone – emboldened by their success
at Castell'Arquato – moved to attack Groparallo and Monte Chino.
However, despite a couple of supply drops in March, they were still
poorly armed, especially compared to the German and Italian militia
troops they came up against, and their attacks were successfully fought
off. Stephen radioed for air support, but the air forces had their hands
full with the battle that was raging along the front and failed to appear.
He felt he had let the partisans down, but he need not have worried: on
the 19th, the enemy abandoned both Groparallo and Monte Chino,
giving the Piacentini another morale-boosting victory.

More and more partisans were now appearing in the open. As in
France the previous summer, it seemed as though almost every young
man in northern Italy was now a partisan. Cosimo Arrichiello, for one,

was far from impressed. Still keeping his head down and biding his time as a farm labourer in the Stura Valley, he was outraged when 'partisans' destroyed all the bridges around Marene, which connected the tiny town to the surrounding villages. Well off the beaten track and away from the main lines of communication in the area, these bridges were used only by locals, most of whom were contadini. 'Apart from the hardship and annoyance that the peasants had to endure,' noted Cosimo, 'there was no justification for such demolition.'[354]

That was as may be, but everyone sensed that both the German occupation and the age of fascism were now inextricably coming to an end, and this gave the young men of northern Italy an increasingly brazen confidence. The General Insurrection was about to catch like wild fire, and retribution was in the air.

Meanwhile, in the Argenta Gap, fighting was heavy and vicious, with the Germans putting up stiff resistance. Argenta itself did not fall until 16 April, and only then after a heavy aerial bombardment. On the 18th, Tom Finney and the 9th Lancers were involved in a particularly heavy attack when all three squadrons pushed north of Argenta and captured a crucial crossing that had only been partially demolished by the retreating Germans. As daylight began to fade, together with the London Irish infantry in support, they attacked the gun lines of the German 42nd Jäger Division. As vehicles and ammunition dumps exploded, sending huge pyrotechnics high into the evening sky, the Lancers forged ahead, overwhelming the German position and capturing more than 450 prisoners. The cost to the Lancers was only two tanks damaged – Tom was amazed they had come through the day's fighting with such light casualties. It was, he readily admits, 'very scary'.

Ray Saidel, his time as an infantryman over, entered the battle on the 17th, when Combat Command B, led by Colonel Hamilton Howze, was moved up on the left of the 10th Mountain Division, passing through the small town of Tolé – where Gianni Rossi had captured German plans of the Gothic Line more than ten months before. Ray was now part of 'Task Force C', and as they pushed northwards towards Modena their progress was slowed by German rearguards.

Lieutenant Bob Wiggans was also now at the front. Eighty-fifth Infantry Division had been in army reserve, but on the morning of the 18th, relieved units of the 10th Mountain and 1st Armored Divisions west of the Reno. They immediately went into action, but resistance was light and their advance rapid – so much so that in Bob's D Company of the 1st Battalion, 338th Infantry, they outran their mobile kitchens and his men missed three meals on the trot. Recognising the importance food played in the morale of his men, he eventually took a jeep and drove back down into the valley and onto Highway 64, and some six miles back he eventually found the food wagon. With some help, Bob managed to tow it back up to his men. They then ate their three missed meals one after the other.

By evening on the 19th, they had reached the edge of the great mountain chain and were looking out across the northern plains. It was a magnificent sight, but one Bob could feel little excitement about. 'It should have been exhilarating coming down off the Apennines into the Po Valley,' he noted. 'But I looked across the lush valley to see the snow-capped Alps, and my heart sank. I just knew I couldn't fight up another mountain.'[355] Little did he realise just how completely German resistance was beginning to disintegrate.

Hans Golda, on the other hand, was starting to sense the writing on the wall. His and his men's lives had become one of crossing rivers, making a stand, firing a few salvos, then falling back once more amidst the mayhem of retreat. They were now, by the 19th, near Budrio, to the north-east of Bologna, and that day Hans lost yet another of his men when a shell landed right in front of their latest command post. Hans hurried over when he heard the news. 'There were bits of flesh sticking to the door,' he noted. 'Gomolka's chest had been torn to pieces; nothing could be done. One of my best men was dead.' He was distraught; they all were. With his men gathered despondently around him, he handed out a round of cigarettes. 'I knew that in such moments,' he wrote, 'these were little sticks of light that worked miracles.'

News was hazy and based on rumour rather than fact, but it all seemed to be bad: the Tommies had crossed the Reno to the north; infantry were pouring back; others were moving forward. 'A real German front of defence no longer existed,' scribbled Hans, who was becoming increasingly desperate for new orders from regimental headquarters. 'Our patience,' he noted, 'was sorely tested by the hours of waiting and the hours of not knowing what was happening.'[356]

The same day, the South Africans pushed forward towards Bologna. 'Vado just a shell,' said Dick Frost of the town where the Stella Rossa had carried out one of their first attacks a year before. 'Passed many dead horses along a very dusty road and had great difficulty in crossing the Reno by ford.'[357] There were no bridges left.

William Cremonini had been back in his home town of Bologna, along with his comrades in the Bir el Gobi Company. One of their companies, led by Captain Pifferi, had been at the front, just south of the city at Pianoro, and Barnini's men, including William and Roberto Vivarelli, had been due to join them at their positions. On the 20th, however, stragglers from Pifferi's company began reaching Bologna – the rest, it seemed, had either been either killed or taken prisoner.

The same day, they also heard that the Germans had already withdrawn from the city. At 7.30 p.m. orders arrived telling them to retreat too, although where to was not clear. Sending most of their equipment and material on a truck back to Milan in order to lighten their load, they set out northwards on foot, the last Axis troops to leave Bologna. 'When we retreated,' says William, 'I passed within 200 metres of my front door. But I didn't stop at my house; I carried on retreating. For me, even if the war had gone on another ten years, I would have gone on fighting – out of honour, because that was what I thought was right.'

The Germans had been pushed back all along the front, and although the line was still intact it was clearly about to fall apart. It was an impossibly difficult time for von Vietinghoff. He had asked Hitler's permission to withdraw to the Po on 14 April, but his request had yet again been refused. Five days later, he braced himself to defy Hitler and sound the retreat regardless. On the 20th, the signal was given to all his forces to fall back to the Po; then in the evening he informed the Führer. Hitler, raving in his bunker with the ruins of Berlin above him, replied that local breakthroughs were no reason for a general retreat, and that any commander who entertained thoughts of defeat would be dealt with most severely. The die, however, had already been cast; and von Vietinghoff knew it was already far too late to save his forces.

At dawn on the 21st, it was Polish troops arriving from the Via Emilia who first entered Bologna, rather than the Americans, British and South Africans. And the partisans were already there to greet them. General Clark immediately broadcast the news to the world, this time including the efforts of all his troops. 'The 15th Army Group has today liberated Bologna from the Germans,' he announced. 'The American Fifth Army and the British Eighth Army now stand inside the gateway to the Po Plain, poised to destroy the Germans.'[358]

Another back in his home town that day was Gianni Rossi, entering with the OSS unit he had joined after recovering from his wounds. Cornelia Paselli was also in Bologna; she and her younger sister, Giuseppina, had been living there with an aunt for several months. When they saw the Allied troops and partisans streaming victoriously through the streets, Cornelia and her sister hugged one another and began to cry. Their tears were not of joy, however, but of grief. 'What was there to be happy about?' she says. 'We had lost our mother, our father, our brother and sister. Our friends. What a stupid waste the whole war had been. If they had managed to end it, why did it have to start in the first place?'

THIRTY-NINE

The End of the War in Italy
21 April–2 May 1945

On 18 April, General Karl Wolff saw Hitler for the last time, talking with him in the Führer bunker in Berlin. Wolff had seen with his own eyes that there was no hope left for Berlin, and so told the Führer that he had now established a direct opening to the White House. It was, of course, a whopping lie, but in any case made no difference; Hitler had told him that German forces could keep going for another two months along a line from Prague to the capital. 'Well, I said to myself,' said Wolff, 'when the Gods strike and wish to destroy someone, they strike him with blindness.'[359] He immediately headed back to Italy, where on 22 April he went to an urgent meeting at von Vietinghoff's headquarters. Other senior Nazis were also there including Ambassador Rahn and Gauleiter Hofer. 'Hundreds of thousands of German soldiers,' von Vietinghoff told them, 'are waiting for the words from me that will save their lives. Time is running out.'[360] In that case, Wolff told them, they should conclude a surrender straight away. He had been to see Kesselring on his way to Berlin. Now Commander-in-Chief West, with authority over all German troops in Western Europe, Kesselring had been keen to conclude a peace, but had insisted on the approval of the Führer. Wolff reported this now, and claimed that Hitler had indeed given him that authority. They key was to act quickly and decisively.

It was not to be, however, as the senior Germans in Italy began openly bickering over possible terms. Von Vietinghoff wanted an 'honourable' surrender; Hofer wanted south Tyrol to remain in Austrian hands. This was absolute fantasy, as Wolff was well aware, and not until early morning on the 23rd was it agreed that he should head to Switzerland straight away, this time with two plenipotentiary negotiators from von Vietinghoff's staff.

*   *   *

Without the mountains to protect them, the German army poured northwards, now, more than ever, at the mercy of the overwhelming Allied air forces. On the 20th, Hans Golda and his 8th Battery managed to cross the River Reno and begin firing in support of the 278th Infantry Division. At seven in the evening, as dusk was falling, they were then told to make for the town of Bondeno on the River Panaro, some six miles to the northwest. About to fire their last salvo and get going, news reached them that Bondeno had already fallen. Now only the west was open. Hans looked at his men. They were exhausted, their faces black with dust and smoke. He passed round some wine to fortify them before they set off again, but at that moment, British shells began to rain down towards them. One by one, Hans had his men load up and drive off; as ever, he made sure he was the last to leave.

They rendezvoused in the town of Sant' Agostino, and then continued towards Finale Emilia on the River Panaro. Two-and-a-half miles short of the bridge, they met with total gridlock, nose to bumper vehicles, carts, and guns, stuck on the road and prevented from moving off it by deep ditches either side. 'It made a pathetic picture,' noted Hans. 'In the direction of Finale we cold hear the sounds of battle. Officers of all levels were wandering around. Nobody took any decisions.' Apparently, a band of partisans had blocked the only bridge.

Hans now decided to try and do something about it. Ordering his men to prepare their nebelwerfers, he then tried to make the necessary calculations to hit the partisans. It was, of course, a huge gamble. Would their salvoes hit the enemy, or their own closely packed columns? It was a risk he felt he had to take. 'I must say,' wrote Hans, 'that I had never before felt as pale or shaken so much as I did at that moment, as the tubes stared into the night and the gunners waited for the order to fire. I stood in the corner of an empty shed, whispered in God's name and yelled out, The whole battery – fire!'

His gamble, it seemed, had paid off. In a matter of minutes, the traffic was moving forward again. 'Everywhere, witnesses told us with enthusiasm about the great effect of our salvo,' he recorded. 'It had landed right in the middle of the target.' Eventually, they reached the wooden bridge themselves, which wobbled under the strain as they crossed; then they pushed on through the night. 'Every minute was precious,' noted Hans. 'We had to get as far away as possible before the Jabos came.'[361]

*   *   *

Friedrich Büchner and his anti-tank company reached the River Po on the night of 21/22 April. The remnants of the 98th Division and those of the 21st had converged on the tiny village of Ro, six miles north-west of Ferrara. The scene was one of chaos and abandonment. Friedrich felt almost stupefied by what was happening. 'We'd been retreating daily for twelve days,' he says. 'There wasn't any feeling left.' The bridge at Ro had been destroyed, so the troops had to cross via a makeshift boat bridge. 'We couldn't cross by day because of the Allied planes,' Friedrich explains, 'so every night we had to reassemble it then in the morning take it to pieces again.' It took three days to get the 98th and 21st Divisions across. They had to leave all their equipment apart from those guns mounted on half-tracks. Lots of men, impatient after waiting so long to cross the boat bridge, tried to swim. But the Po was wide and had strong currents. Large numbers drowned in the process.

Once on the other side, Friedrich and his colleagues continued their journey north. He and fifteen others managed to get a ride on a truck, but the majority were not so fortunate. Both on the banks of the Po and along the roads heading north, abandoned German equipment littered the roads.

Hans Golda and his men reached the Po on the 22nd. Houses and vehicles were burning brightly. A whole stand of wagons flamed fiercely. Dead horses hung from their harnesses. Hans managed to find the regimental HQ and reported that he and his entire battery had arrived. 'Only a tired thank you was the answer to my report,' he noted. 'I looked hopelessly from one face to the other; in each one was the deepest despondency.' Then he realised the horrifying truth – there was no way for them to get their equipment across the river. For Hans, who had managed to keep his equipment safe throughout the entire campaign, and who had struggled at great risk to himself and his men for the past few days to bring his werfers and ammunition this far, this was a devastating blow.

His men were every bit as shocked, but with heavy hearts they first destroyed their ammunition, then set the werfers into firing positions, Hans ordering Leutnant Petzinger to cover their backs until the following morning. He was then to destroy them and follow behind. In the meantime, however, they had to find a way to get across. They too saw men drowning and heard the cries of those being sucked under by the currents. A heavy depression now took hold of Hans. Their next task was to destroy their vehicles, which they did by driving them into the water. 'It was a scene to break your heart,' noted Hans. 'The drivers cried like children.'

Gradually dawn spread across the river, revealing the full scale of the carnage. The river still teemed with soldiers trying – and often failing – to swim across. He was still unsure what to do, but there were rumours of ferries operating further up the river and so he decided they should try and find one of these. Gathering his men and a number of those from the 9th Battery, they headed along the river and eventually, three miles on, reached a large ferry carrying ambulances and wounded across, and by good fortune managed to get a ride across. 'Our spirits were at zero when we looked back at the other bank,' wrote Hans. 'The long, burning columns of tanks blown up, the many plumes of smoke – each of which was the grave of a valuable vehicle. With a last, painful look, we said goodbye.'[362]

As Hans Golda was crossing the Po, General Wolff was speeding on his way to Switzerland, accompanied by his two negotiators for the German surrender in Italy, Oberstleutnant Hans-Lothar von Schweinitz of von Vietinghoff's staff, and Obersturmbannführer Eugen Wenner, one of his own adjutants. Also with them was Baron Parilli. Unbeknown to them, however, Dulles' instructions not to talk further with Wolff or any of his representatives still stood; instead permission from Washington was needed to allow two Swiss diplomats to begin talks on behalf of the Allies.

The next day – 24 April – and with still no word back from Washington, Wolff lost patience, and announced he was leaving his two negotiators in Switzerland and heading back to Italy. In fact, he had been called to Milan where Standartenführer Dollmann had managed to negotiate an armistice with the CLNAI through the mediation of Cardinal Schuster. A meeting between Wolff and the CLNAI had been part of the deal – a ploy by Dollmann to buy time until an agreement had been made with the Allies.

It was now 25 April. Mussolini, who had left Gargnano under his own steam while Wolff was away, had also gone to Milan hoping to be able to surrender to the Socialists. He had known for some time that the end was just around the corner, and had admitted as much nine days before when he had spoken with a journalist for the last time. 'Interview or testament?' he had asked his interviewer.

The mediator was once again Cardinal Schuster, who had arranged for the Duce to be present at the same meeting with the CLNAI as Wolff and Dollmann. Meeting the Cardinal at the city's Curia, Mussolini offered to surrender on the condition he be allowed to retreat to the Valtellina accompanied by 3,000 Blackshirts. The CLNAI delegation, including General Cadorna, then arrived, but before talks could get underway, the meeting was interrupted by a number of Fascist *gerarchs*, Marshal Graziani, included, who told Mussolini that Wolff had been negotiating all along without his knowledge. 'They have always treated us like slaves,' erupted a furious Mussolini, 'and now at the end they have betrayed me!'[363] How Graziani and his cohorts found out is unclear, but the Cardinal now confessed this was indeed true. With that, Mussolini walked out. A room of refuge that the Cardinal had prepared for him was to remain unused.

The same day, the CLNAI called for a general strike in Milan, the signal that the General Insurrection was to begin. Stephen Hastings and his Piacentino partisans began battling their way towards Piacenza, and strikes also took place in Turin and Genoa, though in the cities there were only light clashes and sporadic fire-fights; still poorly armed, partisans were understandably nervous about exposing themselves to heavy fighting while large numbers of German and Fascist troops remained in the city.

Even so, there was considerable confusion amongst the Axis forces still in Milan and other cities. Most of the men of Bir el Gobi Company had managed to make it back to Milan and to Pavolini's base at the Villa Necchi, and in the afternoon a number of them accompanied their commander as he tried to go to the Pirelli tire factory to talk to the strikers. They were shot at, however, and unable to get near. 'No one in Milan seemed to know the true situation,' wrote Roberto Vivarelli, 'but we knew we were completely routed.'[364]

William Cremonini had earlier been sent to Maderno to bring back equipment for the Company from their headquarters. He would never now manage to rejoin them, however, for on the evening on the 25th the Company decided to surrender to the CVL. The Germans were pulling out of the city, and Pavolini was planning to head to Como to join Mussolini. Only eleven members of the Company decided to stay with him – of whom Roberto Vivarelli was one.

Early the next morning, Roberto set off with Pavolini. Theirs was a straggling line of vehicles, but despite being fired upon they made it safely to Como. There they learned that Como was about to be taken by the partisans; a truce was in place until 3.30 p.m. Pavolini then called Roberto and the remaining Blackshirts together and told them they must now look after themselves and try to save their skins. It was the last Roberto ever saw of him.

In the meantime, General Wolff had deliberately missed the meeting with the CNLAI in Milan, and instead had reached an SS office on the western shores of Lake Como late on the night of the 25th. By the morning, Marshal Graziani had arrived to see him, seeking protection from the SS. Graziani was as incensed as Mussolini about the surrender negotiations, but nonetheless Wolff still eventually persuaded him to sign away the authority for von Schweinitz and Wenner to negotiate on behalf of the RSI.

By now, however, Wolff's lakeside villa was surrounded by partisans, and only by frantic telephone calls to his Swiss negotiators and the intervention of an American OSS agent, were the partisans called off and Wolff allowed to leave safely. It was now the early hours of 27 April, and still the surrender had not been agreed. And with every minute that passed, more people were being killed.

Mussolini was now heading northwards towards the Valtellina. In hot pursuit was Pavolini, and on the trail of both was Elena Curti, who was especially concerned about the Fascist Party commander. 'I was,' she admits, 'a little in love with him.'

Learning he had already passed through Como and had headed further north, she took a bicycle and followed, finally catching up with him in the tiny village of Argegno, nine miles beyond Como on the western banks of the lake. Delighted to see her and touched by her obvious devotion, Pavolini invited her to join him in his armoured car as he and a number of his Blackshirts journeyed further north still, to the town of Menaggio, where most of the Fascist leadership, Mussolini included, were now hiding in an old school that had been converted into a barracks.

Early the following morning, 27 April, the convoy continued the journey north towards the Alps, accompanied by a number of German troops. Elena was once again travelling in Pavolini's armoured car. After an hour, at Pavolini's insistence, Mussolini joined them. 'You're here too?', he said, seeing Elena and sitting down next to her.

The convoy made good progress until they reached the village of

Musso. Just beyond, on a straight stretch of road, two felled trees barred their way. 'We've had it,' Elena thought to herself. It was a classic partisan ambush. But they moved the trees without incident, and continued again until the armoured car struck a three-pronged nail and punctured a tyre. They had no choice but to try and repair it and soon after partisans appeared. Carrying a white flag, the German commander began talking with them, explaining they were merely trying to head home through the Alps. The talks continued. Meanwhile, in the armoured car, the tension was rising. Neither Elena nor anyone else knew what was going on. Not even Mussolini. His mistress, Clara Petacci, appeared, as did various Fascist leaders, until eventually the German commander re-turned and told them that they, the Germans, were being allowed to go on their way, but that the partisans would not let any Italian go further. He offered to take Mussolini, and only Mussolini, with him, so long as the Duce agreed to put on a German uniform. 'I will go,' Mussolini decided eventually, then Elena heard him mutter under his breath, 'because I trust the Germans more than the Italians.'

When he had gone a stunned silence fell over those left behind. Elena felt distraught – at the void left by her father's departure and by the realisation that they were now alone. Pavolini looked shaken, then eventually announced they should try and turn around and find another route to the Alps. Before they had got going again, however, gunfire opened up. Pavolini grabbed a white flag and showed it through the spy hole of the car. The firing stopped and the Fascist Party secretary and the others in the armoured car gingerly clambered out. Quickly, Elena began trying to tear up as many documents as she could, but when she eventually looked out of the car to see what was going on, everyone had gone. Feeling abandoned and scared, she spotted two men from their convoy lying dead nearby and realised that she faced two choices: either to leave by the front of the car with her hands in the air, or to jump out of the back and make a run for it. 'I decided to jump,' she noted. 'I said a prayer, thought for an eternal minute about the life I had lived, bade farewell to my loved ones and, trying to be brave, I launched myself.'

No sooner had she picked herself up than she heard someone shout at her to put her hands up. Coming over to her, the partisan discovered she was carrying a gun. 'It was her! It was her!' he yelled to his mates. Confused, Elena did not understand what they were talking about. Another partisan intervened, ordering the others to leave her alone. Seizing her chance, Elena pleaded with him that she had merely hitched a ride in the armoured car; that she was nothing to do with the men inside it. Either the young man believed her or took a fancy to her, but having taken her to Dongo, a town about a mile or so further on, he left her in the town square, telling her she was free to go.[365]

Elena had escaped death by the skin of her teeth, but neither the Duce, Pavolini or Claretta Petacci were so fortunate. When the Germans were searched as they reached Dongo, Mussolini was discovered. Pavolini and the others were taken there too, and the following day, all were shot. Their bodies were then taken to Milan, where, just five months before, Mussolini had made his address to rapturous applause. On 28 April the bodies – sixteen in all – were unceremoniously dumped in the Piazzale Loreto. A crowd soon grew around them. The corpses were kicked, spat on and even urinated over, then strung up on butchers' hooks, upside down, on the girders of a petrol station by the side of the square.

It was on this day too, as had already occurred elsewhere in liberated cities across the north, that partisan reprisals occurred in the city, with horrendous numbers of Fascists, former Fascists and even only supposed Fascists being dragged out of their homes and off the streets and butchered, shot and hanged according to mob law. The following day, Roberto Vivarelli, now in civilian clothes and wandering aimlessly, learned of Pavolini and Mussolini's death. 'I don't know,' he wrote, 'whether I suffered more from grief or indignation.'[366]

Wolff, meanwhile, had met the Swiss diplomats on the border near Como, where he learned that Washington had at last authorised von Schweinitz and Wenner to negotiate. With this news, he was smuggled through Switzerland, across northern Italy, and then down to Bolzano, where von Vietinghoff had since established his headquarters.

It was in the early hours of 28 April that an utterly exhausted Wolff told von Vietinghoff, Rahn, Hofer, and other leading commanders that his negotiators had signed the surrender. This was another lie; they would not, in fact, sign until 2 p.m. on the 29th, but Wolff wanted to impress upon them that there was now no turning back. Von Vietinghoff seemed relieved, although he asked Wolff whether his demands had been met; Gauleiter Hofer also now told them that he wanted to be accepted as the highest German authority in Italy. Wolff was tearing out his hair in frustration. They were finished; it was over, yet men like Hofer were still making insane demands.

Hofer then spoke with Kesselring and told him everything. The

Feldmarschall was appalled, declaring that Wolff and von Vietinghoff had acted without authority and treasonably. Von Vietinghoff was promptly sacked and General Friedrich Schulz appointed in his place. 'What did von Vietinghoff do?' said Wolff. 'He came back and formally handed over to Schulz, and all attempts to keep him to his promises failed.' In addition, he now told Wolff he no longer had the authority to authorise the surrender.

On the 30th, von Schweinitz and Wenner returned, telling Wolff and Schulz that the surrender documents had been signed and that a ceasefire would take effect at 12 p.m. on 2 May. Alexander now wanted Wolff and von Vietinghoff's assurance that they would honour the terms. Increasingly frantic and at the point of despair, Wolff tried to persuade Schulz to give the necessary authorisation instead of von Vietinghoff. Schulz, however, refused to do so without the authority of Kesselring. Wolff rang the Feldmarschall but was told he was not available. He appealed again to Schulz, stressing that 'it would be madness not to conclude the negotiations'. Still Schulz refused to budge. It was a drastic situation requiring drastic measures, and so Wolff played his final card and had General Schulz and his chief of staff, Generalleutnant Menzel, arrested and placed in 'honourable custody'. He then sat down with them again and pleaded with them for the last time. 'I told them we could not carry on as we were,' said Wolff, 'and asked them whether they didn't want to join us again voluntarily.' By soothing them, placating them, and assuring them that by agreeing they would be doing their duty to the Fatherland and the soldiers under their command, they were eventually talked round. With relief coursing through him, Wolff told them, 'Look here, my children, don't let's waste any more time. It's Germany that's at stake, and not individuals. You know all these Army Commanders and I don't. Please see this thing through with me. Get in touch with the Commanders and tell them that my orders are to be strictly carried out.'[367] Schulz and Menzel did so, and the surrender was finally concluded.

While dictators were being executed and secret surrender negotiations carried out, the victorious Allied armies were hurtling northwards. Up to the Po crossing, some 35,000 German soldiers had been taken prisoner, while a further 32,000 had been killed or wounded. The Allies were now pursuing an utterly routed enemy. 'Things were very confused,' says Ray Saidel, who at one point found himself capturing half a dozen trucks full of German infantry. 'We marched these German prisoners up the road,' he says, 'and the partisans were helping us guard them.' A German officer then complained to Ray that the partisans were stealing their belongings, even pulling rings off their fingers. 'I told him that as far as I was concerned,' added Ray, 'they could take the fingers and all, so to shut up.'

Bob Wiggans had reached the Po around noon on the 24th, crossing later that afternoon in a DUKW amphibious craft. Two days later, the 85th 'Custer' Division reached the edge of Verona. 'Moved at dusk along good roads and past hundreds of burnt-out Jerry vehicles,' noted Dick Frost on the 26th. The following day, he was amongst the last of the South Africans to cross the Po south of Legnano. The Americans pushed on north towards the Brenner, while much of Eighth Army, with the New Zealanders and the 6th Armoured Division, hurried towards the north-east and to Trieste.

Away to the west, the battle for Piacenza was reaching its climax, the partisans of the 13th Zone inching their way ever closer to the city. On the 26th, word reached Stephen Hastings that the US 135th Infantry were nearing Piacenza, and so in a captured German staff car, he set out to meet them. 'It was,' he admitted, 'a stupid thing to do.'[368] Bumping into one of their forward patrols, the Americans at first thought they were Germans. Stephen reckoned it was his moment of greatest danger since being parachuted into the mountains.

Although the partisans continued to probe towards Piacenza, the SS troops still in the city were far too well armed for them to risk an all-out attack, and it was not until the Americans sent three Sherman tanks to help that the enemy troops finally packed up and left. On the 29th, the triumphant partisans swarmed into the city; as Stephen noticed, there were suddenly more of them than he had realised. 'At night,' he wrote, 'the streets echoed to fusillades from automatic weapons. Scores were being paid off. Life was, to say the least, uncertain for suspected Fascists. We did our largely ineffective best to calm this down.'[369]

Hans Golda now had gathered around him his own battery, men from the 9th and also a number of infantrymen stragglers. They had managed to bribe some Pioneers to take them across the Adige and had pushed on into the foothills of the Alps, dodging pot-shots from the partisans. In one village, they came across some Fallschirmjäger in the process of stringing up a partisan on a lamp-post for killing one of their men; the war was all but over, but there was to be no mercy from these para-troopers. 'He didn't seem to care as the noose was put around his neck,' noted Hans, 'and as he dangled, he didn't move; didn't even twitch. A strange death.'[370]

They pushed on, exhausted. As they looked up towards the stunning peaks of the Alps, Hans felt strangely lighter of spirit. The surroundings were beautiful; suddenly the death and destruction of the past few weeks seemed behind them.

Not far away was Jupp Klein, still with his company of Pioneers. Under his command were a number of British and American POWs who had been ordered to help his men dig ditches. On 1 May, one of the American prisoners escaped, which upset Jupp greatly. He knew he had to get all the POWs back to their prison camp, or else the SS would make life very difficult for him. Certain the prisoner could not have gone far, he went off to search for the American himself. Entering one house he found only several cowering Italians; then he kicked down the door of the next. There was a young man inside, shivering with fright.

'Where's the American?' Jupp demanded.

'Hitler is dead!' the man told him. 'It came through the radio!'

'Nonsense,' said Jupp.

'It's true, it's true,' the Italian insisted.

Completely stunned, Jupp staggered back to his men, where other Italians confirmed the news. 'I thought, what will become of us? I had in my mind only the Russians,' he says. 'I thought that would be it for Germany. The Russians will come and we will cease to exist.' Later, a detachment of SS troops arrived and took the prisoners away. No one noticed the missing American.

The next morning, Jupp and his men were ordered to go to Bolzano. There they were captured by the Americans and put on trucks with the men who until the day before had been POWs working for him. 'They embraced us,' says Jupp, 'crying, "The War is over! The War is over!"'

The same day, Hans Golda and his band of men reached Ora. There they too learned the news of Hitler's death and that the war was due to end the following day. 'Now we had lost the war,' he noted, 'and we gave ourselves up to our fate.' Soon after, the Americans reached them and they too became prisoners of war.

Meanwhile Friedrich Büchner and his small party of fifteen men had reached the Piave Valley and were nearing the town of Belluno when they stopped for the night at a farmhouse. The following morning, they woke to find themselves surrounded by partisans, who led them up to a sheep hut in the mountains, where there were a further sixty or so captured German troops. On 1 May, they were all taken outside the hut and lined up. 'The Communist leader turned up,' said Friedrich, 'and they pulled out three soldiers who were Russians. They'd been with the 98th Division throughout the campaign in Italy.' The partisan leader then pulled out a machine pistol and shot the first of the three men. 'But he didn't do it properly,' says Friedrich. 'The Russian was lying on the ground screaming.' Nor did he kill the other two outright either. For a further ten minutes, the three men were lying there screaming until they were finally put out of their misery. 'It was terrible,' says Friedrich. 'Absolutely terrible.' It was the day after his nineteenth birthday.

The following morning, the rest were taken back down the mountain and at Belluno were handed over to the Americans.

In Trieste, the situation was impossibly tense. It was clear that Marshal Tito's Communist Yugoslav partisans were going to try and annexe all of Istria, including Trieste, back into Yugoslavia. Alexander immediately ordered his New Zealand troops to rush to Trieste to prevent Tito's men taking command of the city, while it was agreed with the Germans that they would defend Trieste from Tito's men until the New Zealanders arrived. The German garrison stopped the Titoists from entering Trieste on 1 May. 'It was absolutely terrifying,' says Clara Duse. 'We heard shooting. We were really worried about what the Yugoslavs would do.' The following day, and not a moment too soon, the New Zealanders – Tini Glover and the Maori Battalion among them – arrived and took control of the city from their new one-day-old ally. 'And then you should have seen the rejoicing,' says Clara. 'The New Zealanders were kissed and given flowers – we were all so relieved. It was incredible.'

The war in Italy was finally over, exactly twenty months after the Allies first crossed from Sicily onto the Peninsula. It was no small triumph for the Allied men and commanders of the campaign that Italy was the first unconditional surrender by Germany in Europe; VE Day would follow six days later. It was Alexander's second complete victory over the German forces, and as he noted, Britain and her Allies were, at last, 'out of the tunnel of the long, dark years'.

POSTSCRIPT

The same could not be said for Italy – not quite, at any rate. Partisan reprisals against Fascists were savage across the north, where at least 15,000 – and possibly as many as 30,000 – were killed. Predictably, many of the victims had not been Fascists at all, but the merest suspicion, or the say-so of a vindictive neighbour, was often considered evidence enough. Even conservative estimates suggest that there were more killed in this swift and savage blood-letting than during all the rastrellamenti. Civil war is always especially barbaric.

Meanwhile in Trieste and Istria, the situation was far from clear. Some Yugoslav partisans had reached the centre of Trieste on 1 May, and insisted on a dual 'occupation and administration' with the Allied Military Government when the New Zealanders arrived, despite a previous agreement with the Allies to the contrary. American troops also arrived in the area, but neither they nor the New Zealanders were able to stop further reprisals. A staggering number of people accused of being Fascists (even though many were not) were executed – some 4,768 by the second week of June; and despite promising the opposite, the New Zealanders also handed over most of the 7,000 German garrison to the Titoists. A large proportion were also shot. 'All Italians of any standing in Trieste except Yugoslav sympathisers are being arrested,' noted Field Marshal Alexander on 6 May. 'All manpower between ages sixteen and sixty are being conscripted; Italians for forced labour, sympathisers of a military age being armed.'[371] Yet despite knowing this, Alexander was initially reluctant to send his troops in to fight the Yugoslavs. The war was over, after a long and bitter struggle. To ask them to risk their lives again seemed to him an order too far.

Churchill tried to intervene and was prepared to let Allied troops force Tito's men out of Istria entirely. But he needed Truman, the new

President of the United States, to support him. Truman refused, while Stalin suggested a new demarcation line be agreed between Tito and Alexander. Churchill had to acquiesce, and a new border was soon agreed, just to the east of Trieste. Much of Istria – including Clara Duse's childhood home – became part of Yugoslavia. On 12 June, after forty days, Tito's troops began pulling out of Trieste and at last the killing stopped.

There had been so much suffering in Italy during the year and a half of war on its soil. The Allies' final victory was an astonishing achievement, and for bringing such a disparate and exhausted force together and giving it the belief to win the day Alexander and Clark, especially, deserve enormous credit. So too do their air forces, which in their initial blitz gave the men on the ground such a colossal advantage. And, of course, so too do the men on the ground, who had slogged it out for so long, yet somehow found the energy and drive to go the final yard.

No less impressive was the performance of Kesselring and his army. Bereft as they were of air forces and fire power, they nonetheless fought on until almost the bitter end, often in impossibly difficult circumstances. The Italian campaign was never ever less than hard-fought.

From the Allied point of view, controversy has dogged the campaign ever since. Questions remain over whether it was worth it, whether the Allies made too many mistakes, and whether Clark's ego and ambition prevented the Allies from a complete victory in June. On the whole, historians have not been generous. Alexander has been seen as 'lacking grip' – that favoured old phrase – and too easily pushed around by Clark and others. The enormous difficulties facing him, the repeated cuts in manpower and equipment, and the vast challenge of bringing a polyglot force of some seventeen nations together, are often forgotten. That he managed to keep his forces together and fulfil the tasks given him was an incredible achievement that deserves greater credit.

Clark has come in for even stronger criticism, made all the easier by citing his more unpleasant character traits. These, however, are no reason for blaming him for many of the disappointments and frustrations of the campaign. Arrogance and ambition do not necessarily make a man a poor commander. Not only was he tough, forthright, and prepared to make difficult decisions, his operational planning was always superlative, and never was this better demonstrated than in his preparations for the final offensive.

Of course the Allies made mistakes – all commanders do in times of war; so too did Kesselring, who is now considered one of the finest German commanders of the Second World War. The picture never seems as clear at the time as it does in retrospect, but for anyone doubting the formidable task that faced the Allies as they clawed their way up the Peninsula, a visit to Cassino or to the central Apennines, or even a drive from one side of the country to the other should clarify matters; it is easy to be fooled by the soft hills of Tuscany or the plains around Venice.

After the difficulties of geography, the biggest hindrances to the Allies came from the slow initial build-up of supplies, the shortage of amphibious craft that would have enabled stronger outflanking operations, and the withdrawal of seven divisions and substantial numbers of aircraft when the campaign was there for the taking in the summer of 1944. These were decisions made outside the theatre, and caused by difficult and often divisive strategic quandaries in Washington and London.

Yet in many ways the campaign did achieve its ends, and not just for the Allies. Alexander later pointed out that the Italy campaign, despite its secondary status, tied up large numbers of German troops and war materiel that could have been used against the Allies elsewhere. Kesselring, in notes on the campaign written after the war, says the same: that in Italy, Axis forces tied up large number of Allied troops and war materiel that could have been used elsewhere, and indeed this was so. Unfortunately, Italy was invaded by the Allies on the basis of false assumptions – assumptions that were shattered almost as soon as the campaign began. Thereafter it never quite had the Allied chiefs' full support, but nor were they prepared to give up on it entirely. The fall of Rome, when it eventually came, was a great victory, but regardless of the arguments that followed, it was a huge tragedy for all involved, and not least the Italians, that Alexander's forces were not given the kind of support that would have seen them gain victory before the autumn of 1944 – a victory that in the event was denied them by a sliver. The sad fact is that Italy was a terrible place to fight a war. On the German side, casualties were 536,000; on the Allies, 313,500. Total casualties, including Italians, stand at over a million.

The terrible rastrellamenti of the summer and winter of 1944–45 and the bloody reprisals at the end of the war are still the subject of debate and soul-searching in Italy. Possibly, had Pavolini not formed the Blackshirts in July 1944, the partisan reprisals might have been avoided. William Cremonini and others might not agree, but by that time

Mussolini certainly knew the Germans were not going to win the war. So, too, must have Pavolini. Fanatics, however, are often blind, and for all his obvious charisma, Pavolini acted from belief, however warped, rather than from reason.

Despite Allied fears, and despite having the largest Communist Party in the west, Italy did not become a Communist state. Weakened by their concessions to the Allies in the winter of 1944, the political parties of the far left were unable to bring about a revolution. The takeover of northern Italy by the Allied Military Government was swift and the subsequent hand-over of power was, mercifully, peaceful. The Catholic Church, which had remained a powerful force in Italian life both socially and politically, gave its support to the Christian Democrats, who consequently swept to power and remained there for the next thirty years. In 1946, having rejected the monarchy, Italy became a democratic republic, with an elected president as head of state.

Despite the terrible sufferings of those in the south, once the war was over, and once Italy's two halves had been stitched back together, economic recovery was comparatively swift. Reconstruction was aided by the large number of German POWs who remained in Italy: it was German troops, for example, who were largely responsible for rebuilding the monastery at Monte Cassino to something close to its former glory. The fact that Italy's industry in the north survived also played its part. The Allies had been paranoid about a possible scorched-earth policy by the Germans as they retreated. Partisans have ever since claimed they were responsible for preventing this, and indeed, saving power stations and industrial plants had been part of the remit given to them by the Allies. Von Vietinghoff, however, in post-war statements, claimed otherwise, stating categorically that he had forbidden any demolitions except those of absolute military necessity, and to make sure this order was carried out, claimed he had ordered all demolition troops back to the Brenner sector beforehand; certainly that was where Jupp Klein and his men were.

In any case, as von Vietinghoff was quick to point out, no partisan band would have been able to stop them had he wished to carry out such demolitions. 'The troops constantly guarding all important objectives consisted of high-class technicians,' he commented, 'who would have done the job before the first patriot could have been on the spot.' Previous history from earlier in the campaign suggests he was probably right.[372] This is not to denigrate the efforts of the partisans, however, most of whom fought bravely and heroically in impossible circumstances. Indeed, read any German memoir or diary, or speak to any German veteran of the Italian campaign, and they all speak of the enormous menace of the partisans and the debilitating effect they had on German morale in Italy. But even so, poorly trained, and, especially, poorly armed and undernourished men can only achieve so much.

Those who fought and lived in Italy through that last year of war shared different fates. Alexander remained in Italy until 1946, and later became Governor-General of Canada. He made an unhappy foray into politics, briefly joining Churchill's second government, and was given an earldom. He died in June 1969.

Mark Clark became High Commissioner for Austria, and later took over as commander of the United Nations forces in Korea. It was Clark who signed the ceasefire agreement in 1953. Retiring from the army, he became president of The Citadel, the Military College of the South, in Charleston, South Carolina. It was here that he died in 1984. Harold Macmillan continued his life in politics, becoming Conservative Prime Minister of Britain from 1957 to 1963. He resigned due to ill health, but recovered and later became the 1st Earl of Stockton. He died in 1986.

Among the German commanders, General Wolff was captured but escaped trial as an SS general and leading Nazi by testifying against his former comrades at Nuremberg. Released from custody in 1947, he was then arrested and tried for war crimes in 1949, subsequently serving four years, before retiring quietly. He always maintained his hands were clean over the question of the Holocaust, but in 1964 he was arrested and put on trial yet again, accused of knowingly deporting 300,000 Jews from the Warsaw Ghetto to Treblinka in 1943. Found guilty of organising boxcars for the deportation, he was imprisoned again, although released soon after due to poor health. He died in 1984, having led a comfortable and peaceful retirement.

Kesselring was tried and convicted for war crimes, although the sentence of death was commuted to life imprisonment, in part thanks to lobbying by Churchill and Clement Attlee, and then commuted again. Although he oversaw some of the most brutal atrocities witnessed in the entire war in the West, he was released in 1952, and died in 1960. Sturmbannführer Walter Reder, on the other hand, a mere major, and commander of the 16th Waffen-SS Reconnaissance Battalion, was famously tried in Italy for war crimes and spent most of the rest of his life in prison on Gaeta sixty miles south of Rome. He died in 1991. In 2004, a military tribunal in La Spezia condemned three former officers of the 16th Waffen-SS for their part in the massacre at Sant' Anna. In February 2007, ten former soldiers from Reder's Reconnaissance Battalion were also given life sentences *in absentia* for their part in the massacre on Monte Sole. These, and the massacre in the Ardeatine Caves, remain the most notorious of the atrocities committed by the 'NaziFascisti' but sadly, they were only three of more than the 700 committed in Italy.

No one, however, has ever tried to put any of the French colonial Goumiers on trial for the appalling spree of rape and murder they carried out in May 1944. Trawl through the archives of Paris, London and Washington and it is hard to find much mention of these crimes, yet for many of the rape victims, they might as well have been killed. Many found themselves ostracised by their husbands and communities. 'My father got back at the end of the war and hell came into our house,' says 'Anna C'. 'Mummy often cried, even when she was working or when she was on her own. My father started to drink and lost his temper over nothing and became violent. My grandmother died of a broken heart ... When I reached maturity, one day my father said to me: Mind you don't end up like your mother.'[373] This was not untypical. Pasua Pisa's husband came home, but she could no longer bear to 'lie with a man'. Desperate for a child, she went to Rome and to an orphanage, and spotted a baby smiling up at her. She picked him and cuddled him, and took him home. He and his wife now run the farm on top of Monte Rotondo.

Only the longest-serving Allied troops were sent home straight away. The remainder had to stay in Italy until the unrest had settled down, the Istria question had been resolved, and AMG had formally relinquished all authority to the Italian government. Others became part of the Army of Occupation in Austria. Tom Finney made his footballing debut for England in two unofficial internationals against Switzerland, but despite a month's leave in November 1945, remained in the army, and in Italy, until the summer of 1946. Returning home, he finally made his debut for Preston North End and went on to become one of England's greatest post-war footballers. He still lives in the town of his birth.

Stan Scislowski remained in hospital until July 1945. They were difficult months, when he was overcome by a strange depression and a kind of nervous tension, which he has since realised was 'post-traumatic stress'. Leaving hospital, he was posted to a repatriation depot in England and finally returned home to Windsor, Ontario in July 1946, married his childhood sweetheart and had six children. He is now grandfather to nine.

Sam Bradshaw suffered in similar ways to Stan. After recovering from his neck wound, he was posted home. But returning to Merseyside was a traumatic experience. 'It was the worst thing about the war,' he says. 'No one had conditioned me about what to expect.' He had been away four years and in his mind's eye, time had stood still at home; he hadn't expected his mother to have aged so much or his young niece to have grown into a woman. All the people he had once known had gone. The pub was empty and served watered-down beer, so he left and wandered past his old school. 'I sat down and I just broke down,' he says. 'It was terrible and I felt so ashamed. But I was mentally ill; bloody ill. I didn't tell anyone.' He did, however, stay on in the army and was posted to the 3rd Royal Tank Regiment. On arriving in Germany, he was sent to Fallinbostel near Belsen, and was among the first Allied troops to reach the death camp. Sadly, he was too late to save Emilio Sacerdote, who had been moved there in March and who had died soon after – one of 6 million Jews from all over Europe to have died in the Holocaust. After the war, Sam was commissioned – retiring as a major – and later became chairman of the Eighth Army Veterans' Association. Married with seven children, he lives in Wigan.

Ion Calvocoressi was still in Burma, with General Leese, at the war's end. Returning home, he left the army and turned to stockbroking in the City of London. He remained close friends with Sir Oliver Leese, right up until the general's death in 1978. Ion Calvocoressi died in July 2007. Ted Wyke-Smith returned to his pre-war career as an engineer in the British steel industry, where he remained, very successfully, until retirement. Married in 1952, he raised four children and now lives in Devon. Peter Moore was still in Greece when the war ended. Afterwards, he left the army, went to Cambridge University, and then began a long career as a farmer and agricultural adviser. He married and had three sons, and lives just the other side of the Leicestershire border in Derbyshire. Reg Harris was sent back to Italy right at the end of the war, but then left the army and returned home to his wife and son. He continued to work on the same Fonthill estate as his father, eventually becoming buildings manager. He lives in Fonthill still.

After the war, Stephen Hastings joined the Foreign Office, before later becoming an MP and a minister in Margaret Thatcher's government. Knighted, he retired to concentrate on one of his life's passion – horses – both breeding and racing, right up until his death in 2005.

Tini Glover made it home and has lived in or around Gisborne ever since, becoming chairman of a large estate of Maori Land, and exporting squash, sheep, cattle, as well as producing wine. Kendall Brooke was liberated from Stalag VII-A POW camp at Moosburg, north-east of Munich in April 1945, then flown to England and from there eventually made it back to South Africa. His younger brother, however, was not spared. Also serving in Italy, he was killed in the final days of the war. Dick Frost survived, however, and eventually emigrated to England. Ray Saidel went home to New Hampshire, took over a motor-car dealership and, despite being over eighty, still races cars to this day. Bucky Walters became a teacher in New Jersey, while Bob Wiggans went home to his wife and continued his life as a farmer in Upstate New York.

Hamilton Howze remained in the army, rising to become a full general and commanding the US 3rd Army. Earmarked to lead US forces in the projected invasion of Cuba in 1962, he also became a pioneer of army–air mobility during his time as Director of Army Aviation. Later working for the Bell Helicopter Company, he retired to Texas and died in 1998.

Of the airmen, Charles Dills returned home to the States and became an academic, rising to become Professor of Chemistry at Cal Poly in San Luis Obispo, California. It was there that he met his wife, a marine biologist and English teacher. Ken Neill returned to New Zealand where he took over the family farm, before retiring to Christchurch, where he still lives. Ernest Wall was demobbed from the RAF in December 1946 and joined the Scottish civil service. His great passion, however, was hockey, and he became a leading light in the Scottish Hockey Union and spent thirty-two years on the International Rules Board. He was awarded an OBE for services to the sport. Married with two daughters and seven grandchildren, he lives in Peebles, near Edinburgh. Despite his rapid advancement during the war, Cocky Dundas nevertheless left the RAF in 1947, and joined Beaverbrook newspapers. He continued a life in media, eventually becoming chairman of Thames Television before retiring in 1987. Married with three children and seven grandchildren, he died in 1994.

For the Poles there would be no victorious homecoming. After the war, Wladek Rubnikowicz remained in Italy, watching his people's further humiliations from afar. Out of 'sensitivity' to the Russians, the Polish forces were excluded from any of the victory parades in London. Polish troops were also asked not to talk publicly about their experiences in Russia. He left the army in 1946, having risen to lieutenant-colonel, and having become second-in-command of the Polish Officer Cadet School in Lecce. After settling in England, he married and had a daughter, but it was not until 1991 that he finally returned home to Glebokie, the town of his birth. It was no longer in Poland, however, but Belarus.

Some of the German troops also found themselves with no home to return to. Rudi Schreiber's family home was lost to Soviet Russia. He eventually escaped to the west after being nearly shot in Czechoslovakia at the end of the war – his would-be executioner's pistol jammed, allowing Rudi the chance to escape.

After leaving Italy, Georg Zellner had completed a regimental leader course, was promoted to *Oberstleutnant* and took command of a regiment on the Western Front. Wounded, he ended the war in hospital where he was captured by the Americans. Returning home in 1946, he struggled to find work because of his part as a regimental commander in the war. He died in Regensburg in 1969, aged sixty-three.

Franz Maassen was eventually released from POW camp in 1946 and returned home to Düsseldorf, where he continued running the family bakery. 'Only after the war,' he says, 'did I feel human again.' Friedrich Büchner also took over the family slate business on his return from captivity in 1947. Willi Holtfreter survived the war, but found himself stranded in the West. His home, however, was now in the East, and so he crossed the border and returned home to Abtshagen, where he worked in the timber factory until he retired. Hans-Jürgen Kumberg, after helping to rebuild Cassino as a POW, emigrated to Canada. His son later married an Italian. Jupp Klein was sent to a POW camp in Egypt, from where he was recruited by the British for operations in Greece. Later, after returning to Germany, he married and took over his father-in-law's building business, which he still runs. He is also one of the co-founders of the Monte Cassino Foundation, an organisation he set up to promote peace and reconciliation.

William Cremonini managed to survive the reprisals by staying in convents and monasteries and by passing himself off as a repatriated POW from Germany. He eventually returned to Bologna where he was arrested and spent a year in prison. Once freed, he struggled to find a job: his war years always seemed to catch up with him. In 1951, however, his luck turned when he got married and secured a job as a typographer. Roberto Vivarelli managed to make his way back to Milan, and after finding his mother, hid until the dust had settled. Between 1948 and 1951, he was hospitalised with tuberculosis. It was, however, a life-changing experience. As many of the patients were former soldiers with no education and no prospects, an enterprising officer organised courses to educate these men and Roberto became one of the teachers. He later went on to become an internationally renowned professor of history. Elena Curti also survived the war and eventually married and moved to Barcelona where she studied art. Now back in Italy, she remains a well-known artist. Antonio Cucciati returned home from hospital without further recriminations and later started a successful garage and motor dealership. He still lives in the family home in San Colombano.

Not until the war was over was Lupo's fate discovered. His body was found in bushes near Cadotto, where it had lain undiscovered for six months. He had been felled as he, Gianni, and Leone had tried to escape. He remains, however, venerated in the area. At the very top of Monte Sole stands a memorial to the men of the Stella Rossa. Recently someone has daubed in red paint, '*Vie Lupo*' [sic] across it.

There is also a road named after him in Vado, as there is for Gianni Rossi. Gianni became a mechanic in Bologna and eventually retired to Vado, where he still lives. Cornelia Paselli married, had four children, and still lives in Bologna. Carlo Venturi, in Modena at the war's end, returned home to Casalecchio and later became a leading light in the Bologna ANPI, the national partisan association. Iader Miserocchi accompanied Eighth Army all the way to Trento. 'I went,' he says, 'to enjoy the sorry spectacle of a defeated and retreating German army attempt to reach the borders of its own home.' With the war – and his own personal mission – over, he returned to Ravenna. He was not forgotten, however, by the men of the new Italy. Not only was he given the honorary rank of captain, he was awarded the Bronze Medal for Military Valour. 'He was captured and underwent atrocious torture,' ran the citation, 'which he bore without revealing a single detail which might harm his compatriots. As soon as he was freed, he took up arms again against the enemy and, on 4th December, he entered Ravenna in victory, leading his men.' He lives in Ravenna still. Carla Capponi married Paolo, had two children and lived in Rome peacefully for the rest of her life. She died in 2001.

After his twenty-month exile in Piemonte, Cosimo Arrichiello returned home safely to Naples. Unable to settle, however, he followed his father and brother and joined them in Java, before emigrating first to Australia and then eventually to England, where he became a civil servant. He lives there still. Eugenio Corti became – and remains – an acclaimed novelist and author, highly respected to this day in Italy. Clara Duse married a British officer, and with no home to return to, settled with her husband in England, where she still lives. Antonio and Iris Origo continued to live at La Foce, Iris becoming a noted writer and historian. Antonio died in 1976, Iris twelve years later. La Foce thrives, however, and is still lived in by their daughter, Benedetta; its gardens are open to the public on Wednesdays. Italo Quadrelli and his family moved back to Onferno almost immediately after the war passed through and began the painstaking process of rebuilding their farm and livelihood. After the war, Italo became a coach driver. He now lives in the rebuilt town of Gemmano.

Carla Costa was presumably freed at the end of the war. There are several people with that name living in Rome, but none appear to be former German spies. Nor do I know what happened to Hans Golda or Willfried Segebrecht, except that Willfried died in 1994. Hans Golda's remarkable testimony lies in a type-written manuscript in a dusty folder in the German military archives in Freiburg. As such he remains the character he revealed in his memoirs – and thus someone very much still alive.

There is little left in Italy to remind people of the terrible war that took place there. Towns like Cassino, that were completely destroyed, or Rimini, that were 90 per cent destroyed, are conspicuous in Italy – a place of such beauty – for their modernity and sad lack of charm, but most of those towns and villages only partially destroyed have, for the most part, been rebuilt beautifully. It is still possible to see the odd German bunker, or shrapnel blast on a building that had once found itself in the front line, but of the great German defence lines there is almost nothing left. Soon the last of the survivors will have passed on too, and the war will finally be part of a more distant history. But there is one place in Italy where the shadow of war still hangs heavy, and that is Monte Sole. The mountain villages have never been lived in since, and their ruins are slowly but surely being reclaimed by nature. These are beautiful, yet haunting, places, melancholy dripping from the abundant oaks and chestnuts all around. Only one quiet spot seems to have remained much as it was more than sixty years before: the cemetery at Casaglia, where so many were killed – where Cornelia Paselli lost her mother, brother and sister. And on the iron gate, there is always a simple wreath. One day, Italy will be able to forget. But not quite yet.

REFERENCES

Notes have not been made for quotation from any of the people privately interviewed for the research of this book.

1 TNA WO206/4622
2 Lt-General W. Anders, *An Army in Exile*, p. 163.
3 Ibid.
4 Mark Clark Diary, 5/5/1944, Clark Papers, CIT.
5 IWM 80/5/1.
6 Robert Landon Wiggans, 'The Hazardous Trail: Journeys of an Ithaca Boy', MHI.
7 Clark Diary, 11/5/1944.
8 Letter to wife, 10/5/1944, Leese Papers, IWM.
9 Joseph Klein, 'German Parachute Engineer Battalion and the Italian War 1943/45', unpublished memoir.
10 BA-MA MSG1/2817.
11 Wiggans, op. cit.
12 TNA CAB 120/603.
13 BA-MA MSG2/4335.
14 Winston S. Churchill, *The Second World War*, Vol. V, p. 529.
15 J. M. A. Gwyer and J. R. M. Butler, *Grand Strategy*, Vol. III, p. 669.
16 Cited in Michael Howard, *History of the Second World War: Grand Strategy*, Vol. IV, p. xvii.
17 Cited in ibid., p. 208.
18 Cited in John Ehrman, *History of the Second World War: Grand Strategy*, Vol. V, p. 116.
19 Cited in Howard, op. cit., p. 503.
20 Alexander Papers, TNA.
21 MHI MS C-095b.
22 Ibid.
23 Cited in Walter Warlimont, *Inside Hitler's Headquarters*, p. 344.
24 Cited in Ian Kershaw, *Hitler: 1936–1945 – Nemesis*, p. 599.
25 Albert Kesselring, *The Memoirs of Field-Marshal Kesselring*, p. 171.
26 Generalfeldmarschall Albert Kesselring, 'Mediterranean War, Part V', MHI.
27 Omar Bradley, *A Soldier's Story*, p. 307.
28 Dwight D. Eisenhower, *Crusade in Europe*, p. 231.
29 IWM.
30 TNA WO214, Alexander Papers.
31 Field Marshal Lord Alanbrooke, *War Diaries, 1939–1945*, p. 499.
32 TNA CAB 106/707.
33 Eugenio Corti, *The Last Soldiers of the King: Wartime Italy, 1943–1945*, p. 40.
34 Ibid., p. 41.
35 Ibid., p. 100.
36 Ibid., p. 113.

37 Pietro Badoglio, *Italy in the Second World War*, p. 81.
38 Cosimo Arrichiello, *Italian Heartbreak*, p. 273.
39 Cited in Richard Lamb, *War in Italy*, p. 132.
40 Cited in Caroline Moorehead, *Iris Origo*, p. 1.
41 Iris Origo, *War in Val d' Orcia: An Italian War Diary*, 9/9/1943.
42 Ibid.
43 Ibid., 5/5/1944.
44 Arrichiello, op. cit., p. 295.
45 Sir John Slessor, *The Central Blue*, p. 558.
46 Cited in Vincent Orange, *Slessor: Bomber Champion*, p. 130.
47 Hugh Dundas, *Flying Start*, p. 178.
48 Slessor, op. cit., p. 569.
49 Cited in ibid., pp. 570–77.
50 Clark Papers, CIT.
51 Kesselring, *Memoirs*, p. 200.
52 BA-MA MSG2/4335.
53 Ibid.
54 Clark Papers.
55 BA-MA MSG2/4335.
56 BA-MA MSG1/2816.
57 Cited in Nicholas Farrell, *Mussolini: A New Life*, p. 430.
58 Filippo Anfuso, *Da Palazzo Venezia a Lago di Garda*, pp. 343–44.
59 Cited in Lamb, op. cit., p. 86.
60 Cited in F. W. Deakin, *The Six Hundred Days of Mussolini*, Part III of *The Brutal Friendship*, p. 57.
61 Stanley Scislowski, *Not All of Us Were Brave*, p. 130.
62 MHI C-095b.
63 TNA WO204/10181.
64 Carlo Venturi, *Ming Tra i Ribelli*, p. 64.
65 D. C. Quilter (comp. and ed.), *No Dishonourable Name*, p. 78.
66 Statistics provided by the Historiale di Cassino.
67 Clark Diary, 18/5/44.
68 Leese Papers.
69 Wiggans, op. cit.
70 MHI C-064.
71 Scislowski, op. cit., pp. 188–94.
72 BA-MA MSG 2, Hans Golda.
73 Scislowski, op. cit., p. 195.
74 Leese Papers.
75 Clark Diary, 20/5/1944.
76 Sidney T. Matthews Papers, MHI.
77 Cited in Brian Harpur, *The Impossible Victory*, p. 107.
78 Eric Sevareid, *Not So Wild A Dream*, p. 393.
79 Hamilton H. Howze, 'Thirty-Five Years and Then Some: Memoirs of a Professional Soldier', MHI.
80 Sevareid, op. cit., pp. 396–97.
81 Howze, op. cit.
82 Franz Kurowski, *The History of the Fallschirm Panzerkorps Hermann Göring*, p. 267.
83 Howze, op. cit.
84 Sevareid, op. cit., p. 400.
85 Lucian K. Truscott, *Command Missions*, p. 375.
86 Cited in Raleigh Trevelyan, *Rome '44: The Battle for the Eternal City*, p. 265.
87 Leese Papers.
88 Scislowski, op. cit., p. 197.
89 Ibid., p. 199.
90 Ibid., p. 201.
91 Clark Diary, 8/5/1944.
92 Sevareid, op. cit., pp. 400–01.
93 Clark Papers.
94 Howze, op. cit.
95 Cited in Tommaso Baris, *Tra due fuochi*, p. 94.
96 TNA WO 204/9945.
97 DORER 1310.
98 DORER 1307.
99 DORER 1303.
100 DORER 1314
101 DORER 1309.
102 Norman Lewis, *Naples '44: An*

Intelligence Office in the Italian Labyrinth, entry for 28/5/1944.

103 BA-MA MSG2, Hans Sitka.

104 Ibid.

105 Istituto Ferrucio Parri.

106 Message of 28/5/1944, cited in Churchill, op. cit., p. 536.

107 MHI C-064.

108 Sevareid, op. cit., p. 405.

109 MHI C-064.

110 Clark Papers.

111 TNA AIR 49/129.

112 BA-MA MSG2/4335.

113 Leese Papers.

114 Howze, op. cit.

115 Sevareid, op. cit., p. 409.

116 Howze, op. cit.

117 Mark W. Clark, *Calculated Risk*, p. 364.

118 Ibid.

119 Sidney T. Matthews interview with Field Marshal Alexander, MHI.

120 Clark Diary, 5/5/1944.

121 Leese Papers.

122 Ibid., IWM 96/40/1.

123 Kesselring, op. cit., p. 203.

124 IWM 96/40/1.

125 Origo, op. cit., 22/5/1944.

126 Ibid.

127 Origo, op. cit., 6/6/1944.

128 Bonomini, Luigi, et al. (eds), *Riservato a Mussolini: Notiziari giornalieri della Guardia nazionale repubblicana.*

129 Cited in ibid.

130 Ibid.

131 *Il Resto del Carlino*, 6/6/1944, Istituto Ferrucio Parri.

132 TNA WO204/11749.

133 Roberto Vivarelli, *La fine di una stagione*, p. 13.

134 MHI C-064.

135 Kesselring, op. cit., p. 204.

136 BA-MA MSG1/2817.

137 BA-MA MSG2/4335.

138 Cited in Warlimont, p. 416.

139 Cited in General Sir William Jackson, *History of the Second World War: The Mediterranean and Middle East*, Vol. VI, Part I, pp. 301–02.

140 Cited in Maurice Matloff, *Strategic Planning For Coalition Warfare, 1943–1944*, p. 425.

141 TNA WO/214.

142 TNA CAB 106/707.

143 TNA WO 214.

144 Wiggans, op. cit.

145 Clark Papers.

146 Clark Diary, 15/6/1944.

147 Ibid.

148 Leese Papers.

149 DORER 1297.

150 DORER 1317.

151 TNA WO 204/9945.

152 Origo, op. cit., 18/6/1944.

153 TNA WO 235/375.

154 TNA WO 208/4672.

155 BA-MA MSG2/4335.

156 Leese Papers.

157 SANMMH.

158 Ibid.

159 Eugenio Corti, *The Last Soldiers of the King*, p. 101.

160 Cited in Anders, op. cit., p. 187.

161 Corti, op. cit., pp. 133–34.

162 Dundas, op. cit., p. 183.

163 Ibid., p. 184.

164 BA-MA MSG1/2817.

165 Ibid.

166 Origo, op. cit., 21/6/1944.

167 Ibid., 22/6/1944.

168 Ibid.

169 Ibid.

170 Willfried Segebrecht Diary, in 'Im gleichen Schritt und Tritt', 26/6/1944.

171 Ibid.

172 Ibid.

173 SANMMH.

174 Origo, op. cit., 29/6/1944.

175 Lewis, op. cit., 22/10/1944.

176 Sevareid, op. cit., p. 365.
177 Lewis, op. cit., 4/10/44.
178 *US Army in World War II: The Technical Services – The Medical Department: Medical Service in the Mediterranean and Minor Theaters,* p. 257.
179 Lewis, op. cit., 18/4/1944.
180 Sevareid, op. cit., p. 377.
181 Harold Macmillan, *The Blast of War, 1939–1945,* p. 388.
182 Harold Macmillan, *War Diaries: The Mediterranean, 1943–1945,* 8/4/1944 entry.
183 Macmillan, *Blast of War,* p. 388.
184 Ibid., p. 414.
185 Cited in Caroline Moorehead, *Martha Gellhorn: A Life,* p. 251.
186 Martha Gellhorn, *The Face of War,* p. 136.
187 Ibid.
188 Ibid.
189 Macmillan, *War Diaries,* 19/6/1944.
190 TNA WO 214.
191 TNA FO 954/17.
192 Cited in Ehrman, op. cit., p. 355.
193 TNA FO 954/17.
194 Leese Papers.
195 TNA CBA 106/707.
196 Cited in Kesselring, op. cit., p. 207.
197 BA-MA MSG1/2817.
198 Istituto Storico Provinciale della Resistenza, *L'8.a Brigata Garibaldi nella Resistenza,* Vol. I, p. 122.
199 Ibid.
200 Cited in Clark, op. cit., p. 381.
201 Dundas, op. cit., p. 185.
202 BA-MA MSG1/2817.
203 BA-MA MSG2/4335.
204 Cited in TNA WO 208/4672.
205 Ibid.
206 Cited in Lamb, op. cit.
207 Cited in Farrell, op. cit., p. 445.
208 Cited in Deakin, op. cit., p. 187.
209 Ibid., p.188.
210 Memoir of Lieutenant Barnini, Bir el Gobi Company, Museo Reggimentale Giovani Fascisti.
211 SANMMH.
212 Memoir of Lieutenant Barnini.
213 Caroline Moorehead (ed.), *The Letters of Martha Gellhorn,* p. 169.
214 Cited in Luciano Casella, *Tuscany and the Gothic Line,* p. 272.
215 Leese Papers.
216 TNA CAB 106/707.
217 TNA WO 214/34.
218 Leese Papers.
219 Clark Diary, 10/8/1944.
220 MHI CIA-HR70–2.
221 TNA WO 204/7586.
222 Peter Moore, *No Need To Worry: Memoirs of an Army Conscript,* p. 134.
223 Ibid., p. 142.
224 Kesselring, op. cit., p. 228.
225 Lewis, op. cit., 12/8/1944.
226 Lewis, op. cit., 13/8/1944.
227 *Il Resto del Carlino,* 24/8/1944.
228 Ibid., 22/6/1944.
229 TNA WO 204/12694.
230 Ibid.
231 MHI CIA-HR 70–2.
232 TNA HW 12/304.
233 Kirkman Papers, LHCMS.
234 Cited in Rowland Ryder, *Oliver Leese,* p. 187.
235 Winston S. Churchill, *The Second World War,* Volume VI, p. 78.
236 Ibid., p. 105.
237 BA-MA MSG2/4335.
238 Moore, op. cit., p. 154.
239 Ibid., p. 155.
240 Scislowski, op. cit., p. 244.
241 Ibid., p. 246.
242 Ibid.
243 Ibid., p. 256.
244 Gellhorn, op. cit., p. 147.
245 BA-MA MSG2/4335.
246 Anders, op. cit., p. 221.
247 Moore, op. cit., p. 165.

248 General Frido von Senger und Etterlin, *Neither Fear Nor Hope,* p. 273.
249 Clark Diary, 7/9/1944.
250 Corti, op. cit., p. 240.
251 Ibid., p. 248.
252 Wiggans, op. cit.
253 Ibid.
254 Segebrecht Diary, 14/9/1944.
255 Ibid.
256 Dundas, op. cit., p. 189.
257 Ibid., p. 190.
258 Ibid., p. 191.
259 *Gianfranco Moscati Collection*, IWM.
260 Ibid.
261 BA-MA MSG2/4335.
262 Ibid.
263 Ibid.
264 SANMMH.
265 Segebrecht Diary.
266 Cited in Giampietro Lippi, *Il Sole di Monte Sole*, p. 313.
267 Segebrecht Diary.
268 Ibid.
269 Ibid.
270 Von Senger, op. cit., p. 269.
271 Papers, Consorzio di Gestione Parco Storico di Monte Sole.
272 Lewis, op. cit., 20/9/1943.
273 Sevareid, op. cit., p. 388.
274 Ibid.
275 Cited in Norman Kogan, *Italy and the Allies,* p. 86.
276 Lewis, op. cit., 23/9/1944.
277 Cited in John Ehrman, *Grand Strategy*, Vol. VI, p. 37.
278 Macmillan, *War Diaries*, 16/9/1944.
279 Wiggans, op. cit.
280 Ibid.
281 Leese Papers.
282 BA-MA MSG2/4335.
283 Moore, op. cit., p. 183.
284 SANNMH.
285 Anders, op. cit., pp. 232–33.
286 BA-MA MSG2/4335.
287 Ibid.
288 Scislowski, op. cit., p. 295.
289 Segebrecht Diary, 17/10/1944.
290 Clark Diary, 16/10/1944.
291 Kesselring, op. cit., p. 218.
292 TNA CAB 106/707.
293 TNA WO 214/34.
294 Ibid.
295 Scislowski, op. cit., p. 365.
296 Ibid.
297 Istituto Storico Provinciale, op. cit., p. 254.
298 TNA WO 204/11749.
299 Ibid.
300 Moore, op. cit., p. 192.
301 Ibid., p. 193.
302 TNA WO204/7301.
303 Ibid.
304 Ibid.
305 TNA HS 7/61.
306 OSS Donovan Papers – OSS Weekly Report, 18/11/1944, MHI.
307 TNA WO 208/4517.
308 OSS Donovan Papers, 18/11/1944.
309 TNA HS 7/59.
310 TNA HS 7/59.
311 Macmillan, *War Diaries*, 7/12/1944.
312 TNA HS 7/59.
313 TNA WO 204/7301.
314 Gianfranco Moscati Collection, IWM.
315 TNA CAB 121/196.
316 Clark Papers.
317 Sidney Matthews Papers, MHI.
318 Dundas, op. cit., pp. 193–94.
319 Clark Papers.
320 Cited in Hondon B. Hargrove, *Buffalo Soldiers in Italy,* p. 47.
321 Clark Papers.
322 MA-BA MSG2/4335.
323 Scislowski, op. cit., pp. 322–23.
324 SANMMH.
325 Field Marshal Alexander, *The Italian Campaign: 12th December, 1944 to 2nd May 1945*, p. 24.

326 Scislowski, op. cit., p. 339.
327 BA-MA MSG2/4335.
328 SANMMH.
329 BA-MA MSG2/4335.
330 Cited in Ehrman, op. cit., Vol. VI, p. 95.
331 Clark, op. cit., p. 417.
332 Kesselring, op. cit., p. 221.
333 Corti, op. cit., p. 279.
334 Scislowski, op. cit., p. 364.
335 Wiggans, op. cit.
336 Memoir of Lieutenant Barnini.
337 TNA AIR 23/8014.
338 NARA RG 226–154-55.
339 Stephen Hastings, *The Drums of Memory*, p. 112.
340 TNA WO 208/4517.
341 Ibid.
342 Anders, op. cit., p. 251.
343 Wiggans, op. cit.
344 Ibid.
345 Clark, op. cit., p. 414.
346 Clark Diary, 8/3/1945.
347 Ibid., 2/3/1945.
348 Air Historical Branch, 'RAF Narrative: The Italian Campaign 1943–1945, Vol. III.'
349 Dundas, op. cit., p. 200.

350 BA-MA MSG2/4335.
351 Dundas, op. cit., p. 202.
352 SANMMH.
353 Clark Diary, 11/4/1945.
354 Arrichiello, op. cit., p. 372.
355 Wiggans, op. cit.
356 BA-MA MSG2/4335.
357 SANMMH.
358 Clark Diary, 21/4/1945.
359 TNA WO 208/4517.
360 Cited in Jochen von Lang, *Top Nazi,* p. 291.
361 BA-MA MSG2/4335.
362 Ibid.
363 Cited in Nicholas Farrell, op. cit., p. 461.
364 Vivarelli, op. cit., p. 89.
365 Elena Curti, *Il Chiodo a tre punte*, Chapter XIX.
366 Vivarelli, op. cit., p. 91.
367 TNA WO 208/4517.
368 Hastings, op. cit., p. 129.
369 Ibid., p. 130.
370 BA-MA MSG2/4335.
371 TNA WO 214.
372 TNA WO 311/359.
373 DORER 1310.

BIBLIOGRAPHY

Abbreviations used in References

BA-MA   Bundesarchiv-Militärarchiv, Freiburg-im-Breisgau

IWM   Imperial War Museum, London

CIT   The Citadel, Military College of the South, Charleston, South Carolina

DORER   Documenti della Resistenza a Roma e nel Lazio at Istituto Romano per la Storia d'Italia dal Fascismo alla Resistenza, Rome

LHCMS   Liddell Hart Centre for Military Studies, King's College, London

MHI   The Military History Institute, Carlisle Barracks, Pennsylvania

NARA   The National Archives and Records Administration, College Park, Maryland

SANMMH   South African National Museum of Military History

TNA   The National Archives, Kew, London

UNPUBLISHED SOURCES

(a) Archives

Archivo Prov. Le Forlì-Cesena della Associazione Nazionale Partigiani d'Italia, Forlì, Italy

Documents and correspondence of Iader Miserocchi; various self-produced publications: *Sebben Che Siamo Donne... Testimonianze di donne resistenti raccolte da Grazia Cattabriga e Rosalba Navarra*; *Storia ad Sergio* (memoir); *La Battaglia di Biserno 12 Aprile 1944 in due inediti* (pamphlet); editions of *Cronache della Resistenza*

Bundesarchiv-Militär Archiv, Freiburg-im-Breisgau
Karl Burckhardt, diary; Hans Golda, memoir; Karl Loeck, memoir; Hans Sitka, papers and memoir; Georg Zellner, papers and diary; war diary of 4th Fallschirmjäger Regiment

The Citadel, Military College of the South, Charleston, South Carolina
Mark Clark Papers: diaries, records, letters and correspondence, press cuttings

Consorzio di Gestione Parco Storico di Monte Sole, Marzabotto, Italy
Papers, reports and correspondence relating to the Stella Rossa and the massacre on Monte Sole, 29 September–1 October 1944

Gurkha Museum and Archives, Peninsular Barracks, Winchester
Citations of 1/2nd and 1/9th Gurkha Rifles; papers of J. P. Cross

Hazel Braugh Records Center and Archives, The American Red Cross, Lorton, Virginia
American Red Cross oral history of Marguerite (Maggie) Potts

Imperial War Museum, London
Department of Documents: Papers of Sir Oliver Leese, including letters, diary and unpublished memoir; H. A. Wilson, IWM 80/5/1; Collezione Gianfranco Moscati; Captain F. Cox, 88/44/1; Major E. F. P. Armitage, 91/21/1; E. M. Rose, 67/257/1; P. Odner, 99/31/1; Field Marshal Lord Harding, 96/40/1; D. P. H. Wright, 91/26/1; H. Hayes, 84/3/1; Captain D. H. Deane, 95/33/1; A. S. Angus, 93/17/1; Captain A. G. Oakley, 94/41/1; Lt Col. K. Shirley-Smith, 87/31/1; R. I. L. Cunningham, 87/61/1
Sound Archive: Interview transcript, Major Roy Farran, SR 18034

Istituto Ferruccio Parri, Bologna
Editions of *Il Resto del Carlino*, May 1944–May 1945; various CUMER bulletins, reports and correspondence; *Raccolta Bergonzini Luciano*

Istituto Romano per la Storia d'Italia dal Fascismo alla Resistenza, Rome
Documenti della Resistenza a Roma e nel Lazio, including accounts of rapes in Lazio south of Rome and accounts of conditions and experiences during the DIADEM battles

Istituto Storico della R.S.I., Bologna
Documents, letters, press cuttings, photographs and various writings collected and edited by Arturo Conti in *Repubblica Sociale*

Joint Services Combined Staff College Library, Defence Academy, Shrivenham, Wiltshire
Air Historical Branch: 'RAF Narrative – The Italian Campaign 1943–1945', Volume II; 'Notes From the Theatre of War', No 14, Italy; translation of captured German documents: 'The Luftwaffe in Italy'; 'The German Supply Situation', by Colonel Ernst Faehndrich

Liddell Hart Centre for Military Studies, King's College, London
Papers of Lieutenant-General Sir Sidney Kirkman; Papers of Field Marshal Viscount Alanbrooke

The Military History Institute, Carlisle Barracks, Pennsylvania
Army Service Experience Questionnaires: John W. Attwell; George G. Harper; Rufus Johnson; H. Robert Krear; Robert M. Marsh; Robert L. Wiggans
Senior Officers Debriefing Program: General Edward Almond; General Mark Clark; General Hamilton Howze
Memoirs and recollections: John J. Roche, 'Forty Years After'; memoir by Robert M. Marsh; memoir by George G. Harper; H. Robert Krear, 'The Journal of a US Army Mountain Trooper in World War II'; Robert Landon Wiggans, 'The Hazardous Trail: Journeys of an Ithaca Boy'; Hamilton H. Howze, 'Thirty-Five Years and Then Some: Memoirs of a Professional Soldier'
Historical Division: Dietrich Beelitz, 'The Battle of Bologna, Oct 44–Apr 45'; Field Marshal Albert Kesselring: 'German Strategy during the Italian Campaign'; 'Mediterranean War, Part V: Campaign in Italy, Part II'; 'The War Behind the Front: Guerrilla Warfare'; General of the Waffen-SS Max Simon, 'Experience Gained in Combat with Russian Infantry'; 'Italian Theatre: The Fighting in the Bologna-Adriatic Coast Sector'; 'German Rear Area Organization – Italy'; 'Psychological Warfare'; Oberst Ernst Eggert, 'Supply during Allied Offensive May 1944 and Subsequent Fighting to the Apennines'; General Frido von Senger und Etterlin, 'War Diary of the Italian Campaign'
William J. Donovan Papers: 'OSS Situation Weekly Reports'; 'The Contributions of the Italian Partisans to the Allied War Effort'; 'The Resistance Movement in German-Controlled Italy'; 'British Policy in Italy'; 'Italy: Civil Affairs'

Museo Reggimentale Giovani Fascisti, Ponti Sul Mincio, Italy
Memoir of Lieutenant Barnini, Bir el Gobi Company

The National Archives and Records Administration, College Park, Maryland

Unit histories, records, and war diaries: 'Fifth Army – G2 Intelligence, Judge Advocate'; 88th Division; 85th Division; 10th Mountain Division; 34th Division; 135th Infantry Regiment; 1st Armored Division; 13th Armored Battalion; 1st Armored Battalion; 92nd Division; 'Report of Investigation Concerning Loss of Combat Efficiency of the 2nd Battalion, 370 Infantry Regiment, 92nd Infantry Division

OSS files: supply drop details; Professore Piero Ziccardi, 'Zucca' Mission; Alberto Blandi, 'Maria Giovanna' mission

Miscellaneous: Reports on organisation of SS in Italy; Italian SS

The National Archives, Kew, London

Air force: unit histories and Operational Record Books of: 244 Wing, 334 Wing, 235 Squadron, 2 South African Air Force Squadron

SOE: 'SOE activity in Italy, 1941–1945'; F. W. D. Deakin, 'SOE and Italian Resistance, 1941–1945'; Lt Col. Beevor and Lt Col. Pleydell Bouverie, 'History of HQ SOM'; 'Co-Ordination of Air Support for SOE Operations Italy and the Balkans'; Report by Lionel Santi; Nembo Italian Combat Division; Major B.J. Barton, Report on Operation 'Cisco/Red'; Major Roy Farran, 2 SAS Regiment, Report on Operation 'Tombola'; Award of DSO to Major Roy Farran; Michael Lees, Report on Reggio Emilia Partisans; Berti Francesco, Report on Partisan Activity in the Fall of Florence

Army: The Papers of Field Marshal Earl Alexander; various files relating to II Polish Corps; 21 Army Group Memorandum on British Armour; Report of Gothic Line Defences; War Diary of Eighth Army; War Diary of 15th Army Group; War Diary of 78th Division; Regimental War Diaries of 2/5th Battalion Leicestershire Regiment; 3rd Battalion Coldstream Guards; 2/7th Battalion The Queen's Royal Regiment; 9th Battalion Queen's Royal Lancers; 2nd Battalion Rifle Brigade, 10th Battalion Rifle Brigade; 1/2nd Battalion Gurkha Rifles

Voluntary statements by German officers: Otto Baum; Dietrich Beelitz; Alexander Bourquin; Eduard Crasemann; Eugen Dollmann; Otto Heckel; Richard Heidrich; Fritz Hilderbrandt; Karl-Heinz Hol; Herbert Kappler; Hans Keller; Albert Kesselring; Joachim Lemelsen; Eberhard von Mackensen; Alfred Schlemm; Frido von Senger und Etterlin; Max Simon; Heinz Trettner; Heinrich von Vietinghoff; Karl Wolff

Miscellaneous: Reports on war crimes and atrocities by Yugoslavian partisans; documents relating to the David Group; reports of the war crimes trial of Albert Kesselring; interrogations, statements and case relating to Carla Costa; translations of intercepted signals of Japanese ambassador to the RSI; reports on war crimes investigations; report on German reprisals for partisan activity in Italy; Wolff's peace feelers; US Fifth Army reports from CEF HQ; files on Italian Black Brigades; interrogations of and statements by Prince Junio Valerio Borghese

Royal Green Jackets Museum and Archive, Peninsular Barracks, Winchester
Papers of Alex Bowlby

South African National Museum of Military History, Johannesburg
Diary and papers of Dick Frost

(b) Oral History

Werner Eggert, 4th Fallschirmjäger Regiment, 1st Fallschirmjäger Division, interviewed by Katja Elias
Xavier Krebs, Moroccan Tirailleurs, interviewed by Jane Martens
Nainabahadur Pun, 1/2nd King Edward VII's Own Gurkha Rifles, interviewed by Major Peter Ridlington

Interviews conducted by author (preserved at Sound Archive, IWM, London)
Stanislaw Berkieta, 15th Lancers Regiment, 5th Infantry Division, II Polish Corps
Harry Bland, driver, GSO3, Eighth Army Headquarters
Sam Bradshaw, 6 Royal Tank Regiment
Dennis Bray, 225 Squadron, RAF
Kendall Brooke, Royal Natal Carbineers, 6th South African Armoured Division
Friedrich Büchner, 3rd Anti-Tank Company, 98th Infantry Division
Albert Burke, Headquarters, 92nd Infantry Division
Ion Calvocoressi MC, ADC Commanding Officer, Eighth Army
Generale Vittorio de' Castiglioni, No 1 Special Force, SOE
Renato Cravedi, XIII Zone Piacenza partisans
William Cremonini, Bir el Gobi Company, RSI
Antonio Cucciati, Nuotatori e paracadutisti, Decima MAS

Elena Curti, Mussolini's 'eyes and ears' in Maderno, and Ministry of
   Popular Culture, RSI
Anna Del Conte, Italian civilian, Amaseno, Emilia Romagna
Petrus Dhlamini, driver, 6th South African Armoured Division
Charles Dills, 522nd Squadron, 27th Fighter-Bomber Group
Eddie Dunhill, 148 Squadron, RAF
Clara Duse, Italian civilian, Trieste
Ray Ellis, escaped British POW
Lyall Fricker, 260 Squadron, RAF
Ernest Gearing, 7/23rd Medium Regiment, 6th South African Division
Tini Glover, 28th (Maori) Battalion, 2nd New Zealand Division
Reg Harris, 3rd Battalion, Coldstream Guards, 1st Guards Brigade
Sir Stephen Hastings MC, No 1 Special Force, SOE
Willi Holtfreter, III/Jagdgeschwader 53
Professor Sir Michael Howard, 3rd Coldstream Guards
Ines Righi Albano, Servizio Ausiliario Femminile (SAF), Comando
   Provinciale, Guardia Nazionale Repubblicana, Verona
Pat Ives, 4th Reconnaissance Regiment
Howard Jackson, 739th Squadron, 454th Bomb Group, 15th US Air Force
Joseph Klein, Pioneer Battalion, 3rd Fallschirmjäger Regiment
Bill Konze, 3rd Battalion, 349th Infantry Regiment, US 88th Infantry
   Division
Kurt Langelüddecke, Heavy Artillery Troop 602, 1st Fallschirmjäger
   Division
Christopher Lee, 205 Group RAF
Carlo Lucini, XIII Zone Piacenza Partisans
Franz Maassen, 3rd Battalion, 994th Infantry Regiment, 278th Infantry
   Division
Bernard Martin, 148 Squadron, RAF
Leo Mateucci, 8th Garibaldi Brigade Partisans
Cecil Maudesley, MM, 4/13th Frontier Force Rifles, 6th South African
   Armoured Division
Len Meerholz, 1 Squadron, South African Air Force
Iader Miserocchi, Commander 2nd Battalion, 8th Garibaldi Brigade
   Partisans
Glauco 'Gordon' Monducci, Green Flames, Reggio Emilia Partisans and
   Black Owls
Peter Moore MC, 2/5 Leicestershire Regiment
Ken Neill DFC, 225 Squadron, RAF

Nigel Nicolson, Headquarters, Guards Brigade

Helmut Ortschiedt, Medic, 15th Panzer Grenadier Division

Cornelia Paselli, Italian civilian, Monte Sole

Professor Tomasz Piesakowski, 17th Infantry Battalion, 5th Kresowa Division, II Polish Corps

Francesco Pirini, Italian civilian, Monte Sole

Heinz Puschmann, 4th Fallschirmjäger Division

Italo Quadrelli, Italian civilian, Gemmano

George Ramsay, 2nd Battalion, Scots Guards

Gianni Rossi, second in command, Stella Rossa partisans

Wladek Rubnikowicz, 12th Lancers, 3rd Carpathian Division, II Polish Corps

Ray Saidel, 1st Armored Battalion, US 1st Armored Division

Giuseppe 'Pino' Schiavi, XIII Zone Piacenza Partisans

Rudi Schreiber, Pioneer Battalion, 16th Waffen-SS Panzer Grenadier Division

J. W. 'Toby' Sewell, 2/7th Battalion The Queen's Royal Regiment

Gastone Sgargi, Stella Rossa partisan

George Underwood, 381st Bomb Squadron, 310th Bomb Group, 57th Bomb Wing, 12th US Air Force

George Vaughan, 5th Battalion Hampshire Regiment, 78th Division

Carlo Venturi, Stella Rossa and 62nd Garibaldi Partisans

Professor Roberto Vivarelli, Bir el Gobi Company, RSI

Ernest Wall OBE, 24 Squadron, South African Air Force

Edward 'Bucky' Walters, 135th Infantry Regiment, US 34th Infantry Division

Ted Wyke-Smith MC, 214th Field Company, 78th Division Royal Engineers

(c) Diaries, Letters and Memoirs

Blomfield-Smith, Denis, 'Fourth Indian Reflections: Memoirs of a Great Company'

Brodhurst-Hill, David, letters

Calvocoressi, I., 'Diary'

Cox, E. G., 'How We Won World War II, or If Only Hitler Had Known'

Cubitt-Smith, Henry, 'Yadgari'

Eggert, Werner, 'Memoir'

Ellis, Ray, 'Once A Hussar'

Harris, Reg, 'Memoir'

Hinsby, D. F., 148 Squadron, RAF, letters

Hirst, Fred, 'A Green Hill Far Away'

Istituto Storico della Resistenza Forlì, '1943–1944 vita quotidiana . . . par cla strê'

Jackson, Howard, various reminiscences, essays, etc

Klein, Joseph, 'German Parachute Engineer Battalion and the Italian War, 1943/45'

Kumberg, Hans-Jürgen, 'A Paratrooper's Story'

Lampson, Giles, letters

La Rosa, A., 'Storia della Resistenza nel Piacentino' (Amministrazione Provinciale di Piacenza su Iniziativa della Commissione Consiglieri Provinciale Partigiani per la Celebrazione del decannale della Constituzione)

Lowrey, Jerome, various papers

Maassen, Franz, memoir

Reder, Walter, various papers and correspondence

Sear, George, 'A brief history of HMS *Kingston*, a "K" Class Destroyer of WW2'

Sewell, J. W., 'War Diary'

PUBLISHED SOURCES

(a) Official Histories

Blair, Lt Col. C. N. M., *Guerrilla Warfare* (HMSO, 1957)

Boog, Horst, et al., *Germany and the Second World War: Volume IV – The Global Conflict* (Clarendon Press, 2001)

Cody, J. F., *28 (Maori) Battalion* (War History Branch, Department of Internal Affairs, Wellington, New Zealand, 1956)

Coles, Harry L. and Weinberg, Albert K., *United States Army in World War II Special Studies: Civil Affairs – Soldiers Become Governors* (Office of the Chief of Military History, Department of the Army, 1964)

Ehrman, John, *History of the Second World War: Grand Strategy, Volume V* (HMSO, 1956)

—— *History of the Second World War: Grand Strategy, Volume VI* (HMSO, 1956)

Fisher Jr, Ernest F., *United States Army in World War II, The Mediterranean Theater of Operations: Cassino to the Alps* (Center of Military History United States Army, 1977)

Harris, C. R. S., *History of the Second World War: Allied Military Administration of Italy, 1943–1945* (HMSO, 1957)

Hinsley, F. H., *British Intelligence in the Second World War*, Abridged Edition (HMSO, 1993)

Howard, Michael, *History of the Second World War: Grand Strategy, Volume IV* (HMSO, 1972)

—— *The Mediterranean Strategy in the Second World War* (Greenhill Books, 1993)

Jackson, General Sir William, *History of the Second World War: The Mediterranean and Middle East, Volume VI, Part II* (Naval and Military Press, 2004)

—— *History of the Second World War: The Mediterranean and Middle East, Volume VI, Part III* (HMSO, 1988)

Kroener, Bernard R., Muller, Rolf-Dieter, and Umbreit, Hans, *Germany and the Second World War, Volume V: Organisation and Mobilization of the German Sphere of Power* (Clarendon Press, Oxford, 2003)

Lee, Ulysses, *United States Army In World War II: Special Studies – The Employment of Negro Troops* (Office of the Chief of Military History, United States Army, 1966)

Matloff, Maurice, *United States Army in World War II: The War Department – Strategic Planning For Coalition Warfare, 1943–1944* (Office of the Chief of Military History, Department of the Army, 1959)

Matloff, Maurice, and Snell, Edwin M., *United States Army in World War II: The War Department – Strategic Planning For Coalition Warfare, 1941–1942* (Office of the Chief of Military History, Department of the Army, 1953)

Molony, Brigadier C. J. C., *History of the Second World War: The Mediterranean and Middle East, Volume V* (HMSO, 1973)

—— *History of the Second World War: The Mediterranean and Middle East, Volume VI, Part I* (Naval and Military Press, 2004)

Nicholson, Lt Col. G. W. L., *Official History of the Canadian Army in the Second World War: Volume II, The Canadians in Italy 1943–1945* (Edmond Cloutier, 1957)

Orpen, Neil, *South African Forces World War II, Volume V: Victory in Italy* (Purnell, 1975)

Parker, H. M. D., *History of the Second World War: Manpower – A Study of Wartime Policy and Administration* (HMSO, 1957)

Paul, Col. Wilfred J., and Simpson, Albert F., *The Army Air Forces in*

World War II, Volume Three: Europe: Argument To V-E Day, January 1944 To May 1945 (University of Chicago Press, 1951)

Pogue, Forrest C., *United States Army in World War II, The European Theater of Operations: The Supreme Command* (Office of the Chief of Military History Department of the Army, 1954)

Roberts Greenfield, Kent (General Editor), *United States Army in World War II: The War in the Mediterranean: A WWII Pictorial History* (Brassey's, 1998)

(b) Books

Absolom, Roger, *A Strange Alliance: Aspects of Escape and Survival in Italy, 1943–45* (Leo S. Olschki Editore, 1991)

Addison, Paul, and Calder, Angus (eds), *Time To Kill: The Soldier's Experience of War in the West, 1939–1945* (Pimlico, 1997)

Aitken, Tom, *Nowhere to Hide: A Story of Cassino* (Lamberti Federico e Figli Editore, 1994)

Alanbrooke, Field Marshal Lord, *War Diaries, 1939–1945* (Weidenfeld and Nicolson, 2001)

Alexander, Field Marshal, *The Alexander Memoirs, 1940–1945* (McGraw-Hill, 1965)

—— *The Italian Campaign, 12th December 1944 to 2nd May 1945* (HMSO, 1951)

—— *The Paintings of Field Marshal Earl Alexander of Tunis* (Collins, 1973)

Alston, Mike, *Destroyer and Preserver* (Maphigrada Publishing, 1993)

Ambrose, Stephen E., *Eisenhower: Soldier and President* (Pocket Books, 2003)

Anders, Lt-General W., *An Army in Exile: The Story of the Second Polish Corps* (Macmillan, 1949)

Anfuso, Filipo, *Da Palazzo Venezia a Lago di Garda* (Settimo Sigillo, 1996)

Anon., *The Rise and Fall of the German Air Force* (issued by the Air Ministry, 1948)

ANPI, *Testimonianze incise nel Marmo* (Monumenti, Cippi e Lapidi, Piacenza, 1999)

Arrichiello, Cosimo, *Italian Heartbreak: Life Under Mussolini* (The Book Guild Ltd., 2004)

Atkins, Peter, *Buffoon In Flight* (Ernest Stanton Publishers, 1978)

Avagliano, Mario (ed.), *Generazione ribelle: diari e lettere dal 1943 al 1945* (Einaudi, 2006)

Avallone, R., Lottici, M., and Molle, R., *Cassino War Memorial: Le immagini della battaglia* (Herald Editore, 2005)

Awatare, Arapeta, *Awatare: A Soldier's Story* (Huia, 2003)

Bacon, Admiral Sir Reginald, Fuller, Major-General J. F. C., and Playfair, Air Marshal Sir Patrick (eds), *Warfare Today: How Modern Battles are Planned and Fought on Land, at Sea, and in the Air* (Odhams Press Limited, no date)

Bader, Douglas, *Fight For the Sky: The Story of the Spitfire and Hurricane* (Sidgwick and Jackson, 1973)

Badoglio, Pietro, *Italy in the Second World War: Memories and Documents* (Oxford University Press, 1948)

Ball, Edmund F., *Staff Officer With the Fifth Army* (Exposition Press, 1958)

Ball, Simon, *The Guardsmen: Harold Macmillan, Three Friends, and the World They Made* HarperCollins, 2004)

Baris, Tommaso, *Tra due fuochi* (Editore Laterza, 2003)

Barnett, Correlli (ed.), *Hitler's Generals* (Weidenfeld and Nicolson, 1989)

Battaglia, Roberto, *The Story of the Italian Resistance* (Odhams Press, 1958)

Battini, Michele, and Pezzino, Paolo, *Guerra ai civili: Occupazione tedesca e politica del massacre. Toscana 1944* (Saggi Marsilio, 1997)

Bayne-Jardine, C. C., *Mussolini and Italy* (Longman, 1966)

Ben-Ghiat, Ruth, *Fascist Modernities: Italy, 1922–1945* (University of California Press, 2001)

Bentivegna, Rosario, *Achtung Banditen! Roma 1944* (Mursia Editore, 1983)

Beretta, Roberto, *Storia del Preti uccisi dai Partigiani* (Piemme, 2005)

Bertoldi, Silvio, *I Tedeschi in Italia* (Rizzoli, 1964)

Bidwell, Shelford, *Gunners at War* (Arrow, 1972)

Bidwell, Shelford, and Graham, Dominick, *Firepower: British Army Weapons and Theories of War 1904–1945* (George Allen and Unwin, 1982)

Blackwell, Ian, *Cassino* (Pen and Sword, 2005)

Blaxland, Gregory, *Alexander's Generals: The Italian Campaign, 1944–45* (William Kimber, 1979)

Blumenson, Martin (ed.), *Command Decisions* (Office of the Chief of Military History, Department of the Army, 1960)

—— *Mark Clark* (Jonathan Cape, 1985)

Bocca, Giorgio, *La Repubblica di Mussolini* (Mondadori, 1994)

—— *Storia dell'Italia Partigiana* (Mondadori, 1995)

Böhmler, Rudolf, *Monte Cassino: A German View* (Cassell, 1964)

Bonali, Ennio, et al., *Tavolicci e l'area dei tre Vescovi: Una comunità pietrificata della Guerra* (Società Editrice Il Ponte Vecchio, 2000)

Bonomi, Ivanoe, *Diario di un Anno* (Garzanti, 1947)

Bonomini, Luigi, et al. (eds), *Riservato a Mussolini: Notiziari giornalieri della Guardia nazionale repubblicana novembre 1943–giugno 1944* (Feltrinelli, 1974)

Borghese, J. Valerio, *Sea Devils* (Andrew Melrose, 1952)

Bosworth, R. J. B., *Mussolini* (Arnold, 2002)

Bowlby, Alex, *Countdown To Cassino* (Leo Cooper, 1995)

—— *The Recollections of Rifleman Bowlby* (Cassell, 1999)

Bowman, Martin W., *USAAF Handbook, 1939–1945* (Sutton, 2003)

Bradley, General Omar, *A Soldier's Story* (Henry Holt & Co., 1951)

Brett-Smith, Richard, *Hitler's Generals* (Osprey, 1976)

Brookes, Andrew, *Air War Over Italy* (Ian Allen, 2000)

Brooks, Thomas R., *The War north of Rome, June 1944–May 1945* (Da Capo, 1996)

Bryant, Arthur, *Triumph in the West* (Collins, 1959)

—— *The Turn of the Tide* (Collins, 1957)

Budiansky, Stephen, *Battle of Wits: The Complete Story of Codebreaking in World War II* (Penguin, 2000)

Bullen, Roy E., *History of the 2/7th Battalion, The Queen's Royal Regiment, 1939–1946* (Roy E. Bullen, 1958)

Butcher, Harry C., *Three Years With Eisenhower* (Heinemann, 1946)

Byers MC, E. V., *With Turbans to Tuscany* (E. V. Byers, 2002)

Cadorna, Raffaele, *La Riscossa: dal 25 Luglio alla Liberazione* (Rizzoli Editore, 1948)

Campbell Begg, Dr Richard, and Liddle, Dr Peter, *For Five Shillings A Day: Personal Histories of World War II* (HarperCollins, 2002)

Capponi, Carla, *Con Cuore di Donna* (Il Saggiatore, 2000)

Cardozier, V. R., *The Mobilization of the United States in World War II: How the Government, Military and Industry Prepared for War* (McFarland and Company, 1995)

Carver, Michael, *Harding of Petherton* (Weidenfeld and Nicolson, 1978)

—— *The Imperial War Museum Book of the War in Italy, 1943–1945* (Pan, 2001)

Casella, Luciano, *Tuscany and the Gothic Line* (La Nuova Europa, 1983)

Cassinari, Giorgio, *Piacenza nella Resistenza* (TEP, 2004)

Cederberg, Fred, *The Long Road Home: The Autobiography of a Canadian Soldier in Italy in World War II* (General Paperbacks, 1989)

Chessa, Pasquale, *Guerra Civile: Una storia fotografica* (Mondadori, 2005)

Churchill, Winston S., *The Second World War, Volume IV: The Hinge of Fate* (Cassell, 1951)

—— *The Second World War, Volume V: Closing the Ring* (Cassell, 1952)

—— *The Second World War, Volume VI: Triumph and Tragedy* (Cassell, 1954).

Ciano, Galeazzo, *Diary, 1937–1943* (Heinemann, 1947)

Cioci, Antonio (ed.), *Museo del Reggimento Giovani Fascisti Piccola Caprera* (Gianni Iuculano Editore, 2000)

Clark, Lloyd, *The Friction of War: Anzio and the Fight to Free Italy* (Atlantic Monthly Press, 2006)

Clark, Mark W., *Calculated Risk* (Harper and Brothers, 1950)

Clarke, Rupert, *With Alex At War: From the Irrawaddy to the Po, 1941–1945* (Leo Cooper, 2000)

Collotti, Enz, Sandri, Renato, and Sessi, Frediano (eds), *Dizionario della Resistenza* (Einaudi, 2000)

Comitato Regionale per onoranze ai Caduti di Marzabotto, *Marzabotto. Quanti, chi e dove* (Ponte Nuovo Editirice Bologna, 1995)

Corrigon, Gordon, *Blood, Sweat and Arrogance and the Myths of Churchill's War* (Weidenfeld and Nicolson, 2006)

Corti, Eugenio, *The Last Soldiers of the King: Wartime Italy, 1943–1945* (University of Missouri Press, 2003)

Corvo, Max, *OSS Italy 1942–1945: A Personal Memoir of the Fight For Freedom* (Enigma Books, 2005)

Cozzi, Paolo (ed.), *Reder: il regista della inaudite sagre di sangue* (Nuova Graphica, no date)

Cox, Geoffrey, *The Race For Trieste* (William Kimber, 1977)

Cross, J. P., and Gurung, Buddhiman, *Gurkhas At War* (Greenhill Books, 2002)

Curti, Elena, *Il Chiodo a tre punte: Schegge di memoria della figlia segreta del duce* (Iuculano, 2003)

Dallek, Robert, *Franklin D. Roosevelt and American Foreign Policy, 1932–1945* (Oxford University Press, 1995)

Dancocks, Daniel G., *The D-Day Dodgers: The Canadians in Italy, 1943–1945* (McClelland and Stewart, 1991)

Davidson, Basil, *Special Operations Europe* (Readers Union, 1980)

Davis, Kenneth S., *The American Experience of War 1939–1945* (Secker and Warburg, 1967)

Davis, Melton S., *Who Defends Rome?* (The Dial Press, 1972)

Deakin, F. W., *The Brutal Friendship: Mussolini, Hitler and the Fall of Italian Fascism*, (Pelican, 1962)

—— *The Six Hundred Days of Mussolini*, Part III of *The Brutal Friendship* (Doubleday, 1966)

Delaney, John P., *The Blue Devils in Italy: A History of the 88th Infantry Division in World War II* (The Battery Press, 1988)

Del Bravo, Fabio, *La Nostra Gente* (Edizioni Tipografia Artistica Fiorentina)

De Lenardis, Massimo, *La Gran Bretagna e la Resistenza partigiana in Italia (1943–1945)* (Nuovo Istituto Editoriale Italiana, 1945)

De Mattei, Professor Roberto, *Historiale di Cassino* (Literalia, 2005)

D'Este, Carlo, *Fatal Decision: Anzio and the Battle For Rome* (Harper-Perennial, 1992)

Doherty, Richard, *Only the Enemy in Front: The Recce Corps at War 1940–1946* (Tom Donovan Publishing Ltd, 1994)

Dole, Bob, *One Soldier's Story* (HarperCollins, 2005)

Dollmann, Eugen, *The Interpreter* (Hutchinson, 1967)

Duke, Neville, *Test Pilot* (Grub Street, 2003)

Duke, Neville, and Franks, Norman (ed.), *The War Diaries of Neville Duke* (Grub Street, 1995)

Dundas, Hugh, *Flying Start* (Penguin, 1990)

88th Infantry Division Association, *88th Infantry Division: Blue Devils* (Turner Publishing Company, 1992)

Eisenhower, John S. D., *Allies: Pearl Harbor To D-Day* (Da Capo Press, 2000)

—— *Crusade in Europe* (Doubleday & Co., 1948)

Ellis, John, *The Sharp End: The Fighting Man in World War II* (Pimlico, 1993)

—— *The World War II Databook* (Aurum Press, 1995)

Ellwood, David, *Italy, 1943–1945* (Leicester University Press, 1985)

Fabre, Giorgio, *Hitler's Contract* (Enigma Books, 2005)

Flower, Desmond, and Reeves, James (eds), *The War, 1939–1945: A Documentary History* (Da Capo Press, 1997)

Farran, Roy, *Operation Tombola* (Collins, 1960)

—— *Winged Dagger: Adventures on Special Service* (Cassell, 1998)

Farrell, Nicholas, *Mussolini: A New Life* (Phoenix, 2004)

Fleischer, Wolfgang, *An Illustrated Guide to German Panzers, 1939–1945* (Schiffer Publishing, 2002)

Foot, M. R. D., *Resistance: European Resistance to Nazism 1940–45* (Eyre Methuen, 1976)

—— *S.O.E.: The Special Operations Executive, 1940–1946* (BBC Books, 1984)

Ford, Ken, *Battleaxe Division* (Sutton, 2003)

Forty, George, *British Army Handbook, 1939–1945* (Sutton, 2002)

—— *German Infantryman At War, 1939–1945* (Ian Allen, 2002)

—— *IS Army Handbook, 1939–1945* (Sutton, 2003)

Fraser, David, *And We Shall Shock Them: The British Army in the Second World War* (Cassell 1999)

Fussell, Paul, *Wartime: Understanding and Behaviour in the Second World War* (Oxford University Press, 1989)

Galeotti, Domenico, *La Seconda Guerra Mondiale Sull' Appennino Tosco-Emiliano* (Tipolito Pieffepi, 2003)

Garber, Max, and Bond, P. S., *A Modern Military Dictionary* (P.S. Bond Publishing Co., 1942)

Gardinaer, Wira, *The Story of the Maori Battalion* (Reed, 1992)

Garibaldi, Luciano, *Mussolini: The Secrets of His Death* (Enigma Books, 2004)

Gellhorn, Martha, *The Face of War* (Granta, 1998)

Gentile, Emilio, *The Origins of Fascist Ideology, 1918–1925* (Enigma Books, 2005)

Giadresco, Gianni, *Guerra in Romagna, 1943–1945* (Il Monogramma, 2004)

Gilbert, Martin, *Road to Victory: Winston S. Churchill, 1941–1945* (Minerva, 1989)

Ginsborg, Paul, *A History of Contemporary Italy: Society and Politics 1943–1988* (Penguin, 1990)

Gleeson, Ian, *The Unknown Force: Black, Indian and Coloured Soldiers Through Two World Wars* (Ashanti Publishing, 1994)

Gorlitz, Walter (ed.), *The Memoirs of Field-Marshal Wilhelm Keitel* (Cooper Square Press, 2000)

Graham, Dominick, *The Escapes and Evasions of an Obstinate Bastard* (Wilton 65, 2000)

Graham, Dominick, and Bidwell, Shelford, *Tug of War: The Battle for Italy, 1943–44* (Hodder and Stoughton, 1986)

Greene, Jack, and Massignani, Alessandro, *The Black Prince and the Sea Devils: The Story of Valerio Borghese and the Elite Units of the Decima MAS* (Da Capo, 2004)

Grementieri, Carla, *Iris Versari e la Resistenza delle Donne* (Vespignani Editore, 2004)

Gunston, Bill, *Fighting Aircraft of World War II* (Salamander Books, 1988)

Gurrey, Donald, *Across the Lines: Axis Intelligence and Sabotage Operations in Italy 1943–1945* (Parapress Ltd, 1994)

Hamilton MC, Stuart, *Armoured Odyssey* (Tom Donovan Publishing, 1995)

Handel, Michael I. (ed.), *Intelligence and Military Operations* (Frank Cass, 1990)

Hargrove, Hondon B., *Buffalo Soldiers in Italy: Black Americans in World War II* (McFarland and Company, 1985)

Harpur, Brian, *The Impossible Victory: A Personal Account of the Battle for the River Po* (William Kimber, 1980)

Harrison Place, Timothy, *Military Training in the British Army, 1940–1944* (Frank Cass, 2000)

Harris Smith, Richard, *OSS: The Secret History of America's First Central Intelligence Agency* (The Lyons Press, 2005)

Hastings, Major R. H. W. S., *The Rifle Brigade in the Second World War 1939–1945* (Gale and Polden Ltd., 1950)

Hastings, Stephen, *The Drums of Memory* (Pen and Sword, 2001)

Hayward, Brigadier P. H. C., *Jane's Dictionary of Military Terms* (Book Club Edition, 1975)

Heiber, Helmut, and Glantz, David M., *Hitler and His Generals: Military Conferences, 1942–1945* (Enigma, 2003)

Hillson, Norman, *Alexander of Tunis* (W. H. Allen, 1952)

Hogg, Ian V., *The Guns, 1939–45* (Macdonald, 1979)

—— Introduction, *The American Arsenal: The World War II Official Standard Ordnance Catalog of Small Arms, Tanks, Armored Cars, Artillery, Antiaircraft Guns, Ammunition, Grenades, Mines Etcetera* (Greenhill, 1996)

Holmes, Richard, *Battlefields of the Second World War* (BBC Books, 2001)

—— *Firing Line* (Pimlico, 1994)

Hood, Stuart, *Carlino* (Carcanet Press, 1985)

Hooten, E. R., *Eagle In Flames: The Fall of the Luftwaffe* (Brockhampton Press, 1999)

Hope, Michael, *The Abandoned Legion* (Veritas Foundation Publication Group, 2005)

Horne, Alastair, *Macmillan, 1894–1956* (Macmillan, 1988)

Hougen, Lt Col. John H., *The Story of the Famous 34th Infantry Division* (The Battery Press, 1949)

Howe, George F., *The Battle History of the 1st Armored Division – Old Ironsides* (Combat Force Press, 1954)

Howlett, Peter, *Fighting With Figures: A Statistical Digest of the Second World War* (HMSO, 1995)

Hoyt, Edwin P., *The GI's War: American Soldiers In Europe During World War II* (Cooper Square Press, 2000)

Ismay, Hastings, *The Memoirs of General Lord Ismay* (The Viking Press, 1960)

Istituto Storico Provinciale della Resistenza, *L'8.a Brigata Garibaldi nella Resistenza, Vols I and II* (La Pietra, 1981)

Ivie, Tom, and Ludwig, Paul, *Spitfires and Yellow Tail Mustangs: The 52nd Fighter Group in World War Two* (Hikoki, 2005)

Jackson, W. G. F., *Alexander of Tunis As Military Commander* (Batsford, 1971)

—— *The Battle For Italy* (Harper and Row, 1967)

—— *The Battle For Rome* (Batsford, 1969)

Jadecola, Constantino, *Mal'Aria: Il secondo dopoguerra in provincia di Frosinone* (Centro di Studi Sorani 'V. Patriarca' Sora, 1998)

James, Lawrence, *Warrior Race: A History of The British at War* (Abacus, 2002)

Jenkins, Roy, *Churchill* (Pan, 2001)

Jones, R.V., *Most Secret War: British Scientific Intelligence 1939–1945* (Coronet 1979)

Jones, Tobias, *The Dark Heart of Italy: Travels Through Time and Space Across Italy* (Faber and Faber, 2003)

Katz, Robert, *Death In Rome* (Jonathan Cape, 1967)

—— *Fatal Silence: The Pope, the Resistance and the German Occupation of Rome* (Cassell, 2004)

Keegan, John (ed.), *Churchill's Generals* (Abacus, 1999)

—— *The Second World War* (Pimlico, 1997)

Kemp, Anthony, *The SAS At War, 1941–1945* (Penguin, 2000)

Kershaw, Ian, *Hitler: 1936–1945 – Nemesis* (Penguin, 2001)

Kesselring, Albert, *The Memoirs of Field-Marshal Kesselring* (Greenhill Books, 1988)

King, Michael, *Maori* (Heinemann, 1984)

Kippenberger, Major-General Sir Howard, *Infantry Brigadier* (Oxford University Press, 1949)

Klein, Harry (compiled and ed.), *Springbok Record* (South African Legion of the British Empire Service League, 1946)

Kloman, Erasmus H., *Assignment Algiers: With the OSS in the Mediterranean Theater* (Naval Institute Press, 2005)

Knopp, Guido, *The SS: A Warning From History* (Sutton, 2005)

Knox, MacGregor, *Hitler's Italian Allies: Royal Armed Forces, Fascist Regime, and the War of 1940–1943* (Cambridge University Press, 2000)

Kogan, Norman, *Italy and the Allies* (Harvard University Press, 1956)

Kohn, Richard H., and Harahan, Joseph P. (eds), *Air Superiority in World War II and Korea* (USAF Warrior Studies, Office of Air Force History, 1983)

Kurowski, Franz, *The History of the Fallschirm Panzerkorps* (J. J. Fedrowicz Publishing Inc., 1995)

Lamb, Richard, *War In Italy, 1943–1945: A Brutal Story* (John Murray, 1993)

Lang, Jochen von, *Top Nazi: SS General Karl Wolff, The Man Between Hitler and Himmler* (Enigma Books, 2005)

Lees, Michael, *Special Operations Executed* (William Kimber, 1986)

Lett, Gordon, *Rossano* (Hodder and Stoughton, 1955)

Levi, Primo, *If This Is a Man/The Truce* (Abacus, 2005)

Lewin, Ronald, *Ultra Goes to War: The Secret Story* (Penguin, 2001)

Lewis, Laurence, *Echoes of Resistance: British Involvement with the Italian Partisans* (Costello, 1985)

Lewis, Norman, *Naples '44: An Intelligence Office in the Italian Labyrinth* (Eland, 2002)

Lewis, Ted, *I Was No Soldier: An Artist's War Diary* (Steele Roberts, 2001)

Liddell Hart, B. H., *The Other Side of the Hill* (Cassell, 1948)

Linderman, Gerald P., *The World Within War: America's Combat Experience in World War II* (Harvard University Press, 1999)

Linklater, Eric, *The Campaign in Italy* (HMSO, 1951)

Lippi, Giampietro, *Il Sole di Monte Sole* (Edizione ANPI)

—— *La Stella Rossa a Monte Sole* (Ponte Nuovo Editrice Bologna)

Lochner, Louis P. (trans. and ed.), *The Goebbels Diaries* (Hamish Hamilton, 1948)

Loewenheim, Francis L., Langley, Harold D., and Jonas, Manfred (eds), *Roosevelt and Churchill: Their Secret Wartime Correspondence* (Barrie and Jenkins, 1975)

Loy, Rosetta, *First Words: A Childhood in Fascist Italy* (Metropolitan Books, 2000)

Lucioli, Massimo, and Sabatini, Davide, *La Ciociara e le Altre: Il Corpo di Spedizione Francese in Italia, 1943–1944* (Edizioni Tusculum, 1998)

Mack Smith, Denis, *Mussolini* (Paladin, 1983)

Mackenzie, William, *The Secret History of SOE, Special Operations Executive, 1940–1945* (St Ermin's Press, 2000)

Macintosh, Charles, *From Cloak and Dagger: An SOE Agent in Italy, 1943–1945* (William Kimber, 1982)

Macmillan, Harold, *The Blast of War, 1939–1945* (Harper and Row, 1967)

—— *War Diaries: The Mediterranean, 1943–1945* (Macmillan, 1984)

Majdalany, Fred, *Cassino: Portrait of a Battle* (Longmans, 1957)

—— *The Monastery* (John Lane The Bodley Head, 1946)

Martin, G. W., *Cassino to the River Po, Italy 1944–45* (G.W. Martin, 1999)

Mauldin, Bill, *Bill Mauldin's Army* (Presidio Press, 2003)

McCarthy, Michael C., *Air To Ground Battle for Italy* (Air University Press Maxwell Air Force Base, Alabama, 2004)

McGaw Smyth, Howard, *Secrets of the Fascist Era: How Uncle Sam Obtained Some of the Top-Level Documents of Mussolini's Period* (Southern Illinois University Press, 1975)

McNab, Chris (ed.), *German Paratroopers* (MBI Publishing, 2000)

Merewood, Jack, *To War With the Bays: A Tank Gunner Remembers, 1939–1945* (1st Dragoon Guards, 1996)

Michel, Henri, *The Shadow War: Resistance in Europe, 1939–45* (Andre Deutsch, 1972)

Ministero per i Beni e le Attività Culturali, *4 giugno 1944: La liberazione di Roma nelle immagini degli archive alleati* (Skira editore, 2004)

Ministry of Foreign Affairs of the U.S.S.R., *Correspondence Between Stalin, Roosevelt, Truman, Churchill and Attlee During WWII* (University Press of the Pacific Honolulu, Hawaii)

Monducci, Glauco, *Gordon . . . e vennero i giorni del gufo nero* (Edizionie Bertani & C., 1995)

Montanelli, Indro, and Cervi, Mario, *L'Italia della Guerra Civile: 8 settembre 1943–9 maggio 1946* (Biblioteca Universale Rizzoli, 2000)

Montemaggi, Amedeo, *Gemmano: La Cassino dell'Adriatico* (Commune di Gemmano, 1998)

—— *Linea Gotica: Lo sfondamento canadese a Tavullia episodio chiave della Guerra in Italia* (Commune di Tavulla, 1997)

Moore, Peter, *No Need To Worry: Memoirs of an Army Conscript 1941 to 1946* (Wilton 65, 2002)

Moorehead, Caroline, *Iris Origo: Marchesa of Val d'Orcia* (John Murray, 2003)

—— *Martha Gellhorn: A Life* (Vintage, 2004)

—— (ed.), *The Letters of Martha Gellhorn* (Chatto and Windus, 2006)

Moravia, Alberto, *Two Women* (Penguin, 1976)

Morris, Eric, *Circles of Hell: The War in Italy 1943–1945* (Hutchinson, 1993)

Morris, Jan, *Trieste and the Meaning of Nowhere* (Faber & Faber, 2002)

Morton, H. V., *A Traveller in Italy* (Methuen, 1964)

Moseley, Ray, *Mussolini: The Last 600 Days of Il Duce* (Taylor Trade, 2004)

Mountfield, David, *The Partisans: Secret Armies of World War II* (Hamlyn, 1979)

Murphy, Robert, *Diplomat Among Warriors* (Pyramid Books, 1965)

Murray, Williamson, *Luftwaffe: Strategy For Defeat 1933–45* (Grafton, 1988)

Mussolini, Benito, *La Democrazia dalle Pance Piene: Scritti e discorsi della Repubblica Sociale Italiana* (Edizioni FPE Milano, 1967)

Newark, Tim, *The Mafia at War: Allied Collusion With the Mob* (Greenhill Books, 2007)

Newby, Eric, *Love and War in the Apennines* (Picador, 1983)

Newby, Wanda, *Peace and War: Growing Up In Fascist Italy* (Picador, 1991)

Nicolson, Nigel, *Alex: The Life of Field Marshal Earl Alexander of Tunis* (Weidenfeld and Nicolson, 1973)

—— *Long Life: Memoirs* (Weidenfeld and Nicolson, 1997)

O'Donnell, Patrick K., *Operatives, Spies and Saboteurs: The Unknown Story of the Men and Women of WWII's OSS* (Free Press, 2004)

Olsen, Jack, *Silence On Monte Sole* (G. P. Putnam's Sons, 1968)

Orange, Vincent, *Slessor: Bomber Champion* (Grub Street, 2006)

Orgill, Douglas, *The Gothic Line* (W. W. Norton & Company, 1967)

Origo, Benedetta, et al., *La Foce: A Garden and Landscape in Tuscany* (University of Pennsylvania Press, 2001)

Origo, Iris, *Images and Shadows: Part of a Life* (John Murray, 1970)

—— *War in Val d'Orcia: An Italian War Diary, 1943–1944* (Flamingo, 2002)

Overy, Richard, *Why the Allies Won* (Pimlico, 1996)

Owen, Roderic, *The Desert Air Force* (Arrow, 1958)

Parker, Matthew, *Monte Cassino* (Headline, 2003)

Parks, Tim, *Italian Neighbours* (Vintage, 2001)

Parton, James, *Air Force Spoken Here: General Ira Eaker and the Command of the Air* (Alder and Alder, 1986)

Peli, Santo, *Storia della Resistenza in Italia* (Einaudi, 2006)

Peniakoff, Vladimir, *Popski's Private Army* (Cassell, 2002)

Perret, Bryan, *Iron Fist: Classic Armoured Warfare Case Studies* (Arms and Armour, 1995)

Perret, Geoffrey, *There's a War To Be Won: The United States Army in World War II* (Ballantine, 1991)

Petacco, Arrigo, *Riservato Per Il Duce* (Arnoldo Mondadori Editore, 1979)

Piesakowski, Tomasz, *The Fate of Poles in the USSR 1939–1989* (Gryf Publications, 1990)

Pisanò, Giorgio, *Gli ultimi cinque secondi di Mussolini* (Il Saggiatore, 1996)

Pistilli, Emilio, *La battaglia di Cassino: giorno per giorno* (Città di Cassino, 1999)

—— (ed.), *Memoria e Monito* (CDSC Onlus, 2004)

Pogue, Forrest C., *George C. Marshall: Organizer of Victory* (Viking, 1973)

Poprzechny, Joseph, *Odilo Globocnik: Hitler's Man in the East* (McFarland and Company, 2004)

Porch, Douglas, *The Path to Victory: The Mediterranean Theater in World War II* (Farrar, Strauss and Giroux, 2004)

Price, Dr Alfred, *Late Mark Spitfire Aces 1942–45* (Osprey, 1995)

Prien, Jochen, *Jagdgeschwader 53, January 1944–May 1945* (Schiffer Publishing, 1998)

Quarrie, Bruce, *Weapons of the Waffen-SS* (Patrick Stephens Ltd, 1988)

Quazza, Guido, *Resistenza e storia d'Italia: Problemi e ipotesi di ricerca* (Feltrinelli, 1976)

Quilter, D. C. (compiled and ed.), *No Dishonourable Name* (William Clowes and Sons Ltd, 1947)

Ramati, Alexander, *The Assisi Underground* (Allen and Unwin, 1978)

Rees, Laurence, *The Nazis: A Warning From History* (BBC Books, 1997)

Reid, Howard, *Dad's War* (Bantam Press, 2003)

Richards, Denis, and Saunders, Hilary St. George, *Royal Air Force 1939–1945, Volume II: The Fight Avails* (HMSO, 1954)

Ringlesbach, Dorothy, *OSS: Stories That Can Now Be Told* (Author House, 2005)

Ripley, Tim, *Wehrmacht: The German Army in World War II 1939–1945* (Brown Reference Group, 2003)

Rossi, Gianni Scipione, *Mussolini e il diplomatico: La vita e i diari di Serafino Mazzolini, un monarchico a Salò* (Rubbettino, 2005)

Royal Institute of International Affairs, Chatham House, London, *Review of the Foreign Press, 1939–1945: Series A Vol. IX* (Kraus International Publications)

Ryder, Rowland, *Oliver Leese* (Hamish Hamilton, 1987)

Salvadori, Massimo, *The Labour and the Wounds* (Pall Mall Press, 1958)

Saunders, Hilary St. George, *Royal Air Force 1939–1945, Volume III: The Fight is Won* (HMSO, 1954)

Schachermayr, Stefan, *Major Walter Reder: Der Fall des letzten österreichischen Kriegsverurteilten in italienischem Gewahrsam,* (Im Kommissionsverlag bei Verlag Welsermühl, Wels, 1968)

Schmidt, Robert H., *The Forgotten Front in Northern Italy: A World War II Combat Photographer's Illustrated Memoir of the Gothic Line Campaign* (McFarland and Company, 1994)

Schreiber, Gerhard, *La Vendetta Tedesca 1943–1945: Le Rappresaglie Naziste in Italia* (Mondadori, 2000)

Schroth, Raymond A., *The American Journey of Eric Sevareid* (Streerforth Press, 1995)

Schultz, Paul L., *The 85th Division in World War II* (Infantry Journal Press, 1949)

Scislowski, Stanley, *Not All of Us Were Brave* (Dundurn Press, 1997)

Scott Daniel, David, *The Royal Hampshire Regiment, Volume Three, 1918–1954* (Gale and Polden, 1955)

Seago, Edward, *With the Allied Armies in Italy* (Collins, 1945)

Senger und Etterlin, General Frido von, *Neither Fear Nor Hope* (Presidio, 1989)

Sevareid, Eric, *Not So Wild a Dream* (Athenaeum, 1976)

Shephard, Ben, *A War of Nerves: Soldiers and Psychiatrists, 1914–1944* (Jonathan Cape, 2000)

Sherwood, Robert E., *The White House Papers of Harry L. Hopkins, Volume II, January 1942–July 1945* (Eyre and Spottiswoode, 1949)

Short, Neil, *German Defences in Italy in World War II* (Osprey, 2006)

Simpson, J. S. M., *South Africa Fights* (Hodder and Stoughton, 1941)

Slessor, Sir John, *The Central Blue* (Cassell, 1956)

Sloan Brown, John, *Draftee Division: The 88th Infantry Division in World War II* (Presidio, 1988)

Smith, Philip A., *Bombing to Surrender: The Contribution of Airpower to the Collapse of Italy, 1943* (Air University Press, Maxwell Air Force Base, Alabama, 1998)

Somerville, Christopher, *Our War: How the British Commonwealth Fought the Second World War* (Cassell, 2005)

Stevens, Lieut-Colonel G. R., *Fourth Indian Division* (McLaren and Son Ltd., 1948)

Sutherland, Jonathan, *World War II Tanks and AFVs* (Airlife, 2002)

Taylor, John W. R., and Moyes, Philip J. R., *A Pictorial History of the RAF, Volume Two 1939–1945* (Ian Allen Ltd, 1980)

Tedder, Marshal of the Royal Air Force Lord, *With Prejudice* (Cassell, 1966)

Terraine, John, *The Right of the Line* (Hodder and Stoughton, 1985)

Thorpe, D. R., *Eden* (Chatto and Windus, 2003)

Toffoletto Romagnoli, Mary, *Sull' Eccido di Marzabotto: dalla Testimonianza dell' Orsolina Antonietta Benni*, (Edizioni Digi Grafm, 2005)

Tompkins, Peter, *A Spy in Rome* (Weidenfeld and Nicolson, 1962)

—— *Italy Betrayed* (Simon and Schuster, 1966)

Tooze, Adam, *The Wages of Destruction: The Making and Breaking of the Nazi Economy*, (Penguin Allen Lane, 2006)

Townley, Edward, *Mussolini and History* (Heinemann, 2002)

Trevelyan, Raleigh, *The Fortress: A Diary of Anzio and After* (Four Square, 1966)

—— *Rome '44: The Battle for the Eternal City* (Secker and Warburg, 1981)

Truppenkameradschaft, *Im gleichen Schritt und Tritt: Dokumentation der 16. SS-Panzergrenadierdivision 'Reichsführer-SS'*, especially Willfried Segebrecht diary, (Schild-Verlag GmbH, 1998)

Truscott, Lt Gen. L. K., *Command Missions* (Presidio, 1990)

Tudor, Malcolm, *Special Force: SOE and the Italian Resistance, 1943–1945* (Emilia Publishing, 2004)

Tutaev, David, *The Consul of Florence* (Secker and Warburg, 1966)

United Nations War Crimes Commission, *Law Reports of Trials of War Criminals, Volume VIII* (HMSO, 1949)

Van Creveld, Martin, *Fighting Power: German and US Army Performance 1939–1945* (Greenwood Press, 1982)

Various, *Reporting World War II: American Journalism 1938–1946* (The Library of America, 1995)

Venturi, Carlo, *Ming tra i Ribelli* (Edizioni Aspasia)

Vittiglio, Fred, and Fiorillo, Fernando, *Foto di Guerra* (Lamberti Editori Cassino, 1984)

Vivarelli, Roberto, *La fine di una stagione* (Società editrice, 2000)

Voss, Capt. Vivian, *The Story of No 1 Squadron, SAAF* (Mercantile Atlas, 1952)

Wallace, Robert, *The Italian Campaign* (Time-Life Books, 1981)

Warlimont, Walter, *Inside Hitler's Headquarters, 1939–45* (Presidio, 1964)

Westphal, Siegfried, *The German Army in the West* (Cassell and Company, 1951)

Whicker, Alan, *Whicker's War* (HarperCollins, 2005)

White, B.T., *Tanks and Other Armoured Fighting Vehicles of World War II* (Peerage Books, 1975)

Whiting, Charles, *Hunters From the Sky: The German Parachute Corps, 1940–1945* (Cooper Square Press, 2001)

Williamson, Gordon, *Waffen-SS Handbook, 1933–1945* (Sutton, 2003)

Wilmott, H. P., *The Great Crusade: A New Complete History of the Second World War* (Pimlico, 1992)

Windsor, John, *The Mouth of the Wolf* (Gray's Publishing Ltd., 1967)

Wolfe, Robert (ed.), *Captured German and Related Records: A National Archives Conference* (Ohio University Press, 1974)

Wyss, M. de, *Rome Under the Terror* (Robert Hale Ltd, 1945)

Zuehlke, Mark, *The Gothic Line: Canada's Month of Hell in World War II Italy* (Douglas and McIntyre, 2003)

—— *The Liri Valley: Canada's World War II Breakthrough to Rome* (Douglas and McIntyre, 2001)

(c) Pamphlets and Periodicals

Anon., 'Bundestagsdebatte über die Waffen-SS', Der Freiwillige

Anon., 'Der letzte Kriegsgefangene aus dem 2. Weltkreig'

Anon., 'Wahrheit und Gerechtigkeit für den Menschen und Soldaten Walter Reder'

Blumenson, Martin, 'Ike and His Indispensable Lieutenants,' *Army* (June 1980)

Blumenson, Martin, and Stokesbury, James L., 'Mark Clark and the War in Italy', *Army* (May 1971)

Brookes, Wing Commander Andrew, 'Air Power and the Italian Campaign, 1943–1945', *RUSI Journal* (December 1996)

Cardoza, Anthony L., 'Recasting the Duce for the New Century: Recent Scholarship on Mussolini and Italian Fascism', *The Journal of Modern History,* 77 (September 2005)

D'Albac, Air Vice-Marshal J. H., 'Air Aspects of the Campaigns in Italy and the Balkans', *RUSI Journal*

Flores, Jackson, 'Jambocks over Italy', *Air Enthusiast* (January/February 1996)

McAndrew, Dr William J., 'Eighth Army at the Gothic Line: Commanders and Plans', *RUSI Journal* (March 1986)

—— 'Eighth Army at the Gothic Line: The Dog-Fight', *RUSI Journal* (June 1986)

Talamo, Giuseppe, 'La Storiografia sulla Resistenza', *Cultura e Scuola* (luglio–settembre 1964)

(d) Film and Television

Bland, Harry, *A Personal Journey*

CDSC Onlus, *Memoria e Monito: Gli eventi bellicio nel Basso Lazio autunno 1943–primavera 1944*

Huston, John, *San Pietro* (US Army Pictorial Services, 1945)

Il Consorzio di Gestione Parco Storico di Monte Sole, *I testimoni di Monte Sole*

Isaacs, Jeremy, *The World at War* (Thames Television, 1973)

Rossellini, Robert, *Paisa* (1946)

—— *Rome, Open City* (1946)

Whicker, Alan, *Whicker's War* (Channel 4, 2005)

(e) Internet

www.britishpathe.com – news reels from Italian campaign
www.kattoliko.it/corti/vita – biography of Eugenio Corti
www.geocities.com/stanlegion/front.html – articles by Stan Scislowski
www.walkervilletimes.com – articles by Stan Scislowski
www.geocities.com/raf_112_sqdn – photographs of 112 Squadron, RAF

www.members.aol.com/famjustin/Underwoodbio – memoir of George
    Underwood
www.afvinteriors.hobbyvista.com – details of WWII tanks
www.specialcamp11.fsnet.co.uk – details of German prisoners held in
    Special Camp 11
www.hotlinecy.com – interview with Karl Wolff

(f) Maps

Atlante stradale d'Italia, Centro, 1:80,000, Touring Club Italiano
Le Battaglie Della Linea Gotica 1944–45, 1:100,000, Edizioni Multi-
    graphic, Firenze
Italia centrale, Foglio 2, 1:400,000, Touring Club Italiano
Italia meridionale, Foglio 3, 1:400,000, Touring Club Italiano
Italy, Road Atlas, 1:250,000, AA
Italy, Sheets 1–56, 1:250,000, Prepared by the Geographical Section,
    General Staff, No 4230, Published by War Office, 1943
Lazio, 1:200,000, Touring Club Italiano
Parco Nazionale della Foreste Casteinesi Monte Falterona e Campigna:
    I Segnie della Memoria e i luoghi della Resistenza nel Parco, 1:60,000,
    SELCA, Firenze
Parco Storico di Monte Sole, Emmegipi Elaborazioni Cartografiche
A Series of II Polish Corps Aerial Maps, Produced by the 516th Field
    Survey Company, R.E., April 1945
Val d'Orcia, 1:25,000, Edizioni Multigraphic

ACKNOWLEDGEMENTS

I would not have been able to write this book without the help of a great many people, most notably the veterans and their families, who, without exception, gave their time freely and co-operated beyond what could be reasonably expected: Ines Righi Albano, Stanislaw Berkieta, Harry Bland, Sir Nicholas and Lady Nadine Bonsor, Sam Bradshaw, Dennis Bray, Kendall Brooke, Friedrich Büchner, Albert Burke, Ion Calvocoressi, Katherine Calvocoressi, Richard Calvocoressi, Generale Vittorio de' Castiglioni, David Clark, Renato Cravedi, William Cremonini, Antonio Cucciati, Elena Curti, Anna del Conte, Petrus Dhlamini, Charles Dills, Eddie Dunhill, Clara and Cedric Gordon, Ray Ellis, Sue Fellowes, Gareth Fonteneau, Lyall Fricker, Ernest Gearing, Tini Glover, Ian Harris, Reg Harris, Sir Stephen Hastings, D. F. Hinsby, Willi Holtfreter, Professor Sir Michael Howard, Pat Ives, Howard and Pam Jackson, Joseph Klein, Bill Konze, Hans Kumberg, Wolf von Kumberg, Kurt Langelüddecke, Christopher Lee, Jay and Bee Lowrey; Carlo Lucini, Franz Maassen, Bernard Martin, Leo Mateucci, Cecil Maudesley, Len Meerholz, Iader Miserocchi, Glauco Monducci, Nainabahadur Pun, Peter Moore, Ken Neill, Nigel Nicolson, Helmut Ortschiedt, Cornelia Paselli, Professor Tomasz Piesakowski, Francesco Pirini, Aldo Prati, Heinz Puschmann, Italo Quadrelli, George Ramsay, Gianni Rossi, Teresa and Wladek Rubnikowicz, Ray Saidel, Giuseppe Schiavi, Toby Sewell, Gastone Sgargi, George Underwood, George Vaughan, Carlo Venturi, Professor Roberto Vivarelli, Ernest Wall, Bucky Walters and Ted Wyke-Smith.

I would also like to thank the staffs of the various archives who helped with guidance and advice. In particular, I would like to thank: Dr Peter Liddell and Cathy Pugh of the Second World War Experience Centre, Horsforth, Leeds; Dr Christopher Dowling, Richard Hughes, Roderick

Suddaby, Suzanne Bardgett, Sarah Batsford and the team at the Imperial War Museum; Arturo Conti, Signor Minucci and Enrico Persiani at the Istituto Storico RSI; Antonio Cioci and all the former Giovani Fascisti at Piccola Caprera; Giampietro Lippi, ANPI of Bologna, Forlì and Piacenza; Anna Salerno at the Consorzio di Gestione Parco Storico di Monte Sole in Marzabotto; Major Gray at the Green Jackets Museum in Winchester; Professor Monty Soutar of the History Group at the Ministry for Culture and Heritage in New Zealand; Mandeep Singh Bajwa in India; Eric Marenga, Hamish Paterson and Rowena Wilkinson at the South African National Museum of Military History; the archivists at the Military History Institute, Carlisle Barracks; Arthur Blake in South Africa; Susan Robbins Watson at National Headquarters American Red Cross; Jane Yates at The Citadel, South Carolina; Kim Sherwin at the JSCSC Library at Shrivenham.

Thanks are also due to Peter Caddick-Adams and Robert Boyle for their military expertise and advice; to Professor Jeremy Black, James Petrie, and my father, Martin Holland, for reading the manuscript. I would also like to thank Charles Cardozo, Lycia Parker, Margaret Byers, Giles Bourne, James Owen, Peter Riddlington, Jane Martens, John Musgrave, Steve Carter, Caroline Moorehead, James Walker, Guy and Giovanna Waley, Rowland White, Guy Walters, and, in South Carolina, Bill and Marie Pierce.

For this book I owe, as ever, enormous thanks to Lalla Hitchings – and her son Mark – who have tirelessly transcribed all my interviews. I would also not have been able to research or write it without the enormous help of Roddy Bassett, who interpreted my first interviews in Italy and Sarah Rivière, who helped organise interviews in Germany, subsequently interpreted and helped translate them, and especially for her work on the Hans Golda manuscript. I would also like to thank Sarah and her husband, Michael, for putting me up several times in Berlin. Finally, I am especially indebted to Julia Waley for her considerable input and help, accompanying me on many trips around Italy, and translating and transcribing interviews, texts and archival documents, and for her proof reading.

My thanks also go to Trevor Dolby, and at HarperCollins to Arabella Pike, Richard Johnson, Essie Cousins, John Bond, Sarah O'Reilly, Alice Massey, Melanie Haselden, Geraldine Beare, Helen Ellis and Peter Wilkinson; to Kate Johnson for her expert copy-editing, and to everyone else involved in the publication of this book. Thank you also to Jake

Smith-Bosanquet, Clare Conville and everyone at Conville and Walsh, but particularly to Patrick Walsh.

Finally, I would like to thank Rachel and Ned for always being there for me.

ABBREVIATIONS AND GLOSSARY

AAI	Allied Armies in Italy
AFHQ	Allied Forces Headquarters
AMG	Allied Military Government
AMGOT	Allied Military Government of Occupied Territories
ANVIL	Allied invasion of southern France, later renamed 'DRAGOON'
AOK	Armeeoberkommando – the equivalent to an Allied army
AUTUMN FOG (*Herbstnebel*)	German plan for strategic withdrawal of Army Group C to and beyond the River Po, first suggested August 1944
Battalion	infantry unit used in both Allied and Axis armies of around 700–900 men of all ranks
AXIS (*Achse*)	German operation to disarm Italian armed forces the moment the Italians surrendered to the Allies
CAO	(Allied) Civil Affairs Officer
CIL	Corpo Italiano di Liberazione
CLN	Comitato di Liberazione Nazionale
CLNAI	Comitato di Liberazione Nazionale per l'Alta Italia
Corps	a component of an army containing at least two divisions
CUMER	Comando Unico Militare Emilia-Romagna
DAF	Desert Air Force
DIADEM	Allied offensive and advance on Rome, May 1944
DRAGOON	Allied invasion of southern France, known as 'ANVIL' until 1 August 1944
Division	a major tactical and administrative unit of an army containing within its structure all the various forms of arms and services necessary for sustained combat: from infantry, tanks, artillery, engineers – or 'sappers' – to

support troops. Divisions could have different empha-
ses. An armoured division – or in the German army,
panzer division – would have, at its heart, perhaps one
or two armoured brigades, each made up of two tank
regiments, and a lorried infantry battalion made up of
mortar-gun, machine-gun and anti-tank gun teams.
The Germans also had panzer grenadier divisions –
a mixture of armour and infantry, or plain grenadier
divisions – predominantly infantry. Armoured divisions
were usually slightly smaller than infantry divisions –
15,000 men of all ranks, as opposed to around 17,000

FEC	French Expeditionary Corps
FOO	forward observation officer
GAP Central	Gruppi di Azione Patriottica Centrale
GNR	Guardia Nazionale Repubblicana
Goum	a unit of Moroccan *Goumiers*, roughly equivalent to a regular army company
Goumier	an irregular Moroccan soldier recruited from the Berber tribes of the Atlas Mountains
MAAF	Mediterranean Allied Air Forces
MALLORY MAJOR	Allied air operations to destroy bridges across the River Po from July 1944
Maryland	codename for SOE's operation in Italy
MASAF	Mediterranean Allied Strategic Air Force
MATAF	Mediterranean Allied Tactical Air Force
OLIVE	Eighth Army's assault on the Gothic Line, August 1944
OVERLORD	Allied landings in Normandy from 6 June 1944
OSS	Office of Strategic Services
rastrellamento	literally a 'thorough search', but used to describe anti-partisan operations carried out by German and Italian Fascist troops
RCT	Regimental Combat Team – an American formation roughly equivalent to an infantry brigade
RSI	Repubblica Sociale Italiana
SHINGLE	Allied landings at Anzio from 22 January 1944
SIM	Servizio Informazione Militare – the Italian military intelligence branch
SOE	Special Operations Executive
STRANGLE	Allied air operation to destroy German rail, road and

sea communications south of Pisa–Rimini line, March to May 1944

Sicherheitsdienst the SS intelligence service

TAC Tactical Air Command

Tabor the French colonial equivalent of a brigade of irregular infantry

tedesco *Italian for a German* (pl. *tedeschi*). Allied troops in Italy sometimes referred to German troops as 'Teds'

GUIDE TO RANKS

Officers

BRITISH ARMY	WEHRMACHT	SS AND WAFFEN-SS	RAF
Field Marshal	*Feldmarschall*	*Reichsführer*	Marshal
General	*Generaloberst*	*Oberstgruppenführer*	Air Chief Marshal
Lieutenant-General	General	*Obergruppenführer*	Air Marshal
Major-General	*Generalleutnant*	*Gruppenführer*	Air Vice Marshal
Brigadier/Brig-Gen	*Generalmajor*	*Brigadeführer*	Air Commodore
		Oberführer	
Colonel	*Oberst*	*Standartenführer*	Group Captain
Lieutenant-Colonel	*Oberstleutnant*	*Obersturmbannführer*	Wing Commander
Major	Major	*Sturmbannführer*	Squadron Leader
Captain	*Hauptmann*	*Hauptsturmführer*	Flight Lieutenant
Lieutenant	*Oberleutnant*	*Obersturmführer*	Flying Officer
Second Lieutenant	*Leutnant*	*Untersturmführer*	Pilot Officer

Non-Commissioned Officers

BRITISH ARMY	WEHRMACHT	SS AND WAFFEN-SS
Warrant Officer 1	*Stabsfeldwebel*	*Stabsscharführer*
Warrant Officer 2	*Oberfeldwebel*	*Hauptscharführer*
QM Sergeant	*Feldwebel*	*Oberscharführer*
Staff Sergeant	*Unterfeldwebel*	*Scharführer*
Sergeant	*Unteroffizier*	*Unterscharführer*
Corporal	*Obergefreiter*	*Rottenführer*
Lance-Corporal	*Gefreiter*	*Sturmmann*
Private	*Schütze*	*Schütze*

INDEX

AAI *see* Allied Armies in Italy
Abruzzi Mountains 53, 57
Abtshagen 70
Abwehr 305, 306, 307, 368, 425
Abyssinia 199
ACC *see* Allied Control Commission
Adriatic 40, 47, 54, 56, 226, 292, 293, 294, 295, 300, 342, 399, 427, 475, 503
Adriatic Coastland 94, 194, 195
Adriatic Front 103, 358, 369, 418
Advisory Council for Italy 245
Aegean 27, 29, 36, 46, 55, 321
AFHQ see Allied Forces Headquarters
Alatri 175
Alban Hills 127, 149, 151, 158, 160, 161, 215
Albert Line 222, 224, 226–40, 259, 262
Alexander, Gen. Sir Harold xxxix, 39, 41, 47, 48, 82, 83, 85, 127, 133, 134, 165, 171, 181, 182, 184, 220, 240, 245, 271, 319, 347, 423, 528
  assessment of 529–30
  at Cassino 9, 13, 14, 21, 23, 31
  at Dunkirk 406
  attempts to train Italian 'combat groups' 346
  and breaking of the Gothic Line 279, 293–5, 298
  character of 44–5
  cross-Adriatic plan 426–7, 428
  death of 532
  family background 42–3
  and final offensive 505
  and German surrender 524
  military career 43–4
  and Operation ANVIL debate 208, 211–13, 253–7, 259
  and the partisans 445, 446, 447, 450
  promoted Field Marshal 454
  radio broadcast 188
  relationship with Clark 158–9, 161, 162–3, 454–5
  setbacks 475–6
  and shortages of men and ammunition 258, 363, 400, 427–8, 428, 454
  and slowing of Allied advance 225–6
  and spring offensive 495, 496, 497
  and surrender of German forces 501
  tactical skills 41, 45, 50–2, 79, 131, 141–3, 459, 466–8
Alexandria 39, 200
Algeria 25, 26, 166
Algiers 484
Allen, Brig.-Gen. 151
Allied airforce 3, 70, 71–80, 104, 133, 147–8
Allied Armies in Italy (AAI) xxxix, 3, 17
  15th Army Group 46, 292, 454, 514
Allied Chiefs of Staff 476
Allied Control Commission (ACC) 244, 245, 250, 307, 395, 397
Allied Forces 9, 48
Allied Forces Headquarters (AFHQ)
  Algiers 244, 245, 247, 312, 395, 446, 484

Allied Military Government (AMG) 216–17, 245, 246, 307, 308, 395, 397, 398, 447, 484, 533
Allied Military Government of Occupied Territories (AMGOT) 244
Almond, Gen. Ned 457–8, 491, 492
Alpine Approaches 94
Alps 30, 41, 94, 211, 255, 256, 281, 494, 513, 522, 526
Altamura, Francesco 308
Altenstadt, Oberst von 32
AMG *see* Allied Military Government
AMGOT *see* Allied Military Government of Occupied Territories
Anders, Gen. Wladyslaw 7, 8–9, 82, 226, 238, 272, 274, 335, 405, 406, 413, 488–9
Anglo-Boer War 218
Aniene 202
Anti-Inflation Committee 397
Anzio xl-xlii, 10, 11, 13, 22, 29, 49, 50, 51, 104, 126, 131, 142, 151, 158, 159–60, 174, 181, 208, 213, 215, 479
Apennines 29, 47, 169, 211, 259, 262, 292–3, 294, 347, 363, 369, 400, 406, 426, 480, 495, 513, 530
Apuan Mountains 289, 311, 313, 444, 456, 462
Aquino 104, 132, 133
Arada 234 jet aircraft 497
Arce 139, 153, 171
Arcioni, Amedeo 120
Arctic Circle 5–6, 46
Ardeatine Caves xliv-xlv, 288–9, 533
Ardennes 475, 487
Arezzo 268, 277, 278
Argegno 521
Argenta 496, 505, 510
Argenta Gap 496, 508, 512
Army Air Staff 74
Arnhem 475
Arnold, Gen. 'Hap' 214
Arrichiello, Cosimo 57–9, 64–7, 193–4, 311, 511–12, 538
Artena 149, 163, 174
Atlantic 46

Attlee, Clement 532
Auditore 337
Aurunci Mountains 14, 40, 69, 83, 84, 86, 128, 132, 140, 165
Auschwitz 475
Ausente Valley 86
Ausoni Mountains 67, 142, 150, 165
Ausonia 86, 216
Austin, Sgt. Stan 404
Austria 36, 94, 170, 256, 281, 494, 504
Avanguardisti (Fascist youth organisation) 61
Avezzano 203
Axis forces 12, 25, 26, 34–5, 38–9, 61, 287, 391, 395, 488, 514

Baade, Generalmajor Ernst-Günther 32, 36, 85
Badoglio, Marshal Pietro 35, 39, 55, 56, 57, 122, 200, 244, 249–50, 295, 448
Bagno di Lucca 340
Bagno di Romagno 264, 412
Bagnoregio 222
Bailey bridges 82–3, 88–9, 133, 156, 164, 222, 369, 416–17, 424, 478
Bailey, Donald 88
Balilla (Fascist youth organisation) 61
Balisti, Major Fulvio 62
Balkans 26, 27, 29, 35, 36, 47, 55, 76, 254, 255, 257, 345, 356, 447, 483, 504
Balsamo, Pasquale xxxiii-xxxv
Baltic 70
Bardine 314, 374
Bardo 59
Bari 56, 123, 188, 312, 346, 453
Barman, Capt. 146–7
Barnini, Lt. 285, 288, 481–2, 500, 514
Bartocci, Enzo 288
Barton, Maj. John 441–3, 444, 450–2
Bastardo 298, 299
Bastia 509
Bastico, Gen. 39
Battle of Kursk 370, 387
Battle of the Rivers 362, 399
Bayreuth 38

BBC Radio London 124
Bedell-Smith, Gen. 51
Beerlitz, Oberst Dietrich xliii, 259
Belgium 202, 370
Belgrade 495
Bellaria 495
Belluno 94, 526–7
Belmonte Castello 128
Belsen 534
Belvedere 236
Belzec 195
Benevento 307–8, 346, 399
Benni, Sister Antonietta 373, 384
Bentivegna, Rosario 'Paolo' 152, 153,
    178, 537
  and Via Rasella attack xxxiii, xxxvi, xl,
    xlii
Berchtesgarden 32
Berne 487
Bernstorff, Countess Ingeborg Maria
    von 101
Bettola 222
Bialystock 5–6, 195
Bidente Valley 264, 413
Bittner, Maj. 238
Blackshirts 368, 443, 480, 520, 521, 530
Blasi, Guglielmo 152
Bletchley Park 16–17
Blommen, Capt. Paul 272–4
Bocale, Leonardo 215
Böhmler, Oberst Rudolf 478
Bologna 62, 64, 113, 116, 118, 189, 191,
    212, 265, 267, 294, 342, 347, 355,
    363, 367, 369, 372, 374, 406, 417,
    418, 426, 427, 441, 459, 462, 466,
    468, 495, 500, 513, 514, 537
Bologna Province 193
Bolti family 65, 67
Bolzano 94, 453, 498
Bondeno 517
Bonomi, Ivanoe 122 and note, 250, 295,
    395, 396, 447, 448–50
Bordeno 450
Borghese, Prince Valerio 60, 200–1
Borgo Santa Maria 329
Bosco Chiese Nova 478
'Bowling Alley' xli

Bra 58–9, 65
Bradley, Gen. Omar 44
Bradshaw, Sgt. Sam 324–6, 337–8, 391,
    534
Brann, Gen. 151
Bray, Fg Off Den 461
Bray, Wilf 299
Brazil 258
Brazilian Expeditionary Forces 298, 347,
    456
Brenner Battles 494, 497–8
Brenner Pass 94, 281, 370, 504, 525
Brescia 62
Brigate Nere (Black Brigades) 283–6,
    309–11, 310–11, 313, 356, 446
Brindisi 123, 188
British Army Commands and Forces
  Army Groups
    11th Army Group 405
    18th Army Group 44
  Armies
    First Army 298
    Eighth Army 13–15, 14, 16, 17n, 25,
      26, 32, 44, 47, 48, 50, 51, 81, 82, 132,
      133, 134, 135, 141, 153, 157, 164,
      165, 171, 176, 182, 183, 203, 217,
      219, 222, 258, 271–2, 292, 293–4,
      295, 298, 317, 319, 320, 342–3, 344,
      360–1, 363, 369, 371, 372, 405–6,
      419, 424, 427, 432, 459, 462, 466–7,
      496–7, 509–10, 514, 525, 537
  Corps
    Royal Armoured Corps 493
    V Corps 225, 317–18, 325, 326, 336,
      359, 406, 407, 433, 504
    X Corps 51, 53, 87–8, 165, 406, 412
    XIII Corps 81, 87, 132, 153, 156, 164,
      171, 182, 217, 219, 258, 272, 295,
      317, 347, 348, 400, 431, 493, 509
  Divisions
    1st Division 43
    4th Division 127, 423, 433
    4th Indian Division xxxix, 14, 19, 21,
      87, 325, 336, 358, 467
    5th Division 476
    6th Armoured Division 87, 89, 156,
      525

British Army Commands and Forces
Divisions – *cont.*
8th Indian Division 14, 19, 21, 85, 87, 89, 412
10th Indian Division 269–70, 291, 439
46th 'Midlands' Division 10, 298, 317, 325, 326, 336, 343, 359, 409, 439, 462
52nd Division 165
56th Division 336, 343, 362, 363
78th Division Royal Engineers 19, 87, 88, 89, 109, 222, 400, 509
Brigades
19th Indian Brigade 14, 15
24th Guards Brigade 223, 228, 347, 401
38th Infantry Brigade 109
139th Infantry Brigade 359
Regiments
1st Grenadiers 127
1st King's Royal Rifles 422
1/9th Gurkha Rifles xxxix, 337
2/5th Leicester Regiment 298, 299, 324, 326, 328, 336, 359, 360, 408
2/5th Queen's 344
2nd Artillery Group 346
2nd Coldstream Guards 127
3rd Coldstream Guards 223, 228–9, 267–8, 286, 430, 493
3rd Royal Tank Regiment 534
4/11th Sikhs 337
5th Sherwood Foresters 298
7th Queen's Hussars 226
9th Queen's Royal Lancers 494, 509, 512
184th Artillery Regiment 53, 225
Argyll and Sutherland Highlanders 15, 21
Grenadier Guards 247, 291
Irish Guards 42
Royal Tank Regiment 325
Scots Guards 484
Miscellaneous
312th Field Security Service 168, 241
British Liaison Officers (BLO) 484
British War Office 88

Broadhurst, Harry 174
Brooke, Gen. Alan, Chief of Imperial General staff 25, 27, 47, 48, 50, 212, 255–6, 400
Brooke, Lt. Kendall 217–18, 219, 223, 347, 401, 404, 411–12, 430, 431, 435–7, 535
Bruce, Maj. 292
Brünn 169
Brussels 427
Büchner, Friedrich 498–9, 505, 518, 526–7, 536
Budrio 513
Buffarini-Guidi, Guido 93
Bühler, Unterscharführer 352
Bulgaria 340
Burke, Master Sgt. Albert 457–8, 467, 492
Burma 43, 144
Burns, Gen. 177, 318
Byelorussia 253

C-in-C Mediterranean Air Command 75
'Cab Rank' 74, 75
Ca' Bregade farmhouse 114
Ca' di Durino 378
Ca' Dizzola 379
Cadorna, Gen. Rafaele 56, 311, 312, 445, 520
Cadotto 375, 378, 381–2, 384, 537
Caesar Line 126–7, 141, 158, 160, 164, 171, 173, 177, 183
Cagnano 270
Cairns, Lt.-Col. Bogardus 163
Cairo 44, 180, 405, 484
Caldeon, Earl of 42
Calvocoressi, Capt. Ion 81–2, 127–8, 134, 291–2, 319, 342–4, 405, 534
Calzorlari, Francesco 315
Camp Shelby (Mississippi) 15
Campania 246
Camugnano 401
Canadian Forces 107, 125, 132, 133, 153, 156, 164, 317, 318, 328, 334, 335–6, 359, 362, 393, 406, 407, 473, 476

Divisions
 1st Canadian Division 89, 136, 419
 5th Armoured Division 103, 156,
  164, 176, 460, 466
Brigades
 11th Infantry Brigade 103
Regiments
 5th Armoured Regiment 135
 No 3 Canadian Infantry
  Reinforcement Unit 103
 Perth Regiment 103, 135–6, 157,328,
  329, 419, 466, 468, 473
Canèr, 2nd Lt. 346
Capponi, Carla 'Elena' xxxiii, xl, 59–60,
  152–3, 178, 537
Caprara 375
Capri 78, 246
Capron, Eric 336
Carabinieri 65, 95, 168, 194, 220, 285, 425
Carducci, Nello 288
Carpena 433
Carretta, Signor 398
Caruso, Pietro 398
Casa Raggi 490
Casablanca Conference (1943) 26, 28
Casadei, Adriano 310
Casaglia 191, 379, 385, 539
Casale 62
Casalecchio 354, 537
Casalecchio di Reno 113, 114
Casarino 478
Caserta 31, 76, 104, 188, 395, 399
Cassino xxxvi-xxxvii, 47, 49, 50, 51, 71,
  75, 85, 106, 112, 125, 127, 128, 136,
  175, 182, 200, 215, 216, 228, 274,
  335, 346, 431, 530, 536, 538
 1st battle xxxvii, 10, 18
 2nd battle xxxvii
 3rd battle xxxvii, 17, 18
 4th battle xxxvi-xl, 3–22, 8, 32, 53,
  82–91, 123
Cassino Front 103
Castel Bolognese 460
Castel di Masino 481–2, 500
Castel Massimo 106
Castel San Pietro 417, 418
Castellaro 372

Castell'Arquato 502, 511
Castellina 276
Castelluccio 64
Castiglione 269, 473
Castiglione dei Pepoli 372
Ca' Termine 378
Cattolica 302, 334
Cavaglia 481
Cavendish, Lady Dorothy 247
Ca' Veneziani 21, 119, 191, 367
Caviglia, Marshal Enrico 60
CBS News 143, 144, 150
Cecina 272, 281
Cephalonia 60
Ceprano 104, 106, 133, 158, 163
Cerpiano 373, 379, 384, 385
Cerratina 225
Cerreto 346, 477
Cesena 370, 371, 418, 419
Ceserano 313
Cetona 223
Chianciano 221, 228, 234
Chianti 267
Chianti Hills 276, 286
Chienti River 238, 253
China 144
Chiusi 219–20, 239
Chrostek (Polish soldier) 253
Churchill, Oliver 312
Churchill, Winston 7, 23, 25, 26, 27, 28,
  30, 31, 46, 47, 153, 171, 210, 211,
  247, 248, 249, 250, 254–7, 298,
  319–20, 335, 395–6, 428, 446–7,
  454, 528, 532
Ciano, Count Galeazzo 96, 246
CIL see Corpo Italiano di Liberazione
  under Italian Forces with Allied
  Armies
Cisterna 13, 143
Civil Affairs Officer (CAO) 216, 217
Civilian Training Program (US) 77
Civitavecchia 22, 213
Civitella 222
Clark, Gen. Mark W. xxxix, 10, 25, 26,
  45, 46, 47, 55, 82, 84, 86, 131, 133,
  146, 172, 293, 363, 476
 and allowing of troops into Rome 219

Clark, Gen. Mark W. – *cont.*
  assessment of 529
  and attack on Bologna 372
  character of 104, 454–5
  death of 532
  and fall of Rome 178–83
  and final offensive 510, 514
  frustration and anger of 423–4
  and the Gothic Line 141–4, 294, 295,
    342
  and Italian partisans 266–7
  lines of attack 158–64
  manpower problems 257–9, 347, 428,
    456
  near-fatal plane crash 213–14
  on the Negro soldier 492
  and Operation ANVIL debate 211,
    214, 253–4
  plans for Spring offensive 495–7
  and Poland 489
  relationship with Alexander 455
  relationship with Leese 16, 271–2
  renewed offensive 400–1, 405, 407,
    459
  and Serchio offensive 466–8
  tactical skills 12–14, 15, 25, 26, 160,
    171, 173–4, 183
Clark, Renie 174
CLN *see* Comitato di Liberazione
  Nazionale
CLNAI *see* Comitato Liberazione
  Nazionale per l'Alta Italia
CLNE *see* Comitato di Liberazione Nord
  Emilia
'Clover II' mission 485–6
Coastal Command 72, 257
Colle del Carnaio 265
Colli Laziali 158, 159
Collina 411
Colonello (Italian partisan) 377, 379,
  382
Comando Unico Militare Emilia-
  Romagna (CUMER) 267, 312,
  355–6, 367, 484
Combined Chiefs of Staff 212–13,
  254–7
Comitato di Liberazione Nazionale

(CLN) 122, 123, 153, 178, 248–9,
  250, 355, 447, 448–50
Comitato di Liberazione Nord Emilia
  (CLNE) 486
Comitato Liberazione Nazionale per
  l'Alta Italia (CLNAI) 267, 311, 312,
  445, 446, 447, 448, 450, 486, 501,
  519, 520, 521
Communists 226, 312, 335, 398, 399,
  413, 447, 502
Como 521
Comrie, Col. Murray 218
Conca River 359
Conca Valley 343
Concordia 443
contadini 190–1, 220, 375
Contignano 187, 231
Corbari, Silvio 310
Corfu 60
Cori 13, 148, 159–60
Coriano Ridge 338, 343, 359, 360
Corinaldesi, Virgilio Pallottelli 99
Corps of Volunteers of Freedom (CVL)
  311, 312, 313, 445, 447, 450, 486,
  520
Corsica 29, 268, 279, 353, 414
Corti, Lt. Eugenio 53–6, 57, 225, 226–7,
  250–1, 346, 477, 538
Costa, Carla 197–8, 305–7, 367–8, 369,
  425–6, 434–5, 538
Coulter, Gen. 348
Cowles, Virginia 289
Cremonini, Sgt. William 61–2, 197, 285,
  287, 288, 356–7, 481–2, 514, 520,
  530, 536–7
Crete xxxvii
Crichton, Maj. 239, 430
Crisaldi, Umberto (Il Vecchio) 355 and
  note, 375, 378
Croatia 94, 202
Croce, Benedetto 295
Croce (village) 343, 359
cross-Channel invasion 26, 27, 30
Cucciati, Angela Curti 97, 98
Cucciati, Antonio 200–1, 500, 505, 537
CUMER *see* Comando Unico Militare
  Emilia-Romagna

Curti, Elena 97–9, 287–8, 488, 521–3, 537

CVL *see* Corps of Volunteers of Freedom

D-Day 79, 183, 202, 208, 209, 210, 252, 490

David, Col. Tomaso 197–8, 305, 307, 368

De Gasperi, Alcide 398

De Gaulle, Gen. Charles 214, 254, 319

Decima MAS (X Flottiglia Mezzi d'Assalto) 60, 200–201, 311, 356, 505

  Nuotatori e Paracadutisti (NP) 500

Devers, Gen. 428

Diamond, Norm 393

Dickson, AVM William 74, 174–5, 291, 455

Dill, Field Marshal Sir John 209–10, 454

Dills, Capt. Charles 76–8, 104–5, 148, 280–1, 353, 392, 535

Dink (German gunner) 87

Dodecanese Islands 29, 46

Dollmann, Standartenführer 519, 520

Dolomites 94, 453

Donets Basin 36

Dongo 523

Dönitz, Grand Admiral Karl 41

Dresden 71

Dulles, Allen 487, 500, 501, 519

Duncan, Gregory 147

Dundas, Gp Capt Hugh 'Cocky' 73–4, 75, 174–5, 227–8, 268–9, 291, 353–4, 455, 495, 504–5, 508–9, 535

Dundas, John 73–4

Dunkirk 43, 406

Duse, Clara 194, 195, 315, 345, 474–5, 527, 529, 538

Düsseldorf 409

Duxford 74

Eaker, Gen. Ira 70, 72, 75, 76, 78

EAM/ELAS 448, 454

East Africa 72

East Prussia 478, 498

Eastern Allies 34

Eastern Front 18, 36, 207, 253, 340, 370, 386, 387, 499

Eastern Mediterranean 76

Eden, Anthony 153

Egypt 25, 72, 218, 274, 321, 414

Eisenhower, Gen. Dwight D. 11, 12, 25, 26, 44, 50, 51, 56, 209, 211, 214, 254, 256, 427, 475, 497

El Alamein 14, 26, 34, 44, 48, 60, 81, 217

Ellis, Capt. John 327

Emilia Romagna 222

Empoli 347

Enfidaville 61

Enrico (partisan) 464–5

Eritrea 324–5

Esperia 86, 128, 131, 216

Ethiopia 93

Europe-first policy 24–6

Everard, Peter 299

Faenza 347, 462, 499

Far East 25, 46, 144

Fargo 77

Farinacci, Roberto 93

Farnocchia 290

Fasano 101

Fascist Federation 199

Fascist Party 118, 284, 285, 311, 448–50

Fascist Police 446

Fascist *squadristi* 93, 283, 284

Fascist Youth Organisation 93

Fascists/Neo-Fascists 93–7, 113, 114, 121, 122, 170, 189, 193, 196, 220, 226–7, 264, 266, 314, 354, 357–8, 368, 443, 448, 451, 464, 500, 523, 528

  see also Young Fascists

Ferentino 165

  refugee camp at 216

Ferrara 443, 518

Feuerstein, General 32, 84

Figline Valdarno 278

Finale Emilia 517

Finney, Tom 493–4, 509, 512, 533

Firenzuola 287, 349, 400
First World War 11, 38, 43, 49, 72, 94,
    101, 116, 183, 196, 217, 299, 329,
    357, 373
  Battle of Loos 43
  Gallipoli 51
  Passchendaele 43, 44
  Somme 43
  Vimy Ridge 329
  Western Front 47, 183, 247, 321, 359
Fisher, Maj. 454
Fiume 94, 123
Florence 63, 115, 272, 278, 285–8, 293,
    294, 300, 305–7, 347, 414, 415–16,
    425, 461, 488
Flossenbürg concentration camp 453
Foggia 30, 46, 494
Foglia 326, 328
Fondazza 113
Fondi 135, 150, 167
Fondouk 146
Fonso (Italian partisan) 120
Forlì 116, 264, 310, 347, 406, 418, 419,
    426, 432–4, 438, 458
Forme D'Aquino 153
Formia 131, 150
Forsinone 167
Fosso Munio 466
France 25, 26, 27, 28, 38, 41, 47, 50, 71,
    81, 165, 202, 208, 209, 213, 214,
    254, 256, 268, 279, 281, 302, 320,
    340, 352, 356, 363, 370, 414
Franchi (real name Sogno) 485–6
Francis, Maj. Peter 401
Franco-Italian Armistice Commission
    32
Frederick, Gen. 178–9
Free Polish Forces 7
French Army Commands and Forces 14,
    134, 161
French Expeditionary Corps 83, 84, 131,
    132, 142, 150, 165–6, 214, 274
  Goums 14, 166, 390–1, 533
French Riviera 26, 27
Freyberg, Gen. xxxix, 274
Frömming, Major 139
Frosinone 22, 106, 390–1

Frost, Cpl. Dick 222, 239, 286, 347, 363,
    411, 465–6, 511, 513, 525, 535
Futa Pass 189, 347
Futte, Pte. 430

Gabbiano di Monzuno 314
Gabbro 273
Gaeta 131, 135, 532–3
Gambut 321
Gammell, Gen. 255
GAP Central (Gruppi di Azione
    Patriottica Centrale) xxxiii, 152, 442
Gardelletta 118, 119, 190, 191, 381, 384,
    465
Gargnano 92, 97, 101, 368, 519
Garibaldi brigades 122 and note
Gävernitz, Gero von 500
Gellhorn, Martha 252–3, 288–9, 305, 332
Gemmano 196, 338–40, 343–4, 358–63,
    538
Genazzano 161
Genghis Khan Line 416, 459, 477
Genoa 64, 193, 281, 340, 520
Genovese, Vito 245–6, 307
Genz, Egon 420–1, 422
Genzano 215
George VI, King 291
German Forces
  Army Groups 78, 202
    Army Group B 35, 40
    Army Group C 41, 169, 426, 456, 476
    Army Group Reserve 85
    Centre 36
    Kurland 478
    Southwest xlii-xliii, 41
  Armies
    AOK 10: 12, 16n, 21, 32, 41, 51, 84,
      106, 107, 125, 126, 127, 132, 133,
      141, 142, 143, 158, 161, 162, 165,
      171, 172, 176, 203, 206, 207, 300,
      301, 324, 334, 341, 371, 418, 426,
      496
    AOK 14: xl, xliii, 16n, 50, 127, 132,
      135, 160, 161, 172, 174, 177, 179,
      183, 202, 202–3, 206, 259, 348, 371,
      417, 426, 454

Corps
  1st Fallschirmjäger Corps 349
  14th Panzer Corps 32, 33, 84, 106,
    125, 132, 165, 172, 177, 232, 236,
    340, 372, 417
  51st Mountain Corps 32, 84, 85, 89,
    125–6, 172
  76th Panzer Corps 324, 338, 417,
    454, 508
Divisions
  1st Fallschirmjäger (Parachute)
    xxxvii, 84, 90, 108, 125, 132, 171,
    228, 286, 300, 302, 324, 372, 374,
    417, 418, 478
  3rd Panzer Grenadier Division 232
  4th Fallschirmjäger Division 144,
    348, 371
  15th Panzer Grenadier Division 84,
    106, 132
  16th Waffen-SS Panzer Grenadier
    Division 127, 202, 232, 235–6, 272,
    289–90, 313, 341, 342, 372, 373,
    374, 401, 405, 417, 422, 454, 477,
    532
  20th Luftwaffe Field Division 221,
    232
  21st Division 518
  26th Panzer Grenadier Division 127,
    132, 329, 348, 354
  29th Panzer Grenadier Division 135,
    137, 343, 348, 417, 497
  44th Infantry Division 84, 85, 106,
    165
  71st Division 86, 106, 132, 324, 336
  90th Panzer Grenadier Division 85,
    89, 104, 132, 362, 401, 417, 459,
    462, 503
  94th Division 19, 86, 106, 132
  98th Division 336, 466, 499, 518
  114th Jäger Division 394, 408
  232nd Infantry Division 491
  278th Infantry Division 369, 370,
    423, 433, 466, 517
  305 Infantry Division 132
  334th Infantry Division 163, 169,
    206, 228, 374
  356th Infantry Division 343, 433

  362nd Infantry Division 172, 373
  715th Infantry Division 163–4, 348,
    371
  Fallschirm-Panzerkorps Hermann
    Göring 149, 163, 172, 173,
Regiments
  2nd Bavarian Foot Artillery
    Regiment 38
  3rd Fallschirmjäger Regiment 21, 139
  4th Fallschirmjäger Regiment 18,
    109, 203, 286, 417–18
  8th Werfer Battery 22, 85, 126, 140,
    517
  9th Battery 320, 418, 519, 525
  16th Artillery 374
  35th SS-Panzer Grenadier Regiment
    237, 373
  36th SS-Panzer Grenadier Regiment
    373, 374
  994th Infantry Regiment 371, 418–19
  East Grenadier Regiment 169, 170,
    374, 375
  HG Artillery 149
  Panzer Grenadier 141
  3/SS Police Regiment Bozen xxxiv,
    xlii
  Waffen-SS 169, 232–3, 384
  Wehrmacht Flak-Regiment 105 374
  Werfer Regiment 56 140
  Werfer Regiment 71 22, 85, 126, 206,
    228, 277–8, 302, 320, 343, 360, 418,
    459
Battalions
  16th Waffen-SS Panzer
    Reconnaissance Battalion 236, 349,
    352, 372, 373, 374, 377, 422
  2/16th SS-Pioneer Battalion 16 233
  H G Armoured Reconnaissance
    Battalion 149–50
  Fallschirmjäger Pioneers 18, 89–90,
    91, 92, 108, 126, 128, 130, 133, 139,
    153, 233, 233, 332, 348, 455, 484,
    489
  German High Command (OKW) Berlin
    xliii, 35, 39, 41, 95, 127, 158, 169,
    202, 207–8, 259, 282, 301, 368, 416,
    459, 476

German Intelligence Service 22, 198, 367–8
German Sudetan Freecorps 170
Ghandi (Italian soldier) 482–3
Ginestreto Ridge 328
Giogo Pass 347, 348, 349
Gioiella 228
Giuseppina (Italian child prostitute) 308
Glander, Alfred 429–30
Glebokie 5
Globocnik, General Odilo 195, 315
Glover, Tini 274–7, 362, 463, 527, 535
GNR see Guardia Nazionale Repubblicana (GNR)
Golda, Oberleutnant Hans 22, 85, 87, 126, 140, 153, 174–6, 206, 221, 228, 277–8, 302, 320, 333–4, 343, 360–2, 407–8, 418, 437–8, 459–60, 468–9, 473, 508, 513, 517, 518–19, 525–6, 538
Gomolka (German soldier) 513
Göring, Hermann 38, 232
Gorizia 99
Gothic Line (Green Line) 207 and note, 212, 213, 257, 259, 262–3, 265, 278, 289, 292–5, 300–2, 319–32, 334, 335–6, 340, 342, 347, 348–9, 359–63, 373, 424, 428, 431, 439
Goumiers (irregular Moroccan soldier) 14, 20, 151, 166–8, 390–1
Goums (unit of Morroccan Goumiers) 14, 166, 390–1, 533
Gova 451
Gradara 333–4
Gran Sasso 57, 92
Grappallo 502
Graziani, Marshal Rodolfo 93–4, 95, 282, 283, 284, 300, 362, 456, 520
Greece 27, 29, 34, 35, 399, 428, 447–8, 449, 454, 484, 495
Grizzana Morandi 374
Grizzano 375
Groparallo 511
Groppallo 485–6
Group Ops Officers 280–1
Gruenther, Gen. Al 162–3, 295
Gruppo SA 198 and note

Guardia Nazionale Repubblicana (GNR) 95, 101, 113, 189, 193, 198, 264, 265, 282, 283, 285, 314, 315, 356, 451
Gubbio 221
Guderian, Feldmarschall 207
Guingand, Gen. Freddie de 51
Gulf of Genoa 209, 300
Gustav Line xxxvii, xl, 12, 14, 22, 40, 47, 51, 76, 83, 85, 86–7, 91, 96, 103–10, 125, 126, 128, 131, 158, 213
Guzar 7

Hackenholt, Lorenz 195
Harding, Gen. Sir John 45, 51, 83, 131, 142, 158, 182, 183, 271, 291, 293, 294, 424, 446
Harmon, Gen. 151
Harris, Sgt. Reg 223, 228–9, 239, 267–8, 286, 429, 432, 465, 493, 534
Hartmann, General 84, 86, 106
Hastings, Capt. Stephen 484–6, 501–2, 511, 520, 525, 534–5
Hawkesworth, Gen. 'Ginger' 326–7
Hays, Maj.-Gen. George P. 476
Heidrich, General Richard 302
Hemingway, Ernest 252
Hermann (POW) 189
Hermes (South African POW) 119
Herr, General 138, 417, 454, 509
Heydrich, General Reinhard 102
Heysham, Group Captain David 74
Highway 6 319
Highway 64 491, 513
Hill 131 (near Spigno Ridge) 86
Hill 445 (near Monte Cassino) xxxix
Hill 609 (Tunisia) 146
Himmler, Reichsführer Heinrich 101, 169, 232, 487, 501
Hitler, Adolf 24, 32, 39, 41, 57, 60, 127, 158, 169, 173, 202, 207, 212, 232, 255, 256, 416, 418
authority and power of 33–4
death of 526
and ending of hostilities 487–8, 516

failure of plot against 340
and final assault 514
health of 33, 36
irrational behaviour of 36–7
meeting with Mussolini 283
orders reprisals for Via Rasella attack
  xliii–xliv
prosecution of war 33–6
and raising of New Italian Army 95
and refusal to accept responsibility for
  mistakes 34
relationship with Mussolini 92, 93, 94
told of situation in Italy 259, 262
Hitler Line see Senger Line
Hitler Youth 61, 71, 107, 369–70
HMS Valiant 200
Hofer, Gauleiter Franz 94, 516, 523
Hoffmeisterx, Gen. Bert 329
Holfreter, Leutnant Willi 70–1, 76, 105,
  227, 536
Hoppe, Generalleutnant Harry 370–1
Howze, Col. Hamilton 145–6, 148–50,
  151, 162, 163, 175, 177, 178, 183,
  231, 341, 342, 512, 535
Hungary 127, 202, 256, 345

Il Vecchio see Crisaldi, Umberto
Imola 372, 400, 462
Imperial General Staff 255
Impruneta 286
India 405
Innsbruck 494, 495
Insom, Giorgio 485
Iraq 72
Irrawaddy River 43
Istria 94, 528, 533
Italian Action Party 122, 447
Italian Air Force (Regia Aeronautica) 59,
  116
Italian Forces with Allied Armies 35,
  53–60, 95, 447
  Army of Liguria 362, 456
  Italian Royal Army 57, 295, 313
  Corpo Italiano di Liberazione (CIL)
    53, 225, 226, 248, 272, 318, 346
  Motorised Corps 59

Ariete Division 56
Nembo Division 225, 226–7
Italian Forces with German Armed
  Forces
  Bir el Gobi Company 62, 285, 287,
    311, 356–7, 480–3, 513–14, 520
  Folgore Division 60
  Giovani Fascisti Bologna Battalion
    61
  Monte Rosa Division 467
  Nembo Division 60
Italian Communist Party (PCI, Partito
  Communista Italiano) 116–17, 121,
  248, 249, 355, 531
Italian Navy 59–60
Italian New Republican Army 95, 120,
  226, 310, 456, 467
Italian partisans 60, 196, 235, 370, 520
  1st Division Piacenza 485
  Justice and Liberty Division 485
  Modena Division 267
  Prati Division 485
  8th 'Romagna' Garibaldi Brigade 116,
    118, 121, 265, 406, 412–13, 432,
    433, 458
  10th Garibaldi Brigade 290, 312
  19th Giambone Brigade 357
  28th Garibaldi Brigade 458–9, 493
  36th Garibaldi 493
  62nd Garibaldi Brigade 312, 354
  Majella Brigade 226
  Stella Rossa brigade 115, 120–4,
    170–1, 189–90, 267, 302–3,
    312–15, 336, 348, 354, 355 and
    note, 367, 373, 374–5, 385, 386,
    388–9, 413, 429, 484, 513, 537
  2nd Battalion 116, 264, 412, 432
  Susa Alpine Battalion 357
  and apparent retreat of the Germans
    373
  assessment of 531–2
  attacks on 111, 187, 221–2, 356–8,
    374–5, 377–82, 383–92, 481–3
  and battle for Forlì 432–4
  breaking up of 354–5
  brutality of 194, 388–9, 527
  burying of 268

Italian partisans – *cont.*
  effectiveness of 169–71, 188–90,
    220–1, 264–7, 302–3
  and final offensive 511–12
  in Florence 305
  increased activity of 311–16
  and liberation of Bologna 367
  living conditions 441–2
  in Lucca 342
  politicisation of 355–6
  raids for food 192–4
  recruitment to 113–24, 169
  support for 188, 190, 190–2, 264, 266,
    356, 386, 483–6
  tensions with royalist troops 226–7
  terror attack in Naples xxxiii-xxxvi,
    xlii-xlv
Italian Secret Service 188
Italy
  administration in 92–102, 196–7,
    243–51, 396
  Allied agreement to invade 23–31
  anti-Semitism in 357
  armistice in 54–69, 57, 62, 113, 188,
    194, 247, 265
  black market in 193, 216, 242–3,
    245–6, 360, 397, 398
  bombing of 75–80, 104–6, 137–8, 187,
    188, 191, 215, 227–8, 230, 234–5,
    349, 353–4, 358, 361, 392, 399, 400,
    409, 412, 442, 508–9, 510–11
  concentration camp in 195
  economic crisis in 396–8
  executions and massacres in xliv-xlv,
    96, 115, 188, 195, 221–2, 265,
    288–90, 314–15, 379–82, 383–92,
    443, 523, 526, 528
  food shortages in 53, 152–3, 191–4,
    216, 307
  forcible evacuations in 215
  living conditions in 66–8, 139, 195–6,
    242–6, 307–8, 384, 395
  patriotism in 197–201
  prostitution in 243
  rape and pillage in 166–8, 222–3, 226,
    390–2, 443, 485, 533
  reconstruction in 395–9, 531–2

refugees in 215–17, 235, 358–9
resistance in *see* Italian partisans; Stella
  Rossa
Risorgimento 66, 245
Itri 131

Jackson, Col. 490–1
Jäger, Adam 361
Japan 24, 43
Jesi airfield 319, 414, 478
Jock (Scots POW) 119, 189
Jodl, Generaloberst Alfred xliv, 35
Johnstone, Maj. 442
Joint Chiefs of Staff 475
Jones, Lt. Geoffrey 'Wacky' 229, 239
Juin, Gen. 83, 132, 134, 165, 179, 214,
  231, 271, 406

Kappler, SS Obersturmbannführer
  Herbert xliii, xliv
Karlsbad 282
Karoton (Russian partisan) 303
Kazakhstan 8
Keitel, Feldmarschall Wilhelm 35, 95,
  169, 282
Kesselring, Feldmarschall Albert xl, xlii,
  xliv, 12, 32, 45, 48, 51, 55, 60, 86,
  141, 142–3, 160, 183, 220, 232, 258,
  372, 423, 459
  Allies assumptions concerning 293,
    294, 295
  anti-partisan activities 169, 221–2,
    265, 282, 356, 374–5, 377–82, 386,
    389, 444, 487
  assessment of 530
  and blowing of bridges 286
  caught off guard 21–2
  character of 37, 42
  constraints on 416
  critical position of 369
  declares Rome an 'Open City' 94, 178
  diplomatic and organisational skills 39
  and evacuation of troops from Sicily
    36
  family background 37–8

forces in disarray 134–5
and German retreat 158, 207–8, 213,
    286, 341
and German surrender 501, 516, 523–4
and the Gothic Line 255–6, 259,
    300–2, 324
and government of Italy 100
and Italian guerrillas 111
and lines of supply 302–3
and possibility of defeat 417
problems for 202–3
and reinforcement of AOK 14 206–7
seriously injured in an accident 426
and spring offensive 476–7, 497–8
tactical skills 37, 39–41, 49, 78–9,
    84–5, 106, 125–7, 149, 172–3,
    262–3, 269, 334, 347, 417–18
tried and convicted of war crimes 532
views on treatment of Italy 92–3
wartime appointments 38–9
and withdrawal from the Albert Line
    239
Keyes, Gen. 177, 178
Kingcombe, Gp Capt. Brian 175, 455
Kirkman, Gen. Sidney 87, 182, 292, 317,
    347, 424, 478–9
Kirkuk 8
Klein, Leutnant Joseph 'Jupp' 18, 89–90,
    91, 104, 107–9, 126, 128–30, 139,
    233, 300, 324, 362, 387, 478, 526,
    536
Kluge, Feldmarschall von 36
Koch, Pietro 152
Kretzschmann, Hermann 112, 115
Kumberg, Hans-Jürgen xxxvii-xxxix, xlii,
    18, 109–10, 133–4, 171, 175, 203,
    206, 228, 324, 417, 464, 478, 536
Kurz, Hauptmann Hans 371, 419, 421,
    433–4, 438–9

La Cantina 328
La Foce estate 63, 188, 219–20, 223,
    230–1, 232, 234–5, 238, 538
La Quercia 314, 465
La Spezia 200, 462, 464, 533
Labico 176

Lagaro 375
Lake Bolsena 106, 149, 213, 222, 257
Lake Bracciano 227, 231
Lake Comacchio 493, 496, 503, 505, 508,
    509
Lake Como 521
Lake Garda 62, 92, 94, 101, 283, 284
Lake Nemi 215
Lake Trasimeno 207, 228, 269, 277
Lampson, Capt. Giles 180–1
Lanuvio 148, 172
Lanzo 358
Latvian Army 43
Law, Guardsman 429
Lazo Torinese Valley 357
Le Marche 346
Leandro (child refugee) 191
Leese, Gen. Sir Oliver 8, 9, 13, 14,
    16–17, 21, 51, 81, 82, 91, 127, 134,
    141–2, 153, 164, 165, 175, 182, 213,
    215, 217, 222, 258–9, 271–2, 291,
    292–5, 303, 318, 319, 335–6, 343,
    359, 363, 405–6, 534
Leese, Margie 17, 134
Legnano 525
Lemelsen, General Joachim 206–7, 221,
    341, 347–8, 349, 372, 426, 433, 454,
    466, 503
Lemie 357
Lemnitzer, Gen. Lyman 501
Lenola 167
Lepini Mountains 160, 161, 165, 175
Lerch, Christian 195
Levant 72
Levola 358
Lewis, Norman 168, 241–2, 243, 307–8,
    390, 398–9
Liano 418, 437–8, 468
Libya 25
Liguria 209
Linaro 412
Liri Appendix 14, 21, 88
Liri River 10, 15, 85, 136, 164
Liri Valley xxxviii, 4, 9, 14, 17n, 20, 22,
    32, 40, 49, 83, 85, 87, 89, 91, 93,
    107, 125, 131, 132, 134, 142, 143,
    153, 164, 181, 293, 335

Livorno 273, 274, 479
Ljubljana 212, 254
Ljubljana Gap 94, 255
Lombardy 54
Longo, Luigi 311, 447
Loos, Obersturmbannführer 374
Lowrey, Sgt. Jerome 231, 342, 479
Lubianka prison 8
Lucca 289, 342, 417
Lucky Luciano (gangster) 245
Luftwaffe 21–2, 38, 42, 62, 70, 71, 202,
  370
  Air Force
  2nd Air Fleet 38
  Group
  III/JG53 ('Pik As') 71, 227
  Squadron
  9th Staffel (squadron) 105
  Fighter Reserve 71
Lugano 445, 446
Luigia (farmer's daughter) 299–300
'Lupo' see Mario 'Lupo' Musolesi

MAAF see Mediterranean Allied Air
  Forces
MASAF see Mediterranean Allied
  Strategic Air Forces
MATAF see Mediterranean Allied
  Tactical Air Forces
Maassen, Unteroffizier Franz 294,
  369–71, 387, 388, 408–10, 418–22,
  429–30, 432, 433–4, 438–9, 536
McCreery, Lt.-Gen. Sir Richard 51, 406–7,
  423, 462, 476, 495, 496–7, 509–510
Macdonald, Lt. 325–6
Macerata 252
Macmillan, Harold 182, 245, 247–50,
  254, 257, 395, 396, 397, 399, 400,
  447, 449, 532
McNair, Gen. Lesley 11
McNarney, Gen. 447
McRorie, Pete 157
Maderno 62, 99, 284, 285, 286, 287, 368,
  480, 500, 520
Magnami, Ferruccio (Giacomo) 355n
Mahuika, Lt. 463

Malta 70, 71, 475, 495
Malta, Siege of 37
Mälzer, Gen. Kurt xlii, xliii
Mandola 443
Mantova 280
Manual of Military Hygiene 128
Marauders 460, 494
'March of Youth' 61
Marene 65, 512
Marseille 254
Marshall, Gen. George 11, 23, 28, 29,
  214, 254, 342, 475, 476, 489, 492
Martinelli, Mario 425
'Maryland' (SOE operations in Italy)
  188
Marzabotto 377
Marziolo, Col. 485–6
Mascarenhas, Gen. 456
Mason, Special Agent Gordon 426, 434
Mason-Macfarlane, Gen. Sir Noel 245,
  250, 395
Massa 456, 461
Massa-Carrara 374–5, 388
Massa-La Spezia 415
Mauri, Pietro 264
Mauthausen concentration camp 374
Mazelin, Troop Sgt. Lester 273, 274
Mazzini, Giuseppe 121
Medicina 418
Mediterranean 34, 44, 46, 47, 72, 208,
  210, 244, 245, 335, 475, 494
Mediterranean Allied Coastal Air Forces
  73
Mediterranean Allied Forces (MAAF)
  70, 71–2, 73, 75
Mediterranean Allied Photographic
  Reconnaissance Wing 73
Mediterranean Allied Strategic Air
  Forces (MASAF) 73, 75, 76, 504
Mediterranean Allied Tactical Air Forces
  (MATAF) 73, 147, 257, 352–3
Mediterranean Command 444
Mediterranean strategy 25–31, 35, 50
Meldola 432, 433
Menzel, Generalleutnant 524
Mercato Saraceno 413
Messina (city) 36

Messina, Straits of 36
Metauro River 324, 326
Michalski, Iwo 238
Middle East 8, 24, 25, 44, 50, 222, 298,
    320–1, 400, 476, 493
Mignano Gap xxxvii, 40, 46
Milan 94, 98, 122 and note, 198, 199,
    306, 311, 367–8, 480, 481, 488, 514,
    519, 520, 523
Mingardi, Lorenzo 374
Minturno Ridge 14, 16
Mirandola 441, 443
Miserocchi, Iader 116, 117–18, 122, 190,
    264, 265, 412–13, 432, 433, 458–9,
    493, 537
Mobile Observation Room Unit 74
Modena 443, 451, 537
Molotov, Vycheslav 23, 25
Monastery Hill xxxviii, 9
Mondaino 336
Monte Altuzzo 348, 349, 399, 400
Monte Artemisio 172, 173
Monte Battaglia (Battle Mountain) 372
Monte Belmonte 417
Monte Cairo xxxviii, 17
Monte Calderaro 418
Monte Calvi 236, 237
Monte Cassino xxxvii, 8, 9, 10, 18, 40,
    49, 75, 82, 89, 91, 106, 125, 127–8,
    139, 531, 536
Monte Castellaro 464
Monte Castello 456
Monte Cerere 418
Monte Chino 511
Monte Colombo 360
Monte della Mandrone 131
Monte Faito 20
Monte Grande 417, 418, 424, 464,
    489–90
Monte Grande d'Aiano 491
Monte Grosso 406
Monte Luro 333
Monte Maio 10, 40, 83, 165
Monte Oggioli 303
Monte Pastore 189
Monte Pezze 411, 430, 473
Monte Rotondo 67, 137, 533

Monte Salvaro 417, 479
Monte San Terenzo 314, 388
Monte Santa Maria Tibernia 270
Monte Savaro 384
Monte Sole 113, 121, 123, 170, 189, 190,
    191, 192, 267, 314, 354, 367, 372,
    373, 374, 375, 379, 380, 384, 385,
    401, 422, 437, 465, 466, 473, 491,
    493, 511, 537, 538
Monte Sorrate xliii
Monte Stanco 404, 411
Monte Trocchio 19
Monte Vigese 404, 411
Montecalderado 464
Montecalvo 337
Montecchio 329
Montefiore 139
Monteluro 302
Montepastore 189
Montepulciano 63, 219, 220, 221, 234–5,
    238
Montgomery, Gen. Sir Bernard 44, 47,
    48, 50, 81, 85, 174, 180, 181, 208,
    222, 259, 475
Monticelli 348, 349
Montilgallo 408
Moore, Capt. Peter 298–300, 324,
    326–8, 336, 359–60, 408, 439–40,
    453–4, 534
Morandi, Italo *see* Vailati, Bruno
Morciano 338
Morocco 25, 26, 166
Morolo 167
Moroni, Antonio 54
Mount Vesuvius 15
Mountbatten, Admiral Louis 81
Movimento Giovanile Repubblicano
    (Fascist youth organisation) 199
Munich 57
Münker, Leutnant 420–1
Murphy, Robert 247, 249
Murrow, Edward R. 144
Musolesi, Guido 121
Musolesi, Mario 'Lupo' 115, 119, 120,
    121, 122–4, 171, 189, 267, 302, 303,
    312–13, 314, 354–6, 367, 373,
    374–5, 377–8, 444, 537

Musso 522

Mussolini, Benito 30, 35, 39, 57, 61, 63,
    66, 196, 246, 248, 314, 368, 399, 531
    attitude towards Jews 357
    and daughter Elena 97–9
    escape, capture and death of 519–23
    fall of 92, 96–7, 116, 121, 198
    and forming of Brigate Nere 283–4
    health of 92, 94
    as isolated figure 99–100
    as journalist 97, 196–7
    mistresses 97
    and the partisans 445
    political passion 97
    and raising of a New Army 95–6
    reclusiveness of 488
    relationship with Hitler 92, 93, 94,
        282–3
    sphere of control 94–5
    suggests counter-offensive 467

Mussolini Canal 147

Mussolini, Rachele 97

Naples 12, 15, 30, 39, 40, 57, 59, 66,
    125, 145, 150, 168, 242–3, 245, 252,
    353, 400, 479, 538
    Via Rasella attack xxxiii–xxxvi, xlii, 152

National Committee for the Liberation
    of Upper Italy (Comitato di
    Liberazione Nazionale per l'Alta
    Italia, CLNAL) 122

Nazis 36, 94, 101, 195, 340, 387, 448,
    532

Neal, Don 393

Neill, F Lt Ken 414–16, 461–2, 464–5,
    478, 535

Neo-Fascists see Fascists/Neo-Fascists

Nepia, Cpl. 276

Netherlands 38, 370

Nettuno 53, 143

Neureither, Unteroffizier 422

New Zealand Forces xxxix, 217, 274,
    275–6, 286, 407, 462–3, 509, 525
    Battalion
    28th (Maori) Battalion 275–6, 362,
        527

Niccioleta 221

Nicoletti, Liliana 123

Niryan-Mar Gulag 6–7

No 1 Special Force (SOE) see under
    Special Operations Executive (SOE

Normandy 47, 165, 174, 181, 202, 208,
    209, 252, 254, 256, 340

North Africa 12, 25, 26–8, 28, 34, 35,
    38–9, 48, 51, 61, 62, 68, 71, 73, 74,
    80, 81, 94, 145, 217, 218, 231, 280,
    325, 406, 479

Nure Valley 485–6

Nuremberg 532

Office of Strategic Services (OSS) 123,
    188, 190, 264, 311, 313, 356, 444,
    446, 448, 484, 487, 500, 514, 521

Olare 339

Omaha Beach 252

Onferno 138, 139, 196, 304, 358

Onore e Combattimento (Neo-Fascist
    youth movement) 197–8

Operation ANVIL 31, 208–14, 240,
    253–7, 257–9, 293

Operation AUTUMN FOG 301

Operation AXIS 36, 57

Operation DIADEM 9–11, 36, 76, 82,
    182, 210, 217, 317, 390, 391, 466,
    476, 494

Operation DRAGOON 279, 340

Operation MALLORY MAJOR 280, 281

Operation OLIVE 295, 317, 359, 406

Operation OVERLORD 28, 30–1, 50,
    208, 245, 255, 257

Operation Reinhardt (1942) 195

Operation SHINGLE xl, 11

Operation STRANGLE 51, 76, 78–9, 152

Operation TORCH 11

Ora 526

Organisation Todt 79, 85, 112, 118, 189,
    301, 302, 385, 412, 445

Origo, Marchese Antonio 62–4, 66,
    187–8, 219–20, 230–1, 234–5,
    238–9, 538

Origo, Iris 62–4, 187–8, 219–20, 230–1,
    234–5, 238–9, 538

Ortona xxxvii
Orvieto 219–20, 257, 293
OSS *see* Office of Strategic Services
Ostiglia 280
Ottani, Agostino (Sergio) 355n

Pacific 46, 209, 211, 476
Pajetta, Gian Carlo 447
Palermo 246
Palestine 218, 298, 299, 321, 414
Paniora, Lt. 463
Pantelleria 298
Parilli, Baron 500, 519
Paris 340, 427
Parker, Maj. 14–15
Parma 281
Parri, Ferruccio 311, 445, 446, 447, 501
Partito Repubblicano Fascista (PRF)
    (Neo-Fascist Party) 93
Paselli, Angelina 382, 383, 385
Paselli, Cornelia 190–1, 192, 193, 367,
    373–4, 375, 379–82, 383, 385, 465,
    515, 537, 539
Paselli, Gigi 381, 383
Paselli, Giuseppe 191
Paselli, Giuseppina 191, 381, 383, 385,
    515
Paselli, Luigi 191
Paselli, Maria 191, 381, 383
Paselli, Virginio 191, 367, 373, 379, 382,
    385
Passau 19
Patton, Gen. George 44
Pavolini, Alessandro 62, 92, 93, 95, 96,
    283–4, 285, 305, 309, 311, 446, 488,
    500, 520–3, 530, 531
Pearl Harbor 15, 25
Pelle, Tommaso 216
Pellizzari barracks 57, 58–9, 65
Peninsular Base Section (PBS) 246
Peretola airfield 414, 415
Persia 8, 72
Perugia 268, 291, 353
Pesaro 317, 335
Pescara 56, 225, 414
Petacci, Clara 97, 522, 523

Petzinger, Leutnant 518
Phoenix, Lt. 334
Piacenza 485, 485–6, 501, 502, 511, 520,
    525
Pianoro 514
Piave Valley 526
Pico 131, 132, 134, 141
Piedimonte 8, 125, 128, 153
Piemonte 67, 287, 311, 356, 538
Pienza 63
Pietermaritzburg 218
Pieve di Rivoschio 265
Pifferi, Capt. 514
Pignataro 85, 88, 90, 128, 136
Piper Cub 177, 213–14
Pirini, Francesco 384–5, 465
Pisa (city) 149, 189, 232, 341, 342, 392,
    456
Pisa, Pasua 67–9, 137–8, 150–1, 166,
    533
Pisa-Rimini Line 31, 112, 207, 208, 254
Pistoia 340, 347, 352, 425
Piumarola 88
Pius XII, Pope 102
Pizzoni, Alfredo 447
Po Plain 514
Po Valley 30, 47, 424, 513
Poggia Renatico 62
Point 111 (Montecchio) 329, 331
Point 131 (Cassino) 19–20
Point 512 (Monte Sole) 435
Point 593 (Monte Cassino) 107
Poland 5, 7, 54, 195, 340, 370, 413,
    488–9
Poletti, Col. Charles 246, 288
Polish Air Force 73
Polish Forces 3–4, 7–8, 9, 20–1, 82, 87,
    91, 106, 110, 132, 153, 272, 288,
    504, 509
  Corps
    II Polish Corps 3, 4, 8, 226, 238, 253,
        335, 405, 406
  Division
    3rd Carpathian Division 4, 8, 413
  Regiments
    12th Polish Lancers 4–5, 8, 9, 21,
        106, 110

Polish Home Army 335
Pontecorvo 85, 109, 131, 132, 133, 134,
    140, 141, 142
Pontine Marshes 40, 148
Popski's Private Army 459 and note
Porta San Paolo 60
Portal, Charles, Chief of Air Staff 72
Potenza 54
Predappio 406
Preece, Bill 336
prisoners-of-war (POWs) 64, 119, 189,
    265, 266, 343, 387, 390, 396, 437,
    439, 442, 443, 451, 464, 490–1, 503,
    526, 528, 531, 536
Prunaro di Sopra 378
Prützmann, General 101
Psychological Warfare Executive (PWE)
    242–3, 312
Pyramid of Cestius 60

Quadrelli, Dino 196
Quadrelli, Italo 138–9, 196, 304, 358,
    538
Queen Elizabeth 200
Questura 118
Quinan, David 430
Quiney, Guardsman Arthur 430
Quintavalle (driver of Elena Curti)
    288
Quisil Ribat Oasis 8

Radicofani 231, 232
Rahn, Dr Rudolph 93, 100, 111, 283,
    314, 501, 516, 523
Rainer, Dr Friedrich 94
Rapido River 10–11, 14, 127, 145, 160,
    172
Rastenburg xliii
Ravenna 116, 117, 373, 427, 458–9, 460,
    496, 500, 537
Rawson, Ian 336
Red Army 27, 335, 497
Red Cross 63, 188, 235, 246, 305, 307,
    337
Reder, Sturmbannführer Walter 237–8,

314, 349, 373, 374, 375, 377, 385,
    386, 532–3
Reggio 245
Reggio Emilia 442
Reggio Palace (Caserta) 31
Regia Aeronautica 70
Remagen 497
Reno Valley 267, 302, 372, 373, 375, 401,
    456, 491, 495, 510
Repubblica Sociale Italiana (RSI) 96, 97,
    98, 100, 111, 117, 119, 193, 194,
    196–7, 201, 242, 244, 284, 368,
    500
Republic of Domdossola 444
Ribbentrop, Joachim von 487
Ricci, Renato 93, 95
Ricciarelli, Vitterio 288
Richardson, Alec 51
Richtofen, Feldmarschall Wolfram von
    70
Rieti 203, 206
Rimini 189, 195, 293, 340, 342, 343, 346,
    353, 361, 362, 406, 478, 538
Rino (Italian partisan) 377
Rioveggio 372–3, 373, 375, 377
Risiera di San Saba (Trieste) 195, 315
River Adige 301, 427, 477, 478, 525–6
River Arda 502
River Arno 278, 286–7, 289, 305, 306,
    340, 341, 347, 456
River Ausa 362
River Conca 334, 336, 342, 343
River Don 53
River Foglia 326
River Garigliano 10, 14, 15, 20, 82, 87,
    88
River Lamone 460, 462
River Melfa 153, 157
River Orcia 231
River Panaro 517
River Pechora 6
River Piopetta 88, 89
River Po 279–80, 281, 301, 302, 369,
    427, 441, 480, 495, 498, 518, 519,
    524, 525
River Reno 113, 114, 189, 479, 495, 509
River Riccio 103

River Ronco 418, 419, 420, 422, 423, 434
River Rubicon 362, 369, 407 and note, 408
River Santerno 459, 466, 505
River Savio 264, 265, 418, 419
River Secchio 443
River Senio 463, 466, 468, 499, 500, 504
River Setta 367, 377
River Tiber 202, 206, 213, 215, 217, 225, 307, 398
River Volturno 46
Ro 518
Roberto (Italian soldier) 482
Roccastrada 232, 233
Rocco, Lino 123–4
Röffner (German soldier) 418
Rogge, Peter 387
Romagna 116, 189, 190, 264, 304, 347, 412
Romagna Mountains 265, 443
Romania 76, 345
Rome 9–11, 22, 23, 28, 31, 35, 39, 40, 41, 47, 48, 51, 55, 56, 60, 67, 84, 86, 93, 94, 112, 125, 143, 147, 149, 152–3, 158, 161, 165, 171, 174, 214, 231, 232, 250, 288, 306, 346, 397, 425, 445, 475, 478, 530, 533
  Allied capture of 177–83, 197, 200, 202, 211, 225
Rommel, Feldmarschall Erwin 26, 29, 34, 35, 37, 38, 39, 40, 41
Roosevelt, Franklin D. 23, 25–6, 47, 77, 183, 248, 250, 257, 295, 335, 395–6, 428, 454, 510
Roseberry, Col. 445, 446
Rosignano 272, 273
Rossi, Gianni 115, 118–19, 120–4, 171, 312, 314, 354, 373, 375, 377–8, 384, 385, 417, 512, 515, 537
Rossi, Leone 354, 375, 377–8, 537
Route 64 401
Route 65 347, 372, 400
'Rover David' 74–5
Rowe, Blackie 330
Royal Air Force Mediterranean and Middle East 72

Royal Air Force (RAF) 73, 321, 412
Commands
  Bomber Command 72
  Fighter Command 37
Group
  5 Group 72
  205 Group 345
Wing
  239 Wing 174
  244 Wing 174–5, 227, 268, 291, 353, 455, 495, 505, 509
  324 Wing 74
  334 Wing 483
  344 Wing 123
  Typhoon fighter-bomber wing 74
Squadron
  56 Squadron 74
  225 Squadron 414–15, 478
Desert Air Force (DAF) 73, 74, 174–5, 268, 333, 361, 455, 465, 495, 504
Royal Australian Air Force 73
Royal Navy 112
Rubnikowicz, Wladek 4–7, 8–9, 9, 21, 106–7, 110, 238, 252, 253, 335, 413, 478, 489, 535
Rumania 340
Runstedt, Feldmarschall Gerd von 498
Russia 36, 38, 43, 53–4, 71, 108, 156, 170, 253, 256, 294, 370, 386–7, 389

Saar 107
Sacerdote, Emilio 357–8, 453, 534
Saidel, Pte. 1st Class Ray xl-xli, xlii, 145, 231–2, 234, 341–2, 479, 512, 524–5
Salerno 12, 12–13, 29, 33, 40, 45, 46, 55, 56, 74, 158, 197, 390, 415
Salerno, Gulf of 39
Salò 94, 99
Saludecio 338
Sammarchi, Olindo 120
San Bernardo 64–5
San Fortunato Ridge 343, 359, 360, 362
San Gemini 206
San Giorgio 128
San Mamante 385
San Marcello Pistoiese 349, 425

San Martino 377
San Pietro 62
San Terenzo 374
Sant' Angelo 85
Sant' Anna 290, 533
Santa Maria 141
Santa Maria Infante 86, 390
Santa Maria a Vico 168
Santa Sofia 265, 413
Sardinia 26, 29, 55, 60
Sarsina 116, 264, 412, 413
SAS 484
Sasso Marconi 374
Sassoleone 424
Sassoon, Siegfried 359
Sauckel, Gauleiter Fritz 112
Savage, Andrew 239, 430
Savignano 407
Savio Valley 413
Savioia, Admiral di 200
Schelasin, Rottenführer 372
Schlemm, General 374, 386
Schmidkuntz, Hauptsturmführer 379
Schmidt, Schütze 140
Schreiber, Rudi (pseud) 233, 274, 313,
    341, 388, 478, 536
Schulz, General Friedrich 524
Schuster, Cardinal 487, 519, 520
Schweinitz, Oberstleutnant Hans-Lothar
    von 519, 521, 523, 524
Schwerin, General von 508
Scislowski, Stan 103–4, 135–7, 140–1,
    156–8, 164, 165, 175, 328–9, 330,
    331–2, 337, 393–4, 419, 430, 431,
    460–1, 463, 466, 468, 473–4,
    477–8, 533–4
SD (Sicherheitsdienst, SS Security
    Service) xliii, xliv, 100
Second Front 14
Segebrecht, Hauptsturmführer Willfried
    236–8, 262, 272, 314, 352, 372–3,
    375, 377, 378–9, 381–2, 384, 386,
    422–3, 538
Selborne, Lord 446
Senger (Hitler) Line 51, 107, 125,
    126–7, 128, 130, 132, 133–4, 139,
    140–2, 153, 157, 158

Senior Civil Affairs Officer (SCAO) 166
Serchio Valley 456, 467, 491
Serra, Miranda 197
Serraggia 279
Sessford, Cpl. 432
Setta River 113, 114, 119
Setta Valley 170, 190, 267, 302, 314, 372,
    373, 422, 465
Sevareid, Eric 143, 144, 147, 150, 162,
    173, 177, 179–80, 246, 252, 390
Sezze 158
Sforza, Count Carlo 248, 249, 250, 448,
    449, 450
Sicily 12, 18, 26, 34, 36, 39, 44, 51, 74,
    80, 81, 108, 146, 197, 298, 398, 527
Siena 199, 200, 276, 292, 392, 405, 427
Sikorski, Gen. 7, 8
Simon, Generalleutnant Max 374, 386
Sitka, Unteroffizier Hans 169–70, 374,
    375
Slessor, AM Sir John 72, 75, 76, 78, 79, 447
Sobibor 195
SOE see Special Operations Executive
Sonthofen 36
Sosabrowski, Gen. 413
South African Air Force 73
    24th Squadron 320, 321, 414, 460, 494
South African Forces 218, 228, 352, 401,
    405, 422, 525
  Divisions
    6th South African Armoured
        Division 217, 218, 223, 274, 347, 431
  Brigades
    12th Infantry Brigade 217, 218, 405
  Regiments
    1st City/Cape Town Highlanders 412,
        511
    Imperial Light Horse 401
    Royal Natal Carbineers 217, 218, 222,
        286, 347, 363, 401, 404, 411, 465,
        510
Soviet Union 6–7, 24, 130, 202, 413,
    488, 489
Spanish Civil War 118, 122, 252, 447
Spata, Anna 305–6
Spazzol, Arturo 310
Special Operations Executive (SOE) 188,

264, 265, 311, 312, 356, 441, 444,
  445, 446, 448, 484, 486, 501
No 1 Special Force (SOE in Italy) 188,
  265, 441, 446
Speer, Albert 111
Spigno Saturnia Ridge 19, 86
Spoleto 493
SS (*Schutzstaffel*) 92, 101, 194–5, 232–3,
  282, 283, 284, 285, 309, 358, 368, 437,
  444, 453, 487, 500, 525, 526, 532
Stalin, Josef 8, 23, 47, 335, 528
Stalingrad 27, 32, 35, 370
Stanco 405, 411
Stangl, Franz 195
Stazzema 290
Steccola 378
Steeve (South African POW) 119, 189
Stella Rossa brigade *see under* Italian
  partisans
Stimpson, Secretary of War 281
Stockdale, Peter 299
Stralsund 70
Stura Valley 64–5, 67, 193, 512
Subiaco 161, 175
Sudetenland 169
Suez Canal 39
Sugano (Italian partisan) 267, 354
Supreme Allied Commander 447
Supreme Allied Commander
  Mediterranean 72, 399
Surk, Walter 408–9, 410
Switzerland 357, 500, 501, 519, 523

Tactical HQ (British) 82
Talbot, Lt. 494–5
Tanassy, Maj. Emil 148
Tavarnelle 292, 342, 425, 434
Tavoletto 337
Tavolicci 265
Tedder, Air Chief Marshal Sir Arthur 75
Tehran Conference (1943) 30–1, 47
Teramo 226
Terni 206
Terracina 135, 148, 150
Third Reich 112, 194, 195, 212, 498, 510
Thunderbolts 148

Tiber Valley 269
Timpkes, Maj. 22
Tito, Marshal 356, 399, 483, 527, 528–9
Todt, Fritz 112
Togliatti, Palmiro 248, 249
Tolé 189, 315, 512
Tossi, Gianni 189–90
Toussaint, General Rudolf 100
Treblinka 195, 532
Trento 94
Trevine 269
Trieste 94, 127, 194–5, 255, 315, 345,
  525, 527, 528
Truman, Harry S. 528–9
Truscott, Maj.-Gen. Lucian 13, 142, 151,
  159, 161, 162, 172, 454, 466, 476, 495
Tunisia 25, 27, 34, 37, 39, 44, 48, 145,
  146, 231, 298, 342, 414, 454
Turin 58, 64, 65, 193, 201, 309, 356, 520
Tuscania 105, 214
Tuscany 29, 62, 63, 200, 221
Tyrol 94, 516
Tyrrhenian coast 235, 272, 503
Tyrrhenian Sea 131, 236

Ubaldo, Don 379
Ukraine 101
Ultra 16–17
Umberto, Prince 249, 449
Umbria 298, 299, 493
Union of South Africa 217
United Nations 395
United States Army Command and
  Forces xli, 11–12, 15, 16, 19, 25, 86,
  146, 231, 272, 330, 479
  Armies
    Third Army 535
    Fifth Army xxxix, 10, 12, 13, 14, 16,
      17n, 19, 46, 51, 83, 104, 131, 132,
      133, 134, 141, 142, 145, 150, 160,
      174, 179, 181–2, 202, 206, 213, 216,
      217, 219, 222, 231, 257, 258, 271,
      293–4, 295, 342, 346–7, 348, 363,
      369, 371, 405, 406–7, 417, 423, 424,
      427, 431, 432, 435, 459, 462, 464,
      466, 475, 495, 496–7, 510, 514

United States Army Command and
    Forces – *cont.*
  Corps
    II Corps 14, 83–4, 86, 87, 134, 142,
      148, 150, 161, 165, 174, 177, 178,
      213, 216, 347, 400, 495, 510
    IV Corps 236, 347, 401
    VI Corps xl, 12, 13, 51, 142, 143,
      144, 145, 148, 149, 150, 151,
      159–60, 161, 162–3, 171, 172, 174,
      176, 214, 219, 258
  Divisions
    1st Armored xli, 143–4, 151, 161,
      233–4, 272, 335, 341, 342–3, 347,
      362, 363, 401, 423, 479, 510, 512
    Combat Command A (CCA)
      145–6, 147, 231, 341
    Combat Command B (CCB) 145,
      151, 401, 510, 512
    3rd Division 11, 162, 174
    10th Mountain Division 476, 480,
      491, 495, 497, 510, 512
    34th 'Red Bull' Division 146, 161,
      172, 179, 236, 237, 272, 274, 289,
      347, 401, 417, 422, 423
    36th 'Texas' Division 10, 14, 131,
      143, 145, 161, 172, 236
    45th Division 161
    82nd Airborne Division 55, 56
    85th 'Custer' Infantry Division 14,
      15, 16, 19, 83, 131, 347, 348, 349,
      371, 399, 400, 479, 512, 525
    88th 'Blue Devils' Infantry Division
      14, 15, 177, 371, 372, 417
    91st Division 347, 349
    92nd 'Buffalo' Division 163, 258,
      298, 341, 456–8, 461, 465, 467,
      491–3, 503
  Regiments
    1st Armored Regiment 231
    3rd Infantry 143–4, 161, 176
    13th Armored 145, 148
    133rd 236
    135th Infantry 146, 236, 272, 525
    338th Infantry 15, 86, 131, 179, 349
    370th Regimental Combat Team 341,
      342, 347

    442nd 'Nisei' Infantry Regiment 236,
      491–3
    509th Airborne Combat Team 161
  Battalions
    1/338 Infantry 19–20, 135, 512
    3/338 Infantry
    1st Provisional Rifle Company
      479
    2/370th Infantry 492
  Miscellaneous
    1st Special Force 143–4, 147, 161,
      174, 177, 178
    306th Counter Intelligence Corps
      Detachment 425, 434–5
    Howze Force 148–50, 151, 162, 163,
      174, 176, 177, 231
  US Army Air Force (USAAF) 21, 73,
    77
  Air Force
    Eighth Air Force 72
    Fifteenth Air Force 46, 345
  Air Command
    12th (later renamed 22nd) Tactical
      Air Command 73, 279, 268, 302,
      414, 475, 504
  Group
    27th Fighter-Bomber Group 76,
      77–8, 104, 148, 279, 292
    33rd Fighter Group 280
  Wing
    51st Troop Carrier Wing 73, 483
    57th Bombardment Wing 73
  Squadron
    522nd 148
Urbino 235
Uzbekistan 7, 8

Vado 113, 123, 170, 367, 422
Vailati, Bruno (real name Italo Morandi)
  265–6, 412, 432, 443
Val d'Arda 485
Val di Viù 356–7
Val d'Orcia palazzo 62–4, 187, 188,
  219–20, 220, 221, 228, 230–1
Val d'Ossola 444
Val Trebbia 485

Valiani, Leo 445, 446
Valli di Comacchio 373
Vallo Torinese 356
Valmontone 13, 143, 148, 149, 151, 158,
    160–1, 162, 163, 165, 171, 172,
    175–6, 183, 211, 215
Valtellina 500, 520
Vatican 153
Vavallero, Gen. 39
VE Day 527
Veggio 473
Velletri 149, 160, 161, 163, 172, 173, 215
Venafro 21
Venturi, Carlo 113–15, 121, 124, 170,
    189, 267, 354, 537
Vergato 479, 510
Verona 64, 96, 370, 450, 494, 498, 499,
    525
Versari, Iris 310
Via Adriatica 318, 335
Via Appia (Route 7) 40, 158
Via Aurelia 236
Via Casilina (Route 6) 18, 40, 89–90,
    103, 104, 105, 106, 130, 132–3, 139,
    143, 147, 151, 153, 160, 161, 163,
    164, 165, 172, 175, 178, 182, 183,
    217, 219
Via Emilia (Route 9) 369, 406, 439, 459,
    462–3, 496, 514
Vichy regime 12, 25
Victoria, Queen 42
Vienna 57, 255
Vigese 401
Vigo 401
Villa Cora (Florence) 415
Villa Feltrinelli 97, 283, 368
Villa Necchi 480, 520
Vittorio Emanuele III, King 35, 53, 56,
    122, 200, 247–50, 346, 449, 488
Vivarelli, Roberto 198–200, 392, 480–1,
    514, 520–1, 523, 537
Vivarelli, William 514
Vokes, Maj.-Gen 103
Volelli, Oder 315
Volturno 299
Von Mackensen, Generaloberst Eberhard
    xl, xliii, 135, 160, 173, 202, 206

Von Senger und Etterlin, General
    Fridolin 32–3, 34, 36, 84, 106,
    125–7, 131, 132, 141, 165, 172, 183,
    232, 340, 388
Von Tippelskirch, General Kurt 454
Von Vietinghoff, Generaloberst 21, 32,
    36, 106, 107, 125, 126, 141, 158,
    160, 203, 207, 301, 302, 324, 360,
    369, 416, 417–18, 426, 454, 456,
    459, 462, 476, 498, 501, 514, 516,
    523–4, 531
Vyshinsky, Andrei 248

Walker, Gen. 10, 172
Wall, F Sgt Ernest 320, 321, 361, 414,
    460, 494–5, 535
Walters, Sgt. Edward 'Bucky' 146–7,
    179, 236, 272–4, 347, 535
Wanoa, Sgt.-Maj. 463
Warsaw 5, 195, 335
Warsaw Ghetto 532
Warsaw Uprising 413
Washington Conference (1941) 24
Wehrmacht 282, 283, 384
Wenner, Oberstrumbannfüjrer Eugen
    519, 521, 523
West Point 11
Western Allies 34, 413, 475, 487
Western Desert 484, 485
Western Front 170, 487, 494, 498, 499,
    536
Westphal, Gen. Siegfried xlii, xliv, 32, 51
White, 'Chalky' 485
White Flame (Fascist youth
    organisation) 200
Wick, Helmut 74
Wiggans, Lt. Bob 15–16, 20, 86, 131,
    131–2, 135, 179, 213, 348–9, 399,
    400, 479–80, 489–90, 512–13, 525
Wilcockson, Maj. 441, 451
Wilson, Gen. Sir Henry Maitland
    'Jumbo' 50, 208–14, 245, 255, 256,
    259, 399, 447, 454
Winter (Bernhardt) Line 47
Wirth, Christian 195
Wolff, General Karl xlii, 100, 100–2,

169, 187, 282, 283, 313, 444, 445–6, 487–8, 500–1, 516, 519, 520, 521, 523, 524, 532
Wolfsschanze (Wolf's Lair) xliii, 283
Wyke-Smith, Lt. Ted 19, 88, 127, 133, 156, 222, 416–17, 424, 478, 534

Yalta Conference (1945) 488–9, 495
Young Fascists 61, 197–201
  see also Fascists

Yugoslavia 90, 194, 199, 356, 399, 427, 483, 527, 528

Zanelli, Italian Fascist 117
Zavatti, Dr Silvio 310
Zellner, Major Georg 18–19, 87–8, 104, 106, 128, 137, 165, 203, 220, 229–30, 262, 269–70, 275, 536
Ziegler, General Heinz 426, 454
Zuckerman, Professor Solly 75